DOING RESEARCH ON CRIME AND JUSTICE

DOING RESEARCH ON
CRIME AND JUSTICE

EDITED BY

ROY D. KING AND EMMA WINCUP

OXFORD

UNIVERSITY PRESS

OXFORD

UNIVERSITY PRESS

Great Clarendon Street, Oxford OX2 6DP

Oxford University Press is a department of the University of Oxford.
It furthers the University's objective of excellence in research, scholarship,
and education by publishing worldwide in

Oxford New York

Athens Auckland Bangkok Bogotá Buenos Aires Calcutta
Cape Town Chennai Dar es Salaam Delhi Florence Hong Kong Istanbul
Karachi Kuala Lumpur Madrid Melbourne Mexico City Mumbai
Nairobi Paris São Paulo Singapore Taipei Tokyo Toronto Warsaw

with associated companies in Berlin Ibadan

Oxford is a registered trade mark of Oxford University Press
in the UK and in certain other countries

Published in the United States
by Oxford University Press Inc., New York

British Library Cataloguing in Publication Data

Data available

Library of Congress Cataloging in Publication Data

Data available

ISBN 0–19–876540–1

Typeset by RefineCatch Limited, Bungay, Suffolk
Printed in Great Britain
on acid-free paper by
TJ International Ltd., Padstow, Cornwall

DEDICATION

This book is dedicated to

Seren and Branwen
and
Emma Wincup and Arthur and Bessie Davis

PREFACE

The idea for this book was conceived when we were colleagues together at the Centre for Comparative Criminology and Criminal Justice at the University of Wales, Bangor. In one of our regular meetings to discuss research agendas one of us remarked on how little guidance there had been when she was a PhD student about the real process of doing criminological research. Somehow the insights of even the most knowledgeable and experienced supervisors, thrown into discussions during supervisions or thesis committee meetings, do not have the same gravitas as words on the printed page, and yet the words on the printed pages of methodology textbooks and research monographs made all too little reference to the lived experience of researchers doing their research. Indeed all too often the textbooks are written as though research is not a lived experience at all, but simply the application of techniques developed by others and which have been deemed right for one or another style of research.

Emma's remarks reminded the other editor of his first experience of social research: examining the case records of probationers vaguely searching for clues as to possible explanations for their delinquency, in fulfilment of the under-graduate dissertation requirements for a sociology degree at the University of Leicester. Indeed he was not much wiser when subsequently invited by his eminent PhD supervisor, the late Jack Tizard at the MRC Social Psychiatry Research Unit, to study patterns of long-stay hospital care for children. Being parachuted in to fieldwork situations can be an extremely daunting business—and no amount of reading can fully prepare one for it. That sense of wondering what one has embarked on, and how one is going to go about it, indeed why one is there at all, has probably beset generation after generation of research work-ers. The strong will always survive, but it was a long time before he realized that at bottom the research process was essentially about finding things out and trying to understand what it is that one has discovered. Research methods and techniques are an aid in that process but are sometimes wrapped in mystique and it is easy to believe that they should be used like a recipe book. There are, of course, circumstances in which a rigorous application of technique is essential. But there are others where improvisation is the order of the day. The measure of the good researcher comes in judging the difference between these situations and having the flexibility to deploy the best approximation one can find to make the maximum possible use of what, in the social world, are always unique circumstances and opportunities.

The original title for this volume was going to be *The Honest Criminologist's Guide to Doing Research on Crime and Justice* (*in homage to Norval Morris and Gordon Hawkins*). Hardly any of the established authors contributing to Parts

One, Two, and Three of this volume had a formal research training. Most had learned what they know through trial and error in the school of hard knocks and some of them are battle-scarred. When they were invited to contribute to this volume in ways which got beyond the conventional accounts in method-ological appendices and in ways that also reflected some of their own real experiences of the research process, most readily embraced the idea of express-ing themselves as 'honest criminologists'. All of these authors, some now approaching the end of their careers, are actively involved in passing on what they have learned either to graduate students or to younger colleagues, or both, in their respective fields of expertise. However, there seemed much to be gained from bringing that wealth of expertise together in a single volume for the benefit of those approaching criminological or criminal justice research for the first time, be they undergraduates taking their first fumbling steps on the road to discovery, or one of an increasing number of practitioners in the criminal justice field who are becoming both research-literate and research-active, or perhaps especially graduate students or neophyte professional researchers.

By contrast most of the authors contributing to Part Four will have had some formal research training as part of their doctoral studies. Some of these authors are already on their third or fourth post-doctoral research projects, whereas others have only recently emerged from their *viva voce* examinations—in one case since writing the first draft of his chapter for this book. The careers of these contributors have been forged in a very different political, economic, and social climate from that in which their supervisors started out twenty or thirty years earlier. And they work within a discipline which has changed almost beyond recognition. Among these contributors will be some of the movers and shakers of criminology in the coming years: and the sharpness and recency of their experience can be expected to resonate with those of the generation to come. If we are right then there will be everything to be said for revisiting these areas in subsequent editions: to create periodic benchmarks on the state of the discipline.

In editing this volume our biggest debt, of course, is to our contributors. The volume stands or falls on what they have had to say. Many produced their chapters under enormous pressure, not least the pressure of the research pro-cess itself: the need to manage research centres and institutes, the continuing need to compete for research funds, and, for the authors in Part Four, the need to establish independent research careers. Given the level of commitments it is not surprising that the process was more time-consuming than our original schedule proposed. It is sometimes hard to know who feels guiltier in this process: editors for nagging people about deadlines or contributors for missing them. But we hope the task has been worthwhile and we are grateful to Michaela Coulthard and Myfanwy Milton at Oxford University Press for having confidence in the project and being patient with the delays.

Several others have contributed to the shaping of this volume in various ways, sometimes without knowing it. Some of these are acknowledged in the dedication (fittingly in a book that deliberately spans the generations to Emma Wincup's grandparents and Roy King's grandchildren). Others include colleagues at the Centre for Comparative Criminology and Criminal Justice, especially Claire Davis our Research Administrator who organized an initial conference of the contributors in Bangor in September 1998 and has worked closely with the editors throughout. And, of course, our students, especially our graduate students.

Thanks also to our copy editor, Kate Elliott, who reminded us of the importance of grammatical correctness and produced many improvements.

ROY D. KING   EMMA WINCUP
Bangor, July 1999   Cardiff, July 1999

SHORT CONTENTS

CONTENTS

NOTES ON CONTRIBUTORS

Carole Adams is Lecturer in Criminology and Research Methods in the School of Social Science at Middlesex University.

John Baldwin is Professor of Judicial Administration and Director of the Institute of Judicial Administration in the Faculty of Law at the University of Birmingham.

Anthony Bottoms is Wolfson Professor of Criminology at the Institute of Criminology at Cambridge University.

Lynn Hancock is Lecturer in Criminology in the School of Social Science at Middlesex University.

Dick Hobbs is Professor of Sociology in the Department of Sociology and Social Policy at the University of Durham.

Carolyn Hoyle is a Research Officer at the Centre for Criminological Research at the University of Oxford.

Roy D. King is Professor of Criminology and Criminal Justice and Director of the Centre for Comparative Criminology and Criminal Justice (4CJ) at the University of Wales Bangor.

Mike Maguire is Professor of Criminology and Criminal Justice at Cardiff University.

George Mair is Professor of Criminal Justice in the School of Law, Social Work and Social Policy at Liverpool John Moores University.

Pat Mayhew is Head of the Patterns of Crime section in the Crime and Criminal Justice Unit of the Research, Development, and Statistics Directorate at the Home Office.

Bonny Mhlanga is Research Fellow at the Centre for Criminology and Criminal Justice at the University of Hull.

Rod Morgan is Professor of Criminal Justice in the Department of Law at Bristol University.

Patricia Rawlinson is Lecturer in Criminology and Criminal Justice at the Centre for Comparative Criminology and Criminal Justice (4CJ) at the University of Wales Bangor.

Robert Reiner is Professor of Criminology in the Law Department at London School of Economics.

Karen Sharpe is Senior Lecturer in Police Studies, Centre for Police Research and Education, School of Social Sciences, University of Teesside.

Catrin Smith is Lecturer in Criminology and Criminal Justice at the Centre for Comparative Criminology and Criminal Justice (4CJ) at the University of Wales Bangor.

Sandra Walklate is Professor of Sociology in the Department of Sociology at Manchester Metropolitan University.

Julia Wardhaugh is Lecturer in Criminology and Criminal Justice at the Centre for Comparative Criminology and Criminal Justice (4CJ) at the University of Wales Bangor.

Dave Whyte is a Researcher at the Centre for Criminal Justice in the School of Law and Applied Social Studies at Liverpool John Moores University.

Emma Wincup is Lecturer in Criminology and Criminal Justice in the School of Social Sciences at Cardiff University.

LIST OF TABLES

LIST OF FIGURES

INTRODUCTION

Roy D. King and Emma Wincup

Problems of law and order, crime, and the criminal justice process have never had so much attention as in the last few years. If they are to be properly understood and appropriately addressed they must be effectively researched in ways that are theoretically grounded, methodologically secure, and practically based. How well these problems will be tackled in future will depend upon new generations of criminologists able to learn from what has gone before.

The growth of interest in problems about crime and justice has been mirrored by a burgeoning of courses on these subjects in the universities. Once taught only as a postgraduate discipline, criminology now figures increasingly in undergraduate courses and many universities have introduced criminology and criminal justice degree schemes at single or joint honours level. The future would-be researcher is nowadays likely to have had her or his interest first aroused in the context of doing an undergraduate project or dissertation on a criminological or criminal justice topic.

The need for greater rigour in the research training process has been a recurring theme on the part of research councils which now require university departments, or increasingly faculties, to meet stringent criteria for their research training programmes for postgraduate students. Although we hope that the apprenticeship model of research training will long continue it now forms a smaller part of the process than heretofore, with increasing emphasis being placed on classroom teaching in research methods.

There are, of course, several textbooks to which new researchers may turn where they can discover the technical details of how to conduct research using particular methods or how to interpret particular kinds of data. But there are no books which deal at all comprehensively or authoritatively with the broad sweep of the research process in criminological and criminal justice settings, or which convey the changing pattern of what it has been and what it is now like actually to engage in that process in the real-world settings in which research is carried out. This book aims to fill that gap.

In this introduction we first set out the structure of the book and the over-arching rationale. We then try to highlight what seem to be the central messages of our contributors and to point up the recurring themes.

RATIONALE FOR THIS BOOK

Part One of the book raises issues that track across all specialized areas within criminology and criminal justice, and anyone contemplating work within these fields needs to have a mind to them. The first chapter is predicated upon our belief that, at some level, theory is inseparable from the research process in whatever field it is carried out. The second recognizes that all research is conducted within a political context which exercises constraints not only upon what research is funded, but also how and by whom it is carried out. In view of the general significance that these chapters would have across the board, our contributors here were given a fairly free rein about how, and at what length, they might best develop their arguments.

Part Two is divided substantively into broad sub-areas in terms of research on crime, criminals, and victims: and Part Three is similarly sub-divided into substantive areas of research on criminal justice agencies and institutions. It might seem slightly unusual to focus a book dedicated to the research process on substantive areas, rather than upon styles of research, methodological themes or techniques, or the stages of the research process from design, through data collection and analysis, to writing up. However, it is our strongly held belief that students come into research not from an interest in methods and techniques but either because they have an interest in an area of study but may not be quite sure just what it is that interests them; or because they are fired up about problems and issues in the real world—about what happens in criminal gangs or in police stations, about how victims are treated by the police, or prisoners by prison staff. It is also our belief that there is more to be gained from connecting the research process to real situations in which it takes place than from attempting to crystallize it out into a series of more abstract (and less interesting) procedures.

Our dividing up of the field is inevitably somewhat arbitrary, and of course we could have done it in other ways. There are problems of boundaries—for example between researching street criminals and researching white-collar and professional criminals. There are problems of possible gaps and omissions— for example it could be argued that researching juveniles or women offenders, or drugs or gangs, or crime prevention (and no doubt many others) might have merited separate attention. But in a book of reasonable length some limits have to be imposed, and we saw a danger of the book becoming too repetitive if the same methodological issues were rehearsed in more and more sub-divisions. To some degree it was possible to overcome some of the problems of overlap, and possible omission through discussion at a conference of contributors at the outset, and through the circulation of preliminary outlines.

We were somewhat more prescriptive in regard to the contributions in Parts Two and Three. Within fairly tight word limits we asked contributors to give the neophyte researcher a brief overview of the main themes, topics, or problems researched in their area of expertise, how those had been defined in terms of theoretical traditions and perspectives, and what had been the main styles of research adopted. However, the intention was not to provide a state-of-the-art review of research but simply to set some signposts. The main task was to provide a more than usually reflexive account of the art and craft of doing research, drawing upon the contributors' own experience, in ways that might provide some comfort and succour to those about to embark on the same process themselves. Finally contributors were asked to give some indication of the prospects for future research as they saw it, and to suggest some key references for further reading. We emphasized that this was not intended to be so prescriptive as to become a straitjacket—and it can readily be seen that not all contributors have followed the guidelines in all respects—including one of the editors. Nevertheless, we hope that each of these chapters in its own way will provide a good starting off point for those about to put their toes in the water.

The contributions to Part Four are very different—both from each other and from what has gone before. We recognized from the outset that the political, economic, intellectual, and research training context had changed dramatically over the last quarter of a century: but that nevertheless the new generation of researchers—in so many ways more sophisticated and certainly better prepared than the generations before them—experienced the same kinds of problems as they came to terms with the research process and what it meant to them as upwardly mobile academics and as people. We took soundings on what were some of the more interesting pieces of research recently completed, mostly for PhD or immediately post-doctoral research, and asked this new, or newer, generation of scholars to reflect specifically on the experience of turning what they had read in books into the reality of research on the ground. In selecting contributions for Part Four we had a mind partly to plug some of the substantive gaps earlier in the book, and partly to try to obtain representative coverage of the kind of work that was currently being undertaken. We hope that their recent and often vividly described experiences will demonstrate to would-be researchers: the excitement, the loneliness, the ups and downs, but in the end the sheer satisfaction of doing research as one moves from principles to practice.

OVERVIEW

In the first chapter of Part One Tony Bottoms takes up the challenge of exploring the relationship between theory and research in criminology. He quotes a
colleague who commented that:

Far too many of my graduate students over the years have had difficulty in reaching for
a theoretical perspective with which they could make sense of what they have done after
the event, let alone guide them before or during the research process.

There is no doubt that for many postgraduate research students getting to grips
with theoretical concerns is a daunting task, and, as Bottoms notes, 'an
impatience with theory from those wanting simply to "get on with the job" of
reducing crime, or of running a just and efficient criminal justice system' can
certainly act as a deterrent for large numbers of professional researchers. A
recurring theme elsewhere in this book, but developed particularly by Rod
Morgan in Chapter Two, is the extent to which the Home Office, as the largest
funder of, and the largest customer for, criminological research, dictates the
research agenda, and it should come as no surprise that that agenda is couched
in practical, policy-relevant concerns rather than in terms of the theoretical
development of an academic discipline. But, as Bottoms rightly points out,
'there are no theory-neutral facts' and once one has grasped this then 'virtually
no issue is so trivial as to be without the potential for fruitful theoretical
reflection if one approaches it aright'. As he and his colleagues have shown in
their own research, the practical concerns of officials with the problem of
control in prisons, for example, can be reconceptualized in terms of theories
of order and legitimacy with benefits both to our theoretical understanding of
what goes on in prisons and for prisons policy. In the long run that must always
be the case. The problem with the funding of much research today is that there
is no long run. Even so there is probably no research so short-lived, small-scale,
or so defined in practical terms that it could not be sharpened by reference to
some theoretical framework.

Moreover, the process is two way. Bottoms contends, in ways that we fully
endorse, that there is a real world available for observation and that theoretical
criminologists, even at the most general level and no matter how impatient they
become with the minutiae of empirical research, have to grapple with the
theory/research relationship because ultimately all theory is connected with
the empirical world. And, as Morgan notes, the real difference between British
criminology and its European counterparts is that British empirical research
has thrown up an extraordinary wealth of data with which British theoreticians
can and do have to interact. European theorizing on crime problems tends to be
more abstract precisely because there is a lack of data with which to connect.

Bottoms argues that there are real grounds for optimism about the future of criminological research because there have been major advances in our understanding of the relationship between theory and research. After a discussion of the common obstacles that get in the way of a serious confrontation with the problems of relating theory to research (and vice versa), Bottoms reviews some lessons to be drawn from the ways in which different kinds of criminologists have conceptualized the theory/research relationship. He then develops a more formal exposition of the theory research/relationship through an attempted reconciliation of the hypothetico-deductive logic of Merton and the inductive grounded theory of Glaser and Strauss using a version of Layder's adaptive theory. In a well worked out example of the approach, though in fact it predated Layder's formulation, Bottoms provides a vivid demonstration of the interaction between theory and research in the field of environmental criminology which could well serve as a model for research in other areas of the field. One of the most intriguing elements in Bottoms' contribution is his illustration of the way in which empirical research can be brought to bear even on normative theories.

In delineating the extent to which the Home Office has become the dominant player in criminological research, Morgan raises important questions about the way in which research is commissioned, particularly the need for wider publicity, greater transparency, and perhaps above all a strong peer review process if the best research is to be done and the best value is to be gained. Nevertheless, he notes that some strong element of political control of state-funded research is inevitable and has always been present. At the same time, he notes that there are a number of ways in which research can be carried out without funding and without formal access, simply because some elements of crime and the criminal justice process are open to public view. He also points out that there are several other sources of funding—apart from the Home Office and Economic and Social Research Council (ESRC)—which are relatively untapped.

In Part Two of the book contributors attempt to cover the variety of approaches to research on crime, criminals, and victims. Pat Mayhew, one of the principal architects of the distinguished British Crime Survey, and a pioneer of the rather more difficult, and perhaps even dubious, art of conducting international crime surveys, writes as a researcher whose career has been spent within what was originally the Home Office Research Unit and, after various reorganizations, has become the Home Office Research, Development and Statistics Directorate. Her comprehensive review of the possible purposes of victim surveys is followed by a consideration of methodological issues. There is no doubt that one of the most important sources of data to which Morgan referred and about which British criminologists can theorize to their hearts' content has been the British Crime Survey. Consideration is now being given to whether its regular sweeps should become annual. Yet there is an inherent dilemma at the centre of the crime survey rationale: on the one hand there is a natural desire on the part of researchers to revise and refine their questions, not least to take account of what previous sweeps have shown, but on the other hand the 'trend line' is one of its major strengths, especially as counting rules for police classifications change. Large-scale national surveys require large-scale resources, the more so in the light of developments such as computer assisted personal interviewing (CAPI) which has been used in the last three sweeps of the BCS. But if national surveys are likely to remain beyond the reach of university-based researchers, local crime surveys have performed an important role in the development of British criminology, and a rather different one from national surveys, and have received a boost from the Crime and Disorder Act 1998. Mayhew discusses many of the ways in which victim surveys can be expected to contribute to future research.

As Mike Maguire points out in Chapter Four criminologists, these days, spend very little time talking to or researching street criminals—the perpetrators of small-time thefts, burglaries, assaults, vehicle crimes, and acts of vandalism which make up the bulk of offences recorded annually in Criminal Statistics. As research agendas have switched from explaining crime to the management of risk, the process of talking to criminals has become an oddly neglected art. Maguire argues for a righting of the balance and, after reviewing the main traditions of research on offenders, then writes with refreshing candour of the lessons to be learned from looking back at one's early, and often rather fumbling, apprenticeship as a criminological research worker. Some of the issues discussed by Maguire—the need to prevent research from becoming unfocused and fragmented, and the need for good and detailed contemporaneous note-taking, for example—involve lessons that can be quickly learned (and in today's climate of tighter management of funded research are less likely to happen). Others—such as how one manages a research role in relation to criminals whilst conducting appreciative, ethnographic research in real-world settings are matters which go to the heart of the research process—and on which several of the contributors to Part Four have interesting things to say.

Maguire cautions that anyone trying to repeat this kind of ethnographic research—which involved, among other things, talking to offenders in pubs and clubs—might face a more risky situation. In the world of serious professional and organized crime comprehensively reviewed by Dick Hobbs in Chapter Five it is even more difficult to study criminals in their natural settings because 'serious criminals seldom offer themselves for examination unless there is a film deal involved, and once located it must always be remembered that they are hardly obliged to tell the truth'. Once having been invited to 'fucking come and see me, fucking write about me you fucking long streak of fucking useless. . . . Professor fucking Thunderbirds Brains' Hobbs also notes that there is no requirement for such criminals to be polite. Politeness is one thing, personal safety is another. One researcher was murdered when he turned his attention from hustling to organized crime. Not surprisingly some have tried to study professional criminals from within the comparative safety of custodial environments, but such efforts all too easily switch studies of professional criminals into studies of prisoners. In a world where the political economy of crime now links street drug dealers with private armies in the Far East, and market traders with Asian sweat shops producing counterfeit designer labels, the process of differentiating serious offending into neat conceptual categories becomes a kind of academic conceit, argues Hobbs. It also means that researchers must exploit any opportunity to glean data that becomes available.

If Hobbs argues that the attempt to separate out different categories of criminals is conceptually a somewhat arbitrary process, Sandra Walklate initially wonders whether there are any serious methodological issues in researching victims of crime which are different from the mainstream of criminological research. Although interviews with victims can become highly emotionally charged and may involve a different and supportive relationship between researcher and respondent (and may sometimes raise additional ethical questions—see the discussion of Hoyle's contribution below). Walklate contends that in other respects the research questions are not unlike those in other kinds of research. After reviewing the various styles of research on victims Walklate provides an account of her own struggle to relate empirical discovery and conceptual development outside the positivist paradigm in ways that echo the discussion by Bottoms.

In Part Three contributors examine the research process within the context of research on criminal justice agencies and institutions. In a comprehensive review Robert Reiner explores research conducted on the police from within academic institutions, official government-related bodies, and think tanks and pressure groups, as well as by journalists. In an important discussion of the relationship between the researcher and the police, Reiner discusses the crucial problem of access to the police for research purposes, not just from his own position as an 'outside-outsider' but for researchers in other situations. Like other writers throughout this volume Reiner notes that access is not just negotiated once but is constantly re-negotiated throughout the research. He draws attention to the acceptable and unacceptable conditions which gatekeepers might wish to impose upon research as well as the importance for researchers to become conscious of how they might be viewed by their subjects and the impact this might have on their findings (for which purpose Reiner took to carrying index cards to note down different perceptions of himself by others). Noting the changing agenda of police research Reiner makes a plea which mirrors Maguire's, namely for more direct observational studies of police work.

If gaining access to the police is difficult and accessing professional criminals dangerous to life and limb, accessing the more hidden processes of court work and decision-making and then writing about them can prove dangerous to one's career. Ironically, the public nature of courts means that they offer a research site which requires no specially negotiated access and may not even require large-scale resources. But the real work of the courts—the way in which cases are shaped before trial, the negotiations which lead to guilty pleas, or the deliberations of the jury room or the reasons for particular sentencing decisions by judges—are hidden from public view. Special difficulties confront the research worker in accessing such processes, and in Chapter Eight, after an analysis of the main approaches which have been adopted in studying the work of the criminal courts, John Baldwin discusses his own work with Mike McConville on plea-bargaining more than twenty years ago as a case study in the politics and ethics of research. It is impossible to exaggerate the importance of guilty pleas to the functioning of the criminal courts. Baldwin and McConville's research findings—uncovered in the course of a Home Office funded study of jury trials—suggested that some innocent defendants who had been expected to go to trial had been induced, in the main by their own barristers, to plead guilty. When research findings challenge powerful vested interests the going can get very tough indeed for researchers who stick to their task. Baldwin raises important questions for researchers which are all too rarely aired in public—though others in this volume also address them—namely, to what extent can a researcher be justified in being less than candid with respondents about the objectives of a study, knowing that full disclosure would produce guarded or distorted responses. There are no easy answers, but the discussions here and elsewhere in this book provide food for thought.

George Mair, though now at Liverpool John Moores University, conducted research for some sixteen years as a member of the Home Office Research (and Planning) Unit. Not surprisingly a central question he addresses is who pays the piper? Whilst acknowledging that the Home Office has shaped the research agenda on community penalties, just as it has on other matters, he never felt that his work was subject to censorship, although on one occasion he came close to withholding his name from the title page. It would be foolish to deny that there are political pressures surrounding what is researched and what (and when) findings are published. But, as Morgan noted in Chapter Two, the Research Unit has a distinguished record of publications and its researchers are held in high international regard. Few researchers working from within the Home Office, however, can have had the same freedom which university-based researchers have been able to achieve whilst still being funded by the Home Office. Maguire and Baldwin, as we have seen, managed to have considerable freedom of action over what they were able to do, if not in the publication of Mair findings (albeit for different reasons) and King in Chapter Ten reports similar scope to develop his early research in Albany even though the Research Unit lost interest when comparative data could not easily lend support to the supposed justifications for existing policies. Though these examples are drawn from the days which long pre-dated the process of tendering for Home Office contracts Bottoms and colleagues have been able to develop prison research quite flexibly, within a general remit, from the late 1980s and into the 1990s. Nevertheless, King would argue that it helps in doing prisons research if one has independent funding from bodies such as the ESRC because prison staff are frequently as suspicious of Home Office intentions as are prisoners, and it puts the ownership of the results beyond dispute.

Mair concludes that, for the most part, research into community penalties has followed fairly mundane paths, using predictable methodologies, and with little direct impact upon policy or practice. By contrast prison research has been more innovative both in methods and in testing out theoretical approaches. In part this results from the unique situation in custodial settings whereby researchers have more or less simultaneously and more or less continuously to negotiate access to both staff and prisoners, whose complex interactions with each other typically form the subject matter under investigation. Not surprisingly Roy King pays particular attention to the considerations which affect the successful negotiation of an acceptable research role and suggests a number of nostrums for the conduct of research in prisons.

The contributions to Part Four raise many issues of interest to the neophyte researcher. Readers may notice that, whereas eight of the ten contributors to Parts One, Two, and Three of this volume are male, eight out of the ten contributors to Part Four are female (and will draw their own conclusions from that). Not surprisingly, reflections upon gender and relationships figure prominently in their accounts of research although these do not always play out in expected ways.

Julia Wardhaugh discusses the interconnections between personal biography and choice of research topic, and then, by conceptualizing participant observation as two dimensions with different degrees of 'participation' and observation ranging from the 'covert' to the 'overt', shows how it was necessary to adopt different positions in three scenarios drawn from her ethnographic research on street homelessness. Catrin Smith and Emma Wincup explore the similarities and differences in the various stages of the process of 'breaking in' to their research locations—respectively women's prisons and bail hostels for women. Working within a political and policy context which shaped both their roles and their access, they develop a provisional categorization of the kinds of relationships which they were able to establish with respondents. 'Paddy' Rawlinson addresses not just the pros and cons of being a mature student breaking into the research world of academe but also the dilemmas facing a Western woman researcher getting by in the extraordinarily intimidating research environment surrounding organized crime and its control in Russia—where managing sexuality was at a premium. The problems of managing sexuality were also at the heart of Karen Sharpe's street-corner research with prostitutes, punters, and the police—though she was as likely to be spat on by other women as she was propositioned by men. Any new researcher—and not just those working in exceptionally difficult research locations—will take comfort both from the refreshingly candid fieldnotes which Sharpe quotes to illustrate her anxieties before she was able to establish some kind of rapport, and also from the eventual outcome—though research is not for the faint-hearted.

Lyn Hancock, working under the auspices of the Leverhulme Special Research Fellowship Scheme, developed a comparative study of two inner-city neighbourhoods. Unlike the earlier work discussed by Bottoms, which compared areas in Sheffield in a series of matched pairs one of which had high crime rates and the other low crime rates, Hancock's research locations were both high crime-rate areas. Would-be researchers would do well to think through the relative merits of these contrasting approaches. In keeping with many other researchers, including Bottoms, she sought to keep the identities of both individuals and communites anonymous, though this contrasts markedly with the stance adopted by King on prisons. It may be that there is scope for further discussion about the practical and ethical implications of anonymity, and hasty commitment to politically correct codes of practice for research workers may stifle creativity in the search for respectability.

Carole Adams also had problems in relation to the management of sexuality in the conduct of her research on suspects in their dealings with the police and lawyers, and her best guesses as to the appropriateness of dressing up and dressing down for different respondents were sometimes confounded in the event. She also addresses the critical issue which no researcher can avoid, the extent to which one becomes concerned about or involved with the subjects of one's research. The fact that researchers are also people, neglected in textbooks on research methods, is stubbornly reflected in the reported experiences of almost all our contributors. Carolyn Hoyle's findings on her study of domestic violence incurred the wrath of vested interests reminiscent of the reaction to Baldwin and McConville's work on guilty pleas, except that in her case the vested interests were those of radical feminists who lacked the institutional power of the legal profession. Nevertheless, standing by one's data in the face of the onslaught of concerted criticism which attacks the person and the methods without confronting the findings can be excruciatingly uncomfortable. Hoyle's work raises crucial ethical questions about when one accepts non-response for what it is, and how far it is acceptable to be economical with the truth and perhaps even to lie in the search for otherwise unobtainable data.

Bonny Mhlanga's study of the role of ethnic factors in decisions made by the Crown Prosecution Service was conducted with the support of an Economic and Social Research Council Post Doctoral fellowship. He deployed the techniques of multivariate analysis to explore the relationship between Crown

Prosecution Service (CPS) decisions and the ethnic origins of defendants, whilst simultaneously taking into account the influence of gender, age, socio-economic status, area of residence, primary offence and those taken into consideration (TICs), and several other factors. Somewhat surprisingly the results showed that ethnic minority defendants were more likely than white defendants to receive 'favourable' outcomes from CPS lawyers. Mhlanga argues that it is necessary to think through in a theoretically informed way to potential outcomes before collecting data if one is able to make sense of them at the analysis stage, but he also argues for the need for the use of more qualitative techniques in any future research in this area to get at the reasoning of CPS lawyers in reaching their decisions. Finally, Dave Whyte speaks to a somewhat different problem from the usual concern with the Home Office hegemony over research: namely the influence of powerful, but high-risk, industries over research into health and safety. As an independent academic pursuing his doctoral research he discusses the difficulties of an outsider gaining access to managers and workers within the off-shore oil industry as well as the reluctance of officials from regulatory bodies such as the Health and Safety Executive to co-operate.

PART 1
THEORY AND POLITICS IN CRIMINOLOGY

1

THE RELATIONSHIP BETWEEN THEORY AND RESEARCH IN CRIMINOLOGY

Anthony Bottoms

INTRODUCTION

In accepting the challenge of writing a chapter on the relationship between theory and research in criminology, I am streetwise enough to know that I invite at least two lines of criticism. The first line of criticism is likely to be marshalled mainly by theoreticians, who will point out that the relationship between theory and research has been understood in many different ways by different kinds of criminologists over the decades. Such critics may then argue that there is no possibility of providing, within a chapter of this length, any adequate overall account of all the different possible ways of conceptualizing theory–research linkages in criminology, let alone some of the deeper issues that are raised by these contrasting approaches (for example, the competing epistemological and/or ontological assumptions that may be embedded within differing accounts of the theory/research relationship). As a consequence of these difficulties, the critics will go on to suggest, this chapter will almost inevitably be weighted towards the author's own understandings of the relationship between theory and research, and their own research practice (and this would be so whoever the chapter-author happened to be).

Let me say straight away that I plead guilty to these charges. A full survey of all possible ways of understanding the theory/research relationship in criminology is simply not possible within the framework of this chapter, and inevitably this does produce some weighting of the text towards my own understandings and practice. It is only fair that readers should be warned of this bias from the outset.

The second line of criticism might be raised by a rather more miscellaneous group of critics. I shall call it the 'pragmatic division of labour' criticism, and it can perhaps be reasonably characterized in the following four propositions:

i.   Doing good empirical criminological research is very difficult, and requires certain quite advanced skills and training.
ii.   Doing good theoretical criminology is also very difficult, and requires its own rather different skills and training.
iii.   Life is short, and there is no time for everyone to master everything. Moreover, human beings differ quite substantially in their skills and capabilities (for example, some who are adept at unravelling the intricacies of Michel Foucault's theoretical arguments will have no idea how to interpret the results of a multivariate statistical analysis; and the same is also true in reverse).
iv.   Therefore, let everyone do what she/he is good at, in a pragmatic division of labour, and criminology will flourish.

It is not at all difficult to empathize with some of the sentiments underpinning such arguments. It is certainly the case, for example, that people differ in their skills and aptitudes, and that no-one has all the necessary skills to be a fully rounded criminologist. Hence, there has to be some division of labour among criminologists.

And yet, I would argue, there is a significant danger in the 'pragmatic division of labour' approach, a danger that the new generation of criminologists should take very seriously. This danger can perhaps best be understood by focusing upon two key propositions which I take to be unassailable, and upon which the remainder of this chapter is founded. Key Proposition I (KP I) holds that, whether one likes it or not (and some do not like it much), some engagement with theory is inevitable if one is to practise social science (including criminology) at all. Neither the natural nor the social world can be neutrally observed and reported upon by the research analyst, for we always approach all our empirical observations through some kind of theoretical understandings. As Sir Karl Popper (1968: 107n) famously put it: 'observations . . . are always *interpretations* of the facts observed; they are *interpretations in the light of theories*' (emphasis in original). To demonstrate this point, Popper, when teaching, sometimes simply asked his lecture audience to 'observe'. The students, of course, invariably replied: 'But *what* shall we observe?', thus making Popper's point for him (see Magee 1973: 33).

But while KP I asserts that criminologists cannot avoid theory, Key Proposition II (KP II) asserts that there is indeed a real world, and that criminologists cannot avoid engagement with that world, whether they like it or not (and some do not like it much). The implication of KP I is that we always see the world only through a set of theoretical spectacles which can be called *interpretations* or *constructions*; and this has given rise to a social science approach called 'constructivism' which—up to a point, quite rightly— emphasizes the need to examine carefully the constructions or interpretations that social actors, including social scientists, bring to their observations of the natural and social world. It is not hard to see that, if taken to extremes, constructivism quickly runs into difficulties. Since all observations are, admittedly, 'constructions', some have argued that empirical research findings are therefore always simply another 'construction', with no particular claim to validity. Some constructivists have themselves not flinched from spelling out the implications of this view:

[Data] derived from constructivist inquiry have neither special status nor legitimation; they represent simply another construction to be taken into account (Guba and Lincoln 1989: 45).

A position of this kind is one that is, in epistemological terms, relativistic: that is to say, it maintains that 'there is no such thing as objective knowledge of realities independent of the knower' (Flew 1979: 281). And if one adopts epistemological relativism, there is ultimately no point in doing social science (or indeed natural science) at all. That is because, from a relativist standpoint, we can never say that theoretical account A gives a truer picture than theoretical account B of (say) how interrogations are conducted in a given police station: all we can say is that theorist A is offering one account, and theorist B another.

In contradistinction to relativism, KP II holds that there is a real world available for observation, and that we can observe it with greater or less accuracy. Although we can never make observations except through one or another pair of theoretical spectacles ('interpretations') that does not mean that we can never judge which of two interpretations is nearer the truth. To take a famous example from the British criminological literature, in the early 1980s the county of Nottinghamshire had a very high recorded crime rate, notwithstanding that it is not one of Britain's major metropolitan areas. David Farrington and Elizabeth-Ann Dowds (1985) set out to investigate whether Nottinghamshire was indeed an exceptionally criminal county. To do this, they took two comparison areas (both, like Nottinghamshire, non-metropolitan counties in the Midlands), and then carried out a victimization survey in all three areas, together with careful analyses of the recording practices of the separate police forces for the three areas. The researchers' conclusions were, in a nutshell: first, that the incidence of crime in Nottinghamshire was indeed somewhat higher than that in the other two counties, but not so much higher as the officially recorded crime figures would lead one to believe; and, secondly, that various aspects of police recording practices in Nottinghamshire had led to a higher official recording of criminal incidents than was the case in the other two counties. Farrington and Dowds's methodology, in this study, was rigorous enough to persuade criminologists from a variety of different theoretical orientations that the conclusions of the study were, broadly, to be trusted; in other words, that the account the researchers had provided of crime levels in Nottinghamshire was nearer to the truth than was the apparent message of the officially-recorded crime figures. That did not mean that Farrington and Dowds's data were in all respects 100 per cent accurate (survey data never are); and certainly their data were not based on theory-neutral observations. But the research design, and the researchers' subsequent implementation of that design, was sufficiently strong to suggest that the research results were convincing.

If (as I contend) both KP I and KP II are true, then three things follow. First, anyone attempting empirical research in criminology must inevitably grapple to some degree with the theory/research relationship, because there are no theory-neutral facts, and theory is therefore inextricably involved in the process of data-gathering and data-interpretation. But, secondly, anyone attempting to write theoretical criminology must also grapple with the theory/research relationship (even if their preference is to analyse the relevance for criminology of the so-called 'general social theorists'—Foucault, Giddens, Habermas etc.). This is because there is a real world that is available for observation and interpretation, and an important test (though not the only test) of any theoretical account will be whether it interprets that real world more accurately and convincingly than do other theoretical accounts—for which purpose, the results of empirical research will have to be taken into account by the theorist. Indeed, as Derek Layder (1998: 94) has recently and challengingly argued, 'all theory is connected with the empirical world (although variably in terms of level of abstraction), *otherwise it would not qualify as "social theory" in the first place*' (emphasis added). Thirdly, it is important to realize that acceptance of both KP I and KP II necessarily entails that there is a genuine possibility of cumulation of knowledge in criminology. I recognize that, in the current climate of social science in Britain, such a claim is contentious; but if there is a real world that is (to an extent) knowable independently of the knower, then it must be possible through careful empirical research and insightful theorization gradually to understand more about that world. Personally, I have no difficulty whatever in accepting the claim that knowledge can be cumulative, because in the course of my own professional career huge advances have been made in criminological knowledge—for example, in the fields of understanding official crime statistics, criminal careers, repeat victimization, and policing studies. Further advances in knowledge in these and other fields will certainly follow.

The preceding paragraph argues that all criminologists need to grapple to some degree with the theory/research relationship, from which it follows that the 'pragmatic division of labour' approach, in its full-blown form, is ultimately not a sustainable option (although, as previously argued, some division of labour will inevitably remain). Yet many, perhaps especially at graduate student level, will find this conclusion rather daunting, and certainly difficult. As one experienced empirically-oriented criminologist put it to me in a private note when he knew that I was preparing this chapter:

Far too many of my graduate students over the years have had difficulty in reaching for a theoretical perspective with which they could make sense of what they have done after the event, let alone guide them before or during the research process.

Looking back to earlier stages of my own academic career, I can easily recall difficulties of this kind in doing my own research. But there is good news at hand for the new generation of criminologists. In my judgement, substantial progress has been made by social scientists in the last twenty years in conceptualizing the theory/research relationship. There are, therefore, surer guiding lights available to the present generation of graduate students than existed for their predecessors. Moreover, once one really grasps that there are no theory-neutral facts, then virtually no issue is so trivial as to be without the potential for fruitful theoretical reflection if one approaches it aright. To take an example from the field of prison studies, when I was myself conducting extensive field-work in a borstal institution in my first research project (see Bottoms and McClintock 1973) I can recall being bored by some of the minutiae of the institutional regime that were fairly frequently debated in the meetings of borstal staff that I attended as a research observer. Such details, I then thought, were important for the borstal staff, but not for the criminological researcher, who must concentrate on more substantively important things (the treatment programme being offered, how inmates responded to this programme, and so on). Ironically, however, as I shall briefly indicate later in this chapter, some of my recent work in the field of prison studies (Sparks, Bottoms and Hay 1996) emphasizes the huge importance, for a theoretical understanding of prisons as institutions, of the minutiae of everyday prison routines.

The remainder of this chapter is divided into four main parts. In the first section I offer a brief discussion of some of the common obstacles faced by any criminologist wanting to treat the theory/research relationship seriously. In the second section I attempt to draw some lessons from the past, through a consideration of some of the ways that different kinds of criminologists have, historically, conceptualized the theory/research relationship. The third section provides a somewhat more formal exposition of what I take to be the key approaches to the theory/research relationship, and an attempted reconciliation of some of their main features. In the final section I offer an example of the theory/research relationship from one sphere of criminological work—environmental criminology—in which I have myself been engaged.

COMMON OBSTACLES

It might be helpful to begin with some more pragmatic observations. For the truth is that, however much lip-service is paid to the importance of the theory/research relationship, there are also powerful forces working against younger researchers as they try to develop their own understandings of the interconnections between theory and data, and to develop the skills necessary to handle these interconnections. I shall briefly deal with five of these common obstacles in this introductory section.

I. DISCIPLINARY SPECIALIZATION

The first obstacle is that, naturally enough, younger researchers wish to make their way in the world. And all too often, it seems, successful academic careers are based on narrow specialization—or at any rate, to get one's first permanent academic job one needs to present oneself as a specialist of a particular kind (for example, a theorist, or a quantitative researcher used to handling large data sets). These pressures can certainly militate against the development of a rounded understanding of theory/research relationships.

II. DISCOURAGEMENT OF THEORY BY 'PRACTICAL PEOPLE'

The second obstacle is perhaps a particular problem in the sphere of criminology. University colleagues from other academic specialisms are frequently surprised when I tell them that I give more papers to non-academic audiences than I do to specialist academic seminars or conferences; but, in the nature of the case, a whole host of non-academic people are potentially interested in what criminologists have to say (politicians, Home Office officials, judges, magistrates, police, prison staff, probation officers, victims, crime prevention panels, journalists—the list is endless). And there is undoubtedly, in many instances, an impatience with theory from those wanting simply to 'get on with the job' of reducing crime, or of running a just and efficient criminal justice system. This impatience can sometimes manifest itself in two rather different ways. The first—not without some justification in the case of some theorists—is exasperation at the complex language often employed by theoreticians, who may seem to the lay person to be spinning complex webs of words that really mean very little. The second form of impatience is that when the theorist tries to 'boil down' what he/she is trying to say in an accessible form, this may be hailed by the lay audience as 'a statement of the obvious'. Faced with such a 'double whammy', it is important not to lose one's nerve. The point is this: if social theory is to illuminate the social world, then it ultimately *has to* 'make sense' to people who inhabit that world (or at any rate, to those who inhabit that world and have their wits about them); for if it does not, then the theory is failing in its task of explanation. But once a theoretical issue is grasped by a layperson, it can indeed seem 'obvious', precisely because it does help to make sense of the lived world as experienced by that person. To avoid charges of 'stating the obvious' (and for other reasons both more and less reputable), theorists have therefore been prone to take refuge in their own special languages. To an extent, that is necessary in order to be precise in one's theorization; but it can certainly also make theory seem inaccessible to the practical person.

There are no easy solutions to these difficulties. I would, however, like to share some optimistic (though admittedly anecdotal) experiences from the recent past. I have recently been engaged in the advanced academic training of senior managers in the police and prison services (generally speaking, area commanders and equivalent in the police service; prison governors and equiva-lent in the prison service). To my surprise, when I have introduced to such groups some aspects of my own work on late modernity theory as applied to criminology (see Bottoms and Wiles 1995), or structuration theory as applied to the understanding of prison life (see Sparks, Bottoms and Hay 1996), there has been widespread interest—and certainly more interest than such topics would normally evoke from, say, Home Office officials. The reason for this contrast, I believe, is that senior Home Office officials are apt to understand the world in terms of a set of discrete analytical problems to be solved; hence, a given problem can, to an extent at least, be analysed in isolation from its wider context. By contrast, a senior manager in command of a police division or a large prison inevitably realizes that there are many *interconnections* between different parts of the complex world that they are supposed to 'manage'. They would like to have some fuller understanding of these interconnections, and that is precisely what theoretical frameworks, when adequately understood and internalized, can begin to provide.

III. PIGEONHOLING

The third obstacle to sophisticated criminological work embracing both theory and empirical data is what I shall call 'pigeonholing'. There are two versions of this—'methodological pigeonholing' and 'theoretical pigeonholing'.

By 'methodological pigeonholing', I mean the tendency to assume that cer-tain sorts of research methods 'go with' particular kinds of theoretical approach, to the exclusion of other kinds of data. So, for example, ethnographic research studies naturally use research methods of a qualitative kind, such as participant and non-participant observation, extended interviews, and so on. From within this research perspective, it is not too hard to develop the view that quantitative data are at best irrelevant, or at worst potentially misleading, because they fail adequately to reflect the real on-the-ground contexts of the meanings of social life in a given milieu. But this is unhelpful pigeonholing. In fact there is no reason at all why a primarily ethnographic study should not be assisted by quantitative data. For example, two colleagues and I pursued a qualitative sociological study of two maximum security prisons (Sparks, Bottoms and Hay 1996). There was reason to suspect, from observational and interview data in one of the prisons (which ran a deliberately 'relaxed' regime for principled reasons), that the degree of freedom afforded to the prisoners, while it had important advantages, also facilitated behaviour such as the easy formation of gangs and cliques, and the possibility of 'hidden' violence to certain inmates, carried out in one of the rather large number of poorly-supervised locations in the prison. Collection of quantitative data about recorded major incidents in the prison, about the frequency of use of alarm bells, and about head injuries treated in the prison hospital all tended to confirm the picture originally derived from qualitative sources (see Sparks, Bottoms and Hay 1996: ch. 7). An example in the reverse direction (of quantitative data-patterns about communities and crime that led on to fruitful and confirmatory ethnographic work) is given in the final section.

In my view, the mental barriers that some qualitative researchers have set up against the use of quantitative data, and the equivalent barriers set up by some quantitative researchers against qualitative research data, have been some of the most unhelpful features of the British criminological landscape in the last quarter-century. There are signs that these barriers are now being overcome; for the future health of the subject, let us hope so, since there is no justifiable reason for them.

I need say less about 'theoretical pigeonholing', by which I mean attitudes of a kind which assert or believe, explicitly or implicitly, that because a particular person adheres to a theoretical standpoint other than one's own, their writings necessarily contain little of interest. (We have all heard, in casual conversations with off-duty academics, statements of the kind that since X or Y is a Marxist/positivist/etc., they have nothing useful to say.) One might have hoped that criminologists knew enough about the unintended effects of labelling to avoid this kind of pigeonholing, but sadly this has not always been the case.

IV. ECLECTICISM AND SYNTHESIS

A further obstacle to a creative and constructive relationship between theory and empirical research comes from a confusion between eclecticism and synthesis. The confusion is usually implicit rather than explicit, but it is nevertheless very important in obstructing progress.

Theories in criminology are quite often rather partial in their coverage: we cannot, for example, seriously expect 'labelling theory' or 'strain theory' to explain all criminality, even though in certain specific circumstances such the-ories have much to offer. This limited coverage of particular theories would not matter in the least if, in criminology, there were a widespread 'culture of openness'—that is, a culture of being open to the insights offered by many theories, and being willing to consider their possible contribution to social-scientific explanation within a particular set of circumstances. Unfortunately, criminologists have not always advocated or upheld such a culture, and at least in the past there have been some unhelpful 'turf wars' between adherents of certain different theories, in which on occasion the participants have seemed more eager to score points off one another than patiently to try to explain the social phenomena under investigation.

The culture of openness advocated above could and should lead to a process of theoretical *synthesis*, that is, 'the composition or combination of parts or elements so as to form a whole' (first definition of 'synthesis' in *Longman's Dictionary of the English Language*). But good synthesis is difficult. What is much easier is a somewhat unthinking *eclecticism*. Flew's (1979) dictionary of philosophy defines eclecticism as 'the principle or practice of taking one's views from a variety of philosophical and other sources', sometimes in ways 'that make no strenuous effort to create intellectual harmony between discrete elem-ents' (p.24). So defined, eclecticism is clearly different from (and much more pragmatic than) synthesis, and some eclectic approaches are indeed intel-lectually disreputable because they do not seriously attempt 'to create intel-lectual harmony between discrete elements'. Sadly, this justified suspicion of eclecticism has too often led to an unthinking rejection of synthesising approaches.

I remain an unrepentant advocate of serious attempts at synthesis, for the reasons that I gave in a 1993 paper (Bottoms 1993: 59):

Scholars from many different intellectual traditions and nationalities have struggled with the explanation of crime; much of what they have written may now be seen as ephemeral or mistaken, but many have left valuable insights of one kind or another. Each of us, as St. Paul put it in another context, tends to 'see through a glass, darkly' (I Corinthians xiii, 12): it would be surprising, therefore, if only one of us (or one particu-lar school) had grasped the whole truth, and it would accordingly seem appropriate to seek to synthesise the valuable findings and insights of various scholars, even those of very different disciplinary backgrounds, or of different political persuasions from our own. As Anthony Giddens (1984: xxii) puts it, if ideas or data seem 'important and illuminating, what matters much more than their origin is to be able to sharpen them so as to demonstrate their usefulness, even if within a framework which might be quite different from that which helped to engender them'.

It is worth noting that in the passage quoted above, Giddens speaks of *ideas or data* that seem important and illuminating. A good synthesis seeks to weld theory and data together in an ongoing cumulative search for the truth. That is a task of a very high order; I shall discuss possible procedures for this task in a later section of this chapter.

V. THE PROBLEM OF CONCEPTUAL HEGEMONY

Even if methodological and theoretical pigeonholing is avoided, and even if a research worker is in principle happy to work towards synthesis, there remains a further obstacle that may impede the optimum development of the relationship between theory and research. I shall call this obstacle 'the problem of conceptual hegemony'.

I shall illustrate this problem from experience during a recent research project. Colleagues and I were commissioned by the Home Office to carry out a literature review on whether, and if so in what circumstances, more severe sentences deter crime. As part of our report, we wrote a section that attempted a thorough conceptual analysis of policies of general deterrence, i.e. any intendedly deterrent policy that aims to reduce future offending among the public at large through fear of the possible consequences (von Hirsch *et al.* 1999, section 3). Within that analysis, we emphasized that deterrence, based as it is on fear as the motive for avoiding a given action, is a *subjective* concept;[1] and we then set out five conditions that we argued are *stipulative* (i.e. logically necessary) for the successful achievement of marginal general deterrence in an individual case. To give a flavour, the first of these five conditions was said to be that where an intendedly general deterrent policy has been freshly introduced, 'a potential offender must realise that the probability of conviction or the severity of punishment has changed'.

Some of the most sophisticated recent studies of general deterrence have been conducted by econometricians (for references, see von Hirsch *et al.* 1999: section 6). Econometricians work with aggregate data, and, as we pointed out in our report:

general deterrence, as a policy aim, is designed to produce an *aggregate* crime-preventive effect . . . Thus a net deterrent effect may be achievable even if only a portion of the intended audience alters its behaviour through fear of the consequences— provided that the effect on this group suffices to reduce the offence rate, and provided also that there are no substantial countervailing effects (von Hirsch *et al.* 1999: 6).

We asked an econometrician friend to look at our draft report. He had no difficulty with our emphasis on aggregate effects, but he could see no purpose in the stress on the subjective character of deterrence. His intellectual training

---

[1] To be more precise: 'Criminal deterrence (being concerned with fear of penal consequences) is subjective in two senses. First, it depends not on what the certainty and severity of punishment actually are but on what potential offenders *believe* that they are . . . Second, criminal deterrence depends not only on what potential offenders believe the sanction risks to be, but on how they evaluate those risks in terms of their subjective disutilities' (von Hirsch *et al.* 1999: 6, emphasis in original).

was to work in a certain way, using certain models and approaches: to him, therefore, studying deterrence was a question of looking for aggregate effects. Without being in any way hostile to other approaches to the subject, he initially could not see the point of them. He certainly did not expect us to reply, as we did, that in our view the subjective character of general deterrence was ultimately more fundamental for the research analyst than is the fact that general deterrence policies are designed to produce aggregate effects (see generally von Hirsch *et al.* 1999).

Our econometrician colleague was not alone. All of us, as researchers, have our preconceptions and preoccupations that can produce conceptual hegemonies, and corresponding blind spots. That is why the early exposure to others of one's preliminary research findings and tentative theorizing, in a non-threatening atmosphere, can often be so very beneficial to the constructive development of research.

LESSONS FROM THE PAST

In this section, I shall attempt—necessarily very briefly and perhaps therefore a little crudely—to sketch how, historically, various kinds of criminologists have dealt with the theory/research relationship. From this rapid survey, some helpful leads for the creative linking of theory and research can, I think, be developed.

CLASSICISM

Classicism is, perhaps, the earliest kind of criminology that is still seriously read as a potential contribution to contemporary debates. The most celebrated classicist authors are Cesare Beccaria and Jeremy Bentham, as between whom there are not only many similarities, but also important differences (see Hart 1982). Classicists were essentially political theorists, writing about the principles that should govern how crime is to be dealt with by the state (on classicism see, for example, Radzinowicz 1966: ch. 1). There is thus, within classicism, an important reminder that 'crime', as a concept, is not simply descriptive of a certain kind of human behaviour (as is, for example, the concept of 'running'). Rather, by defining a given behaviour as a 'crime', a society attaches to that behaviour an important element of *societal censure* (see Sumner 1990); and the acts that are censured in this way can and do vary from society to society, and in any one society over time. Thus, crime is ultimately a *normative category*, and significant debates can be, and need to be, generated in any given society not only about what kinds of conduct ought to be defined as 'criminal' (the content of the criminal law); but also about the processes by which alleged crimes ought to be investigated and proved (criminal procedure) and, if proved, punished (penology). Classicists excelled at this kind of normative theorization, but they also sometimes made empirical assertions, some (though by no means all) of which were later shown to be false. These empirical assertions were not based on any kind of systematic research, but rather upon common-sense observations and armchair reflections. Thus, classicists' understanding of the relationship between theory and research was by modern standards deficient, because they carried out no empirical research. But their emphasis upon systematic normative theorization is something to which contemporary criminology could very usefully return.

NATURAL SCIENCE-BASED POSITIVISM

In the second half of the nineteenth century, the successes of natural science and engineering were everywhere apparent (from Darwin to the railway network, audacious bridge-building, and advances in medical science). Not surprisingly, bold pioneers in psychology, psychiatry, and sociology sought to apply the natural-scientific approach to the study of human behaviour. At that date, 'the natural scientific approach' was defined as including a strong emphasis on *observations*, a *neutral* and *dispassionate* approach on the part of the scientist, and an assumption that *causal laws* of behaviour could be discovered (in short, *positivism*). In what was to become a very famous aphorism, contrasting the positivists with their classicist predecessors, it was declared that 'the classical school bade men study justice, but the positivists bade justice study men' (see Radzinowicz 1999: 19). In other words, the positivists insisted that the classicists' armchair theorization would no longer serve. Criminologists must get out into the world, and study criminals, criminal areas, and criminal justice scientifically; and policymakers must then take serious account of what the criminologists had found.

When I began to study criminology in the early 1960s, the specific theories of Cesare Lombroso (the first major criminological positivist) were long since discredited, but Lombroso was still widely revered as the founder of the so-called 'scientific approach' to criminology, then the dominant paradigm in the field. Many of the approaches to the study of criminology that have developed since the late 1960s have been a reaction of one sort or another to positivism; and, since that is the case, it is worth spelling out in some detail here the main assumptions of this so-called 'scientific approach'. These can be characterized as follows:

i.   It was assumed that the methods of natural science could and should be unproblematically applied to the social world (while making allowance, of course, for the fact that the context was empirically different). Since such methods were taken to include assumptions of determinist causation, it was assumed that human behaviour should be studied within a determinist framework.

ii. It was assumed that the foundation of all science, natural and social, was 'sense-data', i.e. facts that could be observed with our senses. Such sense-data were assumed to be directly accessible to the scientific observer, who would report on them dispassionately. Thus, the bedrock of science was theory-neutral facts, carefully collected by the scientist. These foundations to knowledge ('real facts') were seen as much surer than the 'metaphysical speculations' of the classicists.

iii. It was assumed that there was a sharp distinction between 'facts' and 'values'. The former were open to scientific observation and verification; the latter were not, but were instead dependent upon 'taste' or personal preferences. Indeed, in philosophical circles influenced by scientific positivism it was in the 1950s and early 1960s quite a commonly-held view that rational discussion about substantive moral principles was impossible. Together with the emphasis on empirical observation (see above), all this represented a complete break with the assumptions of the classicists (whose work was therefore sometimes characterized, in derogatory tone, as 'pre-scientific').

iv. Positivism had an admitted difficulty with the concept of 'crime', given that what was 'criminal' in a given society was defined by those in power, and that societies differed, sometimes markedly, in what kinds of behaviour they defined as 'crimes'. All this seemed to be very far from the stable and 'natural' *explanandum* (phenomenon to be explained) apparently required for a fully 'natural-scientific' criminology. This important difficulty was usually evaded by positivists through an intellectual fudge to the effect that only some kinds of crimes (murder, theft, etc.) constituted the core subject-matter of criminology, and that these were the 'natural crimes', in contradistinction to other kinds of 'administrative' crimes.

v. Because of its desire to follow as closely as possible the methods of the natural sciences, positivist criminology that focused on the explanation of criminal behaviour was and is primarily concerned 'with how accurate facts can be obtained and how theory can thereby be more rigorously tested' (Glaser and Strauss 1967: 1). That is to say, the ideal research method was seen as an initial collection of facts, the formulation—by logical processes—of a theory in the shape of a formal hypothesis, and then the rigorous testing of that hypothesis, to verify or falsify it. If a modified hypothesis then seemed necessary in the light of the results of the first testing, then that hypothesis (Hypothesis B) was formulated and formally tested—and so on. This is a process that has been aptly described

as the *hypothetico-deductive approach*, and I shall have more to say about it
in the next main section of this chapter.

vi.   Not all criminological research, of course, is concerned with the explan-
      ation of criminal behaviour; for example, quite a lot of it is concerned
      with evaluating the success or otherwise of various criminal justice inter-
      ventions such as community policing or intendedly rehabilitative pro-
      grammes in prisons. True to their core beliefs, positivist criminologists
      turned once again to natural science to provide a model for their evalu-
      ative work, and this was found especially in the 'clinical trial' experimental
      method widely used in scientific medicine. So positivists advocated, for
      example, the random allocation of research subjects as between two
      'treatments' (e.g. intensive probation and ordinary probation), in an
      endeavour to eliminate spurious outcomes resulting from pre-treatment
      differences between the experimental and the control groups. (For advo-
      cacy of the random allocation method in criminological evaluation, see
      for example Farrington 1983).
vii. The positivists' preference for methods akin to the natural sciences, for the
      hypothetico-deductive approach to explanatory research, and for the
      experimental method in evaluative research, all combined to produce a
      powerful preference for quantitative over qualitative data.

Every one of the above assumptions has been questioned, often heavily, in post-
1970 criminology. Space precludes any detailed treatment, but let a few things
be said quickly. It is now widely held that social science is not the same as
natural science, essentially because its subjects are human beings who can
attribute meaning to the situations in which they are placed, and may therefore
react to and possibly alter those situations (see, e.g., Giddens 1984). Theory-
neutral sense-data are now seen as impossible to obtain (see the introduction to
this chapter). There has been a major revival in normative theorization about
the political and moral worlds since 1970, beginning with the work of Rawls on
the concept of justice (see, e.g., Rawls 1972; Skinner 1990). On any objective view,
'crime' has to be seen as a non-natural category of behaviour, crucially
definitionally dependent on the censuring processes of a given society. The
hypothetico-deductive approach to explanation, and the positivists' preference
for quantitative data, were both frontally challenged by Glaser and Strauss as
long ago as 1967 (see further below). And the intellectual hegemony of the
experimental and quasi-experimental approach to evaluation research, though
it has lasted longer in mainstream criminology than have most of the legacies of
positivism, has recently been powerfully challenged by Pawson and Tilley 1997
(see further below). None of the above remarks should be taken to mean that
the positivist paradigm in criminology is dead, for it manifestly is not. But the
paradigm is unquestionably much more severely open to question than it was

in, say, 1965. We thus now need to sketch briefly some of the alternative theoretical approaches that have been developed, with special reference to their differences from positivism, and also to their understanding of the theory/research relationship.

But a final word about positivism needs to be added. In some criminological circles, the term 'positivism' is now never used without strongly pejorative connotations. This is descriptively unhelpful, but more importantly it can serve to deflect attention from the strengths of the so-called 'scientific approach' in criminology. Whatever the defects of positivism (and it has many), it has bequeathed to contemporary criminologists a fine tradition of careful observation of the natural and social worlds, and a tradition also of the scientist's duty to report his/her research data dispassionately, even if he/she finds them personally unwelcome. For those of us who argue that there is an external world which is in principle capable of being described (albeit not without difficulties), these are important legacies.

ACTIVE-SUBJECT SOCIALLY-ORIENTED CRIMINOLOGIES

Stuart Henry and Dragen Milovanovic (1996: 17–18) have suggested a very useful way of classifying mainstream criminological theories, along two dimensions. In the first dimension, theories are characterized according to the extent that they view human beings as *active subjects* (that is, do they have the capacity to create and shape their own world, or are they constrained and determined in their behaviour by their individual biology and upbringing and/or by the social world that surrounds them?). In the second dimension, theories are characterized according to whether they see human behaviour as primarily *individual* or primarily *social*. Each of these dimensions is perhaps best understood as a continuous distribution, but for heuristic purposes both can be usefully treated as dichotomies. When this is done, mainstream criminological theories are seen as divided into four principal types, namely: (i) active-subject individually-oriented theories; (ii) active-subject socially-oriented theories; (iii) passive-subject individually-oriented theories; and (iv) passive-subject socially-oriented theories. The positivist tradition, in its various manifestations, is of course the main—although not the only—exemplar of the third and fourth ('passive subject') types.[2] The first and second types, however, require further discussion. I will start with the second type (active-subject socially-oriented criminologies), since it is from this tradition that some of the sharpest challenges to positivism have been articulated. Within this kind of criminology, I

---

[2] Positivism is often understood to be associated particularly with an individually oriented approach. It is therefore important to emphasize that, in the history of criminology, there have been a number of socially-oriented positivist approaches, including for example strain theory, subcultural theories, and functionalism.

shall focus especially upon the contributions of the ethnographic approach, and of social constructivism.

There is a long and distinguished tradition of ethnographic work of a criminological kind; for example, in the inter-war period members of the Chicago School of Sociology famously championed the ethnographic tradition, and their work included some criminological research, especially by Clifford Shaw. This earlier tradition was drawn upon in the revival of ethnographic work in criminology that took place as the hegemony of positivist criminology was increasingly threatened after the mid-1960s (for a seminal text, see Matza 1969; for examples of subsequent British criminological work of an ethnographic kind, see for example Foster 1990, Rock 1993).

By comparison with positivism, ethnography has very different emphases in three particular respects. First and most obviously, its preference is for carefully-nuanced reportage, based on deep immersion in the life-worlds of the subjects being studied; hence ethnography has a preference (usually a strong preference) for qualitative rather than quantitative data. Secondly and relatedly, ethnography places much more emphasis than does positivism on the meaning of social actions to actors, and on their detailed understandings of particular social contexts. Thirdly, therefore, the ethnographic approach emphatically rejects the view that social science can be studied in the same way as natural science, for the phenomena studied in natural science do not attribute meaning to their life-worlds as human beings do. These three attributes of the ethnographic approach all contain important correctives to the positivist tradition. They lead, collectively, to a particular strength of the ethnographic tradition, rarely found in other kinds of criminology; namely, its ability to uncover some of the deep cultural meanings and normative bonds which are often so important in everyday social life.

As regards the theory/research relationship, it has to be said that writers in the ethnographic tradition are generally speaking rather suspicious of theoretical generalizations. For them, the particular contexts of specific social situations are all-important, and they therefore tend sometimes to have difficulty in generalizing from these particulars. In so far as they do generalize, they have a strong preference for the *inductive* rather than the *deductive* approach to theory-construction: that is to say, they prefer to build theory 'upwards' from an understanding of specific social situations, rather than formally testing hypotheses (the 'inductive *vs.* deductive' debate is more fully considered in the next main section).

The social constructivist approach is often in practice closely linked to ethnography. However, for analytical purposes at least, it is worth separating the two. Ethnography differs from positivism especially in emphasizing the meaning content of actions to actors. Social constructivism shares that view, but takes it further, pointing out that each of us has frames of understanding within which we view the natural and social worlds, and emphasizing the need to 'unpack' carefully each actor's framework of understanding. Everyone has had the experience of watching a particular social event or action, and then realizing that the event has been understood completely differently by a different observer. (This is perhaps most familiar in situations where a child and an adult together watch a situation developing.) The social constructivist stresses the need to understand ('deconstruct') carefully the 'social constructions' which each of us uses in observing and participating in social life. 'By being witness to the day-to-day reasoning of their research subjects, by engaging in their life-world, by participating in their decision-making' (Pawson and Tilley 1997: 21), as well as by careful interviewing of the research subjects about their understandings of the world, a detailed picture of actors' 'social constructions' can be assembled. Thus, social constructivism differs from positivism especially in denying the existence of theory-neutral facts, and in seeking to deconstruct the world-views through which different social actors view particular events and activities.

In the introduction to this chapter it was noted that social constructivism could sometimes develop into an unhelpful position of epistemological relativism. While such views must be vigorously contested, there is much to be gained from milder versions of social constructivism. The challenge, which I shall take up later in this chapter, is to incorporate such insights into a non-relativistic intellectual framework within which the cumulative generation of knowledge remains possible.

ACTIVE-SUBJECT INDIVIDUALLY-ORIENTED CRIMINOLOGIES

In the 1980s and 1990s, a number of versions of active-subject individually-oriented criminology have come to the fore. These criminologies are similar to the ethnographic approach in emphasizing that human beings make real choices, rather than being seen (as in the positivist tradition) as simply the end-product of various biological, familial, and social forces and influences working upon them. But this kind of criminology nevertheless differs markedly from ethnography in emphasizing primarily the reasoning/rational dimensions of human decision-making, rather than normative bonds and cultural contexts. In this respect, active-subject individually-oriented criminologies resemble the classical tradition of Beccaria and Bentham, and it is because of this that they are sometimes referred to as 'neo-classical' approaches.[3]

Three main strands within this kind of criminology can usefully be distinguished. The first is the economic approach to crime and punishment, which has been built upon a seminal article by the leading economist Gary Becker

[3] It is, however, important to distinguish these kinds of neo-classical explanatory approaches from neo-classical normative theorizing in criminology, such as desert theory.

(1968). (For references to more recent works in this tradition, see for example Pyle 1995.) The second strand is rational choice theory, which has itself developed in part out of the now extensive body of work on 'situational crime prevention' (see generally Clarke 1995; Cornish and Clarke 1986). The third strand is 'routine activities theory', which has many similarities with, but also some important differences from, rational choice theory (see Felson 1998; Clarke and Felson 1993).

All three of these strands have made important contributions to criminology. They have demonstrated beyond reasonable doubt that subjects' choices can sometimes be read as containing elements of prudential rationality. This can often be seen most clearly using aggregate data, from which prudential rationality can be inferred—for example, in an early study which showed that vandalism by bus passengers occurred much more frequently on the (unsupervised) upper deck. The situational crime prevention and routine activities approaches have also brought firmly to criminologists' attention the role of opportunity in the ætiology of crime; and, conversely, that if opportunities are restricted then reductions in criminality will often take place (see the discussion in Clarke 1995). These advances, however, have been made at the cost of a somewhat decontextualized view of the human subject, as for example the ethnographic work of Wright and Decker (1994) on active burglars has clearly demonstrated. Similarly, the routine activities approach has strongly emphasized choices made at the site (or potential site) of a criminal act, but it has to a very large extent ignored the biographical histories and social understandings of the potential offenders who might actually be faced with such choices.

There is thus a paradox within much active-subject individually-oriented criminology, and it is one that is perhaps of special importance to the subject matter of this chapter. These criminologies stress the importance of the active subject, but—with some honourable exceptions—they often show a real reluctance to investigate in detail the actual choices made by the active subject within specific social contexts. The explanation of this paradox is not hard to uncover: for if one incorporates into one's theoretical approach a presupposition of rationality, then it can very easily be assumed that that presupposition does not itself require empirical investigation. That is especially likely to be the case when some empirical research (notably aggregate research) clearly suggests that this presupposition of rationality contains at least some validity.[4] The justified stress on the reasoning subject within this kind of criminology (an emphasis not available in most other criminological traditions) thus may have an unfortunate tendency to inhibit empirical research on the ways in which subjects' more abstract and prudential reasoning processes may interact with

---

[4] This, of course, is why the discipline of economics has built its analyses primarily upon rational choice models. The over-simplicity of such models has, however, led to criticisms within the field of economics itself: see, for example, the work of Paul Ormerod (1994, 1998).

other features of their lives, such as the structural and cultural contexts which they inhabit.

POLITICAL-ACTIVIST CRIMINOLOGIES

Anyone acquainted with the development of criminology in Britain since 1970 will be aware that many proffered analyses have been quite explicitly politically-activist in their approach to their subject matter. This is most obviously true of Marxist-oriented criminologies, feminist criminologies, and the theoretical movement known as 'left-realism' (on which see Young 1997).

This category of criminology overlaps with Henry and Milovanovic's four-fold typology of mainstream criminologies, because—as these authors make clear—political-activist criminologies can be (i) active-subject socially-oriented (as is, for example, left realism), (ii) active-subject individually-oriented (liberal feminism), and even (iii) passive-subject socially-oriented (some versions of Marxism). From the point of view of the present chapter, there are however some distinct points to be made by drawing specific attention to political-activist criminologies, since the explicit element of political activism within such theories obviously raises some rather special issues about the relationship between theory and research in criminology.

Part of the strong legacy of positivism to British (and other) criminology has been a deep suspicion, in many 'mainstream' criminological circles, about any kind of political or moral engagement on the part of criminologists. (Within the positivist tradition, such an engagement was, as we have seen, denigrated as 'unscientific'.) That view must however now be regarded as unsustainable. For the concept of 'crime' itself, and the kind of criminal justice system that a given society develops, must necessarily be the product of political and moral choices. Moreover, even the most careful, dispassionate, and rigorous criminological research can have political consequences. As Henry and Milovanovic (1996: 7) point out, the often suggested dualism between 'theory' and 'practice' is in certain respects intrinsically false, since, as Paulo Freire (1972: 77) put it, 'there is no true word that is not at the same time a praxis. Thus, to speak a true word is to transform the world'. Or perhaps we should more modestly say: 'to speak a true word is *potentially* to transform the world'.

Political-activist criminology thus has the major merit of reminding us that doing research and theory in criminology is itself inevitably linked to the political landscape, whether the criminologist likes this or not (see further the chapter by Rod Morgan in this volume). In that sense, political-activist criminology returns criminology to its roots in classicism, where the normative dimensions of the subject were explicitly emphasized. Doing criminology, in short, necessarily entails some engagement with normative issues, and it is for that reason that a brief discussion of normative theory is included later in this chapter.

The above comments, however, do not mean that all political-activist criminology is to be celebrated. For, as Key Proposition II claims, there is a real
world available for observation, and we can observe it with greater or less
accuracy. And very often, political-activist criminologies make *empirical assertions* in support of their chosen cause (they are indeed more or less obliged to
do so, since in the modern world many people will be unconvinced by a given
moral/political case unless it is supported by empirical data as well as moral/
political argument). Those empirical assertions then need to be rigorously
tested, in exactly the same way as other empirical assertions—as do the
counter-assertions of an empirical kind offered by moral/political opponents of
the original activists. Any criminologist with any length of experience will have
seen examples of political advocacy (perhaps by a criminal justice pressure
group) where inconvenient empirical data are temporarily 'forgotten', or even
where strong empirical assertions are made in an attempt to forward the political cause, notwithstanding a distinctly weak empirical base to the argument.
Even professional criminologists have been known to engage in this kind of
tactic. But to move in this direction is dangerous, for it can, at worst, subordin-
ate scholarship to political goals. And to do this is to move decisively and
disastrously away from the search for truth. Many will remember John Rawls's
argument on the opening page of his classic book on justice:

Justice is the first virtue of social institutions, as truth is of systems of thought. A theory
however elegant and economical must be rejected or revised if it is untrue; likewise laws
and institutions no matter how efficient and well-arranged must be reformed or abolished if they are unjust (Rawls 1972: 3).

This passage is most often cited for its emphasis on the primacy of justice
within normative debates; but in every way as important is Rawls's emphasis on
the primacy of truth as a criterion when one is seeking to explain the natural
and social worlds.

AN OVERVIEW

Table 1.1 attempts to summarize much of the argument of this section, by giving
an overview of some of the principal features—positive and negative—of the
five kinds of criminology that the section has examined. If the arguments so far
presented have merit, then obviously in thinking about the relationship
between theory and research in criminology we will wish particularly to make
use of, and perhaps to develop, the various items listed in the column headed
'Positive Features'. At this point in the argument, however, we need to remember the previously-made distinction between eclecticism and synthesis. Simply
selecting items from the 'Positive Features' column, and jamming them
together in a random fashion, will not constitute a synthesis. We will need some

Table 1.1: Summary of Some Positive and Negative Features of Five Approaches to Criminology

		Positive Features	*Negative Features*
1.	Classicism.	Emphasis on the normative dimension within criminology.	No empirical research.
2.	Natural science-based positivism.	Careful and precise observations.	Assumption of equivalence of natural and social science.
		Scientific detachment.	Assumption of theory-neutral facts.
			Weak ability to handle the normative dimension within criminology.
3.	Active-subject socially-oriented criminologies.	No assumption of theory-neutral facts.	Sometimes shies away from theoretical generalizations.
		Careful observations based on immersion in the social world.	Can relapse into relativism.
		Emphasis on meaning of social actions to actors and especially on cultural/normative social bonds.	
		Emphasis on need to deconstruct actors' frames of reference.	
4.	Active-subject individually-oriented criminologies.	Emphasis on reasoning powers of subjects, and of constraints on individual action.	Over-emphasis on individual rational choice; decontextualization of human subjects.
5.	Political-activist criminologies.	Emphasis that research and knowledge is itself part of a political process.	Political goals can override search for truth.

principled and defensible procedures for synthesis, and it is this kind of problem that the next section addresses.

THE THEORY/RESEARCH RELATIONSHIP: SOME KEY APPROACHES

In some ways, this section constitutes the heart of the chapter, since it is the section within which the relationship between theory and research is most formally considered. But the space available necessarily means that I cannot here engage in a full and formal treatment of these important matters; and in any case, my expertise lies in the doing of criminological research rather than in specialist consideration of methodological issues. I shall, accordingly, here simply flag a number of key topics arising from the formal literature on the theory/ research relationship, with appropriate pointers to more specialist sources for further reading.

GENERAL SOCIAL THEORIES

Let me begin with what I shall call 'general social theory' (or 'GST').[5] This is the kind of theory that usually most interests and excites theoretical criminologists, but unfortunately, at least until recently, it has often seemed remote and baffling to empirical researchers, with the result that they have not mined the resources of this kind of theory as fully as might have been expected. It is to be hoped that the new generation of criminological researchers will develop this important linkage much more fully in the future.

A 'general social theory' has been usefully described by Layder as a theoretical approach that 'has a very broad explanatory remit and concerns itself *either* with whole societies and the processes involved in their development, *or* with very general aspects of social reality such as the relationship between agency and structure or macro and micro levels of analysis' (Layder 1998: 14, emphasis added). A good example of general social theory that is well known to criminologists can be found in the work of Michel Foucault. Although he sometimes wrote on directly criminological issues (most famously the prison: see Foucault 1979), it is clear both from his major writings themselves and from interviews that Foucault was less concerned with crime and punishment *per se*

---

[5] There is no agreed terminology for this kind of theory. The term 'grand theory' is sometimes used, but (in English anyway) this has unhelpfully pejorative undertones. 'Macro-level theory' is another possibility, but this misleadingly suggests that GST has nothing to say about micro-social phenomena. 'General social theory' is an adaptation of Layder's (1998) 'general theory'.

than he was with broad issues of power, the diffusion of disciplinary mechanisms throughout social systems, and so forth; and these matters are themselves understood within some rather special epistemological frameworks. Like most general social theorists, Foucault adopts a number of terms that have a special meaning within the totality of his theoretical scheme: these include, for example, the concept of 'discipline' itself, the concept of 'the examination' (see Foucault 1979: 184–94), and, in his later works, the concept of 'governmentality' (see Burchell, Gordon and Miller 1991; Garland 1997).

Of course, many other GST approaches have been of interest to criminologists. David Garland's (1990) *Punishment and Modern Society*, for example, in setting out 'to provide a rounded sociological account of punishment in modern society', explored the Durkheimian, Weberian, and Marxist traditions in social theory, as well as the work of Foucault and other more modern writers. In recent years, the GST approaches that have been most drawn upon in criminological work are perhaps Marxism (of various types), feminism (of various types), critical theory, psychoanalytic theory (from Freud to Lacan), Giddens's 'structuration theory', poststructural theories (including Foucault), and various theories of 'late modernity' and 'postmodernity' (on which see Henry and Milovanovic 1996).

GST approaches have sometimes been dismissed as being too ethereal, and too far removed from everyday realities, to be of any practical value to the empirical researcher (see, e.g., Gregson 1989). But, in my judgement, to take this view is a serious mistake. For example, some general social theories are (see above) particularly concerned with 'whole societies and the processes involved in their development', and it must obviously be the case that any GST with useful insights into the nature of a given 'whole society' might contain ideas that can be fruitfully employed (or adapted) to analyse particular structures or processes within that society. Other GSTs are concerned to analyse 'very general aspects of social reality such as the relationship between agency and structure', and again it is likely that such theories, if they contain true insights, could have considerable potential for enriching many research projects, even those that at first glance appear to be severely practical and policy-oriented.

By way of a concrete example of some ways in which general social theory can enrich empirical research, let me briefly describe the use that colleagues and I made of Giddens's (1984) 'structuration theory' in a Home Office-funded research project on issues of control and order in two long-term maximum-security prisons. The central brief of our research was 'to describe accurately and to explain the nature of control problems [in long-term prisons] and the conditions leading to their emergence' (Sparks, Bottoms and Hay 1996: 98). To tackle this problem, we decided to focus on the issue of *how day-to-day order is maintained* in a maximum-security prison, reasoning that this would give us a better theoretical base from which to understand how specific 'control problems' (in the Home Office's language) might emerge. Although we wrote our technical report for the Home Office with virtually no mention of structuration theory, we had from an early point in the research been intrigued by at least two matters which increasingly seemed to us to link up with Giddens's GST approach. These were, first, an awareness that 'the complexity and refinement of what prison officers do often goes unremarked because there seems to be no vocabulary for talking about it' (Sparks, Bottoms and Hay 1996: 73); and secondly, that in the prison *everyday routines* seemed to play a key part in the maintenance of order, notwithstanding that they had been largely neglected by many (though not all) earlier prison sociologists. These two issues, it seemed to us, linked respectively to Giddens's concept of 'practical consciousness' (which 'consists of all the things that actors know tacitly about how to "go on" in the contexts of social life without being able to give them direct discursive expression': Giddens 1984: xxiii); and to Giddens's emphasis on routine activity 'as crucial both to the reproduction of social life, and to the fending away of personal anxiety and insecurity' (Bottoms, Hay and Sparks 1990: 86). From these beginnings, we then attempted a more wide-ranging and systematic assessment of how structuration theory might play a part in the explanation of the maintenance of order in prisons (Sparks, Bottoms and Hay 1996: 69–84), though structuration theory was never our only theoretical resource in this quest.

Yet despite these kinds of constructive possibility, there are some real potential difficulties which the empirical researcher might encounter when considering the relevance of any given GST for his/her research problem. One possible strategy for such a researcher might be described as that of 'wholesale adoption', that is, a decision 'to employ the whole package of concepts and underlying assumptions [of a given GST] to provide a ready-made "explanation" of the [research] findings' (Layder 1998: 23). But a researcher who chooses a 'wholesale adoption' approach potentially faces a double set of problems. The first is that, when she comes to present her research findings, she may find herself being forced to become a last-ditch defender of every detailed feature of the chosen GST—a position in which she is unlikely to feel comfortable. (She adopted the theory, after all, simply in order to make better sense of some of her research findings; and, not being a general social theorist herself, she very likely did not at that point think through every analytical detail, and potential criticism, of the GST in question.) The second potential problem with the 'wholesale adoption' approach is that it may blind the researcher to some aspects of the emerging research findings themselves. Obviously, *some* of the research findings will fit well with the chosen GST (or the researcher would not have been attracted to that theory in the first place); but other findings might very easily be much harder to link sensibly to the GST in question. It is clearly important that the researcher remains alive to the disjunctions between any given GST and the emerging research results, as much as to the congruences between them;[6] but this may be very hard to achieve if there has been a whole-sale adoption of a given GST.

An alternative to 'wholesale adoption' is of course the 'selective adoption' of concepts from one or more GSTs as a way of seeking to enrich the theoretical explanation of the topic being studied. Such a strategy would avoid the prob-lems outlined above; but it can bring other problems in its wake. In particular, as Layder (1998: 23) points out, there exists the unfortunate possibility 'of wrenching concepts out of their wider theoretical context [in the work of a general social theorist] and thus inadvertently disfiguring their meaning'. A further, and related, potential problem is that, in a search for synthesis, one might pluck one or two key concepts from several different GST sources, with-out adequate awareness of the theoretical incongruities that might thus be set up. If this occurs, one will finish up with a poorly-thought-through eclectic approach, rather than an adequate synthesis.

Yet despite these dangers, the 'selective adoption' approach potentially has several advantages. In the first place, given appropriate theoretical awareness, it becomes possible to draw fruitfully upon several different concepts from differ-ent GSTs (and not just one). This is likely to be seen by many empirical researchers as the most useful way of utilizing GST, given such researchers' quite reasonable focus upon specific problems of explanation in their chosen empirical field. Moreover, a 'selective adoption' approach does not necessarily entail any large-scale importation into the research analysis of an extensive 'apparatus of abstract concepts' (Giddens 1991: 213); rather, it allows the researcher, if she wishes, to use GST concepts in 'a sparing and critical fashion' that, hopefully, really can illuminate the social phenomena being studied. Equally, however, a researcher who considers that a given GST (say, feminist or Marxist theory) offers the truest account of 'very general aspects of social reality' may, in a 'selective adoption' approach, use that GST extensively, but not exclusively or uncritically.

It follows from the preceding paragraphs of this subsection that the best way for empirical researchers to use concepts from general social theories is select-ively, but with appropriate sensitivity to the overall theoretical contexts within which the concept(s) were first generated. Yet this suggestion, though attractive, is nevertheless quite daunting for the beginner, because it places upon the researcher a requirement that he/she should ideally be sufficiently familiar with the GST(s) in question to be able to use concepts derived from them selectively and confidently, yet in an accurate and appropriate way. Hence it is important

---

[6] For example, in *Prisons and the Problem of Order* (Sparks, Bottoms and Hay 1996), my colleagues and I fully acknowledged the importance and subtlety of much of Foucault's analysis of the prison, but we argued that claims for his 'superior understanding of the internal ordering of prisons' could not be sustained in the light of contemporary evidence about the way that prisons function (p.65).

for the neophyte researcher to check out—maybe with a supervisor, or perhaps with someone who is an expert on general social theory—whether or not the proposed use of a given general social theorist's concept is indeed appropriate in the relevant research context. The neophyte researcher will also find helpful, in this regard, the increasing number of introductory texts on individual general theorists (such as Foucault or Habermas) and on certain general GST approaches (such as feminism and late/post-modernity theory).

Implicit in the foregoing discussion is one important point which requires emphasis. When we speak of 'the relationship between theory and research'— the central topic of this chapter—we most naturally think of how theory and data can best be brought together in the service of true explanation. But we need also to recognize that any serious treatment of the theory/research relationship has to take account of the fact that there is normally a range of competing theories (including competing GSTs) available to the researcher in developing an explanation. Part of the researcher's choice of theory must depend on the fit between data and theory, but part of it must also depend upon the analytical coherence of the different theoretical concepts deployed in the overall explanation. Hence, it is necessary for the researcher to pay close attention to the precise content of the theoretical concepts deployed, and to ensure that these can be utilized in conjunction with one another without analytical discordance.

The preceding comments will hopefully encourage more empirical researchers to consider the constructive and creative use of concepts from GST within their future research projects. But to achieve this, they will also need methodological procedures that will encourage such an approach. As we shall see in the next three subsections, serious engagement with GST has in the past hardly been prominent in most formally-prescribed methodological procedures, but that state of affairs is now changing for the better.

HYPOTHETICO-DEDUCTIVE THEORY

In this and the next two subsections, I shall address directly the relationship between theory and data in empirical research. Traditionally, there have been two main (and very distinct) approaches to this topic, which I shall call respectively 'hypothetico-deductive theory' and 'grounded theory'. (The word 'theory' in this connection has sometimes caused confusion, but the usage is so well established that it would be perverse to change it here. The confusion has arisen because it is sometimes assumed that in speaking of 'theory', the reference is to some kind of substantive theory, rather than to a proposed methodological approach.)

In practice, however, many empirical criminological researchers, including myself, have utilized neither of the two classical approaches in their pure form, but rather some mixture or amalgamation of them. Hence the importance of

Derek Layder's (1998) recent book, which explicitly attempts to provide a coherent new methodological synthesis that, among other things, incorporates some features of both hypothetico-deductive theory and grounded theory, while also being fully aware of the theoretical dissonance between these two approaches in their originally-stated forms. Layder calls his proposed new approach 'adaptive theory', and I shall consider it after briefly discussing the two older approaches.

A classic formulation of hypothetico-deductive theory is that by Merton (1967). Layder (1998: 16) usefully summarizes Merton's argument:

[Merton] argued that although we develop our initial ideas about a research problem through empirical observations of some social phenomenon (like rates of suicide in different societies), we then construct a possible theoretical explanation for the phenomenon through a logical, deductive process, which is consistent with the known facts. Research then proceeds on the basis of finding more facts and information about the topic, area or problem in question in order to 'test-out' the original hypothesis. The unearthing of evidence through empirical research either confirms the initial theoretical ideas or disconfirms them, leading to their reformulation or abandonment. [It is argued that] the more theory is tested-out in this manner, the more likely it is that supportive evidence will be found and this can lead to a relatively stabilized body of theory which can help to illuminate other research in the area.

As is clear from the above description, in Merton's approach the underlying procedural logic is *deductive* rather than *inductive*. Merton's own account of his proposed methodological approach emphasizes especially the importance of 'middle-range theory' in social scientific explanation, and it is easy to see why. For in hypothetico-deductive theory we start with some limited factual observations, and then we try to formulate a careful hypothesis that will explain these observations; subsequently, we test and revise this hypothesis. Almost inevitably, this process results in theories about particular social institutions (marriage, bureaucracy, prisons, etc.), particular kinds of action (e.g. committing suicide; taking illegal drugs), or particular kinds of social aggregate (e.g. cities *vs.* rural areas). Such theories are significantly different from (and obviously more restricted in scope than) the general social theories discussed in the preceding sub-section.

A number of justified criticisms can be levelled at hypothetico-deductive theory. One, which follows directly from the comment in the previous paragraph, is that the hypothetico-deductive approach finds it very difficult to engage with general social theory at all.[7] Secondly, once the 'hypothesis-formulation' stage has begun, the approach may tend unduly to restrict the researcher's focus. That is because, at this stage, the emphasis is all upon

---

[7] This is not simply a question of neglect by hypothetico-deductive theorists, but arises from a logical difficulty in the way that hypothetico-deductive theory has been conceptualized. See further Layder (1998: 138).

refining the hypothesis, hence fresh data that might make one want to think again about the framework underpinning the original formulation might not be very actively sought by the researcher—and, even if discovered accidentally, might not be very carefully thought about. And thirdly, because the hypothetico-deductive approach places particular emphasis on 'verifying' or 'falsifying' a hypothesis, there has been a tendency for researchers of this kind strongly to favour quantitative as opposed to qualitative data sources, to the point where the latter are quite often accorded only a very secondary status by researchers following hypothetico-deductive procedures.[8]

Despite these drawbacks, hypothetico-deductive theory has important merits. It emphasizes, rightly, that theory is involved from a very early stage in the research process. It encourages careful and precise formulations of theoretical ideas (in the shape of hypotheses to be tested); and it requires the rigorous testing of theoretical ideas against relevant data where this is appropriate and feasible. These are all very positive attributes that need to be nurtured in the development of empirical research.

GROUNDED THEORY

So-called 'grounded theory' is an approach formulated by Glaser and Strauss (1967) in conscious opposition to hypothetico-deductive theory. Where hypothetico-deductive theory emphasizes a deductive approach and quantitative data, grounded theory prefers an inductive approach and the prioritising of qualitative data.

In the first paragraph of their book, Glaser and Strauss tell their readers that they wish to further 'the discovery of theory from data—systematically obtained and analyzed in social research'. Two pages later, they elaborate this statement:

Theory in sociology is a strategy for handling data in research, providing modes of conceptualization for describing and explaining. The theory should provide clear enough categories and hypotheses so that crucial ones can be verified in present and future research. . . . The theory must also be readily understandable to sociologists of any viewpoint, to students and to significant laymen. Theory that can meet these requirements must fit the situation being researched, and work when put into use. By 'fit' we mean that the categories must be readily (not forcibly) applicable to and indicated by the data under study; by 'work' we mean that they must be meaningfully relevant to and be able to explain the behavior under study . . . .
To generate theory that fills this large order, we suggest as the best approach an initial,

---

[8] A fourth important criticism of a more technical nature is that, despite the apparently rationalist foundations of hypothetico-deductive theory, the most important formulations of this approach, such as Merton's (1967), have in fact been heavily dependent on empiricist criteria of knowledge at certain key points: see Layder (1998: 137–8).

systematic discovery of the theory from the data of social research. Then one can be relatively sure that the theory will fit and work. And since the categories are discovered by examination of the data, laymen involved in the area to which the theory applies will usually be able to understand it, while sociologists who work on other areas will recognise an understandable theory linked with the data of a given area (Glaser and Strauss 1967: 3–4).

The principal method advocated by Glaser and Strauss to further the discovery of grounded theory is that of 'comparative analysis', an approach that they say places 'a high emphasis on *theory as process;* that is, theory as an ever-developing entity, not as a perfected product' (p. 32). Thus, for example, beginning perhaps with just a few observations, the researcher aims constantly to work outwards from the data, in an endeavour to *generalize* from one kind of situation to another, or to *define differences*, and thus gradually to generate and refine theoretical statements. To be maximally effective, this approach requires one to be extremely systematic in the sequential selection of comparative examples, so as constantly to try to achieve a progressive elaboration or refinement of the theory (a process described as 'theoretical sampling'). In this way, Glaser and Strauss hope, one can generate both 'substantive theory' ('theory developed for a substantive, or empirical, area of sociological inquiry') and 'formal theory' ('theory developed for a formal or conceptual area of sociological inquiry'). Overall, 'the design involves a progressive building up from facts, through substantive to grounded formal theory' (p. 35).

Glaser and Strauss are clear about what they see as the advantages of this approach, as compared with hypothetico-deductive theory:

Verifying a [hypothetico-deductive theory] generally leaves us with at best a reformulated hypothesis or two and an unconfirmed set of speculations; and at worst a theory that does not seem to fit or work . . . [grounded theory] gives us a theory that 'fits or works' in a substantive or formal area (though further testing, clarification or reformulation is still necessary) since the theory has been derived from data, not deduced from logical assumptions (pp. 29–30).

Additionally, they argue, the use of a hypothetico-deductive approach unduly *restricts* subsequent empirical work to verificatory processes, and blunts the researcher's sensitivity to the full range of theoretical possibilities in the patterns of data.

There is no doubt that some of these ideas have considerable merit. There are, however, at least three significant difficulties with grounded theory, as formulated by Glaser and Strauss. The first is that, by speaking of 'the discovery of theory from data', these authors unjustifiably assume the existence of theory-neutral facts. Hence, a key element of their whole approach is, from the outset, theoretically flawed. Secondly, and relatedly, Glaser and Strauss's procedures virtually by definition preclude an empirical researcher from incorporating

elements of GST into his/her analysis. Thirdly, Glaser and Strauss's prioritization of qualitative data seems as unjustified as does the hypothetico-deductive
theorists' prioritization of quantitative data.

If we now stand back and consider this brief discussion of hypothetico-
deductive theory and grounded theory, it would seem that what is needed is an
approach to the theory/research relationship that can incorporate at least the
following features:

i.   a firm acceptance that there are no theory-neutral facts, and that the
      process of empirical research is therefore inextricably involved with
      theoretical issues from the outset of the inquiry. (Because of the date at
      which they were first formulated, neither hypothetico-deductive theory
      nor grounded theory truly grasps the full implications of this crucial
      point.)

ii.   a willingness to refine and test hypotheses rigorously where appropriate,
      but not in such a way that one becomes blind to the implications of fresh
      data that do not readily 'mesh' with the pre-existing line of inquiry.

iii. a willingness to employ to the full the benefits of the 'comparative analy-
      sis' method of grounded theory, while nevertheless accepting the two key
      points listed above.

iv.   an unwillingness to foreclose inquiry too quickly, recognizing with Glaser
      and Strauss that theory is indeed always a 'process . . . an ever-developing
      entity'.

v.   a constant willingness and ability to be open to the relevance of concepts
      from general social theories at all stages of the developing theoretical
      analysis.

vi.   a genuine willingness to utilize appropriately both quantitative and
      qualitative data-sources.

While a number of empirical researchers have, in their research practice,
developed methodological approaches that do indeed fully incorporate all the
above points, we have until recently lacked any formal theoretical statement of
such a methodological approach. Hence the importance, in my judgement, of
Layder's (1998) recent book entitled *Sociological Practice*, in which he puts
forward what he calls the 'adaptive theory' approach to the theory/research
relationship. I would not wish to defend every proposition that Layder offers
in this volume (my stance is that of 'selective adoption', not 'wholesale
adoption'!); and I certainly do not suggest that his formulations are incapable
of improvement. But Layder's text does offer us, I believe, a definite advance in
the formal statement of a fruitful approach to the theory/research relationship.

ADAPTIVE THEORY

I shall devote little space here to any formal summary of Layder's proposed 'adaptive theory' approach. That is partly because the main outlines of Layder's approach will already be apparent from the discussion in the preceding subsection; and partly also because in the final section of this chapter I shall discuss an example from criminological research that adopted, implicitly, an 'adaptive theory' procedure. To give a flavour of Layder's approach, however, it is worth quoting the core of his answer to the question: 'what is adaptive about adaptive theory?'. This runs as follows:

So the adaptive part of the term is meant to convey that the theory simultaneously contains two fundamental properties. First, that there is an existing theoretical scaffold which has a relatively durable form since it adapts reflexively rather than automatically in relation to empirical data. Secondly, this scaffold should never be regarded as immutable since it is capable of accommodating new information and interpretations by reconfiguring itself. Thus, although the extant 'theoretical elements' are never simple empiricist 'reflections' of data, they are intrinsically capable of reformulating ('adapting' or 'adjusting') themselves in response to the discovery of new information and/or interpretations of data which seriously challenge their basic assumptions. Such reformulations may involve only minor modifications . . . but they may also require fundamental reorganization, such as either abandoning an existing category, model or explanation, or creating new ones, depending on the circumstances (Layder 1998: 150–1).

Additionally, it is I think important to make two comments that link 'adaptive theory' procedures to some of the preceding discussions in this chapter. The first of these comments is formal/analytical; the second is criminological.

The formal/analytical comment relates to the issue of inductive *vs.* deductive research procedures. Layder (1998: 135) fully recognizes that his 'insistence that adaptive theory employs both deductive and inductive procedures' could be read by some as an attempt to combine what might well be regarded 'as "incompatible" premises or underlying assumptions'. Layder's important response to this objection is worth quoting extensively:

My usage of [the terms induction and deduction] does not invoke the idea that *in the final analysis* theory has *either* to be produced exclusively in a deductive manner *or* solely within an inductive frame of reference . . . In terms of adaptive theory both forms of theory-generation, construction or elaboration are permissible within the same frame of reference and particularly within the same research project and time frame. . . . I regard induction and deduction as frameworks of ideas—discourse and the practices they embody—which are potentially open to each other's influence. Thus it is not only a matter of allowing their dual influence on theory-construction, but also of allowing their mutual influence on each other. Moderate (rather than extreme) definitions of these terms will allow for this. As epistemological anchorages neither induction nor deduction can be understood as prior or privileged in terms of their influence—neither must have a fixed starting point as the most basic premise of knowledge production.

Induction and deduction must be conceived as equally important and mutually influential approaches to knowledge, according to different empirical and theoretical circumstances. These latter will reflect the ongoing nature of particular research projects (Layder 1998: 136, emphasis in original).

My final—and explicitly criminological—comment on adaptive theory takes us back to the preceding main section in this chapter (on 'Lessons from the Past'), and in particular to Table 1.1. In discussing Table 1.1, I suggested that we needed methodological procedures that would allow us to make full use of the 'positive features' identified in column 1 of the Table, but that this needed to be achieved not eclectically, but within some 'principled and defensible procedures for synthesis'. My argument would now be that the adaptive theory framework potentially provides exactly such 'principled and defensible procedures'. But it does not automatically do so—much depends on the individual researcher's understanding and skills as a research project unfolds.

THE THEORY/RESEARCH LINKAGE IN EVALUATION RESEARCH

The preceding subsections have dealt with various approaches to the theory/research relationship, focusing on the central problem for social science, namely that of the explanation of social phenomena. But there is of course in criminology a somewhat differently-focused kind of research, namely evaluation research, which at least in some of its forms has been much more concerned with comparing the outcome-effectiveness of different programmes (of crime prevention, intended rehabilitation, etc.) than with explanation.

Undoubtedly the dominant paradigm in evaluation research in criminology has been the experimental or quasi-experimental approach (see Cook and Campbell 1979). The classical research design used in this approach is the so-called 'OXO' design, summarized in Table 1.2. One of the key methodological preconditions in such designs is the effective equivalence of subjects in the experimental and control conditions, to be achieved either by the random allocation of subjects or by appropriately stringent methods of statistical control. Thereafter, only the experimental group is exposed to the programme being evaluated (e.g. a neighbourhood watch programme, or a

Table 1.2: The Classical Research Design for Experimentally-based Evaluations

	Pre-test	Treatment	Post-test
Experimental group	O_1	X	O_2
Control group	O_1		O_2

cognitive-behavioural rehabilitation programme), and the subsequent behaviour of subjects in both experimental and control conditions is assessed in the post-test context. Pawson and Tilley (1997: 33) well summarize the methodological thinking behind designs of this kind:

The key stroke of logic in this classical design is that, being identical to begin with, the only difference between the experimental and control group lies in the application of the initiative. Any difference in behavioural outcomes between the groups is thus accounted for in terms of the action of the treatment. If the researcher has managed to put into place this regime of manipulation, control and observation, then we require no further information to infer that treatment (cause) and outcome (effect) are linked.

Experimental and quasi-experimental evaluation researchers quite often speak of this approach as 'testing a null hypothesis'. That is to say, the formal hypothesis being tested in the research is that the various (experimental and control) programmes do not differ in their outcomes; if a significant difference in outcome is in fact found, then the null hypothesis has been falsified. It is not difficult to see, from this language, that the experimental/quasi-experimental evaluation research tradition is, in the policy/evaluation sphere, logically very closely akin to the hypothetico-deductive approach in explanatory research.

It is therefore hardly surprising that some of the main criticisms levelled at the experimental/quasi-experimental approach are rather similar to those levelled at hypothetico-deductive theory. First, it is claimed that the experimental/quasi-experimental approach sometimes makes no serious attempt to explain why a given programme appears to 'work'; it simply measures comparative outcomes (though this critism does not apply to the better quasi-experimental designs). Secondly, it is claimed that all too often in experimental evaluations replication studies are conducted which fail to confirm the original results, at least in the form or to the degree suggested by the first study; and this criticism is of course uncomfortably reminiscent of Glaser and Strauss's comment that hypothetico-deductive theory generally 'leaves us with at best a reformulated hypothesis or two and an unconfirmed set of speculations' (see above).

The experimental/quasi-experimental approach to evaluation research has recently been strongly criticized by Pawson and Tilley (1997), who describe themselves as following an alternative, 'scientific realist' approach to evaluation. Interestingly, one of these authors' main emphases is upon the need *to explain* any outcome results found in evaluation research. For this purpose, they claim that, in evaluation studies, from an explanatory point of view it is always the case that 'outcomes follow from mechanisms acting in contexts' (p. 58); or, putting the matter more mathematically (p. xv):[9]

---

[9] I have followed Pawson and Tilley's mathematical notation here, though I suspect that the addition sign should more appropriately be represented as a multiplication sign.

Mechanism (M) + Context (C) = Outcome (O)

Hence, Pawson and Tilley speak of 'CMO configurations', and suggest that 'the task of a realist evaluation is to find ways of articulating, testing and refining conjectured CMO configurations' (p. 77).

In my judgement, Pawson and Tilley's emphasis on the importance of explanation within evaluation studies is a useful corrective to the relative neglect of this issue by some experimental/quasi-experimental researchers. It is much less clear, however, that the authors' hostility (not too strong a word) to the experimental approach is justified. We have previously noted that, in explanatory research, the hypothetico-deductive approach has certain merits, as has the grounded theory approach. An important strength of Layder's 'adaptive theory' approach to explanation is that it aims (among other things) to incorporate the strengths of both these approaches, within a theoretically coherent framework. The point cannot be pursued in detail here, but it seems likely that an 'adaptive-theory'-type approach to evaluation research, combining the strengths of the experimental approach and the 'CMO configuration' approach, could similarly have much to commend it. As with adaptive theory, this would also have the merit of creatively conjoining quantitative and qualitative data in an evaluation context.

IS THE THEORY/RESEARCH LINKAGE RELEVANT TO NORMATIVE ANALYSIS IN CRIMINOLOGY?

I claimed earlier that 'doing criminology' necessarily entails some engagement with normative issues. Given such a claim, at least some brief attention to normative theorization in criminology seems appropriate.

Normative theory seeks principled answers to 'ought' questions. For example, the question 'ought possessing cannabis to be a crime?' is known to be controversial. The serious normative theorist, in trying to answer such a question, will among other things seek to consider what justifies societies in deeming any given act to be criminal; she would then consider whether the possession of cannabis seems to meet the criteria for appropriate criminalization that have been specified. This second stage might well involve the use of empirical information, for example about any harmful effects that cannabis may have on health.

This kind of theorization is thus subtly different from explanatory research, where both theory and data are used conjointly in a search for true explanations of social phenomena. Normative analysis is not engaged in a search for truth in quite the same way: rather it attempts a rational and principled exploration of the moral/political justifications for a given course of action. There can be no doubt, however, that doing normative theory can involve very searching and difficult intellectual analysis (as for example recent discussions of the concept of mercy in criminal justice have clearly shown: see, e.g., Murphy and Hampton 1988; Harrison 1992; Walker 1995). And, sometimes, empirical research can help to take forward these normative discussions (in the case of mercy, the debate was enriched by Walker's empirical investigation of how the Court of Appeal in England had used this concept in decided cases). Hence there can be an important element of theory–research linkage in normative research, but this is not quite the same kind of linkage as in explanatory research.

A good illustration of these points can be found in a recent PhD project completed at Cambridge University. Parts of the 1991 Criminal Justice Act were clearly influenced by desert theory (on which see, e.g., von Hirsch 1986). Among other things, the Act imposed on courts in England and Wales the requirement that, when passing a sentence including one or more 'community orders' (i.e. probation orders, community service orders, curfew orders, etc.), 'the restrictions on liberty imposed by the order or orders shall be such as in the opinion of the court are commensurable with the seriousness of the offence, or the combination of one or more offences associated with it'(s.6(2)(b) of the Criminal Justice Act 1991).

Susan Rex (1997) carried out a qualitative PhD research project that sought to explore the on-the-ground reality of the probation order, as perceived by both probationers and probation officers, in the context of the new legislative provision. One of her main conclusions was that, in the probation order, a mechanical counting of 'contact hours' as 'restrictions on liberty' missed the point. There were indeed restrictions placed on probationers, but these centrally arose from the *demands for change* in the offender's behaviour that both probation officers and probationers understood as the central purpose of the probation order (and that sometimes required considerable effort from the probationer). For example, being on probation could involve a strong sense of *limited privacy* (as a necessary corollary of the demands for change); and the sheer length of the probation order (with an accompanying sense of 'being under surveillance') could sometimes be seen by probationers as restrictive, notwithstanding low contact hours per month.

It seemed clear that, in these respects, the probation order was significantly different from the community service order (although Rex herself did not empirically investigate the latter, relying instead on previous research accounts). The CSO usually involved, in total, more contact hours between the offender and the probation service, but it was typically completed within a shorter number of months. Moreover, it seemed clear from the empirical evidence that 'the supervision which is the whole point of probation is entirely different from the supervision involved in community service, where it is the offender's performance of a task (rather than the offender him or herself) which is being supervised' (Rex 1997: 116).

In a recent article, I sought to analyse several aspects of Andrew von Hirsch's version of desert theory (Bottoms 1998). The article was, therefore, primarily intended as a contribution to normative analysis. In one section of the paper, I used Susan Rex's research results extensively, and I concluded as follows:

on the basis of Rex's research, it seems fairly clear that section 6(2)(b) of the Criminal Justice Act 1991, with its attempt to provide a unified desert-based 'penalty-scale' for community sentences based on 'the restrictions on liberty imposed by the order or orders' makes sense only if the phrase 'restrictions on liberty' is interpreted in a very different way for different community orders (Bottoms 1998: 74–5).

In short, normative analysis in criminology had been significantly assisted by careful empirical research.

It will be clear from the preceding argument that normative analysis is emphatically not the unscientific pursuit that positivism made it out to be. It can involve extremely intricate philosophical analysis, and this analysis can intersect with, and be illuminated by, empirical research at many points. Hence, the theory–research linkage is important in normative analysis, just as it is in doing explanatory work in criminology (though given the different purposes of normative and explanatory analyses, the theory–research linkage necessarily manifests itself in different ways). Normative analysis has not often been included in previous discussions of the theory/research relationship in criminology: in the future it needs to be more centrally located in such discussions.

AN EXAMPLE OF THE THEORY/RESEARCH RELATIONSHIP

In this final section, an example of the theory/research relationship is offered, illustrating some aspects of the preceding argument. The example concerns research into areal differences in crime rates, and shows in particular how different empirical research methods (quantitative and qualitative) can be used in harmony to develop and refine a theoretical concept. It also offers an example of an implicitly 'adaptive theory' approach, although the work involved was completed some time before the publication of Layder's (1998) text on adaptive theory.

In the late 1960s, I was privileged to be appointed as the first specialist lecturer in criminology at Sheffield University. The university had officially designated criminology as one of its 'growth-point' areas, and I was encouraged, with the help of a research assistant, to develop research in the subject.

It seemed sensible to begin with a study that investigated general aspects of crime in the city of Sheffield, as a background to later and more detailed research. So a project on 'urban crime in Sheffield' was developed, to try to make a further British contribution to the so-called 'ecology of crime' tradition. When we commenced this study, we had no specific hypotheses to test: given the circumstances in which the research was conceived, it was 'ground-clearing', developmental research. Not surprisingly, therefore, when the then newly-published inductivist methodology of Glaser and Strauss (1967) came to attention, it was enthusiastically received, notwithstanding some of its already-apparent weaknesses (see Bottoms 1973), and notwithstanding that we were already committed to a more quantitative research programme than Glaser and Strauss would have encouraged.

In the first year of the research, as well as collecting very detailed data on crime and offenders in the city, we read as widely as we could both in the 'communities and crime' research literature, and more generally in urban sociology.

One specific aspect of urban sociology that quickly interested us was culled directly from Rex and Moore's (1967) then recently-published study of Commonwealth immigration to Sparkbrook, Birmingham. Rex and Moore noted that new immigrants to the city were heavily constrained in their choice of housing, partly by market forces (the costs of owner-occupation, building societies' practices concerning mortgage eligibility, etc.), but also partly by the bureaucratic eligibility rules of the local authority as regards access to council housing. These various housing constraints significantly influenced the kinds of area within Birmingham where immigrants could realistically settle.

From these observations, Rex and Moore developed the theoretical concept of the 'housing class'. They suggested that 'there is a class struggle over the use of houses and *this class struggle is the central process of the city as a social unit* (Rex and Moore 1967: 273, emphasis added). In so arguing, they were following Max Weber's suggestion that any market situation (which Rex and Moore conceptualized as including the differential placement of various social groups *vis-à-vis* systems of bureaucratic allocation) will lead to the emergence of struggles which could be deemed 'class struggles'. In postulating the existence of these 'housing classes', the authors did not of course deny that a family's position in the housing market depends in significant part upon income, and is therefore intimately linked to the labour market. However, they went on to insist:

it is also the case that men [*sic*] in the same labour situation may come to have differential degrees of access to housing, and *it is this which immediately determines the class conflicts of the city as distinct from the workplace* (Rex and Moore 1967: 274, emphasis added).

Although we were aware, from an early date, of some conceptual criticisms of the appropriateness of Rex and Moore's use of the term 'housing *class*' (see, e.g.,

Pahl 1970), as potential urban criminological researchers we were extremely interested in the 'struggle for housing' framework embedded in Rex and Moore's discussion. We were therefore keen to explore whether this idea could be more specifically developed within a criminological context.

It is worth noting in retrospect (though we did not fully realize it at the time) that at this stage we had already departed from Glaser and Strauss's methodological prescriptions. The 'struggle for housing' idea had come, not from our own data, but from an external theoretical source. However, although the theoretical idea attracted us, we still had not thought through whether it could be made to 'work' in a criminological context, and our overall methodological strategy remained inductivist.

It had already been decided that our first analyses were to be largely statistical, involving especially multivariate analyses of the relationships between census data for Sheffield and recorded crime and offender data for the city for the same year (this research is fully reported in Baldwin and Bottoms 1976). Within the framework of a macro-level statistical study of this kind, we could necessarily operationalize the 'housing class' (or 'housing conflict') concept only in a very crude fashion. But we did our best. From census data, information was available on the percentage of households in each census enumeration district (or 'ED') that were owner-occupiers, 'council tenants' (i.e. local authority housing), or held their properties through a private-market rental agreement. (These were, at the time, the only important kinds of housing tenure in England.) For simplicity of analysis, we therefore classified all EDs into four main types; namely, EDs in which over 50 per cent of the households were respectively owner-occupiers, council tenants, or renting privately; and so-called 'mixed' EDs in which no single tenure type was predominant.

Without going into detail here, there were enough tenure-type differences in the subsequent multivariate statistical analyses to suggest that the 'housing struggle' concept was worth pursuing further in a criminological context (Baldwin and Bottoms 1976).

Up to this point, the research had had a whole-city focus. To develop the emerging ideas in greater depth, it was obviously necessary to select certain specific local areas for closer attention. Given the apparent importance of the 'housing conflict' idea, we decided, as a deliberate tactic, to focus attention at this stage on areas that seemed similar in many respects, including housing tenure, but that differed substantially in recorded crime and offender rates. In taking this step, we were very much influenced by Glaser and Strauss's prescriptions as regards *theoretical sampling*, which they define as 'a process of data collection for generating theory whereby the analyst . . . decides what data to collect next . . . in order to develop his theory as it emerges. The process of data collection is *controlled* by the emerging theory' (Glaser and Strauss 1967: 45, emphasis in original). I am bound to say, however, that in real life the decision did not feel anything like as well-organized as this quotation suggests. Given Rex and Moore's theorization, and the results of our own first-stage analyses (Baldwin and Bottoms 1976), we very much wanted to pursue the 'housing conflict' concept in a criminological context, but there seemed nevertheless to be a fairly large element of 'stepping into the unknown' as we selected the districts for specific, small-area analysis.

We selected seven areas in particular for further analysis (see Bottoms, Mawby and Walker 1987 for details). The basic idea was to choose pairs of areas that seemed similar in housing terms, but that differed substantially in recorded crime and offender rates. Three such pairs were identified:

i.   An adjacent pair of pre-Second World War low-rise council housing areas, one with high crime/offender rates, and one with low;

ii.   An adjacent pair of post-Second World War high-rise council housing areas, one with high crime/offender rates, and one with low.

iii.   A non-adjacent pair of predominantly privately-rented areas (but also containing other tenure types). One area had very high crime and offender rates, and was then the city's principal area for prostitution; the other area had low crime and offender rates.

Finally, an owner-occupier low-crime and offender rate area was added; no satisfactory high crime/offender 'pairing' for this area could be identified.

It is important to notice that we had come this far in the research design without, so far, investigating in detail whether the crime/offender rate differences found might simply be the product of artificialities in the officially-recorded crime data.[10] That possibility was, therefore, the obvious next step in the analysis, and was duly undertaken in the seven areas, partly through a very thorough analysis of how the police data had come to official attention; partly by investigating alternative indices of deviance in the areas (such as police 'command and control' data, and data from the licensing authority on television licence evasion); and partly by carrying out a victimization survey. (On the first two sources see Mawby 1979; on the third see Bottoms, Mawby and Walker 1987.) The results of all this work were perhaps surprisingly uniform: for the most part, the officially-recorded crime rate differences between the selected pairs of areas seemed to be reflecting real behavioural differences between the areas.

Obviously at this stage a more detailed on-the-ground analysis was called for. For simplicity, I shall here discuss how this was undertaken only in respect of the first pair of areas listed above, i.e. the pre-Second World War council

---

[10] This might seem strange to the contemporary generation of criminologists, for whom victimization surveys are a routine part of the criminological landscape. However, the period I am here describing (the mid-1970s) was several years before the first sweep of the British Crime Survey. The victimization survey that we carried out in the seven local areas in Sheffield at that time was in fact only the second victimization survey ever to be completed in Britain.

housing pair. This pair of areas we called Gardenia (the high-crime estate) and
Stonewall (the low-crime estate).

We were able to investigate the demography of these two areas quite carefully,
with results that were fairly spectacular. The areas were of similar social class
composition (as judged by the Registrar-General's social class categories), and
they were also similar in their gender and age composition, mean household
size, and unemployment rates. Yet their crime rates, by whatever measure one
judged them, were very different. These findings were, of course, potentially of
very special interest in relation to Rex and Moore's original theorization. Here
were two areas that were in demographic and occupational (or labour market)
terms very similar indeed; hence their crime rate differences could not be
attributed to the standard factors of social class, age, etc. Could they, then, be
explicable in 'housing class' (or related) terms, that is, viewing competition for
housing (as Rex and Moore did) as 'the central [social] process of the city as a
social unit' (see above). And if so, how was that reconcilable with the fact that
the two areas had been selected for detailed research analysis precisely because
they were both, in formal terms, of similar housing status, i.e. pre-Second
World War low-rise council housing areas?

We progressed the explanation from this point primarily through the work of
an ESRC-funded PhD student, Polii Xanthos. She carried out detailed ethnographic work on the two estates, and she also investigated in some depth—
through access to the files of the local authority's Housing Department—how
processes of housing allocation and transfer on the estates were related to other
social processes, including criminality (Xanthos 1981). Briefly, these investigations showed that both Gardenia and Stonewall had begun life as 'select' estates
with good reputations; that sometime in the early post-war period Gardenia
had 'tipped'; that a number of aspects of social life in Gardenia (especially one
part of it) were now significantly different from social life in Stonewall; that, in
particular, there was a subcultural network of families (many interrelated by
marriage) in south-east Gardenia, many of the male members of whom had
criminal records; that these social patterns, once established, were essentially
buttressed by aspects of the local authority's housing allocation system; and
that these choices incorporated both prudential and cultural dimensions (see
generally Bottoms, Mawby and Xanthos 1989; Bottoms, Claytor and Wiles 1992).

From these various research strands, we eventually formulated what in Glaser
and Strauss's terms would be called a *substantive theory*, outlining the putative
relationship between housing markets and the 'community crime careers'
(Reiss 1986) of small residential areas. Our final and formal statement of this
theory is set out schematically in Figure 1.1. It has three central features:

i.   It emphasizes that in a given housing market context, the kinds of indi-
       viduals and families that will move into a given residential area will not be

Figure 1.1: Relationship between the Potential Effects of the Housing Market and Residential Community Crime Careers

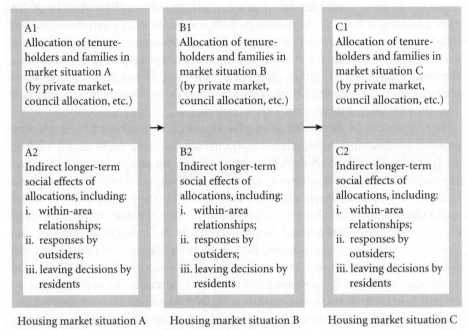

Housing market situation A   Housing market situation B   Housing market situation C

Source: Bottoms, Claytor and Wiles (1992)

random, but rather will be heavily influenced by aspects of the market situation as it applies to that particular area (e.g. price; public sector allocation rules; perceived desirability in the eyes of potential movers-in; etc). (See A1 in Figure 1.1.)

ii. Next, the housing market context can have crucial secondary social effects—in terms of, for example, the nature of the relationships which subsequently develop in an area; responses by outsiders (including social control agents, potential residents, etc.); and leaving decisions by residents (on which see Taub, Taylor and Dunham 1984). (See A2 in Figure 1.1.)

iii. Finally, the housing market context itself might change (see Figure 1.1, columns B and C). This might occur for macro-economic or macro-social reasons unconnected to specific features of life in a given residential area;[11] or it might occur because some of the indirect social effects (see A2 in Figure 1.1) themselves alter aspects of the area's housing market position, e.g. its perceived desirability.

---

[11] Such processes have significantly affected many British council estates in the 1990s: see for example the very interesting discussion in Power and Tunstall (1995) on how local improvements on unpopular estates were working against the grain of broader national and regional changes in housing markets.

It should additionally be emphasized that, although this model was developed originally with special reference to public sector housing in Sheffield, it is intended to be a formal model of much more general applicability. Thus, for example, although the point cannot be pursued in any detail here, the model is believed to be applicable to the case studies of crime victimization in selected areas of Chicago, as set out in Taub, Taylor and Dunham (1984). Back in Britain, the model has received explicit support in Hope and Foster's (1992) analysis of changes in criminality over time in a council estate in a northern city (see also Pawson and Tilley 1997: 94–103).

In retrospect, the methodological procedures that we adopted in developing this line of research can be seen as similar in many ways to those later described by Layder as 'adaptive theory'. Rex and Moore's 'housing class' concept had provided the original inspiration for what, after detailed research, became a middle-range formal theory about the relationship between the housing market and subsequent criminality in any given area. Along the way, some features of the original theorization were dropped (notably the concept of the housing *class*); and, since we were working in a criminological context which Rex and Moore did not address, it was necessary to adapt and develop their theoretical approach (which, in its original form, paid little attention to any longer-term behavioural consequences arising indirectly from the operations of the housing market). These alterations to the conceptualization took place as the end-result of a series of methodological steps, involving a constant process of theoretical readjustment as data from a wide range of sources (from multivariate statistical analysis to ethnography) became successively available.

In conclusion, we can usefully reflect on this example in the context of some of the wider themes previously discussed in this chapter. Here, two issues are perhaps of special relevance. First, at one level, Figure 1.1 might be regarded by some as a 'statement of the obvious', because once one has grasped its message, that message is indeed basically a simple one. I once presented an earlier version of Figure 1.1, with appropriate supporting data and argument, to a Scandinavian audience. In the subsequent discussion, a senior Scandinavian criminologist commented that the thesis was at the same time both simple and one with profound implications. Leaving aside the important but minority problem of the homeless, he commented, 'everyone has to live somewhere, but as criminologists we have not paid enough attention to the wider social implications of this simple point'. That comment, of course, very accurately reflected, in a criminological context, some of the theoretical concerns that had led John Rex and Robert Moore to formulate their original 'housing class' concept.

But scholarship always moves on, and this leads me to my final point. Rex and Moore's theorization was developed in the late 1960s. In the 1970s, there was a marked revival of interest in urban sociology in Europe, particularly emphasizing macro-social perspectives. In 1982, one commentator described

Rex and Moore's work as having been carried out in a Weberian tradition, concentrating on 'the observable distributions of urban resources'. But, he went on, this type of work, 'although useful in understanding local processes, did not address the growing significance of national and international developments in shaping particular urban developments' (James Simmie, Editor's Preface in Elliott and McCrone 1982). In other words, if one is not careful, the 'urban resources' approach can become too parochial in its scope. That comment is undoubtedly to an extent justified, yet it has its own dangers. Certainly 'national and international developments' are often crucial to an understanding of local processes, as indeed is witnessed by the very rapid processes of deindustrialization in Sheffield since our first criminological research studies were conducted there. (For some comments on Sheffield as a 'rustbelt city', in the context of the general social changes of late modernity, see Bottoms and Wiles 1995.) But these wider developments in no way render redundant the processes described in Figure 1.1: they simply require them to be understood in a fresh context. As Glaser and Strauss (1967: 32) emphasized thirty years ago, theory is 'an ever-developing entity, not . . . a perfected product'. One of the things that makes theory 'ever-developing' is that there is a continuing dialectical relationship between emergent theories and changes in the social world. Given that we live in a rapidly-changing social world, we can therefore be sure that in the coming years there will be much further material with which to consider the relationship between theory and research in criminology.

REFERENCES

BALDWIN, J., and BOTTOMS, A. E. (1976). *The Urban Criminal.* London: Tavistock.

BECKER, G. S. (1968). 'Crime and Punishment: An Economic Approach'. *Journal of Political Economy* 76: 169–217.

BOTTOMS, A. E. (1973). 'Methodological Aspects of Classification in Criminology'. *Collected Studies in Criminological Research* (Council of Europe), 10: 27–76.

—— (1993). 'Recent Criminological and Social Theory: The Problem of Integrating Knowledge about Individual Criminal Acts and Careers and Areal Dimensions of Crime', in D. P. Farrington, R. J. Sampson, and P-O. H. Wikström (eds.) *Integrating Individual and Ecological Aspects of Crime.* Stockholm: National Council for Crime Prevention.

—— (1998). 'Five Puzzles in von Hirsch's Theory of Punishment', in A. Ashworth and M. Wasik (eds.), *Fundamentals of Sentencing Theory.* Oxford: Clarendon Press.

—— CLAYTOR, A., and WILES, P. (1992). 'Housing Markets and Residential Community Crime Careers: A Case Study from Sheffield' in D. J. Evans, N. R. Fyfe, and D. Herbert (eds.), *Crime, Policing and Place.* London: Routledge.

—— HAY, W., and SPARKS, J. R. (1990). 'Situational and Social Approaches to the Prevention of Disorder in Long-Term Prisons'. *The Prison Journal* 70: 83–95.

BOTTOMS, A. E., and McCLINTOCK, F. H. (1973). *Criminals Coming of Age*. London: Heinemann.

—— MAWBY, R. I., and WALKER, M. A. (1987). 'A Localised Crime Survey in Contrasting Areas of a City'. *British Journal of Criminology* 27: 125–54.

—— —— and XANTHOS, P. (1989). 'A Tale of Two Estates', in D. Downes (ed.), *Crime and the City*. London: Heinemann.

—— and WILES, P. (1995). 'Crime and Insecurity in the City', in C. Fijnaut, J. Goethals, T. Peters, and L. Walgrave (eds.), *Changes in Society, Crime and Criminal Justice in Europe* Vol. 1, *Crime and Insecurity in the City*. The Hague: Kluwer.

BURCHELL, G., GORDON, C., and MILLER, P. (eds.) (1991). *The Foucault Effect: Studies in Governmentality*. London: Harvester Wheatsheaf.

CLARKE, R. V. G. (1995). 'Situational Crime Prevention', in M. Tonry and D. P. Farrington (eds.), *Building a Safer Society*. Chicago, Ill.: University of Chicago Press.

—— and FELSON, M. (eds.) (1993). *Routine Activity and Rational Choice*. New Brunswick: Transaction Publishers.

COOK, T. D., and CAMPBELL, D. T. (1979). *Quasi-Experimentation*. Chicago, Ill.: Rand McNally.

CORNISH, D. B., and CLARKE, R.V.G. (eds.) (1986). *The Reasoning Criminal*. New York: Springer.

ELLIOTT, B., and McCRONE, D. (1982). *The City: Patterns of Domination and Conflict*. London: Macmillan.

FARRINGTON, D. P. (1983). 'Randomized Experiments on Crime and Justice', in M. Tonry and N. Morris (eds.), *Crime and Justice: An Annual Review of Research*, Vol. 4 Chicago, Ill.: University of Chicago Press.

—— and DOWDS, E. A. (1985). 'Disentangling Criminal Behaviour and Police Reaction', in D. P. Farrington and J. Gunn (eds.), *Reactions to Crime*. Chichester: John Wiley.

FELSON, M. (1998). *Crime and Everyday Life* (2nd edn.). Thousand Oaks, Calif.: Pine Forge Press.

FLEW, A. (ed.)(1997). *A Dictionary of Philosophy*. New York: St. Martin's Press.

FOSTER, J. (1990). *Villains: Crime and Community in the Inner City*. London: Routledge.

FOUCAULT, M. (1979). *Discipline and Punish: The Birth of the Prison*. Harmondsworth: Penguin Books.

FREIRE, P. (1972). *Pedagogy of the Oppressed*. Harmondsworth: Penguin Books.

GARLAND, D. (1990). *Punishment and Modern Society*. Oxford: Clarendon Press.

—— (1997). '"Governmentality" and the Problem of Crime: Foucault, Criminology, Sociology'. *Theoretical Criminology* 1: 173–214.

GIDDENS, A. (1984). *The Constitution of Society*. Cambridge: Polity Press.

—— (1991). 'Structuration Theory: Past, Present and Future', in C. Bryant and D. Jary (eds.), *Giddens' Theory of Structuration: A Critical Appreciation*. London: Routledge.

GLASER, A., and STRAUSS, A. (1967). *The Discovery of Grounded Theory*. Chicago, Ill.: Aldine.

GREGSON, N. (1989). 'On the (Ir)relevance of Structuration Theory to Empirical Research', in D. Held and J. B. Thompson (eds.), *Social Theory of Modern Societies: Anthony Giddens and His Critics*. Cambridge: Cambridge University Press.

GUBA, Y., and LINCOLN, E. (1989). *Fourth Generation Evaluation*. London: Sage Publications.

HARRISON, R. (1992). 'The Equality of Mercy', in H. Gross and R. Harrison (eds.), *Jurisprudence: Cambridge Essays*. Cambridge: Cambridge University Press.

HART, H. L. A. (1982). *Essays on Bentham*. Oxford: Clarendon Press.

HENRY, S., and MILOVANOVIC, D. (1996). *Constitutive Criminology*. London: Sage Publications.

HOPE, T., and FOSTER, J. (1992) 'Conflicting Forces: Changing the Dynamics of Crime and Community on a "Problem Estate"'. *British Journal of Criminology* 32: 488–504.

LAYDER, D. (1998). *Sociological Practice: Linking Theory and Social Research*. London: Sage Publications.

MAGEE, B. (1973). *Popper*. Glasgow: Fontana/Collins.

MATZA, D. (1969). *Becoming Deviant*. Englewood Cliffs, NJ: Prentice-Hall.

MAWBY, R. I. (1979). *Policing the City*. Farnborough: Saxon House.

MERTON, R. K. (1967). *On Theoretical Sociology*. New York: Free Press.

MURPHY, J. G., and HAMPTON, J. (1988). *Forgiveness and Mercy*. Cambridge: Cambridge University Press.

ORMEROD, P. (1994). *The Death of Economics*. London: Faber.

—— (1998). *Butterfly Economics*. London: Faber.

PAHL, R. E. (1970). *Whose City?* London: Longmans.

PAWSON, R., and TILLEY, N. (1997). *Realistic Evaluation*. London: Sage Publications.

POPPER, K. (1968). *The Logic of Scientific Discovery*. London: Hutchinson.

POWER, A., and TUNSTALL, R. (1995). *Swimming Against the Tide: Polarisation or Progress on 20 Unpopular Council Estates, 1980–1995*. York: Joseph Rowntree Foundation.

PYLE, D. J. (1995). *Cutting the Costs of Crime*. London: Institute of Economic Affairs.

RADZINOWICZ, L. (1966). *Ideology and Crime*. London: Heinemann.

—— (1999). *Adventures in Criminology*. London: Routledge.

RAWLS, J. (1972). *A Theory of Justice*. London: Oxford University Press.

REISS, A. J., JR. (1986) 'Why are Communities Important in Understanding Crime?' in A. J. Reiss, Jr. and Michael Tonry (eds.), *Communities and Crime*. Chicago, Ill.: University of Chicago Press.

REX, J., and MOORE, R. (1967). *Race, Community and Conflict*. London: Oxford University Press.

REX, S. (1997). 'Perceptions of Probation in a Context of "Just Deserts"', unpublished PhD thesis, University of Cambridge.

ROCK, P. (1993). *The Social World of an English Crown Court*. Oxford: Clarendon Press.

SKINNER, Q. (ed.) (1990). *The Return of Grand Theory in the Human Sciences*. Cambridge: Cambridge University Press.

SPARKS, R., BOTTOMS, A. E., and HAY, W. (1996). *Prisons and the Problem of Order*. Oxford: Clarendon Press.

SUMMER, C. (ed.) (1990). *Censure, Politics and Criminal Justice*. Milton Keynes: Open University Press.

TAUB, R. P., TAYLOR, D. G. and DUNHAM, J. D. (1984). *Paths of Neighborhood Change*. Chicago, Ill.: University of Chicago Press.

VON HIRSCH, A. (1986). *Past or Future Crimes*. Manchester: Manchester University Press.

—— BOTTOMS, A. E., BURNEY, E. and WIKSTRØM, P-O. (1999). *Criminal Deterrence and Sentence Severity*. Oxford: Hart Publishing.

WALKER, N. D. (1995). 'The Quiddity of Mercy'. *Philosophy* 70: 27–37.

WRIGHT, R. T., and DECKER, S. H. (1994). *Burglars on the Job*. Boston, Mass.: Northeastern University Press.

XANTHOS, P. (1981). 'Crime, the Housing Market and Reputation: A Study of Some Local Authority Estates in Sheffield', unpublished PhD thesis, University of Sheffield.

YOUNG, J. (1997). 'Left Realist Criminology: Radical in its Analysis, Realist in its Policy', in M. Maguire, R. Morgan, and R. Reiner (eds.), *The Oxford Handbook of Criminology* (2nd edn.). Oxford: Oxford University Press.

2

THE POLITICS OF CRIMINOLOGICAL RESEARCH

Rod Morgan

INTRODUCTION

By the time this chapter is published the largest programme of criminological research ever undertaken in the United Kingdom will have been launched. This research is part of the government's Crime Reduction Strategy. The New Labour (as it wishes to be known) administration, elected in May 1997, succeeded in displacing a Conservative government which had been in power for eighteen years. New Labour won in part by persuading the electorate that it, and not the Conservative Party, could successfully deliver 'law and order'. It promised to be 'tough on crime, tough on the causes of crime', though on the hustings, and during its first months in office, it was the first part of this populist equation that was emphasized. Now that New Labour, backed by the largest parliamentary majority of recent years, has settled into government, ministers are beginning publicly to face up to the crime and criminal justice complexities and dilemmas they have inherited. Sound-bite 'law and order' politics are gradually giving way to the subtle compromises which arise from the difficult policy choices that are dictated by the responsibilities of office. Crime, and what to do about crime, is among the government's top policy priorities. If New Labour are to win a second or third period in office their senior tacticians believe they must succeed, or have the appearance of succeeding, on the 'law and order' front for two principal reasons. First, because they know that the public at large is overwhelmingly preoccupied by crime (Mirrlees-Black and Allen 1998). And, secondly, because 'law and order' has traditionally been the Labour Party's electoral Achilles' Heel. Criminological research is about to be pressed into service, because the Labour Party needs to establish its governmental credentials. But the criminological research that it will commission will be of a particular type and will be linked to New and not Old Labour concerns. It will thus illustrate a fundamental truth, namely, that criminological *research* is inescapably political and in recent years has become increasingly impregnated by party politics, more so than criminology itself. The aim of this chapter is to explain why this is so and to draw out some of the political connections that frame the UK cottage industry of criminological research. In the course of telling the story I shall refer to some of my own experience of working in this field of research.

SETTING THE CRIMINOLOGICAL SCENE

Whatever criminology is about it is inescapably about crime. From time to time critics argue that much criminological work is theoretically impoverished, and that crime would be better contemplated within wider horizons—social strati-fication, socialization and role theory, social justice, and so on. Such critics suggest that the study of crime and our responses to it should be part of a broader commitment to the development of fundamental social or normative theory, and as part of that ambition sometimes disclaim the title criminology because of its allegedly customary technicist limitations. But these flailings have so far been largely in vain and the polemical essays in which they are endlessly pursued are often circular and, in the final analysis, banal in their attempted reformulations (for recent examples, see Henry and Milovanovic 1994; Loader 1998). Criminology, as entrepreneurial gambit, occupational title, and disciplin-ary descriptor, thrives despite the predilection of its practitioners to claim for their own contribution some prefix—*new, radical, left, critical, realist, left-utopian*—signifying enquiring purity, theoretical significance and social rele-vance while attaching to the work of others a label—*positivist, administrative, jobbing, right, right-utopian*—signifying political subservience or corruption, theoretical impotence or social irrelevance. Why? Any account of the politics of current criminological research needs briefly to begin with the socio-economic context within which criminology as it is taught in places of higher education continues to burgeon.

As we enter the new millennium Britain is arguably a more fractured society than at any point since the Second World War. This is the consequence of a paradox. Modernity has increased the degree to which we share a common politico-cultural infrastructure the language of which endorses citizenship, democracy, public accountability, equality of opportunity, collective and individual justice, and so on. Almost everyone: has the vote; has access to elementary education free at the point of delivery; derives information and entertainment from national mass media; benefits from the state-provided safety net of a National Health Service; and, if unemployed, sick or of pension-able age, has the assurance of transfer payments which will minimally provide shelter, put clothes on backs, and food in bellies. Moreover, we are all citizens of a state that has signed up to international human rights conventions and, in the Human Rights Act 1998, has incorporated those obligations into domestic law. It was not so previously. Yet whereas two thirds to three quarters of us live comfortably or luxuriously, enjoying unprecedentedly high incomes and a cornucopia of consumer choice—new and more powerful cars, second holidays and homes, electronic gadgetry, designer fripperies, and pre-packaged all-the-year-round exotic foods brought to our out-of-town supermarkets from every corner of the globe—the other one quarter to one third of the population live in poverty and insecurity which in the latter decades of the twentieth century has in relative terms grown progressively more acute (Hutton 1996).

According to the latest government statistics our unprecedented prosperity is less and less equally shared: income inequality has grown during the last twenty years more in Britain than in almost all other developed countries including the USA (Treasury 1999, para. 2.03). The proportion of the population living in households with income below half the national average—the generally accepted definition of relative poverty—is now twelve million, three times the number in 1979 and encompassing approximately a quarter of the population. This relative poverty is both persistent—families are trapped within it—and geographically concentrated. It is explained largely by technological change and shifting labour market conditions, combined with demographic changes and increased determination by successive governments to control or cut public expenditure and not to pursue redistributive fiscal policies. There is less and less call for unskilled workers and their relative earnings have declined. Long-term unemployment has increased. Low-paid part-time employment has increased. Whereas a majority of the population now live in multiple-earner households, 18 per cent of the population live in workless households. In areas like Mersey-side the figure is 28 per cent and examination of the small area data reveals significantly higher figures. These growing inequalities are reinforcing and inter-generational. A third of our children, four million in all, are living in relative poverty, three and a half times the number in 1979 (Treasury 1999, para. 3.20). Children brought up in relative poverty are significantly more likely to fail at school and the absence of educational qualifications is the greatest handicap for those entering the more competitive labour market.

Some of these themes are the enduring stuff of social stratification. However, being unemployed and living in relative poverty at the beginning of the new millennium is not the same experience as it was at the end of the nineteenth century or the Great Depression of the 1920s. Today virtually every household and child's head has images piped into it of what one writer has termed the 'carnival of wealth and self-indulgence' (Davis 1998: 175) which a large propor-tion of the population takes for granted. The cultural and political solidarity of the working classes—a term now considered quaint—has all but evaporated.

The nuclear family, let alone the extended family, has for a large proportion of households fallen apart. Young mothers struggle alone to bring up a growing proportion of children in relative poverty and more and more old people live out their days in uncared-for solitude. Poverty today is concentrated in several thousand sink estates, the residual legacy of our post-War commitment to public housing. These are the sites repeatedly identified by studies of socio-economic disadvantage in contemporary Britain. Here are the geo-coded and mapped hot-spots identified by the new generation of local authority planners preparing the crime and disorder audits required by the Crime and Disorder Act 1998. The poverty indicators—high unemployment, a high proportion of single-parent households and families dependent on income support, many children entitled to free school meals, households without access to a motor vehicle, children leaving school without qualifications, and so on—generally correspond to the sites in which are concentrated the community safety alarums—high police-recorded crime, high incidence of domestic violence, evidence of drug abuse, many addresses of known offenders, permanently excluded school pupils, children on the at-risk register and attenders at hospital accident and emergency departments. Every major city has its stigmatically deprived 'symbolic location', but the major conurbations in the rust-belt zones have swathes of housing, mostly local-authority-owned, where hopelessness thrives and in which alienation is the engine driving the substantially drug-related property crime from which Britain now suffers. It is too early to take comfort from the stabilization and modest fall in police-recorded crime that has occurred since 1992 (Home Office 1997), indeed there are already warnings that the lull is over.

The almost relentless growth in property crime of recent decades has affected the whole country—rural areas, small towns, provincial cities, and major con-urbations. But crime is most prevalent in those urban areas where the multiply disadvantaged dwell. And at the heart of this growth and concentration lies an uncomfortable structural truth. Britain is now a more unequal and disaffected society than for many a year and crime, together with victims' fear of and anger about crime, is the generally recognized and principal symptom of our social disarray. It is not an exaggeration to suggest that the incidence of predatory crime in contemporary Britain is symptomatic of a slow-burning socio-economic civil war. It is the flip-side of the complacent acceptance by the majority of the population of a prosperity based on blatant inequality and social injustice fostered by the progressive abandonment over two decades of civic responsibility in favour of privatized protection.

This state of affairs is partly the consequence of global technological change bearing down on a nation that was the crucible of the industrial revolution. Traditional sources of employment—agriculture, fishing, mining, and large-scale manufacturing—have massively declined and large sections of the workforce have almost literally been thrown on the scrap-heap. Several of the geographical zones in which those redundant workers have been concentrated have become rust belts. Yet successive governments have pursued policies which have exacerbated the strains of this transition. Britain under the Conservative governments of the 1980s proudly boasted of leading Europe towards privatization, deregulation, and the creation of a more 'flexible' labour market—that is, a labour market in which the workforce is less protected, less well trained, and less invested-in. Fiscal policies were adopted based on the proposition that whereas the already well-rewarded apparently needed the *incentive* of greatly increased incomes (both earned and retained after tax), the disadvantaged needed the *spur* of reduced state benefits in order that the dependency culture be undermined. The wealthy were made more wealthy and the poor poorer. Those with jobs worked longer and longer hours while those without jobs, particularly the rising generation of long-term unemployed youth, had time to kill.

It was to middle-income Britain, relatively thriving, but nevertheless anxious about the pitfalls and tensions abounding in the new deregulated market place, that the major political parties made their pitch. This was the constituency to which New Labour promised to be 'tough on crime' and undertook not to reverse the reduced taxation policies to which the Conservatives had moved during the course of eighteen years. On the one hand New Labour used the language of social inclusion and restorative justice, and preached the virtues of public services and holistic social policy. On the other it appeared willing to continue dismantling a welfare state based on the concept of citizenship through social equality, in favour of marketization and criminal justice measures designed to control the socially troublesome outwith the new stakeholder fraternity. That is, New Labour seemed willing to maintain the trend from modernity—assimilation and incorporation—to post-modernity—separation and exclusion (Young 1998).

LAW AND ORDER POLITICS

In 1979 the Conservatives promised the electorate that if elected they would cut public expenditure virtually across the board but increase spending on 'law and order' services. This stance was fundamental to the radical project on which the Conservative government thereafter embarked. It capitalized on traditional Conservative strengths and Labour weaknesses as far as a sizeable proportion of the electorate were concerned. That this was so was tacitly acknowledged by the Labour Party after its electoral defeat in 1993. An essential part of the transition from Old to New Labour involved the Labour Party distancing itself from what were perceived to be the law and order skeletons in their cupboard.

The strength of the Conservative Party has traditionally been its capacity to signify oneness with the bastions of British sovereignty—the monarchy and the aristocracy, property, the armed forces, the institutions of the educated elite, the land, and the law (Parkin 1967; see also Honderich 1990). By contrast the Labour Party has traditionally grounded its appeal on cautiously challenging these institutions and assumptions: it has laid claim to the values of community and redistributive justice. After the Second World War this cleavage offered distinctive choices in most areas of social policy—taxation, education, health, housing, and so on. On the one hand one could vote for progressive taxation and high quality, more-or-less-free-at-the-point-of-delivery, comprehensive public services: on the other for self-reliance within the competitive market place backed up by basic, selective, and means-tested state provision. Through-out most of the twentieth century, however, the pursuit of Labour Party ideals has meant that activists, or groups closely allied to the Labour Party, from time to time became involved in skirmishes with the law and the courts. This was necessary, for example, to achieve recognition of trade unions more than a century ago and again during the 1980s to defend their rights and interests, most conspicuously during the miners' dispute of 1983–4. Parallel acts of civil disobedience have periodically engaged Labour Party supporters pursuing pro-test or reformist agendas ranging from the Campaign for Nuclear Disarmament in the 1960s to poll-tax resistance in 1989–91.

Although the Labour and Conservative parties have seldom taken radically distinctive policy stances on 'law and order' issues, their general ideological positioning has meant that they tend to be drawn to different explanations of crime and disorder. The Conservative Party typically assumes that crime is the product of individual pathology and the breakdown of established patterns of authority. The Labour Party tends to assume that crime is the product of structural forces, in particular inequality and lack of legitimate opportunity. It follows that its party projects have been different. For Labour the task has been to *connect* the phenomenon of crime to socio-economic policy: the Conserva-tives have been keen to *disconnect* these phenomena (Downes 1989). For Labour these connections provide *explanations*, whereas for Conservatives they provide *excuses* and serve to undermine the rule of law itself.

During the 1970s and 1980s, a period during which there was growing public concern about crime, the Conservatives were able rhetorically to underline their commitment to the rule of law and Labour's alleged unreliability in this sphere by recording and trotting out a catalogue of incidents illustrating the willing-ness of Labour Party supporters to break the law or speak ill of it and its enforcement agents. It is this aspect of Old Labour that New Labour has striven, successfully it would appear, to put behind it. New Labour wishes now to be seen as the party that will best protect citizens against crime—to be the *real* party of law and order—and, given that the 1980s was a decade of inexorable growth in recorded crime and almost unprecedented civil disorder (industrial disputes, inner city riots, and public protests), the better guarantor of the Queen's Peace. This is best exemplified by: the Prime Minister's and Home Secretary's support for 'zero-tolerance policing' (see Dennis 1997); their backing while in Opposition, and implementation since coming to office, of the key provisions of the Crime (Sentences) Act 1997 (thereby, with reference to presumptive minimum four-year prison sentences for third-time burglary convictions, effectively endorsing Conservative Home Secretary Michael Howard's claim that 'prison works'); and their adoption of a series of tough measures, particularly in relation to youth justice, in the Crime and Disorder Act 1998.

It is true that the Crime and Disorder Act 1998 also incorporates a number of measures which open up a range of possibilities for crime prevention in a holistic sense. The Morgan Report (Home Office 1991), whose key recommendations the Conservative government rejected, has been dusted off and local authorities are now statutorily required to prepare Crime and Disorder Strategies based on a partnership approach between all the key agencies. However, it is noteworthy that having initially adopted the all-encompassing language of community safety (see Hughes 1998, ch. 6) New Labour has in the end preferred the narrower, tougher term 'crime and disorder' and local authorities have unequivocally been told that there is to be no additional core funding for their crime preventive work. Instead there will be specific crime preventive initiatives funded by central government, but the general planning process is to be paid for out of the crime prevention savings achieved (Home Office 1997, para. 34). Thus despite the setting up within the Prime Minister's Office of a Social Exclusion Unit, and the allocation of £800 million over three years for a *New Deal for Communities* programme involving the planned regeneration of seventeen 'pathfinder' deprived areas, New Labour's toughness regarding the 'causes of crime' appears so far to be narrowly conceived. The previous Conservative government's public expenditure limits have been broadly endorsed and taxation is not to be increased. It follows that despite such measures as the introduction of a modest minimum wage, there is to be no radical income redistributive programme. The increased income and wealth inequalities of recent years are not to be reversed. Poverty will not diminish except to the extent that prudent management of the economy generally serves to generate economic growth and reduce unemployment.

As far as the causes of crime and disorder are concerned tough love is to be applied in a largely individualistic sense according to tough-minded criteria. The policy language is couched entirely in terms of managerial control rather than social equity or collective justice. Crime *hot spots* are to be identified and short-term *risk assessments* made so that there can be *targeted interventions* subject to *cost-benefit evaluations* of effectiveness. The programme is to be backed up by research. Indeed there is to be more funded criminological research than ever before: but it is to be research conforming to the prescriptions of New Labour governance.

This emphasis is nowhere better illustrated than in the Report of the New Labour-dominated House of Commons Home Affairs Committee on *Alternatives to Prison Sentences* (1998). The tone of the report is tough-minded and the approach managerialist. Thus, the Committee concludes that the objective of crime prevention would not be well served by the courts making significantly greater use of imprisonment than is currently the case. But the Committee also gives a good deal of attention and support to the propositions that, when the pattern and rate of offending in England and Wales are taken into account, some offenders not currently imprisoned arguably should be and non-custodial sentences generally have no better record for preventing recidivism than does imprisonment. Indeed, they argue that when proper allowance is made for undetected offences committed by offenders subject to non-custodial penalties during the period that they are subject to those penalties, then imprisonment might be judged more effective than the alternatives. Like the pot which can be described as either half-full or half-empty, non-custodial and custodial sanctions can be compared either (or both) in terms of their roughly equivalent effectiveness or ineffectiveness. They can also be compared in terms of their relative cost in public expenditure and human liberty, in which case non-custodial penalties come out as clear winners. But that opportunity is not taken by the Home Affairs Committee.

The Committee accepts that imprisonment is the proper disposal for dangerous and/or persistent offenders. Although it recommends that community alternatives be used for other offenders, it insists that these alternatives be made more effective and take an overtly punitive form in which sentencers and public are likely to have confidence. The Committee is highly critical of much non-custodial practice. It is 'astonished' at the general absence of assessment of the effectiveness of community sanctions and 'alarmed' at the low level of compliance by local probation services with the national standards for supervision and the enforcement of orders laid down centrally by the Home Office. It is persuaded by the evidence that community programmes based on what are now referred to as 'what works?' principles (broadly, cognitive-behavioural approaches that are proportionate to the actuarial assessment of risk posed, which require the active participation of the offender, which are skills-oriented, employment-focused, and so on) offer a more cost-effective long-term response to much offending than imprisonment (see McGuire and Priestley 1995; Vennard, Sugg and Hedderman 1997). But it insists that these programmes be carefully targeted, strictly enforced, and rigorously evaluated. And it 'deplores' the cosy language of 'clients' and so on that the Probation Service has traditionally employed. It recommends, for example, that the Community Service Order be renamed the Criminal Work Order, a recommendation to which the Home Secretary has since acceded. It is reported (*Guardian*, 14 April 1999) that Mr Straw is also considering re-naming the Probation Service—the Criminals Correction Agency perhaps?

THE CRIMINOLOGICAL ENTERPRISE

In 1993–4 I was jointly responsible for putting together a criminological reader which has become, with its second edition, a standard text in the UK (Maguire, Morgan, and Reiner 1997). In the preface we noted the extraordinary development during its relatively short life of criminology in higher education as a taught subject and research enterprise. In the space of little more than forty years criminology has been transformed from being the focus of a few lone pioneering figures to a major academic industry, large-scale and organized as far as teaching is concerned and expansive, though still largely cottage, with respect to research. In the 1950s there were virtually no undergraduate courses, and those who began to teach the subject at postgraduate level had remarkably little research material on which to draw in preparing their courses. Today virtually none of the ninety universities in the UK is without undergraduate options in criminology (or some application of criminology or criminal justice) and many now have specialist taught postgraduate courses. There are a score or more criminology-related university research centres avidly competing for the funds available from the Home Office, the Economic and Social Research Council (ESRC), the major charitable research foundations, and, increasingly, the local authorities and statutory services. The *Howard Journal* and *British Journal of Criminology* have been joined by half a dozen others whose content is largely or partially devoted to criminology articles. Several leading publishers carry substantial lists of titles devoted to criminology.

This extraordinary growth is not surprising. The 'law and order' services— police, social services, Crown Prosecution Service, the courts, probation, and prisons—have grown enormously in terms both of personnel and budget. In 1998–9 total government expenditure on 'public order and safety' in England and Wales amounted to nearly £17,000 million. The police service alone employed almost 183,000 personnel (officers and civilians) compared to just over 81,000 in 1958–9. The Prison Service employed over 42,000 staff compared to fewer than 6,000 in 1958–9. This official account does not tell anything like the full story, however. The burgeoning commercial security industry is estimated now to be significantly larger than that of the state police (Jones and Newburn

1998) and the senior ranks of the security services are drawn substantially from the state police and other law and order services. The latest recruits to this expanding *corps* of 'law and order' players are the district council community safety officers responsible for co-ordinating the Crime and Disorder Strategy documents now required of every local authority by the Crime and Disorder Act 1998. Short and distance-learning courses are already sprouting to meet this new market opportunity.

The evidence suggests that criminology is an intrinsically attractive subject as far as an expanding proportion of social science and law students is concerned. It addresses questions that are of general public interest and concern and it covers incidents and processes—crime and punishment—that provide the subject matter of a high proportion of news coverage and popular entertainment. When student applicants to universities are asked during interviews to talk about some aspect of social policy or law that has attracted their interest and thought, most focus on some aspect of crime or criminal law. The topics are accessible and in the air. Criminology has also become of straightforward utilitarian career value. Recruits to the law and order public services are increasingly expected to have some familiarity with the criminological theory and practice that inform practical crime prevention, social work, policing, sentencing, and so on. Criminology is the product of contemporary governance and increasingly services it through the recruitment and training of personnel. It was ever thus, but has become more so. Much of the debate in criminological texts about the shifting contours of *administrative, radical, critical* criminology and so forth represent real changes of theoretical emphasis and substantive interest in what and how academic criminologists teach and undertake research (van Swaaningen 1997). But it has always been the 'government project' (Garland 1997) that has driven the expansion of the discipline, even though the 'government project' marginally changes from time to time in tone, method and direction. Nowhere is this more apparent than in the funding of criminological research.

THE INFRASTRUCTURE AND PROCESS OF CRIMINOLOGICAL RESEARCH

THE HOME OFFICE

If size and influence are the criteria then any institutional account of criminological research in Britain must begin with the Home Office Research, Development and Statistics Directorate (HORSD, as the former Home Office Research Unit and other more specific research groups within the Home Office are now known).The HORSD is the largest single employer of criminological researchers in the UK. At any one time there are upwards of 100 of them and the number is currently being greatly increased. Not all are graduates who have studied criminology either as an undergraduate option or as a postgraduate specialism. Several have backgrounds in a variety of social sciences ranging from economics to geography and psychology and are new to the areas of crime prevention, policing, and criminal justice on which most HORSD work is focused. Moreover, because the HORSD has the largest criminological research budget in Britain, a budget used both in-house and to commission research from the academic community, market research companies, and, increasingly, management consultants, the Directorate is intermittently the employer of outsiders, including a considerable number of academic criminologists based in universities. It exercises the natural influence of paymaster, actual and potential—grants hoped for as well as received. Thus when the Directorate organizes open days to announce research programmes, as it did in December 1998 to discuss the evaluation of the current Home Office Crime Reduction Programme, or in January 1999 to discuss the evaluation of the Drugs Programme, it is inundated with requests from academics anxious to have a seat at the table from which crumbs might fall. Such events are always over-subscribed.

Like all institutionally powerful paymasters HORSD inspires both sycophancy and disdain. The HORSD lies in a chain of command that begins with the Home Office policy divisions and ultimately ends up close under the thumb of ministers. The criminological fraternity is, at best, insecure about its identity as impartial scholar, and some sections like to see themselves as spokespersons of the oppressed caught in the expanding trap of criminal justice. Not surprisingly academic reactions to the Directorate can sometimes be extreme. Those academic researchers, and criminological centres, who regularly undertake contracts for HORSD are sometimes the object of scarcely disguised contempt from other criminologists who wear their radical-critical pretensions conspicuously on their sleeves.

It is widely contended, and not just by the radical outsiders, that most Home Office-funded criminological research is:

i. almost entirely atheoretical *fact gathering*—how many crimes are not reported? How many crimes probably are committed by persons arrested (or probably not committed by persons imprisoned)? What drugs are consumed by young people arrested and not arrested? What is the level of compliance of offenders sentenced to one court order as opposed to another? And so on;

ii. is *narrowly focused*—generally on a recent spending or administrative initiative or piece of legislation;

iii. and is designed to be, and in its final product invariably is, *policy-friendly.*

Which is to say that it is: *empirical*; generally *quantitative* (the emphasis being on measuring the easily measurable); increasingly incorporates a *cost-benefit* assessment; overwhelmingly *short-termist*—designed to answer the question whether whatever is being evaluated is having an immediate impact; and *uncritical*, in the sense that it does not question general government policy but merely it reports whether the evidence collected supports the continuation of one policy tactic as opposed to another.

To the extent that this typification is correct—and I suggest that though it largely is, it is nonetheless not the whole story—it should not be a cause for surprise and is certainly no scandal. It was ever thus. The Home Office serves an elected government more or less carrying out manifesto commitments. HORSD's customers are the Home Office policy divisions serving political masters whose primary interest is confirmation that the policies they are pursuing are working so that the public at large, given whatever hopes and fears they entertain, can be persuaded that they made the correct choice at the last General Election and will make the same choice at the next. This is not to say that the HORSD criminological research programme is a political charade. It is not. Its design and delivery are methodologically demanding and professionally competent—indeed it enjoys a substantial international reputation in that regard—and it is characterized by a high level of integrity with respect to reliability and validity. The HORSD has over the years been an unrivalled source of apprenticeship for leading researchers many of whom have since left the Home Office and taken up senior academic posts in university departments of criminology. Moreover, a significant proportion of the research undertaken *within* the HORSD, as well as *for* the HORSD, is published in the same academic journals which carry the work of scholars not aspiring to Home Office funding. Nevertheless, the HORSD research programme is ultimately managed for political ends—to enhance the reputation of the political party in government. That means that at best it aims at the fine-tuning of policy, not challenging it and certainly not discrediting either it or the agencies that deliver it and for which the government is responsible to Parliament. This is a fact of Home Office life. Only when the ministerial thumb is pressed too firmly on the HORSD programme—Michael Howard, the Conservative Home Secretary from 1992–7, arguably exercised a baneful hands-on influence (and at one point even considered disbanding the Directorate) which stimulated an unprecedented exodus of research staff—is the discomfort within HORSD as palpable as that more generally felt without.

The significance of the HORSD research programme, and the tensions surrounding it, are well illustrated by the arrangements for New Labour's £250 million *Crime Reduction Programme*—for which a separate evaluation budget of £25 million is nominally attached over the next three years—and the evaluation of other criminal justice initiatives announced by the government. The latter include: the youth justice provisions in the Crime and Disorder Act 1998 and the work of the Youth Justice Board established to oversee the working of those provisions (an overall budget of £85 million over three years); the drugs prevention programme in both prisons and the community (a budget of £211 million over three years); additional resources for the Probation Service (including £56 million to pilot, evaluate, and implement the Drug Treatment and Testing Order); and additional resources for the Prison Service to provide prisoner programmes, resources which the new Director General of the Prison Service has said will substantially be devoted to developing the literacy, numeracy, and employment skills of young offenders in the Young Offender Institutions.

Precisely what all this adds up to in terms of a criminal justice research budget is as yet unclear, but it emphatically represents during the period 1999–2002 a significant increase on the HORSD spend during the period 1991/2–1996/7 when the Home Office research budget ranged between £10.9 and £14.8 million *per annum*. The bulk of the HORSD budget has always been spent in-house on research officers who both carry out research and supervise projects contracted to external researchers. It is notable that thirty-six of the eighty-seven pieces of work making up the HORSD programme in 1998–9 were being conducted by outsiders. Not all of this work constitutes research (several projects concern the development and application of the police funding formula and others the preparation of factual digests on criminal justice for practitioners, for example) and a good deal is not criminological (various pieces of work on the voluntary sector, the Passport Agency, the Fire Service, value for money in Home Office spending, and so on). But the bulk of it is criminological, and ranges from the latest sweep of the British Crime Survey—now a biennial commitment—to the urine testing of arrestees (if US precedent is any guide, likely to become a perennial exercise), to another round of the 1953 Cambridge Delinquent Development cohort, to more transient concerns such as the evaluation of the use made of new police stop and search powers under the Criminal Justice and Public Order Act 1994 and the effectiveness of using Community Service Orders for fine defaulters and electronic monitoring for bailees under the Crime (Sentences) Act 1997.

The budget allocated for the evaluation of the current *Crime Reduction Programme* will certainly be criminological and the research will probably be characterized by precisely those features described above which are held by many commentators to represent the theoretical poverty of much HORSD work. Consider the following.

A relatively new aspect of Home Office research is the evaluation of government-promoted policy initiatives in which the participants are criminal justice providers—police forces, probation services, individual prisons, young offender teams, local authority-based crime prevention partnerships, and so on—who must themselves competitively bid for the privilege of taking part. At least £32 million over the next three years, for example, is to be spent on a *targeted policing* programme (Home Office 1999a). The forty-three police forces in England and Wales were invited to submit bids and eleven projects, out of the approximately seventy submitted, have been shortlisted and are to be funded. A second tranche of projects is to be funded during 1999–2000. The attractions of participation for chief constables are obvious: by this means they can secure, say, half a million pounds additional funding for their force *and* advance their reputation as pioneers of good practice. The problems targeted by the eleven shortlisted bids include everything from rural crime, to markets in stolen goods, to alcohol-related violence in entertainment zones, to offences committed by absconders from community homes to prolific illicit drug-related crime. The bidders—local police forces in partnership with local authorities, probation and social services, health authorities, and whichever other agencies are deemed relevant—have been informed that they must spend their budgets by April 2002. This date, it should be noted, is approximately the latest by which the government must prepare for the next General Election. Planning for initiatives must be based on the plausible proposition that the intervention can be made to work in terms of a reduction in police-recorded crime, or other indicators (such as hospital accident and emergency injury admissions, public self-report surveys, and so on) which give a more comprehensive picture of the incidence of crime. Independent evaluation will demonstrate whether or not the initiative works within the timescale of the project. The evaluations will be undertaken by consortia of academic criminologists. Their attentions are directed to the need to identify:

i.   *inputs* (the additional human, physical, and financial resources used to undertake the project); the *costs* being the monetary value of the inputs;
ii.   *outputs*—the direct products of the implementation process arising during the implementation period;
iii.   *impacts*, the initial results of the outputs attributable to the intervention which serve to disrupt the causes of the criminal events;
iv.   *outcomes*, the consequences of the intervention both during and subsequent to the implementation, the key outcomes being those that relate to the stated objectives of the intervention and the *benefits* being the monetary value of the outcomes attributed to the intervention (Home Office 1999b, 7).

The other components of the government's *Crime Reduction Programme*—the *domestic burglary project*, the *short-term prisoner resettlement project*, the *fine enforcement project*, and so on—have the same methodological strictures attached to them. The government is looking for interventions which have immediate results—'a quick real impact' (Home Office 1999a)—and which can be shown to have cost benefits capable of being mainstreamed, that is replicated by other policing and criminal justice agencies. This is a long way from the evidence of growing structural socio-economic inequality, and the sense of social injustice which accompanies it, with which we began this chapter and on which many radical criminologists wish to concentrate their attentions. Though the *Crime Reduction Programme* claims to combine short-term interventions with long-term work to tackle the causes of crime and though it is true that there are references in the *Programme* to the need to reduce social exclusion (school exclusions and dealing more effectively with domestic violence, for example), the bulk of the Home Secretary's message, and the associated spending concerns targeting offenders and managing them more effectively. One does not have to be particularly cynical to see the possibility of this leading to more rather than less social exclusion in the form of custodial penalties—a continuation of a trend which has seen the prison population rise by more than 50 per cent during the period 1992–8 (Morgan and Carlen 1999).

It is for precisely this reason that the work of the HORSD is controversial, and the controversy is, if anything, growing rather than diminishing in intensity. There are two principal reasons for this: first, because there has been some tightening in the manner and degree to which the Home Office exerts control over the delivery of its research programme; secondly, because the field of academic criminology has itself expanded and because academic criminologists are working in a higher education climate in which there is increased pressure to publish so-called original research and gain externally-funded research contracts. Increased Home Office control over the research agenda is the corollary of the party politicization of 'law and order' policy described above. Because governments now commit themselves prior to election to specific 'law and order' programmes, instead of relying on the recommendations of various 'expert' advisory bodies (Royal Commissions, statutory or *ad hoc* policy standing committees, and so on) once they had been elected, the content and outcome of criminological research now has greater party political salience. Nowadays Home Office-funded contracts are generally: more specific in their content; of shorter duration; subject to closer supervision; covered by stricter rules of confidentiality; and subject to firmer control regarding the use of data and the content and publication of research results. Furthermore, most contracts are now obtained through a tendering and competitive bidding process that places the external researcher in a more subservient position, constantly second-guessing the will of the Home Office policymakers. This represents a tightening of the reins, not a sea change, however. Undertaking research for the Home Office was never a liberal experimental playground, not if one wanted to work for the Home Office again. The reason there is increased, and critical, academic awareness of the Home Office reins is that the Home Office budget now looms so large in the consciousness of university-based criminologists and that all university departments are under increasing pressure to secure external research funding.

Now that the *big* criminological research initiative associated with the Home Office *Crime Reduction Programme* is under way, tender documents are being published, co-operative research consortia are being put together between universities, contracts jockeyed for, bids submitted, agreements signed and field-work begun. It is a frantic process driven not by an academic agenda—though the formation of the *Programme* has arguably itself been influenced by the broader academic debate. Instead it is a political programme of which different sections of the academic criminological fraternity are simultaneously disdainful and calculatingly and opportunistically respectful. Before the next General Election is announced there will almost certainly be a deluge of articles deploring the narrow, technical, evaluative studies that the Home Office will fund. And this critical outpouring will emanate from centres of learning whose post-graduate students will nevertheless be familiarized by their tutors with the research initiatives pursued by the government, and who will themselves largely be destined for the services delivering the programmes subject to attack. Which is to say that those who wield the critical pens will mostly be involved, indirectly if not directly, in the controversial research enterprise that sustains, as it has always sustained, criminology in the field of higher education. To the extent that criminology is a discipline prostituted to government it is because criminology is indissolubly a normative discipline. Normative because criminology, uniquely among the branches of social science, has as its subject matter and built into its title a social problem—crime. And crime is a category which is politically and not academically determined. No amount of obscurantist language and arcane conceptual recategorization can evade this fundamental nexus.

My own view and experience of the Home Office research enterprise is more nuanced than that set out above. I would emphasize the following points.

i.   even were this or any other government to commit itself to the economic policies that might begin to close the socio-economic gulfs that have opened up over the last twenty years, or promote more inclusive social policies, there would nevertheless continue for the forseeable future to be a major crime problem about which the public would continue to demand from their politicians that something be done;

ii.   any good government would, in response to these short-term pressures, adopt an evidence-based substantive approach, rather than purely symbolic measures, to placate the public. This would involve targeting those forms of crime, and those criminals most prolifically responsible for it, that most worry the public;

iii. given that no government, in the short term at least, can greatly change those structural factors which motivate people to commit crime, any sensible government must concentrate on those factors which affect the objective opportunity to commit crime (*objective* opportunities which are *subjectively* interpreted as opportunities) and the likelihood of being apprehended and proceeded against by the authorities. Furthermore, any responsible government must approach these issues from a cost-benefit standpoint;

iv. the Home Office programme offers a large number of criminologists, working both in-house and out-house, unrivalled apprenticeship opportunities to engage in research which, however narrowly conceived, is nevertheless methodologically rigorous. Moreover, once the Home Office has given its approval to a research project, it is always open to an imaginative and critically minded researcher to view the data collected within a broader theoretical frame of reference; that is, once the ball has been picked up, there are few real limits to the distance one can run with it. If Home Office-funded research projects are limited in their outputs and outcomes (to use the language deployed above) this typically has more to do with self-censorship or the interpretative failure of academic researchers to realize and seize opportunities than any constraints imposed by the Home Office. The catalogue of criminological books, and articles in scholarly criminological journals, incorporating sophisticated theoretical contributions for which funding originally came from the HORSD is substantial (it would be invidious to cite particular examples);

v. it can never be stressed too often that those authors who engage in more abstract theorizing about the social construction of crime and the form of reactions to it are dependent for most of their insights on the wealth of empirical data that the HORSD has largely been responsible for amassing. These data, collected through processes too often derided, are the clay and straw that make the bricks which both make for an accountable criminal justice system and permit it to be effectively challenged and analysed. Anyone who has spent time engaged in discussions with academic criminologist colleagues from other European jurisdictions—France, Italy, Spain, Greece, for example—will be aware that their critiques are typically theoretically abstract for want of practical knowledge about how their criminal justice systems operate in practice. That is, their theoretical edifices are often a sign of weakness rather than strength.

I am not suggesting that the Home Office encourages radical critiques: it does not. Or that the Home Office does not attempt to constrain what it regards as unruly or embarrassing prodigies: it does. Ministers, and their civil servant concierges, generally do their best to suppress, temporarily at least, research findings that ruffle policy assumptions or programmes. Most senior criminologists who have undertaken work for the Home Office during their careers, or who have been dependent on the key criminal justice agencies for access to data, have tales to tell of obstruction, attempted suppression, delays in publication, and so on. It is the research equivalent of traffic calming, even if some of the tales have to be taken with a pinch of salt, which is to say that there are often two sides to the stories. Some academic criminology researchers, as the exchanges between researchers in the pages of scholarly journals testify, are not above claiming findings that their data scarcely warrant. However, the truth about most criminological research is that very few pieces of work are either so categorical in their conclusions, or so broad in their implications, that they have the capacity seriously to discomfort ministers and governments. We are for the most part easily swept aside. Furthermore, a good deal of Home Office policy-making is taken in spite of, rather than because of, criminological research findings (the classic case in recent years being Mr Howard's claim that 'prison works' with the result of his rhetoric being the substantial rise in prison numbers).

In conclusion, a few words about the process by which HORSD contracts are obtained. Though it is the case that practically all HORSD research contracts now have to be bid for by competitive tender, the process by which academic researchers get invited to bid is far from transparent, and there is currently no peer review of, or academic representation within, the process through which contracts are allocated. Furthermore, the Home Office equivalent of Chinese walls between contractors and contractees invite suspicions rather than confidence. Let us take these issues briefly in turn.

First, it seems often to be a matter of chance whether individual academic researchers are informed about a research tender. Speaking from personal experience, I have sometimes heard about a tendering process only after the closing date for bids has passed. On other occasions I have been telephoned by someone within HORSD and asked if I would be interested in tendering for a particular contract which I may or may not have heard was in the offing. There is, as far as I am aware, no national Home Office notice board through which all research criminologists can discover, well before the date by which bids must be submitted, that certain contracts are to be let. This seems both unfair and inefficient. One has the impression that to know what research is to take place one must develop an inside track, be in the know, cultivate contacts within HORSD.

Secondly, it is far from clear why bids are won or lost and how decisions are made. Sometimes one is told an approximate 'ball park' budget for a particular bid. Sometimes one is given no guidance at all. Sometimes there are rumours, colleagues having allegedly been given a hint about how much money is to be allocated. Thus, when the process is over, one wonders how important the cost of a bid is in the decision to award it. And, sometimes, when one sees the text of a winning bid, one is at a loss to know what it was about the bid that won the day. Unlike the process whereby ESRC grants, and charitable foundation grants, are allocated, there is no independent peer review, unless one judges the researchers employed within the HORSD always to be the appropriate peer reviewers, a proposition which stretches credulity. This is less than satisfactory.

Thirdly, as was noted above, there has been a substantial exodus of researchers from HORSD to the universities in recent years. And many of these ex-HORSD personnel are now among the largest recipients of HORSD contracts. The process is not unlike the manner in which senior Treasury and Defence Department civil servants resign their posts only to take up, within a matter of weeks or months, senior banking or defence industry directorships, and begin trading with their former colleagues. Moreover—and I count myself among these ranks—if one is well-known to senior HORSD personnel one may be invited to act as a research consultant overseeing the delivery of a contract by a fellow academic, or assessing the quality of competitive bids from the major criminal justice services for initiative development money, and then being invited to bid for the evaluation of those same policy initiatives. This smacks of insider trading and is at odds with the appearance of transparent fairness which the competitive tendering process is designed to convey. Or, to take a personal experience which occurred a few years before the competitive tendering process was initiated, I once contacted the Research Unit to outline some research I was interested in undertaking with a view to Home Office funding. I was informed that matters would best progress if I set out my ideas on paper, which I did. The next thing I knew was that the research officer I initially contacted within the Research Unit had himself gained approval, on an in-house basis, to undertake almost exactly the same project which I had submitted. There is need for some ethical protocols to be developed here.

THE ECONOMIC AND SOCIAL RESEARCH COUNCIL (ESRC)

The ESRC is quantitatively the second most important port of call for the potential criminological researcher and, for those not wishing to engage in policy-related research, by far the most important. Criminology is among the many areas of work that the ESRC covers, though there is no specific allocation of its budget to this topic. Indeed the electronic catalogue of research work it has funded over the years cannot even be interrogated employing this title to see precisely how much criminology research has been funded. The position is roughly as follows.

The ESRC currently has a spending budget of £65 million, of which approximately one third (£23 million) is used to fund postgraduate studentships and two thirds (£42 million) research projects. Though the work of the ESRC is criticized for being increasingly influenced by government policy, with user panels and user interests (industry, the civil service, the principal state services, and major professions) more and more represented in its counsels (Hillyard and Sim 1997), the research themes that the ESRC has announced it is pursuing are nevertheless remarkably broad and inclusive:

Economic Performance and Development
Environment and Sustainability
Globalisation, Regions and Emerging Markets
Governance, Regulation and Accountability
Technology and People
Innovation
Knowledge, Communication and Learning
Lifespan, Lifestyles and Health
Social Inclusion and Exclusion

(ESRC 1997 and http://www.esrc.ac.uk)

Though it is not clear where *justice* fits in to the ESRC programme—and there is possibly a good case for *Justice* being a theme—it will no doubt be said in the ESRC's defence that justice, like equality and other values, informs, or is capable of informing, several or all of the substantive themes that the Council has set out. Certainly a good deal of criminological work fits neatly within three of these themes, namely Governance, Regulation, and Accountability; Lifespan, Lifestyles, and Health; and Social Inclusion and Exclusion.

What is clear is that in recent years a significant number of ESRC student-ships and a reasonable part of the research budget has been allocated for work that can broadly be described as criminological. Furthermore, the breadth of this work—both theoretically and empirically—has been far greater than that sponsored by the HORSD.

The ESRC disburses money for research through *programmes*—designated and advertised collections of work tied to a dedicated budget for a particular time period—and in *response* to unsolicited applications. Applicants have a statistically better chance of succeeding in getting money by using the response mode than applying through programmes, though it is questionable whether those likelihoods can reasonably be compared. Anyone who has had any involvement in ESRC decision-making—I have acted as a peer reviewer on many occasions and chaired the steering committee for a criminology research programme—knows that solicited applications to programmes and unsolicited applications are *not* of like quality. When the ESRC publicly announces that it invites research applications for a particular programme it is typically inundated with applicants climbing onto the latest bandwagon: a high proportion of applications are from persons with little or no experience in the relevant field advancing poorly thought-out off-the-top-of-the-head plans. By contrast unsolicited applications more typically come from researchers who have thought long and hard about whatever it is they are proposing. This being the case a large question mark has to be placed over the ESRC's current policy of allocating an increasing proportion of its research budget to programmes.

During the last fifteen years there have been several predominantly criminological ESRC research programmes. There is currently a *Violence* programme, described as central to the Council's theme of *Social Inclusion and Exclusion.* It is funded over five years to the tune of £3.6 million. Twenty out of the more than 241 applications were funded by the commissioning panel, following the usual two-stage process. Applicants were initially invited to submit a brief outline and costing of projects. From these a small number—though on this occasion more than three times as many as were eventually funded—were invited to develop and flesh out new bids in more detail. Each bid was subject to peer review by at least two independent academic criminologists, with nominated members of the commissioning panel being asked to look closely at particular applications falling within their area of expertise. Exactly the same process was adopted by the 1993–7 programme on *Crime and Social Order*—the steering committee for which I chaired—to which £3.2 million was allocated: this comprised twenty-one projects. In the 1980s there were research programmes on *Crime and Criminal Justice* and *Policing and the Public.*

ESRC programmes tend generally to be somewhat eclectic in spite of their thematic pretensions. Thus the *Crime and Social Order* programme included projects which were contemporary as well as some which were historical; some focused on Britain and others on international comparisons; there were projects concerned with purely conceptual issues whilst others tracked the implementation of particular policies; some comprised large-scale surveys and others small-scale case studies; and projects utilized econometric, geographical, psychological, anthropological, and sociological approaches and techniques. The topics ranged from: an Anglo-French comparison of criminal justice, to the recreational use of drugs by young people, to the social, political, and moral context of fear of crime, to the connection between the use of steroids and violence and the growing use of private security and CCTV. The range of the findings can be seen from three collections of material arising from the programme: a special issue of the *British Journal of Criminology* (1999) devoted to the historical studies, a collection of essays on aspects of crime and order in Britain at the end of the millennium (Carlen and Morgan 1999) and a much larger collection of essays stimulated by programme participants at an international conference, involving both British and other European criminologists, organized by members of the Programme Steering Committee (Ruggiero, South and Taylor 1998). The current *Violence* programme is similarly diverse in character with projects historical and contemporary, comparative and case study, domestic, institutional, and public, racial and age-related. An early product of the *Violence* initiative will also be a special issue of the *British Journal of*

Criminology, this time devoted to emotionality and the process of doing research on violence.

At any one time several other ESRC programmes are likely to include at least a minority of research projects of a criminological nature. Thus the current *Youth, Informal Economy* and *Aging* programmes each contain criminological projects and it is very likely that the *Future Governance* and *Democracy* programmes, currently being commissioned, will do so also. In addition there is a substantial sprinkling of criminological research projects funded as a result of unsolicited applications. If the ESRC database (*ESRC Regard*, maintained by the University of Bristol and accessible from the ESRC website—www.esrc.ac.uk) is interrogated thematically then the keyword *crime*, for example, throws up sixty research award holders during the period 1983 to the present day which were *not* part of any programme. Other keywords—*deviance, policing, criminal justice, delinquency*, and so on—would no doubt generate a longer list. The sixty listed *crime*-related projects amount to an investment of approximately £3.4 million in *addition* to the criminological research programmes. The range of their size and content is well illustrated by the eight non-programme current awards listed. They include £8,780 to Middlesex University for a seminar series on the Crime and Disorder Act 1998 and £371,984 *towards* (funding has also been obtained from the Scottish Office and other sources) the largest longitudinal cohort study ever mounted in the UK to look at offending being organized by the University of Edinburgh. Other studies comprise: £12,417 for a study of social networks and social exclusion (Keele University); £100,113 for a study of attrition of child sexual cases in the criminal justice system (Universities of Huddersfield and Manchester); £38,488 for a study of witnesses with learning disabilities (Universities of Liverpool and Manchester); £165,651 for a study of identification and verification of faces captured on video (University of Stirling); £37,299 for a study of child daycare policy by local authorities (University of Essex) and £75,790 for a study of racial violence in Greater Manchester (Lancaster University). These eight projects, the combined budget for which exceeds £0.8 million, suggests that there is plenty of scope for criminologists to gain funding for research projects that do not fall within the scope of programmes, elastic though the latter often are.

It is also worth noting that some of the non-programme projects funded by the ESRC over the last fifteen years have been conducted by scholars relatively early on in their academic careers, the products from which have been books and articles that are recognized now as key studies within the criminological literature. Moreover, many ESRC-funded projects—programme and non-programme—have provided the first step on the academic career ladder for newly graduating criminologists.

OTHER SOURCES OF RESEARCH FUNDING

Britain is enormously rich in the number of charitable foundations it possesses: many of these foundations fund research and a good many give money for work—either research or initiatives that can be subject to evaluation—on aspects of crime and criminal justice, though most will absolutely *not* fund work which is also being submitted for a postgraduate qualification. Most readers will be familiar with the largest of these foundations—Nuffield, Rowntree, Leverhulme, and so on—but there are a good many others whose names are less familiar but whose identities can be discovered by consulting the *Charities Yearbook*. Moreover, in addition to the government departments and agencies *other* than the Home Office which occasionally fund research of a criminological or socio-legal character—principally the Department of Health, the Lord Chancellor's Department, and the Prison Service—there is a growing body of work, admittedly mostly small-scale—funded by local services and local authorities. A good many district councils, for example, undertook their crime and disorder audits in the autumn of 1998 (as required by the Crime and Disorder Act 1998) with the assistance of academics or market research companies, if they did not contract out the work completely. Many police forces, most of which have a limited in-house research capacity, also commission pieces of work or actively seek research partners as the corollary of bidding for central government funding for this or that initiative. Needless to say, however, everything said above in relation to the HORSD applies also to research undertaken for other branches of the central and local state: if anything more so. This type of research is for the most part narrow and policy-oriented in scope.

Nevertheless, it is easy to underestimate the potential of non-mainstream sources of funding. Scanning through my own *cv* I find that in addition to the traditional ESRC and Home Office grants I have also had commissions or funding from: the Mental Health Foundation, Wiltshire Probation Service, the Nuffield Foundation (on several occasions), the Rowntree Trust, the Police Foundation, the Law Society, the Airey Neave Foundation, the Ford Foundation, and the Avon and Somerset Police. The Airey Neave Foundation, about which I confess I had never heard before approaching them on the recommendation of a colleague in 1992, provided me with a substantial sum (£42,000) which enabled me and a colleague to travel widely throughout Europe studying the *modus operandi* and impact of an international human rights body (Evans and Morgan 1998; Morgan and Evans 1999). I mention the fact because I think that most academic criminologists seldom look beyond the usual suspects for research funding: I believe there is greater scope for support both locally and Europe-wide than is commonly imagined.

CONCLUSION

Direct HORSD criminological research spending, and increasingly government policy-influenced ESRC research spending, involves several million pounds annually flowing into academic criminology centres, the bulk of it to the major centres that, as a result, are also the principal academic employers of criminological researchers and the major postgraduate training grounds in criminology. There are exceptions to this rule—universities that have substantial postgraduate courses but which attract little or no Home Office money, and *vice versa*—but they are exceptions. The Home Office agenda and budget is the piper that calls many of the dominant tunes played in contemporary criminology.

Given that, directly or indirectly, the state is the principal *employer* both of criminology and criminologists, it is scarcely surprising that the major expansion of criminology in the 1980s and 1990s has coincided with its partial retreat from the macro issues of social stratification, wealth and income distribution, and social justice to the narrower managerialist concerns of risk assessment (Feeley and Simon 1992), secondary and tertiary crime prevention (Brantingham and Faust 1976), and the cost effectiveness of one form of government intervention compared to another (Jefferson and Shapland 1994). Needless to say—though this is not an issue on which I have focused in this chapter—the power of the state as the provider of funds is even greater when it comes to data access, an issue which is discussed in some detail by other contributors to this volume. The courts, the Crown Prosecution Service, the police, and the Prison Service have always run relatively tight ships when it comes to allowing criminologists permission to set up their anthropologist huts in judges' retiring rooms, prosecutors' filing rooms, custody suites, and prison landings. Within the last year, undertaking research, *at the behest* of the Home Office, on the use made of victims' statements by criminal justice decision-makers, we were required to agree, at the insistence of the Lord Chancellor's Department, that questions not be asked of judges about particular cases (Morgan and Sanders 1999). This is an advance on the situation fifteen years ago (Ashworth *et al.* 1984)—at least we were allowed to *talk* to judges, and they were more than willing to talk to us—but the restriction is nevertheless an indication of the continuing preoccupation of the state with control over data which might elucidate how decisions are actually made.

Criminology is called on to assist the processes by which felons might be better identified (the ESRC has recently funded two major projects concerned with the facial recognition of individuals through CCTV surveillance) or individually targeted, risk-assessed, and treated (the bulk of the Home Office Crime Reduction Programme), but there is much less encouragement for projects that

consider crime in terms of broader social and economic policy or which examine closely the quality of justice distributed by criminal justice decision-makers.
Thus though New Labour appears committed to an evidential approach to
'what works?'—a commendable advance on the previous Conservative
administration, during the latter years of which a good deal of policy was made
in apparent defiance of the research evidence—the question 'what works?' is
nevertheless asked and required to be answered in individualistic and narrowly
conceived terms (see Raynor and Vanstone 1997). That is, the question is posed
within the parameters of prevailing government policy. This is the research
context in which the newly graduating criminologist researcher is likely to
undertake his or her first fieldwork. But there is nothing to inhibit the budding
critic or the seasoned campaigner from using the multiplicity of criminological
data collected by these means, and attaching them to the broader socio-
economic data streams, in order to demonstrate, or suggest, that there is
another interpretation or pathway. The great fortune of the British criminologist is that he or she inhabits a domain in which there is more than enough
data available for secondary analysis. And there are no access problems to be
overcome for this task.

REFERENCES

ASHWORTH, A., GENDER, E., MANSFIELD, G., PEAY, J., and PLAYER, E. (1984). *Sentencing in the Crown Court: Report of an Exploratory Study*. Oxford University Centre for Criminological Research, Occasional Paper No. 10.

BRANTINGHAM, P. J., and FAUST, F. L. (1976). 'A Conceptual Model of Crime Prevention', *Crime and Delinquency* 22: 130–46.

BRITISH JOURNAL OF CRIMINOLOGY (1999). Special Issue on *Histories of Crime and Modernity* edited by A. Davies and G. Pearson, 39, 1.

CARLEN, P., and MORGAN, R. (eds.) (1999). *Crime Unlimited? Questions for the New Millennium*. Basingstoke: Macmillan.

DAVIS, N. (1998). *Dark Heart: The Shocking Truth about Hidden Britain*. London: Vintage.

DENNIS, N. (ed.) (1997). *Zero Tolerance: Policing a Free Society*. London: Institute of Economic Affairs.

DOWNES, D. (1989). 'Only Disconnect: Law and Order, Social Policy and the Community' in M. Bulmer, J. Lewis, and D. Piachaud (eds.), *The Goals of Social Policy*. London: Unwin Hyman.

ESRC (1997). *Thematic Priorities: Update*. Swindon: Economic and Social Research Council.

EVANS, M. D., and MORGAN, R. (1998). *Preventing Torture: A Study of the European Committee for the Prevention of Torture and Inhuman or Degrading Treatment or Punishment*. Oxford: Clarendon.

FEELEY, M. M., and SIMON, J. (1992). 'The New Penology: Notes on the Emerging Strategy of Corrections and its Implications'. *Criminology* 30: 452–74.

GARLAND, D. (1997). 'Of Crimes and Criminals: The Development of Criminology in
    Britain' in M. Maguire, R. Morgan, and R. Reiner (eds.), *The Oxford Handbook of
    Criminology* (2nd edn.). Oxford: Oxford University Press.

HENRY, S., and MILOVANOVIC, D. (1994). 'The Constitution of Constitutive Criminology: A
    Postmodern Approach to Criminological Theory' in D. Nelken (ed.), *The Futures of
    Criminology*. London: Sage.

HILLYARD, P., and SIM, J. (1997). 'The Political Economy of Socio-Legal Research' in P.A.
    Thomas (ed.), *Socio-Legal Studies*. Aldershot: Dartmouth.

HOME AFFAIRS COMMITTEE (1998). *Alternatives to Prison Sentences*. London: HMSO.

HOME OFFICE (*Morgan Report*) (1991). *Safer Communities: The Local Delivery of Crime
    Prevention through the Partnership Approach*. London: Home Office.

—— (1997). *Getting to Grips With Crime: A New Framework for Local Action*. London:
    Home Office.

—— (1999*a*). *Reducing Crime and Tackling its Causes: A Briefing Note on the Crime
    Reduction Programme*. London: Home Office.

—— (1999*b*). *Crime Reduction Programme: Analysis of Costs and Benefits—Guidance for
    Evaluators*. Research Development and Statistics Directorate. London: Home Office.

HONDERICH, T. (1990). *Conservatism*. London: Hamish Hamilton.

HUGHES, G. (1998). *Understanding Crime Prevention: Social Control, Risk and Late
    Modernity*. Buckingham: Open University Press.

HUTTON, W. (1996). *The State We're In*. London: Vintage.

JEFFERSON, T., and SHAPLAND, J. (1994). 'Criminal Justice and the Production of Order and
    Control: Criminological Research in the UK in the 1980s'. *British Journal of Criminology*,
    34: 265–90.

JONES, T., and NEWBURN, T. (1998). *Private Security and Public Policing*. Oxford:
    Clarendon.

LOADER, I. (1998). 'Criminology and the Public Sphere: Arguments for Utopian Realism' in
    P. Walton and J. Young (eds.), *The New Criminology Revisited*. Basingstoke: Macmillan.

MAGUIRE, M., MORGAN, R., and REINER, R. (eds.) (1997). *The Oxford Handbook of
    Criminology* (2nd edn.). Oxford: Oxford University Press.

McGUIRE, J., and PRIESTLEY, P. (1995). *Reviewing 'What works?': Past, Present and Future*.
    Chichester: Wiley.

MIRRLEES-BLACK, C., and ALLEN, J. (1998). *Concern about Crime: Findings from the 1998
    British Crime Survey*. Research Findings No. 83, London: Home Office.

MORGAN, R., and CARLEN, P. (1999). 'Regulating Crime Control' in P. Carlen and R. Morgan
    (eds.), *Crime Unlimited? Questions for the 21st Century*. Basingstoke: Macmillan.

—— and EVANS, M. D. (1999). *Protecting Prisoners: The Standards of the European
    Committee for the Prevention of Torture in Context*. Oxford: Clarendon.

—— and SANDERS, A. (1999). *Final Report for the Home Office on the Uses to Which Victim
    Statements are Put*. Bristol: University of Bristol.

PARKIN, F. (1967). 'Working Class Conservatives: A Theory of Political Deviance'. *British
    Journal of Sociology* 18: 278–90.

RAYNOR, P., and VANSTONE, M. (1997). *Straight Thinking on Probation. The Mid-Glamorgan
    Experiment*. Centre for Criminological Research, Probation Studies Unit Report No 4.
    Oxford: Oxford Centre for Criminological Research.

RUGGIERO, V., SOUTH, N., and TAYLOR, I. (eds.) (1998). *The New European Criminology:
    Crime and Social Order in Europe*. London: Routledge.

TREASURY (1999). *Tackling Poverty and Extending Opportunity: The Modernisation of Britain's Tax and Benefit System, Number Four.* London: HM Treasury.

VAN SWAANINGEN (1997). *Critical Criminology: Visions from Europe.* London: Sage.

VENNARD, J., SUGG, D., and HEDDERMAN, C. (1997). *Changing Offenders' Attitudes and Behaviour: What Works?* Research and Statistics Directorate Research Study No. 171. London: Home Office.

YOUNG, J. (1998). 'From Inclusive to Exclusive Society: Nightmares in the European Dream' in V. Ruggiero, N. South, and I. Taylor (eds.), *The New European Criminology: Crime and Social Order in Europe.* London: Routledge.

PART 2

RESEARCH ON CRIME, CRIMINALS, AND VICTIMS

3

RESEARCHING THE STATE OF CRIME: LOCAL, NATIONAL, AND INTERNATIONAL VICTIM SURVEYS

Pat Mayhew

INTRODUCTION

Victim surveys (or crime surveys as they are sometimes called) are relatively new in criminological research, the result of advances in survey methodology and improved facilities for computer analysis. Most typically, they ask house-holders directly about their personal experience of victimization, whether or not they reported what happened to the police. They thus offer a measure of crime a distance apart from police records, of which more below. I know of no full list of the main victim surveys, but in 1987 prior to the start of the International Crime Victimization Survey (ICVS) programme, I logged surveys at national or state level in about two dozen countries. The number of local surveys can only be guessed at.

This chapter looks at the rationale for different types of victim surveys and discusses some of the main differences in the ways they have been conducted. With respect to national surveys I concentrate most on the British Crime Survey (BCS). This is partly because I have been closely involved with it, but also because it is important for benchmarking reasons, has recently used innovative computer technology, and has in large part 'contoured' the victim-ization debate. Some mention is also made of the ICVS, with which I have also been involved. The approaches taken by local surveys are illustrated mainly by reference to UK studies. I have not personally been involved in local surveys, but I have reviewed many. The emphasis throughout is less on the substantive results of surveys than on important methodological issues (though see *Further Reading* for those who want a broad overview). Overriding attention is paid to representative household surveys, since these are the main genre. Some mention is made of surveys of ethnic minority populations, children, and women as victims of domestic violence and sexual crime. The methodology of household surveys has been adapted to look at non-household targets and some mention is also made of these.

THE DEVELOPMENT OF VICTIM SURVEYS

NATIONAL SURVEYS

National surveys took hold in the main first. The earliest major household survey was carried out in the United States for the President's Crime Commission in the 1960s (Ennis 1967). This was followed in 1972 by the first round of what is now called the National Crime Victimization Survey (NCVS), which has been conducted annually since (see Rand (1998) for latest results). In Europe, the first large-scale survey was in Finland in 1970, with the well-known London study by Sparks, Genn and Dodd (1977) following shortly after. The first British Crime Survey (BCS) was conducted in 1982 in England and Wales (Hough and Mayhew 1983), and Scotland (Chambers and Tomb 1984). The BCS in England and Wales has now been conducted seven times, the last sweep in 1998. After the 1982 sweep in Scotland, surveys have been done three times more, the last in 1996 (see MVA Consultancy 1998). National surveys have been done, in many other countries, including Canada, Australia, the Netherlands, and Switzerland.

THE INTERNATIONAL CRIME VICTIMIZATION SURVEY

A recent development has been standardized, fairly small-scale household surveys in a number of countries, through the ICVS programme. Surveys in about twenty industrialized countries have been conducted in 1989, 1992, and 1996, with some countries participating more than once (see Mayhew and van Dijk 1997 for latest results). Surveys have also been carried out in over fifty countries in transition and developing countries, usually at city level, through a programme directed by the United National Interregional Criminal Justice Research Institute (UNICRI) in Rome (see Zvekic 1998 and Alvazzi del Frate 1998 for results).

The ICVS was set up because comparisons of figures of offences recorded by the police are problematic due to differences in the way the police define, record, and count crime. And since most crimes the police know about are reported by victims, police figures can differ simply because some crimes are reported more often in some countries than others. Critically, though, the ICVS used the same questionnaire and analysis methods to produce more equivalent results than follow from comparisons of independently organized surveys. The importance of differences in survey methodology for influencing the count of victimization is returned to.

Although some reference is made to the ICVS, this chapter does not deal with the practicalities of mounting victim surveys in different countries. International surveys are logistically difficult, and not to be recommended without good financial backing, guaranteed interest in host countries, and willingness on the part of organizers to involve themselves in tedious technical oversight to ensure consistency. International surveys have other special problems, too, regarding the ownership of results, and how and when results are released (crime 'league tables' can be sensitive).

While the victim surveys mentioned above were in the main 'bespoke' ones, in some countries victimization questions have been included in surveys with other main perspectives. In the UK, perhaps the earliest use of victimization questions was in a 1966 OPCS survey about moral attitudes (Durant, Thomas and Willcock 1972). The General Household Survey has also carried questions on burglary since 1973 (see Office of National Statistics 1998). Victimization questions are now also relatively common in regular polls conducted by MORI, Gallup etc., as well as in fact-gathering polls by magazines and newspapers. (The form of the questions vary widely, and often give only crude measures.)

Household victim surveys at national level set out specifically to provide an *overview* of victimization risks and (typically) attitudes to crime. Sample sizes are usually such as to preclude much interregional analysis. There is none within the ICVS, where sample sizes are modest even at country level. The NCVS, which has by far the largest sample size of any current victim survey (at the moment 80,000 people are interviewed a year), presents results according to the size of the locality in which the respondent lives, but stops short of providing estimates for given cities. The lowest level of analysis in the BCS is the eleven Government Office Regions in England and Wales, although by combining data from different sweeps risks for different types of area can be documented using the ACORN classification of neighbourhood types.[1]

LOCAL SURVEYS

In the UK, the first important local survey was done in London by Sparks, Genn and Dodds (1977). Two other local surveys predated the first BCS: in Sheffield

---

[1] ACORN stands for 'A Classification of Residential Neighbourhoods' (CACI Ltd). This assigns each home in the country to one of 17 neighbourhood groups or 54 neighbourhood types according to the social and housing characteristics of its immediate area as measured by the 1991 Census. There are a few other so-called commercial 'geo-demographic profile' classifications available based on the same principles as ACORN—Mosaic and Pinpoint are others.

(Bottoms, Mawby and Walker 1987) and in Mosside comparing black and white residents (Tuck and Southgate 1981). After this, there was a crop of local victim surveys concerned to highlight the scale of crime in particular high-crime areas: e.g. in Merseyside (Kinsey 1985; Kinsey, Lea and Young 1986), in Islington (Jones, Maclean and Young 1996; Crawford *et al.* 1990) and in a few London boroughs (London Borough of Newham 1987; Painter 1992). Like the BCS, their purpose ranged wider than just charting levels of risk, as discussed later.

One important category of local surveys is those conducted to evaluate crime prevention programmes, looking at 'before and after' risks (and perceptions of risk). They are often intended to complement the picture from recorded crime figures which could potentially change simply because programmes often encourage reporting. A prime example of 'evaluation surveys' are those done as part of the large-scale evaluation of Phase 1 of the Safer Cities programme targeted at burglary (Ekblom, Law and Sutton 1996). The surveys covered areas targeted for action, as well as areas in comparison cities. They looked at victimization experience before and after Safer Cities action, fear of crime, changes in security behaviour, and whether people were actually aware of burglary action having been taken (they were surprisingly unaware as it happened). The effectiveness of improved street lighting has also been tested with local victim surveys, to assess both changes in risks and feelings of security (see Painter 1996 for a review).

Police forces are required by the Audit Commission to measure the quality of policing services and by the Police Act 1996 to assess what people feel about policing objectives and priorities. There is much variation in what is done and how frequently (Chatterton, Langmead-Jones and Radcliffe 1997), but some forces use local sample surveys to canvass views. These have also been of interest to local councils which indeed have sometimes funded surveys as part of a political bid for more locally accountable policing, for example the Newham victim survey (London Borough of Newham 1987), and the survey focused on women carried out by Manchester City Council Police Monitoring Unit (see Hoffman 1996: 67–71). Some of the surveys done by the police and local authorities have covered victimization and reporting to the police as additional topics. Few results are widely available, but levels of reporting to the police often emerge higher than in the BCS—perhaps because the police are identified as sponsors.

Local victim surveys are likely to become a growth industry as a result of the statutory duty for crime audits to be carried out in the context of the local crime prevention partnerships required by the Crime and Disorder Act 1998. Some anticipated features of these surveys are taken up at the end of the chapter.

COMMERCIAL VICTIM SURVEYS

Some victim surveys have looked at non-household targets. For convenience, they are called commercial crime surveys here, although this fudges their coverage somewhat. An elementary point about them is that they fill a gap in police statistics, which do not usually allow *types of target* to be singled out within legal offence categories. (Theft from shops is an exception in England and Wales.) Surveys have not been the only methodology used for assessing commercial crime: some studies have used administrative or 'head office' records. These are useful for gathering information held centrally, although they omit crimes not reported to the head office, and do not usually look at factors that put some premises at greater risk than others, such as location, size, and opening hours.

There was a set of commercial surveys in the early NCVS programme covering burglary and robbery in businesses and selected non-governmental organizations (US Department of Justice 1976). However, these were discontinued when it was found that most incidents were reported to the police. More recently, the Dutch have espoused commercial surveys (e.g., van Dijk and van Soomeron 1992).

In Britain, risks to commercial premises have been assessed through a number of *ad hoc* surveys. These have covered the crime problems of building societies and banks (Austin 1988; Gill and Matthews 1994), post offices (Ekblom 1987), small shops (Ekblom and Simon 1988; Hibberd and Shapland 1993), chemists' shops (Laycock 1984), a large shopping centre (Phillips and Cochrane 1988), and industrial estates (Johnston *et al.* 1994). Gill (1993) looked at risks for nearly 350 small holiday accommodation businesses, using a postal questionnaire, while Levi (1988) used the same methodology to study fraud against businesses. A survey of 3,000 retailing and manufacturing premises was conducted by the Home Office in 1993 (Mirrlees-Black and Ross 1995). Outside the commercial sector, Smith (1987) did an exploratory study of victimization among hospital staff in a large general hospital.

Commercial victim surveys have often been small in scope (the NCVS Commercial Surveys were by far the largest). I know of no recent sample surveys that have been repeated to examine trends over time. Rather, commercial surveys have usually been done to illustrate the *nature* of the crime problem in a particular sector, or its extent in a *local* area. Mirrlees and Ross (1995) were unusual in estimating the number of total crimes against retailers and manufacturers in England and Wales, by grossing up their survey estimates. The only other grossed-up totals of the volume of crime and financial losses have usually been for retailers, on the basis of 'head office' records (see, for example, British Retail Consortium 1999).

OTHER SURVEYS

Young populations Most household surveys have taken samples of adults, usually those aged 16 or more. Younger respondents are generally omitted because of the need to negotiate parental permission, and because they are not seen to be necessarily good respondents for reporting on household crime, or general household matters such as income levels. However, several surveys in the USA have focused on students, finding them at high risk (see, for example, Kaufman *et al.* 1998). The experiences of the younger respondents in the NCVS are covered by Whitaker and Bastian (1991): 12- to 15-year-olds were less at risk than those aged 16 to 19, and suffered less serious incidents. An early Dutch survey looked specifically at the links between offending and victimization among teenagers, claiming that victimization could lead to 'compensatory' offending (van Dijk and Steinmetz 1983).

In Britain, bullying in schools has attracted attention from researchers who have found it widespread (see, e.g., Farrington 1993; Pitts and Smith 1995). A few surveys, some of them administered in schools, have looked at wider forms of childhood victimization in particular localities (notably, Mawby 1979; Anderson *et al.* 1994; Hartless *et al.* 1995). Within the Home Office, the 1993 Youth Lifestyle Survey (currently being repeated) carried victimization questions alongside those on self-reported offending among 14–25-year-olds (Graham and Bowling 1995). The 1992 BCS carried an additional sample of 1,350 12- to 15-year-olds, selected from children in homes where an adult was interviewed for the main BCS. Using a self-completion written questionnaire, they were asked about victimization and harassment away from home since the beginning of the 1991 summer holidays—a period of about six to eight months. Briefly, the results confirmed the findings of local studies: that young teenagers experienced high levels of incidents covered by the survey, although many were not seen as serious. Few incidents came to the attention of the police, and many were not reported to parents or teachers either. For crime types that can be compared across age groups, the 12–15-year-olds experienced more thefts of property than those aged 16 or over. Their risks of theft from the person and assaults away from home were higher than for adults aged 20 or over, but fairly comparable to those for 16–19-year-olds (see Aye Maung 1995a for full results).

Asking children about sexual and violent behaviour within the home raises obvious difficulties, and a more common approach to estimating such childhood victimization has been to ask adults about their early experiences. Finkelhor (1994) reviews studies on sexual abuse from a number of countries including that by Baker and Duncan (1985) in Great Britain.[2] A principal feature

---

[2] The special component on the 1994 BCS covered sexual victimization from age 16 onwards. The component in the 1996 BCS on domestic violence also covered the same age range.

of results is their variability. Differing response rates and, above all, differing questions explain this in the main.

Surveys of women's experience of domestic violence and sexual victimization There has been a raft of local UK surveys concerned with measuring women's experience of domestic violence, sexual crime, and harassment, as well as some important recent national developments in the USA *via* the NCVS (Bachman and Saltzman 1995) and bespoke surveys in Canada (Johnson and Sacco 1995), Australia (Australian Bureau of Statistics 1996), and New Zealand (New Zealand Ministry of Justice 1996).

The main feature of the surveys done to date has been their differences in approach, both as regards the samples taken and the sorts of questions asked. This has resulted in such widely different estimates of the extent of victimization that comparisons between them are, frankly, fruitless. This is likely to remain the case. Percy and Mayhew (1997) review many of the surveys on sexual victimization, and looks in detail at reasons for the disparity in estimates. Mirrlees-Black (1999) does the same for surveys covering domestic violence.

There is little doubt that an academic industry will continue to thrive on studies of crime against women. 'Bespoke' surveys are likely to be more favoured, as it is recognized that the weakest point of 'general purpose' victim surveys is poor measurement of crimes between offenders and victims known to each other. With these, one robust approach would be to 'cut one's losses' and accept that conventional survey techniques will fail to do justice to related-party crime, where respondents are highly likely to be reticent with interviewers. The obvious difficulty here is the presentational one of ignoring an important area of offending, especially as it is poorly covered in police statistics because of low reporting rates. The alternatives are to provide clear 'health warnings' about the estimates produced, or to employ improved methods of data collection. A recent approach taken in the BCS is reported on later.

WHAT HOUSEHOLD VICTIM SURVEYS ARE ABOUT

Victim surveys of householders have served five main purposes, although their relative importance varies somewhat according to the survey being done. They are:

i.   to provide an alternative measure of crime to offences recorded by the police;
ii.   to look at levels of reporting to the police and why crimes are not reported;

iii.   to give information on crime risks in a way police figures allow much less
       well;
iv.   to flesh out the nature of victimization from crime;
v.   to take up other crime-related issues.

Each of these is explored a little below. After this, I turn to the question of how
well surveys measure what they set out to.

VICTIM SURVEYS AS AN ALTERNATIVE MEASURE OF CRIME

Victim surveys essentially try to measure the 'real' extent of victimization by
asking people about crimes whether or not they were reported to the police.
Many surveys do this to emphasize the widespread nature of victimization,
simply noting the extent of unreported crime along the way as it were. Relatively few try and estimate the 'real' number of household burglaries, say, compared to the number recorded by the police. The ICVS, for instance, does not
attempt any comparison between its survey estimates of crime and recorded
crime figures.[3] Nor do most national surveys in other countries. Results from
the NCVS, for instance, are not set alongside the police Uniform Crime Reports
in any precise way, although occasionally long-term trends from the two
measures are shown (see, e.g., Bureau of Justice Statistics 1993).

There are a few exceptions in the UK surveys. Sparks, Genn and Dodd (1977)
attempted a match in survey and police figures for London, while the first
Islington survey also made some comparisons (Jones, Maclean and Young
1986). The Farrington and Dowds' (1985) survey assessed whether victimization
risks in Nottinghamshire supported the picture from crimes recorded by the
police, in which Nottinghamshire topped the force league. (It showed that levels
of victimization were only slightly higher than in two adjacent counties, with
other data suggesting that high recorded crime in Nottinghamshire was largely
attributable to distinctive recording practices.) The early surveys in different
parts in Sheffield also acted as a check on the picture gained from police figures
(Bottoms, Mawby and Walker 1987).

The BCS has been in the business of attempting a fairly tight comparison
between police figures and its own risk estimates. Offences are classified, according to police rules, on the basis of detailed information in a 'Victim Form'
rather than through affirmative answers to 'screener' questions (discussed more
below). The process of matching BCS offence categories with those of the police
allows for comparisons of trends in crime according to the two sources, with
the BCS risk estimates grossed up to provide national England and Wales totals,

---

[3] Although at the time of the first ICVS sweep, van Dijk, Mayhew and Killias (1990) made a very
rough assessment of how far the two measures were in line, taking levels of reporting into account.

and with some adjustment made to police figures to maximize comparability.[4] At least this is done for a sub-set of 'matchable' offences.[5] The matching process allows some estimate of what is an evident 'recording shortfall' between the number of offences estimated to have been *reported* to the police and the actual number *recorded* (this being part of the 'dark figure' of crime, additional to offences not reported at all).[6] The 1998 BCS showed, for instance, that whereas 44 per cent of 'matchable' crimes uncovered by the survey were said to have been known to the police, the number of recorded incidents was only 54 per cent of the estimated number reported—albeit suggestive rather than precise figures.[7] The considerable extra work involved in linking police and survey figures has undoubtedly increased the value of the BCS information, but the more parsimonious approach of letting survey results speak for themselves is probably the way forward for most victim surveys.

Figure 3.1 (See page 100) illustrates the points above by showing the overlap between survey and police counts. While I do not suggest that the relative size of the counts is accurate, it illustrates how some types of crime will be captured by both counts, some by only one, and some by neither. Within the coverage they take, victim surveys capture such incidents as respondents are *prepared to talk about* that fall within what can be called a *nominal* definition of crime: incidents which strictly could be punished, even if perhaps not doing so. In contrast, the police record a more *operationally* defined set of incidents: those which come to their attention, which they feel merit official attention, and which meet their organizational demands for reasonable evidence. For many incidents, the public and the police will agree about what is 'crime'. Agreement will be poorest for less serious incidents, and where there is most discretion for taking legal action—and this is important in helping to explain the gap between reported and recorded crime. In any event, when surveys are repeated over time, as the BCS has been, a broader count of incidents is necessary to reveal whether there are reporting and recording changes over time.

There is another distinction worth noting in the approaches taken by victim surveys as regards what incidents are counted. Many surveys essentially leave the task of defining crime to the respondent. They use quasi-legal terms in asking 'screening' questions to determine whether a respondent had been

[4] For instance, crimes against those under 16 are excluded as they are not covered by the survey; and recorded vehicle thefts are adjusted to exclude commercial vehicles.

[5] Some offences cannot be matched as they are not regarded as notifiable offences and are therefore not counted by the police (e.g., common assaults); others are recorded by the police in broad categories spanning offences against both institutional victims and private individuals.

[6] The number of incidents reported to the police is estimated by multiplying the *proportion* of BCS incidents said to have been reported by the total BCS count.

[7] There is a sampling error on the survey estimates of 'experienced' and 'reported' crime. Some of the apparent shortfall will also reflect inevitable differences in the way offences are classified in the BCS and by the police, although in principle the same rules are followed.

Figure 3.1: Comparing Survey Data and Police Counts of Crime

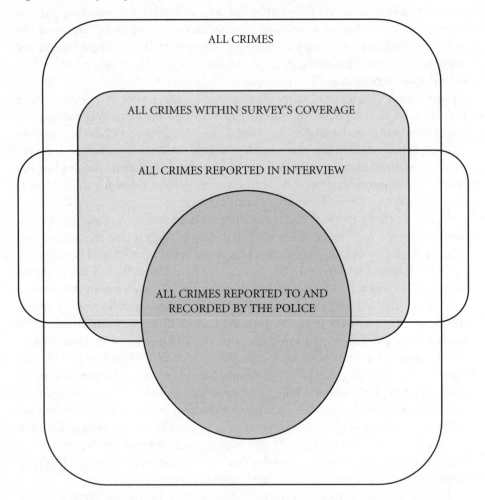

ALL CRIMES

ALL CRIMES WITHIN SURVEY'S COVERAGE

ALL CRIMES REPORTED IN INTERVIEW

ALL CRIMES REPORTED TO AND
RECORDED BY THE POLICE

'burgled' for instance; and they apply no checks on respondents' definitions. They give a count of crime, therefore, as defined by the sampled population. (Examples here are the Australian surveys, the ICVS, and virtually all of the local UK surveys.) In contrast, some surveys (the BCS and the NCVS are examples) trawl for possible crimes incidents through similar screening questions, but surveyors *post hoc* define these as crimes (or not) using more detailed information, as explained above. In the BCS for instance, between 5 and 10 per cent of incidents mentioned in screener questions are discounted as 'crimes' (the figure has varied by sweep somewhat). This is because the details given do not suggest any genuine criminal misbehaviour, or the crime is 'out of scope' of the survey, or it is clear that the police would not have recorded a crime (e.g.

because the perpetrator is clearly mentally ill). Moreover, between 10 and 30 per cent of incidents from particular screening questions are classified under offence types different from those suggested by the screener questions (Aye Maung 1995*b*). These differences in approach are important when comparing crime counts from different surveys.

One issue for victim surveys is how far to stray from measuring burglary, car crime, assault etc. to encompass incidents which fail to meet the criteria of a criminal offence but which can be unpleasant, if not frightening. Sexual and racial harassment falls into this category, as well as abusive verbal behaviour at work and in public places. Experience of such harassment is of interest in its own right, but it is also seen as potentially important in explaining patterns of fear of crime (e.g. Painter 1992).

Local surveys are often considered to have done more on this measurement front, although in fact a variety of different types of harassment have been covered by the BCS since the 1984 sweep, including racial harassment (e.g. Aye Maung and Mirrlees-Black 1994; Percy 1998), sexual harassment (e.g. Hough 1995), verbal abuse at work (Aye Maung and Mirrlees-Black 1994), obscene telephone calls (e.g. Buck, Chatterton and Pease 1995), and—in the 1998 BCS— 'road rage'.

There are no special problems in designing questions to cover 'lower level' harassment, and it is appropriate to analyse experience of them in much the same way as 'conventional' victimization. Two points can be made however. First, harassment may be more part of a continuing process than discrete one-off events (cf. Bowling 1993). Trying to tally the number of incidents, then, is less suitable than assessing broad levels of exposure, taking into account that few people avoid being subject to uncivil behaviour at some time or other. Second, and related to this, is the issue of what stands as *relevant* victimization here. This is a matter of choice, of course, but too broad a coverage of everyday petty harassment can lead to over-inclusivity if it is simply added to more unequivocally 'criminal' victimization. Thus, one of the difficulties of comparing estimates of sexual victimization from different national and local surveys stems from the different thresholds they have taken as regards relevant incidents (see Percy and Mayhew 1997). The same point applies to the experiences of ethnic minorities as regards racially motivated crime and harassment (see, e.g. Percy 1998).

REPORTING CRIME TO THE POLICE

Asking what goes unreported to the police, and why not, has been a feature of most victim surveys. This has been primarily to show that many incidents of a criminal nature never get to police attention. In the 1998 BCS, for instance, 60 per cent of the crimes interviewers were informed about were said *not* to have become known to the police (Mirrlees-Black *et al.* 1998). As to why the police are not informed, the evidence consistently shows that this is mainly because victims feel the incidents are too trivial or not amenable to police action. But this is not the whole story. Skogan's (1994) analysis of BCS results remains one of the best assessments of the influences on reporting. He showed that intrusiveness, harm, level of loss, and whether or not a loss is insured are most influential, but that related-party incidents go unreported more often. Who the victims are is also relevant. People in urban areas and Afro-Caribbeans report less often taking other factors into account. Older people are more likely to report, and home owners and council tenants are also more likely to do so than private renters. In contrast, other victim characteristics do not have much influence once offence-related factors are controlled for: e.g., gender, access to a telephone at home, or having been a victim in the past. Little in later analysis of the BCS upsets this general picture. An important implication of this for local surveys is that they may uncover a greater disparity in risk between 'bad' and 'good' areas than is indicated by police figures.

CRIME RISKS

A principal focus of household victim surveys has been to show how risks of crime differ. In this they have stolen a considerable march on police data, which provide very little about victims even in terms of gender and age, let alone variables such as social class and household composition. One of the aims of the early local surveys in Merseyside, Islington, and London (see above) was to highlight disparities in risk, discrediting the focus of the BCS on national average figures. The conclusions drawn by these 'left realist' victim surveyors was that crime has a severe impact on those in inner cities, and an even greater one on the less advantaged. The charge laid against the BCS was that it glossed over extensive pocketing of crime (and portrayed fear of crime as irrational along the way). As it happens, the criticisms largely ignored the content of BCS publications, but they achieved currency simply through repetition. Indeed, they continue to do so to some extent (e.g. Walklate 1989; Zedner 1997).

The considerable literature on risks of victimization shows, in very brief summary, that (a) risk variations differ somewhat according to offence type; (b) there is a concentration of risk among the less socially privileged; and (c) the probability of being *repeatedly* victimized is even more unevenly spread than the probability of being victimized at all. The results from the 1998 BCS illustrate all these points with up-to-date information (Mirrlees-Black *et al.* 1998). The phenomenon of repeat (or multiple) victimization is now one of the best-known products of victim surveys, the BCS in particular. Much has been done to document its extent and nature, despite the fact that the usual twelve-month 'recall period' in which respondents report their experiences places an artificial bound on the number of repeat incidents that can be counted. It is likely that there will be demand for future local surveys to identify repeat victimization, and this has some implications for the design of crime counting questions. Pease (1998) gives a good overview of findings about repeat victimization, as well as the strengths and limitations of survey data on it.

THE NATURE OF VICTIMIZATION

The police of course have a lot of information on the nature of crimes they know about. Little of it is routinely reported, although it can be accessed by criminologists for special studies. In principle, victim surveys are an additional way of charting the nature of victimization. The BCS for instance currently reports on levels of injury in assaultive crime, whether offenders were under the influence of drink or drugs, where and when offences occurred, how burglars got into a house, and the costs of victimization (e.g., Mirrlees-Black, Mayhew and Percy 1996; Budd 1999).

How far victim surveys can unpick the nature of crime depends on their size: larger national surveys produce more crime incidents on which to generalize. It also depends on the number of questions asked, and the number of incidents which are followed up. Some surveys extrapolate from details of the 'last' incident of a particular type (the ICVS does this for instance). This is efficient in reducing interviewing time, but risks bias in so far as respondents choose a 'last' incident which is most salient to them, and on which they have most to say.

Asking a large number of questions about the nature of victimization is of questionable value in smaller surveys since they will produce too few incidents for reliable analysis. The costs of crime, for instance, are made up of damage and theft losses (at least), and account should be taken of losses recompensed through insurance. Several questions are needed to untangle these costs well. Sound conclusions about when and how different crimes happen are also difficult to draw from small samples, and it is probably better to try and access local police information. Insufficient incidents are also a problem for looking at what was stolen (which requires a *long* code list), and where property was stolen from. Probably the most useful question for smaller surveys is the victim's relationship to offender(s), since this will highlight some of the extent of related-party crimes, and usefully explain reporting patterns. The emotional and practical effects of crime are also worth documenting since available police information is poor, and they add to the picture of the impact of victimization. Questions about how far victims feel they contributed to what happened (through lax security or provocation, for instance) can be illuminating, but are more often than not avoided for fear of 'victim blaming'.

OTHER CRIME-RELATED ISSUES

It is expensive to arrange interviews with respondents in order to discuss their experience of crime. Having paid the price, nearly all victim surveys use the opportunity to delve into other crime-related issues. The BCS rotates the topics it looks at. The 1998 sweep, for instance, covered fear of crime, attitudes to the police, security behaviour, attitudes towards sentencing and the criminal justice system, attitudes to juvenile offending, witnessing crime, and knowledge of Victim Support. Since 1992, the BCS has also looked at knowledge and use of illicit drugs (see Ramsay and Spiller 1997 for latest results). Probably the two most popular topics in local surveys have been fear of crime and attitudes to the police, although I know of no good synthesis of their findings.

HOW WELL DO VICTIM SURVEYS COUNT?

THE VICTIM SURVEY COUNT

The first obvious point to make is that household victim surveys do not measure all 'crime': their coverage is not wide enough. Crimes against commercial and public sector targets are omitted for instance, as well as 'victimless' crimes such as drug possession. Homicide is obviously not counted, since no victim is available. And it is difficult to cover fraud, since many people will not be aware they have been victimized.

A second difficulty is that no sample survey represents the population adequately. Household sampling frames exclude potentially high-risk groups such as the homeless or those in non-household accommodation. Other respondents prove impossible for interviewers to locate at home, and others refuse to be interviewed because of concerns about the validity of a survey, lack of time or interest. The main concern here is that victimization rates for non-respondents may be higher than for those who do respond (and see Aye Maung (1995b) for a discussion of the effects of non-response in the BCS).

Thirdly, as only a sample of the population is questioned, findings are subject to sampling error. The BCS is large by the standards of most surveys, but even many of its estimates are imprecise, in particular for rare crimes such as robbery and serious assault. The error range on victimization figures from smaller local surveys will be considerable, and will greatly limit respectable analysis of changes over time or between groups.

Fourthly, victim surveys are prone to undercount 'offences' which are either on the borderline of what people actually regard as criminal (e.g., pub fights), or which they might be reluctant to talk about because the offender is known.

Sexual and domestic offences are the most obvious examples, as already mentioned.

Fifthly, there is also a set of more specific limitations that arise from asking people to *remember* experiences of crime and locate them accurately in time. One concern here is whether forms of victimization which are more repetitive in nature can be readily located in limited time frames as discrete and def-initionally tidy events. This bears in particular on domestic and sexual violence, as well as on many forms of harassment—if these are a focus. Genn's (1998) essay on crime on a London housing estate remains the best illustration of how conventional victim survey counting methods fail to justice to the chaotic lives of victimized (and victimizing) women.

This apart, most of the work done on how accurately people remember incidents of victimization has been in relation to the NCVS (see Skogan 1986 and Sparks 1991 for reviews), although the London study is also relevant. The overall conclusion is that response biases work, on balance, to *undercount* survey-defined offences, but with differential losses across crime categories. Thus, in checks where people have been asked about offences *known* to have been reported to the police, more trivial crimes (e.g., minor thefts, vandalism, and some assaults) are less likely to be recalled in interview. More serious incidents are more likely to be, on the other hand, and indeed may even be over-counted, as more salient events tend to be pulled forward in time. The count of crime from victim surveys, then, is both incomplete and biased.

MEMORY PROMPTS

An elementary but little regarded point about how accurately surveys measure victimization bears simply on the number of screener 'prompts' that are offered (for instance, whether respondents are reminded about incidents whereby someone with a right to be in the home might have stolen something, and whether someone (without right of entry) might have tried to get in, and whether someone might have got in and not stolen something—all as well as whether entry was achieved and something was stolen). Essentially, the more prompts, the more criminal victimization will be counted—since different screeners will jog the respondent's memory in different ways. There is a good case for saying 'more is better' as far as screener questions are concerned. (For example, separate screeners about attempted and completed burglaries will produce a higher count than a single screener meant to cover burglary incidents of all kinds.) Using a more restricted set of screener questions, moreover, runs the risk of respondents 'forcing' incidents into a screener which *nearly* taps what happened, thereby contaminating what the screener is meant to be meas-uring. The main danger of using an expansive array of screeners is that respondents can report on the same incident in response to different screener questions (despite being instructed not to do so). This is difficult to detect unless screeners' questions are followed through with additional questions on the event being recalled, which allows double-counting to be identified.

CURRENT RESEARCH METHODOLOGY

No attempt is made here to review exhaustively the methodology of different victim surveys, or to explore all the technical pros and cons of different approaches. Rather, I restrict myself to a broad overview of the main methods used, and signal some of the most important technical considerations to do with these. There is an element of 'horses for courses' in choosing how to do a survey, with timescales and available funds being constraining factors. A general point is that whatever methods are used, victim surveys are popular. Crime is salient for a wide raft of the population, and when people have been victimized they are usually only too willing to answer questions about it.

SAMPLING

Most victim surveys want to document the experience of 'ordinary' people, wherever they come from. The two most obvious household sampling frames, therefore, have been Electoral Registers (ERs) or the Small Users Postcode Address File (PAF). The advantage of ERs is that they are readily accessible, a consideration that may be particularly relevant for local authority victim surveys in the future. Also, they allow a sample of *named* individuals to be picked beforehand (at least from those aged 18 or older), which is useful if introductory letters are to be sent beforehand, a procedure to be recommended. However, it is now well established that ERs under-represent key victim groups: young people, the unemployed, ethnic minorities, and those in rented accommodation (Todd and Butcher 1982). PAF lists all postal delivery points, and represents the fullest register of household addresses since almost all households have a delivery point, or letterbox. One disadvantage of PAF (a relatively small one) is that there is some mismatch with the 'large users' PAF which means that the proportion of ineligible addresses tends to be higher. The lack of a list of named occupants also means that any introductory letter can only be sent to the 'Occupant', who may or may not be the household member one is really after. (Note that most surveys pick one randomly selected householder, mainly to reduce the interview burden for selected households. Both the BCS and ICVS do this, although the NCVS in the USA questions all household members aged 12 or more about personal crime, with one main respondent covering household crime.)

Different sampling decisions can apply if the focus is on particular high interest groups (e.g., women, the elderly, children, the disabled, ethnic minorities, etc.). Some groups can be picked up from representative sampling frames, although they may need to be augmented—by residential homes, for instance, for an elderly population. A sufficiently large initial sample will produce enough numbers for some special groups: the 1998 BCS, for instance, identified about 1,400 people with a limiting disability. But without an initially large sample, one would need to resort to other sources—disability payment records perhaps.

The experience of ethnic minorities with regard to victimization and harassment is likely to remain of interest. Normal samples will produce insufficient numbers for reliable analysis so that special sampling techniques need to be employed. The usual one goes under the term 'focused enumeration' (see Brown and Ritchie 1981). The BCS has regularly carried an ethnic minority 'booster sample' (see, e.g., FitzGerald and Hale 1996; Percy 1998), and victimization and harassment are covered in the Policy Studies Institute's survey of ethnic minorities in Britain (see Modood *et al.* 1997 for latest results). Some local surveys have also covered ethnic minority populations (notably, London Borough of Newham 1987, and the first and second Islington crime surveys (respectively, Jones, MacLean and Young 1986; Crawford *et al.* 1990). Victimization levels are generally higher than for whites, although to a large degree this can be explained by demographic, social, and residential factors which increases their risks. This needs to be adequately taken into account in analysis.

Covering the victimization experience of children and teenagers is possible, but it is wise to get parental consent, and conventional victimization questions need to be adapted to reflect the day-to-day experiences of the young and to bring into scope behaviour which some children (especially younger ones) may not appreciate is 'criminal', offensive, or anti-social. Asking children about abusive behaviour within the home raises obvious ethical problems.

MODE OF INTERVIEW

There are three main possibilities as regards the way in which victimization can be measured: mail questionnaires (least frequently used and dealt with only briefly here), telephone interviews (of growing popularity), and face-to-face personal interviews (most frequently used and the most flexible).

Mail surveys The advantage of mail (or postal) surveys is that they are relatively cheap. The disadvantages are that they rarely achieve high response rates. They also restrict what sort of questions can be asked, for one because average (and low) literacy levels have to be accommodated. Low response might not necessarily be a problem if those who *do* respond are representative. There is good reason to doubt this. Those with 'something to say', particularly the more literate, may be particularly likely to take the trouble to complete a mail questionnaire.

Telephone surveys The use of telephone interviews in victim surveys in the UK is now growing, and some surveys carried out by the police have used them. Most telephone surveys use Computer Assisted Telephone Interviewing (CATI) where the questionnaire is a computer program which specifies the questions, the range, and the structure of permissible answers, and the routing instruction which determine which questions are asked, and in what order.

The Home Office Commercial Crime Survey used CATI, because telephone interviews were regarded as more acceptable to busy managers (Mirrlees-Black and Ross 1995). It used the British Telecom business database as its sampling frame. Pilot work however confirmed the need to send an introductory letter to identify the person in the best position to answer the questions, and to allow that person to collate information before the telephone interview took place. CATI was also used in most countries taking part in the ICVS.

Telephone interviews are less suitable for long interviews, and response rates tend to be lower, for one because it is easier to refuse an interview over the phone. Telephone interviews are less culturally acceptable in some countries than others, and the UK is one. Another major issue concerns the representativeness of telephone owners. Although telephone penetration in this country is now very high (96 per cent) overall, it is lower for households in some areas and of some types (Beerten and Martin 1999). Finally, a major problem with telephone interviews is the lack of a suitable sampling frame to draw a nationally representative probability sample (quota samples are less of a problem). Telephone directories are of limited use as more than a third of households have ex-directory numbers, and true random digit dialling (RDD) cannot be used as yet because of an irregular telephone numbering system—though a variant of RDD was used in England and Wales and Scotland in the ICVS. Ownership of other communication links such as answerphones, fax, and internet are all likely to increase too, and this will add to the problems of contacting householders by phone.

As against all this, telephone surveys are cheaper, involve less effort for interviewers, and allow good centralized supervision. They also allow for more standardization of questionnaire administration, which was a key advantage in the ICVS for instance. There may be a role, too, for follow-up telephone interviews with respondents who have initially taken part in a face-to-face interview. This could be useful for tracking changes in attitudes over time, for instance, or for assessing how long the effects of victimization last.

Face to face interviews Victim surveys in this country have mainly used face-to-face interviews. This is partly because they usually offer higher response rates, and partly because of what I see as an inherent suspicion in this country about the 'respectability' of telephone surveys. Face-to-face surveys allow more complex questioning than self-completion postal questionnaires. They also allow scope for interviewer ratings. For instance, the physical condition of the respondent's home or immediate neighbourhood can be noted, or even whether a burglar alarm or other obvious security devices are visible. Interviewer ratings seem less often used outside the BCS than they might be, although they can provide useful analysis variables.

Face-to-face interviews are most expensive, although costs are more competitive where interviews are only within a local area. Some local surveys have tried to contain costs further by using student interviewers, special constables, or even police officers. It would be over-pious to say that these are not to be recommended, but obviously proper training is needed, especially as a young student might not present the image of a 'professional' interviewer. There is also the problem that police personnel cannot conceal their identity, and when a survey is about crime it is hard to think that this does not introduce bias.

The use of Computer Assisted Personal Interviewing (CAPI) in face-to-face interviews is rapidly replacing paper-and-pen interviewing (PAPI) for larger surveys. The general consensus of the methodological literature (see, e.g., Martin and Manners 1995; de Leeuw and Nicholls 1996) is that CAPI improves data quality (mainly through automating routing, in-built range and consistency checks, and minimizing missing data). It also facilitates more complex questionnaire design, and allows for randomization of question order and response categories to avoid well-known order effects. CAPI increases the speed of results once interviews are completed, though this is offset by longer questionnaire development time. With large surveys, CAPI can be cheaper than PAPI if the initial hardware is in place and interviewers are already trained. But costs are higher for one-off or small surveys, due to high programming and testing costs. CAPI has been used in the last three sweeps of the BCS.

For victim surveys, there are three particular considerations. First, the evidence suggests that respondents may well answer more frankly in CAPI than in PAPI mode. This is possibly because computers enhance the appearance of professionalism of interviewers, and that being involved with the screen and keyboard, interviewers appear more neutral to respondents. (Questioning of sensitive issues through the use of *self-keying by respondents themselves* is discussed below.) Secondly, CAPI does not cope well at the moment with producing a readily understandable paper version of the questionnaire. This is a considerable drawback in seeing how the questionnaire is shaping up, and in distributing versions of it to interested parties. Thirdly, the initial costs of hardware and interviewer training make it unlikely that many local survey agencies—let alone university researchers—will be in a position to use CAPI. Market forces will undoubtedly come into play, though, so that smaller agencies may have to merge or subcontract data collection to larger 'CAPI-ready' organizations.

One by-product of CAPI in victim surveys is the potential to allow respondents to use the computer themselves to answer questions of a particularly sensitive nature. This technique is known as Computer Assisted Self Interviewing (CASI) and has been used in the last three sweeps of the BCS with respondents aged 16–59—to cover self-reported drug-taking (three times), sexual victimization (twice), being offered and buying goods known to be stolen (once), and domestic violence (once). Results were encouraging. Few respondents needed help from interviewers and few refused (indeed many positively enjoyed self-keying). More pertinently, for topics covered by existing BCS questions, much higher rates of admissions emerged in CASI mode (see Mirrlees-Black 1999 for domestic violence results; Percy and Mayhew 1997 for sexual victimization; and Ramsay and Spiller 1997 for drug-taking). One explanation for this is that respondents may feel that answering a 'black box' affords greater privacy than showcards or a self-completion pen-and paper questionnaire (used previously for drug taking). It could also be that the technical formality of a computer screen prompts more thoughtful and honest answers. In any event, self-keying techniques are clearly a major breakthrough as regards getting a more complete count of the sensitive topics which have been poorly covered by victim surveys up until now.

SOME OTHER ISSUES

Survey sponsors Who sponsors a victim survey can be important. The BCS is introduced as a Home Office survey. The high response rate it achieves (79 per cent in 1998, and 83 per cent 1996) may reflect the 'status' of the sponsor, but it may be that some people feel that participation is required—even though the advance letter and 'doorstep' introductions stress that it is voluntary. As a generalization, it is likely that response will be higher in surveys sponsored by agencies which respondents see as in a position to influence change. This bodes well for local authority/police surveys. It bodes less well for surveys presented as serving the interests of university researchers.

Crime prevention questions One problematic area of questioning in victim surveys is about household crime prevention. Being asked by unknown interviewers whether there are high-quality door and window locks, a burglar alarm installed, or the number of hours (and even which hours) the house is left empty provokes a wary reaction from many respondents who become concerned about the authenticity of the survey. Asking these questions in telephone interviews is particularly problematic. A careful introduction to the questions is needed, and respondents should be given the choice to miss them out altogether if they feel uncomfortable. Not covering the questions at all is probably less of a loss than might be imagined. Some respondents tend to exaggerate security 'just in case' the information is passed on. And—more important—assessing the effectiveness of security (which is usually the purpose) is complicated. One needs to compare security levels of (i) non-victims, (ii) victims at the time they were victimized, and (iii) victims currently. This is because many people will upgrade security after a burglary, so that simple comparisons of non-victims and victims will show the latter to better protected. Moreover, security coverage is highly related to income that is itself related to risk; assessing security patterns therefore needs to take income into account.

Question order Questionnaire designers are probably less aware than they should be of the implications of where in a questionnaire a particular item is placed. It is usually recognized that surveys should start with some not overly important 'warm-up' questions, and that those high-priority questions should not be put at the end, because some respondents may have drawn a halt before then. Question position, however, can be quite important for influencing observed frequencies. This is important both for comparing the results of similar questionnaires over time, and for comparing results from independently organized surveys.

One example from BCS relates to attitudes to the police. All sweeps have included one general question: 'taking everything into account, would you say the police in this area do a good job or a poor job?' In 1988, the question was included twice—a simple mistake! The question was first asked early on, and for half the sample it was also asked halfway through a set of questions on contacts with the police, late into the interview. The results are interesting. Among those asked the question twice, 66 per cent gave the same rating, but 22 per cent gave a more *positive* rating the second time of asking (a smaller 13 per cent gave a less favourable rating). There is little obvious explanation, except perhaps that having become more sensitized to crime issues as the questionnaire proceeded, respondents became more sympathetic to the demands on the police.

Another example is from the 1994 BCS in relation to a question on women's fear of rape. In previous sweeps, the 'worry about rape' question was in a battery of fear questions near the beginning of the questionnaire. In 1994, the 'worry' questions were split into two, and some—including the rape question— were put much later in the questionnaire, along with new questions of fear of non-criminal misfortunes. In the 1992 BCS, 30 per cent of women said they were very worried about rape, whereas 22 per cent said this in 1994. (When there was no question order change, the percentage reporting that they were worried about crime increased.) Tentatively, one might suppose that greater worry is registered in a more 'off-the-cuff' answer early on in the questionnaire before women have gone through questions which remind them of the mundanity of most criminal victimization. In any event, though, it is clear that measurement can be sensitive to question position.

FUTURE RESEARCH

A notion worth dispelling first is that victim surveys can realistically be developed to reveal the full extent of the 'dark figure' of crime. Household surveys only cover selected crime types, and they are much easier to do with adult samples, which leaves aside victimization of children. Those living in institutions could be better covered than to date, and the Office of National Statistics is developing a Communal Establishment survey which might provide a vehicle for this. But it is hard to envisage that adequate samples can be taken from the large number of different types of institutions that exist, and the residents of some may be poorly equipped to answer relevant questions anyway. The problem of estimating crime against the private and public sector is also one of adequately covering the plethora of targets: hospitals, hotels, schools, banks, car parks, shipyards, transport firms, and government offices, etc. Even for businesses, the best available sampling mechanism—the BT Business Database—is poorer than that available for households. By the same token it gives a poorer base for grossing up survey estimates for particular commercial sectors. Some crimes against businesses will also be resistant to measurement through surveys: companies are particularly resistant to saying much about fraud for instance.

The BCS is now well entrenched as the national survey in England and Wales, and consideration is currently being given to doing annual sweeps. There is a case to be made that it needs an overhaul, not least because of what it has itself shown about measurement issues. The difficulty is that the BCS trend line is one of its major strengths, and all the more so as the new 'counting rules' for police classification of crimes, introduced in 1998, will severely upset the continuity of the police measure. However, changing BCS techniques is highly likely to alter its count of crime, as illustrated earlier in various ways. A further sweep of the ICVS is planned for early 2000.

LOCAL SURVEYS

The statutory requirement for crime prevention partnerships between the police, local authority, and other agencies introduced in the Crime and Disorder Act 1998 promises a sea change as regards the demand for local victim surveys. Local problems of crime and disorder are meant to be identified on the basis of sound information, and monitored by the same. Surveys are one obvious way of collecting this information—although of course there are others (see Hough and Tilley 1998). Some features of these local surveys can be anticipated:

i.   They will obviously be geared to local crime issues, and the substance of surveys will vary to the extent that local crime problems differ across local authorities (they may not do much).

ii.   It is likely that there will be a demand for local surveys to cover experience of disorderly conduct and 'everyday' harassment. Repeat victimization, too, is now such a 'buzz word' that surveys which fail to cover it will not be regarded well.

iii. Cost constraints will mean that 'quick and dirty' survey solutions are attractive. For instance, self-completion questionnaires in local newspapers will appeal although the representativeness of those who reply will be poor. Even if representative sampling is done, it is likely to be done on insufficiently large samples given that those who are paying will have become used to polls of typically 1,000 people being used to predict election results for instance. The confidence limits of representative samples of this size are not too problematic for measuring very broad patterns. But they allow little analysis of sub-groups, and will be inadequate to compare the results of one sweep with another. Such comparisions are likely to be demanded by local partnerships. (On a sample of 1,000, for instance, the change in the overall burglary risk in an area would need to be about a full 50 per cent up or down before it could be said to be statistically significant.)

iv.   Partnerships are likely to want to test what the public wants in the way of prevention programmes and policing priorities. As Hough and Tilley (1998) point out, however, people may be poorly informed about what is best, or may not have thought hard enough about it to give a considered view (though this will not prevent them from offering a response). It is best for respondents to be made fully aware of the full range of competing demands on the police. It is even better if they are asked to give answers which take account of opportunity costs: e.g. that more patrolling (a consistent favourite) might mean fewer resources available to tackle drunken driving. Possibly focus groups are better for unpicking public expectations of policing (Bradley 1998 reports a useful study on these lines).

v.   There will be considerable interest in fear of crime and how it affects 'quality of life'. (This has already become apparent in the context of the development of national and local Sustainable Development Indicators.) Conventional fear of crime questions have been subject to particular academic scrutiny (see, e.g., Hale 1966) and there should be scope for improvement here. Measuring the effect of crime on people's quality of life will need imaginative questions and benchmarking against the effects of other social stresses. It is more difficult than might be supposed to see how people's lifestyles are negatively affected by crime when the choices they make (e.g., about whether or not to go out at night) reflect several considerations in practice, and when some choices reflect rational good sense rather than dysfunctional fear.

vi.   Surveys may often be the best way of measuring crimes against businesses and other organizations, so that researchers and survey companies will need to get up to speed on drawing good samples and achieving respectable response.

vii.   There may be interest in victims' interactions with and knowledge of *local* offenders, and this may raise special problems of confidentiality and 'getting people to talk'.

viii. There is likely to be demand for *repeated* surveys. As said, this will require adequate sample sizes to track trends in victimization levels reliably (assessing attitude change is less demanding in sample size terms.) There will also be more need for tight consistency in repeated surveys than is usually appreciated. As seen, question order at the very least can influence responses. The addition of new topics (or the deletion of old ones) might also unbalance responses in a way that undermines comparability across survey sweeps.

SUGGESTIONS FOR FURTHER READING

There are several 'victimology' overviews. Useful ones are Karmen (1990), *Crime Victims: An Introduction to Victimology*, and Fattah (1991), *Understanding Criminal Victimisation*. A more 'left realist' perspective is Mawby and Walklate (1994), *Critical Victimology*. The first part of Zedner's (1997) essay on 'Victims' in *The Oxford Handbook of Criminology* covers some of the same ground as in this chapter, with more emphasis on the results of the UK surveys rather than the methodology. Koffman (1996) also gives a good overview of the UK crime surveys.

There are numerous textbooks on how to design and conduct surveys and the lessons are entirely applicable to victim surveys. A recent one in the UK is *Survey Research* by Sapsford (1999). Hough and Tilley's (1998) guidance on *Auditing Crime and Disorder* (ch. 2) covers many of the same issues about policing and victim surveys as here and provides some illustrative costings for different types of surveys. Nicholas Fyfe's (1997) report for the Scottish Office on *Designing Police User Surveys* is also useful.

Richard Sparks' (1981) long essay on the methodological problems of victim surveys remains unrivalled, but there is also coverage in Coleman and Moynihan (1996).

REFERENCES

ALVAZZI DEL FRATE, A. (1998). *Victims of Crime in the Developing World.* Publication 57. Rome: UNICRI.

ANDERSON, S., KINSEY, R., LOADER, I. and SMITH, C. (1994). *Cautionary Tales.* Aldershot: Avebury.

AUSTIN, C. (1988). *The Prevention of Robbery at Building Society Branches.* Crime Prevention Unit Paper 14. London: Home Office.

AUSTRALIAN BUREAU OF STATISTICS. (1996). *Women's Safety—Australia 1996.* Canberra: Autralian Bureau of Statistics.

AYE MAUNG, N. (1995a). *Young People, Victimisation and the Police: British Crime Survey Findings on Experiences and Attitudes of 12 to 15 Year Olds.* Home Office Research Study 140. London: Home Office.

—— (1995b), 'Survey Design and Interpretation of the British Crime Survey' in M. Walker (ed.), *Interpreting Crime Statistics.* Oxford: Oxford University Press.

—— and MIRRLEES-BLACK, C. (1994). *Racially Motivated Crime: A British Crime Survey Analysis.* Home Office Research and Planning Unit Paper 82. London: Home Office.

BACHMAN, R., and SALTZMAN, L. E. (1995). 'Violence Against Women: Estimates from the Redesigned Survey'. *Bureau of Justice Statistics Special Report.* Washington, DC: Bureau of Justice Statistics.

BAKER, A. W. and DUNCAN, S. P. (1985). 'Child Sexual Abuse: A Study of Prevalence in Great Britain'. *Child Abuse and Neglect* 9: 457–67.

BEERTEN, R., and MARTIN, J. (1999). 'Household Ownership of Telephone and Other Communication Links: Implications for Telephone Surveys'. *Survey Methodology Bulletin, No. 44.* London: Social Survey Division, Office of National Statistics.

BOTTOMS, A. E., MAWBY, R. I., and WALKER, M. (1987). 'A Localised Crime Survey in Contrasting Areas of a City'. *British Journal of Criminology* 27: 125–54.

BOWLING, B. (1993). 'Racial Harassment and the Process of Victimisation: Conceptual and Methodological Implications for the Local Crime Survey'. *British Journal of Criminology* 33: 231–50.

BRADLEY, R. (1998). *Public Expectations and Perceptions of the Police.* Police Research Series Paper 96. London: Home Office.

BRITISH RETAIL CONSORTIUM (1999). *Retail Crime Survey 1998.* London: British Retail Consortium.

BROWN, C., and RITCHIE, J. (1981). *Focussed Enumeration: The Development of a Method of Sampling Ethnic Minorities.* London: Social and Community Planning Research.

BUCK, W., CHATTERTON, M., and PEASE, K. (1995). *Obscene, Threatening and other*

Troublesome Calls to Women in England and Wales: 1982–1992. Research and Planning Unit Paper 92. London: Home Office.

BUDD, T. (1999). *Burglary of Domestic Dwellings: Findings from the British Crime Survey*. Statistical Bulletin 4/99. London: Home Office.

BUREAU OF JUSTICE STATISTICS (1993). *Highlights from Twenty Years of Surveying Crime Victims*. Washington, DC: US Department of Justice.

CHAMBERS, G., and TOMBS, J. (eds.) (1984). *The British Crime Survey: Scotland*. A Scottish Office Social Research Study. Edinburgh: HMSO.

CHATTERTON, M. R., LANGMEAD-JONES, P., and RADCLIFFE, J. (1997). *Using Quality of Service Surveys*. Police Research Series Paper 23. London: Home Office.

COLEMAN, C., and MOYNIHAN, J. (1996). *Understanding Crime Data: Haunted by the Dark Figure*. Milton Keynes: Open University Press.

CRAWFORD. A., JONES, T., WOODHOUSE, T., and YOUNG, J. (1990) *The Second Islington Crime Survey*. London: Centre for Criminology, Middlesex Polytechnic.

DE LEEUW, E., and NICHOLLS, W. (1996). 'Technological Innovations in Data Collection'. *Sociological Research Online, 1, 4. <http://www.socresonline.org.uk/socresonline/1/4/ leeuw.html.*

DURANT, M., THOMAS, M., and WILLCOCK, H. D. (1972). *Crime, Criminals and the Law*. London: HMSO.

EKBLOM, P. (1987). *Preventing Robberies at Sub-Post Office*. Crime Prevention Unit Paper 9. London: Home Office.

—— and SIMON, F. (1988). *Crime and Racial Harassment in Asian-run Small Shops*. Crime Prevention Unit Paper 15. London: Home Office.

—— LAW, H., and SUTTON, M. (1996). *Safer Cities and Domestic Burglary*. Home Office Research Study 164. London: Home Office.

ENNIS, P. H. (1967). *Criminal Victimization in the United States: A Report of a National Survey. US President's Commission on Victimization and Administration of Justice. Field Studies II*. Washington, DC: US, Government Printing Office.

FARRINGTON, D. P. (1993) 'Understanding and Preventing Bullying' in M. Tonry (ed.) *Crime and Justice: A Review of Research, Vol. 17*. London: University of Chicago Press.

—— and DOWDS, E. A. (1985) 'Disentangling Criminal Behaviour and Police Reaction' in D. P. Farrington and J. Gunn (eds.), *Reaction to Crime: The Public, the Police, Courts, and Prisons*. Chichester: John Wiley.

FATTAH, E. A. (1991). *Understanding Criminal Victimization*. Scarborough, Ontario: Prentice Hall Canada Inc.

FINKELHOR, D. (1994). 'The International Epidemiology of Child Sexual Abuse'. *Child Abuse and Neglect* 18: 409–17.

FITZGERALD, M., and HALE, C. (1996). *Ethnic Minorities, Victimisation and Racial Harassment*. Home Office Research Study 154. London: Home Office.

FYFE, N. (1997). *Designing Police User Surveys*. Edinburgh: Scottish Office (Central Research Unit).

GENN, H. (1988). 'Multiple Victimisation' in M. Maguire and J. Pointing (eds.), *Victims of Crime: A New Deal?* Milton Keynes: Open University Press.

GILL, M. (1993). *Crime on Holiday: Abuse, Damage and Theft in Small Holiday Accommodation Units*. Studies in Crime, Order and Policing: Research Paper No. 1. Leicester: Centre for the Study of Public Order, University of Leicester.

—— and MATTHEWS, R. (1994). 'Robbers on Robbery: Offenders' Perspectives' in M. Gill (ed.), *Crime at Work: Studies in Security and Crime Prevention*. Leicester: Perpetuity Press.

GRAHAM, J., and BOWLING, B. (1995). *Young People and Crime*. Home Office Research Study. 145. London: Home Office.

HALE, C. (1996). 'Fear of Crime: A Review of the Literature'. *International Review of Criminology* 4: 79–150.

HARTLESS, J., DITTON, J., NAIR, G., and PHILLIPS, S. (1995). 'More Sinned Against than Sinning: A Study of Young Teenagers' Experience of Crime'. *British Journal of Criminology* 35: 114–33.

HIBBERD, M., and SHAPLAND, J. (1993). *Violent Crime in Small Shops*. London: Police Foundation.

HOUGH, M. (1995). *Anxiety about Crime: Findings from the 1994 British Crime Survey*. Home Office Research Study 147. London: Home Office.

—— and MAYHEW, P. (1983), *The British Crime Survey: First Report*. Home Office Research Study 76. London: HMSO.

—— and TILLY, N. (1998). *Auditing Crime and Disorder: Guidance for Local Partnerships*. Crime Detection and Prevention Series Paper 91. London: Home Office.

JOHNSON, H., and SACCO, V. (1995). 'Researching Violence Against Women: Statistics Canada's National Survey'. *Canadian Journal of Criminology* 37: 281–304.

JOHNSON, V., LEITNER, M., SHAPLAND, J., and WILES, P. (1994). *Crime on Industrial Estates*. Home Office Crime Prevention Unit Series Paper 54. London: Home Office.

JONES, T., MacLEAN, B., and YOUNG, J. (1986). *The Islington Crime Survey*. London: Gower.

KARMEN, A. (1990). *Crime Victims: An Introduction to Victimology*. Pacific Groves, Cal.: Brooks Cole.

KAUFMAN, P., CHEN, X., CHOY, S. P., CHANDLER, K. A., CHAPMAN, C., RAND, M., and RINGEL, C. (1998). *Indicators of School Crime and Safety*. Washington, DC: US Department of Education and Justice.

KINSEY, R. (1985). *Merseyside Crime and Policing Survey: Final Report*. Liverpool Police Committee Support Unit.

—— LEA, J., and YOUNG, J. (1986). *Losing the Fight against Crime*. Oxford: Basil Blackwell.

KOFFMAN, L. (1996). *Crime Surveys and Victims of Crime*. Cardiff: University of Wales Press.

LAYCOCK, G. (1984). *Reducing Burglary: A Study of Chemists' Shops*. Crime Prevention Unit Paper 1. London: Home Office.

LEVI, M. (1988). *The Prevention of Fraud*. Crime Prevention Unit Paper 17. London: Home Office.

LONDON BOROUGH OF NEWHAM (1987). *A Report of a Survey of Crime and Racial Harassment in Newham*. London: London Borough of Newham.

MARTIN, J., and MANNERS, T. (1995). 'Computer Assisted Personal Interviewing in Social Research' in R. M. Lee (ed.), *Information Technology for the Social Scientist*. London: UCL Press.

MAWBY, R. I. (1979). 'The Victimisation of Juveniles: A Comparative Study of Three Areas of Publicly Owned Housing in Sheffield'. *Journal of Research in Crime and Delinquency* 10: 93–113.

—— and WALKLATE, M. (1994). *Critical Victimology*. London: Sage.

MAYHEW, P., and VAN DIJK, J. J. M. (1997), *Criminal Victimisation in Eleven Industrialised Countries: Key Findings from the 1996 International Crime Victimisation Survey*. The Hague: Ministry of Justice, Department of Crime Prevention.

MIRRLEES-BLACK, C. (1999). *Domestic Violence: Findings from a New British Crime Survey Self-Completion Questionnaire.* Home Office Research Study 191. London: Home Office.

—— and ROSS, A. (1995). *Crime against Retail and Manufacturing Premises: Findings from the 1994 Commercial Victimisation Survey.* Home Office Research Study 146. London: Home Office.

—— BUDD, T., PARTRIDGE, S., and MAYHEW, P. (1998). *The 1998 British Crime Survey, England and Wales.* Statistical Bulletin 21/98. London: Home Office.

—— MAYHEW, P., and PERCY, A. (1996). *The 1996 British Crime Survey, England and Wales.* Statistical Bulletin 19/96. London: Home Office.

MODOOD, T., BERTHOUD, R., LAKEY, J., SMITH, P., VIRDEE, S., and BEISHON, S. (1997). *Ethnic Minorities in Britain: Diversity and Disadvantage.* London: Policy Studies Institute.

MVA CONSULTANCY (1998). *The 1996 Scottish Crime Survey.* Scottish Office Central Research Unit. Edinburgh: The Scottish Office.

NEW ZEALAND MINISTRY OF JUSTICE (1996). *New Zealand Women's Safety Survey.* http://www.justice.govt.nz/pubs/reports/1996/victims.

OFFICE OF NATIONAL STATISTICS (1998). *Living in Britain: Results from the 1996 General Household Survey.* London: Stationery Office.

PAINTER, K. (1996). 'Street Lighting, Crime and Fear of Crime: A Summary of Research' in T. Bennett (ed.), *Preventing Crime and Disorder.* Cambridge: Institute of Criminology.

—— (1992). 'Different Worlds: The Spatial, Temporal and Social Dimensions of Female Victimization' in D. J. Evans, N. R. Fyte, and D. T. Herbert (eds.), *Crime Policy and Place.* London: Routledge.

PEASE, K. (1998). *Repeat Victimisation: Taking Stock.* Crime Detection and Prevention Series paper 90. London: Home Office.

PERCY, A. (1998). *Ethnicity and Victimisation: Findings from the 1996 British Crime Survey.* Home Office Statistical Bulletin 6/98. London: Home Office.

—— and MAYHEW, P. (1997). 'Estimating Sexual Victimisation in a National Survey: A New Approach'. *Studies in Crime and Crime Prevention* 6: 125–50.

PHILLIPS, S., and COCHRANE, R. (1988). *Crime and Nuisance in the Shopping Centre: A Case Study in Crime Prevention.* Crime Prevention Unit Paper 16. London: Home Office.

PITTS, J., and SMITH, P. (1995). *Preventing Bullying in Schools.* Crime Detection and Prevention Series Paper 63. London: Home Office.

RAMSAY, M., and SPILLER, J. (1997). *Drug Misuse Declared in 1996: Latest Results from the British Crime Survey.* Home Office Research Study No. 172. London: Home Office.

RAND, M. (1998). *Criminal Victimization 1997: Changes 1996–7 and Trends 1993–7.* Washington, DC: US Department of Justice.

SAPSFORD, R. (1999). *Survey Research.* London: Sage.

SKOGAN, W. G. (1994). *Contacts between Police and Public: Findings from the 1992 British Crime Survey.* Home Office Research Study 133. London: HMSO.

—— (1986). 'Methodological Issues in the Study of Victimisation' in E. Fattah (ed.), *From Crime Policy to Victim Policy.* London: Macmillan.

SMITH, L. J. F. (1987). *Crime in Hospitals: Diagnosis and Prevention.* Crime Prevention Unit Paper 7. London: Home Office.

SPARKS, R. (1981). 'Surveys of Victimisation: An Optimistic Assessment' in M. Tonry and N. Morris (eds.), *Crime and Justice: An Annual Review of Research, Vol. 3.* London: University of Chicago Press.

—— Genn, H., and Dodd, D.J. (1977). *Surveying Victims.* London: John Wiley.

Todd, J. and Butcher, B. (1982). *Electoral Registration in 1981.* Office of Population Censuses and Surveys. London: HMSO.

Tuck, M. and Southgate, P. (1981). *Ethnic Minorities, Crime and Policing.* Home Office Research Study 70. London: HMSO.

US Department of Justice (1976). *Criminal Victimization in the United States, 1976.* A National Crime Survey Report. Washington, DC: US Government Printing Office.

Van Dijk, J. J. M. and Steinmetz, C. (1983). 'Victimization Surveys: Beyond Measuring the Volume of Crime'. *Victimology: an International Journal* 8: 291–301.

—— and van Soomeron, P. (1992). *Criminaliteit en de Detailhandel.* The Hague: Dutch Ministry of Justice.

—— Mayhew, P. and Killias, M. (1990). *Experiences of Crime across the World: Key Findings of the 1989 International Crime Survey.* Deventer: Kluwer.

Walklate, S. (1989) *Victimology: The Victim and the Criminal Justice Process.* London: Unwin Hyman.

Whitaker, C., and Bastian, L. (1991). *Teenage Victims: A National Crime Survey Report.* Washington, DC: US Department of Justice.

Zedner, L. (1997), 'Victims' in M. Maguire, R. Morgan and R. Reiner (eds.), *The Oxford Handbook of Criminology.* (2nd edn.). Oxford: Oxford University Press.

Zvekic, U. (1998). *Criminal Victimisation in Countries in Transition.* Publication 61. Rome: UNICRI.

4

RESEARCHING 'STREET CRIMINALS': A NEGLECTED ART

Mike Maguire

INTRODUCTION

Criminologists nowadays spend surprisingly little of their time talking to 'criminals'. Previous generations probably did so a little more, but the majority of encounters were formal interviews with samples of convicted offenders in prisons or probation offices, usually to apply psychological tests or to elicit quantifiable data about their backgrounds. It has thus always been relatively unusual for researchers to get to know their subjects well, to meet them in less artificial settings, and to allow them to talk about crime and criminality at length in their own terms. It has been even rarer—for readily understandable reasons—for researchers to get close enough to criminal groups to learn in detail about (still less to observe) how they plan and commit illegal acts.

Criminologists as a body probably deserve criticism for this situation, which has left some important gaps in knowledge at the heart of the subject. Over the last twenty years, the scope, depth, and funding of crime-related research have grown enormously, benefiting from new computerized data sources in police and criminal justice agencies, as well as (since 1982) from the regular 'sweeps' of the British Crime Survey. However, this growth has been unbalanced, with some significant shifts in focus. We now know far more about patterns of offences and their physical circumstances (for overviews, see Maguire 1997; Bottoms and Wiles 1997), but this has not been matched by comparable advances in our understanding of the people responsible for most of these offences. For example, we still know relatively little about how they make decisions on where and when to commit (or not to commit) particular kinds of crime, or how they perceive the risks involved: such knowledge is not only of academic interest, but is potentially valuable for the development of crime prevention strategies. Equally, penal policy has seen a broad shift away from interest in 'rehabilitating' individual offenders, towards methods of categorizing them according to their 'level of risk' and the development of strategies—

including surveillance, curfews, and preventive prison sentences—to 'manage' that risk (Feeley and Simon 1992; O'Malley 1998): advocates of these new approaches tend to pay little attention to what offenders think or why they commit crime.

Importantly, too, these shifts in focus have been accompanied by declining attention among criminologists to some of the central theoretical questions (for example, about 'explaining crime' or the 'transmission of criminal values') which preoccupied their predecessors. Despite the overall expansion of research, many basic theories of crime remain largely untested empirically, thus inhibiting their refinement and development—and, ultimately, the progress of criminology as an academic discipline. To counteract this, more direct and detailed knowledge about criminal groups and the relationships between their members could stimulate re-thinking about, for example, sub-cultural or social learning theories, which have been largely neglected for years. And even those more recent theories which stress the importance of situation, environment, or opportunity—such as rational choice theory (Cornish and Clarke 1986) and routine activities theory (Felson 1994)—would benefit from studies of the actual decision-making behaviour of offenders.

In sum, there is a strong case for 'righting the balance' in current patterns of criminological work, by encouraging—and allocating more funding to—research with offenders. In particular, it will be argued here—with due recognition of the practical, ethical, and personal safety limitations—there is a need for more qualitative research using ethnographic or participant observation methods. The use of such methods has a long, if precarious, tradition within the discipline, which has been kept alive through several generations by small numbers of highly skilled—and in some cases very brave—individual researchers. Most of these have been passionate advocates of the value to criminology of ethnographic fieldwork with offenders, sometimes in the face of hostility from 'mainstream' criminologists who have attacked it, variously, as 'unscientific', 'too risky', 'too difficult', or 'immoral' (for a selection of arguments on both sides, see, for example, Sutherland and Cressey 1960; Polsky 1971; Hobbs 1988; Wright and Bennett 1990; Hobbs and May 1993; Wright et al. 1992).

The main focus of this chapter will be upon the perpetrators of so-called 'volume crime': the generally small-time thefts, burglaries, assaults, vehicle crimes, and acts of vandalism which make up the bulk of offences recorded annually in Criminal Statistics. Research on those involved in more serious and 'organized' crime is discussed by Dick Hobbs in the next chapter. This distinction is somewhat arbitrary, and some overlaps are inevitable. Indeed, as Hobbs points out, individuals can oscillate between quite different modes of offending, which leads Hobbs to question the validity of dividing them into separate categories at all. Even so, most commentators would agree that, while the boundaries are certainly fuzzy, there are different levels of criminal organization (distinguished, for example, by their complexity, resources, or capacity to enforce discipline or subvert criminal justice processes) and that relatively few offenders ever take part in criminal enterprises at the 'higher' levels.

Our main interest here, then, is in what writers have variously called 'ordinary', 'run of the mill', or 'street' criminals, or (emphasizing the frequency of both their criminal activities and their court convictions) 'persistent' or 'recidivist' offenders. The police—and many offenders themselves—tend either to use general slang terms such as 'villains' or to refer to categories based on criminal specialisms ('burglars', 'car thieves', 'fighters', 'street dealers', etc.). None of these labels is entirely satisfactory (for a discussion of their relative merits, see Maguire and Bennett 1982: 63–6), but it is difficult to find one suitable term for what is in reality a very broad category with unclear boundaries and diverse membership. It is also important to stress that—despite their lack of precision—social classifications of this kind are often more useful to researchers than classifications created on the apparently more 'objective' basis of official criminal records: the latter only reflect people's interactions with the criminal justice system, which may be merely one factor among many in the construction of their social identity as 'criminals'.

The basic shape of the chapter is as follows. It begins with a brief historical overview of the main kinds of research which have been carried out with offenders, relating these to broad shifts in criminological theory and penal policy, and to consequent changes in the kinds of research question which have been asked. This is followed by discussion of some illustrative examples of studies (of 'criminal networks', 'burglars', 'street kids', and 'gangs') which have relied heavily on field research and have used a range of qualitative methodologies, from semi-structured interviewing to 'participant observation'. As will quickly become clear, I am not a specialist in qualitative methodology, let alone an expert ethnographer, and I do not intend to venture into the sophisticated theoretical debates which have developed among sociologists in these areas over the last fifteen or so years (see, for example, Fielding and Fielding 1986; Atkinson 1990; Sayer 1992; Morse 1994). Rather, the focus here will be firmly upon my own and other researchers' experiences of practical issues which arise in the course of fieldwork with offenders. The first two studies discussed are research projects in which I was involved as a young fieldworker in the 1970s. It is interesting (if a little painful) to look back on one's own early fumbling attempts, and I have highlighted my mistakes as well as lessons I learned from them. These two studies also provide striking evidence of how much the policies and practices of funding bodies have changed since the 1970s. The remainder are chosen to illustrate some of the most creative and resourceful approaches which have been adopted in qualitative research on offenders, all of them showing that it is possible to achieve a great deal more in this direction than pessimists perennially suggest.

RESEARCH ON OFFENDERS: A HISTORICAL PERSPECTIVE

In criminology, as in any other area of social research, it is important to place any discussion of research methods within the context of the kinds of questions to which answers are sought. Very different kinds of research questions tend to be asked at different periods, depending upon fashions and developments in theory, current policy concerns, the priorities of funding bodies, and so on. Research on offenders has been particularly affected by broad shifts of these kinds, and it is instructive to consider it briefly from a historical perspective.

While they have intersected considerably since the 1960s, British and American criminology followed somewhat different tracks between the 1920s and the 1960s, and it is fair to say that over this period, the interesting and innovative studies of offenders came almost exclusively from the United States. As will be illustrated presently, these came mainly from the application of sociological methods and approaches to the study of crime, challenging the then pervasive influence of psychiatry and psychology. In Britain, by contrast, criminology continued to be dominated almost entirely by the latter disciplines. One of the main consequences of this was that there was relatively little variation from what are now usually referred to as 'positivist' approaches to research.

Positivism has taken many forms, but what they have in common is a view of 'criminality' as a characteristic of individuals. The fundamental task of criminologists was thus widely perceived to be to search for the 'causes of crime', interpreted as discovering why some people become 'criminal' and why others do not. This was generally combined with a belief that the only appropriate methodology was one based on 'scientific' principles: mainly, that samples of 'criminals' should be compared in a systematic way with equivalent samples of 'non-criminals', in order to identify any statistically significant differences between them. Armed with this knowledge, it was argued, policy-makers would be able to devise more effective ways to reduce crime. However, the kinds of factors on which criminologists focused their analyses changed over time, influenced less by a process of accretion of 'scientific knowledge' than by their own disciplinary backgrounds, prevailing political philosophies, fashions, and developments in theory. Thus early interest in crude physical differences (e.g. skull or body shape) gave way to searches for psychological differences, differences in upbringing and/or differences in social circumstances. Over the years numerous claims were made to have discovered the key causal factor (or combination of factors): the huge diversity of characteristics found by different researchers to be positively correlated with possession of a criminal record included possession of an extra chromosome, extraversion, low intelligence, a broken home, maternal deprivation, poor housing, and lack of education. However, not only were there always high numbers of exceptions to any 'rule' that could be constructed from these findings, but it was clearly dubious to translate statistical association into causality. By the late 1960s, the tide had turned against this kind of research, which became increasingly viewed as a fruitless quest for 'the holy grail'. Within a few years, it had become relegated to marginal status, as young criminologists with backgrounds in sociology successfully spread the message that 'criminality' was a social construction and could not be analysed as though it were a 'scientific fact' (for a critical history of positivist research, see Taylor *et al.* 1973). I shall return presently to this sea change in the discipline and its methodological implications.

The narrow positivist research tradition also remained strong in criminology in the United States between the 1920s and 1960s—notably in the massive longitudinal studies of samples of offenders carried out by Glueck and Glueck (1950)—but it was generally eclipsed by the more imaginative work of those who adopted a sociological approach to the study of crime. Broadly speaking, these writers saw the causes of crime as structural rather than individual, residing in phenomena such as the rapid growth of cities, social inequality, or blocked opportunities (see, e.g., Shaw 1931; Merton 1938; Cohen 1955; Cloward and Ohlin 1960). They were thus less interested in the individual characteristics of offenders than in their place in the social structure and their relationships to other social groups. Many also saw interactions between offenders—particularly in the shape of 'gangs' or criminal 'sub-cultures'—as a major factor in the facilitation of crime, perpetuation of criminal attitudes, and transmission of criminal skills.

The consequences of these kinds of theoretical interests for research methodology were that, instead of adopting the quasi-laboratory method of, as it were, applying a series of scientific 'tests' to samples of captive 'subjects', American criminologists began to look for ways of studying the attitudes and behaviour of criminal groups 'on the streets'. Admittedly, most still relied primarily upon interviews with individual offenders to obtain relevant information, but these often formed part of a quite different methodology. For example, to answer questions about the activities of gangs, it clearly made less sense to construct a representative sample of, say, prisoners with a certain number of previous convictions, than to try to find and speak to members of the gangs in a particular area, be they convicted or unconvicted and in custody or outside: this might entail the creation of 'snowball' samples, where one interviewee recommends another person for the researcher to speak to, and so on. Again, the questionnaires used were often deliberately loosely structured, aimed at maximizing the acquisition of qualitative data and capturing the viewpoint of the offender rather than the pre-judgements of the researcher.

The influence of sociology also encouraged experimentation with a variety of more adventurous and imaginative research methods and new sources of data.

The period in which this flowered most strongly was in the 1920s and 1930s, through the work of the so-called 'Chicago School' of criminology. Although associated with some significant theoretical developments—particularly 'social disorganisation theory' and the (now largely discredited) 'ecological' model of the development of cities and their crime patterns (Park *et al.* 1925; Shaw 1931)—the work of the Chicago-based criminologists was equally, if not more, important in the contribution they made to the development of methodology in the subject. Several had previously worked as journalists, and their first instinct in conducting research was simply to get out into the streets and find out for themselves what was happening, using whatever sources of information they could acquire.

A classic example was Frederic Thrasher's (1927) study, *The Gang*, which used a combination of observation, interviews, life histories, casual discussions, newspaper reports, personal documents, census data, and court records to draw a comprehensive picture of youth gangs in Chicago. Although some of the reported findings were dubious—especially the claim to have identified precisely 1,313 separate gangs!—the methodology had a hugely liberating effect on criminology. Other well-known innovative studies of offenders from this era, both based primarily upon constructing life histories from lengthy interviews, include Clifford Shaw's *The Jack-Roller* (1930) and Edwin Sutherland's *The Professional Thief* (1937).

Although the Chicago school withered after the 1930s, and most of the major American criminologists devoted their energies to theoretical debates, a number of individuals continued the Chicagoan traditions by producing high-quality empirical studies of 'street criminals'. In some cases, they went further than their predecessors, spending long periods in the company of groups of offenders and using methods which might be called 'participant observation'—though the researchers did not actually participate in crime (further comments will be made later about what kinds of research activity are covered by this and alternative terms). The majority involved work with youth gangs (e.g. Whyte 1943; Yablonsky 1962; Liebow 1967), but in my view one of the most interesting and original was Ned Polsky's (1971) first-hand account of the lives of adult pool-room hustlers and of the Greenwich Village 'beat scene'. His book contains an excellent discussion of 'dos and don'ts' in this kind of research, as well as a polemical defence of field research with adult criminals, repudiating criticisms from other American criminologists.

Meanwhile, studies of this kind remained very rare in Britain. However, just as the Chicago school had earlier 'liberated' American criminology, a number of young sociologists began in the late 1960s to attack the positivist tradition in British criminology, producing at the same time some excellent new kinds of studies of offenders—or, as they preferred to call them, 'deviant' groups. Building on the insights of the American labelling theorists (e.g. Becker 1964), these 'deviancy theorists' emphasized the point that 'criminals' do not constitute a 'natural' category, but are people labelled as such as a result of complex social and legal processes. One consequence of this viewpoint was that researchers set out to explore the 'social construction' of crime and deviancy in the everyday world, including the reactions of the people who become labelled as deviant. A good example is Jock Young's (1971) study of drug-takers, which charts a process of 'deviancy amplification' as the subjects, who regard drug-taking as a relatively harmless recreational pursuit, are demonized by more powerful social groups and react in turn by escalating their deviant behaviour. A similar process was demonstrated in Stan Cohen's (1972) classic study of 'mods and rockers' on seaside beaches. The methodology for such studies was eclectic and qualitative, using anything from observation of, and lengthy discussions with, members of the groups in question, to cuttings from popular newspapers—the central aim being to analyse how different social groups understood and defined the situation in question.

The general term most commonly used today to describe this kind of research is 'ethnographic', although I still particularly like David Matza's (1964) concept of 'appreciative' research. This does not imply that the criminologist is an admirer of those he or she studies, but simply that a key feature of the approach is (at least temporarily) to suspend judgement and observe and listen to offenders—in a sense, to allow them to 'tell their own story'. The data obtained may be used—as with the deviancy theorists—to develop or support criminological theories, but the researcher often set outs without a clear hypothesis to test: rather, in the mode of many social anthropologists, he or she may aim to develop theoretical insights as they emerge out of the fieldwork (another term often used in this context is 'grounded theory', a concept originally applied by Glaser and Strauss 1967). Equally, if interviews are conducted, they are likely to be relatively unstructured, allowing the offender to give as free an account as possible. It would be wrong to think of this as a haphazard process, with no testing of the ideas or the data obtained. On the contrary, methodologists have developed quite sophisticated sets of principles and techniques, such as 'reflexivity' and 'progressive focussing', to ensure that ethnographers approach their research in as rigorous a manner as possible (see Hammersley and Atkinson 1995; Atkinson 1990; Hobbs and May 1993; Fielding 1993). However, at the end of the day, the success of this kind of research hinges on the personal qualities of the researcher, whose key tool is his or her imaginative insight.

Rather like the Chicago school some forty years earlier, the 'deviancy school' produced a number of excellent research monographs within a short period, the supply then drying up as the sense of unity dissolved and its members struck out in a variety of directions. Many, in fact, moved away quickly from 'hands on' research with offenders, towards study of the institutions which 'create' criminals and which influence the ways we think about crime and criminality: the government, the law, the police, the courts, and the media. This institutional focus soon extended to interest in, for example, the 'occupational cultures' of criminal justice agencies and to debates about their accountability. By the mid-1970s, studies in which offenders (or deviant groups) were a central focus of the research, had become quite a rarity in Britain.

Meanwhile, as criminologists were turning away from both positivist methodologies and fieldwork-based studies of deviant groups, the key funding agency for policy-related research, the Home Office Research Unit, was also beginning to lose interest in offenders as an object of study and it, too, soon struck out in a number of new directions. First, under the leadership of Ron Clarke in the late 1970s and early 1980s, the Unit directed its attention and its research funds away from seeking ways to 'rehabilitate' offenders, towards finding ways of manipulating the environment (e.g. through target hardening or design) to reduce opportunities for the commission of crime (see, e.g., Mayhew *et al.* 1976; Clarke and Mayhew 1980). The central research question thus became whether or not a particular prevention practice 'worked': how it affected offenders' thoughts or attitudes was of only minor interest. Secondly, with the Conservative governments of the 1980s insisting strongly upon 'value for money' in the public sector, the Home Office began to commission more research on the effectiveness and accountability of criminal justice institutions. And thirdly, from 1982 onwards, the investment of a large proportion of the Home Office research budget in the British Crime Survey stimulated greater attention both to patterns of victimization and to the views and experiences of crime victims—at the same time boosting the profile and status of quantitative research methods (especially the statistical manipulation of large data sets) at the expense of more qualitative methods. While some theoreticians and radical criminologists initially wished to steer clear of the 'policy-oriented' research funded by the Home Office, the huge amounts of new knowledge it generated about crime patterns, victims, and the performance of criminal justice institutions could not be ignored and, together with similar developments in the United States, eventually propelled these topics into centre stage of academic debates (for further discussion, see Maguire 1997).

These shifts of focus in the main funding body further accelerated the already declining interest among university-based researchers in conducting studies of offenders. Over the late 1970s and the 1980s, most criminologists came to see their standard sources of data, not as interviews with samples of offenders, but as published documents and statistics, public surveys, agency records, or interviews with policy-makers, managers, and practitioners. An increasing number (myself included), also turned their attention to crime victims, getting involved with the British Crime Survey or local victim surveys, or conducting interviews in victims' homes. When offenders were interviewed, it was often simply to provide some form of 'consumer feedback' on the performance of a particular agency: for example, to obtain prisoners' views of complaints procedures (Maguire and Vagg 1984), or suspects' experiences of the safeguards introduced by the Police and Criminal Evidence Act 1984 (Brown *et al.* 1992). Moreover, despite the continuing rapid growth of criminology as an academic subject in the 1990s, there have been few signs that a new generation of ethnographers is champing at the bit to study offenders 'in the wild'.

It can be seen from the above review that, throughout the history of their discipline, most criminologists' personal contact with offenders in the course of research has been much less direct and less frequent than outsiders might expect. In Britain, the history of such contacts can be broadly divided into a long period of interviewing 'captive' offenders in order to collect personal and psychological data about them and, after a brief flurry of innovative, 'appreciative' studies of 'deviant' groups based on a variety of fieldwork-based methods, a twenty-five-year period in which (with a few noble exceptions, to be discussed later) contact has been minimal. Moreover, although there is a stronger and longer tradition of qualitative studies of offenders in the United States, the situation there over the last twenty-five years has been similar to that in Britain. In other words, in the remainder of this chapter, which looks in more detail at studies which focus in some depth on offenders' activities, lifestyles, and attitudes, it should be kept in mind that we are describing a minority tradition in criminology, the exception rather than the rule.

RESEARCH WITH OFFENDERS: SOME CONCRETE EXAMPLES

It is now time to look in a more concrete fashion at some of the practical issues which arise in conducting research with offenders. I am going to concentrate here on the 'appreciative' styles of research referred to above, in which the main objective is to find out (and develop explanations of) how offenders think and behave outside custody, rather than on aims and methodologies associated with 'positivist' approaches to criminology.

I shall begin with some comments about my own experiences of this kind of research, with burglars and with other persistent property offenders, in fieldwork conducted during the 1970s. Although I have often subsequently interviewed offenders for other purposes (such as to canvass their opinions about complaints systems or the parole system) it was only in the two studies described that the focus of the research was on their lifestyles and criminal activity: since then, like many other criminologists, I have been drawn increasingly into studies of the agencies which respond to crime, rather than of the perpetrators. Secondly, I shall refer to some studies in which other academics have engaged in research with offenders which comes closer to 'participant observation' than I was able (or sought) to achieve.

A STUDY OF 'CRIMINAL NETWORKS'

I certainly do not put forward the first study as a shining example: through my fault as much as anyone's, it became too unfocused and fragmented, and its eventual output was limited to the unpublished official research report, a few working papers, and a conference paper (Webster and Maguire 1973). In the present-day climate in which funding bodies have to demonstrate 'value for money' in the research they commission, this would rightly have been seen as an insufficient return on their investment. Nevertheless, from a purely selfish point of view, it was extremely interesting and educative to work on, generated some original (if only half-formed) ideas which influenced my later writing, and raised some important practical, methodological, and ethical issues. It also—unusually for this kind of research—focused on adult, rather than juvenile, offenders. Hence, while it may serve here partly as a salutary lesson on mistakes to avoid in field research, it had strong redeeming features and I look back on it essentially as a 'good try' at an extremely difficult piece of research.

I was employed on the project as a research assistant to Douglas Webster, of Salford University. Having just completed a postgraduate degree in social anthropology, this was my first 'real job'. It was a substantial study, employing me full-time and two other researchers part-time for nearly four years. The main aim of the research, which was funded by the Social Science Research Council (the predecessor of the ESRC), was to explore the nature of 'criminal networks' in three medium-sized British towns. There was no immediate policy objective and the project was not shaped by any clear theoretical perspective: despite the long time-scale, it was essentially experimental and exploratory in character, and we were given a great deal of latitude to alter our approach as the study progressed (again, one would be unlikely to find this degree of tolerance from present-day funding bodies).

The rationale for the research was as follows. It was well known that every sizeable town contains a number of persistent property offenders who see the town as their home and who usually return to live there (and often re-offend there) after any prison sentence. It was also clear that many of these are familiar faces to the local police and to each other. However, little was known about how such people relate together: how often and in what contexts they meet, whether they form cohesive groups (or 'sub-cultures'), how much they help or support each other, how they gain reputations as (un)reliable or (in)competent criminals, how they handle disputes, and so on. A starting assumption of the study (based on Douglas Webster's previous experience) was that the best broad description of their inter-relations was of loose 'networks' rather than 'groups': rather like an 'old boy network' of ex-public school pupils, individuals would be able to call upon others for collaboration, help, or services when they needed them, and would be able to verify their '*bona fides*' to those they did not know by means of a verbal 'reference' from mutual acquaintances. Our main task was to explore the nature and parameters of such networks and to develop insights into how they 'worked'.

I was made responsible for most of the work in one of the three towns ('Southtown'), about thirty miles from where I lived. As I was employed full-time, I was expected to work in a more intensive, field-oriented style than my two part-time colleagues, who were based in towns in Scotland and the north of England, and it was planned that eventually their findings would be used to support or complement mine in an integrated document. In the event (another disappointing aspect of the study) the research took rather different directions in each of the three towns and we failed to produce any coherent conclusions from the study as a whole. Consequently, I shall concentrate here only on my own research in Southtown.

The first important decision to be made was how, and to what extent, to involve the local criminal justice agencies, and especially the police, in the study: clearly, they had a great deal of information about offenders which would be valuable to us, but if I developed close relations with them, there was a danger that local offenders would doubt my independence (or even regard me as a police informer) and hence not give me the necessary trust and co-operation to achieve the aims of the study. Vice versa, of course, there was a risk that local police officers or members of other criminal justice agencies would not trust someone who was 'associating with criminals' and would not willingly assist the research. Such problems have been seen as quite acute by some researchers: for example, Richard Wright and Scott Decker, in their study of burglars 'in the wild', decided 'not to use contacts provided by the police or probation officers, fearing that this would arouse the suspicions of offenders that the research was the cover for a sting operation' (Wright *et al.* 1992). As it turned out, however, my own concerns on these scores were allayed more easily than expected, and I managed to maintain good relationships with both 'sides', without hiding from either the fact that I was talking to the other. Early on, I was introduced to the governors of two local prisons and to local court administrators, probation managers, and senior police officers, all of whom promised assistance and access when it was needed for research purposes. It was also agreed with the police that I would not be asked or expected to pass on any information I might gather about any of the individuals I spoke to. The importance of this to my credibility with offenders was fully understood, and the agreement was respected throughout. (Of course, if I had ever picked up any information about a very serious crime—which, thankfully, I did not—the situation might have had to be reviewed.) Equally, I made it clear to offenders that the study had official co-operation, but that anything they told me would remain confidential. On the whole, they seemed to accept my assurances, and I can recall very little open suspicion about my motives or truthfulness (further comment on these issues will be made later).

The main research strategy adopted was a dual one: on the one hand, to use court and police records to identify and interview an initial sample of male offenders with a substantial number of previous convictions in the town and, on the other, to use a 'snowball' method, following up any recommendations to speak to particular people. The 'interviews' that resulted were very varied in duration, frequency, style, subject-matter, and location. In some cases, they led on to research which was closer to 'participant observation'. I interviewed some people in prisons, some in probation offices, some in their homes, and others in pubs, clubs, or cafes. Some interviews lasted only a few minutes, others for hours. Some were relatively formal, others were wide-ranging conversations. Some offenders I saw only once, others I got to know well and met several times. I was also sometimes invited to go for a drink with small groups in pubs and, on two or three occasions, in people's homes. While these were chiefly social gatherings, I also managed to use them partly as informal 'focus groups'. At other times, I went on my own to pubs or cafes where I knew that offenders frequently 'hung out', hoping to meet someone I knew and be introduced to others. Although this happened occasionally, in most cases the visits were unproductive and I sometimes felt very uncomfortable, knowing nobody and not knowing what to do (do you walk up and introduce yourself to a group of strangers who you think may be 'criminals'?).

I should confess at this point that, although I had studied social anthropology and had some vague knowledge of the standard anthropological technique of recording 'field notes' when staying with remote tribes, I (like most of my contemporaries) had had absolutely no formal training in social research methods. I therefore had to learn everything through a combination of 'apprenticeship' and experimentation. I began by accompanying Douglas Webster, who was an experienced fieldworker with exceptional interviewing skills, on four or five visits to probation offices and pubs to meet offenders whom he knew from previous research in the town; from then on, I was on my own. In retrospect, this had both advantages and disadvantages. On the one hand, it gave me confidence in my own abilities, and I think also it made me less inhibited and more creative in my approach to tackling difficult research questions than I would have been if I had first studied methods in an abstract fashion from textbooks. On the other hand, I made a number of mistakes, especially in insufficient awareness of the need to tailor data collection and recording in the field to the process of analysis and writing. Where interviewing was concerned, I soon developed my own style, which—while not necessarily a model I would urge others to follow—has always worked for me in terms of putting people at their ease and 'getting them to talk'. Although sometimes advised otherwise, I decided early on never to use a tape-recorder, even in prison interviews, as it could damage the crucial trust I had to build up with those I spoke to. I generally took notes in my own version of shorthand or speed-writing (more accurately described as 'scribble'), although I did not try to write down everything. My basic aim was to record any points that appeared to me to be important, or any statements that would make useful quotations. Even then, I quickly acquired the habit of writing only at times which would not interrupt the 'flow' of important parts of the conversation: this entailed remembering points or sentences for some minutes and writing one thing while speaking about something else. I also made it a general rule that if people gave me sensitive information about, for example, recent offences they had committed (and it was surprising how many openly volunteered information about such matters), I would make no written record of this. Indeed, as far as possible, I tried to discourage them from giving me this kind of information at all.

Perhaps the key lesson I learned, quite early on, was that the best way of establishing a good relationship with interviewees was to be completely honest about who I was, what I was doing, and why, and—importantly—not to hide the fact that I had access to information about them from the local police, prison records, and so on. I also answered honestly any general questions they had about the research (though I refused to tell them what other individuals had told me). Despite some uninformed portrayals of them, most offenders are anything but naïve, and can quickly sense any attempt to dissimulate. Moreover, I was sometimes seen going into the local police station, and if I had pretended not to have any contact with the police, the attempted deception would soon have become common knowledge. Of course, whether they believed my assurances of confidentiality is a different matter, but my impression was that, despite occasional initial suspicion, most appeared to trust me to a considerable extent by the end of the interview. The establishment of trust was helped by one or two other factors. One was that, as I got to know some offenders quite well, they let it be known that I was 'alright', and as time went on, many of those I came to interview had already heard about the study and that I could be trusted. A second factor was that I discouraged people from telling me about recent offences for which they had not been caught. I was aware that, if they happened to be arrested for such offences shortly after speaking to me, it could be thought that I had passed on information to the police. I explained this to several interviewees, and they understood the point.

It might seem strange that offenders would volunteer such information, but this was not an uncommon experience. Of course, some of their accounts may have been inventions, some may have been 'planted' to test whether I would pass them on, and some offenders may simply have calculated that, even if I turned out to be a 'police spy' and informed on them, the police were unlikely to have enough evidence to prove a case against them. However, the important general point to emerge from this experience is that, provided that one follows some basic rules on confidentiality, this somewhat 'hybrid' form of research—a mix of semi-formal interviewing and (something approaching) participant observation, in which frequent contact is maintained with both offenders and the police—is not only feasible, but can produce some very rich data. Quite contrary to my initial expectations, I found that most offenders were open, friendly, and interested in the study, and were often anxious to tell me a great deal more than I required for the research. Indeed, several tried hard to persuade me to write their 'life story'.

This is not to say that there were no risks involved. Personal safety was certainly an issue, and I was always conscious that, despite all my assurances, somebody in the 'criminal world' might take serious exception to the research. Fortunately it never happened, but I was clear in my own mind that if I received any threats or warnings, I would modify what I was doing, or even give up the research entirely. Perhaps one reason that I was tolerated is that I did not get close to offenders at the more 'professional' end of the spectrum, nor asked in any detail about connections with criminals in London or other large cities. Our focus was very much upon local networks and what one might call 'run-of-the-mill' offenders. Although many of those I spoke to were prolific offenders and had committed some serious crimes, I never had any sense that I was dealing with groups which were 'organized' to the extent of having mechanisms in place to protect their secrets from outsiders—nor, indeed, that they felt any overriding need to do so. I am well aware, however, that anyone attempting to repeat this kind of study today might face a much more risky situation. In the intervening years, criminals have become more mobile, they are arguably more likely to be violent, and, as Hobbs (this volume) points out, drug dealing has permeated the crime world at all levels: those asking a lot of questions about local criminal networks might soon inadvertently find themselves defined as a threat to some major interests.

A second risk which deserves attention is that of the researcher getting too close to the offenders being studied. There was one occasion on which, following an evening spent with two offenders in a pub, I was invited to watch them do a 'job', in order, as they put it, to see what it was 'really like'. Like the classic tabloid journalist, I 'made my excuses and left', but the experience made me very aware of the risk of being swept along by the natural curiosity which every researcher possesses and crossing one of the ethical boundaries which it is vital to maintain strictly in this kind of research. Some of the offenders I saw several times were very likeable, but—especially after this experience—I was always careful to maintain a clear 'distance' in our relationship. This was helped, it is worth noting, by my need to drive thirty miles home each evening, rather than spend the night in the town (the driving could also be used as a legitimate excuse for not drinking heavily). But more generally, I became more aware of the need for conscious setting of limits, or 'line drawing'. This is an extremely important principle in research with criminals. While they have drawn the line at different points, field researchers have been almost unanimous that it is vital to define that line clearly both to oneself and to the offenders. Ned Polsky went a great deal further than most, admitting openly that he was prepared, in the cause of 'science', consciously to break the law by witnessing illegal acts. The researcher, he wrote:

must make the moral decision that in some ways he [sic] will break the law himself. He need not be a 'participant' observer and commit the criminal acts under study, yet he has to witness such acts or be taken into confidence about them and not blow the whistle. That is, the investigator has to decide that when necessary he will 'obstruct justice' or have 'guilty knowledge' or be an 'accessory' before or after the fact, in the full legal sense of those terms (Polsky 1971: 138).

Even so, he stressed as heavily as anyone the need to be absolutely clear about the limits to which one is prepared to go:

You must draw the line, to yourself and to the criminal. Precisely where to draw it is a moral decision that each researcher must make for himself in each research situation . . . You need to decide beforehand, as much as possible, where you wish to draw the line, because it is wise to make your position on this known to informants rather early in the game. For example, although I am willing to be told about anything and every-thing, and to witness many kinds of illegal acts, when necessary I make it clear that there are some such acts I prefer not to witness . . .
Letting criminals know where you draw the line, of course, depends on knowing this yourself. If you aren't sure, the criminal may capitalize on the fact to manoeuvre you into an accomplice role . . . I have heard of one social worker with violent gangs who was so insecure, so unable to 'draw the line' for fear of being put down, that he got flattered into holding and hiding guns that had been used in murders (Polsky 1971: 130–1).

Others have taken a different view of the acceptable limits. Yablonsky (1965), for example, argued that one should not conduct field research with adult crim-inals at all, as it was both immoral and amounted to 'romantic encouragement of the criminal'. Moreover, while he undertook some important field studies of juvenile offenders, where he saw fewer ethical problems, he argued even there that the researcher should act as a 'social worker' at the same time as an ethnographer, adopting what he called the 'dual role of practitioner-researcher' (Yablonsky 1965: 56). At the other extreme, one of the most interesting approaches has been that of Adler (1993), who undertook a 'participant observer' study of some fairly high-level drug dealers, in which she witnessed numerous illegal deals, often without letting some of those involved know that she was a researcher (she was taken in tow by a drug dealer friend, and many of those she met assumed that she, too, was a dealer).

Before leaving the 'networks' study, it is worth making one or two more comments about techniques of data collection and analysis. First of all, while the interviews were deliberately wide-ranging, allowing a full exploration of each offender's perceptions of the size and nature of 'criminal networks' in the town, they also included some tightly structured elements. One such was a chart on which each interviewee was asked to represent graphically his relation-ships with significant others (the initial sample was all male, and I am ashamed to say I cannot recall interviewing any female offenders through the 'snowball'). This chart consisted of a series of concentric circles with the interviewee located at the centre spot. The latter was then asked to draw a number of lines from the centre point outwards, each one representing a relationship, friendship, or acquaintanceship with one or more people: the shorter the line, the more sig-nificant that person or group of people was perceived to be in the interviewee's life. (No pressure was put upon them to attach names to the lines, although some did.) The nature of these relationships was also explored in discussions. It is worth noting in passing that the exercise was often helpful in terms of 'break-ing the ice' and engaging interviewees' interest: as a general rule, interviews are improved by using some devices which allow 'hands on' participation and visual representation of concepts. More importantly, though, analysis of a large number of these charts helped the research team to gain a sense of, for example, the relative closeness of offenders to family members and to 'criminal' or 'straight' friends; or to calculate the average number of other persistent offenders whom each interviewee regarded as close to them. This provided some evidence on the question of whether criminal networks are primarily about the facilitation of crime, or whether they are also important as a form of social support (the findings might also have been used to explore aspects of 'differential association' theory, although we never pursued this).

Of course, techniques of this kind are very crude, and the results could only be used as broad indicators, but they provided at least some systematic support for (or challenges to) other conclusions emerging from interviews and con-versations with offenders. This is a general lesson I have subsequently carried into many other studies: bringing as many different sources of evidence as possible to bear on any particular question—i.e. what is usually called 'triangulation'—is one of the most valuable of all basic approaches to research in the criminological field. One is almost always dealing with topics on which there is no absolutely reliable information, but if findings from a number of different methods (however weak they may be individually) all point clearly in the same direction, one can have a great deal more confidence in making general statements.

A second comment concerns sampling. This was essentially a qualitative study, and the main purpose of constructing an initial 'sample' of offenders for interview—the selection criteria being a minimum number of previous convictions in the town for property offences—was simply to make contact with a substantial number of local persistent offenders in a rapid and efficient fashion. While, based on their answers to a number of questions which were always asked in interviews, some quantitative statements could be made about this group, it became clear that they could not be regarded as a representative sample of members of 'criminal networks' in the town. Some were very much 'loners', others (despite their records) spent very little time in the town, and so on. By the same token, others we met through the 'snowball' method, or were told about, were well-known figures in the town and clearly part of local 'criminal networks', but had very light criminal records or most of their convictions were elsewhere. It was also interesting sometimes to find that a person said to have a reputation as a 'good villain' had numerous convictions for very petty offences: in such cases, it was not always easy to decide whether it was the reputation or the record that was misleading. In other words, although they are a good starting point, it is important to recognize that criminal records are not always a good guide to people's actual behaviour. This kind of mismatch between social and official categorizations of people is an issue which confronts criminologists on many occasions, and is one that should always be borne in mind when constructing samples or interpreting quantitative data based on samples drawn from criminal justice records. (A striking illustration of the point is the finding of Wright *et al.* (1992) that, among a sample of 'active burglars' outside custody which they constructed through a snowball method, only around 25 per cent actually turned out to have any convictions for burglary!)

My final comment here concerns the nature of the data we collected and the problem of analysis. Although, as noted above, a certain amount of the interview data could be quantified (percentages of interviewees answering particular questions in particular ways, average numbers of 'criminal' and 'straight' acquaintances drawn on the chart, and so on), this provided only indicative findings. The study was essentially a qualitative one, and relied primarily upon the strength of the interview material and the insights of the researchers. Perhaps the most successful outcome was the production of what we referred to as 'concerted criminal activities' (Webster and Maguire 1973). These were careful reconstructions of how particular groups of offenders had come together for a period of time and successfully committed a series of offences, before eventually the 'bubble burst' when someone made an error and arrests followed. In these cases, I managed to interview all or most of those involved, went into considerable detail, and developed good insights into the nature of criminal collaboration. Apart from this, however, the interviews turned out to be less productive in terms of final output than I had hoped or expected when conducting them. On reflection, principally through lack of training in qualitative research techniques, many were too unfocused, and I did not record the conversations carefully enough. Hence, although the interviews generated a swathe of ideas, when it came to writing sections of papers on a particular theme or idea I often had available only large numbers of brief notes on the topic from different interviews, together with a few 'pithy quotations', rather than a full record of some in-depth discussions about it.

I took two general lessons from this experience. First, rather than trying to 'cover everything', I should have been more mindful of focusing the interviews upon themes which would be central to the papers which would be the product of the research—including, that is, new themes which emerged in the course of fieldwork. As one experienced researcher once told me in relation to data collection for commissioned research (a piece of advice I have often followed since), 'the best tip is to imagine the final report and work backwards'. Secondly, even if it was difficult to write things down during the interview, I should have been much more diligent in writing up full notes immediately afterwards (I could also perhaps have experimented with tape recording in suitable cases, although I still remain instinctively resistant to this). These points are even more pertinent to present-day qualitative research, where computer packages such as Nudist or The Ethnograph are available to assist the systematic analysis of conversation.

It can be seen from the above account that I was very 'spoiled' in my first introduction to criminological research. Our research team was given a great deal of freedom to explore the topic, a long period of time, considerable resources, and wide-ranging access to institutions and their records. Times have since changed, and such luxuries are rare in a research funding context which has become dominated by short-term projects and risk-averse decision-makers striving to obtain 'value for money'. It might be argued, of course, that the relative unproductivity of the networks project is a good illustration of why 'gambles' should not be taken with unfocused exploratory studies, but even if we did not make the best use of opportunities we were given, I would still argue that some gambles of this kind are necessary if creativity is to be maintained in research. Sadly, there are few posts for young researchers today which offer the time or the flexibility to explore issues through genuine ethnographic fieldwork with offenders: perhaps their best chance of doing so now lies in study for a doctorate, though of course this is likely to be handicapped by limited resources. The other way in which I was 'spoiled' is less defensible, but is anyway much less likely to occur today: namely, that a largely untrained researcher was let loose, with minimal supervision, on a difficult and risky type of fieldwork. From my own point of view, being 'thrown in at the deep end' and allowed to learn by my mistakes was an invaluable experience for my future career, but at the same time it undoubtedly contributed to the relative failure of the project in terms of its focus and output.

STUDIES OF BURGLARS

The second project I shall describe—much more briefly—is a three-year study of burglars and burglary, funded by the Home Office and conducted between 1976 and 1979 by me and Trevor Bennett at the Centre for Criminological Research in Oxford University. I shall also comment on a subsequent innovative study by Dr Bennett (Bennett and Wright 1984) which took the study of burglars forward in a new direction.

While Home Office research funding practice is nowadays characterized by the tendering of short-term contracts to conduct pre-designed studies on topics relevant to immediate policy concerns (see Morgan, this volume), in the mid-1970s the Home Office Research Unit was still prepared to invest in longer term and more fundamental research in response to proposals from academics. The Unit was very supportive of the idea of a broad look at the subject of residential burglary—until then a surprisingly neglected topic—although, as always, it was keen to see significant use made of quantitative methods, as well as to receive specific policy recommendations based on the findings. The ultimate value of the proposal, from the funder's viewpoint, was the collection of information to inform the design of more effective policies to prevent residential burglary. The fieldwork was designed principally to find out more about how burglars chose their targets and committed their offences, to identify any common patterns of burglary through the analysis of police data, and to canvass the views and experiences of victims. We are concerned here only with the offender element of the project, but it is worth mentioning that when the resulting book was published (Maguire and Bennett 1982), the findings from the interviews with victims attracted far more attention than the chapters on offenders—in itself an interesting comment on the priorities of criminology in the 1980s.

Due to my previous experience and my involvement in its design, I was the senior research officer on the project, but Trevor Bennett—who brought with him the benefit of a Master's degree in research methods—proved to be an extremely able partner and we worked in practice as a pair, sharing the field-work duties between us. Our work was officially supervised by the Director of the Centre (Dr Roger Hood), but he had other major projects to concern himself with, and paid us the compliment of trusting us to carry out the research with only periodic meetings to review progress and reassure himself that all was going well.

As the study of burglars comprised only one element of what was a large and complex study, we adopted a less ambitious methodology than in my previous work with offenders. We simply went into a local prison and, with the

Governor's permission, went on to the landings and let it be known, first to staff and subsequently to prisoners, that we wished to 'talk to house burglars'. As inmates were recommended to us, we asked them if they were prepared to be interviewed in confidence, and most agreed. They were, in turn, asked to recommend others, and by a 'snowball' process—which became more effective as the 'grapevine' spread the news that we were harmless—gradually extended our list of interviewees. Some, indeed, approached us and volunteered their assistance. This selection strategy seemed to 'work', in that over a period of about four months we eventually conducted forty lengthy interviews with people who clearly had considerable experience of burgling residential property (we rejected a few other interviews with 'time wasters', particularly from the early stages of the process, but the great majority of interviews turned out to be productive). All forty admitted having broken into at least twenty homes, and the majority over 100. Most, too, described themselves first and foremost as 'burglars', although they also had other forms of crime on their records. The interviews generally lasted for at least an hour, and some prisoners were seen more than once.

For these interviews we used a semi-structured questionnaire, divided into a number of clear themes. Although still allowing a great deal of freedom for discussion under each theme, this ensured that our interviews were generally more focused than those I had conducted in the previous study, with a specific set of topics to explore. For one thing, we were interested in shedding more light on questions raised by our other interviews with victims and by our analysis of geographical patterns of burglary from police records: for example, how persistent burglars reacted to crime prevention 'devices' (such as alarms, window locks, dogs in the house, and so on) or why disproportionate numbers of burglaries seemed to occur just off main roads or close to junctions. Such questions had both theoretical and practical implications. We also explored more systematically some of the themes which had begun to emerge from the 'networks' study, such as the nature of relationships between burglars (focussing, for example, on questions such as how long they tended to 'work' with the same 'partners', or how strong were professed principles such as 'not stealing from your own kind' or 'never grassing'). The result was much more manageable and focused material, which was eventually used in what I consider one of the best chapters of the resulting book (Maguire and Bennett 1982: ch. 3). At the conclusion of this study, following the submission of the report to the Home Office, Trevor Bennett left to take up a post in Cambridge, but I fortunately obtained an extension to my contract to expand the 'burglars' element of the study, and in particular to follow up one particular man we had found, who had been unusually successful as a burglar, stealing large amounts of antiques and jewellery over several years before being apprehended, and who was willing to describe his experiences to me in detail. (I also took the opportunity over this period to begin incorporating the text of our report into a more general book on burglary.) This man, 'Peter Hudson', was serving a long prison sentence, and was eventually transferred to a distant training prison, but I continued to visit and interview him at length. We went through his life together in a systematic way, concentrating on a different period each time. Although I still did not use a tape recorder (though I now partly regret not having done so, so rich was his account), I wrote lengthy notes, asking him to pause if I could not keep up. He was also an excellent writer himself, and prepared for my visits by writing accounts of particular incidents. In the end, I built up a great deal of material which not only gave me insights into the practice of professional burglary, but an excellent chronological account of how my informant—who did not have a 'criminal' family background—had moved through various stages of criminal behaviour to acquire the exceptional level of skill and the 'connections' he needed to become a specialist country house burglar. His 'story' was eventually incorporated into the book as a complete chapter (Maguire and Bennett 1982: ch. 4).

This intensive method of studying criminal lifestyles—usually known as the 'life history' method—has been used to excellent effect by a number of writers, some of whom have based whole books around one person's account, rather than merely one chapter (as mentioned earlier, two of the best examples are Shaw's (1930) study of an adolescent 'jack-roller' and the story of 'Chic Conwell', Sutherland's (1937) 'professional thief'; more recent examples include the study by Klockars (1975) of the life of a receiver). It has the advantage of introducing a strong dynamic element into one's understanding of offenders, enabling one to locate an individuals' behaviour and attitudes within a broader socio-historical framework and making changes over time (and the reasons for those changes) much clearer. It also allows one to develop a relationship with the offender in which he or she may allow the researcher to probe much more deeply than is possible in 'one off' interviews into issues and incidents that are discussed. There remains, of course, the perennial criticism made of qualitative research, but above all of research based on single case studies, that the person is not 'typical', and that therefore one cannot generalize from the findings. The simplest response to this is that other kinds of studies can be used to test how frequently any particular phenomenon occurs: the aim of this kind of research is to gain greater insight into and understanding of one example—in a sense, to seek a 'deeper truth' (for a useful discussion of the main arguments for and against the method, see Faraday and Plummer 1979). It is, however, the case that the success of the life history method depends heavily, not only upon the skills of the interviewer (not least, to keep the subject from 'rambling', while at the same time avoiding interrupting too frequently or steering the conversation too strongly), but upon finding the 'right person' to study. It is important that the person studied is reasonably articulate, and can recall and describe incidents in detail. It is also important to avoid people who are 'plausible liars' and who exaggerate or invent accounts in order to boost their ego. It is wise for this reason to seek independent corroboration of at least some of what the subject says. In the above case, I had the benefit of reading evidence given at 'Peter Hudson's' trial which made it clear that the offences he had committed were exceptional in both scale and skill. I also spoke to his wife (to whom I gave a lift to the prison to visit him) at some length, which gave me another perspective on his life. Beyond that, I could only use my own judgement of his character, together with tests of 'internal consistency', to decide whether what he was telling me was true. Over our several meetings, I felt that I got to know him quite well, and on occasion he revealed a vulnerable side to his outwardly stoical and good-humoured character: this, again, gave me more confidence in the accounts he was giving me.

Before leaving my own work and moving on to comment on Trevor Bennett's later study, I shall digress briefly to round off the story of my own involvement in research on offenders. In broad terms, the burglary study marked the beginnings of my transition from an enthusiastic, if somewhat disorganized, young fieldworker, keen to follow up new ideas in all directions, to a much more pragmatic and 'hard-nosed' career researcher, aware of the need to tailor research proposals and fieldwork to match the policies and requirements of funding bodies and to deliver a timely and professional 'product'. Anyone contemplating a career in criminology will come face-to-face with these kinds of realities, but the path I chose brought me up against them more sharply and more quickly than colleagues who moved into lectureships at an early age. In my case, the burglary project was the last study in which I pursued my original interest in the lifestyles and behaviour of 'street criminals' to any significant degree. Subsequently, my decision to continue for some years as a 'contract researcher' at the Oxford Centre, rather than to seek a lecturing post (where I might at least have continued such research on a small scale in my spare time), dictated that I move away from offender studies entirely.

Following the burglary study, I spent another ten years at the Centre, where the principal source of funding was Home Office grants and all researchers were 'only as good as their last research report' in the competition to land a new grant and a hence a new fixed-term contract of employment. On reflection, although I was quite successful and often enjoyed the very different kinds of research that I learned to conduct, I perhaps stayed too long. Over that period, the Home Office Research Unit not only virtually ceased to fund studies of offenders, but moved towards a position where funding decisions were almost exclusively driven by narrow short-term policy concerns, and where the objectives, substance, methods, and (ever shorter) time-frames of research projects were increasingly rigidly determined in advance by civil servants. Having earlier been self-critical about the lack of rigour and focus in the networks study, I should also admit here that, by the time I left Oxford, I had the quite different concern that so much time spent in policy-driven research was limiting my opportunities and capacity to engage in broader academic debates. It was not until I moved in 1989 to a lectureship post that I was able to regain a significant sense of academic freedom and, relieved of the need to apply for one grant after another, found more time and greater stimulus to write in a reflective style. This is not at all to say that I have repudiated policy-oriented research, which—despite the abovementioned trends—can sometimes be innovative and intellectually challenging, as well as influential and important. My experience at Oxford gave me the skills to deliver a 'professional product' in the form that government funders require, and I have continued at intervals to bid for research money from the Home Office as well as from other sources. The difference is that this is by choice rather than necessity, and with a view to integration with broader academic interests. In conducting such research, the basic aim should be to deliver two quite different types of product, both to the highest possible standards: first, to produce a succinct, publishable report in straightforward language to answer the funder's original research questions; and subsequently, to incorporate elements of the acquired knowledge and material into publications aimed at an academic audience.

Returning now to burglars, I shall finish this section with a few comments to draw the reader's attention to what I consider to be one of the best British studies of offenders to emerge in the last twenty years, Bennett and Wright's (1984) neatly titled book *Burglars on Burglary*, as well as to one of the best American studies of burglars, Wright and Decker's (1994) *Burglars on the Job* (although they have an author in common, the two studies are very different). The first of these—one of the last major offender-centred studies to be funded by the Home Office—was not 'ethnographic' in the normal sense of the term, but used a number of innovative and cleverly designed research techniques to tackle the central questions which the authors had set themselves. Their main interest was in burglars' decision-making processes, and their implications both for theories of deterrence and for the (then highly fashionable) policies of situational crime prevention which were being developed in the Home Office.

The authors constructed an interview sample of male convicted burglars over the age of 16, drawn from both prison and probation service records, the principal criterion being that they must be currently serving a prison sentence, or be on probation for, an offence of burglary. (As noted earlier, this does not mean that the sample can be regarded as representative of 'burglars' as a whole, but we shall not dwell on the point here.) The innovation in the study lay in the use of a number of techniques to explore systematically with the burglars how they decided when and where to offend. For example, in order to identify 'situational cues' used by offenders in their choice of targets, they showed the interviewees video recordings of a variety of streets and buildings, filmed at walking pace to simulate someone going along each street on foot. The offenders were asked to rate each building in terms of its potential as a target, at the same time 'thinking aloud' to explain their reasoning. The researchers also used still photographs and lengthy semi-structured interviews (each lasting two to four hours) to explore other aspects of decision-making. These methods allowed both quantitative and qualitative analysis, and contributed significantly to thinking about both deterrence and crime prevention.

Wright and Decker's (1994) study was also aimed at exploring the factors which burglars take into account when contemplating an offence, but the authors used rather different methods for selecting their subjects and obtaining data. They employed a 'snowball' method right from the start, avoiding all contact with criminal justice agencies. They began by hiring an ex-offender who was now attending university, but who still had many contacts from his 'previous life' (a similar approach was used successfully by Laurie Taylor (1985) in researching his book on London criminals, *In the Underworld*). With his help, the researchers contacted a number of offenders on the streets of St Louis, Missouri, interviewing them and asking them to refer them on to others. They provided a 'sweetener' in the shape of a $25 fee for being interviewed, which they concluded to have been an excellent investment, although by no means the only reason why they received good co-operation: normally, they point out, offenders have to keep much of what they do secret, and they can find it enjoyable and even 'therapeutic' to talk freely to an independent person who poses no risk to them (from my own experience, I concur with this fully). They did not pay for 'referrals', but found that some offenders were taking 'cuts' from the interview fees of those they referred! In terms of their main research objectives, one of the most successful aspects of their methodology was to take Bennett and Wright's idea further and, rather than relying on videotapes, actually to walk the streets with their burglar interviewees, asking them to assess the potential of properties as targets. Finally, as noted earlier, another important outcome of this study was the finding that the majority of the self-confessed 'burglars' they contacted by means of the above method had no convictions for burglary.

PARTICIPANT OBSERVATION: STUDIES OF YOUNG OFFENDERS ON THE STREETS

I finish this chapter with necessarily very brief accounts of two of the British studies of offenders which have come closest to what has traditionally been referred to as 'participant observation'. It is worth noting in passing that this term is not an entirely satisfactory description of what is done in the course of field research, and that various writers have suggested alternative terms or sub-classifications. For example, Gold (1969) distinguishes between 'observer-as-participant', 'participant-as-observer', and 'complete participant' techniques (the last being the rarest and most controversial, raising ethical and legal issues as well as carrying greater personal risks), while Collins (1984) challenges these distinctions as misconceived, preferring the general term 'participant comprehension'. However, our purpose here is to look at what was done in the studies in question, rather than label it. Both concerned young offenders, rather than adults, which perhaps made the researchers' tasks a little easier, but both are nevertheless impressive examples of what can be achieved by good ethnographers with the necessary time, resourcefulness, and discretion to conduct research of this kind. Both were conducted in the late 1960s.

The first is the study by Howard Parker (1974) of a loosely structured group of male 'street kids' in a deprived area of Liverpool, who were frequently involved in offences such as theft from cars, shop and warehouse burglary, and low-level dealing in marijuana. As implied in the title, *View from the Boys*, the main aim was to present their delinquent activities, and other aspects of their lives, through the eyes of the young people themselves. Parker sums up his methodology as 'knocking around with a group of adolescents', on the streets and in the local pubs. He first got to know several of the group—who were mainly around 16–17 years old—when employed as a community youth worker in a holiday centre for disadvantaged city children, continuing to see them afterwards in the city. Subsequently, having taken up a university research post which allowed him the time and freedom to carry out his own independent research in addition to his other commitments (sadly, another luxury rare today!), he decided to make a systematic study of the group. The role he adopted comes closer than that of most other field researchers to what Gold (1969) called 'complete participant'. To a considerable extent, he set out to present himself to his subjects as being 'one of them' and, indeed, claims that his relationship with them was primarily one of 'friendship':

By the time I came down town I was established as OK—that is, amongst other things, boozy, suitably dressed and ungroomed, playing football well enough to survive and badly enough to be funny, 'knowing the score' about theft behaviour and sexual exploits . . .
I am still a regular at the Roundhouse [the area where the boys gathered] and hope to continue to be, for I enjoy the friendship I like to think I have there. Such friendship has been the basis of the whole study . . . Perhaps to those who have attempted a depth-participant observation study such sentiments will seem less irrelevant. All I can say is that this study would not have survived without such reciprocity (Parker 1974: 16).

Moreover, he conducted the research in a fairly 'covert' manner, letting it be known only that he was 'at the university', and pretending that he was studying (in a critical manner) 'the police and the courts', rather than the behaviour of the boys on the streets. He also tried to demonstrate to the boys that his loyalties

lay entirely with them, and passed various 'tests' to prove this. More contro-
versially, going even further than Polsky, he admits in the book to participation
in property offences by acting as a lookout or receiving part of the proceeds,
although he drew the line at actually stealing himself. In a passage that many
ethnographers would interpret as an admission to having 'gone native', he
attempts to justify this position by claiming that many others in the area
behaved similarly:

My position in relation to theft was well established. I would receive 'knock off' and 'say
nothing'. If necessary I would 'keep dixy' [keep watch], but I would not actually get my
hands dirty. This stance was regarded as normal and surprised nobody; it coincided
with the view of most adults in the neighbourhood (Parker 1974: 219).

In terms of data collection and recording, he admits (as I did earlier in relation
to the 'networks' study) to mistakes in choosing what to write down in what
form:

In retrospect, I was too selective in recording data. I did not take enough time in
keeping my fieldwork diary, especially in recording what I considered mundane events.
Quite often I would be obsessed with a small conversation piece to the exclusion of
other events. Had I been more concerned with detailed writing earlier on I would have
probably hit upon ongoing social processes more rapidly than I did. My general
conclusion here therefore is that keeping a detailed and accurate diary may be of great
significance (Parker 1974: 223).

However, this clearly proved to be less of a handicap to Parker than it was in my
case, almost certainly because, by being so deeply immersed in the street life of
the boys, he was able to recall and draw on a great many more experiences than
I could. He also had the advantage of a fairly small and clearly defined group of
subjects, who spent most of their time in a small geographical area, helping him
to create a tight focus for his written product. The resulting book is rich in
material, ideas, and insights, and is valuable not only for its description of 'life
on the streets', but for his efforts to relate his observations to previous theoretical explanations of 'juvenile delinquency' and crime-oriented 'subcultures'
(none of which he found entirely satisfactory).

The final study I shall mention is James Patrick's *A Glasgow Gang Observed*
(Patrick 1973). In contrast to the Liverpool 'street kids', whom Parker (1974: 64)
describes as 'a network, a loose-knit social group', Patrick was in no doubt that
his subjects constituted a 'gang' (or, as its members referred to it, a 'team'): one
of many named gangs in the slum areas of Glasgow in the late 1960s. In locating
his study within a wider literature, then, we should look less towards the well-
known sociological theories of delinquency, subcultures, and so on, than
towards the sizeable body of work—most of it American, and much of it based
on field research—which has grown up on the specific phenomenon of street
gangs. A recurrent theme in this literature—and one which is central to

Patrick's study—is the violence of gang members, which receives considerably more attention than other forms of crime in which they may engage (see, e.g., Bloch and Niederhoffer 1958; Yablonsky 1962; Liebow 1967; Keiser 1969; Miller 1975; for more recent general overviews of gang literature, see Spergel 1990; Huff 1996; Maguire 1996; Klein 1998).

Generally speaking, British criminologists have paid little attention to street gangs, and many have claimed either that they do not exist in this country in anything like the American form, or that they are a rare and fleeting phenomenon. Indeed, Gibbens and Ahrenfeldt (1966) once reported that a research project on gangs had to be abandoned because none could be found! However, Patrick argues that Glasgow is a major exception, possessing a combination of structural conditions—notably, 'long traditions of slum housing and violence'—which are, as he puts it, 'conducive to ganging' (Patrick 1973: 169).

What is almost unique about Patrick's field research with the 'Young Team' is that it was totally covert. Patrick, a college lecturer, spent his summers as a teacher in an Approved School. One day, he was invited by one of the pupils, a gang member, to come with him during a home leave to see 'how it really is'. Between them, they devised a plan to conceal his identity from the rest of the gang, presenting him as an older boy from the Approved School who had no family. They returned together to the gang's area at intervals over a period of four months, during which Patrick joined the gang and got to know many of its members, in the process witnessing a considerable amount of serious violence. He eventually described his experiences in detail in the book, albeit having to leave out many incidents and disguising all names and places, including his own (James Patrick is a pseudonym). Moreover, he never revealed what he had been doing to the Approved School, nor to other authorities. Unfortunately from our point of view, he declines 'for legal reasons' to describe his methodology in any detail, or to discuss the many ethical and other issues arising from it. However, much can be inferred from reading his accounts of meetings and incidents: quite clearly, although he did not commit violent acts himself, he got very close to the 'action', and felt concerned enough about his own safety on the one hand, and police interest on the other, to want to wait a considerable time (and to take legal advice) before publishing a truncated account.

The bulk of the book is descriptive, written in a style accessible to ordinary readers, albeit infused with Glasgow dialect and slang, but it ends with an academic discussion of its implications for theories of gang delinquency and violence. Interestingly, he leans towards the unfashionable view, held by Yablonsky but by few other sociologists at the time, that the core members of gangs tend to be pathologiocallly disturbed, the gang providing a vehicle through which they can express their violent feelings.

CONCLUDING REMARKS

It is hoped that this chapter has provided at least a flavour of what it is like to conduct fieldwork with persistent offenders, particularly outside the safety of prisons or probation offices, as well as illustrating the range and variety of methods which have been used to try to obtain a closer and more realistic picture of how they think and behave when contemplating or committing crimes. Such research is relatively unusual, and even then has been confined principally to studies of young offenders rather than adults (with very few exceptions, too—one being Anne Campbell's (1984) excellent work on girl gangs—studies of female offenders are sadly lacking). It has to be recognized that it is both difficult and time-consuming, carries a variety of tangible risks (including physical harm and being drawn into criminal activity oneself), and is by no means always successful. Even so, if carried out with forethought and preparation, and with full awareness of the risks, it can be rewarding and productive in terms of both description and the development and testing of theory.

A number of themes and issues have emerged in the course of the discussions of individual studies. On some of them, there seems to be no strong consensus: for example, there are successful examples of both 'covert' and 'overt' fieldwork; some researchers (such as Parker) have tried consciously to become 'one of the boys' by dressing similarly or drinking heavily, while others have maintained some social distance in such matters; and some have avoided any relations at all with 'authority' while others have kept in touch with local agencies. On other issues, however, there is fairly clear agreement, and some important lessons can be drawn. For example, while they may disagree on where it is appropriate to draw it, most researchers underline the need to 'draw a line' in terms of one's willingness to observe or play a part in illegal activities. Again, promising and maintaining confidentiality are generally seen as essential. Where research techniques are concerned, most agree on the value of the 'snowball' method of creating interview samples or expanding contacts—a popular approach being to secure one or two strong 'allies' at the outset (whether friends such as Parker's companions from the holiday centre, or a hired 'guide' such as the man employed by Wright *et al.*). They also agree on the need for comprehensive field notes; and (the hardest lesson I learned in the 'networks' study) the need to maintain a clear focus to the study, rather than trying to achieve too much.

Finally, on a more general note, I would support the view that, while the majority of modern criminologists have moved in other directions, largely neglecting the direct study of offenders, it is very important to the health of the discipline that the traditions of field research built up by the Chicago School and kept alive by a relatively small number of individuals, are maintained by new generations of academics. Without this correcting influence, it is all too easy for those studying crime to lose their sense of reality and begin to perceive offenders not as people, but merely as 'problems' or 'numbers' (or, indeed—though much less common now than in the 'left idealist' years of the 1970s—as romanticized figures resisting the injustices of capitalist society). Certainly, from a personal point of view, the few years I spent in research of this kind—albeit not entirely successful, as well as falling far short of the full-blown 'participant observation' of writers like Parker and Patrick—gave me an excellent introduction to criminology. Perhaps above all, they impressed upon me the heterogeneity and complexity of the 'criminal world' and the variety of people who become involved in it: the consequent realization that there are no simple 'solutions' has undoubtedly influenced my thinking ever since.

SUGGESTIONS FOR FURTHER READING

There are a number of good general methodological books on ethnography and participant observation, including Hammersley and Atkinson's *Ethnography: Principles in Practice* (Routledge, 1995), Burgess' *In the Field* (Allen & Unwin, 1984) and Hobbs and May's edited collection *Interpreting the Field: Accounts of Ethnography* (Clarendon, 1993). Victor Jupp's textbook, *Methods of Criminological Research* (Unwin Hyman, 1989) is useful in placing this kind of study within a specifically criminological context, but goes into relatively little detail. For discussion of the special issues and problems involved in researching offenders in the field, it is best to go direct to some of the studies mentioned in this chapter, in which the authors include detailed accounts of how they undertook their fieldwork. In particular, I would pick out the Appendix in Parker's *A View from the Boys* (David and Charles, 1974), the methodological paper by Wright *et al.*(1992) in the *Journal of Research in Crime and Delinquency* (29: 148–61), and the third chapter of Polsky's *Hustlers, Beats and Others* (Pelican, 1971:115–47). Finally, while the rest of the methodology is not described in detail, it is interesting to read the first four sections of Patrick's *A Glasgow Gang Observed* (Eyre Methuen, 1973), in which the author describes his initial introductions to the gang and their violent behaviour.

REFERENCES

ADLER, P. (1993). *Wheeling and Dealing: An Ethnography of an Upper-Level Drug Dealing and Smuggling Community*. New York: Columbia University Press.

ATKINSON, P. (1990). *The Ethnographic Imagination: Textual Constructions of Reality*. London: Routledge.

BECKER, H. (ed.)(1964). *The Other Side: Perspectives on Deviance*. New York: Free Press.

BENNETT, T., and WRIGHT, R. (1984). *Burglars on Burglary: Prevention and the Offender*. Aldershot: Gower.

BLOCH, H.A., and NIEDERHOFFER, A. (1958). *The Gang: A Study in Adolescent Behaviour*. New York: Philosophical Library.

BOTTOMS, A., and WILES, P. (1997). 'Environmental Criminology' in M. Maguire, R. Morgan, and R. Reiner (eds.), *The Oxford Handbook of Criminology* (2nd edn.). Oxford: Oxford University Press.

BROWN, D., ELLIS, T., and LARCOMBE, K. (1992). *Changing the Code: Police Detention Under the Revised PACE Codes of Practice*. Home Office Research Study No. 129. London: HMSO.

BURGESS, R. (1984). *In the Field*. London: Allen & Unwin.

CAMPBELL, A. (1984). *The Girls in the Gang*. New York: Basil Blackwell.

CLARKE, R., and MAYHEW, P. (1980). *Designing Out Crime*. London: HMSO.

CLOWARD, R., and OHLIN, L. (1960). *Delinquency and Opportunity: A Theory of Delinquent Gangs*. Chicago, Ill.: Free Press.

COHEN, A. (1955). *Delinquent Boys: The Culture of the Gang*. New York: Free Press.

COHEN, S. (1972). *Folk Devils and Moral Panics*. London: Paladin.

COLLINS, H. (1984). 'Researching Spoon-bending: Concepts and Practice of Participatory Fieldwork' in C. Bell and H. Roberts (eds.), *Social Researching*. London: Routledge and Kegan Paul.

CORNISH, D., and CLARKE, R. (eds.) (1986). *The Reasoning Criminal: Rational Choice Perspectives on Offending*. New York: Springer.

FARADAY, A., and PLUMMER, K. (1979). 'Doing Life Histories'. *Sociological Review* 27: 773–98.

FEELEY, M., and SIMON, J. (1992). 'The New Penology: Notes on the Emerging Strategy of Corrections and its Implications'. *Criminology* 30: 449–74.

FELSON, M. (1994). *Crime and Everyday Life*. Thousand Oaks, Cal.: Pine Forge.

FIELDING, N. (1993). 'Ethnography' in N. I. Gilbert (ed.), *Researching Social Life*. London: Sage.

—— and FIELDING, J. (1986). *Linking Data*. Beverly Hills, Cal.: Sage.

GIBBENS, T., and AHRENFELDT, R. (eds.) (1966). *Cultural Factors in Delinquency*. London: Tavistock.

GLASER, B., and STRAUSS, A. (1967). *The Discovery of Grounded Theory*. Chicago, Ill.: Aldine.

GLUECK, S., and GLUECK, E. (1950). *Unravelling Juvenile Delinquency*. London: Routledge and Kegan Paul.

GOLD, R. (1969). 'Roles in Sociological Field Investigation' in G. McCall and J. Simmons (eds.), *Issues in Participant Observation*. Reading, Mass.: Addison-Wesley.

HAMMERSLEY, M., and ATKINSON, P. (1995). *Ethnography: Principles in Practice*. London: Routledge.

HOBBS, D. (1988). *Doing the Business: Entrepreneurship, The Working Class and Detectives in the East End of London*. Oxford: Oxford University Press.

—— and MAY, T. (eds.)(1993). *Interpreting the Field: Accounts of Ethnography*. Oxford: Clarendon.

HUFF, C.R. (ed.) (1996). *Gangs in America*. Thousand Oaks, Cal.: Sage.

JUPP, V. (1989). *Methods of Criminological Research*. London: Unwin Hyman.

KEISER, R. (1969). *The Vice Lords: Warriors of the Streets*. New York: Holt, Rinehart & Winston.

KLEIN, M. (1998). 'Street Gangs' in M. Tonry (ed.), *The Handbook of Crime and Punishment*. Oxford: Oxford University Press.

KLOCKARS, C. (1975). *The Professional Fence*. New York: Macmillan.

LIEBOW, E. (1967). *Tally's Corner*. Boston, Mass.: Little, Brown.

MAGUIRE, M. (ed.) (1996). *Street Crime*. Aldershot: Dartmouth.

—— (1997) 'Crime Statistics, Patterns and Trends: Changing Perceptions and Their Implications' in M. Maguire, R. Morgan, and R. Reiner (eds.), *The Oxford Handbook of Criminology*. (2nd edn.). Oxford: Oxford University Press.

—— in collaboration with BENNETT, T. (1982). *Burglary in a Dwelling: The Offence, the Offender and the Victim*. London: Heinemann Education.

—— and VAGG, J. (1984). *The 'Watchdog' Role of Boards of Visitors*. London: Home Office.

MATZA, D. (1964). *Delinquency and Drift*. New York: Wiley.

MAYHEW, P., CLARKE, R., STURMAN, A., and HOUGH, M. (1976). *Crime as Opportunity. Home Office Research Study No. 49*. London: Her Majesty's Stationery Office.

MERTON, R. (1938). 'Social Structure and Anomie'. *American Sociological Review* 3:672–82.

MILLER, W. (1975). *Violence by Youth Gangs and Youth Groups as a Crime Problem in Major American Cities*. Washington, DC: Department of Justice.

MORSE, J. (ed.) (1994). *Critical Issues in Qualitative Research Methods*. Thousand Oaks, Cal.: Sage.

O'MALLEY, P. (ed.) (1998). *Crime and the Risk Society*. Aldershot: Ashgate.

PARK, R., BURGESS, E., and MCKENZIE, R. (eds.) (1925). *The City*. Chicago, Ill.: University of Chicago Press.

PARKER, H. (1974). *View from the Boys: A Sociology of Down-Town Adolescents*. Newton Abbot: David and Charles.

PATRICK, J. (1973). *A Glasgow Gang Observed*. London: Eyre Methuen.

POLSKY, N. (1971). *Hustlers, Beats and Others*. Harmondsworth: Pelican.

SAYER, A. (1992). *Method in Social Science: A Realistic Approach*. London: Hutchinson.

SHAW, C. (1930). *The Jack-Roller: A Delinquent Boy's Own Story*. Chicago, Ill.: University of Chicago Press.

—— (1931). *Delinquency Areas*. Chicago, Ill.: University of Chicago Press.

SPERGEL, I. (1990). 'Youth Gangs: Continuity and Change' in N. Morris and M. Tonry (eds.), *Crime and Justice: An Annual Review* 12: 171–267.

SUTHERLAND, E. (1937). *The Professional Thief: By A Professional Thief*. Chicago, Ill.: University of Chicago Press.

—— and CRESSEY, D. (1960). *Principles of Criminology*. Philadelphia, Penn.: Lippincott.

TAYLOR, I., WALTON, I., and YOUNG, J. (1973). *The New Criminology*. London: Routledge and Kegan Paul.

TAYLOR, L. (1985). *In the Underworld*. Oxford: Blackwell.

THRASHER, F. (1927). *The Gang: A Study of 1,313 Gangs in Chicago*. Chicago, Ill.: University of Chicago Press.

WEBSTER, D., and MAGUIRE, M. (1973). *Why Can't You Guys Get Organised Like That?*

Criminal Organisation, Partial Organisation and Disorganisation in Medium-Sized British Towns. Paper to Fifth National Conference on Teaching and Research in Criminology, Cambridge, 4–6 July 1973.

WHYTE, W. (1943). *Street Corner Society*. Chicago, Ill.: University of Chicago Press.

WRIGHT, R., and BENNETT, T. (1990). 'Exploring the Offender's Perspective: Observing and Interviewing Criminals' in K. Kempf (ed.), *Measurement Issues in Criminology*. New York: Springer.

—— and DECKER, S. (1994). *Burglars on the Job: Streetlife and Residential Break-ins*. Boston Mass.: Northeastern University Press.

—— DECKER, S., REDFERN, A., and SMITH, D. (1992). 'A Snowball's Chance in Hell: Doing Fieldwork with Active Offenders'. *Journal of Research in Crime and Delinquency* 29: 148–61.

YABLONSKY, L. (1962). *The Violent Gang*. New York: Macmillan.

—— (1965). 'Experiences with the Criminal Community' in A. Gouldner and S. Miller (eds.), *Applied Sociology*. New York: Free Press.

YOUNG, J. (1971). *The Drugtakers*. London: Paladin.

5

RESEARCHING SERIOUS CRIME

Dick Hobbs

INTRODUCTION

The aim of this chapter is to highlight the methodological issues pertinent to the study of serious crime, in particular organized, professional, and white-collar crime. These three ill-defined but interlocking areas constitute criminal activity that covers an extremely broad spectrum of crime. Their apparent exclusivity is an academic distinction, based upon specialisms developed not on the street, or the boardroom, but in the academy. The problematic nature of these terms has been discussed at length elsewhere (Hobbs 1997a). This chapter will acknowledge the specific disciplinary and research traditions that inform our understanding of these forms of criminal action that are often hidden from our gaze, whilst acknowledging their lack of empirical exclusivity.

For the most part professional, organized, and white-collar criminals conduct their business in private, and it is often only after the intervention of the criminal justice system that we are able to attempt any analysis or understanding of the contexts and motives that drive them. However, the fact that they are not readily in the public gaze should not detract from the basic reality of this category of crime, and the methodologies available to researchers vary enormously. At one end of the scale retrospective studies offer the opportunity to analyse, with the benefit of hindsight and with minimal personal risk, serious criminality, and certainly the best of these studies remind us that crime can only be understood by comprehending the socio-economic context in which it is enacted. For as Chambliss (1978: 2) has noted, '[c]rime is not a by-product of an otherwise effectively working political economy: it is a main product of that political economy'.

ORGANIZED CRIME

HISTORICAL WORK ON ORGANIZED CRIME

The battle over the origins of organized crime is one being constantly fought, and historians have utilized archive data, such as police and judicial reports, economic evidence, pamphlets, diaries and biographies (Emsley 1997: 61–5), to disinter the professional and organized criminal. However, a serious and somewhat obvious disadvantage of working with archives is that they are the product of elites and their attendants, and the tendency is likely to be to slew the data towards the poor and low level property criminal, and away from the crimes of the powerful. As Sharpe (1999: 1–58) argues, data derived solely from literary evidence and the fears of government are far from infallible guides to reality, and considerable care then must be taken in unpacking data which tends to be biased towards control agencies, presenting a window on their, rather than the deviant's world (Atkinson 1990: 169–74).

Both historians and social scientists have analysed forms of pre-capitalist criminality that bear comparison with contemporary notions of organized crime. For instance, studies of the Elizabethan era suggest that pirates (Browning and Gerrassi 1980), who acquired from the state a licence to plunder, carried out the establishment and maintenance of British colonies. In time, as with contemporary entrepreneurs and captains of industry, their activities were fully legitimated before they gained entree to the Elizabethan elite (Sherry 1986). Naturally this particular form of organized crime became outmoded as commercial cultures came to dominate pre-industrial Britain, and piracy became a threat to legitimate trade, yet succeeded in leaving behind powerful traces of corruption within both government and commerce (Rankin 1969).

Historians, using both primary and secondary sources, indicate that criminal activities including corruption, political insurrection, and violence, went hand-in-hand with the exploitation of natural resources, and were responsible for the establishment of many of America's major industrial and commercial empires (Abadinsky 1990; Bell 1953; Block and Chambliss 1981; Loth 1938; Myers 1936; Sinclair 1962).

Hobsbawm (1972) called upon national and regional monographs, poems, and ballads to develop a schema consisting of three types of bandit; noble robbers, avengers, and resistance fighters. His notion of 'social banditry' remains valuable to this day, particularly when considering public attitudes to organized crime. The Mafia is the most well-known 'brand' of organized crime, and the use of the term has become an imprecise shorthand for organized crime groups, and is often applied by journalists in particular to criminals of ethnic origin. However, studies concerned with the roots of the original (Sicilian) Mafia carried out both in Europe and the USA tend to be sceptical of the simplistic international conspiracy theories (Sterling 1994) that tend to dominate popular images of organized crime. Instead they emphasize the complexity of the phenomena in terms of cultural divergence and in the light of a specific political/economic context. For instance Albini (1971), in his study based upon archival data and interviews with confidential informants in Italy and the USA, denied the existence of an international hierarchical criminal conspiracy, and stressed the importance of patron–client relationships within the context of Sicilian society. Hess (1973) utilized Sicilian archives, the transcripts of trials, and police reports and, like Albini, found no evidence of a Mafia organization. Instead he emphasized the role of the Mafia as a method; a method employed by Mafiosi, who via violence would enforce the authority of absentee landlords, while acting as middlemen and ensuring the continuation of traditional contractual arrangements. Hess also maintained that self-help promoted by self interest amongst individual Mafioso could often be mistaken for organizational solidarity.

Blok (1974), an anthropologist and social historian, spent two and a half years living in a Sicilian village, supplementing his archival research with interviews and conversations. Blok indicated that Mafiosi emerged as mediators not only between landowners and peasants, but also between a weak and distant central government which opposed feudalism, but lacked a monopoly over physical force, and the land owners who sought to retain their long-standing privileges. However, Blok rejected the notion of the Mafia as an organization or secret society. Lacking organization and co-ordination they filled a power vacuum by operating independently as violent entrepreneurs (see Arlacchi 1986).

The history of organized crime in Britain As Sharpe (1999) indicates, organized crime seems to have been a feature of British society from Elizabethan times onwards and British studies of professional criminals, some of them displaying elements of organization, indicate a wide range of activities. Sources for this kind of research sometimes rely heavily upon archives of the emergent criminal justice system, and even given the obvious constraints, such sources cannot be ignored. However, McMullen (1984) questions their value, pointing out that they do little to reconstruct the organizational or cultural features of crime, and his careful study of non-official sources suggests that organized and professional crime in sixteenth- and seventeenth-century London was typified by the formation of confederations of units of criminality, particularly within the stolen property market. Yet the problems of adopting an alternative, yet essentially uncritical, use of popular sources such as contemporaneous literature, are apparent in for instance the work of Salgado (1977), resulting in a view of Elizabethan criminality that is both picaresque and highly professional (see Rawlings 1992).

Historians usefully highlight the market place that emerged from the early years of British urbanization as crucial; creating, for instance, a demand for game which in turn led to a flourishing trade (Munsche 1981; Hay 1975). Similarly, smuggling not only fulfilled a need, but also was an activity that required organization (Winslow, cited in Hay 1975). Further, both smuggling and poaching forged links between rural and urban cultures that echoed the shift from rural to urban economic dependency, and required 'some degree of a division of labour; an intelligence and information system; and a sophisticated network for distributing the goods in question' (Sharpe 1999: 151). The activities of dealers in stolen goods have attracted the attentions of British historians (McMullan 1984; Tobias 1974), and a complex theft, and corruption organization was central to the career of the infamous 'fence' of stolen goods Jonathan Wild (Defoe 1901; Howson 1971).

By the eighteenth century, professional and organized criminals, armed with a range of criminal strategies from petty theft and violence to fraud, were firmly established in Britain. They took root not only in London where the market place was most affluent (Low 1982) and the regimentation of the emerging working class was at its most ineffective (Stedman Jones 1971), but also in coastal, rural, and provincial areas (Styles 1980). Historians have been extremely active in explaining how criminal practice was often affected by changes in the law (Hay 1975; Munsche, 1981). They have also reminded contemporary commentators that rapid changes in criminal trends are not the exclusive prerogative of the modern world (Lloyd Baker 1889: 23), as well as pointing out that moral panics generated by violent criminals are not exclusively twentieth-century phenomena (Sindall 1990). Criminal organizations, according to British historians, comprised 'network(s) of people known to operate, on occasion at least, outside the law, and to whom support and assistance might be given more or less casually, by like minded persons' (Sharpe 1999: 154). But this definition clashes with traditional images emanating from the USA.

The history of organized crime in the USA A dominant explanation of organized crime is to lay blame at the feet of one causal agent, or often one ethnic group, so that the rest of society can feel purged of responsibility. As a historian of organized crime Alan Block has few peers but he has succeeded in questioning many of the myths and assumptions regarding the ethnic origins of American organized crime (e.g. Block 1978). By referring to a range of primary sources including Senate documents, government Crime Commissions, personal documents, newspaper archives, confidential surveillance reports, and law reports (Block 1983), he has consistently argued for more rigour in the analysis of both traditional organized crime and the serious crime community that has replaced it.

As a vivid tableau of organized crime Chicago in the 1920s and 1930s has no rivals. It has fascinated historians with a consistent focus upon the prohibition era, which lasted from 1920–33 (see Kyvig 1979), and its aftermath. The reciprocity of criminal and emergent capitalist forces that was indicated by historians of piracy, also apparent in the taming of the American wilderness (Brown 1991), was now a major feature of an urban frontier engorged with immigration, poverty, and a corrupt political machine (Landesco 1968). During prohibition street criminals of all nationalities were able to take a step up the 'queer ladder of social mobility' (Bell 1953: 133), offering an alternative mode of advancement to ethnic groups who found legitimate routes blocked by the inflexibility of normative society (Haller 1971, 1985; Block 1983).

Historical analysis has shown us that the inevitable repeal of prohibition enabled organized crime to burrow into every aspect of American social and economic life (Kobler 1971; Woodiwiss 1993). For as one of the more influential historians of the era has explained, in order to exploit prohibition to the full criminals had to become expert in banking, insurance, business takeovers, the chemical and cosmetic industries, transport, shipping, the copper, corn, and sugar markets, as well as bottling and labelling industries (Haller 1985: 142). Consequently in an echo of both the pirate era and the Wild West, when the gunslinger became the lawman and republican stalwart (Brown 1991), '[t]he old clear line between underworld and upper-world became vague and easily crossed' (Fox 1989: 51).

Despite the lack of rigour apparent in many accounts of contemporary organized crime (Inciardi, Block and Halliwell 1977), some historians of this era nevertheless managed to uncover facts concerning structures and relationships that are totally consistent with contemporary empirical accounts. In particular as Haller (1971) has indicated in his analysis of the 'Capone Mob', organized crime is in fact an ever-changing series of partnerships in illicit goods and services. In common with many other historians, Haller utilized the archives of newspaper and local religious and governmental bodies, as well as the Internal Revenue Service files, Federal documents, law reports, and other documents, to develop his analysis of crime and vice during the prohibition era.

John Landesco (1968) wrote contemporaneously of this tumultuous era, and his work represents the first field study of organized crime. Landesco's work in Chicago (first published in 1927) formed part of the Illinois Crime Survey, and utilized an unusual mixture of methodologies. He locates organized crime as an essentially local phenomenon that both mirrors and complements the legitimate world, especially the business world. Landesco pointed out that in Chicago political corruption was endemic, and central to the functioning of organized criminality. The social disorganization prevalent in poor areas of the city was regarded as the key to comprehending organized crime, which provided a scarce role model for young working class men.

ORGANIZED CRIME: COMMISSIONS, SPIN OFFS, AND CRITICS

In 1950 Senator Estes Kefauver chaired the Special Senate Committee to investigate organized crime in the United States, placing the subject unambiguously into the political arena. For Kefauver, organized crime was a national conspiracy run by 'a sinister criminal organization known as the Mafia . . . originating in the island of Sicily' (US Senate 1951: 2). The committee decided that organized crime was 'the expression of a moral conspiracy aimed at the vitals of American life' (Block 1983: 123). Its conclusions, however, were based upon the unsubstantiated evidence of law enforcement witnesses, and failed to provide sufficient evidence of a nationwide ethnic conspiracy (Moore 1974). Nevertheless, 'alien conspiracy theory' became a highly influential American obsession which can be observed in the outpourings of specialist police units to this day (Hobbs 1998). The work of the Kefauver Committee has been subjected to detailed critical scrutiny by a number of academic researchers (Bell 1953; Block 1983; Moore 1974).

For many years, the bedrock of evidence for the existence of a national criminal conspiracy was the work of the Kefauver Committee and the testimony of Joseph Valachi. Valachi turned government informant when he discovered that he was to be murdered by New York's Genovese crime family of which he was a member. Already in prison, he killed an innocent prisoner believing him to be his nominated assassin, thus making himself a candidate for the death penalty. Valachi appeared before the US Senate Sub-Committee on Investigations (the McClellan Committee) in 1963 declaring the existence of an hierarchical Italian-American crime organization called La Cosa Nostra. He went on to describe a bloody feud alleged to have taken place in 1931, the Castellammarese War, which resulted in sixty fatalities and led to the formation of the 'new' Mafia (Cressey 1969; Maas 1968; Turkus and Feder 1951). Subsequently both the Castellammarese War and the existence of a hierarchical criminal organization called La Cosa Nostra (a term that nobody had heard before Valachi's testimony) has been disproved countless times, and Valachi's testimony has been totally discredited (Block 1978, 1983; Hawkins 1969).[1]

Valachi's flawed testimony has informed many of our impressions of the structure of organized crime, despite the fact that 'he either withheld facts that should have been known to him or deliberately lied' (Peterson 1983: 425; cf Potter 1994: 31–4). Valachi's evidence failed to implicate many friends and business acquaintances (Salerno and Tompkins 1969), and claimed that La Cosa Nostra prohibited drug dealing (the formal brief of the McClellan Commission was to investigate the role of organized crime in the drug trade), while his

[1] Hawkins (1969) has suggested that Valachi's understanding of La Cosa Nostra was similar to the level of understanding that a petrol station attendant would have of the inner workings of corporate decision-making in a major oil corporation.

enemy and former employer Vito Genovese was clearly active in the drug trade. Most importantly as Potter points out, '[p]rior to Valachi's testimony, the Federal Bureau of Narcotics had only 225 special agents assigned to its operations. The Bureau's successor agency, the Drug Enforcement Administration has 2000 agents' (Potter 1994; see also Messick 1973 for the most sceptical slant on the Valachi testimony).

The 1967 Task Force on Organized Crime provided further elaboration on the theme of the nationwide Cosa Nostra conspiracy, continuing to rely heavily upon Valachi's testimony. The bulk of the evidence was provided by public officials, citing corruption as a major, but impossible to quantify, problem. The emphasis was now on gambling rather than drugs, and the Task Force predictably emphasized the lack of resources and poor co-ordination that plagued police agencies in their fight against organized crime. They recommended strategic intelligence systems, specialized organized crime units, special prosecutors, the introduction of The Racketeer Influenced and Corrupt Organizations (RICO) section of the Organized Crime Control Act (Jacobs *et al.* 1994), and permanent investigating commissions.[2] However the assignment set by the Task Force for Donald Cressey, to outline the structure of organized crime in the USA, led to him emerging as the most influential and controversial academic scholar of organized crime.

As a member of the 1967 Presidential Task Force, Cressey elaborated on Valachi's 1963 testimony, and described a strict Italian/American bureaucratic hierarchy of organized criminality similar in many ways to legitimate business corporations. According to Cressey, twenty-four 'families' were governed by a Commission (Cressey 1969: x–xi), constituting a shadow administration governing a nationwide criminal conspiracy with a monopoly over serious crime, and placing legitimate democratically sanctioned institutions at risk via the corruption of public officials (Cressey 1967, 1969; cf. O'Brien and Kurins 1991). Cressey also accepted in totality Valachi's belief that the Castellammarese War was a crucial incident in the history of organized crime (Cressey 1969, ch. 3).

Confirming media and law enforcement myths, Cressey loaded flimsy uncorroborated evidence into the mould of a highly structured, codified national criminal conspiracy of Italian Americans (Hawkins 1969; Morris and Hawkins 1970; Smith 1975). Further, the level of cohesion that Cressey assumes existed within organized criminal operations (Anderson 1979: 33) coincided with the perceptions of police managers, but is fiercely denied by independent empirical studies. These studies emphasize flexibility (Lupsha 1981), multiple relationships driven by the quest for personal gain (Albini 1971: 288), inter-ethnic

---

[2] Gardiner's study of 'Wincanton' (1970) was a study connected to the Task Force, and remains an excellent example of the use of case-study techniques when applied to a community. Also recommended is Gary Potter's contemporary analysis of 'Morrisburg' (1994), a study that emphasizes the constantly mutating, multifaceted nature of illegal enterprise.

co-operation (Block 1983, ch. 2), and a non-monopolistic, essentially fragmented market place in which it is impossible to gain a monopoly (Reuter 1984;
Reuter and Rubinstein 1978).

The loose categories constituting the subject matter of this chapter are
highly emotive forms of criminality, and the state's efforts to police and
control them have become increasingly politicized. The policing of organized
and professional crime is a public issue that has witnessed the selective presentation of police work as organized, structured, and effective, and to this
end it has been argued that law enforcement agencies have sought out forms
of criminality that mirror the organizational hierarchies of policing (Reuter
1986). As Chambliss points out, 'the law enforcement system maximises its
visible effectiveness by creating and supporting a shadow government that
manages the rackets' (1978: 92). As we can see governmental efforts in the
USA regularly confirm this trend, but Britain is not immune from such
tendencies.

In the UK successive governments have ignored any analysis of the scale of
organized crime, and this is particularly problematic given the massive investment that the state has made in combating the problem. (For a brief overview
of the policing of organized crime in the UK see Hobbs and Dunnighan 1999.)
However, in 1995 the Home Office funded a questionnaire-based pilot study to
explore the nature of organized crime in Britain (Dunnighan and Hobbs 1996).
Problems of co-operation between police and other agencies, as well as jeal-
ousies between various branches of the police immediately became apparent.
The researchers lost control over both the questionnaire design and distribution, and as a result the findings regarding the extent and nature of British
organized crime, including its location, and the nature of its activities were so
flawed as to make the report of limited use to either academics or policy-
makers. With the agreement of the authors the report was never published. This
is indicative of what can happen when academics place themselves in the political arena between policy-makers and police agencies, vying for a slice of what is
becoming a very large pie.

Largely as a result of Kefauver and Valachi, the link between ethnicity and
organized crime became the focus for many scholars. Ianni's (1972) book in
particular should be regarded as an example of how a qualitative study, which
ignores the lure of state-sponsored data can tease out the realities of organized
criminality. Ianni's study based on three years of fieldwork is a valuable and
highly practical ethnographic inquiry, consisting of overt fieldwork at family
gatherings and private dinners, as well as interviews with informants, and the
result lends some empirical credibility to Bell's 'queer ladder' thesis (Bell 1953).
Ianni's later work (1974) supports some aspects of a later official report
(President's Commission 1987) by indicating that new ethnic groups were
taking over from Italians. However, with a quarter of a century of hindsight,

Ianni's prediction of the emergence of a Black Mafia (Ianni 1974) seems somewhat misdirected.

Lupsha (1981; 1983) analysed the available literature and sought out by unspecified means, data on the date and place of birth, and year of arrival in the USA of major organized crime leaders and their associates. He found that the overwhelming majority were 'American born or raised' (Lupsha 1981: 8) and cast some doubt upon the notion of ethnic succession. Contrary to Ianni's predictions, Italians were not giving up crime. Rather they were 'withdrawing from street and direct front line operations' (Lupsha 1981: 5), whilst remaining prominent in organized crime. The multi-ethnic networks described in Block's (1983) historical study also contradict the ethnic succession thesis.

Despite the distinctly 'American' nature of organized crime which was identified in the 1920s by Landesco (Landesco, 1968), interest in ethnic variations on the nature of organized crime groups has not disappeared. Methods employed in these studies vary enormously. Chin (1996), utilizing like Ianni his own ethnic background, interviewed sixty-two Chinese gang members to supplement his previous work that focused upon extortion (Kelly, Chin and Fagen 1993). His findings indicate a complex set of relations based upon underclass adolescents, who, unlike gang members from other ethnic groups, form street gangs which are closely affiliated to organized crime groups. The research rejects the notion of a monolithic hierarchical criminal cartel (Booth 1991), and acknowledges the role of a small number of Tong or secret society members who act as mentors for Tong affiliated gangs (see also Chin 1990; Joe 1994).

YOUTH GANGS AND ORGANIZED CRIME

As far back as Thrasher's groundbreaking study (1927), the links between youth gangs and organized crime have been noted by researchers, and many of these writings indicate that, given the problems inherent in gaining access to organized crime groups, an official role as a community worker or activist can enable trust to be built up in order for observations and interviews to be carried out. These studies suggest that contemporary youth gangs are not that dissimilar to the street gangs of the 1920s and 1930s as exemplars of the evolving nature of organized crime in relation to ethnic origins, class, and territory (Lacey 1991, ch. 3).

The studies by Hagedorn (1988) and Vigil (1988) were based upon their roles as community activists. Hagedorn, working closely with an ex-gang leader, was able to interview forty-seven gang members, while Vigil (1988) gained access to gangs via his role as a local activist sharing many core biographical features with gang members. His Los Angeles study features life histories, qualitative interviews, the use of key informants, and participant observation as the basis of the research strategy that located 'multiple marginality' as the basis of gang membership (Vigil 1988). Hagedorn identified economic conditions as the dynamic for gang activity which includes drug dealing (see the comparative ethnography of three inner city neighbourhoods in New York by Sullivan 1989).

A similar commitment was shown by Moore (1978) who used Chicano ex-convicts as research associates in a study which stressed the isolation of Mexican Americans from mainstream socio-economic life, and underlined the importance of the territorially based, violent, drug-dealing gangs. In the absence of legitimate institutions such gangs constitute alternative neighbourhood governments. (Decker and Van Winkle 1996; cf. Sanchez-Jankowski's 'local patriotism' 1991: 99). In a similar vein, Taylor carried out research on entrepreneurial imperialism within the drugs trade (Taylor 1990), by returning to his old neighbourhood with a team of researchers recruited from his own security and investigation company (see Padilla 1992).

PROFESSIONAL CRIME

ACCESSING PROFESSIONAL CRIMINALS

Most of the studies mentioned above required a great deal of commitment, skill, empathy, and tenacity on the part of the researchers in order to bring them to fruition, but in many cases the initial access was gained via some official or semi-official role. Because of their high visibility at school and in the criminal justice system, youths have always been vulnerable to academic intrusion of some form. In contrast, committed adult offenders specializing in acquisitive crime are somewhat more difficult to access, particularly in their natural setting. Criminals, when encountered on their own ground, have no investment in advancing the academic enterprise, and in many cases the success or failure of a project hinges upon the ability of the researcher to develop good personal relationships. As a consequence this type of work can make considerable demands upon the personal lives of researchers as they trawl areas of society left well alone by most academics.

Sutherland's (1937) study provided academe with a means of engaging with professional crime, and is widely regarded as a classic of criminological research, bringing the life history interview method to the fore (see also Inciardi 1976 and Chambliss's poignant 1972 study). Chic Conwell, the subject of Sutherland's study, introduces readers to a narrative of his criminal career as part of a distinct behaviour system located within loosely organized but cohesive groups sharing technical skills, and an ideology conferring status through a process of differential association.

However, although subsequent work on professional crime has constituted an ongoing debate with Sutherland, most studies of this category of offender have involved interviewing incarcerated professional criminals, or in some cases analysis of police-generated documents (Mack 1964). For instance, Lemert (1958), who interviewed seventy-two prisoners serving sentences for cheque forgery, and three forgers outside the confines of prison, found that cheque forgers were loners possessing few skills, and questioned the entire notion of professional crime as a separate form of criminal activity (Sharpe 1999: 150–4). Similarly, Einstadter (1969) interviewed twenty-five convicted robbers on parole, and twenty-five convicted robbers while incarcerated, and had access to their criminal records and other relevant material generated by the criminal justice system. Although he found that practical skills were common amongst this group, and that they shared many beliefs, some crucial aspects of Sutherland's model were missing, notably a system of tutelage or apprentice-ship to provide a route into the profession.

Shover (1973) indicated that burglars were somewhat closer to Sutherland's classic model of the professional thief than either the cheque forger or the armed robber. However, contrary to Sutherland, he claims that it is not non-instrumental cultural bonding based upon common occupational status, but the exigencies of burglary that necessitates the creation of networks of depend-ency. Shover recognizes a central dilemma in researching this category of crim-inal. On the one hand, this is a group of criminals whose occupational status generally requires men to deploy strategies designed to deter, rather than invite, attention. As a consequence, if a reasonable sized sample and the safety of the researcher are priorities, then interviewing incarcerated criminals is a legitim-ate and prudent tactic (Shover interviewed forty-seven, and administered ques-tionnaires to a further eighty-eight inmates). On the other hand Shover argues that if criminals are studied when they are no longer active then there is a real danger that the study of incarcerated offenders may produce studies of prison inmates (Sutherland and Cressey 1970: 68). To this end, Shover was careful to interview an additional seven non-incarcerated burglars or former burglars, one former fence, and one very peripheral associate of a gang of former bank robbers (Shover 1973: 500).

This combination approach to the problem of accessing professional crim-inals is common amongst scholars (see Letkemann 1973), and is an acknow-ledgement of the problems of locating and researching active criminals. For instance, Luckenbill (1981) reconstructed patterns of compliance in armed robbery via the use of case documents, including police reports and victim and witness statements, which were supplemented by interviews with victims and offenders. He discovered that the primary problem for the robber is the main-tenance of compliance via a series of transactions involving four interrelated tasks: establishing his presence, transforming the setting into 'the robbery frame', transferring the goods to the robber, and finally leaving the scene.

Gibbs and Shelley (1982) provide a candid discussion of one of the problems of the over-reliance upon criminal justice documents when it comes to identifying professional criminals, for these documents are dependent upon police action, and the whims of criminal justice procedure. As a result their quest to recruit serious commercial thieves for interview garnered a sample of only eleven. However, the authors defend prison-based studies, pointing out prison is part of the common experience of professional criminals, and that prison itself 'spawns self inventory' (Gibbs and Shelley 1982: 307). Likewise K. Levi's (1981) case study of an incarcerated hitman, which discusses the methods and motives of a professional criminal specializing in the commodification of death, provides data that it would almost certainly be impossible to glean from free world studies.

The Presidential Commission Task Force into professional crime (President's Commission 1967) adopted a very different set of strategies from the equivalent investigation of organized crime. Its report shows a considerable awareness of the available academic literature and, like all post-1937 studies, is written very much in the shadow of Sutherland. Limited original research was carried out in four cities, and the researchers' time was split equally between criminal justice personnel, such as police and prosecutors, and professional criminals themselves. A total of fifty offenders were interviewed, of whom approximately two thirds were in prison at the time of interview. This study, which was carried out in almost indecent haste during the summer of 1966, was, of course, aimed primarily at informing crime control strategies. However, it proved insightful, particularly in the way in which it questioned the orthodoxy established thirty years earlier by Sutherland, by stressing the importance of 'hustlers', who engage in an extensive range of criminality, and show little propensity for a shared consensus with other hustlers. The notion of a cohesive behaviour system is therefore rejected (see Letkemann 1973).

On a quite different scale, Holzman (1983) studied career property offenders in state prisons and involved interviews with nearly 9,000 prisoners. Mysteriously, the study excluded drug addicts, and expressively as opposed to instrumentally violent offenders, but it refuted the notion of full-time commitment to crime and highlighted the numerical dominance of part-timers, or 'moonlighters'.

To a great extent, studies of professional crime have tended to be theoretically driven by debates with Sutherland. This is remarkable given the apparently limited scope of this classic work, not to mention its vintage. However it does point to the enduring fascination of actual engagement with criminality. Engaging with professional criminals in their natural habitat however, is difficult, dangerous, and often impractical for those wishing to avoid the vicious but tantalizing ambiguities of life amongst the visceral economics of committed villains. But it is a possibility. As one informant, not a man well versed in the intricacies of empirical sociology, enthused, '[y]ou fucking come and see me, fucking write about me you fucking long streak of fucking useless. Come and

put this in a fucking book fucking Professor fucking Thunderbirds Brains'
(Hobbs 1995: 86). Invitations to carry out ethnographic research do not have to
be polite.

ETHNOGRAPHIC STUDIES OF PROFESSIONAL CRIMINALS

What Block (1991a) terms the 'serious crime community' constitute a hidden
population *par excellence*. As a consequence this community is an ideal arena
for ethnographers, particularly when the researcher possesses a biography
which in some way affords them special access. Yet even for these privileged
few, the field is a dangerous place. For instance Ken Pryce, the author of a
groundbreaking ethnography of Caribbean hustling culture in Bristol (1979),
was murdered when he turned his attention to organized crime.

Biker gangs have emerged in recent years as important players in the
organized/professional crime market, and Wolf's (1991) ethnography required
that he become totally immersed in biker culture (acquiring the club name of
'Coyote') producing a genuinely appreciative study of a classic deviant
subculture.

Patricia Adler's study of upper level drug dealers and smugglers required, at
least initially, some pre-academic familiarity with the subject.[3] The project was
based upon six years of fieldwork with sixty-five dealers and smugglers, and
their assorted friends and family, who were part of a culture that is 'secretive,
deceitful, mistrustful, and paranoid' (Adler 1985: 110). Hedonism was the norm
as life was lived as a party (Shover and Honaker 1992). The 1993 edition of
Adler's book features fresh material including an illuminating 'where are they
now' feature on some of the original sample.

Chambliss entered the field to examine how organized crime touches every
stratum of American society (1978: 14), and is closely linked to the legitimate
political economy and, in a similar vein, a study of British professional and
organized criminals carried out in the 1990s (Hobbs 1995) was based on
intensive fieldwork with professional criminals at work and at play, and is
complemented by interviews. As a consequence this study lurches from thick
description of the contemporary habitats of British professional criminals to
retrospective accounts provided by the offenders. The study emphasizes the
shift towards an entrepreneurial criminal culture that mirrors shifts in the
legitimate worlds of industry, commerce, and work.

Bourgois (1995) in his ethnography of the cultural context of crack dealing in
Spanish Harlem spent three years living in El Barrio. The value of ethnographic
methods is apparent in the way in which serious criminality is portrayed within
a framework of economic rather than pathological depravity. Despite being a

---

[3] Hobbs in his ethnographic study of East London (1988), although outside the rubric of this
chapter, does make some useful comments on carrying out research on familiar ground.

white male he succeeded in befriending Puerto Rican crack dealers, overtly and sympathetically documenting extraordinary levels of violence, racism, and sexism in and around the local crack house. Terry Williams' two ethnographies of the crack trade (1989; 1992) also show how valuable ethnography can be in demystifying criminality amongst minority groups, examining in fine detail the entrepreneurial culture which, via the drug trade, prevails amongst citizens of late modern inner-cities (see also Mieczkowski 1990). While Dunlap *et al.*'s (1994) case study of a female crack dealer, establishes that the role of women in the drug trade has close parallels with their role in the legitimate economy (see also Bourgois and Dunlap 1992; Dunlap *et al.* 1990).

The focus of Klockars' (1974) study is Vincent, who is a dealer in stolen goods. Klockars closely observed Vincent at home and at work where '[e]verybody's looking for a bargain' (Klockars 1974: 62). The book is a clearly-written account of a criminal businessman's life which benefits greatly from an excellent methods chapter that is extremely honest regarding in particular the problems of access faced by ethnographers. Another excellent study of the fence at work is that of Cromwell, Olson and Avery (1993) which was conducted partly from the back room of the fence's place of business.[4]

Wright and Decker have in two groundbreaking studies dealt with many of the problems of accessing and gleaning data from active criminals outside the context of the criminal justice system. They studied the 'cognitive script(s)' of both residential burglars (Wright and Decker 1994: 204; see also Cromwell *et al.* 1991) and armed robbers (Wright and Decker 1997), by buying the services of an ex-offender who could access burglars and armed robbers. The subsequent establishment of trust led to a 'snowball' referral effect (Langer 1977; Wright *et al.* 1992), and interviews with 105 and eighty-six offenders respectively were completed. The authors paid their informants for their time, and accompanied the offenders to the site of some of their recent crimes. Elsewhere (Hobbs 2000) I have suggested that this methodology constitutes a remarkable use of ethnographic interviewing technique, lending the study an ethnographic sensibility, that would have been lacking in more orthodox studies that rely upon some form of criminal justice or corrections referral.

BIOGRAPHY, AUTOBIOGRAPHY, AND TRUE CRIME

Given the hidden nature of most serious crime, researchers must exploit any opportunity to glean data that becomes available. Biographies, autobiographies, and true crime or non-fictional accounts make money, and the lucrative and populist end of this market should not be ignored. In the USA this is an

---

[4] In a similar study, Heyl (1979) charts the career of 'Anne', who after ten years as a prostitute becomes the madam of her own establishment. The stress is upon the management of a deviant enterprise that has much in common with legitimate business.

enormous market, and although I will concentrate primarily upon British examples, a few American works must be mentioned. Hohimer's (1981) review of his career as a burglar and the problems that he encountered with organized crime is a fascinating piece of work, while Cummings and Volkman (1992) give an interesting description of the career of a major organized crime figure, John Gotti. John Wideman's (1985) *Brothers and Keepers* gives a vivid and highly personal account of his brother's criminal career as an armed robber and murderer, its effect on his family but, most importantly, the hedonistic attractions of serious crime. The best of this genre succeeds in providing some of the dirty details missing in most academic studies, particularly those reliant upon criminal justice sources, which by definition suffer from a deep moral entrenchment on behalf of the state. For criminal life can be rewarding in more than pecuniary terms, which is why Pileggi's (1987) *Wise Guy*, a biography of gangster Henry Hill, is so valuable. Later used as the basis for the film *Goodfellas*, the book shows how for organized criminals '[l]ife is lived without a safety net' (1987: 39. See also Pileggi 1995).[5] Studies of British professional and organized crime are so rare that without biographies, autobiographies, and true crime books, the bookshelf is almost bare. Generally they portray a huge London bias, and a world dominated by small-scale neighbourhood-based coalitions based upon theft (Hill 1955) and extortion (Pearson 1973). For all their valuable insights they can be sentimental and nostalgic (Kray 1991; Kray and Kray 1989), but the better studies, like their counterparts in the USA, certainly convey the attractions of a life of crime (Benney 1936), the dynamics of masculinity at its heart (McVicar 1979), the role of violence (Fraser 1994), and the importance of reputation, even within instrumental networks of criminal entrepreneurs (Foreman 1996).[6]

Major era-defining crimes have gone virtually unrecorded by British academics, and while books written by journalists are often over-dependent upon criminal justice materials, police press releases, and the account of police officers who became their drinking companions, they do represent a detailed record of events. For instance, to name but a few, the Great Train Robbery (Read 1979[7]), the pre-supergrass era of bank robbery (Ball *et al.* 1978), and the Brinks-Mat robbery (Hogg *et al.* 1988). These vivid accounts of criminal reality have received little, if any, attention from criminologists, who disregard their 'bread and butter' (Shover 1996: xiii), in preference to bloodless, essentially elitist abstraction, or administrative audits of criminal justice effectiveness.

[5] Neal Shover's use of this form of data has a longstanding role in his various works and is discussed in Shover (1996: 189–96).

[6] Two interesting 'true crime' overviews, are Campbell (1991), whose book is based upon a BBC TV series, and Morton (1993).

[7] The dangers of working with informants who, as one public school and Oxbridge-educated academic explained to me, 'may not be gentlemen' is also apparent in Read's book. He was persuaded by some of the robbers that a notorious Nazi commando leader was the mastermind behind the robbery (Read 1979: 53–69, 291–312. See also Biggs 1981: 217–30).

WHITE-COLLAR CRIME

The research reported in this chapter has a distinct class bias, focusing on the criminal exploits of the lower orders; those operating not only outside the law, but also outside the confines of normative acquisitive arenas. White-collar crime can take the researcher closer to the ambiguous heart of business, and away from the ghettoes that are the foci of most researchers' endeavours.

The term white-collar crime was initially formulated by Sutherland (1949) to describe crimes of the respectable, and the middle and upper classes. He illustrates 'the possibility of divergence between legal, social and political definitions of criminality—but in doing so reminds us of the artificiality of all definitions of crime' (Nelken 1994: 366). Indeed the entrepreneurship of the working class (Hobbs 1988) is seldom regarded as ambiguous because it is locks rather than stocks that are being violated for profit, and this brief section will highlight research methodologies that mark a continuum between the ghetto and Gordon Gecko.[8]

From the working condition of domestic help (Aubert 1952) to a corporate-inspired disaster that led to loss of life and long-term chronic health maladies for an entire community (Pearce and Tombs 1993), white-collar crime covers a vast, and probably the most threatening, array of criminality. The range of evidence available suggests that, as a number of contemporary experts have energetically commented (Ruggiero 1996; Slapper and Tombs 1999), the spectrum of enterprise (Smith 1980) that encompasses our vices is not exclusive, for it also encompasses the daylight worlds of production, employment, and fiscal endeavour. This arena of criminality sets a range of unique conundrums before the researcher that are not apparent in the relatively simple worlds of theft, violence, and vice.

Throughout this chapter I have stressed the dangers of an over-reliance upon official sources when researching serious crime, as this would merely contribute further to the impression that the lower orders have a monopoly on crime (see also Jenkins 1987). However, Sindall's (1983) provocative study of nineteenth-century middle-class crime, involving an analysis of London, Birmingham, and Manchester court records, suggests that the nineteenth-century middle classes were more criminal than their working-class counterparts.[9] The tantalizing possibility that the overwhelming criminological tendency to stress the crimes of

---

[8] The problem of definition that is apparent in both organized and professional crime is far greater in the area of white-collar crime. This is a chapter concerned with research, and will give a brief description of methods used to investigate this broad area. However, recent books by Green (1990), Croall (1992), and Slapper and Tombs (1999) are recommended as excellent introductions to the field.

[9] Sindall has been criticized by Radzinowicz and Hood for reaching such sweeping conclusions from so small a sample (1986: 117).

the lower orders may be a gross misrepresentation of societal deviance is one of the most important achievements of scholars of white-collar crime. Further, in relocating the genesis of crime within a socio-commercial context, the researcher discovers a context that also encompasses the wider arenas of professional and organized crime.

As Perkin has noted, the mid-nineteenth-century explosion of industrialism created 'a new world and vocabulary of ingenious crime, which could only be perpetrated by businessmen' (1969: 442), and historians of business have recognized this (Cottrell 1980; Davenport-Hines 1986; Kennedy 1987). Robb's (1992) focus was British white-collar crime between 1845 and 1929, and he used the reports of Parliamentary Select Committees and Special Commissions, parliamentary returns featuring bankruptcy reports, criminal statistics, Inland Revenue reports, and a whole range of statutes relating to commercial regulation. Robb also used court documents and company records. A range of Victorian biographies, business and political texts, periodicals and newspapers, novels, plays, and poetry supplemented these archives. His study indicates that the phenomenon was 'the soft underbelly of the modern British economy' (1992: 181), and that *laissez-faire* economics contrived the same structural and ideological factors that created both legitimate wealth and the accumulation of fortunes founded on deceit for both established and emerging elites.

For Sutherland (1949), white-collar crime was organized crime. He studied retrospective documentation relating to seventy of Americas largest companies, and fifteen public utilities, finding a range of criminal offences that were essentially occupational (Green 1990), and often relating to activities that were breaches of civil or administrative law.[10] Despite refuting class-based theories of crime, Sutherland's theory situates differential association at its core, which may explain the trend amongst academics for seeking out the motivation for upper-world crime rather than its methods and practices.

Clinard (1952) studied the wartime 'black market' from within the Office of Price Administration where he was working. His study of regulation, primarily utilizing official documents, stressed differences in the personalities of offenders (Clinard 1952: 285–389), yet supported Sutherland's thesis by locating violations of rationing and economic control regulations as criminal offences. Clinard also established that these violations, which were carried out principally by businessmen, were sufficiently widespread to threaten the war effort (Clinard 1952: 28–50).

Wartime restrictions imposed upon civilians was also the focus of Hartung's (1950) study examining the data provided by regulatory agencies dealing with

---

[10] The uncut version of Sutherland's study, featuring the authentic names of offending organizations, was not published until 1983.

the wholesale meat industry in Detroit, and stressed the discrepancy between the lenience of the penalty and the seriousness of the crime. Studying this form of crime and its regulation from within regulatory and enforcement agencies using interviews and observations has been continued in the work of Hawkins (1984), Hutter, (1988), and Shapiro (1984).

Cressey (1953) employed the method of analytical induction to interviews with 133 convicted embezzlers for his study of the criminal violation of financial trust. He discovered that trusted persons became embezzlers when they have a combination of a non-shareable financial problem, the necessary knowledge to carry out the fraud, and a stock of suitable rationalizations. Quinney's (1963) study of fraud amongst retail pharmacists also used interviews with offenders and non-offenders, and concluded that professionalism produced controls which acted as a constraint against deviance, while business-orientated persons were not affected by such constraints.

Most of these studies, whether they required analysis of documents or interviews with offenders, were conducted retrospectively, and were therefore somewhat removed from the enacted environment of the offence. Direct engagement with offending organizations and individuals, as in the fields of professional and organized crime is possible (Braithwaite 1984; Geis 1968; Nelken 1983), but rare. Further, the problem for most scholars who attempt to operate without this level of engagement is that most white-collar/corporate crime researchers have an academic training based upon sociology, and know nothing of economics and little of law (Geis 1974: 281).[11] Consequently, it is argued that this is a highly specialized field requiring knowledge that is derived from a range of disciplines, and researchers working in this field often have to employ an array of investigative devices. Braithwaite (1984) is one such researcher who has been responsible for influential studies of corporate malpractice by invoking an array of interviews with those in and out of offending companies, including the disaffected who had left and therefore had a story to tell. He also used trial data, company documents lodged with regulatory agencies, government investigations, and congressional hearings. This use of multiple methodologies is the most common thread to be found running through empirical studies of this form of crime.

However, those who have carried out much of the more efficient unwrapping of white-collar and corporate deviance were able to maintain field relationships with criminals and enforcers over considerable periods of time, and across several research projects. Mike Levi's study of long-firm fraud (1981) is probably as close to an ethnography of fraud as we are likely to get. He carried out an intensive study of court records, and conducted interviews with businessmen,

---

[11] Indeed Vaughan (1983) found that her status as a sociologist barred her from access to corporate data on malpractice.

police, prosecutors and defence personnel, and judges. He also observed four trials and interviewed fraudsters both in and out of prison.[12]

Reliance upon police or regulatory agencies can be problematic, not least due to the lack of any control over their selection of targets; as Geis (1974: 281) argues '[n]obody is tapping the phones of General Motors'. Consequently what Pearce calls 'crimes of the powerful' (Pearce 1976) often appear to be nothing of the kind, as so much research upon various areas of fraud mirrors trends discussed above, in its tendency to be based upon criminal justice-generated data, indicating a disproportionate amount of offending amongst individuals (or firms) of low social status.[13] This is clearly indicated by, among others, Nelken's (1983) study of residential landlords, and most devastatingly by Cook's (1989) use of her status as an ex-governmental worker to make a comparative study of the way that the state deals with welfare and income tax fraud.[14] Yet criminality amongst the business community has been continually unravelled by skilled researchers engaging with the business world and its inhabitants (Punch 1996), in the same way that ethnographers of youth (Parker 1974), of deprived ethnic communities (Bourgois 1995), and working-class neighbourhoods (Hobbs 1988) discovered deviance to be normal, indeed central to the functioning of the culture.

Yet Levi's (1987) analysis of fraud trials between the Second World War and 1987 clearly shows that, with only one exception, establishment figures with 'insider' status have not been prosecuted. Indeed accessing such persons is a major conundrum for researchers. The specialized expertise required to penetrate the financial world, let alone understand how it works, is a major barrier for researchers (Levi 1987). The multiplicity of methods utilized by scholars to unpack such massive crimes as the BCCI fraud (Passas 1994) is marked by a constant shifting from public to private sources; from documentation to conversation. National security issues are encountered, and the very foundations of sovereign states exposed as commercially criminogenic (Block 1991a; 1991b).

CONCLUSION

To continue, we are now living in the future, and to continue to differentiate between the various forms of serious offending featured in this chapter is an

[12] Like Braithwaite's work, Levi's huge body of work deserves far more attention than this brief review can afford it. However, although much of this work is concerned with regulation rather than the crime *per se* (1987), his work on a range of fraud-related issues including the victims of fraud (Levi and Pithouse forthcoming), and the sentencing of white-collar criminals (Levi 1989) shows a deep empirical commitment.

[13] For an excellent discussion of this point see Croall (1992), especially ch. 3.

[14] See also Clark's (1989) clear and readable discussion of insurance fraud.

otherworldly academic conceit. The political economy of contemporary crime links street dealers with private armies in the Far East, market traders in provincial cities with sweat shops producing counterfeit designer clothing in Asia, and weekend cocaine, ecstasy, and amphetamine users with both rogue governments and men of marketable violence all over the globe. This argument has been partly acknowledged by scholars concerned with transnational organized crime.

Transnational organized crime (see Calvi 1993; Godson and Olson 1993; Labrousse and Wallon 1993; Sterling, 1994; Williams 1993; Williams and Savona 1995) has replaced the cold war narratives that dominated the concerns of many political scientists, and it is no coincidence that their interest in crime is also now shared with cold war warriors from the security services (Hobbs and Dunnighan 1999). The sources informing this genre are problematic, often reliant upon mass media sources, and reports emanating from national and international enforcement agencies. Consequently this research trend should be approached with some scepticism (Naylor 1995), as it persists with little hindrance from empirical evidence (Hobbs 1998).

In many ways little has changed since Kefauver in the ability of government agencies to generate politically appropriate research agendas and, as with Kefauver, at the core of discussion on transnational crime are various alien conspiracies the evidence for which is reliant solely upon police-generated data. For instance threat assessments contrived by the National Criminal Investigation Service (NCIS) have concentrated upon Triads, Yardies, Russians, Colombians, Italians, and Turks (NCIS 1993a; 1993b). As Ruggiero (1996) has indicated, the relationship between business crime and criminal business is much closer than a quick sideways glance at both the crime statistics and criminology textbooks would suggest. Therefore identifying aliens as the principal organized crime threat to British society is a device that lets more than a few 'dodgy geezers' off the hook.

A detailed analysis of the empirical truth inherent in such a trend is inappropriate here, but it must be stressed that the complexity of serious crime makes some reliance upon police-generated material inevitable. However this should be matched by the ability to decode and utilize unofficial tales from the cops' canteen and the senior officers' dining room, the corporate boardroom, and the public bar: the ideal being an intimacy with the ties that bind corporate malpractice and economic deviance to the cultural inheritance of traditional visceral practices (Hobbs 1995; 1997b).

The complexity of serious crime will lead the researcher to some as yet undiscovered destinations, and the journey will require rather more than a passing acquaintance with new technology (Norris, Moran and Armstrong 1998), specialized legal knowledge (Slapper and Tombs 1999), and multilingual skills (Rawlinson 1996; see also Rawlinson this volume). Yet as Hobbs (1997b) and Ruggiero (1995) argue, the organization of criminal labour mirrors trends in the organization of legitimate labour, and the complexity of contemporary serious crime should not concentrate upon width at the expense of quality. For the criminal market, like its legitimate partner in profit, functions within networks of small flexible firms rather than monolithic hierarchies, and a range of research strategies should develop to mirror this range. In cinematic terms, a cross between the *Lavender Hill Mob* and *Goodfellas* would be preferable to *The Godfather*.

Historical studies of cultures and socio-economic processes using a range of archive and interview techniques will continue to provide a context for our understanding of contemporary villainy. Due to the resources at their disposal, co-operation with criminal justice and other government agencies is inevitable, particularly for those concerned with macro studies of global criminal trends and processes interacting with international markets. However, as I have already indicated at length, any product of the state, and particularly those products derived from unaccountable agencies concerned with justifying their own budgets, needs to be carefully handled.[15]

Documentary trawls through legal records and case histories, though products of the criminal justice and legal professions, are vital, albeit flawed, tools that can provide key pieces to the jigsaw; particularly in reconstructing financially complex, corporate deviation or cases that cross international and legal jurisdictions. Interviewing serious crime personnel in prison, although fraught with problems, can be useful when large data sets of what would otherwise be difficult to locate, hazardous to engage groups are required. Ethnography is difficult, for serious criminals seldom offer themselves for examination unless there is a film deal involved and, once located, it must always be remembered that, by definition, they are hardly professionally obliged to tell the truth. Further, both the routine discreet and subtle abstraction of some forms of serious crime in the 'suites', and the extreme violence that can be all too apparent at the 'street' end of the market, can render ethnographic techniques less likely to be utilized in certain arenas rather than others. Yet some social scientists (not all would describe themselves as criminologists) have been successful in using ethnographic techniques to research serious crime. Such a method is ideal if the aim is an understanding of the detailed cultural mechanisms of a segment or segments of the market. Alternatively, variants on the method can be used to complement any of the above techniques.

To add a personal note to this review, ethnography's limits are reached at the boundaries of specific and discreet social worlds, whether they be boardrooms or bar rooms. Large data sets relating to criminality cannot be derived from

---

[15] A health warning also needs to be posted upon the outpourings of those crime correspondents who derive most of their stories from press handouts provided by the police. This practice is particularly prevalent amongst provincial media personnel who are often used by the police to conduct public relations campaigns.

ethnographic engagement, and the archives and gulags of official knowledge via collaborations with criminal justice agencies soon beckon to even the most partisan adherent of Robert Park's instruction to his students to 'go get the seat of your pants dirty in real research' (Becker, cited in McKinney 1966: 71). Personal experience indicates that working with criminal justice agencies is no less real, but the researcher is more likely to become expert in the culture of the police or prisons than in the methods, maladies, mergers, markets, and murders of contemporary serious crime.

However, this vastly under-researched matrix of legality (Block 1996) constituting both the criminal labour force (Ruggiero 1996), and the mutating processes of enterprise crime (Van Duyne and Levi 1991) will continue to pose challenges to future researchers. The favoured method will inevitably involve compromise, which, given the difficulties inherent in such projects, should be regarded, not as a weakness, but as a feature of researching ground that does not give up its pay load cheaply. Further, the complexity of the ground and its highly contested nature make the discovery of a single definitive theoretical tool suitable for all forms of organized, serious, professional, white collar, and corporate crime little more than a textbook fantasy of armchair ideologues and criminologists and political scientists with aspirations beyond the academy.

The focus of future research must be the various strata of a market place that mirrors official economies in its application of a relentless logic to an unpredictable volatile environment: an environment that is policed by control agencies who deal with both the usual suspects and new arrivals with a sense of 'déjà vu crossed with amnesia' (Thomas 1989).

SUGGESTIONS FOR FURTHER READING

The curse of cynical middle age tempts this researcher to advise prospective students of this disparate field to arm themselves with a degree in accountancy, a Master's degree in computer studies, fluency in at least three languages, the writings of Robert Park, a liver transplant, a Doctorate in International Relations, a private income, and a shotgun licence. However, even armed with such a package the following books will be invaluable.

Sharpe (1999) and Inciardi *et al.* (1977) provide excellent introductions to some of the historical possibilities of historical research. An introduction to Alan Block's historical work across the entire field can be found in Block 1978; 1983; 1994. Hobbs (1995) provides an overview of the research relating to professional crime and Taylor (1999), Ruggiero (1996), and Ruggiero and South (1995) situate professional and organized criminality within the contemporary political economy of crime. Adler (1995) and Bourgois (1995) have written exemplary ethnographies of this somewhat rugged field, and Ned Polsky's (1971) warnings to fledgling researchers will never go out of date. Wright and Decker's (1994; 1997) highly pragmatic studies of working criminals show every sign of evolving into a criminal saga of survival among the most desperate of post-industrial populations, with current work in progress relating to robberies from drug dealers. At the other end of the 'spectrum of enterprise', anything written by Levi will carry with it commercial sensibilities rare outside an open prison (Levi 1998; Levi and Nelken 1997).

REFERENCES

ABADINSKY, H. (1990). *Organized Crime* (3rd edn.). Chicago, Ill.: Nelson Hall.

ADLER, P. (1985 and 2nd edn. 1993) *Wheeling and Dealing: An Ethnography of an Upper Level Drug Dealing and Smuggling Community.* New York: Columbia University Press.

ALBINI, J. (1971). *The American Mafia: Genesis of a Legend.* New York: Appleton-Century-Crofts.

ANDERSON, A. (1979). *The Business of Organized Crime.* Stanford, Cal.: Hoover Institute Press.

ARLACCHI, P. (1986). *Mafia Business: The Mafia Ethic and the Spirit of Capitalism.* London: Verso.

ATKINSON, P. (1990). *The Ethnographic Imagination.* Routledge: London.

AUBERT, V. (1952). 'White Collar Crime and Social Structure'. *American Journal of Sociology* 58, 263–71.

BALL, J., CHESTER, L., and PERROTT, R. (1978). *Cops and Robbers.* London: Andre Deutsch.

BELL, D. (1953). 'Crime as an American Way of Life'. *The Antioch Review* 13: 131–54.

BENNEY, M. (1936). *Low Company.* (Facsimile edn). Caliban Books: Sussex (1981).

BIGGS, R. (1981). *His Own Story.* London: Sphere.

BLOCK, A. (1978). 'History and the Study of Organized Crime'. *Urban Life* 6: 455–74.

—— (1983). *East Side-West Side: Organizing Crime in New York, 1930–1950.* Newark, NJ: Transaction.

—— (1991a). *Masters of Paradise.* New Brunswick, NJ.: Transaction.

—— (1991b). *The Business of Crime.* St. Paul, Colo.: Westview Press.

—— (1994). *Space Time and Organized Crime.* New Brunswick, NJ.: Transaction.

—— (1996). 'Oil, Gas, Diamonds, Gold and Organized Crime'. Paper presented to the ASC Annual Meeting, Chicago, Ill.

—— and CHAMBLISS, W. (1981). *Organizing Crime.* New York: Elsevier.

BLOK, A. (1974). *The Mafia of a Sicilian Village.* New York: Harper.

BOOTH, M. (1991). *The Triads.* London: Grafton.

BOURGOIS, P. (1995). *In Search of Respect.* Cambridge: Cambridge University Press.

—— and DUNLAP, L. (1992). 'Exorcising Sex-for-Crack Prostitution: An Ethnographic Perspective from Harlem' in M. Ratnet (ed.), *Crack Pipe as Pimp: An Eight City*

Ethnographic Study of the Sex for Crack Phenomenon. Lexington, Mass.: Lexington Books.

BRAITHWAITE, J. (1984). *Corporate Crime in the Pharmaceutical Industry*. London: Routledge and Kegan Paul.

BROWN, R. M. (1991). *No Duty to Retreat*. New York: Oxford University Press.

BROWNING, F., and GERASSI, J. (1980). *The American Way of Crime*. New York: G.P. Putnam and Sons.

CALVI, F. (1993). *Het Europa van de Peetvaders. De Mafia Verovert een Continent*. Leuven: Kritak Balans.

CAMPBELL, D. (1991). *That was Business, This is Personal*. London: Mandarin.

CHAMBLISS, W. (1972). *Box Man*. New York: Harper and Row.

—— (1978). *On the Take*. Bloomington, Ind.: Indiana University Press.

CHIN, K. (1990). *Chinese Subculture and Criminality*. Westport, Conn.: Greenwood.

—— (1996). *Chinatown Gangs*. New York: Oxford University Press.

CLARKE, A. (1989). 'Insurance Fraud'. *British Journal of Criminology*. 29: 1–20.

CLINARD, M. (1952). *The Black Market*. New York: Holt, Rinehart and Winston.

COOK, D. (1989). *Rich Law, Poor Law*. Milton Keynes: Open University Press.

COTTRELL, P.L. (1980). *Industrial Finance, 1830–1914*. London: Methuen.

CRESSEY, D. (1953). *Other Peoples Money: A Study of the Social Psychology of Embezzlement*. Glencoe, Ill.: The Free Press.

—— (1967). 'The Functions and Structure of Criminal Syndicates' in *Task Force Report: Organized Crime*. President's Commission on Law Enforcement and the Administration of Justice, Washington, DC: US Government Printing Office.

—— (1969). *Theft of the Nation: The Structure and Operations of Organized Crime in America*. New York: Harper and Row.

CROALL, H. (1992). *White Collar Crime*. Milton Keynes: Open University Press.

CROMWELL, P., OLSON, J., and AVERY. D. (1991). *Breaking and Entering: An Ethnographic Analysis of Burglary*. Newbury Park, Calif.: Sage.

—— —— —— (1993). 'Who Buys Stolen Property: A New Look at Criminal Receiving'. *Journal of Crime and Justice* 56: 75–95.

CUMMINGS, J., and VOLKMAN, E. (1992). *Mobster*. London: Warner.

DAVENPORT-HINES, R.P.T. (ed.) (1986). *Speculators and Patriots*. London: Frank Cass.

DECKER, S., and VAN WINKLE, B. (1996). *Life in the Gang*. Cambridge: Cambridge University Press.

DEFOE, D. (1901). *The King of the Pirates, Including the Life and Actions of Jonathan Wild*. New York: The Jason Society.

DUNLAP, E., JOHNSON, B., and MANWAR, A. (1994). 'A Successful Female Crack Dealer: Case Study of a Deviant Career'. *Deviant Behaviour*, 15: 1–25.

—— —— SANABRIA, H., HOLLIDAY, E., LIPSEY, B., BARNETT, M., HOPKINS, W., SOBEL, I., RANDOLPH, D., CHIN, K. (1990). 'Studying Crack Users and their Criminal Careers'. *Contemporary Drug Problems*, Spring, 121–4.

DUNNIGHAN, C., and HOBBS, D. (1996). *A Report on the NCIS Pilot Organized Crime Notification Survey*. London: Home Office.

EINSTADTER, W. (1969). 'The Social Organisation of Armed Robbery'. *Social Problems*, 17: 64–83.

EMSLEY, C. (1997). 'The History of Crime and Crime Control Institutions' in M. Maguire,

R. Morgan, and R. Reiner (eds.), *The Oxford Handbook of Criminology* (2nd edn.). Oxford: Oxford University Press.

FOREMAN, F. (1996). *Respect*. London: Century.

FOX, S. (1989). *Blood and Power: Organized Crime in 20th Century America*. New York: William Morrow.

FRASER, F. (1994). *Mad Frank*. London: Little, Brown.

GARDINER, J. (1970). *The Politics of Corruption: Organized Crime in an American City*. New York: Russell Sage Foundation.

GEIS, G. (1968). 'The Heavy Electrical Equipment Anti-Trust Cases of 1961' in G. Geis (ed.), *White-Collar Crime*. New York: Atherton Press.

—— (1974). 'Avocational Crime' in D. Glaser (ed.), *Handbook of Criminology*. Chicago, Ill.: Rand McNally.

GIBBS, J., and SHELLEY, P. (1982). 'Life in the Fast Lane: A Retrospective View by Commercial Thieves'. *Journal of Research in Crime and Delinquency*, 19: 299–330.

GODSON, R., and OLSON, W. (1993). *International Organized Crime: Emerging Threat to U.S. Security*. Washington DC.: National Strategy Information Center.

GREEN, G.S. (1990). *Occupational Crime*. Chicago, Ill.: Nelson-Hall.

HAGEDORN, J. (1988). *People and Folks: Gangs, Crime and the Underclass in a Rustbelt City*. Chicago, Ill.: Lake View.

HALLER, M. (1971). 'Organized Crime in Urban Society: Chicago in the Twentieth Century'. *Journal of Social History* 5.

—— (1985). 'Bootleggers as Businessmen: From City Slums to City Builders', in D. Kyvig (ed.), *Law, Alcohol, and Order: Perspectives on National Prohibition*. Westport, Conn.: Greenwood.

HARTUNG, F. (1950). 'White Collar Offences in the Wholesale Meat Industry in Detroit'. *American Journal of Sociology* 56: 25–34.

HAWKINS, G. (1969). 'God and the Mafia'. *The Public Interest* 14: 24–51.

HAWKINS, K. (1984). *Environment and Enforcement: Regulation and the Social Definition of Pollution*. Oxford: Clarendon Press.

HAY, D. (1975). 'Property, Authority and the Criminal Law', in D. Hay *et al.*, *Albions Fatal Tree*. London: Allen Lane.

HESS, H. (1973). *Mafia and Mafiosi: The Structure of Power*. Lexington, Mass.: D.C. Heath.

HEYL, B. S. (1979). *The Madam as Entrepreneur*. New Brunswick, NJ: Transaction.

HILL, B. (1955). *Boss of Britain's Underworld*. London: Naldrett Press.

HOBBS, D. (1988). *Doing the Business: Entrepreneurship, Detectives and the Working Class in the East End of London*. Oxford: Clarendon Press.

—— (1995). *Bad Business*. Oxford: Oxford University Press.

—— (1997*a*). 'Criminal Collaborations' in M. Maguire, R. Morgan, and R. Reiner (eds.), *The Oxford Handbook of Criminology*. (2nd edn.). Oxford: Oxford University Press.

—— (1997*b*). 'Professional Crime: Change Continuity and the Enduring Myth of the Underworld'. *Sociology*, 31: 57–72.

—— (1998). 'The Aliens Are Not Coming: Organized Crime as a Local Problem'. *International Journal of Risk, Security, and Crime Prevention*, 3: 139–46.

—— (2000). 'Deviance' in P. Atkinson and S. Delamont (eds.), *The Sage Handbook of Ethnography*. London: Sage.

—— and DUNNIGHAN, C. (1999), 'Organized Crime and the Organisation of Police

Intelligence' in P. Carlen and R. Morgan (eds.), *Crime Unlimited, Post Modernity and Social Control*. London: Macmillan.

HOBSBAWM, E. (1972). *Bandits*. London: Pelican.

HOGG, A., McDOUGALL, J., and MORGAN, R. (1988). *Bullion Brinks-Mat*. Harmondsworth: Penguin.

HOHIMER, F. (1981). *Violent Streets*. London: Star.

HOLZMAN, H. (1983). 'The Serious Habitual Property Offender as Moonlighter: An Empirical Study of Labour Force Participation Among Robbers and Burglars', *Journal of Criminal Law and Criminology* 73: 1774–92.

HOWSON, G. (1971). *Thief Taker General*. New York: St. Martins Press.

HUTTER, B. (1988). *The Reasonable Arm of the Law?* Oxford: Clarendon Press.

IANNI, F. (1972). *A Family Business: Kinship and Social Control in Organized Crime*. New York: Russell Sage Foundation.

—— (1974). *Black Mafia: Ethnic Succession in Organized Crime*. New York: Simon and Schuster.

INCIARDI, J. (1976). 'The Pickpocket and his Victim'. *Victimology*, 1: 141–9.

—— BLOCK, A., and HALLOWELL, L. (1977). *Historical Approaches to Crime*. Beverly Hills, Cal.: Sage.

JACOBS, B., PANARELLA, C., and WORTHINGTON, J. (1994). *Busting the Mob: United States v. Cosa Nostra*. New York: New York University Press.

JENKINS, P. (1987). 'Into the Upperworld? Law, Crime and Punishment in English Society'. *Social History* 12: 93–102.

JOE, K. (1994). 'The New Criminal Conspiracy? Asian Gangs and Organized Crime in San Francisco'. *Journal of Crime and Delinquency* 31: 390–415.

KELLY, R., CHIN, K., and FAGEN, J. (1993). 'The Dragon Breathes Fire: Chinese Organized Crime in New York City'. *Crime Law and Social Change* 19: 245–69.

KENNEDY, W.P. (1987). *Industrial Structures, Capital Markets and the Origins of British Economic Decline*. Cambridge: Cambridge University Press.

KLOCKARS, C. (1974). *The Professional Fence*. London: Tavistock.

KOBLER, J. (1971). *Capone: The Life and World of Al Capone*. Greenwich, Conn.: Fawcett.

KRAY, R. (1991). *Born Fighter*. London: Arrow.

—— and KRAY, R. (1989). *Our Story*. London: Pan.

KYVIG, D. (1979). *Repealing National Prohibition*. Chicago, Ill.: University of Chicago Press.

LABROUSSE, A., and WALLON, A. (eds.) (1993). *La Planete des Drogues*. Paris: Seuil.

LACEY, R. (1991). *Little Man*. New York: Little, Brown.

LANDESCO, J. (1968). *Organized Crime in Chicago* (2nd edn.). Chicago, Ill.: University of Chicago Press.

LANGER, J. (1977). 'Drug Entrepreneurs and Dealing Culture'. *Social Problems* 24: 377–86.

LEMERT, E. (1958). 'The Behaviour of the Systematic Check Forger'. *Social Problems*, 6: 141–9.

LETKEMANN, P. (1973). *Crime as Work*. Englewood Cliffs, NJ: Prentice Hall.

LEVI, K. (1981). 'Becoming a Hit Man: Neutralization in a Very Deviant Career'. *Urban Life*, 10: 47–63.

LEVI, M. (1981). *The Phantom Capitalists*. London: Gower.

—— (1987). *Regulating Fraud*. London: Tavistock.

—— (1989). 'Suite Justice: Sentencing for Fraud'. *Criminal Law Review* 420–34.

—— (1998). 'Perspectives on Organized Crime: An Overview'. *The Howard Journal of Criminal Justice*. 37: 335–45.

—— and NELKEN, D. (1997). *The Corruption of Politics and the Politics of Corruption*. Oxford: Blackwells.

—— and PITHOUSE, A. (forthcoming). *Victims of White Collar Crime*. Oxford: Oxford University Press.

LLOYD BAKER, T.B. (1889). *War With Crime*. London: Longman.

LLOYD, H. (1963). *Wealth Against Commonwealth*, ed. by T. Cochran. Englewood Cliffs, NJ: Prentice-Hall.

LOTH, D. (1938). *Public Plunder: A History of Graft in America*. New York: Carrick and Evans.

—— (1982). *Thieves Kitchen: The Regency Underworld*. London: Dent.

LUCKENBILL, D. (1981). 'Generating Compliance: The Case of Robbery'. *Urban Life*, 10: 25–46.

LUPSHA, P. (1981). 'Individual Choice, Material Culture, and Organized Crime'. *Criminology* 19: 3–24.

—— (1983). 'Networks Versus Networking: Analysis of an Organized Crime Group', in G. Waldo (ed.), *Career Criminals*. Beverly Hills, Cal.: Sage.

MAAS, P. (1968). *The Valachi Papers*. New York: Putnam's.

MACK, J. (1964). 'Full-time Miscreants, Delinquent Neighbourhoods and Criminal Networks'. *British Journal of Sociology*, 15: 38–53.

McKINNEY, J. (1966). *Constructive Typology and Social Theory*. New York: Appleton-Century-Crofts.

McMULLAN, J. (1984). *The Canting Crew*. Rutgers, NJ: Rutgers University Press.

McVICAR, J. (1979). *McVicar By Himself*. London: Arrow.

MESSICK, H. (1973). *Lansky*. New York: Berkeley Publishing Company.

MIECZKOWSKI, T. (1990). 'Crack Distribution in Detroit'. *Contemporary Drug Problems* 17: 19–30.

MOORE, J. (1978). *Homeboys: Gangs, Drugs, and Prison in the Barrios of Los Angeles*. Philadelphia Penn.: Temple University Press.

MOORE, W. (1974). *Kefauver and the Politics of Crime*. Columbus, Ohio: University of Missouri Press.

MORRIS, N., and HAWKINS, G. (1970). *The Honest Politician's Guide to Crime Control*. Chicago, Ill.: University of Chicago Press.

MORTON, J. (1993). *Gangland: London's Underworld*. London: Warner Books.

MUNSCHE, P. (1981). *Gentlemen and Poachers*. Cambridge: Cambridge University Press.

MYERS, G. (1936). *History of Great American Fortunes*. New York: Modern Library.

NATIONAL CRIMINAL INTELLIGENCE SERVICE (1993). *An Outline Assessment of the Threat and Impact by Organized/Enterprise Crime Upon United Kingdom Interests*. London: NCIS.

—— (1993). *Organized Crime Conference: A Threat Assessment*. London: NCIS.

NAYLOR, R. (1995). 'From Cold War to Crime War'. *Transnational Organized Crime*, 1(4): 37–56.

NELKEN, D. (1983). *The Limits of the Legal Process: A Study of Landlords, Law and Crime*. London: Academic Press.

—— (1994). 'White Collar Crime', in M. Maguire, R. Morgan, and R. Reiner (eds.), *The Oxford Handbook of Criminology*. Oxford: Oxford University Press.

NORRIS, C., MORAN, J., and ARMSTRONG, G. (1998). 'Algorithmic Surveillance: The Future of Automated Visual Surveillance' in C. Norris, J. Moran and G. Armstrong (eds.), *CCTV, Surveillance and Social Control*. Aldershot: Ashgate.

O'BRIEN, J., and KURINS, A. (1991). *Boss of Bosses*. New York: Simon and Schuster.

PADILLA, F. (1992). *The Gang as an American Enterprise.* New Brunswick, NJ: Rutgers University Press.

PARKER, H. (1974). *View from the Boys, A Sociology of Down Town Adolescents.* Newton Abbott: David and Charles.

PASSAS, N. (1994). 'I Cheat, Therefore I Exist? The BCCI Scandal in Context' in W. M. Hoffman *et al.* (eds.), *Emerging Global Business Ethics.* Westport, Conn.: Quorum Books.

PEARCE, F. (1976). *Crimes of the Powerful.* London: Pluto.

—— and TOMBS, S. (1993). 'Ideology Hegemony and Empiricism: Compliance Theories and Regulation'. *British Journal of Criminology* 30: 423–43.

PEARSON, J. (1973). *The Profession of Violence.* London: Granada.

PERKIN, H. (1969). *Origins of Modern English Society 1780–1880.* London: Routledge and Kegan Paul.

PETERSON, V. (1983). *The Mob: 200 Years of Organized Crime in New York.* Ottawa, Ill.: Green Hill.

PILEGGI, N. (1987). *Wise Guy.* London: Corgi.

—— (1995). *Casino.* New York: Simon and Schuster.

POLSKY, N (1971). *Hustlers, Beats and Others.* Harmondsworth: Pelican Books.

POTTER, G. (1994). *Criminal Organizations.* Prospect Heights, Ill.: Waveland Press.

PRESIDENT'S COMMISSION ON LAW ENFORCEMENT AND ADMINISTRATION OF JUSTICE (1967). *Task Force Report*, Chapter 7, 'Professional Crime', Washington, DC: US Government Printing Office.

PRESIDENTS COMMISSION ON ORGANIZED CRIME (1987). *The Impact: Organized Crime Today.* Washington DC: US Government Printing Office.

PRYCE, K. (1979). *Endless Pressure: A Study of West Indian Lifestyles in Britain.* Harmondsworth: Penguin.

PUNCH, M. (1996). *Dirty Business.* London: Sage.

QUINNEY, R (1963). 'Occupational Structure and Criminal Behaviour: Prescription Violation by Retail Pharmacists'. *Social Problems* 11: 179–85.

RADZINOWICZ, SIR L. AND HOOD, R. (1986). *A History of English Criminal Law*, Vol. 5, *The Emergence of Penal Policy.* London: Stevens.

RANKIN, H. (1969). *The Golden Age of Piracy.* New York: Holt, Rinehart and Winston.

RAWLINGS, P. (1992). *Drunks, Whores and Idle Apprentices: Criminal Biographies of the Eighteenth Century.* London: Routledge.

RAWLINSON, P. (1996). 'Russian Organized Crime: A Brief History'. *Transnational Organized Crime*, 2: 28–52.

READ, P.P. (1979). *The Train Robbers.* London: Coronet.

REUTER, P. (1984). *Disorganized Crime.* Cambridge Mass.: MIT Press.

—— (1986). 'Methodological and Institutional Problems in Organized Crime Research'. Paper prepared for the conference on Critical Issues in Organized Crime Control. Washington, DC: The Rand Corporation.

—— and RUBINSTEIN, J. (1978). 'Fact, Fancy, and Organized Crime'. *The Public Interest*, 53: 45–68.

ROBB, G (1992). *White Collar Crime in Modern England.* Cambridge: Cambridge University Press.

ROEBUCK, J., and JOHNSON, R. (1962). 'The Jack of All Trades Offender'. *Crime and Delinquency* 8: 172–81.

RUGGIERO, V. (1995). 'Drug Economics: A Fordist Model of Criminal Capital'. *Capital and Class*, 55: 131–50.

—— (1996). *Organized and Corporate Crime in Europe*, Aldershot: Dartmouth.

—— and SOUTH, N. (1995). *Eurodrugs*. London: UCL Press.

SALERNO, R., and TOMPKINS, J. (1969). *The Crime Confederation*. Garden City, NY: Doubleday.

SALGADO, G. (1977). *The Elizabethan Underworld*. London: Dent.

SANCHEZ-JANKOWSKI, M. (1991). *Islands in the Street: Gangs in American Urban Society*. Berkeley, Cal.: University of California Press.

SHAPIRO, S. (1984). *Wayward Capitalists*. New Haven, CT: Yale University Press.

SHARPE, J. (1999). *Crime in Early Modern England 1550–1750*. London: Longman.

SHERRY, F. (1986). *Raiders and Rebels*. New York: Hearst Marine Books.

SHOVER, N. (1973). 'The Social Organization of Burglary'. *Social Problems*, 20: 499–514.

—— (1996). *Great Pretenders*. Boulder, Colo.: Westview Press.

—— and HONAKER, D. (1992). 'The Socially Bounded Decision Making of Persistent Property Offenders'. *The Howard Journal*, 31: 276–93.

SINCLAIR, A. (1962). *The Era of Excess: A Social History of Prohibition Movement*. Boston, Mass.: Little, Brown.

SINDALL, R. (1983). 'Middle-Class Crime in Nineteenth-Century England'. *Criminal Justice History* 23–40.

—— (1990). *Street Violence in the Nineteenth Century*. Leicester: Leicester University Press.

SLAPPER, G., and TOMBS S. (1999). *Corporate Crime*. London: Longman.

SMITH, D. JR. (1975). *The Mafia Mystique*. New York: Basic Books.

—— (1980). 'Paragons, Pariahs, and Pirates: A Spectrum-Based Theory of Enterprise'. *Crime and Delinquency*, 26: 358–86.

STEDMAN-JONES, G. (1971). *Outcast London*. Oxford: Oxford University Press.

STERLING, C. (1994). *Crime Without Frontiers*. London: Little Brown.

STYLES, J. (1980). 'Our Traitorous Moneymakers' in J. Brewer and J. Styles (eds.), *An Ungovernable People*. London: Hutchinson.

SULLIVAN, M. (1989). *Getting Paid*. Ithaca, NY: Cornell University Press.

SUTHERLAND, E. (1937). *The Professional Thief*. Chicago, Ill.: University of Chicago Press.

—— (1949). *White Collar Crime*. New York: Holt, Rinehart and Winston.

—— and CRESSEY, D. (1970). *The Principles of Criminology* (8th edn.). Philadelphia, Penn.: Lippincott.

TAYLOR, C. (1990). *Dangerous Society*. East Lansing, Mich.: Michigan State University Press.

TAYLOR, I. (1999). *Crime in Context*. London: Polity.

THOMAS, J (1989). 'Computer Hackers'. Paper given at the Annual meeting of the American Society of Criminology, Reno, Nevada.

THRASHER, F. (1927). *The Gang*. Chicago, Ill.: University of Chicago Press.

TOBIAS, J.J. (1974). *Prince of Fences: The Life and Crimes of Ikey Solomons*. London: Valentine Mitchell.

TURKUS, B., and FEDER, S. (1951). *Murder, Inc.: The Story of the Syndicate*. New York: Farrar, Straus and Young.

UNITED STATES SENATE (1951). *Special Committee to Investigate Organized Crime in Interstate Commerce*. New York: Didier.

VAN DUYNE, P., and LEVI, M. (1991). 'Enterprise Crime in the Netherlands and the UK'. Paper presented at the British Criminology Conference, York.

VAUGHAN, D (1983). *Controlling Unlawful Organizational Behaviour*. Chicago, Ill.:
    University of Chicago Press.
—— (1992). 'The Micro Macro Connection' in K. Schegal and D. Weisbund (eds.), *White
    Collar Crime Reconsidered*. Boston, Mass.: North Eastern University Press.
VIGIL, J. (1988). *Barrio Gangs: Street Life and Identity in Southern California*. Austin Tex.:
    University of Texas Press.
WIDEMAN, J. (1985). *Brothers and Keepers*. New York: Penguin.
WILLIAMS, P. (1993). 'Transnational Criminal Organizations and National Security'.
    Survival, 36: 96–113.
—— and SAVONA, E. (eds.) (1995). 'The United Nations and Transnational Organized
    Crime'. *Transnational Organized Crime*, 1 (3).
WILLIAMS, T. (1992). *Crack House*. Reading, Mass.: Addison-Wesley.
—— (1989). *The Cocaine Kids*. Reading, Mass.: Addison-Wesley.
WINSLOW, C (1975). 'Sussex Smugglers' in O. Hay *et al.* (eds.), *Albions Fatal Tree*. London: Allen
    Lane.
WOLF, D. (1991). *The Rebels: A Brotherhood of Outlaw Bikers*. Toronto: University of Toronto
    Press.
WOODIWISS, M. (1993). 'Crime's Global Reach', in F. Pearce and M. Woodiwiss (eds.) *Global
    Crime Connections*. London: Macmillan.
WRIGHT, R., and DECKER, S. (1994). *Burglars on the Job*. Boston, Mass.: North Eastern
    University Press.
—— (1997). *Armed Robbers in Action: Stick-Ups and Street Culture*. Boston, Mass.: North
    Eastern University Press.
—— REDFERN, A., and SMITH, S. (1992). 'A Snowball's Chance in Hell: Doing Fieldwork with
    Active Residential Burglars'. *Journal of Research in Crime and Delinquency* 29: 148–61.

6

RESEARCHING VICTIMS

Sandra Walklate

INTRODUCTION

My first foray into conducting research into victims of crime was as a part of a team which failed to win the contract to conduct the Merseyside Crime Survey. As a part of that process it became known, locally, that someone 'at the poly' was interested in engaging in such research and I was contacted by a then Senior Probation Officer, George Murphy, who was involved in a Liverpool Victim Support Scheme. He wanted someone to get a feel for how the scheme was working and what victims thought of what they were trying to do. All of that was during 1982–4. It was a salutary experience moving from bidding for over £100,000 for a research contract to conducting a piece of work in one's spare time, but it was also a highly rewarding one. That move was certainly a turning point for me both academically and personally. Over the next ten years I forged strong links with Victim Support on Merseyside, ultimately becoming the deputy chairperson of the Liverpool Crown Court Witness Support Scheme. During that time my views about victims, victimization, and the criminal justice response to such experiences changed considerably.

At the beginning of the 1980s academic and political interest in the victim of crime was in its early stages and was fuelled by a view that the impact of crime, though varied, was not to be taken lightly. My own experience of interviewing victims in Liverpool within three weeks of their victimization confirmed that view and added weight to the minimalist argument to take the needs of victims into account and the maximalist argument for victims' rights. Arguably both positions conferred a special status on victims of crime. However, as the decade progressed, culminating in the first Victims' Charter in 1990, I became less convinced that this 'special status' could usefully inform either policy or research. As a consequence, when I was asked to write this chapter on researching victims I was presented with a real dilemma; why accord researching victims of crime such a status from a research point of view or any other? Surely the issues facing researchers of crime victims were the same issues facing anyone attempting to research any substantive criminal justice issue? On reflection, of course, such a view is not entirely an accurate one. For example, the emotional impact of victimization for some victims may present itself as part of what it is necessary to handle in an interview situation with a researcher. Moreover, in some circumstances the researcher may become an important source of information and/or support for the victim (see, for example, comments of this kind made by Shapland, Wilmore and Duff 1985). However the impact of factors such as these varies markedly from individual to individual, making it difficult either to generalize or predict when it might be necessary to take such issues into account. This raises some questions not only about the policy possibilities, which may or may not be derivable from victim-centred research, but also the extent to which such issues are the same as or different from research centred in different ways. I have, of course, reached this position over a long period of time. I hope this chapter will provide some clues as to how and why I would now challenge the presumption that victims *per se* occupy a special status within criminal justice research.

The aims of this chapter are threefold: first, to explore what methodological questions are raised by engaging in research on victims of crime; secondly, to relate such questions to the broader conceptual problems embedded within the (sub)discipline of victimology; and thirdly, to situate the research, and the research findings on criminal victimization, within a broader political context. In addressing these aims, one of the central concerns of this chapter will be to raise the question whether or not there is anything particular about the experience of criminal victimization which renders researching victims of crime distinctive in any way from other substantive areas of research. This will be approached through a critical reflection on and examination of a two-and-a-half-year research project on the 'fear of crime' completed in August 1996. But first it will be useful to offer a brief overview of the different theoretical perspectives available to researchers concerned with victims of crime and the connections between those theoretical perspectives and different styles of research.

THEORY AND PRACTICE IN VICTIMOLOGY

In many ways the emergence and development of the (sub)discipline of victimology parallels that of criminology. Early victimological work was concerned to identify different types of victims much in the same way that early criminological work endeavoured to identify different types of criminals. Original concerns such as these reflect the extent to which victimology was as embedded in the processes of differentiation, determinism, and pathology as

was criminology (Roshier 1989). These concerns, and their subsequent development, have led commentators to identify different theoretical strands of
criminological thought broadly categorized as positivist, radical, and critical
victimology by Mawby and Walklate (1994). It will be of value to say a little
about each of these, as well as feminism and victimology, since each leads the
research agenda in different directions.

POSITIVISM AND VICTIMOLOGY

The label 'positivist' victimology was initially assigned to a range of victimological work by Miers (1989). He identified the key characteristics of this kind of
work in the following way: '[t]he identification of factors which contribute to a
non-random pattern of victimisation, a focus on interpersonal crimes of violence, and a concern to identify victims who may have contributed to their own
victimisation' (Miers 1989: 3). In other words this version of victimology is
centrally concerned to identify patterns of victimization, the regularities and
precipitative characteristics of victimizing events, and thereby to produce victim typologies. It is a view of the data-gathering process which privileges traditional conceptions of science and scientific objectivity and, as a consequence,
has been very influential in setting the victimological research agenda along a
particular path. That path has, for the most part, been characterized (though
not exclusively) by the use and development of the criminal victimization
survey.

Since a more detailed discussion of criminal victimization survey methods
and findings is given by Mayhew in this volume, it is sufficient to say here that
this kind of victimological work has made an important contribution in identifying and understanding the nature and extent of most conventional forms of
criminal victimization; that is, its patterning and regularity. Much of that survey work has been informed by the lifestyle conceptual framework as developed
by Hindelang, Gottfredson and Garofalo (1978) which has also facilitated the
analysis of such survey data to explore both the risk from and the impact of
crime. The findings that such analyses reveal have been summarized by Mawby
and Walklate (1994: 55) in the following way:

Quantitative findings such as these, then, are not without their uses. They can,
and do, inform policy and have arguably made their own unique contribution
to the movement from crime prevention to victimization prevention (Karmen
1990).

Although there are beneficial qualities which can be identified in positivist
victimology, such work reflects a research agenda which is nevertheless conceptually and empirically impoverished. Such limitations shape the focus and
understanding of the 'victim' in very particular ways. This statement requires
fuller exploration. Positivist victimology is concerned to identify regularities

Table 6.1: Risk and Impact of Criminal Victimization

	High Risk	High Impact
class/status	poor, living in privately rented housing	
gender	males	females
age	young	elderly/not young
marital/family status	divorced; those living in households with no other adults	

(Keat and Urry 1975). It reflects a traditional view of science and the scientific knowledge-gathering process which is concerned to separate that which is knowable—the observable, the measurable, and the objective—from that which is not knowable—belief. Hence the methodological focus on the construction of victim typologies and the search for patterns of victimization through the use of the criminal victimization survey. This process, positivist victimology presumes, equips us with objective, measurable information. This does not mean that such information is without its applied uses, in the spheres of either politics or policy. The development of the criminal victimization survey was clearly influential in placing the question of criminal victimization on the political and policy agendas. Moreover, the use to which such information has been put has, on occasions, been quite clear: in one context to downplay the risk of crime (Hough and Mayhew 1983) and in another to emphasize the risk of crime (see, e.g., the President's Task Force on Victims of Crime 1982).

Despite the value to be attached to the empirical findings which positivist victimology has generated, there are important limitations. Such work is limited because, for the most part, it focuses our attention primarily on what has been called 'conventional crime' (Walklate 1989), as illustrated in the definition of positivist victimology offered by Miers (1989). This work also often takes the meaning of the term 'victim' itself to be self-evident, either as a consequence of the identification of individual suffering or as defined by the legal framework. One gets little sense from within this strand of victimological work of how the state (including the law) actively contributes to the victims we see or do not see, or of the ways in which individuals may actively resist, campaign against, or survive the label 'victim'. This is a direct consequence of the methodological restrictions which derive from positivism and it results in research which focuses on incidents rather than processes, and on measuring the surface manifestation of regular patterns of behaviour as opposed to their underlying causes. Some would argue that the research agenda emanating from radical victimology addresses some, if not all of these issues.

RADICALISM AND VICTIMOLOGY

Whilst the presence of a radical victimology can be traced back to the discipline's early days this radical strand takes on its most substantial form in the 1960s. Essentially a radical victimology, somewhat paralleling (again) a radical criminology, concerns itself with 'victims of police force, the victims of war, the victims of the correctional system, the victims of state violence, the victims of oppression of any sort' (Quinney 1972: 315). In other words, for Quinney all of these victims could be rendered visible by calling into question the role of the capitalist state in defining the social construction of both the offender and the victim. This broader definition of victimology has been associated by Elias (1986) with the whole question of human rights. Indeed, Elias goes so far as to argue that the standards of human rights can provide victimology not only with its definitional framework but also with 'more objective measures of victimization' (Elias 1985: 17). With the possible exception of the work of Reiman (1979) and Box (1983), this rhetorical brand of victimology has done little to establish an empirical body of knowledge. There has, however, been another version of a radical victimology, the impact of which has been somewhat more substantial.

The emergence of radical left realism within criminology and victimology during the 1980s had an impact in the United Kingdom and elsewhere in its determination to take the victim of crime seriously. Young (1986: 23–4) calls for an 'accurate victimology' which starts with the 'problems as people experience them' and embraces an understanding of the geographically and socially focused distribution of criminal victimization. This position has argued that it has embraced the concerns of feminism (Young 1988); an issue to which we shall return. The research findings emanating from this work, and their policy implications, need to be put into the broader political context in which the Labour Party sought to recapture the high ground in the law and order debate from the Conservative Party. So what kind of research has emanated from this version of radicalism that is relevant to researching victims of crime?

Radical left realism uses the same research tool as positivism: the criminal victimization survey. The use of that tool, however, is informed by different theoretical concerns. Radical left realism is committed to geographically and socially focused surveys. In other words its research agenda endeavours to incorporate that which is already known about the patterning of victimization according to age, sex, class, and race. As a consequence it has been very successful at offering a much more detailed picture and analysis of who are the victims of crime (being particularly more successful, for example, at uncovering incidents of racial and sexual harassment than national victimization surveys). It has also included some efforts to explore an understanding of disproportionate victimization in the area of 'commercial crime' (Pearce 1990). However, the use of the same research instrument as positivist researchers highlights an important tension in radical left realism. That tension emanates from this version of victimology's use of the term 'realism'. What is to be understood by the term realism is an issue to which we shall return; suffice it to say at this juncture that radical left realism's understanding and application of this concept are partial and have the cumulative effect, according to Smart (1990), of a latent slippage into positivism.

In general terms, radicalism within victimology endeavours to shift the conceptual framework of the discipline from one which is primarily concerned with victims of crime as defined by the law to one in which the law, the application of the law, and the state are all considered to be problematic. For the most part this has resulted in a rather simplistic reading of the relationship between the law and social class on the one hand and the role of the state on the other (Sumner 1990). Perhaps as a result, radical victimology has failed to develop a coherent research agenda which can usefully explore these issues. In many ways, from the concerns of Elias (1985) with human rights as a universal standard of objective measurement through to the tensions emanating from the radical left realist use of the criminal victimization survey, the agenda which has been set under the radical umbrella has failed to break away from the hold of positivism. A resolution to some of these tensions has been suggested by the emergence of what has been called critical victimology. However, before considering the relevance of that framework to researching victims of crime it is important to say something about the role of feminism in these debates.

FEMINISM AND VICTIMOLOGY

The marginalization of feminism by victimology has been commented on by several writers. Rock (1986), for example, implies that this has occurred to a certain extent in the choices made by feminists themselves who have regarded the concept of 'victim precipitation', so central to much conventional victimological work, as 'victim blaming' not only in its everyday usage but in the way it has been translated in the courts as 'contributory negligence' (Jeffries and Radford 1984). Some aspects of this uneasy relationship between victimologists and feminists are epitomized in their respective use of the terms 'victim' and 'survivor'. The genealogy of the term 'victim' itself connotes the sacrificiant who was frequently, female and the word itself, when gendered as in French, is denoted as female. Feminists, recognizing the power of such a linguistic heritage, regard the term as emphasizing passivity and powerlessness in contrast to what they argue is the active resistance to oppression that most women display in their everyday life in order to survive. Hence the feminist preference for the term 'survivor'. But of course, whilst these terms are often presented as oppositional, experientially speaking they frequently are not. It is as possible to think in terms of an active or passive victim as it is to identify an active or passive survivor. Indeed, an argument can be mounted which presents these concepts as capturing different elements of the same process (Walklate 1993) and moreover are embedded in women's own experiences of their day-to-day lives (Kirkwood 1993). However, the challenge posed by feminism to victimology runs much deeper than this conceptual debate.

In some respects, feminism challenges the very heart of the conventional victimological agenda. That challenge comprises a different understanding of the relationship between what it is to be researched and how that research process might be put into place. Such work challenges the implicit acceptance by the social sciences in general, and victimology in particular, that it is possible to engage in objective value-free research and consequently raises the major fundamental question of what counts as knowledge. The details of this debate need not concern us here, but suffice it to say that what has been considered rational and a rational knowledge production process has from the feminist viewpoint all too often reflected a white, male, middle class, heterosexual view of what counts as legitimate (Harding 1991). Hence the feminist commitment to empirical work conducted 'by women, with women, for women'. In relation to the substantive area of victimology a commitment to a stance of this kind has real consequences indeed.

As the preceding discussion makes clear feminist work is not in and of itself centrally concerned with criminal victimization, yet many of the areas and issues with which feminists have concerned themselves, and campaigned against, are very much about criminal victimization. Rape, domestic violence, child abuse, are all areas in which feminist informed work has achieved much in documenting both the extent and the impact of such events on women's lives. Much, though by no means all, of the empirical work which has documented these events has been qualitative rather than quantitative, although Russell's (1990) seminal work on rape in marriage is a highly notable exception. The findings associated with this work differ from those of more conventional victimological work in two ways. First, they present the safe haven of the home as a significant arena in which to understand criminal victimization, and secondly they postulate an underlying mechanism which produces the surface manifestation of this kind of patterning of criminal victimization, namely patriarchy. Although there is a danger inherent in feminist work which can leave the impression that women are 'victims' and men are not (Walklate 1995, ch. 2), this consideration of feminism returns us to the question of what alternative conception of the knowledge-gathering process might set a different kind of agenda for research on victims of crime. In this context it returns us to the question of what can meaningfully be understood by the term realism.

CRITICAL VICTIMOLOGY

Efforts have been made to construct an alternative agenda for victimology incorporating an understanding of both feminism and realism by Mawby and Walklate (1994) through the proposal of a critical victimology. The term critical has been used in a number of different ways to articulate an agenda for victimology (see, e.g., Miers 1990; Fattah 1991). However, the version of critical victimology proposed by Mawby and Walklate (1994) endeavours to address the problematic aspects of both positivist and radical victimology in three ways; by building on the achievements of radical left realism, through an understanding of scientific realism, and in adopting Giddens' (1984) theory of structuration. This view of victimology demands that we move beyond the mere appearance of things towards understanding what generates that appearance and to ask the question: what constitutes the real?

In order to understand the nature and impact of social reality it is necessary to search underneath the 'mere appearances' associated with positivism and to posit mechanisms by which those appearances are produced. Leaning on Giddens' theory of structuration, endeavours to research the 'real' need to take account of a number of different processes which contribute to the construction of everyday reality: people's conscious activity, their 'unconscious' activity, the unobserved and unobservable mechanisms which underpin daily life, and the intended and unintended consequences of people's action. In other words this kind of theoretical starting point privileges process over incidence and argues for duality rather than dualism. As such it is reminiscent of some feminist concerns (Harding 1991) and provides one way of beginning to understand the dynamism between the structural location of women (victimization) and women's negotiation of that structural location (survival). So structuration theory, and the desire to understand the complexity of human interaction through time and space, demands a research agenda which is both longitudinal and comparative, and which breaks down the barriers between quantitative and qualitative techniques (Pawson 1989). In the context of victimology this kind of starting point postulates the importance of understanding the processes which go on behind our backs, which contribute to the victims (and the crimes) which we 'see' as well as those we do not 'see', in order fully to understand the 'lived realities' (Genn 1988) of criminal victimization. Clues to a research agenda informed in this way are offered in Mawby and Walklate (1994). This form of victimology makes no special claims to privilege one form of knowledge over another. Indeed, its only special claim would lie in the requirement to recognize the political nature of the knowledge production process. It is this view of the knowledge production process which underpins the discussion of the research project which is the focus of concern in the next section.

To summarize: these different versions of victimology set the question of researching victims of crime in quite different ways. Positivist approaches focus on criminal victimization as it is conventionally understood and are concerned to map the patterning of such experiences. Much has been learned about the nature and impact of crime generated by this kind of work albeit from within a limited frame of reference. The impact of radical victimology is a little more difficult to assess. Some versions of this kind of work have been impactive in a more polemical than empirical fashion, though the work of the radical left realists has certainly played its part in widening the debate and consideration of who are the victims of crime. Feminist work, though marginalized by victimology, has also played its part in encouraging a much wider understanding of the nature and impact of crime even though criminal victimization was not its main focus of concern. It is clear that without this feminist input understanding the nature and impact of particular crimes, especially violent crimes, would be significantly impoverished. Each of these approaches has also been differently utilized in the political domain to downplay or highlight the plight of the crime victim at different historical moments. What is now without question, however, is that no political voice is likely to talk about the problem of crime without addressing the concerns of the victim. Victimology in all its various guises has played a significant part in that process of recognition.

However, taking these approaches together it is easy to see that the methodological questions associated with researching victims of crime are very similar to those raised by any social scientific research. These are: how to address the all-pervading influence of positivism in the social sciences, how to resolve the resultant perceived tensions between qualitative and quantitative research, and how to come to terms with the interconnections between research and politics. There are ways of resolving some of these tensions and such a resolution is implied in the discussion which follows.

THEORY INTO PRACTICE

COMMUNITY SAFETY, PERSONAL SAFETY, AND THE FEAR OF CRIME

In this section I shall consider the extent to which the ideas implicit in a critical victimology outlined above can be translated into a meaningful research agenda and how that agenda might be realized. The project under discussion was funded under the ESRC's Crime and Social Order Initiative from February 1994 to August 1996. It must be said that this was not a project necessarily envisaged as being informed by victimology *per se* though it was situated in two high crime areas, which we came to call Oldtown and Bankhill, and was concerned to address the fear of crime in those areas. However, it has also to be said that the methodological ideas of a critical victimology were implicit, if not explicit, throughout the proposed work. What follows is a resumé of, and commentary on, that work.

When this project was conceived its concerns were centrally located within the 'fear of crime' debate. That debate has moved through a number of phases over the last twenty-five years; from the fears constructed in relation to the perceived rising phenomenon of 'black crime' in the 1970s, through the questioned rationality and/or irrationality of people's fears characteristic of the debate during the 1980s (a debate in which the criminal victimization survey played a central part), to the more focused attention on community safety in the 1990s. In the context of that changing debate this project sought to situate an understanding of the 'risk from' and 'fear of' crime in a comparative local urban context. We wanted to understand how people who lived, worked, and went to school in these localities constructed their own responses to such 'risks' and 'fears'. There were two key concepts which underpinned this concern; the notion of 'ontological security' and that of 'community'.

Giddens (1991: 44) suggests that:'[a]ll individuals develop a framework of ontological security of some sort based on routines of various forms. People handle dangers and the fear associated with them in terms of emotional and behavioural formulae which have come to be part of their everyday behaviour and thought'. For Giddens, managing our 'ontological security' is a central problem of late modern society. In part, he argues, this is a consequence of the extent to which 'the risk climate of modernity is [thus] unsettling for everyone: no-one escapes' so that as individuals we 'colonise the future' (Giddens 1991: 124–5) in order to manage (though not necessarily reduce) our anxieties. In the particular context of managing crime and its associated fears and anxieties some of those management processes may be articulated in our understandings of how, when, and where we feel safe. This research project was interested in exploring those processes.

This study also centred on the role of the community, and people's relationship to their community, as a mediating factor in the management of their ontological security. Given that these communities under investigation were also high crime areas, this presumption reflects the historical, sociological, and criminological focus on the inner city (the zone of transition) and its assumed socially disorganized and dangerous nature of that part of the city (Shaw and McKay 1942). Moreover, the communities under investigation appeared, on the basis of local knowledge, to be responding differently to their socio-economic circumstances. This was, therefore, also a comparative study of the validity of the notions of disorganization and dangerousness in these particular settings.

Against this general theoretical framework, the research had five main objectives with regard to these two communities:

i. to document and analyse lay perceptions of 'risk' and 'safety' in a variety of social contexts: on the street, in the workplace, at school, at home.
ii. to document and analyse professional perceptions of 'risk' and 'safety'.
iii. to document and evaluate the nature of formal policy interventions.
iv. to document and evaluate the informal policy processes.
v. to assess the future trajectory of policy processes.

The research used a variety of different research techniques to meet these varied objectives. As we were concerned to explore the 'lived realities' (Genn 1988) of the people in these two locations the research process endeavoured to obtain a feel for and remain sensitive to local issues as local people experienced them. To this end the research, informed by the ideas of methodological pluralism, reflected an empirical strategy which deployed both qualitative and quantitative techniques.

Methodological pluralism, sometimes referred to in the North American literature as triangulation, reflects a view of the research process which privileges neither quantitative nor qualitative research techniques. It is a position which recognizes that different research techniques can uncover different layers of social reality and that the role of the researcher is to look for confirmations and contradictions between those different layers of information. So, for example, for the first stage of our data-gathering process we walked our two research areas with police officers, we frequented the public houses, and we engaged in in-depth interviews with a variety of people working in the localities. Then, on the basis of this information, we produced a criminal victimization survey instrument and conducted a survey in each area, and on the basis of this experience moved into focus group discussions with survey participants. So, as a research process, we were always moving between quantitative and qualitative data looking for ways of making sense of the different layers of social reality in these two areas which were being revealed to us.

It is also important to note at this juncture, that all the members of the research team were female, which, for this kind of work and for the projects funded under this ESRC initiative, was unusual. However, given the nature of some of the issues which came to light during the course of this project, especially the importance attached to the presence of the criminal gang in one of the areas, the fact that we had an all-female research team may arguably have been advantageous. The strong working-class chauvinism of localities like these meant that both men and women talked to us, including those active in criminal activity, perhaps feeling that we posed no threat to them. Moreover, all the members of the research team had pre-existing connections with the locations under investigation; one of us had lived in one of the research areas for three years, another was engaged in voluntary work in one of the locations, and the third had formal links with those charged with the responsibility for implementing community safety strategies in these areas. These links equipped the team with different levels of prior knowledge about the locations under study, some of which certainly facilitated access.

The first six months of the project were spent gaining an in-depth knowledge of the areas by interviewing professional and semi-professional workers in both locations, through ethnographic work (walking around the areas, going to the pubs, going to local meetings), and regular analysis of the local newspapers. Twenty-six interviews were completed with professional and semi-professional workers in each of the areas (fifty-two interviews in total). From this knowledge we were able to build a detailed picture of each of the locations; a knowledge which formed the backcloth against which we conducted our house to house survey of residents. The conduct of that survey built on this knowledge in several ways.

The criminal victimization survey which we conducted comprised tried and tested questions taken from pre-existing criminal victimization surveys amended to take account of our own more localized concerns. It was administered by groups of Salford University students working in pairs, trained by us, to take account of local police advice on such work in these locations and being mindful of the experience of a Home Office sponsored survey conducted a few months earlier. These latter two comments require a fuller explanation.

First, during the time we spent with police officers in each of these locations at the start of this research we learned a good deal, from a policing perspective, about the timing and the placing of criminal activity in these areas. So, for example, we were advised to go out in some streets before 11 a.m. (whilst all the 'baddies' were still in bed) and, certainly as initial strangers to the locations always go out in pairs, and never carry anything which could obviously or easily be snatched. This advice we passed on to our interviewers. (Indeed, one of the research team always acted as supervisor whilst the interviewers were working, noting who went where, for how long, especially if they were invited in to a house.) Secondly, a couple of months prior to the implementation of our survey, the Home Office had chosen one of our locations to do some survey work into witness intimidation. It had used a professional survey company to conduct this work and it very quickly became common knowledge that within four days (some say two) that these interviewers had been 'asked' to leave the estate. It transpired that this was more than rumour as it was commented on in the Home Office's own report from that project (see Maynard 1994). The research on intimidation was intimidated. Both of these sources of information clearly fed the conduct of our own research.

The interviewers we used were not stereotypical university students. They were all mature with northern connections; some were from Salford itself. And although they were going into houses with traditional survey instruments we ensured that the students remained sensitive to the process they were engaging in. We trained the interviewers to pay particular attention to the importance of informality and of asking questions as if they were a part of a conversation. We asked them to be fairly informal in their dress and not to carry clip boards or briefcases but to carry the questionnaires around in plastic bags. This was done as a way of trying to increase their safety on the streets as well as helping the respondents feel more relaxed and confident about the process.

The survey's sampling technique was one which might be called a targeted random sample. Our initial work in these two locations had alerted us to the way in which each of the areas under investigation was differently structured for the people who were living and working there. From the information gathered during our six months of ethnographic work we learned that it was possible to identify nine smaller localities in Oldtown and thirteen in Bankhill. As a result the individuals who actually participated in our survey were chosen at random but in a context in which we had ensured that each separate locality was equally represented. This process generated a total of 596 completed interviews (we had a target of 600 completed interviews) and our sample of respondents closely represented the demographic profile of the areas. We conducted interviews at different times during the day and different days of the week.

One of the purposes of the house-to-house survey was to help decide how focus groups might be constructed and to identify local people who might be willing to participate in them. On the basis of this we held focus group discussions with twenty-one residents of Oldtown and with twenty-nine residents in Bankhill during the next six months. Following on from this work we identified three localities in each ward as 'typical case' studies for further in-depth work. In each of these localities we sent out a postal questionnaire to all the businesses, and other organizations in existence there with a view to capturing a picture of their experiences of working in these areas. A total of 100 community groups and 219 businesses were contacted. These contacts were supplemented with telephone interviews with respondents where there was an expressed willingness on the part of the respondents to do this. In parallel with this activity we collected and analysed police command and control data for our two research areas for the month of January 1995, and conducted in-depth interviews and focus group work with officers patrolling these two wards. This involved a total of eighteen officers of varying ranks. In addition we held eight focus group discussions with 13–15-year-olds in each of the local secondary schools. Ethnographic work continued throughout the course of the study, exemplified by regular attendance at police–community consultative meetings, other local forums as well as continued analysis of the local press. Wherever possible in the last six months of the work we attended local policy group meetings both to disseminate our initial findings and also as a means of establishing some critical feedback on our work.

COMMENTARY

Whilst the preceding discussion offers an overall descriptive outline of what was done, and why, it says little about the process which took place. That process is an important dimension to any research project and is often difficult to capture. However, there are a number of elements to the process of conducting this research project upon which it is important to offer some reflective comment: the kind of comment not often made available in the research methods books.

The interaction between empirical discovery and conceptual development This research began its life concretely situated within the 'fear of crime' debate, and for the first six months of its life that debate continued to fuel its concerns. However, a significant moment of change occurred during the conduct of the criminal victimization survey. This survey was conducted in parallel in Oldtown and Bankhill, in August and September 1994. During the course of that process the student interviewers, who were debriefed after every session of interviewing, reported to us that the survey questions appeared to be working in Bankhill but not Oldtown. When pressed further as to what was meant by this the students told us that people in Oldtown were saying that the questions we were asking did not make any sense to them because 'you were alright round here if you were local'. The students had been instructed to record any response they received to the questions asked, whether or not they matched a particular category, and it became clear that this sense of being 'alright' was being offered often enough for us to re-think whether or not our conceptual apparatus was appropriate. A return to some of the more qualitative interview and ethnographic work, alongside this response to some of the survey questions, led us to consider the extent to which the concept of trust might be a more useful analytical tool than those we had originally adopted. On further analysis we are happier with what this kind of analytical framework can reveal about how people manage their lives in high-crime areas than that proffered by either the notions of 'fear', 'risk', or 'safety' (see in particular Evans, Fraser and Walklate 1996). When this concept was applied to the data relevant to Bankhill it was found to be equally illuminating though differently expressed (see Evans and Walklate 1999 for a much fuller exposition of this argument).

The serendipity of empirical information Again, as the description of the research process offered here implies, this work was primarily conceived in terms of people's experiences of crime and criminal victimization. We had not originally envisaged being concerned with offending behaviour *per se* nor with offenders. However, a shooting incident in Bankhill during the course of conducting our survey led to a minor local demonstration directed at the police handling of this incident which subsequently established, in a very clear way, the role and importance of one criminal gang in particular. The nature of the local knowledge and the contacts of one of the researchers led to a very useful interview with the spokesperson for this criminal gang and provided a further, and unpredicted, important source of information about the nature of crime and criminal victimization, especially in Oldtown. The importance of that information was subsequently validated by the data we gathered from the businesses in that location. Given that this was not a piece of research concerned centrally with the nature of criminal gang activity the opportunities for exploring this dimension of life in these two areas was not taken further. Arguably, however, without the local acceptability of one of the researchers, the sex of the research team, and the particular incident which occurred, the importance of this aspect of community life in these two areas may not have been grasped.

Exploring conceptual subtleties When this research was originally conceived, and the research proposal initially put together (in 1993) little attention was paid to the viability or otherwise of the concept of victim or victimization. Broadly put, there existed considerable tension between victimology's use of the term 'victim' and the feminist use of the term 'survivor' discussed earlier in this chapter. These two terms are in some respects also reflected in the conceptual usage of the terms 'fear' and/or 'safety'. During the focus group discussions, which were guided but never led, the subtleties of such terms were explored more fully. The starting point for the group discussion was some photographs of the research locations. We asked what people thought of the photos and of living in the area. We hoped they would talk about crime, victimization, and the fear of crime. They frequently did. In that context we could identify people who were not victims, but felt themselves to be; people who were victims and did not see themselves in those terms; and organizations which were both seen to be and actually were victims rather than victimizers. This aspect of the research process would benefit from further exploration. It is clear, however, that without the use of the focus group technique a good deal of subtle, nuanced understanding would have been lost.

Controlling dissemination Part of the research process as described above was very much concerned with dissemination. To this end we allocated six months of the research time to this and produced two reports, one for Oldtown one for Bankhill, which were distributed to all who had participated in the research and which were made freely available to any appropriate local forum. Our research findings were used by a range of local organizations. Despite these efforts, and the goodwill which we felt had been established during this process, a report produced in the local press in the summer of 1996 significantly soured these relationships. Our first article from the research was published in the *Sociological Review* in August of that year and a conscientious local reporter read it and produced a rather more sensational newspaper article on its contents. Needless to say that newspaper reporting paid significantly more attention to the presence and impact of the criminal gang in one of our localities, much to the chagrin of the City Council, than we had. No amount of persuasion would convince the officers of the council that we had played no part in the newspaper report and letters were exchanged between the City Council, the ESRC, and the Director of the Initiative under which this research had been funded. It reminded the researchers of the old adage from Howard Becker that a good piece of research will make someone angry. It was fortuitous that the month of August 1996 also saw the end of the project.

It is important for researchers to keep in mind the sensitivity and the sensitive nature of this kind of research and the sensibilities of those involved as respondents. In particular one has to be mindful that people who live in high-crime areas can feel victimized by the research whose intention might nevertheless be to work with them and to improve things for them: there are greater, usually economic, interests at stake for the locally powerful trying to bring business and work to an area. To deny the problems which exist, however, is not perhaps the best way of addressing these sensibilities; to look for the possibilities for change might be a more useful option.

Lessons from this research process What lessons might be learned from this research process in the context of researching victims as a whole? First this research, arguably, highlights very effectively the stranglehold that positivist-oriented work and its commitment to the use and deployment of the criminal victimization survey, has had on both criminology and victimology. That hold has significantly defined the parameters of the fear of crime debate in such a way that it has become almost commonplace to link fear with risk. Yet, as this research illustrated, a subtly nuanced and locally informed use of the same technique, though arguably differently informed at a methodological level, revealed the value of quite a different conceptual apparatus within which to locate an understanding of people's fears. Secondly, aspects of this research are challenging to the concept of victim. It is clear that being identified or identifying oneself as a victim is neither an easy nor a straightforward process; nor is it gendered. In other words it is important not to presume that either femininity or masculinity affords in and of itself management techniques for coping with victimization (for discussion of this last point see Evans and Walklate 1999, chs. 2 and 3). A fuller appreciation of the process of victimization and an understanding of how such processes are or are not attributed and/or embraced would seem to be a valuable area for further investigation. Finally, for the purposes of this discussion, what this case study has hopefully highlighted is a sense of the research process. We started this project concerned with the fear of crime. We finished, we hope, with a better understanding of community dynamics and how these fuel, or do not fuel, people's fears. Such a process can be viewed rather like Sherlock Holmes' 'dog in the night time'; it was the *absence* of the dog's barking which led him to solve the crime in the *Hound of the Baskervilles*. Negative results encouraged us to think again about the data-gathering process and its conceptual validity.

CONCLUSION

This chapter has tried to demonstrate the way in which theory and method are interlinked within victimology, the way in which the different theoretical frameworks presented define the scope for researching victims of crime in different ways, and the kinds of methodological issues which result. One of the key themes is, by implication, the way in which the conceptual vision of social reality, in this context the nature and extent of criminal victimization, informs how any research agenda proceeds, and consequently both what is included and what is excluded from those research findings. It is probably clear to the reader that this author now favours comparative, longitudinal studies, because of their capacity to capture some aspects of social reality over time and space, and because they permit a process to develop between the researcher, the researched, and the research findings. The project, offered as an empirical illustration of a research agenda focused on high-crime areas, presents some insight into how both structuration theory and realism might be made to work. In that process the project started in one place and finished in another and yet simultaneously met most of its objectives. Recapturing that process now is difficult; as is capturing the process of victimization. However, in researching victims of crime there is arguably much more to be learned from trying to film the whole picture than continuing to take snaphots.

END PIECE

It may now have become clear to the reader why this author no longer thinks there are any special issues raised in the course of researching victims of crime. Yes, some interviews may be more emotionally charged, and sometimes the researcher is an important source of information and support. But are these special questions to be taken account of in the research process? The questions raised, it would seem to me, are those raised by any piece of empirical work in any substantive area; does the methodology fit that which is to be researched; is the researcher listening to the data; is the researcher reflecting upon the interaction between the theory and the data? If the answer to these questions is yes then it goes almost without saying that one is treating one's research subjects with respect, that is providing support and information: dealing with people sensitively. And in a sense this is all that victims of crime would desire from the criminal justice system and the policy process: not to be made special, but to be treated with respect.

SUGGESTIONS FOR FURTHER READING

As far as researching victims of crime is concerned I would recommend Sparks, Genn and Dodd (1977), *Surveying Victims*. This study paved the way for the development of the criminal victimization survey in England and Wales and discusses all the major methodological pitfalls associated with that technique. As a follow-on from that research, the essay by Genn (1988) on 'Multiple Victimisation' in Maguire and Pointing (eds.), *Victims of Crime: a New Deal?* (Milton Keynes: Open University Press) raises some fundamental questions about researching victims of crime. And finally, Russell (1990), *Rape in Marriage* (Bloomington, Ind.: Indiana University Press) offers a sound analysis not only of a feminist informed survey but also of the relationship between conceptual clarity and research technique.

REFERENCES

Box, S. (1983). *Power, Crime and Mystification*. London: Tavistock.

Elias, R. (1985). 'Transcending our Social Reality of Victimization: Towards a New Victimology of Human Rights'. *Victimology*, 10: 6–25.

—— (1986). *The Politics of Victimisation*. Oxford: Oxford University Press.

Evans, K., Fraser, P., and Walklate, S. (1996). 'Whom can you trust? The Politics of "Grassing" on an Inner City Housing Estate'. *Sociological Review*, 44: 36–80.

—— and Walklate, S. (1999). *Zero Tolerance or Community Tolerance? Managing Crime in High Crime Areas*. Aldershot: Ashgate.

Fattah, E. (1991). *Towards a Critical Victimology*. London: St. Martins Press.

Genn, H. (1988). 'Multiple Victimisation' in M. Maguire and J. Pointing (eds.), *Crime Victims: A New Deal?* Milton Keynes: Open University Press.

Giddens, A. (1984). *The Constitution of Society*. Oxford: Polity Press.

—— (1991). *Modernity and Self Identity*. Oxford: Polity Press.

Harding, S. (1991). *Whose Science? Which Knowledge?* Milton Keynes: Open University Press.

Hindelang, M. J., Gottfredson, M. R., and Garofalo, J. (1978). *Victims of Personal Crime: An Empirical Foundation for a Theory of Personal Victimisation*. Cambridge, Mass.: Ballinger.

Hough, M., and Mayhew, P. (1983). *The British Crime Survey*. Home Office Research Study, 76. London: HMSO.

JEFFRIES, S., and RADFORD, J. (1984). 'Contributory Negligence or Being a Woman? The Car Rapist Case' in P. Scraton and P. Gordon (eds.), *Causes for Concern*. Harmondsworth: Penguin.

KARMEN, A. (1990). *Crime Victims: An Introduction to Victimology*. Pacific Grove, Cal.: Brooks Cole.

KEAT, R., and URRY, J. (1975). *Social Theory as Science*. London: Routledge.

KIRKWOOD, C. (1993). *Leaving Abusive Partners*. London: Sage.

MAWBY, R., and WALKLATE, S. (1994). *Critical Victimology: The Victim in International Perspective*. London: Sage.

MAYNARD, W. (1994). *Witness Intimidation: Strategies for Prevention*. Police Research Group Paper 55. London: HMSO.

MIERS, D. (1989). 'Positivist Victimology: A Critique'. *International Review of Victimology* 1: 3–22.

—— (1990). 'Positivist Victimology: A Critique Part 2'. *International Review of Victimology* 1: 219–30.

PAWSON, R. (1989). *A Measure for Measure: A Manifesto for Empirical Sociology*. London: Routledge.

PEARCE, F. (1990). *Second Islington Crime Survey: Commercial and Conventional Crime in Islington*. Middlesex Polytechnic: Centre for Criminology.

PRESIDENT'S TASK FORCE ON VICTIMS OF CRIME (1982). *Final Report*. Washington, DC: US Government Printing Office.

QUINNEY, R. (1972). 'Who is the Victim?' *Criminology* 10: 309–29.

REIMAN, J.H. (1979). *The Rich Get Rich and the Poor Get Prison*. New York: John Wiley.

ROCK, P. (1986). *A View from the Shadows*. Oxford: Clarendon Press.

ROSHIER, B. (1989). *Controlling Crime*. Milton Keynes: Open University Press.

RUSSELL, D. (1990). *Rape in Marriage*. Bloomington, Ind.: Indiana University Press.

SHAPLAND, J., WILMORE, J., and DUFF, P. (1985). *Victims in the Criminal Justice System*. Aldershot: Gower.

SHAW, C., and McKAY, H. (1942). *Juvenile Delinquency and Urban Areas*. Chicago Ill.: University of Chicago Press.

SMART, C. (1990). 'Feminist Approaches to Criminology; Or Post-modern Woman Meets Atavistic Man' in L. Gelsthorpe and A. Morris (eds.), *Feminist Perspectives in Criminology*. Milton Keynes: Open University Press.

SPARKS, R. F., GENN, H., and DODD, D. (1977). *Surveying Victims*. London: John Wiley.

SUMNER, C. (1990). *Censure, Politics and Criminal Justice*. Milton Keynes: Open University Press.

WALKLATE, S. (1989). *Victimology: The Victim and the Criminal Justice Process*. London: Unwin Hyman.

—— (1993). 'How Do We Help Them? Responding to Victims of Sexual Assault'. Paper presented to the International Congress of Criminology, Budapest, August.

—— (1995). *Gender and Crime*. London: Harvester Wheatsheaf.

YOUNG, J. (1986). 'The Failure of Criminology: The Need for a Radical Realism' in R. Matthews and J. Young (eds.), *Confronting Crime*. London: Sage.

—— (1988). 'Risk of Crime and Fear of Crime: A Realist Critique of Survey Based Assumption' in M. Maguire and J. Pointing (eds.), *Victims of Crime: A New Deal?* Milton Keynes: Open University Press.

PART 3

RESEARCH ON CRIMINAL JUSTICE AGENCIES AND INSTITUTIONS

7

POLICE RESEARCH

Robert Reiner

INTRODUCTION: WHAT IS POLICE RESEARCH?

The meaning of the term 'police' is notoriously problematic. Because most research on the police has had a practical policy agenda it has taken for granted the police institution as it exists in contemporary society. Historical studies of the origins of modern police organizations might have been expected to raise the issue of what policing is, but for the most part they have also limited themselves to an account of the emergence and development of specific institutional forms. Since Maureen Cain first drew attention to this failure to make the concept of police problematic (Cain 1979) some studies have attempted to analyse the ideas of police and policing. Indeed the term 'policing' has increasingly replaced 'police' in the titles of publications, as a gesture of recognition that modern police forces are but one historically specific variant of the array of policing processes found in different forms of social order. Nonetheless most studies still tacitly assume that contemporary forms exhaust the meaning of 'police'.

This chapter will review and analyse the nature of research on police and policing. It falls into four parts. The first will consider the fundamental concepts of 'police' and 'policing' which bound the field. The second will chart historically the development of research on police and policing, and identify the different strands of research which have emerged. Part three looks at some of the key methods that have been used to study police and policing. Finally, I present some conclusions in part four and critically examine the future of research on policing and the police.

THE CONCEPTS OF 'POLICE' AND 'POLICING'

'Policing' connotes a set of social processes, whilst 'police' has come to refer more specifically to a particular kind of institution, with the primary function of 'policing' (Reiner 1997: 1003–8).[1] Policing may be carried out by a variety of social institutions, agents, or mechanisms, not just the police. Specialized police institutions are not found in all societies, but emerge only with high levels of social complexity (Schwartz and Miller 1964; Robinson and Scaglion 1987; Robinson et al. 1994). 'Policing' is arguably a universal requirement of any social order, but specific police institutions are not.

Policing is an aspect of the wider concept of social control, which has itself got a tortuous history (Cohen and Scull 1983; Hudson 1997; Sumner 1997). Originating in American conservative functionalist sociology in the early twentieth century, social control became a central concept of radical criminology in the 1960s and 1970s, reversing its political connotations but retaining a functionalist sub-text. Most generally social control encompasses the array of formal and informal processes which define and reproduce social order. The concept easily becomes circular and question-begging, for every aspect of a society can be represented as having some control function(s), at least in the very broad sense of contributing to how things are. This plasticity can be avoided only by limiting the definition of social control to specific types of institution or process. To avoid what he caustically criticizes as a 'Mickey Mouse' concept, Cohen proposes restricting its reference to 'the organised ways in which society responds to behaviour and people it regards as deviant, problematic, worrying, threatening, troublesome or undesirable' (Cohen 1985: 1–2).

The idea of policing is clearly a close relative of social control, and raises the same issues of interpretation. Some writers explicitly equate the concepts, but this fails to identify the specificity of what is ordinarily understood to be policing. Policing is distinct, for example, from punishment, and from the wider processes creating or reproducing the conditions for social order, such as childhood socialization or religion—although the 'preventive' role of policing may in some conceptualizations begin to encroach on these.

Policing is a specific sub-set of control processes, directed at preserving and reproducing security and social order by particular means. These are primarily surveillance and investigation to detect potential or actual deviations and initiate sanctions in response, and the gathering and analysis of information about risks to security and order. At the same time policing involves the symbolic representation of social authority through its processes of surveillance and capacity for sanctioning. Policing activities are intended to achieve security and order, but whether they do so is always an open empirical question. Policing may be more or less successful in achieving its objectives. It may also be evaluated differently by people with varying social interests, positions, and

---

[1] The term 'police' itself used to have a much broader connotation than the contemporary usage. It originally encompassed all the internal aspects of governmentality (Foucault 1979). In 18th-century Europe there flourished a 'science of police' covering the gamut of issues relating to the welfare and happiness of populations (Pasquino 1978; Reiner 1988; Garland 1997: 25–6).

values: the policed can be expected to perceive it differently from those who police.

The term 'police' has come to be associated with a historically specific way of performing policing functions (Rawlings 1999). It refers to state organizations employing professionals who are trained and equipped as specialists in policing. Such bodies are characteristic of all modern societies, although they came into being through somewhat different historical trajectories according to variations in culture and political circumstances in different countries. In many places, for example in most of Europe, they originated explicitly as agencies of the state (Mawby 1991). In Great Britain and North America they were represented as having some continuity with earlier forms of communal self-policing, and have had more ambiguous relationships to the central state (Robinson 1979; Reiner 1992a, chs. 1 and 2; Emsley 1996). In many other countries which were once colonies of imperial powers (including Ireland) they originated as instruments of colonial domination (Brogden 1987; Palmer 1988; Waddington 1999: 24–6). There is debate about whether the emergence of police forces in the modern form was a functional necessity because of problems and conflicts generated by industrial capitalism and urbanization, or whether they were primarily a cultural symbol of modernism (Monkkonen 1981). In any event specialist police organizations employed by the central and/or local state have become ubiquitous in contemporary societies.

In earlier societies, however, policing functions were performed by institutions and processes of a diverse kind, albeit not for the most part by specialist professionals. It has always been true in modern societies as well that policing is carried out in many ways by ordinary citizens themselves, apart from the importance of their co-operation for the working of state police organizations (Shapland and Vagg 1987, 1988; Fielding 1987). There continue to be a variety of forms of volunteer policing bodies, with different relationships of harmony or conflict with the professional police themselves, such as the Special Constabulary, neighbourhood watch schemes, the Guardian Angels, and vigilantism (Leon 1989; Gill and Mawby 1990; Bennett 1990; McConville and Shepherd 1992; Johnston 1992). It has also always been the case that a variety of state institutions carry out policing functions in particular places or contexts, such as the British Transport Police, the Ministry of Defence Police, the Atomic Energy Police, and various parks constabularies. Such bodies have been referred to as 'hybrid' police (Johnston 1992: ch. 6). There has also been a private policing sector throughout the history of modern societies (Spitzer and Scull 1977; Shearing and Stenning 1987).

In addition, of course, modern societies continue to be policed by many aspects of social relationships and institutions which do not have any overt policing role, such as families, peer groups, workplaces, religious organizations, clubs, fashions, the mass media, professional associations, and other regulatory bodies. Even the least likely settings have policing embedded in their architecture, routines, symbols, and general staff, as Shearing and Stenning's seminal study of Disney World demonstrates (Shearing and Stenning 1984). The distinctive characteristic of the police is thus not that they have the monopoly of policing in modern societies, or even of policing's ultimate resource, legitimate force (Bittner 1974; Waddington 1999). It is that they are employed by modern states to be specialist professionals organized on a permanent basis for policing, with specific training and capacity for the use of legitimate coercion and force if necessary.

Despite the existence of a plethora of other policing processes and institutions the police had until recently become so dominant symbolically that they monopolized the concept of policing, not only in popular culture but in the research of most academic criminologists. That this is no longer the case is partly because of the work of some pioneering researchers (notably Spitzer and Scull 1977; Shearing and Stenning 1983; South 1988; Johnston 1992) but more fundamentally because of changes in policing itself. In the last quarter century of the second millennium profound social changes have been occurring, suggesting to many a qualitative break in the development of the world order analogous to the rise of industrial capitalism itself. There are many competing attempts to characterize and analyse this supposed break, and indeed some questioning of the novelty or profundity of contemporary change. However, whether or not we are entering a new postmodern, globalized, risk society and information age (Beck 1992; Giddens 1994; Bauman 1997; Castells 1996, 1997, 1998), or just a later stage of capitalist modernity (Callinicos 1989; Hirst and Thompson 1996; Panitch and Leys 1999), there is certainly a major transformation of crime, control, and policing. In many parts of the world 'lawlessness and crime have so destroyed the social fabric that the State itself has withdrawn' (Cohen 1997a: 234). In such areas there is the threat of a 'new barbarism' involving 'the collapse of political order as represented by functioning states' (Hobsbawm 1994: 53).

Whilst not threatened by such extremes of atomic meltdown most industrial societies, including Britain, are experiencing profound shifts in the modalities of social control. This is evident in all aspects of criminal justice policy, but is particularly marked in policing. Over the last two centuries modernism has involved an optimistic project of gradually increasing incorporation of all sections of society into a common status of citizenship in terms of legal, political, and social rights, although enjoyment of these has never been remotely equal (Marshall 1950; Bulmer and Rees 1996). In the last quarter of the twentieth century this long-term trajectory of gradual inclusivism has been set into reverse, as inequalities of all aspects of material and cultural existence have widened rapidly (Hutton 1995; Levitas 1998). An increasing proportion of the population is qualitatively excluded from the way of life of the majority, and economic insecurity is experienced increasingly by most of the population. The consequences for crime and order of this social earthquake are profound (Young 1997*a* and 1997*b*; Taylor 1997; Davies 1998; Currie 1998).

Policing has become embedded in a plethora of environmental, spatial, architectural, and technological modes of achieving and protecting spatial exclusion of the burgeoning new 'dangerous classes' from the castles of consumerism in which the more privileged strata live, work, and play, the advent of what has aptly been called a 'new feudalism' (Shearing and Stenning 1983). The privileged flit between 'security bubbles' in 'cities of quartz' guarded not so much by police or other specialized security personnel as by more or less subtle forms of physical and social barrier (Davis 1990; Bottoms and Wiles 1997: 349–54). States and populations have to adjust to permanent high crime levels, learning a variety of tactics for minimizing the risks or the harm of victimization (Garland 1996). Although there is much can-do political talk of more effective, knowledge-based crime prevention or reduction, and frequent crackdowns, no prospect is envisaged of returning to earlier levels of recorded crime (Nuttall *et al.* 1998). The police have to compete with an increasing array of rival, mainly private, security organizations within an increasingly competitive 'pick'n'mix' policing industry (South 1988; Johnston 1992; Reiner 1997: 1039; Jones and Newburn 1998). At the same time they are subject to increasing managerial and financial forms of accountability from governments seeking to achieve value-for-money 'business-like' policing (Morgan and Newburn 1997; Leishman *et al.* 1996). Effectiveness and cost-benefit research are inscribed increasingly into the routine practices of policing, and police forces become collectors and processors of information about risk and insecurity for an array of public and private organizations (Ericson and Haggerty 1997). More and more research is conducted by, rather than on or for, the police (Brown and Waters 1993; Brown 1996).

THE DEVELOPMENT OF POLICE RESEARCH

Police research only began in Britain in the 1960s. The dearth of earlier work is largely a reflection of the much smaller extent of social science research of any kind. In Britain in particular empirical work in criminology began to proliferate only after the late 1950s, following the establishment of the Home Office Research Unit and the Cambridge Institute of Criminology (Garland 1997: 45–51).

The impetus for research on the police in Britain came both from changes in the politics of criminal justice and theoretical developments in criminology, sociology, and law. This parallels the pressures generating the contemporaneous growth of police research in the USA (Reiner 1997: 999–1000). The underlying context was rising concern about crime and disorder, and a growing public questioning of authority. The police became increasingly visible, controversial, and politicized in response to these tensions and pressures. Many academics have been motivated primarily by the intellectual project of advancing the analysis of policing as a mode of control and governance. Nonetheless the politicization of law and order in the last thirty years (Downes and Morgan 1997) has shaped the trajectory of police research (Reiner 1989).

SOURCES OF POLICE RESEARCH

Police research in Britain has emanated from a variety of sources. These include: academic institutions, official government-related bodies, think tanks and pressure groups, and journalists.

Academic research Until recently most police research was carried out by academics in a variety of disciplines, including criminology, sociology, social policy, law, history, psychology, and economics. Several university centres have been established which concentrate on policing studies (such as the Henry Fielding Centre at Manchester, the Institute of Police and Criminological Studies at Portsmouth, and the Scarman Centre for Public Order at Leicester). Policing research and courses are also a mainstay of the many centres for criminology and criminal justice which have burgeoned around the country since the late 1970s. There has been a proliferation of undergraduate and graduate degree courses in criminology and criminal justice, some with 'police' explicitly in their titles, but most with a strong component of policing in their content (and nearly all catering heavily to police students). Several academic journals have been founded (such as *Policing and Society*). Textbooks and monographs on policing are being published at a pace that is no longer possible for even specialists in the field to keep up with.

Official police research The greatest volume of police research today no longer emanates from academe. There has been a rapid growth of research by policy-making bodies and by the police themselves. In the last twenty years the research focus of the Home Office Research and Planning Unit has become increasingly concerned with policing matters. Before 1979 hardly any of its work touched on policing, but during the 1980s police research became a prominent focus of the Unit's research (recently about half its publications have been on police topics (Reiner 1992*b*: 447). In the last decade a specialist Police Research Group[2] (now the Policing and Reducing Crime Unit) has also been set up in the

---

[2] The Police Research Group was an amalgam of parts of the Research and Planning Unit and social science-oriented research carried out by the earlier Police Requirements Support Unit. This had also conducted technological research, which was transferred to the Police Scientific Development Branch (Brown 1996: 182–3).

Home Office, evolving out of the Crime Prevention Unit. Home Office research on policing will get a further large boost of funding from the government's new £250 million Crime Reduction Programme (Home Office 1998).

Official government police research is not confined to the Home Office. Several local government bodies have sponsored police research, especially during the 1980s when several of the radical Labour local authorities that held office in the Metropolitan areas established police monitoring groups which collected information on a regular basis about police practices and policy (Jefferson et al. 1988). These authorities also often financed outside research projects by academics (e.g. Loveday 1985; Kinsey 1984, 1985a, 1985b; Jones et al. 1986; Crawford et al. 1990; Young 1994). Local government-funded police research activity declined after the 1985 Local Government Act which abolished the radical Metropolitan authorities (Loveday 1987, 1991). However, as a result of the Crime and Disorder Act 1998 they will have to become involved in police research once more, albeit in a rather different way. The earlier local government police research was primarily of a critical character. The new model will be conducted in conjunction with the police, and be of a more policy-oriented, cost-benefit kind, directed at achieving the most effective and efficient crime reduction policies tailored to an audit of local circumstances and problems (as mandated by the Crime and Disorder Act 1998 section 6).

A number of government-established quangos have become important producers of police research in recent years. By far the most influential has been the Audit Commission, which has produced a stream of highly influential studies of aspects of police performance aimed at enhancing the value for money of police activities (Audit Commission 1990a, 1990b, 1993, 1996).

Perhaps the most significant growth point in official police research is by the police themselves (Brown and Waters 1993; Brown 1996). This takes a variety of forms. During the 1980s there was a large increase in the number of graduates joining the service, as well as a growth in the number of serving officers taking degrees on a seconded or part-time basis. In the last decade postgraduate degree courses aimed largely (and sometimes entirely) at the police market have proliferated, attracting considerable numbers of officers who have acquired Master's degrees and (sometimes) doctorates. They will have acquired the skills for conducting research, and often some research experience. Occasionally research projects begun by serving police officers as students have resulted in influential publications (such as Holdaway 1983; Young 1991, 1993). A significant number of police officers have in fact made the switch to becoming full-time academic specialists in police research.

Graduates from these police studies courses have been able to provide the personnel for a huge growth in research within police forces, and by central government policing institutions like HM Inspectorate of Constabulary or the Home Office Police Research Group. As recently as the mid-1980s in-house police research departments were mainly one- or two-person operations with little research expertise. Their function was primarily to collate the statistics and information required for such routine publications as the chief constable's annual report and the design of bureaucratic forms. At best their research projects were 'foregone conclusions', evaluations of pet schemes which were designed never to show failure (Weatheritt 1986, 1989). However there is an increasing proportion of force research departments which produce method-ologically sophisticated research on many aspects of policy and practice, some-times coming to critical conclusions (Brown and Waters 1993; Brown 1996). Forces have also on many occasions contracted research from outside agencies (perhaps the best known example is the celebrated Policy Studies Institute research in the early 1980s: Smith, Gray and Small 1983).

Think-tanks and independent research organizations Independent research organizations, notably the Policy Studies Institute (PSI) and the Police Foundation, have made significant contributions to policing research. The Policy Studies Institute had a distinguished record of research on economic and social issues before its first venture into the policing field (Smith, Gray and Small 1983). It subsequently conducted significant work on such topics as developments in police governance (Jones *et al.* 1994; Jones and Newburn 1997); and private policing (Jones and Newburn 1998).

The Police Foundation is a politically independent registered charity with no core government funding. Although it has firm establishment roots (Prince Charles is its president), it has succeeded in maintaining a quality of critical independence and objectivity in its work (Irving and McKenzie 1989; Irving *et al.* 1989; Weatheritt 1986, 1989, 1993, 1998). In addition to a variety of in-house research projects the Police Foundation has sponsored research by academics (e.g. Waddington 1985) and by police officers (e.g. Blair 1985).

The Police Foundation and the Policy Studies Institute joined forces in 1994 to establish an independent inquiry into *The Role and Responsibilities of the Police.* This was explicitly intended to be an unofficial substitute for the Royal Commission on policing, which many commentators inside and outside the force felt was called for by the increasing controversies surrounding the police and their evident decline in public support. It resulted in a significant research-informed report, and several important publications (Police Foundation/Policy Studies Institute 1996; Saulsbury *et al.* 1996; Morgan and Newburn 1997).

In addition to these independent research organizations, several pressure-groups and politically aligned think-tanks have generated influential research-based work on the police. They include Liberty (formerly the National Council for Civil Liberties) which, as well as producing regular reviews of new legisla-tion and policy developments, finances work by academics through its research arm, the Cobden Trust (e.g. Jefferson and Grimshaw 1984). It also commissioned an independent inquiry chaired by Professor Peter Wallington into the policing of the miners' strike in 1984 (although this was disowned by the AGM of the NCCL in 1985 for supposedly straying beyond its brief and commenting on the conduct of the miners as well as the police). It resulted in the most comprehensive study of the dispute (McCabe *et al.* 1988). Other examples of police research by politically-oriented think-tanks include studies of police accountability by the (Labour-leaning) Institute for Public Policy Research (Reiner and Spencer 1993), and zero-tolerance policing by the (Conservative leaning) Institute of Economic Affairs (Dennis 1997).

Journalists Since the beginnings of police research in this country in the early 1960s, studies by journalists have made significant contributions to analysis and debate. These include Whitaker 1964; Laurie 1970; Humphry 1972; Cox *et al.* 1977; Graef 1989; Rose 1992, 1996.[3] The particular hallmark of much of the best journalistic studies has been the ability to probe particular aspects of police malpractice that academics have seldom dealt with.

THE CHANGING AGENDAS OF POLICE RESEARCH

Several stages can be distinguished in the development of British police research, in terms of the evolving focal concerns of different periods. These seem to be related closely to the changing politics of criminal justice. In two earlier surveys of police research in Britain I suggested that four stages could be distinguished: consensus, controversy, conflict, and contradiction (Reiner 1989, 1992*a*). The contradictory stage now seems to have resolved into a period in which research is dominated by a clear (though not unchallenged) crime-control agenda.

The first empirical research on policing by a British academic was Michael Banton's *The Policeman in the Community* (Banton 1964). Like almost all writing on the police at that time it was framed within a celebratory mode, and assumed a primarily harmonious view of British society. It starts with 'the idea that it can be instructive to analyse institutions that are working well in order to see if anything can be learned from their success' (Banton 1964: vii). Banton's work is a clear exemplification of the *consensus* stage of police research.

During the 1970s and 1980s British police research was increasingly character-ized by themes reflecting the growing conflicts in which policing came to be embroiled. During the *controversy* stage of police research in the late 1960s and

---

[3] Many of these, notably Roger Graef and David Rose, have also made very significant contributions through the medium of television documentaries on policing. Roger Graef's celebrated series on Thames Valley in particular is usually credited with having been a major influence on the reform of police procedures for dealing with victims of rape or domestic violence (Hoyle 1998; Gregory and Lees 1999).

early 1970s policing was beset by a flurry of problems, ultimately resulting from growing divisions and declining deference in society generally. The main manifestations were the rise of forms of middle-class political protest, such as CND, the anti-Vietnam War movement, and student demonstrations, a rebirth of industrial militancy, and increasing revelations of police malpractice including corruption scandals on an unprecedented scale, racial discrimination, and other abuses of police powers (Reiner 1992a: ch. 2).

Reflecting these issues an increasing number of academic researchers began working on the police in the late 1960s and early 1970s. Unlike Banton's pioneering work they did not start from palpably consensus assumptions. The key theoretical influences were symbolic interactionism and the labelling perspective, which saw policing as an important process in shaping (rather than merely reacting to) the pattern of deviance through the exercise of discretion (Lambert 1969, 1970; Cain 1971, 1973; Rock 1973; Chatterton 1976, 1979, 1983; Holdaway 1983; Manning 1977, 1979; Punch 1979a, 1979b). Many of the studies also explicitly focused on issues which were at the forefront of the political controversies involving the police, such as racial discrimination (Lambert 1970), the increasing autonomy of the police (Cain 1973, Holdaway 1977); industrial conflict (Reiner 1978a), and corruption (Punch 1985).

The introduction to Simon Holdaway's 1979 collection of essays on the British police, which includes examples of most of the research then being conducted, sums up accurately the focal concern: 'one of the basic themes running through this book . . . is that the lower ranks of the service control their own work situation and such control may well shield highly questionable practices' (Holdaway 1979: 12).

Research tended to be critical of police practice, whatever its institutional base. Whilst academics, journalists, and pressure groups were concerned primarily with police deviance, official government research was pointing out the limitations of policing as a means of controlling crime. A body of research by the Home Office Research and Planning Unit in particular was highlighting the limited impact of traditional police tactics on crime, reflecting a more general 'nothing works' mood about penal policy (Clarke and Hough 1980, 1984; Morris and Heal 1981; Heal et al. 1985).

The issues examined in the controversy stage linked directly to the key focus of the *conflict* stage of police research: accountability—who controls policing? This indicated the increasing politicization of policing in the late 1970s and early 1980s, embodied most vividly in the major urban riots of the early to mid-1980s, the bitter clashes over the 1984–5 miners' strike, and the acrimonious debates about the extensions of the legal powers of the police proposed by the 1981 Royal Commission on Criminal Procedure and embodied—after a tortuous legislative history—in the 1984 Police and Criminal Evidence Act. It also reflected the growth of Marxist and other forms of radical criminology out of the critical questioning of criminal justice initiated by labelling theory. Many academic studies of the police in this period were explicitly Marxist, and almost all the others (including some Home Office research as well as the work spon-sored by radical local authorities) were critical of the police on issues such as racial discrimination.[4] Uniting all the various causes of concern and contro-versy was a critique of the inadequacy of existing mechanisms for holding the police to account, whether as individuals through the complaints process or the courts, or force policy and operations as a whole through the institutions of police governance (Lustgarten 1986).

By the late 1980s a new stage of debate and research on policing was emer-ging, in which a number of tendencies seemed to be in competition, which I labelled *contradictory* (Reiner 1989: 14–15). The key theme of this stage was the growth of an avowed 'realism', across the political spectrum. Most marked in this country was the new 'left realism' advocated explicitly by Jock Young and others (Cowell *et al.* 1982; Lea and Young 1984; Kinsey, Lea and Young 1986; Young 1986, 1988, 1997*b*). This contrasted itself with what it called the 'adminis-trative criminology' of the Home Office and other parts of the criminal justice policy-making circle, and the 'new right' realism associated most clearly with James Q. Wilson in the USA (Wilson 1975). Although clearly these different variants embodied vastly different political and theoretical assumptions, they shared a similar direction of development.

Again the espousal of 'realism' reflected wider developments in both crim-inological theory and criminal justice politics. In criminology this was part of a more general tendency to turn away from grand theory (Jefferson and Shapland 1994). Although some have continued to try and analyse current crime and criminal justice developments theoretically (not least Jock Young, the pioneer of left realism), the momentum was towards research of a policy-oriented and managerialist kind. The common premise was that crime was a serious problem above all for the poorer and weaker sections of society, and research should be directed primarily at developing concrete, immediately practicable tactics for crime control (for parallel arguments about research in the USA see Weisburd, Uchida and Green 1993).

Police research came increasingly to focus on the search for good practice, rather than the issues of police discretion, deviance, and accountability. Increas-ingly police research was moving in the direction of monitoring and evaluating policing initiatives. 'Community policing' became a fashionable rubric around the world (Skolnick and Bayley 1986, 1988; Fielding 1995). It offered to unite the earlier concerns with accountability and the new concern with effective

---

[4] Examples of academic work from a critical perspective in this period include Hall *et al.* 1978; Cain 1977, 1979; McBarnet 1978, 1979, 1981; Brogden 1977, 1981, 1982; Reiner 1978*b* and 1978*c*; Jefferson and Grimshaw 1984; Grimshaw and Jefferson 1987; Scraton 1985. These and contemporaneous studies from non-academic sources are considered more fully in Reiner 1989: 12–14.

policing: accountability was for good, effective policing, which could only be achieved through cultivating community consent.

This was paralleled by a new, although limited, consensus which was emerging in the political sphere. In the early 1980s the parties had become polarized over the police. On the one hand, the police were basking in a prolonged honeymoon period with the Thatcher government. The police were treated as a special case with regard to the drive for 'value for money' and cuts in public expenditure, a loyal police being seen as essential to defeat the 'enemy within' in the shape of militant trade unionism and other expressions of resistance to the economically polarizing consequences of free-market economics. Labour was successfully stigmatized with an anti-law and order label because of its general social democratic interpretations of crime and disorder as at least in part produced by economic inequality and social exclusion, as well as its civil libertarian concerns. In the later 1980s Labour struggled to regain public confidence in its law and order policies, and in particular to repair broken bridges to the police. This process began under Neil Kinnock, but really only began to succeed during Tony Blair's tenure as shadow Home Secretary, when he began to promulgate his famous sound-bite 'tough on crime, tough on the causes of crime'. As Home Secretary, Jack Straw has clearly continued this line (although many would feel that the phrase has shrunk to the first three words only).

During the 1990s there has clearly emerged a new cross-party consensus that the overriding priority for the police must be crime control. This was spearheaded by Kenneth Clarke and Michael Howard, architects of the mid-1990s policy package embodied in the 1993 White Paper on Police Reform, the 1993 Sheehy Report on pay and career structures, and the 1994 Police and Magistrates' Court Act, aimed at creating a 'business-like' police, constrained by market disciplines to achieve efficient and economic delivery of their primary objective, 'catching criminals', as the White Paper put it. New Labour has left this reform package intact, although it has given it a spin in a more sophisticated direction in the 1998 Crime and Disorder Act and its programme for crime reduction (Home Office 1998).

Research is integral to Labour's crime-reduction agenda in general and the role of the police in particular. The driving paradigm for police research now is clearly *crime control*. Both in the USA and Britain there is a resuscitated belief amongst policy-makers and some researchers that policing is a key element in crime control, not only through broader community strategies but through the deterrent strategy of tougher and more directed patrol and detective work (such as the fashion for 'zero-tolerance' policing: cf. Dennis 1997; Weatheritt 1998; Young 1998). There has been explicit rejection of the earlier 'nothing works' pessimism (most explicitly by Sherman 1992, 1993; but see also Bayley 1998; Brodeur 1998; Nuttall *et al.* 1998).

In this new intelligence-driven crime-control paradigm, policing research figures in an integral way. Policy-oriented research is no longer just a matter of *post hoc* evaluation of police initiatives, although the quantity and sophistication of evaluation has (debatably) grown (Bennett 1990, 1991, 1996; Pawson and Tilley 1994; Cohen 1997*b*; Brodeur 1998). The detailed crime analysis and the tailoring of specific local policing responses in conjunction with other agencies which lie at the heart of the problem-oriented (Goldstein 1990) and intelligence-led approaches which the new Labour government is promoting (Jordan 1998; Home Office 1998) require an on-going research capacity within police forces, as well as closer collaboration with policy-oriented researchers outside.

Critical and theoretical work have certainly not disappeared in recent years, in Britain or elsewhere.[5] In Britain, for example, the influential and much debated study by McConville, Sanders and Leng of the impact of recent legal change on policing (McConville *et al.* 1991) is clearly both theoretical and critical (although it has attracted much controversy because of this: cf. Smith 1997, 1998; Travers 1997; McConville *et al.* 1997). There has been a substantial body of work seeking to analyse the impact of the fundamental social changes of post-modernity on policing (Reiner 1992*c*; Sheptycki 1995, 1997; McLaughlin and Murji 1996, 1997; Bottoms and Wiles 1996; Morgan and Newburn 1997; South 1997; Johnston 1998). There has also been a continuing concern with race and gender discrimination by and in the police (Holdaway 1991, 1996; Cashmore and McLaughlin 1991; Heidensohn 1992, 1994; Walklate 1992, 1996; Martin 1996; Gregory and Lees 1999). Nonetheless the extent of such work has been eclipsed by the rapid growth of policy-oriented work on crime control by the police.

THE METHODS OF POLICE RESEARCH

Research on policing and the police has been carried out using the full gamut of social science research methods: overt or covert participant and non-participant observation; surveys; interviewing; field diaries; policy evaluation; analysis of organizational data like calls for service or personnel deployment; documentary analysis of historical or contemporary records and files; analysis of official statistics. This section will focus on some of the methodological issues which are peculiar to, or peculiarly acute in, researching the police. These arise partly out of the nature of police work and organization in general, but

[5] To take some key examples from overseas, in Australia there is Chan's work on changing police culture (Chan 1997) and Dixon on legal regulation of policing (Dixon 1997), and in Canada the work of Shearing, Ericson, and others on theorizing policing in contemporary post-modern or risk societies (Shearing and Ericson 1991; Shearing 1996; Ericson and Haggerty 1997).

assume different forms in different social and historical contexts, and according to the characteristics of the researcher *vis-à-vis* the police.

We have seen that the focal issues addressed in different periods have varied with the changing politics of law and order, and that research has originated from different institutional bases: academe; official government or police organizations; independent research institutions, political think-tanks and pressure-groups; and journalists. Social research always involves an interaction with people in order to generate or obtain data or texts for analysis and reporting to a wider audience. The peculiarities of research on policing derive from special characteristics of police work, the relationship between the researcher and the police, and the purposes of and audience for the report.

THE PECULIARITIES OF POLICING AS A RESEARCH SUBJECT

As argued earlier, policing is an aspect of social control, and there is inevitably overt or potential conflict with those who are policed (Fielding 1991; Kemp *et al.* 1992). Although the legitimacy of policing will vary in different periods and contexts (Reiner 1992*a*, 1992*c*; Waddington 1999) it is bound up ultimately with coercion and force (Bittner 1974). Much policing is dangerous, 'dirty' work: getting people to do what they do not want to, or making them desist from doing what they do want to do. The tactics used for accomplishing this are almost inevitably going to be controversial even if they are legal, and they are frequently of dubious legality or clearly illegal. This indicates one aspect of the peculiar difficulty of police research. Much research is directed at questions of police deviation from the rule of law, and most addresses issues which are extremely controversial—such as the effects of highly contested legal changes like the 1984 Police and Criminal Evidence Act, the 1986 Public Order Act, and the 1994 Police and Magistrates' Court Act (Dixon *et al.* 1989, 1990; McKenzie *et al.* 1990; McConville *et al.* 1991; Brown 1997; Waddington 1994; Jones and Newburn 1997). Such work is clearly seeking to uncover information which the subjects studied might wish to keep secret. At any rate the police studied will inevitably be anxious about how they are going to be represented to other audiences such as the managers or agencies to whom they are accountable. The resulting problems of access and trust are shared with much other social research that has the potential to uncover dangerous knowledge, but the extent of the difficulty is particularly severe in studying policing because of the highly charged nature of its secrets. On some topics the problems of researching the police are virtually insuperable (for example corruption, which has never been observed or discovered directly by researchers, so that studies of it tend to be based on scandals which are already in the public domain: cf. Punch 1985).

There are other aspects of policing which make it especially hard to uncover information which the subjects wish to keep hidden. Since the birth of police research in the 1960s researchers have pointed to the 'low visibility' of everyday police work as a major factor hampering the achievement of effective accountability to organizational supervisors, let alone processes of external accountability (Goldstein 1960). The main modes of police work are uniform patrol and plain-clothes investigation. Both take place outside the organization, away from immediate oversight by managers, with officers generally working alone or in pairs. This gives the rank and file considerable scope for making their accounts of incidents the authoritative ones (Manning 1979; Chatterton 1979), as there is usually no challenging version other than those of the people who are being policed, who are normally low in 'the politics of discreditability' (Box and Russell 1975). The wish to penetrate this low visibility is why participant observation has been the main technique adopted by researchers wishing to analyse the practices and culture of policing (e.g. Banton 1964, Cain 1973; Chatterton 1976, 1979, 1983; Holdaway 1983; Punch 1979a; Kemp et al. 1992). All other methods rely on some sort of account offered by the police themselves (whether in interviews or official documents and statistics), the veracity of which is often precisely the question being studied. Nonetheless many studies have been based on interviewing officers (e.g. Reiner 1978a, 1991; Fielding 1988; Holdaway 1991) or the analysis of records and documents (e.g. Martin and Wilson 1969; Lambert 1970; Punch 1979b; Waddington 1991, 1993; Wall 1998). Many research projects combine different methodological tools, notably observation, interviewing, and documentary analysis (e.g. Lee 1998; Hoyle 1998).

Even with observational work there is the problem of whether the researcher has the trust of the subjects of the research, and how their behaviour may be modified by the presence of a researcher. Trust is unlikely ever to be complete (which is why such extreme deviance as corruption has never been witnessed by observers). In order to maximize trust observers have to spend extensive periods in the field as a means of becoming accepted. This makes observational work extremely time-consuming and labour-intensive. Thus the price of its arguably greater validity is that it is usually based on only a limited number of sites and times, and the representativeness of these will always be problematic.[6]

In addition to the 'low visibility' problem arising from the scattered and dispersed nature of police work, there is the particular skill officers are likely to have in tactics for covering up what they do not want known. Police researchers are investigating subjects whose job it is to investigate the deviance of others. These are problems which have bedevilled attempts to make officers accountable through such mechanisms as complaints systems (Goldsmith 1991; Maguire and Corbett 1991), but they pose similar obstacles for researchers.

[6] The only example of an observational study which was sufficiently well funded for it to be able to mount observations on an arguably representative range of sites was the Black and Reiss study for the 1967 Presidential Committee on Law Enforcement (Mastrofsk et al. 1998). The resources for so large a study are unlikely to be forthcoming again.

Ultimately there is no way of knowing for certain whether what police do in front of observers, or what they say to interviewers, is intended to present an acceptable face to outsiders. I have often tried to reassure myself that I have achieved some degree of trust as an observer or interviewer when I saw or heard things that would cause the subjects embarrassment if they appeared on the front page of the next morning's *Guardian*, or more feasibly if they became known to supervisors or colleagues (Reiner 1978a: 14–15; 1991: 47–9). Occasionally there may be opportunities for triangulation of material from different sources, although which to rely on if they do not confirm each other is problematic. The precise nature of all these difficulties, and the strategies which might help overcome them, vary according to the characteristics and agenda of the researcher, and her relationship to the police.

THE RELATIONSHIP BETWEEN THE RESEARCHER AND THE POLICE

Clearly the material researchers can obtain from the police will be affected by who they are, and their relationship to the force. Brown has usefully distinguished four possible permutations: inside insiders; outside insiders; inside outsiders; outside outsiders (Brown 1996), each of which will typically have different access to police data and material.

Inside insiders are police officers conducting police research, perhaps for a degree or for an official body like a government department or the force itself. In one sense the problems of access to police are eased, especially if the research is officially sanctioned, giving the researcher some power to compel co-operation. However, whilst access problems are different for an inside insider they do not disappear, and indeed in some instances may be particularly acute precisely because the researcher represents a higher authority. The inside insider is usually at an advantage in overcoming the first hurdle of formal access to police sites, but this does not overcome even problems of access altogether, and in some instances may exacerbate them.

It is important to recognize that access to research sites is not achieved once and for all. There are two clearly different stages which can be distinguished, but the latter in particular is really a matter of continuous negotiation. The first access hurdle is the one usually emphasized in research reports: getting formal permission from the authorities who control any access at all to research sites.

The less visible but more important access problem is securing the trust and genuine co-operation of the people in the research site itself, after formal access has been given. This involves continuous negotiation with a set of individuals who may have different interests and perspectives and hence distrust each other, leading to the problem that the achievement of good relationships with some people may itself pose a barrier to achieving this with others. In general the very fact of having official approval for the research can be a difficulty when it comes to being trusted by the research subjects themselves, who may regard the researcher with suspicion as a tool of management. For this reason some researchers avoid the first hurdle of gaining official approval for access, and go straight to the research subjects themselves, cultivating individuals through such methods as snowball sampling. This is problematic if the research wishes to make claims of representativeness, but, as with all research decisions, there are no clear 'right answers'—it all depends on what the researcher is seeking to achieve. With almost all methodological choices there is a tension between getting rich and valid material on the one hand, and the scale and representativeness of the data on the other. This problem may actually be greater for inside insiders than for other researchers.

Apart from the generalized issues of overcoming the inevitable suspiciousness that police may have of anyone outside their immediate work group (and indeed within it), the characteristics and status of researchers will affect their interaction with the research subjects, and influence the results. This is true for inside insiders as much as outside researchers. A black or woman officer doing research on issues of discrimination, for example, will probably generate a different pattern of results from a white male researcher. There is no neutral Archimedean point from which objective data can be collected: the researcher always influences the social interactions that constitute the data. All one can do is seek to be reflexively aware of this and interpret material in the light of the probable biases. I always keep a card in my index box for analysing research material which I call 'perceptions of me' on which I note any remarks indicating how I was seen, to try and understand how this might affect the pattern of results. This kind of awareness of how the researcher structures the findings is as important for inside insiders as any other relationship to the field being studied.

Outside insiders are those officers who conduct police research after deciding to leave or actually leaving the force. A few researchers have been serving officers who systematically analyse their experiences as research material, having privately decided to leave and pursue academic careers. In effect they are covert participant observers, which clearly raises acute ethical issues about potential abuse of trust (Norris 1993). Once they have left the force, their previous inside experience still presents unique advantages and problems compared to complete outsiders. Again, however, the precise nature of the opportunities and hurdles varies according to the researcher's characteristics and relationship to the force. Some will have become alienated from the cultural values of most other officers before leaving, and may well have not enjoyed complete trust from their colleagues even whilst in the force (Holdaway 1983: 8). Others may continue to identify with rank-and-file police culture after becoming academics, and act as interpreters of this to outsiders. The role of the outside insider may range all the way from spy to propagandist, with different impacts on the relationship with those studied and hence on the nature of the information discovered.

Inside outsiders researchers are non-police officers who have official roles within police forces or governmental organizations with responsibilities for policing such as the Home Office. As mentioned earlier there is a small but growing number of civilian researchers employed by police research depart-ments (Brown and Waters 1993; Brown 1996). There are also many civilians conducting research on policing for a variety of government departments (mainly within the Home Office), for local government and for quangos like the Audit Commission. Some outside research is commissioned by forces or government. Like inside insiders police- or government-employed civilian researchers may find it easier to overcome the hurdle of getting formal access to forces. However, such researchers may have acute problems of gaining genuine co-operation and trust from police officers precisely because they represent authority and their findings may have more immediate impact on policy than those of outsiders. It has been suggested that official researchers would tend to be less critical of policing because of lack of distance from and incorporation into the organization (Sheptycki 1994: 130). In fact much inside outsider research has been very critical of both the effectiveness and the justice of police practices (e.g. Clarke and Hough 1980, 1984; Irving 1980; Morris and Heal 1981; Smith *et al.* 1983; Irving *et al.* 1989; Anderson *et al.* 1993; Brown *et al.* 1993). It is probable, however, that inside outsider research will have a policy focus rather than one concerned with developing a theoretical analysis of policing.

Outside outsider studies have until recently constituted the bulk of police research—work conducted by academics and others who are not employed or commissioned by the police or other governmental bodies with responsibility for policing (although in recent years the various kinds of insider research have grown much more rapidly and may well become predominant soon).

Outside outsiders clearly face the greatest barriers in gaining formal access to police forces for research. They have no official status that mandates formal police co-operation and may (often rightly) be perceived as having critical concerns about police malpractice or failure. Nonetheless such work has pro-liferated in the last thirty years, so the barriers are clearly surmountable. The extent of difficulty will vary from time to time according to the political climate amongst the Home Office and police elite. Clearly the potential researcher will have to make a case out in terms of the contribution of the work not only to academic understanding but in policy terms (however indirect). A track record as an established researcher (or the backing of one) is important.

Negotiating access usually involves more than one hurdle. For example, in order to carry out research based on interviews with chief constables in the late 1980s I had to get the agreement and co-operation of the key figures in all the institutions of the police policy elite, including the Home Office, and the

Association of Chief Police Officers (Reiner 1991, ch. 3). This actually took nearly ten years from my first abortive attempt, and depended crucially not only on changes in personnel in the police world, but also the development of my own work which enabled me to forge links with crucially placed individuals. Nor is formal access something which can be taken for granted after it has been given. If the authorities involved discover that the research is leading in directions they are unhappy with, they can of course abort it, as happened in the late 1940s with the first ever sociological study of policing (Westley 1970). Anxiety about the loss of access may be a factor constraining research throughout the study. I remember standing on a station platform in 1987 two days before the General Election, on my way home after an interview with a chief constable who had just told me that during the 1984–5 miners' strike Margaret Thatcher had put pressure on the police to establish an undercover unit to infiltrate trade unions to prove links with Moscow, at a time when there was blanket denial of government intervention in the operational policing of the strike (Reiner 1991: 191). I was sorely tempted to ring a newspaper with the information, but in the end decided that the likely sacrifice of the research, and the career of the chief constable who had confided in me (not to speak of my own) was too high a price to pay for an act of whistle-blowing that probably would not affect the election outcome.

The researcher is likely to have to give certain undertakings such as protecting the confidentiality of individuals or specific forces by guaranteeing anonymity, which probably do not pose any great limitations for work concerned with general policy or analytical issues. What is more problematic is the question of editorial control of the final report. It is common and reasonable to undertake to show a draft for comment to the bodies that allow access. However allowing the organization researched to censor all or even substantial parts of a study undermines any value the research might have as a contribution to knowledge about policing. However it would be legitimate to edit out errors of fact pointed out by the organization, or information that may be unequivocally harmful if published, for example because it could endanger or discourage witnesses or make specific detection methods widely known and hence less effective. I would never be prepared to give such an undertaking myself. It is also the case that there may be methodological restrictions placed on the research, such as not permitting tape-recording. Frequently it will be specified that certain information cannot be sought. For example, on two occasions I was prohibited from asking questions about political opinions when interviewing samples of officers of different ranks (Reiner 1978a, 1991). It is a matter of judgement whether the specific restrictions imposed make it worthwhile continuing with the research.

Although outside outsiders face greater problems of official access the difficulties of gaining the trust of the actual people researched are shared with insiders. They vary according to the same characteristics of different researchers. The researcher's relationship with the different individuals being studied requires constant and delicate negotiation, and also the reflexive awareness of how the subjects' perceptions of the researcher can alter the material. Many researchers have described what amount to initiation rituals or rites of passage before they gain a modicum of acceptance (these are paralleled by the trials imposed on new colleagues in the force before they are incorporated into the group). Common examples include holding your own in extended drinking sessions at bars, pubs, or clubs after shifts of research work (Reiner 1991: 46; 1992b: 124, 276–7). Researchers will be perceived in different ways by the police they are studying, depending partly on their own characteristics and presentation of self, but partly on circumstances within the police context over which they have little or no control. For example during my PhD research I was usually taken to be a student radical who had inexplicably been let loose on the force. However in one division my research period coincided with a Home Office survey and I tended to be mistaken for a 'Home Office spy'. Whether this accounted for the fact that the officers in that division appeared far more conformist than in any other is impossible to say with certainty—it was nicknamed the 'dull' division in the force, and it is hard to disentangle the effects of suspicion of me as a management snoop (Reiner 1978a: 15–16). Although gaining entry is always a problem, and trust needs to be continuously cultivated, many police officers are only too glad to tell you of their views and experiences once initial barriers have been overcome, and exiting may be as problematic as gaining access in some instances.

Recording data is always problematic in policing research. Tape-recording of interviews is clearly the most reliable and convenient method, but frequently raises initial alarm amongst respondents. In my experience this can usually be alleviated by promising to turn off the tape on request from the interviewee if respondents worry about specific replies. This seldom happens because of the momentum generated by the interview once it has begun, but when it does it is of interest in itself to note the points that arouse particular concern. In observational fieldwork tape-recording is almost always impossible. Contemporaneous note-taking is also almost always ruled out by the physical circumstances, and reliance must be placed on memory. Frequent visits to the toilet to jot down very brief reminders for subsequent report writing are helpful—but may raise concerns about the researcher's health.

CONCLUSIONS: THE FUTURE OF POLICING RESEARCH

Policing research has altered fundamentally during its forty-year history. In Britain until the mid-1980s most of it was done by outsiders to policing, and it was motivated primarily by critical and theoretical concerns, even when done by insiders (Holdaway 1989). The methodological problems were primarily those of detectives or spies: how to get information from people who were (often rightly) suspicious of your motives, had much to hide, and much to lose from its discovery. Most researchers came to be more sympathetic to the police as they did their research, but almost always without going native. Understanding the pressures and constraints of police work mellowed all-out hostility or criticism, but researchers' concerns about discrimination and abuses of power remained undiminished.

An interesting study of the impact of police research on researchers demonstrates how these tensions tend to be resolved according to the disciplinary backgrounds of different researchers (Reiss 1968). Dozens of graduate students were recruited as observers for the large-scale study of patrol work conducted for the Presidential Commission on Law Enforcement, and their views on the police were surveyed before and after the fieldwork. At the outset most shared the anti-police consensus then normal amongst students. But after riding along with the dreaded pigs for many hours in the stressful intimacy of patrol cars, the majority became much more positive in their views of police officers. However, their own political views remained as liberal as at the outset. The dissonance between their assessments of the officers as people and the aspects of their practices which the students disapproved of was resolved in a variety of ways characteristic of their disciplinary backgrounds. Law students saw the issue as bad laws enforced by well-meaning police. Management students sympathized with the street cops and saw the problem as bad management. Sociologists attributed undesirable police behaviour to the structural pressures of an unjust social system.

In the last fifteen years relations between the police and academe have been transformed (Reiner 1994). The police have been seen as useful new sources of students and research funding by increasingly cash-pressured academics, whilst the police have sought to religitimate themselves through academic credentials and increasing their own capacity to do research on policy implementation. Thus research is increasingly of a pragmatic kind, governed by the overriding goal of crime reduction. This is being given an enormous impetus by the new Labour government's approach which is based on intelligence-led and problem-oriented approaches to policing and crime control, requiring regular analysis before initiatives and evaluation afterwards (Nuttall *et al.* 1998). The danger is that the necessarily quicker and more focused assessments of specific problems and attempted solutions may not shed light on the low visibility practices of everyday policing. Our basic knowledge of such basic matters as why people join the force, the extent of use of discriminatory language, the way day-to-day decisions about the use of powers are made, and other key aspects of cop culture are based on increasingly out-of-date research like the PSI study conducted in the early 1980s. Replication of the classic observational studies of routine police work is badly needed.

There are many topics crying out for research of the older kind that sought to understand basic practices without being directed to the immediate solution of practical problems. Ultimately such work can provide a better grounding for policy as well. A key example is the construction of criminal statistics. Much research has shown how statistics have frequently been manipulated by the police to provide support for their organizational interests (Young 1991; Taylor 1998, 1999). There is considerable evidence that the pressure to produce results in the new performance indicator-driven culture of police management is driving the police into wholesale massaging of crime figures (Davies 1999: 12). Yet it is nearly two decades since any observational work was conducted on the routine construction of crime data by the police (McCabe and Sutcliffe 1978; Bottomley and Coleman 1981). Much other work of a fundamental kind is necessary, building on what has gone before. We know little, for example, about the social characteristics of those who call upon the police for help by telephone, although there has been a plethora of work on the content of their demands. Yet this is fundamental for understanding the social role of policing.

At present the thrust of research seems to be away from such fundamental and theoretical questions. However it is possible that recent events will force a change. The controversies raised by the publication of the inquiry into the disastrous and shameful investigation of Stephen Lawrence's murder in 1993 (MacPherson 1999; Bowling 1999) have brought back to the forefront of political debate racism and other issues of police malpractice which were being sidelined. It seems that two decades of reform since the 1981 Scarman Report raised similar questions has achieved little if anything. Nor has concern for value for money as exhibited by performance indicators delivered policing of basic competence. Both police research and police reform of a critical and constructive kind are back on the agenda.

SUGGESTIONS FOR FURTHER READING

Few works address the methods of police research as such. However, most research studies include chapters detailing the methods used, why they were chosen, the problems encountered, and how at least some of these were overcome. For examples discussing observational methods see Skolnick 1966; Reiss 1968; Cain 1973; Manning 1977; Punch 1979a; Holdaway 1983; Fielding 1988; Young 1991, 1993; Waddington 1994. On interview-based research see Reiner 1978, 1991. Weatheritt 1989 is a collection of essays considering the value and limits of policy-oriented research. Weatheritt (1985), Brown and Waters (1993), Sheptycki (1994), and Brown (1996) consider the growth of research by the police themselves, and its relative merits and limitations compared with research on the police by outsiders. Smith (1997, 1998), Travers (1997), and McConville, Sanders and Leng (1997), represent a recent series of exchanges about the issues of balancing scholarship and political engagement in research. Pawson and Tilley (1994), Bennett (1996), Cohen (1997b), and Brodeur (1998) are recent assessments of the methodology of evaluation research. Morgan and Newburn (1997) is a succinct analysis of current policing issues. Reiner 1992a, 1997; Leishman et al. 1996; Waddington 1999 are reviews of the content of police research. Reiner 1989 and 1992b are historical accounts of the development of British police research.

REFERENCES

ANDERSON, R., BROWN, J., and CAMPBELL, E. (1993). *Aspects of Discrimination Within the Police Service in England and Wales.* London: Home Office Police Research Group.

AUDIT COMMISSION (1990a). *Calling All Forces: Improving Police Communications Rooms.* London: HMSO.

—— (1990b). *Effective Policing: Performance Review in Police Forces.* London: HMSO.

—— (1993). *Helping With Enquiries.* London: HMSO.

—— (1996). *Streetwise: Effective Police Patrol.* London: HMSO.

BANTON, M. (1964). *The Policeman in the Community.* London: Tavistock.

BAUMAN, Z. (1997). *Postmodernity and its Discontents.* Cambridge: Polity Press.

BECK, U. (1992). *Risk Society.* London: Sage.

BENNETT, T. (1990). *Evaluating Neighbourhood Watch.* Aldershot: Gower.

—— (1991). 'The Effectiveness of a Police-Initiated Fear Reducing Strategy'. *British Journal of Criminology* 31: 1–14.

—— (1996). 'What's New in Evaluation Research?' *British Journal of Criminology* 36: 567–73.

BITTNER, E. (1974). 'Florence Nightingale in Pursuit of Willie Sutton: A Theory of the Police' in H. Jacob (ed.), *The Potential For Reform of Criminal Justice.* Beverly Hills, Cal.: Sage.

BLAIR, I. (1985). *Investigating Rape: A New Approach For Police*. London: Croom Helm.

BOTTOMLEY, A. K., and COLEMAN, C. (1981). *Understanding Crime Rates*. Farnborough: Gower.

BOTTOMS, A., and WILES, P. (1996). 'Crime and Policing in a Changing Social Context' in W. Saulsbury, J. Mott, and T. Newburn (eds.) *Themes In Contemporary Policing*. London: Police Foundation/Policy Studies Institute.

—— and—— (1997). 'Environmental Criminology', in M. Maguire, R. Morgan, and R. Reiner (eds.), *The Oxford Handbook of Criminology*. (2nd edn.). Oxford: Oxford University Press.

BOWLING, B. (1999). *Violent Racism*. Oxford: Oxford University Press.

BOX, S., and RUSSELL, K. (1975). 'The Politics of Discreditability'. *Sociological Review* 23: 315–46.

BRODEUR, J. P. (ed.) (1998). *How to Recognise Good Policing*. Thousand Oaks, Cal.: Sage.

BROGDEN, M. (1977). 'A Police Authority: The Denial of Conflict'. *Sociological Review* 25: 325–49.

—— (1981). 'All Police is Conning Bastards', in B. Fine, A. Hunt, D. McBarnet, and B. Moorhouse (eds.), *Law, State and Society*. London: Croom Helm.

—— (1982). *The Police: Autonomy and Consent*. London: Academic Press.

—— (1987). 'The Emergence of the Police: The Colonial Dimension'. *British Journal of Criminology* 27: 4–14.

BROWN, D. (1997). *PACE Ten Years On: A Review of the Research*. Home Office Research Study 155, London: HMSO.

BROWN, J. (1996). 'Police Research: Some Critical Issues' in F. Leishman, B. Loveday, and S. Savage (eds.), *Core Issues in Policing*. London: Longman.

—— MAIDMENT, A., and BULL, R. (1993). 'Appropriate Skill-Task Matching or Gender Bias in Deployment of Male and Female Officers?' *Policing and Society*. 3: 121–36.

——and WATERS, I. (1993). 'Professional Police Research'. *Policing*, 9: 323–34.

BULMER, M., and REES, A. M. (eds.) (1996). *Citizenship Today: The Contemporary Relevance of T. H. Marshall*. London: UCL Press.

CAIN, M. (1971). 'On the Beat: Interactions and Relations in Rural and Urban Police Forces' in S. Cohen (ed.), *Images of Deviance*. Harmondsworth: Penguin.

—— (1973). *Society and the Policeman's Role*. London: Routledge.

—— (1977). 'An Ironical Departure: The Dilemma of Contemporary Policing' in K. Jones (ed.). *Yearbook of Social Policy in Britain*. London: Routledge.

—— (1979). 'Trends in the Sociology of Police Work'. *International Journal of Sociology of Law* 7: 143–67.

CALLINICOS, A. (1989). *Against Postmodernism*. Cambridge: Polity Press.

CASHMORE, E., and McLAUGHLIN, E. (eds.) (1991). *Out of Order?: Policing Black People*. London: Routledge.

CASTELLS, M. (1996–8). *The Information Age Vols. I–III*, Oxford: Blackwell.

CHAN, J. (1997). *Changing Police Culture*. Cambridge: Cambridge University Press.

CHATTERTON, M. (1976). 'Police in Social Control' in J. King (ed.), *Control Without Custody*. Cropwood Papers 7: 224–57. Cambridge: Institute of Criminology.

—— (1979). 'The Supervision of Patrol Work Under the Fixed Points System' in S. Holdaway (ed.), *The British Police*. London: Arnold.

—— (1983). 'Police Work and Assault Charges' in M. Punch (ed.), *Control in the Police Organisation*. Cambridge, Mass.: MIT Press.

CLARKE, R., and HOUGH, M. (eds.) (1980). *The Effectiveness of Policing.* Farnborough: Gower.

—— and —— (1984). *Crime and Police Effectiveness.* London: Home Office Research Unit.

COHEN, S. (1985). *Visions of Social Control.* Cambridge: Polity Press.

—— (1997a). 'Crime and Politics: Spot the Difference' in R. Rawlings (ed.), *Law, Society and Economy.* Oxford: Oxford University Press.

—— (1997b). 'The Revenge of the Null Hypothesis: Evaluating Crime Control Policies'. *The Critical Criminologist.* 8: 21–5.

—— and SCULL, A. (eds.) (1983). *Social Control and the State.* Oxford: Martin Robertson.

COWELL, D., JONES,T., and YOUNG, J. (eds.), *Policing the Riots.* London: Junction Books.

COX, B., SHIRLEY, J., and SHORT, M. (1977). *The Fall of Scotland Yard.* Harmondsworth: Penguin.

CRAWFORD, A., JONES, T., WOODHOUSE, T., and YOUNG, J. (1990). *The Second Islington Crime Survey.* London: Middlesex Polytechnic Centre for Criminology.

CURRIE, E. (1998). *Crime and Punishment in America.* New York: Holt.

DAVIES, N. (1998). *Dark Heart.* London: Verso.

—— (1999). 'Watching the Detectives: How the Police Cheat in Fight Against Crime'. *The Guardian,* 18 March, 12.

DAVIS, M. (1990). *City of Quartz.* London: Vintage.

DENNIS, N. (ed.) (1997). *Zero Tolerance Policing.* London: Institute of Economic Affairs.

DIXON, D. (1997). *Law in Policing.* Oxford: Oxford University Press.

—— BOTTOMLEY, A. K., COLEMAN, C., GILL, M., and Wall, D. (1989). 'Reality and Rules in the Construction and Regulation of Police Suspicion' *International Journal of the Sociology of Law* 17: 185–206.

—— —— —— —— and —— (1990). 'Safeguarding the Rights of Suspects in Police Custody'. *Policing and Society.* 1: 115–40.

DOWNES, D., and MORGAN, R. (1997). '"Dumping the "Hostages to Fortune"? The Politics of Law and Order in Post-War Britain' in M. Maguire, R. Morgan, and R. Reiner (eds.), *The Oxford Handbook of Criminology* (2nd edn.). Oxford: Oxford University Press.

EMSLEY, C. (1996). *The English Police: A Political and Social History* (2nd. edn.). Hemel Hempstead: Harvester Wheatsheaf.

ERICSON, R., and HAGGERTY, K. (1997). *Policing Risk Society.* Oxford: Oxford University Press.

FIELDING, N. (1987). 'Being Used By the Police'. *British Journal of Criminology,* 27: 63–72.

—— (1988). *Joining Forces.* London: Routledge.

—— (1991). *The Police and Social Conflict.* London: Athlone.

—— (1995). *Community Policing.* Oxford: Oxford University Press.

FOUCAULT, M. (1979). 'On Governmentality'. *Ideology and Consciousness,* 6: 5–23.

GARLAND, D. (1996). 'The Limits of the Sovereign State: Strategies of Crime Control in Contemporary Society'. *British Journal of Criminology* 36: 1–27.

—— (1997). 'Of Crime and Criminals: The Development of Criminology in Britain' in M. Maguire, R. Morgan, and R. Reiner (eds.), *The Oxford Handbook of Criminology* (2nd edn.). Oxford: Oxford University Press.

GIDDENS, A. (1994). *Beyond Left and Right.* Cambridge: Polity Press.

GILL, M., and MAWBY, R. (1990). *A Special Constable.* Aldershot: Avebury.

GOLDSMITH, A. (ed.)(1991). *Complaints Against the Police.* Oxford: Oxford University Press.

GOLDSTEIN, H. (1990). *Problem-Oriented Policing.* New York: McGraw Hill.

GOLDSTEIN, J. (1960). 'Police Discretion Not to Invoke the Criminal Process: Low Visibility
   Decisions in the Administration of Justice'. *Yale Law Journal.* 69: 543–94.
GRAEF, R. (1989). *Talking Blues.* London: Collins.
GREGORY, J., and LEES, S. (1999). *Policing Sexual Assault.* London: Routledge.
GRIMSHAW, R., and JEFFERSON, T. (1987). *Interpreting Policework.* London: Unwin.
HALL, S., CRITCHER, C., JEFFERSON, T., CLARKE, J., and ROBERTS, B. (1978). *Policing the Crisis.*
   London: Macmillan.
HEAL, K., TARLING, R., and BURROWS, J. (eds.) (1985). *Policing Today.* London: HMSO.
HEIDENSOHN, F. (1992). *Women in Control? The Role of Women in Law Enforcement.* Oxford:
   Oxford University Press.
—— (1994). 'We Can Handle It Out Here: Women Police Officers in Britain and the USA
   and the Policing of Public Order'. *Policing and Society.* 4: 293–303.
HIRST, P., and THOMPSON, G. (1996). *Globalisation in Question.* London: Polity Press.
HOBSBAWM, E. (1994). 'Barbarism: A User's Guide'. *New Left Review.* 206: 44–54.
HOLDAWAY, S. (1977). 'Changes in Urban Policing'. *British Journal of Sociology.* 28: 119–37.
—— (ed.) (1979). *The British Police.* London: Arnold.
—— (1983). *Inside the British Police.* Oxford: Blackwell.
—— (1989). 'Discovering Structure: Studies of the British Police Occupational Culture' in
   M. Weatheritt (ed.), *Police Research: Some Future Prospects.* Aldershot: Avebury.
—— (1991). *Recruiting A Multi-Ethnic Police Force.* London: HMSO.
—— (1996). *The Racialisation of British Policing.* London: Macmillan.
HOME OFFICE (1998). *Crime Reduction Programme Prospectus.* London: Home Office
   Research, Development and Statistics Directorate.
HOYLE, C. (1998). *Negotiating Domestic Violence: Police Criminal Justice and Victims.* Oxford:
   Oxford University Press.
HUDSON, B. (1997). 'Social Control' in M. Maguire, R. Morgan, and R. Reiner (eds.), *The
   Oxford Handbook of Criminology.* (2nd edn.). Oxford: Oxford University Press.
HUMPHRY, D. (1972). *Police Power and Black People.* London: Granada.
HUTTON, W. (1995). *The State We're In.* London: Vintage.
IRVING, B. (1980). *Police Interrogation.* Royal Commission on Criminal Procedure Research
   Study No.1. London: HMSO.
—— and McKENZIE, I. (1989). *Police Interrogation.* London: Police Foundation.
—— BIRD, C., HIBBERD, M., and WILLMORE, J. (1989). *Neighbourhood Policing.* London:
   Police Foundation.
JEFFERSON, T., and GRIMSHAW, R. (1984). *Controlling the Constable.* London: Muller.
—— McLAUGHLIN, E., and ROBERTSON, L. (1988). 'Monitoring the Monitors:
   Accountability, Democracy and Police Watching in Britain'. *Contemporary Crises* 12:
   91–107.
—— and SHAPLAND, J. (1994). 'Criminal Justice and the Production of Order and Control:
   Criminological Research in the UK in the 1980s'. *British Journal of Criminology* 34:
   265–90.
JOHNSTON, L. (1992). *The Rebirth of Private Policing.* London: Routledge.
—— (1998). 'Policing Communities of Risk' in P. Francis, P. Davies and V. Jupp (eds.),
   Policing Futures. London: Macmillan.
JONES, T., MACLEAN, B., and YOUNG, J. (1986). *The Islington Crime Survey.* Aldershot: Gower.
—— NEWBURN, T., and SMITH, D. (1994). *Democracy and Policing.* London: Policy Studies
   Institute.

—— and —— (1997). *Policing After the Act.* London: Policy Studies Institute.

—— and —— (1998). *Private Security and Public Policing.* Oxford: Oxford University Press.

JORDAN, P. (1998). 'Effective Policing Strategies for Reducing Crime' in C. Nuttall, P. Goldblatt, and C. Lewis (eds.), *Reducing Offending.* Home Office Research Study 187, London: Home Office.

KEMP, C., NORRIS, C., and FIELDING, N. (1992). *Negotiating Nothing: Police Decision-Making in Disputes.* Aldershot: Avebury.

KINSEY, R. (1984). *The Merseyside Crime Survey.* Liverpool: Merseyside County Council.

—— (1985a). *Survey of Merseyside Police Officers.* Liverpool: Merseyside County Council.

—— (1985b). *Merseyside Crime and Police Surveys: Final Report.* Liverpool: Merseyside County Council.

—— LEA, J., and YOUNG, J. (1986). *Losing the Fight Against Crime.* Oxford: Blackwell.

LAURIE, P. (1970). *Scotland Yard.* Harmondsworth: Penguin.

LAMBERT, J. (1969). 'The Police Can Choose'. *New Society* 14: 364, 430–2.

—— (1970). *Crime, Police and Race Relations.* Oxford: Oxford University Press.

LEA, J., and YOUNG, J. (1984). *What is to be Done about Law and Order?* Harmondsworth: Penguin.

LEE, M. (1998). *Youth, Crime and Police Work.* London: Macmillan.

LEISHMAN, F., LOVEDAY, B., and SAVAGE, S. (eds.) (1996). *Core Issues in Policing.* London: Longman.

LEVITAS, R. (1998). *The Inclusive Society?* London: Macmillan.

LEON, C. (1989). 'The Special Constabulary'. *Policing* 5: 265–87.

LOVEDAY, B. (1985). *The Role and Effectiveness of the Merseyside Police Committee.* Liverpool: Merseyside County Council.

—— (1987). 'The Joint Boards'. *Policing* 3: 196–213.

—— (1991). 'The New Police Authorities'. *Policing and Society* 1: 193–212.

LUSTGARTEN, L. (1986). *The Governance of the Police.* London: Sweet and Maxwell.

McBARNET, D. (1978). 'The Police and the State' in G. Littlejohn, B. Smart, J. Wakeford, and M. David (eds.), *Power and the State.* London: Croom Helm.

—— (1979). 'Arrest: The Legal Context of Policing' in S. Holdaway (ed.), *The British Police.* London: Arnold.

—— (1981). *Conviction.* London: Macmillan.

McCABE, S., and SUTCLIFFE, F. (1978). *Defining Crime.* Oxford: Blackwell.

—— WALLINGTON, P., ALDERSON, J., GOSTIN, L., and MASON, C. (1988). *The Police, Public Order and Civil Liberties.* London: Routledge.

McCONVILLE, M., SANDERS, A., and LENG, R. (1991). *The Case For the Prosecution: Police Suspects and the Construction of Criminality.* London: Routledge.

—— —— and —— (1997). 'Descriptive or Critical Sociology: The Choice is Yours'. *British Journal of Criminology* 3: 347–58.

—— and SHEPHERD, D. (1992). *Watching Police, Watching Communities.* London: Routledge.

McKENZIE, I., MORGAN, R., and REINER, R. (1990). 'Helping the Police With Their Inquiries'. *Criminal Law Review* 22–33.

McLAUGHLIN, E., and MURJI, K. (1996). 'Times Change: New Formations and Representations of Police Accountability' in C. Critcher and D. Waddington (eds.), *Policing Public Order.* Aldershot: Avebury.

—— and —— (1997). 'The Future Lasts a Long Time: Public Policework and the

Managerialist Paradox' in P. Francis, P. Davies, and V. Jupp (eds.), *Policing Futures.* London: Macmillan.

MacPherson, Sir W. (1999). *The Stephen Lawrence Inquiry.* London: The Stationery Office.

Maguire, M., and Corbett, C. (1991). *A Study of the Police Complaints System.* London: HMSO.

Manning, P. (1977). *Police Work.* Cambridge, Mass.: MIT Press.

—— (1979). 'The Social Control of Police Work' in S. Holdaway (ed.), *The British Police.* London: Arnold.

Marshall, T. H. (1950). *Citizenship and Social Class.* Cambridge: Cambridge University Press.

Martin, C. (1996). 'The Impact of Equal Opportunities Policies on the Day-to-Day Experiences of Women Police Constables'. *British Journal of Criminology* 36: 510–28.

Martin, J. P., and Wilson, G. (1969). *The Police: A Study in Manpower.* London: Heinemann.

Mastrofski, S. D., Parks, R. B., Reiss, A. J., Worden, R. E., DeJong, C., Snipes, J. B., and Terrill, W. (1998). *Systematic Observation of Public Police: Applying Field Research Methods to Policy Issues.* Washington, DC: National Institute of Justice.

Mawby, R. (1991). *Comparative Policing Issues.* London: Unwin.

Monkkonen, E. (1981). *Police in Urban America 1860–1920.* Cambridge: Cambridge University Press.

Morgan, R., and Newburn, T. (1997). *The Future of Policing.* Oxford: Oxford University Press.

Morris, P., and Heal, K. (1981). *Crime Control and the Police.* London: HMSO.

Norris, C. (1993). 'Some Ethical Considerations on Field-work with the Police' in D. Hobbs and T. May (eds.), *Interpreting the Field.* Oxford: Oxford University Press.

Nuttall, C., Goldblatt, P., and Lewis, C. (1998). *Reducing Offending.* Home Office Research Study 187, London: Home Office.

Palmer, S. H. (1988). *Police and Protest in England and Ireland 1780–1850.* Cambridge: Cambridge University Press.

Panitch, L., and Leys, C. (eds.) (1999). *Global Capitalism versus Democracy.* Socialist Register 1999. Rendlesham: Merlin Press.

Pasquino, P. (1978). 'Theatrum Politicum: The Genealogy of Capital—Police and the State of Prosperity'. *Ideology and Consciousness* 4: 41–54.

Pawson, R. and Tilley, N. (1994). 'What Works in Evaluation Research?' *British Journal of Criminology* 34: 291–306.

Police Foundation/Policy Studies Institute (1996). *The Role and Responsibilities of the Police: Report of an Independent Inquiry,* London: Police Foundation/Policy Studies Institute.

Punch, M. (1979a). *Policing the Inner City.* London: Macmillan.

—— (1979b). 'The Secret Social Service' in S. Holdaway (ed.), *The British Police.* London: Arnold.

—— (1985). *Conduct Unbecoming: The Social Construction of Police Deviance and Control.* London: Tavistock.

Rawlings, P. (1999). *Crime and Power: A History of Criminal Justice 1688–1998.* London: Longman.

Reiner, R. (1978a). *The Blue-coated Worker.* Cambridge: Cambridge University Press.

—— (1978b). 'The Police, Class and Politics'. *Marxism Today* 22: 69–80.

—— (1978c). 'The Police in the Class Structure'. *British Journal of Law and Society* 5: 166–84.

—— (1988). 'British Criminology and the State'. *British Journal of Criminology* 29: 138–58.

—— (1989). 'The Politics of Police Research' in M. Weatheritt (ed.), *Police Research: Some Future Prospects*. Aldershot: Avebury.

—— (1991). *Chief Constables*. Oxford: Oxford University Press.

—— (1992a). *The Politics of the Police* (2nd edn.). Hemel Hempstead: Wheatsheaf.

—— (1992b). 'Police Research in the United Kingdom: A Critical Review' in N. Morris and M. Tonry (eds.), *Modern Policing*. Chicago, Ill.: Chicago University Press.

—— (1992c). 'Policing A Postmodern Society'. *Modern Law Review* 55: 761–81.

—— (1994). 'A Truce in the War Between the Police and Academe'. *Policing Today*. 1: 30–2.

—— (1997). 'Policing and the Police' in M. Maguire, R. Morgan, and R. Reiner (eds.), *The Oxford Handbook of Criminology* (2nd edn.). Oxford: Oxford University Press.

——and SPENCER, S (eds.) (1993). *Accountable Policing: Effectiveness, Empowerment and Equity*. London: Institute for Public Policy Research.

REISS, A. (1968). 'Stuff and Nonsense About Social Surveys and Observation' in H. Becker, B. Greer, D. Riesman, and R. Weiss (eds.), *Institutions and the Person*. Chicago, Ill.: Aldine.

ROBINSON, C. D. (1979). 'Ideology As History'. *Police Studies* 2: 35–49.

—— and SCAGLION, R. (1987). 'The Origin and Evolution of the Police Function in Society'. *Law and Society Review* 21: 109–53.

—— SCAGLION, R., and OLIVERO, J. M. (1994). *Police In Contradiction*. Westport Conn.: Greenwood.

ROCK, P. (1973). *Deviant Behaviour*. London: Hutchinson.

ROSE, D. (1992). *A Climate of Fear: The Murder of PC Blakelock and the Case of the Tottenham Three*. London: Bloomsbury.

—— (1996). *In the Name of the Law: The Collapse of Criminal Justice*. London: Cape.

SAULSBURY, W., MOTT, J., and NEWBURN, T. (eds.) (1996). *Themes in Contemporary Policing*. London: Police Foundation/Policy Studies Institute.

SCHWARTZ, R. D., and MILLER, J. C. (1964). 'Legal Evolution and Societal Complexity'. *American Journal of Sociology* 70: 159–69.

SCRATON, P. (1985). *The State of the Police*. London: Pluto.

SHAPLAND, J., and VAGG, J. (1987). 'Using the Police'. *British Journal of Criminology* 27: 54–63.

—— and —— (1988). *Policing By the Public*. London: Routledge.

SHEARING, C. (1996). 'Public and Private Policing' in W. Saulsbury, J. Mott, and T. Newburn (eds.), *Themes in Contemporary Policing*. London: Police Foundation/Policy Studies Institute.

—— and ERICSON, R. (1991). 'Culture As Figurative Action'. *British Journal of Sociology* 42: 481–506.

—— and STENNING, P. (1983). 'Private Security: Implications for Social Control'. *Social Problems* 30: 493–506.

—— and—— (1984). 'From the Panopticon to Disney World' in A. N. Doob and E. L. Greenspan (eds.), *Perspectives in Criminal Law: Essays in Honour of John Ll. J. Edwards*. Toronto: Canada Law Book Co.

—— and—— (eds.) (1987). *Private Policing*. Beverly Hills, Cal.: Sage.

SHEPTYCKI, J. (1994). 'It Looks Different From the Outside'. *Policing* 10: 125–33.

—— (1995). 'Transnational Policing and the Makings of a Postmodern State'. *British Journal of Criminology* 35: 613–35.

SHEPTYCKI, J. (1997). 'Insecurity, Risk Suppression and Segregation: Some Reflections on Policing in the Transnational Age'. *Theoretical Criminology*. 1: 303–14.

SHERMAN, L. (1992). 'Police and Crime Control' in M. Tonry and N. Morris (eds.), *Modern Policing*. Chicago Ill.: Chicago University Press.

—— (1993). 'Why Crime Control is Not Reactionary' in D. Weisburd, C. Uchida, and L. Green (eds.), *Police Innovation and Control of Police*. New York: Springer-Verlag.

SKOLNICK, J. (1966). *Justice Without Trial*. New York: Wiley.

—— and BAYLEY, D. (1986). *The New Blue Line*. New York: Free Press.

—— and—— (1988). *Community Policing*. Washington, DC: National Institute of Justice.

SMITH, D. (1997). 'Case Construction and the Goals of Criminal Process'. *British Journal of Criminology* 37: 319–46.

—— (1998). 'Reform or Moral Outrage—The Choice is Yours'. *British Journal of Criminology* 38: 616–22.

—— GRAY, J., and SMALL, S. (1983). *Police and People in London*. London: Policy Studies Institute.

SOUTH, N. (1988). *Policing For Profit*. London: Sage.

—— (1998). 'Control, Crime and "End of Century" Criminology' in P. Francis, P. Davies, and V. Jupp (eds.), *Policing Futures*. London: Macmillan.

SPITZER, S., and SCULL, A. (1977). 'Privatisation and Capitalist Development: The Case of the Private Police'. *Social Problems* 25: 18–29.

SUMNER, C. (1997). 'Social Control: The History and Politics of a Central Concept in Anglo-American Sociology' in R. Bergalli and C. Sumner (eds.), *Social Control and Political Order*. London: Sage.

TAYLOR, H. (1998). 'Rising Crime: the Political Economy of Criminal Statistics Since the 1850s'. *Economic History Review* 5: 569–690.

—— (1999). 'Forging the Job: a Crisis of "Modernisation" or Redundancy for the Police in England and Wales 1900–39'. *British Journal of Criminology* 39: 113–35.

TAYLOR, I. (1997). 'The Political Economy of Crime' in M. Maguire, R. Morgan, and R. Reiner (eds.), *The Oxford Handbook of Criminology* (2nd edn.). Oxford: Oxford University Press.

TRAVERS, M. (1997). 'Preaching to the Converted? Improving the Persuasiveness of Criminal Justice Research'. *British Journal of Criminology*, 37: 359–77.

WADDINGTON, D. (1998). 'Waddington versus Waddington: Public Order Theory on Trial'. *Theoretical Criminology* 2: 373–94.

WADDINGTON, P. A. J. (1985). *The Effects of Manpower Depletion During the NUM Strike 1984–5*. London: Police Foundation.

—— (1991). *The Strong Arm of the Law*. Oxford: Oxford University Press.

—— (1993). *Calling the Police*. Aldershot: Avebury.

—— (1994). *Liberty and Order: Policing Public Order in a Capital City*. London: UCL Press.

—— (1999). *Policing Citizens*. London: UCL Press.

WALKLATE, S. (1992). 'Jack and Jill Join Up At Sun Hill: Public Images of Police Officers'. *Policing and Society* 2: 219–32.

—— (1996). 'Equal Opportunities and the Future of Policing' in F. Leishman, B. Loveday, and S. Savage (eds.), *Core Issues in Policing*. London: Longman.

WALL, D. (1998). *The Chief Constables of England and Wales*. Aldershot: Avebury.

WEATHERITT, M. (1985). *Innovations in Policing*, London: Croom Helm.

—— (1986). *Innovations in Policing*. London: Croom Helm.

—— (ed.) (1989). *Police Research: Some Future Prospects*. Aldershot: Avebury.

—— (1993). 'Measuring Police Performance: Accounting or Accountability?' in R. Reiner and S. Spencer (eds.), *Accountable Policing: Empowerment, Effectiveness and Equity*. London: Institute for Public Policy Research.

—— (ed.) (1998). *Zero Tolerance*. London: Police Foundation.

Weisburd, D., Uchida, C., and Green, L. (eds.) (1993). *Police Innovation and Control of the Police*. New York: Springer-Verlag.

Westley, W. (1970). *Violence and the Police*. Cambridge, Mass.: MIT Press.

Whitaker, B. (1964). *The Police*. London: Penguin.

Wilson, J. Q. (1975). *Thinking About Crime*. New York: Vintage.

Young, J. (1986). 'The Failure of Criminology: The Need for a Radical Realism', in R. Matthews and J. Young (eds.), *Confronting Crime*. London: Sage.

—— (1988). 'Radical Criminology in Britain'. *British Journal of Criminology* 28: 289–313.

—— (1994). *Policing the Streets*. London: Borough of Islington.

—— (1997a). 'From Inclusive to Exclusive Society: Nightmares in the European Dream' in V. Ruggiero, N. South, and I. Taylor (eds.), *European Criminology*. London: Routledge.

—— (1997b). 'Left Realist Criminology' in M. Maguire, R. Morgan, and R. Reiner (eds.), *The Oxford Handbook of Criminology* (2nd edn.). Oxford: Oxford University Press.

—— (1998). *The Criminology of Intolerance*. London: Middlesex University Centre for Criminology.

Young, M. (1991). *An Inside Job*. Oxford: Oxford University Press.

—— (1993). *In the Sticks: An Anthropologist in a Shire Force*. Oxford: Oxford University Press.

8

RESEARCH ON THE CRIMINAL COURTS

John Baldwin

INTRODUCTION

The criminal courts present enticing opportunities to criminological researchers. They are fascinating institutions, the decisions they take are of undoubted public importance, and they sometimes provide scenes of high drama. Politicians frequently invest the courts with almost mystical powers, seeing them as in the front-line in the war on crime. For researchers, the criminal courts have one great advantage over most other institutions within the criminal justice system: they are open to the public and no difficulties of access arise in observing them. Conducting research on the criminal courts need involve no more than turning up with a notebook, finding a convenient vantage point, and watching whatever takes place.

Although much can be learnt about the courts in this way, it will be argued in this chapter that court observation cannot in itself provide answers to many of the questions that one might wish to ask about the operation of the criminal courts. Many of these questions can only be explored with extreme difficulty. Indeed, there are certain no-go areas. It is not possible, for instance, to observe the way that sentencing decisions are reached, and researchers are actually prohibited by law from speaking to people who sit on juries. More serious still, judges, lawyers, and other court personnel have proved in the past to be almost uniquely resistant to social research. Members of the senior judiciary in particular have never been in the least enthusiastic about research, frequently viewing such endeavours as an unwarranted intrusion into matters that should be their business and no one else's.

For those of us who have conducted research in this climate in the past twenty years, the range of topics that we have been able to examine has been severely limited and the methods that we have been obliged to adopt have often been of necessity highly imperfect. Some projects have got off the ground only because researchers have employed considerable ingenuity and inventiveness.

Much of the research has a decided Heath Robinson feel to it, as researchers have devised imaginative strategies in order to overcome the access problems. Although judicial hostility has thawed somewhat in recent years, there is no denying that studying the way that the criminal courts work remains a very tricky undertaking.

The criminal courts have, however, become more accessible to researchers, in part a reflection of the decline in the public standing of the courts following the many miscarriages of justice that were brought to light in the 1990s (Walker and Starmer 1993; Dennis 1993; McConville and Bridges 1994; Wasik, Gibbons and Redmayne 1999: 563–71). One significant consequence of these revelations has been that politicians and policy-makers have become increasingly sceptical about the pontifications of senior lawyers and judges about how the courts are performing. The importance of research on the courts (and the criminal justice system in general) was acknowledged in both the Philips and Runciman Royal Commissions, whose reports were published in 1981 and 1993 respectively. These Commissions, both of which were concerned with issues relating to the operation of the criminal justice system, did much to change attitudes towards research. They not only initiated their own extensive research programmes (opening up in the process numerous new opportunities for researchers) but they also elevated the role of academic research to new heights because they claimed to be basing many of their recommendations upon it. Although there have been many occasions on which policy change has seemed to fly in the face of research findings—and curtailment of the accused's right to remain silent is but the latest example (Hunt and Young 1995–6)—it has nonetheless become much more common in the past decade for major policy changes in the courts to be preceded by some form of evaluative exercise. Even if resistance to research persists in the criminal courts, times are changing and new opportunities are opening up. The commitment of the new Labour government to 'evidence-led' criminal justice policy is likely to reinforce this process.

DESCRIBING THE RESEARCH EXPERIENCE

Although a much more professional approach to criminological research has been evident in recent years, people like myself who have been conducting criminological and related research for a number of years have often received precious little formal research training. I must confess that my own limited skills are in the main the result of long experience, a modicum of reading, and learning about research methods from others with whom I have collaborated. Many of us owe great debts of gratitude to PhD supervisors and other colleagues who have offered advice about technical aspects of doing research and communicated their own enthusiasm for the research enterprise. But this is inevitably a hit-and-miss approach which tends to be reflected in the way we write about research. It is odd that, if one reads the methodology texts or even published monographs, one often forms only a limited impression of what it is like to carry out research. In reading research reports, I am repeatedly struck by how scant is the information provided by many criminologists about the methods and the sampling procedures they have employed. If they bother to give such information at all, it is often relegated to a short paragraph, perhaps only a footnote. The tendency is baldly to state that 'interviews were conducted with a sample of . . . or 'questionnaires were distributed to . . .', and it is unusual for authors to present a copy of the questionnaires or the interview schedules they have used or even to say much about the general nature of the questions they have posed or the procedures they have followed. This makes critical evaluation of results extremely difficult, and most readers are, it seems, remarkably charitable in their willingness to accept results on trust.

Methodo-logical flaws.

One might go further and argue that criminological researchers are guilty of presenting a misleading picture because of their inclination to skate over the problems that they have encountered. I have seen for myself how uneasy officials (whether they be practitioners, civil servants, or representatives of funding bodies) become when researchers seek to report the details of discussions that were assumed to be off the record. This applies even when such exchanges have determined the way that a study has been conducted or influenced the form that a final report has taken. Given the limited published information available, it is not surprising that many people who start out on research are taken aback when they run into difficulties that they could not have foreseen. Any researcher interested in criminal justice issues may find, for instance, that it takes months of painful and frustrating negotiation simply to get a project off the ground, if indeed it gets off the ground at all. Even then, it may well prove impossible to conduct the study along the lines that were originally envisaged. Matters may become even more fraught when questions are raised about the publication of results. While organizations will usually tolerate critical research reports when they are kept private, many baulk at the prospect of public disclosure. There are, however, few descriptions of these common difficulties in the available literature.

EMPIRICAL AND THEORETICAL TRADITIONS

It would be wrong to imply that, because of the serious difficulties that arise in examining the work of the criminal courts, researchers have been put off from examining them. Quite the opposite is true, and numerous criminological studies (probably running into hundreds) concerned with the operation of the

funding determines research ·

criminal courts have been conducted in this country. But the character of this research has been increasingly determined by the interests of funding bodies rather than by researchers themselves. When surveying this huge number of disparate investigations, it is quickly apparent that most have been descriptive in nature, setting out to show how the courts (or, more accurately, particular aspects of their functions) operate in practice. There is nothing necessarily wrong with this since there is great public and political ignorance about the workings of the courts, and the legal mythology that surrounds the courts is remarkable for its endurance. But such emphasis on description, in a situation where funding bodies increasingly call the tune, has meant that only half-hearted efforts have been made by researchers to develop theoretical perspectives in relation to the operation of the criminal courts.

Much court research in this country has been conducted in the context of an empirical and 'reformist' tradition (Low 1978) with issues examined primarily from a legal or a policy perspective. It is not difficult to explain why 'policy-relevant' research is in the ascendancy. Since much of the funding for research on the criminal courts has come, directly or indirectly, from government sources, researchers have not on the whole been encouraged to engage in theoretical flights of fancy. In a general discussion of the development of criminology in the 1980s, Jefferson and Shapland (1994: 268) note how, despite expansion in the size of the research community itself, financial and other pressures within the academic environment have led to the 'growth of "safe", narrowly-focused, policy-relevant research, and a decline in critical research'. This pattern has become more marked in recent years in part as a result of the intense competition for contracts from government departments and from the two Royal Commissions. But, more fundamentally, it is a reflection of the growing insistence of funding bodies that research on the courts be of direct value and relevance to court users and policy-makers. It is, therefore, a sad, but perhaps inevitable, fact that the broad contours of criminological research on the courts reflect to a greater extent the demands of funding bodies, particularly when they are government departments, than the curiosity and the interests of the researchers concerned.

In so far as attempts have been made to develop theoretical perspectives on the workings of the criminal courts, three approaches which stand out as particularly promising and worthy of more sustained application may be briefly mentioned. First, variants of conflict theory have on occasion been used to explain why it is that the economically powerless are unlikely to receive a fair deal from state bureaucracies. It is suggested that courts and legal processes are likely only to reflect, reinforce, even to exacerbate inequalities and that the young, ethnic minorities, the unemployed, the dispossessed, and the poor (who comprise a majority of criminal defendants) are most likely to be disadvantaged in this situation (e.g. Box 1971; Sanders and Young 1994). Secondly, the

traditional representation of the criminal process as concerned with establishing 'truth' has been challenged by authors (e.g. McBarnet 1976; McConville,
Sanders and Leng 1991; Kalunta-Crumpton 1998) who see the 'truth' as being
socially 'constructed' and refracted through the processes of 'interpretation,
addition, substraction, selection and reformulation' (McConville, Sanders and
Leng 1991: 12). On this view, the facts of the prosecution's case are 'constructed'
from competing and malleable accounts presented by the parties. Thirdly, the
concept of 'court culture', originally developed in the United States (Church
1985), has been adapted to explain disparities in procedures and decision-
making from court to court in this country (e.g. Rumgay 1995; Hucklesby 1997).

But such theoretical forays are not common in the literature on the criminal
courts in this country. Much more pervasive is the large quantity of survey
research that has been carried out, much of it simple fact-gathering. There is no
disguising the fact that much research on courts falls squarely within the category of 'administrative criminology' (Sanders 1997a) in that it seeks to provide
management information primarily for use by members of the court bureaucracy, policy-makers, administrators, and others, particularly with a view to
improving the running of the court system. The bulk of this work has emanated, directly or indirectly, from the Home Office, and even a cursory glance at
the many Home Office reports that have been published in the past twenty
years reveals their prevailing character. Statistical tables tend to cover their
pages. As many as thirty tables (or the pie charts or bar diagrams that have to
some extent replaced tables in the 1990s) are by no means uncommon, even in
short monographs. The analysis of results generally owes more to high-level
statistics than to any underlying theoretical paradigm. In most of the reports,
little attempt is made at assessment or criticism. A good illustration of this
stubbornly atheoretical approach is seen in the celebrated Crown Court study
(Zander and Henderson 1993)—an inquiry that was undertaken under the auspices of the Royal Commission on Criminal Justice. This study of the criminal
courts is by far the most extensive ever undertaken in this country and was
based upon thousands of self-completion questionnaires distributed to judges,
prosecution and defence barristers, defence solicitors, the Crown Prosecution
Service, the police, court clerks, defendants, and members of juries. The authors
make no bones about their intentions. 'It was agreed', Michael Zander writes in
his introduction, 'that the report of the study would not include evaluation of
the data nor recommendations. It would simply report the results' (page xvii).
Like Mr Gradgrind in Dickens' *Hard Times*, the authors set out to present the
facts: it is not their intention to seek to understand, explain, or assess, let alone
engage in abstract theoretical speculation.

Although there is a strong view within the criminological community that
there is nothing wrong with conducting research that is closely aligned to the
policy interests of government, there are nonetheless various problems that

need to be recognized. In particular, issues tend to be viewed largely, if not exclusively, from the perspective of policy-makers or court administrators rather than of those on the receiving end of judicial processes. This raises an uncomfortable issue which is central in all criminological research: how have the 'problems' to be investigated by researchers been identified and defined? It is worth digressing to say something about this difficulty, and I shall illustrate it with reference to two of the studies in which I have myself participated. In the first (Baldwin and McConville 1977), Michael McConville and I were interested in the way that defendants in the Crown Court decided to plead guilty, and we raised doubts about the fairness of the pressures to which they were subject. We concluded that the rights of defendants were commonly infringed as efforts were made to induce them to plead guilty. We argued that the most potent pressure was exerted by the defendants' own lawyers, whose arm was strengthened by the sentencing system itself. The emphasis in a good deal of the subsequent writing on this subject has, however, shifted from a preoccupation with defendants' rights to a concern about the administrative problems created by 'cracked trials', especially the way that court resources are wasted when defendants plead guilty after their cases have been listed for trial (see further Bredar 1992; Zander and Henderson 1993: 149–58; Royal Commission on Criminal Justice 1993: 110–14; Plotnikoff and Woolfson 1993). The important point here is that the vantage point from which 'problems' are defined is critical in criminological research.

A further illustration of this difficulty emerged in a study that McConville and I conducted of the outcome of jury cases in the Crown Court (Baldwin and McConville 1979a). The question that the Home Office originally invited us to examine was whether the high rate of acquittal in the Crown Court (which was almost 50 per cent where defendants pleaded not guilty) could be justified and whether, as some prominent commentators (e.g. Mark 1973) were suggesting at the time, it was unreasonably high. We were, however, able to broaden the scope of the enquiry to include all jury cases and, in the final report, we expressed our concern about numbers of wrongful convictions by juries (Baldwin and McConville 1979a: 68–87) which we viewed as a more serious evil than that of perverse acquittal. Ten years later, the revelations about the large number of miscarriages of justice, almost all of which had followed jury trials, provided an unmistakable indication that to examine the problems thrown up by juries exclusively in terms of unacceptably high acquittal rates would have been dangerously misconceived.

One might observe, then, that a main difficulty with research that purports to be based on simple fact-gathering is that 'facts' are not unproblematic or self-evident realities. The 'truth' is not an objective reality waiting to be discovered, but is critically influenced by those with the political power to define the nature of the 'problems' that need to be explored.

THE EXISTING RESEARCH ON THE CRIMINAL COURTS

It is necessary in a chapter of this kind to delineate the main approaches that have been adopted in studying criminal courts in this country. The following discussion is not intended to be a comprehensive review of this body of research literature (for which, see Sanders and Young 1994; Sanders 1997*b*; Ashworth 1997), and a good deal of important work will inevitably be overlooked in the following account. But it is worth attempting to identify the major landmarks in the available research on the courts and to offer a commentary on the main approaches that have been adopted. Five general approaches (which do not fall neatly into watertight compartments) can be identified: the large-scale statistical surveys of courts and court users; studies concerned with 'demythologizing' criminal justice; observation of court hearings; research concerned with the pre-trial 'shaping' of cases for trial, and studies of the deliberative processes of decision-makers.

Statistical surveys of courts and court users Reports are now regularly published on delays in hearing cases in the magistrates' courts; opinion polls are taken of public attitudes towards the courts and sentencers, and surveys are conducted of the reactions of court users to the standard of service offered by the courts. In addition, about twenty studies of the criminal courts have to date been published by the Home Office Research and Statistics Directorate (or its forerunner). These reports deal with a great variety of questions, and the list includes—to pick a few publications on courts almost at random—studies of sentencing practices (Tarling 1979; Moxon 1988; Flood-Page and Mackie 1998), the efficacy of time limits in reducing the delays in bringing cases to trial (Morgan and Vennard 1989), mode of trial decisions (Riley and Vennard 1988; Hedderman and Moxon 1992), decisions to adjourn cases (Whittaker and Mackie 1997), and public attitudes to the courts and sentencing (Hough and Roberts 1998). There have been significant shifts in the way that research has been undertaken by members of the Home Office over the years, and one should not underestimate the value or the importance of this work. Even if there are certain inherent difficulties with policy-driven research, even the most grudging critic would recognize that much Home Office research is methodologically sophisticated, well informed by the relevant literature, and conducted on a larger scale than a lone researcher could possibly achieve. The esteem in which Home Office researchers are held within the criminological community is indicated by the fact that they are amongst the most frequently cited in the standard academic literature (see Cohn and Farrington 1998).

'Demythologizing' criminal justice Since the criminal courts have attracted so much adverse publicity in the past decade, it is not surprising that the focus of much research has been to uncover malfunctioning in courts' operations. Many

studies have indicated that a wide hiatus exists between high legal principle and the daily reality of the administration of justice in the courts—what Sanders (1997a) has labelled 'gap' research. The truth is, as a generation of criminal justice researchers in this country has come to recognize, the operation of the criminal courts can scarcely be said to live up to its own rhetoric. Although the criminal courts espouse certain inalienable values, such as the presumption of innocence, the right of the accused to be tried by a jury of peers, and the requirement that proof be established before an impartial tribunal beyond reasonable doubt, these rights translate in practice into pale shadows in the great majority of cases heard in the criminal courts.

'Demythologizing' criminal justice is now a growth industry. Most of the relevant research has been highly critical in tone as study after study has highlighted serious flaws in courts' operations. It is well established in this literature (Sanders and Young 1994: 249–318) that the criminal courts, in common with other legal institutions, frequently do not work in the ways that the criminal law textbooks describe. Researchers have demonstrated, for example, in relation to the award of legal aid (e.g. Young, Moloney and Sanders 1992), legal representation (e.g. McConville et al. 1994), the discontinuance of weak prosecution cases (e.g. Block, Corbett and Peay 1993; Baldwin 1997), bail (e.g. Brink and Stone 1988; Hucklesby 1997), and plea (e.g. Baldwin and McConville 1977; Baldwin 1985; McConville et al. 1994), that the procedures adopted in the criminal courts fall short of what one would expect from reading the standard legal texts. Rights of defendants, which are assumed to be absolute and non-negotiable, seem in many circumstances to be based on a very flimsy legal foundation indeed. The available evidence (Carlen 1976; McBarnet 1981) indicates that this disparity is likely to be even greater in magistrates' courts than in the Crown Court. 'Magistrates' courts are crime control courts overlaid with a thin layer of due process icing' is how the point is made by Sanders and Young (1994: 304).

Observation of court hearings Despite its immediate appeal, it is curious that few criminologists have spent much time in the courts engaged in prolonged and systematic court observation. One would, for instance, be hard-pressed to find examples of this kind of research in the past five years published in, say, the *British Journal of Criminology* and the *Howard Journal of Criminal Justice*—two mainstream British criminological journals. This is certainly not because such an approach is useless or subject to irremediable methodological flaws. Indeed, where researchers have troubled to spend time in the courts, the exercise has often produced great dividends, and five studies which were based in varying degrees upon court observation—by Bottoms and McClean (1976), Carlen (1976), McBarnet (1981), Darbyshire (1984), and Rock (1993)—provide outstanding examples of what can be achieved simply by watching the criminal courts in action. These studies have contributed in significant ways to an

understanding of the influence of 'court-culture' on decision-making and the [+ive]
importance of examining the relationships that exist between the various court
actors. There have also been a number of other, small-scale but highly illuminating observational studies concerned with the way that complainants, especially those involved in rape trials, and other witnesses are treated in the courts
(e.g. Adler 1982, 1987; Temkin 1987; Lees 1996).

Court observation can, however, be deceptively straightforward, and anyone
who spends time in courtrooms quickly becomes aware of its drawbacks. The
most obvious is that, whatever fascination courts may hold, they are nevertheless subject to lengthy periods of unrelenting tedium. Much of the business of
the criminal courts is, as Bottoms and McClean (1976: 226) noted, 'dull, com-   [-ive]
monplace, ordinary and after a while downright tedious'. There are frequent
periods in any court where little seems to be happening. Delays and adjournments dog the work of the courts, and the consequent administrative inertia
can sap the energy and enthusiasm of even the most committed researcher.
Furthermore, proceedings in courts can be extremely confusing. Much has been
written about the sense of alienation that defendants experience as they confront legal processes and about the way that court procedures are much more
closely attuned to the needs of the professionals than to those of defendants.
The study by McConville *et al.* (1994), concerned with the organization of
criminal defence practices, offers powerful evidence of this and forms part of an
empirical tradition, dating back to the Bottoms and McClean study in the 1970s,
which has drawn attention to the tendency of court professionals to take con-   [power of]
trol of criminal cases, reducing defendants to such a passive and subsidiary   [lawyers.]
position that they become malleable and acquiescent, prepared to accept the
lawyer's view of matters and powerless themselves to influence the course of
events. What is less often noted is that researchers are in a similar position to
defendants. They are not consulted about decisions either, and they may feel a
sense of exclusion, estrangement, and alienation that is comparable to that   [alienation]
experienced by defendants. Researchers are seriously handicapped when they   [of]
are excluded from the significant action, and court procedures can be as baffling   [researchers]
to them as to anyone else as a result.

An even more serious problem with observational research is that open court
proceedings present only the public face of justice. Researchers who sit in court
commonly realize, with a sense of unease, that the really important decisions in
most cases are being taken elsewhere. The sight of judges, jurors, and magistrates traipsing out of court to consider decisions in the privacy of their retiring
rooms is simply the most visible manifestation of this. A much greater problem
for researchers is that many crucial decisions are made by the parties even
before the case reaches the courtroom. Much of what happens in court is
predetermined by what has happened at a number of earlier stages in the
criminal process, particularly what has transpired in the police interrogation

room, in informal discussions between prosecution and defence lawyers (perhaps with the involvement of the judge at a Plea and Directions Hearing), or in private exchanges between defendants and their lawyers. It is in these pre-trial encounters that cases are 'shaped' for the court hearing, with the result that much judicial decision-making consists of little more than ratifying decisions that have already been agreed between the parties in advance of the hearing.

The pre-trial 'shaping' of cases This brings me to the fourth approach to the study of the criminal courts which involves examining off-the-record, pre-trial decision-making. Research along these lines has developed in recognition of the point that, if we are to understand decisions taken within the criminal courts, the influence of pre-trial decision-making needs to be considered. The crucial decision here is the defendant's choice of plea—a decision that is in practice just as likely to reflect the knowledge and bargaining position of the respective parties as the strength of the prosecution's evidence. It has been increasingly acknowledged that judicial decision-making, including sentencing, is influenced by the complex interplay of relations amongst various court actors and that pre-trial decisions taken by police officers, defence and prosecution lawyers, and defendants have a critical bearing upon what happens in court. Although this point was made in the United States half a century ago, it has taken a long time to dawn on researchers in this country. Any understanding of the workings of the criminal courts is, then, incomplete without an appreciation of the pre-trial processes that shape cases for trial.

It is important to recognize that, whatever the rhetoric, the criminal justice system in this country is a very efficient mechanism in generating a high level of guilty pleas (Baldwin and McConville 1977; McConville *et al.* 1994). It is striking that, in many pre-trial discussions, criminal justice rhetoric is subverted and replaced by apparently diametrically opposed values. Many years ago, Bottomley (1973: 84) presciently noted the paradox that, whatever weight is attached to the principle of the presumption of innocence, 'once a person has appeared in court facing a criminal charge many of the subsequent decisions taken by the various parties concerned . . . often seem to be influenced rather by a principle of "assumption of guilt"'. While the common assumption in legal texts is that defendants will plead not guilty and even be tried by a jury, jury trials are in practice the rare exception. No more than 2 per cent of all defendants eligible to be tried by jury are ultimately tried in that way. Over 90 per cent of defendants whose cases reach the courts end up pleading guilty, generally in the lower courts. In these circumstances, there is no contest, no testing of evidence, no calling of witnesses, and no open court trial. At the hearing itself, the prosecution's evidence tends to be dealt with perfunctorily, and, instead of it taking hours or even days to hear witnesses, cases are disposed of in a matter of minutes.

It would be difficult to overstate the importance to the work of the criminal courts of the commonplace observation that the vast majority of defendants plead guilty. The profound legal, moral, and theoretical implications of the guilty plea continue to be unravelled. That so high a proportion of defendants plead guilty at court sometimes comes as a surprise to those unfamiliar with the subject. But why does it happen? How can one explain the rarity of contested trials in courts that are said to be committed to the principle of open-court, adversarial contest? The answer is that pre-trial criminal procedures and the sentencing system in this country are specifically structured to induce defendants to plead guilty. The most potent pressure on defendants is the so-called discount principle in sentencing. This principle, which is bolstered by a long line of decisions by the Court of Appeal (Sanders and Young 1994: 320–8; Ashworth 1998: 267–97), has established that those who plead guilty are entitled to a hefty reduction in sentence. But being well established does not make the principle fair, and doubts might be raised about the blanket application of the principle and whether there is a danger that it might induce innocent as well as guilty people to plead guilty.

It hardly needs to be stated that formidable difficulties face any researcher who wishes to examine the way that guilty pleas are reached. I speak here from personal experience, and later in the chapter I shall present a case study, based on my own experience, to demonstrate how acute the difficulties can sometimes be. Guilty pleas are, *par excellence*, 'low visibility' decisions in that all the interesting exchanges take place off the record, often in hurried and furtive encounters at the doors of the courts. As is clear from a mountain of literature on the vexed subject of 'plea bargaining' in the United States, guilty pleas are frequently determined in bargaining sessions that are at once underhand and unsavoury. Such dealings are, indeed, often deliberately hidden, not just from public view but from that of the courts as well. So how can one possibly examine decisions of this kind where the parties themselves may well have an interest in keeping the procedures strictly private?

There is probably no way that this can be done adequately, and researchers have had to make the best of the limited access that has been granted them. Twenty years ago, Michael McConville and I (Baldwin and McConville 1977) sought to examine these decisions simply by asking a sample of defendants (all of whom had indicated from the start their wish to be tried by jury but pleaded guilty at the last minute) how they came to make what seemed on the surface a rather strange decision. This raises obvious methodological difficulties about the extent to which one can accept at face value what defendants say about their experiences, an issue which will be raised again later. In a subsequent study (Baldwin 1985), I was able to get closer to the negotiations between prosecution and defence lawyers when I was allowed to observe their exchanges (and tape record them) at formal pre-trial reviews in the magistrates' courts. (The pre-trial review is a special procedure used at some courts to allow the lawyers to meet some weeks before trial and determine issues likely to be in contention.) The exchanges between lawyers at pre-trial reviews in the magistrates' courts have also been the subject of subsequent research (Brownlee, Mulcahy and Walker 1994; Mulcahy 1994).

No researcher has got closer to uncovering what happens in these pre-trial stages than McConville and his colleagues (1994) who were able to persuade forty-eight law firms throughout the country to allow them to 'shadow' solicitors as they went about their business and observe the way that they dealt with cases. Although direct observation of this kind is a time-consuming (and therefore expensive) exercise and one that is far from free from methodological problems of its own, the study nonetheless revealed much about solicitor–client interactions that simply could not have been discovered by other methods. The portrayal of the criminal courts not 'as trial venues but as places where defendants can be processed through guilty pleas' (McConville *et al.* 1994: 210) has profound implications for the courts themselves. The somewhat churlish complaint by Brown (1997: 108) that the sample of lawyers that was shadowed in the study was unrepresentative—when representativeness would be all but impossible to achieve in research of this kind—underlines the point that in criminological research there is a danger that even the most imaginative and revealing initiatives may be sacrificed on the high altar of an elusive methodological purity.

Studies of the deliberative processes of decision-makers The clear implication of the above discussion of pre-trial processes is that it is simplistic, even misconceived, to view sentencing in the criminal courts in a vacuum, as if it were a stand-alone decision, uninfluenced by the way that cases are 'constructed' for trial. Sentencing itself should be regarded as being contingent upon the way that cases are prepared for trial and examined within that broad context. The failure to do this in studies of sentencing disparities represents a significant weakness. A number of useful studies have, however, been concerned with decision-making within the courtroom, and this fifth category of research has been concerned to explore the deliberative procedures of judges, magistrates, and juries. Again, the problems that arise in studying such decision-making are formidable. As noted earlier, senior members of the judiciary in this country have never been willing to participate in empirical research projects, tending to regard requests that they do so almost as an impertinence. But this has not meant that their decisions have been entirely immune from research, and, in a few studies, the sentencing patterns of magistrates and judges have been examined, albeit in an anonymous, statistical manner, not on a judge-by-judge basis (Hood 1962, 1992; Tarling 1979; Hedderman and Moxon 1992; Moxon and Hedderman 1994; Flood-Page and Mackie 1998). However, the question of sentencing disparities (according to race, gender, and type of courts), which has preoccupied a generation of researchers in the United States, has been curiously neglected in this country. With the notable exception of the almost single-handed efforts of Roger Hood (1962, 1972, 1992), virtually all the substantial statistical research on sentencing disparities in this country has been done by researchers within the Home Office.

Those who have tried to go beyond the statistics and talk directly to judges have been frustrated. The illuminating case study provided by Ashworth *et al.* (1984) gives a good indication of the depth of judicial hostility to such exercises. Yet judicial distaste for research has not altogether prevented criminologists from involving sentencers in their inquiries, although it has always been lay magistrates rather than the professional judiciary who have participated. One approach has been to interview samples of magistrates about the way they go about sentencing, and at least half a dozen studies have involved such interviews (see Burney 1979; Eaton 1986; Parker, Sumner and Jarvis 1989; Brown 1991; Rumgay 1995; and Flood-Page and Mackie 1998). As Parker, Sumner and Jarvis (1989: 39) argue, it is possible to 'get to the heart of the sentencing decision directly and immediately' by speaking to magistrates, and they were able in their study to develop important arguments about the imperviousness of magistrates' sentencing decisions to outside control from this interview material. In a similar way, Rumgay (1995: 203) used the material she collected from extended interviews with magistrates to find out about 'the traditions and perspectives which guided the collective decision making of this disparate group of [magistrates]' and she drew a number of conclusions about the influence of 'court culture' on local sentencing patterns. It is noteworthy that several of these studies have indicated how the private views and attitudes of lay magistrates may run counter to the spirit of legislation and be reflected in sentencing decisions.

If researchers have experienced difficulties in examining the decisions taken by sentencers, these are slight when compared to the problems they have faced in seeking to examine the operation of the jury system. Jurors themselves are out of bounds because they are prohibited by law from revealing the secrets of the jury room to researchers or anyone else. Section 8 of the Contempt of Court Act 1981 states that 'it is a contempt of court to obtain, disclose or solicit any particulars of statements made, opinions expressed, arguments advanced or votes cast by members of a jury in the course of their deliberations'. Some writers (e.g. Devons 1965) have gone as far as to suggest that the reason that the jury needs such protection is that it would not survive if its deliberations were to be subjected to rigorous scrutiny. Limited dispensation was, it is true, granted to Zander and Henderson (1993) under the auspices of the Royal Commission on Criminal Justice to distribute questionnaires to over 9,000 jurors who sat in Crown Courts throughout the country in two weeks in 1992. Even though the ɔnnaire included very interesting questions about jurors' understanding of evidence and the judge's summing up, the study was much more successful in providing information about jury composition and about the experience of jury service than in increasing understanding of the way that verdicts themselves were reached.

Despite the severe restrictions imposed on researchers in this country, several studies of jury decision-making have nonetheless been conducted. A number of imaginative, if limited, approaches have been adopted, including laboratory re-enactments of jury trials in front of 'simulated' juries (Sealy and Cornish 1973a, 1973b); the employment of 'shadow' volunteers to sit almost literally alongside the real jury in the courtroom (McCabe and Purves 1974; McConville 1991), and examination of other participants' comments on the validity of juries' verdicts (Zander 1974; Baldwin and McConville 1979a; Zander and Henderson 1993: 162–72). Much of this work illustrates the point that, with sufficient ingenuity, no legal institution is truly beyond the reach of research.

A CASE STUDY IN THE POLITICS AND ETHICS OF RESEARCH

I have argued that, in order to understand how courts work, it is not enough simply to observe what happens in open court because so many decisions are determined by the various actors in the pre-trial stages. It is worth examining in greater detail some of the consequences for researchers who seek to investigate the controversial issue of plea negotiation in the criminal courts and to consider the trouble that can ensue when they insist on writing about their findings. Over twenty years ago, Michael McConville and I explored this issue in the Birmingham Crown Court, and, in the process, we raised doubts about procedures commonly adopted at that time in Crown Courts. We were particularly concerned that undue pressures were exerted upon defendants to induce them to plead guilty, and we argued that some innocent defendants were persuaded to plead guilty in court as a result. As comparatively young men at the time, McConville and I were ill-prepared for the concerted attack that was launched on our report. Since the difficulties that arose in this study are still endemic in the research enterprise, it may be instructive to consider our experience as a case study of the pressures to which criminological researchers may be subject.

In the mid-1970s, in a project that was funded by the Home Office, McConville and I were examining the outcome of jury trials in the Birmingham Crown Court. We were, however, frequently frustrated because many of the cases that the court authorities had predicted would be jury trials ended abruptly with defendants pleading guilty at the doors of the court, minutes before the trial was due to start. As an adjunct to our jury study, we decided to try to find out why this was happening. We could not talk to the barristers concerned because the Senate of the Bar, after prolonged but fruitless negotiations with us, had adamantly refused to allow individual barristers to participate in any aspect of our enquiry. We interviewed 121 of the defendants who had been involved in last-minute changes of plea and asked them how they had reached what seemed on the surface a curious decision. The replies we received took us by surprise. With remarkable consistency, the defendants (including a minority who claimed to be innocent of the charges they faced) told us how they had been caught up in various out-of-court deals and how a variety of pressures had been exerted upon them, in the main by their own barristers, to persuade them to plead guilty. It seemed to us that we had stumbled upon the underhand, even shabby, side of the administration of criminal justice, at variance with textbook descriptions of criminal trials in England. Since the subject of plea negotiation had scarcely been raised in the relevant literature in this country (unlike the situation in the United States), we decided to write a book about this aspect of the research.

To say that this book was unwelcome would be a serious understatement, and it was without doubt considered very bad form in many quarters even to raise the subject of plea negotiation, let alone to discuss it in print. Months before publication of our results, McConville and I found ourselves on the receiving end of a ferocious public attack, and we became extremely unpopular amongst senior members of the legal profession and the judiciary. Years later, Sir Thomas Bingham (1993: 323)—when he was Master of the Rolls—described us as being 'the legal equivalent of Salman Rushdie'. In the course of the assault that was launched against us, we were subject to intense pressure from the Bar, the Law Society, and the Home Office to shelve the idea of publication of the book. For over three months, senior members of the legal profession conducted a well-orchestrated campaign in the media intended both to discredit the report (at that stage in draft form) and to raise doubts about our competence and integrity as academic researchers (Baldwin and McConville 1979b).

The first signs of trouble were evident in May 1977 after we had distributed a confidential draft of our report, *Negotiated Justice*, to interested parties for comment some months before publication. Details of our results were leaked to the *Sunday Express*, and its front page headline, 'Do-a-deal barristers in law row', sparked off the controversy. I still remember well the sense of shock at the hostility shown by the legal establishment. Sir David Napley (who was at that time the President of the Law Society and a member of the steering group appointed to advise on the research) appeared on television on the Monday evening following the *Sunday Express* leak to denounce the study. The then

Chairman of the Bar also went into print and dismissed the study as 'a compilation of unsubstantiated anecdotes' and as being no more than 'the tittle-tattle of the cells'. The Senate of the Bar wrote to the Home Secretary urging him to discourage publication of the book which, it was said, would be 'directly contrary to the public interest'. The Chairman of the Criminal Bar Association went even further and, in a front page article in the *Guardian Gazette* (a leading journal for legal practitioners), accused us of being in breach of our contract with the Home Office and of breaking guarantees of confidentiality—slurs that were subsequently retracted and for which a full public apology was made. The Home Secretary, who had made a lengthy statement later in May 1977 about our draft report in the House of Commons, contacted the Vice-Chancellor in our University, the late Lord Hunter, to warn him of the serious consequences to the University if the book were to be published.

Michael McConville and I, in the company of our Dean, were immediately summoned to meet the Vice-Chancellor, and I can still recall with grim clarity the discussion in his rather gloomy, cavernous room. He warned us of the risks of any precipitate move on our part to publish controversial findings of this kind. He instructed us that we were not to go ahead with our publication plans until he had conducted his own enquiry within the University and satisfied himself that the study was sound and that the conclusions that were drawn were reasonably based. He said that he had already contacted three Emeritus Professors and asked them to read the draft report and to comment on it. In the meantime, we were told to have no contact with the press and not to respond to any further attacks upon the study. McConville and I then had to wait for several weeks for the inquiry to be completed. It goes without saying that this was a period of the greatest anxiety for us because we felt that our University careers were in the balance. In the event, the Vice-Chancellor announced that we had been 'vindicated' by the committee's inquiry and that we could after all go ahead with publication. He volunteered (albeit with subsequent misgivings about the offer) to contribute a Foreword to the book.

The point of this lengthy description is neither to rake over old embers of something that happened over twenty years ago nor to gloat over a modest moral victory, still less to gain any frisson of pleasure from retelling a cautionary tale about the risks of engaging in criminological research. The main lesson to be derived from this experience—and this has been reinforced on several occasions in subsequent years—is that seeking to challenge powerful vested interests within the judicial system is a dangerous blood sport and a determination to publish unpalatable results is a high-risk activity. Seeking to tell it 'as it is' may sound fine in the methodological texts but it can prove a painful and costly undertaking, and any researcher who wishes to do so can expect to win few friends or accolades. He or she may, indeed, find that the going gets extremely rough, and public criticism (even public vilification) may in the end be the price that has to be paid if a critical report is to see the light of day.

The easy option is of course to seek to reach an accommodation with critics, and, if a compromise can be reached without sacrifice of principle, then this is a preferred course. But in my experience this is rarely possible, and, to the extent that attempts at appeasement involve the watering down or removal of offending passages in a report, the researcher's own independent status will be violated. Appeasement will undoubtedly smooth the path to publication (and there are in the standard literature an unknown number of reports that have been emasculated in this way) but such a course quickly becomes self-defeating. It is my strong conviction that, unless researchers are prepared to resist the pressures that inhibit the free publication of results, whatever personal cost this may entail, they should not be in the business of conducting academic research. This is not to say that interested parties should be denied an opportunity to comment on the contents of draft reports. On the contrary, they have a right to do so, and researchers have a duty to pay careful heed to points that are made and, if need be, to amend drafts accordingly. However, it is vital, even axiomatic, that the content of any final report should be the researcher's responsibility and no one else's and that all pressure to discourage the publication of results be firmly resisted. But it is also axiomatic that those who are criticized in research reports have themselves an absolute right to respond, and to do so publicly if they wish. For some researchers, acrimonious public debate, in the press and even in a TV studio, is as much part of the hurly-burly of academic writing as coping with unfavourable reviews and hostile rejoinders.

This experience of being on the rough end of criticisms from senior members of the legal profession and judiciary also brought home the acute ethical dilemmas that confront criminological researchers. In particular, the charge was made by senior members of the Bar that, since Michael McConville and I had claimed to have uncovered instances of serious miscarriage of justice and had impugned the integrity of members of the Bar, we ought to reveal the identities of the cases and individuals concerned so that matters could be rigorously investigated. The researcher's responsibilities in this regard are, I would suggest, far from being clear-cut, and I am myself doubtful that there would be any consensus in the criminological community about how far researchers should be prepared to reveal such information. In many situations of this kind, there is, it seems, precious little guidance available to researchers. While all professional criminologists would no doubt agree that the confidentiality of materials must be guaranteed and that respondents must be assured that their anonymity will be respected, other questions commonly arise on which one cannot be so unequivocal. Is a researcher, for instance, ever justified in being less than completely candid with respondents about the objectives of a study, knowing that full disclosure is likely to produce guarded, even distorted, responses? Should people ever be observed without their knowledge, when seeking their permission might have detrimental consequences for the study? Does the moral injunction that we do not distress, annoy, or embarrass participating organizations or individuals extend to the preparation and publication of critical reports? Criminological researchers have operated for many years without a written code of conduct or code of ethics, and the British Society of Criminology has recently published such a code. Although there is a danger that the promulgation of codes of conduct might be seen by researchers as a bureaucratic straitjacket, inhibiting their activities through the adoption of arbitrary or questionable standards, the absence of a code of conduct has nevertheless meant that the resolution of everyday, but acute, ethical difficulties has been treated as a matter for the researcher's own conscience.

CONCLUSION

Reports of research almost always provide a simpler, tidier, and more straightforward account of the process than that experienced by researchers in the field. By the time of publication, the creases have usually been ironed out of reports and the dog-fights that have taken place suppressed or forgotten. For a variety of personal and professional reasons, criminological researchers tend to be reticent about describing the problems that have arisen in the course of their investigations. Indeed, there are few accounts in the standard literature of the kind of problems that any researcher is likely to face in seeking to examine politically sensitive issues or to publish unpopular or unpalatable results.

Those of us who have had long experience of conducting research in and around the courts know something of these problems. In addition, we know how tiresome it can be to negotiate access and how disagreeable it is to encounter the hostility of certain groups to the very notion of 'research'. We have also experienced at first hand the drudgery that is involved in much academic research, the long hours spent sitting on hard benches in courts, the frustrations of wasted days, and the confrontations with disgruntled respondents. And we have found that in the end there is no guarantee whatever that our efforts will be appreciated. Worse still, many of us have had to confront intractable problems at the publication stage, and have come to accept how tough life can get when we become subject to insidious pressures to soften or distort the tenor of our findings.

This is, however, the bleak side of criminological research, and, as someone who has devoted a substantial part of his working life to conducting empirical research—and earned a reasonable living by doing so—I would not in any way wish to present a picture of academic research that is negative or off-putting. There are very many tangible and intangible benefits and privileges attached to conducting academic research, and for my part I have found it to be a uniquely satisfying and worthwhile activity. Criminological researchers are justified in being proud of what they do and of what they can achieve, and they are entitled to be gratified in knowing that their work is read and, on occasion, quoted. Those who have shared this experience also appreciate the fiercely addictive character of academic research and the genuine sense of excitement that attends the discovery of new knowledge.

SUGGESTIONS FOR FURTHER READING

Accounts of research on the criminal courts, as with other areas of criminology, are not noted for the attention they give to methodological issues. However, the following all contain methodological discussions which are likely to be of interest to would-be researchers.

ASHWORTH, A., GENDERS, E., MANSFIELD, G., PEAY, J., and PLAYER, E. (1984). *Sentencing in the Crown Court*. Occasional Paper No 10. University of Oxford. Oxford: Centre for Criminological Research.

JEFFERSON, T., and SHAPLAND, J. (1994). 'Criminal Justice and the Production of Order and Control: Criminological Research in the UK in the 1980s'. *British Journal of Criminology* 34: 265–90.

LOW, C. (1978). 'The Sociology of Criminal Justice: Progress and Prospects' in J. Baldwin and A.K. Bottomley (eds.), *Criminal Justice: Selected Readings*. London: Martin Robertson.

McCONVILLE, M., HODGSON, J., BRIDGES, L., and PAVLOVIC, A. (1994). *Standing Accused: The Organisation and Practices of Criminal Defence Lawyers in Britain*. Oxford: Clarendon Press.

SANDERS, A. (1997). 'Criminal Justice: The Development of Criminal Justice Research in Britain' in P.A. Thomas (ed.), *Socio-Legal Studies*. Aldershot: Dartmouth.

I am very grateful to my colleagues, Dr Adrian Hunt and Mr Stephen Shute, for their advice on an earlier draft of this chapter.

REFERENCES

ADLER, Z. (1982). 'Rape—The Intention of Parliament and the Practice of the Courts'
    Modern Law Review 45: 664–75.
—— (1987). Rape on Trial. London: Routledge and Kegan Paul.
ASHWORTH, A. (1997). 'Sentencing', in M. Maguire, R. Morgan, and R. Reiner (eds.),
    The Oxford Handbook of Criminology (2nd edn.). Oxford: Oxford University Press.
—— (1998). The Criminal Process: An Evaluative Study (2nd edn.). Oxford: Oxford
    University Press.
—— GENDERS, E., MANSFIELD, G., PEAY, J., and PLAYER, E. (1984). Sentencing in the Crown
    Court. Occasional Paper No 10, University of Oxford. Oxford: Centre for Criminological
    Research.
BALDWIN, J. (1985). Pre-Trial Justice: A Study of Case Settlement Procedures in Magistrates'
    Courts. Oxford: Blackwells.
—— (1997). 'Understanding Judge Ordered and Directed Acquittals in the Crown Court'.
    Criminal Law Review 536–55.
—— and McCONVILLE, M. (1977). Negotiated Justice. London: Martin Robertson.
—— and —— (1979a). Jury Trials. Oxford: Clarendon Press.
—— and —— (1979b). 'Plea Bargaining and Plea Negotiation in England'. Law and Society
    Review 13: 287–307.
BINGHAM, SIR THOMAS (1993). 'Twenty-Five Years of the Institute of Judicial
    Administration'. Civil Justice Quarterly 12: 322–5.
BLOCK, B.P., CORBETT, C., and PEAY, J. (1993). Ordered and Directed Acquittals in the
    Crown Court. Royal Commission on Criminal Justice, Research Study No 15. London:
    HMSO.
BOTTOMLEY, A. K. (1973). Decisions in the Penal Process. London: Martin Robertson.
BOTTOMS, A.E., and McCLEAN, J.D. (1976). Defendants in the Criminal Process. London:
    Routledge and Kegan Paul.
BOX, S. (1971). Deviance, Reality and Society. New York: Holt, Rinehart and Winston.
BREDAR, J.K. (1992). 'Moving Up the Day of Reckoning: Strategies for Attacking the
    "Cracked Trials" Problem'. Criminal Law Review 153–9.
BRINK, B., and STONE, C. (1988). 'Defendants Who Do Not Ask For Bail'. Criminal Law
    Review 152–62.
BROWN, D. (1997). PACE Ten Years On: A Review of the Research. Home Office Research
    Study 155, London: HMSO.
BROWN, S. (1991). Magistrates At Work. Milton Keynes: Open University Press.
BROWNLEE, I. D., MULCAHY, A., and WALKER, C.P. (1994). 'Pre-Trial Reviews, Court
    Efficiency and Justice: A Study in Leeds and Bradford Magistrates' Courts'. Howard
    Journal of Criminal Justice 33: 109–24.
BURNEY, E. (1979). J.P.: Magistrate, Court and Community. London: Hutchinson.
CARLEN, P. (1976). Magistrates' Justice. London: Martin Robertson.
CHURCH, T. (1985). 'Examining Local Legal Culture'. American Bar Foundation Research
    Journal 3: 449–518.
COHN, E.G., and FARRINGTON, D.P. (1998). 'Changes in the Most-Cited Scholars in Major
    International Journals between 1986–90 and 1991–95'. British Journal of Criminology 38:
    156–70.

DARBYSHIRE, P. (1984). *The Magistrates' Clerk.* Chichester: Barry Rose.

DENNIS, I. (1993). 'Miscarriages of Justice and the Law of Confessions: Evidentiary Issues and Solutions'. *Public Law* 291–313.

DEVONS, E. (1965). 'Serving as a Juryman in Britain'. *Modern Law Review* 28: 561–70.

EATON, M. (1986). *Justice for Women?* Milton Keynes: Open University Press.

FLOOD-PAGE, C., and MACKIE, A. (1998). *Sentencing Practice: An Examination of Decisions in Magistrates' Courts and the Crown Court in the mid-1990's.* Home Office Research Study 180. London: HMSO.

HEDDERMAN, C., and MOXON, D. (1992). *Magistrates' Court or Crown Court? Mode of Trial Decisions and Sentencing.* Home Office Research Study 125. London: HMSO.

HOOD, R. (1962). *Sentencing in Magistrates' Courts.* London: Stevens.

—— (1972). *Sentencing the Motoring Offender.* London: Heinemann.

—— (1992). *Race and Sentencing.* Oxford: Clarendon Press.

HOUGH, M., and ROBERTS, J. (1998). *Attitudes to Punishment: Findings from the British Crime Survey.* Home Office Research Study 179. London: HMSO.

HUCKLESBY, A. (1997). 'Court Culture: An Explanation of Variations in the Use of Bail by Magistrates' Courts'. *Howard Journal of Criminal Justice* 36: 129–45.

HUNT, A., and YOUNG, R. (1995–6). 'Criminal Justice and Academics: Publish and be Ignored?' *Holdsworth Law Review* 17: 193–227.

JEFFERSON, T., and SHAPLAND, J. (1994). 'Criminal Justice and the Production of Order and Control: Criminological Research in the UK in the 1980s'. *British Journal of Criminology* 34: 265–90.

KALUNTA-CRUMPTON, A. (1998). 'The Prosecution and Defence of Black Defendants in Drug Trials: Evidence of Claims-Making'. *British Journal of Criminology* 38: 561–91.

LEES, S. (1996). *Carnal Knowledge: Rape on Trial.* London: Hamish Hamilton.

LOW, C. (1978). 'The Sociology of Criminal Justice: Progress and Prospects' in J. Baldwin and A.K. Bottomley (eds.), *Criminal Justice: Selected Readings.* London: Martin Robertson.

McBARNET, D.J. (1976). 'Pre-trial Procedures and the Construction of Conviction' in P. Carlen (ed.), *The Sociology of Law.* University of Keele Sociological Review Monograph.

—— (1981). *Conviction: Law, the State and the Construction of Justice.* London: Macmillan.

McCABE, S., and PURVES, R. (1974). *The Shadow Jury at Work.* Oxford: Oxford University Penal Research Unit.

McCONVILLE, M. (1991). 'Shadowing the Jury'. *New Law Journal* 141: 1588 and 1595.

—— SANDERS, A., and LENG, R. (1991). *The Case for the Prosecution.* London: Routledge.

—— HODGSON, J., BRIDGES, L., and PAVLOVIC, A. (1994). *Standing Accused: The Organisation and Practices of Criminal Defence Lawyers in Britain.* Oxford: Clarendon Press.

—— and BRIDGES, L. (1994). *Criminal Justice in Crisis.* Aldershot: Edward Elgar.

MARK, SIR ROBERT (1973). *Minority Verdict.* London: BBC Publications.

MORGAN, P., and VENNARD, J. (1989). *Pre-Trial Delay: The Implications of Time Limits.* Home Office Research Study 110. London: HMSO.

MOXON, D. (1988). *Sentencing Practice in the Crown Court.* Home Office Research Study 103. London: HMSO.

—— and HEDDERMAN, C. (1994). 'Mode of Trial Decisions and Sentencing Differences Between Courts'. *Howard Journal of Criminal Justice* 33: 97–108.

MULCAHY, A. (1994). 'The Justifications of "Justice": Legal Practitioners' Accounts of

Negotiated Case Settlements in Magistrates' Courts'. *British Journal of Criminology* 34: 411–30.

PARKER, H., SUMNER, M., and JARVIS, G. (1989). *Unmasking the Magistrates*. Milton Keynes: Open University Press.

PLOTNIKOFF, J., and WOOLFSON, R. (1993). *From Committal to Trial: Delay at the Crown Court*. Law Society Research Study No 11. London: Law Society.

RILEY, D., and VENNARD, J. (1988). *Triable-Either-Way Cases: Crown Court or Magistrates' Court?* Home Office Research Study 98. London: HMSO.

ROCK, P. (1993). *The Social World of an English Crown Court*. Oxford: Clarendon Press.

ROYAL COMMISSION ON CRIMINAL PROCEDURE (Chairman: Sir Cyril Philips) (1981). *Report*. Cmnd 8092, London: HMSO.

ROYAL COMMISSION ON CRIMINAL JUSTICE (Chairman Viscount Runciman) (1993). *Report*. Cm 2263, London: HMSO.

RUMGAY, J. (1995). 'Custodial Decision Making in a Magistrates' Court: Court Culture and Immediate Situational Factors'. *British Journal of Criminology* 35: 201–17.

SANDERS, A. (1997a). 'Criminal Justice: The Development of Criminal Justice Research in Britain' in P.A.Thomas (ed.), *Socio-Legal Studies*. Aldershot: Dartmouth.

—— (1997b). 'From Suspect to Trial', in M. Maguire, R. Morgan, and R. Reiner (eds.), *Handbook of Criminology* (2nd edn.). Oxford: Clarendon Press.

—— and YOUNG, R. (1994). *Criminal Justice*. London: Butterworths.

SEALY, A. P., and CORNISH, W. B. (1973a). 'Jurors and their Verdicts'. *Modern Law Review* 36: 496–508.

—— and —— (1973b). 'Juries and the Rules of Evidence: L.S.E. Jury Project'. *Criminal Law Review* 208–23.

SHAPLAND, J., and BELL, E. (1998). 'Victims in the Magistrates' Courts and the Crown Court'. *Criminal Law Review* 537–46.

TARLING, R. (1979). *Sentencing Practice in Magistrates' Courts*. Home Office Research Study 56. London: HMSO.

TEMKIN, J. (1987). *Rape and the Legal Process*. London: Sweet and Maxwell.

WALKER, C., and STARMER, K. (1993). *Justice in Error*. London: Blackstone Press.

WASIK, M., GIBBONS, T., and REDMAYNE, M. (1999). *Criminal Justice: Text and Materials*. London: Longman.

WHITTAKER, C., and MACKIE, A. (1997). *Managing Courts Effectively: The Reasons for Adjournments in Magistrates' Courts*. Home Office Research Study 168. London: HMSO.

YOUNG, R., MOLONEY, T., and SANDERS, A. (1992). *In the Interests of Justice?* London: Legal Aid Board.

ZANDER, M. (1974). 'Are Too Many Professional Criminals Avoiding Conviction?—A Study of Britain's Two Busiest Courts'. *Modern Law Review* 37: 28–61.

—— and HENDERSON, P. (1993). *Crown Court Survey*. Royal Commission on Criminal Justice, Research Study No 19. London: HMSO.

9

RESEARCH ON COMMUNITY PENALTIES

George Mair

INTRODUCTION

Reflecting on the research process is a dangerously seductive topic. Every academic researcher has a favourite 'war story' about research, and sometimes these can be not only funny but instructive. The possible drawback is that research can emerge from such accounts as simply an exciting—maybe slightly risqué, even perhaps a little dangerous—way of spending one's time and furthering one's academic career. Research is, of course, exciting but it is considerably more than that; it usually involves much hard work, it can be lonely and boring, and it can take over your life to an uncomfortable extent. Research into community penalties, which is the subject of this chapter, may not have the immediate appeal of some criminological topics (the police or criminals somehow always seem more exciting), but it does have its compensations and I hope that I will be able to demonstrate some of them.

Although for virtually all of its history the probation service which is responsible for most community penalties has remained on the margins of criminal justice both academically and politically, there is a strong case for revisualizing it as being at the heart of the criminal justice process. This is emphatically *not* to envisage it as being centre-stage, as John Patten once viewed it when he was Minister of State at the Home Office in the late 1980s. The choice of metaphor is important: 'centre-stage' implies being in the spotlight and in the full view of the audience; 'at the heart' suggests a more hidden—although absolutely vital—role. It is the latter which characterizes the probation service, whose work remains hidden from the general public in a way in which the work of the courts, the police, and prisons is not.

In this chapter I shall argue that, although there has been a considerable literature focusing on the work of the probation service, the majority of research into community penalties has had negligible impact on policy or practice. Why should this be so? The answer is that the research has been

small-scale, local, fragmented, time-limited and—despite being defined directly
or indirectly by the Home Office—has rarely been an integral part of the policy
process, or been successfully incorporated into practice nationally. I will return
to these points at the end of the chapter.

My focus is on research into community penalties and this imposes some
editorial boundaries. On the one hand I will ignore some key aspects of the
work of the probation service. For example I will not discuss research into
pre-sentence reports (PSRs, or social inquiry reports as they were previously
known). However, it is important to stress that PSRs are a vital weapon in a
probation officer's armoury for two reasons: first, since judges and magistrates read them regularly, they are probably the most significant tool in
building up and maintaining officer credibility in the courts: and secondly,
the reports guide—to a considerable degree—sentencer decisions about the
kinds of offenders who are sentenced to community penalties. Nor will there
be any discussion of the work carried out by probation officers with
prisoners during their time in prison and while under supervision post-
release. Again, however, it should be emphasized that this is a substantial area
of work; 66,000 persons were subject to pre- and post-release supervision in
1997. Another area which will not be further discussed is the history of
community penalties. High-quality historical research into the probation service itself is sadly lacking despite the work of Bochel (1976), Haxby (1978),
and McWilliams (1983; 1985; 1986; 1987); and studies of individual penalties,
including the development of the probation order, simply do not exist. Without detailed, perhaps local, studies of the evolution of community penalties
we lack an important part of the context in which to understand current
policy and practice.

On the other hand two community penalties which are not run by the probation service—the curfew order and the attendance centre order—will be discussed. Whilst neither of these penalties currently deals with many offenders,
they are significant in that they represent a non-probation service inroad into
community penalties. The curfew order particularly has the potential to
become a major player in the community penalty arena and this could have
interesting repercussions for the probation service. Monetary penalties—still
the most commonly used court sentence in this country—will also be
considered.

I have imposed several other arbitrary boundaries on the discussion to keep
it within manageable proportions. First, only research covering adults and
young adults from the age of 17 upwards will be included. Secondly, the work
discussed will be UK-based. And thirdly, I will focus on the post-war period—
indeed, most of the work discussed will come from the last twenty years.

With these considerations in mind I will first discuss some of the general
issues that have formed the background to research into community penalties

in my experience and then discuss some studies of specific penalties. Finally, I will revisit some key issues and set out some points for future work.

KEY BACKGROUND ISSUES

WHO PAYS THE PIPER?

To a considerable extent, the research agenda for community penalties has been, and continues to be, shaped by the Home Office. This has implications for the research process, although I should point out that, at least as far as my own research has been concerned, these have not involved censorship. In the sixteen years I spent in the Home Office Research and Planning Unit (HORPU), the last ten involved in researching community penalties, I never felt that my work was subjected to censorship. So far as I am aware things have not changed since I left the Home Office. Perhaps more radical critics will argue that this was simply unnecessary because I was successfully socialized into the repressive habits of the Home Office and that my work was (and is) self-censored. I can only beg to differ.

Of course, one writes for one's audience; a piece for a tabloid newspaper would read very differently from an article in the *British Journal of Criminology*. With careful management and over time, one learned in the Home Office what the concerns of policy-makers were and one understood how a research report should be written. If I had ever been worried about the integrity of the research being compromised I was quite prepared to insist that my name would not appear on the title page (and the fact that Home Office reports carry authors' names is important). Only once did I feel that I *might* have to go as far as this and that was in connection with the first UK research into electronic monitoring (Mair and Nee 1990). In that case one could sense that the political pressures for a positive result from the trials were considerable, even though no pressure was directed at me. In the event, this remains the only piece of research I ever carried out at the Home Office which was commented on positively by people on both sides of the fence; those in favour of tagging as well as those against it, thought that the report backed up their positions. Perhaps this demonstrates that I am an inveterate trimmer, but I prefer to think that it serves to show that there are usually two sides (or more) to a question and this report brought them out.

Certainly, one's research reports were subjected to a good deal of critical comment from colleagues in the RPU as well as from staff in the relevant policy divisions, but such comments were not the final word. Discussion and negotiation always took place and, on the whole, I think that my work was improved by the scrutiny it received. It may have been time-consuming to redraft; it may—at times—have been annoying to have to respond to policy-makers who knew little about research and insisted on tinkering with carefully crafted sentences, but research reports were more tightly focused and read more clearly as a result.

Research was much more carefully scrutinized during the Michael Howard years (indeed, his junior minister, David Maclean, even proposed closing down the HORPU altogether); more questions were asked about why projects were being proposed, what they were designed to achieve, and research reports were studied in more detail by ministers themselves. Such scrutiny could lead to a 'spin' being put on research, as happened with the first national study of reconviction rates for some considerable time (Lloyd, Mair and Hough 1994), where the press release suggested that prison was the most successful sentence in terms of reconviction rates. The research said no such thing, but its publication coincided with the Howard 'Prison Works' campaign and it was hardly acceptable that the Home Secretary's own researchers should have media coverage for a study which cast doubt on this simple claim.

POLICY DEMANDS AND THE FRAGMENTATION OF RESEARCH

There are two main problems with research being Home Office defined. The first is that policy-makers are not adept at framing research questions. In the final analysis the research process in the Home Office is customer-driven; if a policy division cannot be persuaded to support a research project then it is unlikely to be done. Projects can be proposed by policy divisions or by researchers; in the former case, it is difficult for the researcher to say no, while in the latter a strong case has to be made if the topic is not currently seen as important. The problem with research ideas which originate with policy divisions is that they tend to come in unresearchable terms—'we'd like to know a bit more about . . .', or 'we're having some problems with . . .'. By the time a research project has been stitched together to take account of the initial issues, it can be hard for policy-makers to see how their interests are being served. This is not to argue that policy-relevant (or practice-relevant) research should be solely researcher-driven. What is really required is a much closer relationship between policy-makers and researchers where the latter are treated as equals rather than (as is all too often the case) lesser beings who are called in to help solve a minor technical problem.

The second problem is that research tends to be fragmented and non-cumulative. Research was planned on an annual basis in the Home Office because it was intended to be policy-relevant and policy priorities can change quite suddenly. This did not mean that only projects of twelve months or less could be carried out, although the time-scale for research tended to decrease over the years. The drawback was rather that research topics also changed suddenly, so that having just finished a project on a subject which had raised far more questions than it had answered and invited the development of more focused and pertinent work, one had to move to a completely different topic. There were, therefore, some rather wasted opportunities, and since it can be unsound to base practice on one or two unrelated research studies it will be interesting to see how many of these chickens come home to roost with the new government emphasis on evidence-based practice (Chapman and Hough 1998).

One of the more surprising things about researching community penalties from inside government was just how little basic information the Home Office had. Many of the projects carried out between 1985 and 1995 had first to find out how many examples existed 'out there'. I was amazed to discover, for example, that we first had to find out how many probation day centres there were in the mid-1980s (Mair 1988). Similar fact-finding problems were faced in studies of probation provision for drug misusing offenders (Nee and Sibbitt 1993), of probation motor projects (Martin and Webster 1994), of community-based programmes for sex offenders (Barker and Morgan 1993), and of the ways in which probation services addressed the literacy needs of offenders (Davis *et al.* 1997). If such basic information is not available it becomes impossible to begin to evaluate such programmes. The need to collect such information has implications for research; not just the fact that some kind of sample survey or full census might have to be carried out, but that as a consequence the study might take longer than envisaged and it might cover less ground than had been planned.

A considerable amount of Home Office-funded research is not done in-house but put out to tender, and here the problem arises that tender specifications may be so tightly defined that the scope for being creative in designing the research is narrowed out of existence. Tenders are awarded often on grounds of cost, moderated perhaps by considerations of the track record of the researcher. Obviously, those who fund research have a right to state what they want, but if they design the project themselves they are missing out on potentially more fruitful approaches and innovative ideas. There needs to be some way of striking a balance between defining the project and permitting the bidders to design it.

These background issues which shape research are not necessarily confined to the Home Office: outside funding agencies also often want (and deserve to have) sight of research proposals and reports with the right to comment prior to publication (they may also insist on the right to deny publication); they too may find it difficult to formulate research questions; they too may not have any interest in or the ability to fund longer or follow-up studies (one of the major problems of criminological research—and this applies to other academic disciplines too—is that you get no plaudits for replication studies); and they may not have the kind of information which a researcher assumes they would hold.

ACCESS AND CONFIDENTIALITY

More commonplace (though rarely simple) issues for research such as access and confidentiality are also subject to the Home Office factor. Being in the HORPU made access *in general terms* not a particular problem, but this did not mean that one thereby could study the *specific* probation areas which most needed research. Chief Probation Officers could easily provide reasons for not wanting researchers (perhaps especially those from the Home Office) tramping around their area. All too often the reason given was that they had recently been inspected by Her Majesty's Inspectorate of Probation (HMIP). Given the number of probation areas subjected to some kind of HMIP inspection annually this could make choosing areas for study an extremely prolonged process.[1]

Standard provisions about confidentiality were applied in Home Office research; individuals would not be identified, although matters were much more vague about identifying probation areas. No probation area was anonymized whilst I was working in this field in the Home Office, although other researchers have felt the need—or been requested—to do this (see, e.g. May 1991; Skinns 1990). Naming areas could, no doubt, lead to individual probation staff being identified, but this was never raised as an issue as far as I was concerned. Confidentiality could obviously prove to be more problematic when it was necessary to collect names and dates of birth of offenders for the purposes of access to a national database in order to study previous criminal history and recidivism. Some probation officers worried about providing such information in case it led to some kind of police action. Assurances that there were strict protocols about how such data might be used were, in my experience, always enough for the data to be supplied. However, reaching agreement about linking ethnic data to reconviction studies was much more problematic; this was seen by probation organizations—particularly the National Association of Probation Officers (NAPO) and the Association of Black Probation Officers (ABPO)—as much too sensitive a subject to confront.

One issue which became increasingly difficult to handle was pressure from probation services to be seen to have performed well. During the 1980s, the probation service felt more and more pressure from government to be effective, efficient, and economic, to be accountable for what it did, and to plan and target its work more appropriately (McLaughlin and Muncie 1994). The Audit

---

[1] Graham Smith, HM Chief Inspector of Probation, has recently stated that 'we would expect almost every service to be seen by us for something every year' (House of Commons Home Affairs Committee 1998a), which suggests that, when local inspections are included, some probation areas could well be suffering from inspection fatigue.

Commission, which has become a significant presence in the criminal justice process, published a critical report on the probation service at the end of the decade (Audit Commission 1989). Performance indicators and national standards were introduced at the start of the 1990s. One response to all this pressure was to become defensive and if a Chief Probation Officer agreed to allow research locally there was often a hope that the results would show the service in a positive light. This could lead to the absurd situation whereby the probation service was very keen indeed on the idea of research or evaluation in theory and in public, but when confronted with research findings which suggested that things were not going well was much less enthusiastic.

Pressure for positive results is pervasive and understandable. Many projects are set up with minimal resources and little time to operate 'normally'; researchers are asked to evaluate what are essentially pilot projects, but in the hope (if not the expectation) that a glowing report will show unequivocally positive results. Such a hope is naïve, but the need to find more money is always present, and this is more likely to be forthcoming if the project is judged to be a success by a so-called 'independent' academic. It is hard to blame those who develop and work in such projects for wanting to have some job security, but it is simply not possible to conclude from the study of a *pilot* project that it is an absolute success. Not only are probation services and the like under pressure to demonstrate effectiveness, but this pressure is then transferred to researchers— a move which could have implications for the quality of research carried out, as well as leading to certain researchers being shunned in a tender if they have a reputation for not coming up with the 'right' answers.

This kind of situation is likely to get worse. Increasingly, there is an orthodoxy originating from the Probation Inspectorate that only cognitive behavioural techniques provide the basis for effective probation work. Despite the fact that the strong evidence base which its proponents claim for it does not exist, cognitive behaviouralism is being preached as the gospel for community penalties. This raises the alarming prospect that researchers who do not subscribe to this particular credo will be marginalized in bidding for research, and even that research findings may be interpreted in such a way as to boost cognitive behaviouralist techniques or explain away any possible shortcomings. While the nonsense of 'Nothing Works' (a statement) has at last been rightly seen as an empty formulation, its replacement by 'What Works?' (a question) has not heralded a new openness about effective approaches to community penalties. The answer to the question is invariably cognitive behaviouralism.

In this section I have discussed some of the critical issues forming the backdrop for research that I encountered while based in the Home Office and managing a part of the Research and Planning Unit devoted to researching community penalties. I would not wish to suggest that these issues are peculiar to researching community penalties, or that they only arise in the Home Office.

They are, however, significant issues that have an (often unspoken) impact upon how research is formulated, designed, carried out, and written up. In the next section I will flag up and comment on some of the more important pieces of research that have been carried out into community penalties.

THE 'BEST' OF COMMUNITY PENALTIES RESEARCH

THE PROBATION ORDER

Despite the fact that it has been the bread-and-butter work of the probation service since its beginnings, research into the basic probation order is notable by its complete absence. Probably the main reason for this is the nature of the order: most basic probation orders remain rooted in one-to-one casework between a probation officer and the offender and this takes place in private, behind closed doors, almost always in the probation office. It would be seen as obtrusive, perhaps threatening, and certainly as changing the dynamics of the relationship for a researcher to sit in and observe sessions of this kind. As a result, we know next to nothing about one-to-one casework in practice, a situation which is deplorable.

The first significant piece of probation research (funded by the Home Office), entitled appropriately enough 'The Results of Probation' (Radzinowicz 1958), was a reconviction study. Data on 9,336 offenders (54 per cent juveniles) were collected from the London and Middlesex probation areas between 1948 and 1953 (including a three-year follow-up) with a view to carrying out 'a detailed enquiry into the effectiveness of probation as a method of treatment for offenders'. The main findings were as follows: adults were more likely to succeed than juveniles (success was defined as having completed the order with no reconviction during a follow-up period of three years); women were more likely to succeed than men; probation was especially effective 'in dealing with adolescent and adult first offenders'; its effectiveness decreased, however, when applied to recidivists; and 'in many of the more difficult cases the reinforcement of probation by combining it with conditions of residence has not proved to be particularly effective'. Today, such results from a reconviction study would be unsurprising, but at the time the impact of this study was considerable.

It is worth noting, however, some of the limitations of the study. First, that publication of the results was *eight years* after the last orders in the sample had been terminated. Secondly, there is a real possibility of the sample being biased as it was chosen from only two probation areas and in the immediate aftermath of the war. Thirdly, as more than 90 per cent of the sample had been convicted of offences against property, so there could be no consideration of differences in reconviction rates being associated with different offences. Fourthly, there was no attempt to describe what probation supervision consisted of and precisely how that might reduce further offending, but in that respect the Cambridge study was of its time. Notwithstanding its limitations, this research deserves not to be forgotten as many of its findings remain relevant today.

For a ten-year period beginning in 1966, a major (and concerted) part of the Home Office research effort went into trying to discover what the key factors were in successful probation work (Folkard *et al.* 1966; Barr 1966; Barr and O'Leary 1966; Davies 1969, 1970, 1973, 1974; Sinclair 1971; Folkard *et al.* 1974; Folkard, Smith and Smith 1976). There is little to comment on in terms of the methods used in these studies, but they do demonstrate a considerable commitment by the Home Office to conduct research into probation and how effective it might be. Unfortunately, the final report (Folkard, Smith and Smith 1976) on this research programme which set out the results of the IMPACT (Intensive Matched Probation and After-Care Treatment) experiment was very brief, obviously disappointing ('the results showed no significant differences in . . . reconviction rates . . . therefore producing no evidence to support a general application of more intensive treatment'), and published immediately after the British version of 'Nothing Works' (Brody 1976). As a result, Home Office research into community penalties virtually disappeared; an examination of the two Home Office research series (Home Office Research Studies and Research and Planning Unit Papers) demonstrates just how little research into probation took place between 1976 and 1988.

By the mid-1980s, the probation service was no longer in the business of rehabilitating offenders but diverting them from custody, and the probation order was capable of having additional requirements attached to it. The publication of the Statement of National Objectives and Priorities (Home Office 1984) was the first signal that the Home Office was beginning to take a more controlling approach. Day centres became the flavour of the month, with the addition to the probation order of a condition to attend a designated centre for up to sixty days, and a detailed, long-term evaluation of one such centre was carried out by Peter Raynor (1988). In his study of the Afan Alternative project, Raynor used a variety of methods in an effort to try to capture the complexity of the phenomenon, and looked at several measures of effectiveness. His research still stands as an important attempt to move away from a reliance on reconviction rates as the only measure of effectiveness for a court sentence, and to try to situate a project in its context (the beginnings, perhaps, of what we now refer to as a process evaluation). Interest in day centres was strong and a variety of studies appeared, all trying to assess how far the centres were effective at diverting offenders from custody (among them Mair 1988; Vass and Weston 1990), but all facing the same methodological difficulty—how could one be certain that an offender sentenced to attend a day centre was indeed being diverted from a custodial sentence and not from another non-custodial one?

One particularly interesting study focusing on the probation order in Scotland was carried out in the late 1980s and early 1990s and involved interviewing sheriffs, offenders, and their supervising officers (social workers, as there is no probation service in Scotland) in four courts with varying uses of probation (Ditton and Ford 1994). The aim was to investigate views and attitudes about probation, how and why it was used, what the process of supervision was seen to entail, how orders ended, etc. The significance of this study lies in its pulling together the views of the three main groups involved in probation and it throws up many fascinating insights. Unfortunately, the research is written up in a very sparse style with little methodological information or contextualization, and analysis which—at times—is difficult to relate to the data collected. But that does not detract from the fact this is an ambitious study covering considerable ground, and it is perhaps notable that it was funded by the Scottish Office. Why should such an ambitious piece of work be funded by government when a separate probation service does not even exist in Scotland? And why cannot the Home Office do something along the same lines?

A major Home Office study of intensive probation (Mair *et al.* 1994) which attempted to build on the work of Raynor by using various measures of effectiveness (including an assessment of the costs involved—an aspect of research which has become increasingly important, and which to do properly requires skills that most social researchers lack) as well as carrying out a process evaluation, was crippled by a loss of policy interest in the initiative and the lack of support for a reconviction study. Such a study could have suggested vital links between models of intensive probation and reconviction rates—an association which is hinted at in a reconviction study of day centres (Mair and Nee 1992; for a twelve-month reconviction study of one intensive probation project see Brownlee 1995).

Increasingly, research is trying to look at the association between reconviction rates and types of programme, but this is a complex topic which so far has not been well served. The original studies, describing the programmes and how they operate, tend to be published well in advance of the reconviction studies. This can mean that any relationship between the two is difficult to grasp. It is also now commonplace for the reconviction study to be carried out by different (Home Office-based) researchers, which raises the question of how process and outcome can be linked satisfactorily. Reconviction studies are often published in summary form in the *Research Findings* series and it is difficult to raise complex issues in just four pages. Examples of this can be found in the case of a study of motor projects—which resulted in the issuing of a Home Office guidance to probation services (Martin and Webster 1994; Sugg 1998; Home Office Probation Circular 1998); and in a project studying community-based programmes for sex offenders (Barker and Morgan 1993; Beckett *et al.* 1994; and Hedderman and Sugg 1996).

More promising as a research strategy is the approach followed by Raynor and Vanstone (1994; 1996) in their detailed investigation of the STOP (Straight Thinking On Probation) programme in Mid-Glamorgan. A complex evaluation study has been designed which will aim at making links between the operation and organization of the programme and its outcomes. So far, only short reports have been published, but it is to be hoped that a full-length book will appear eventually, as such long-term research strategies are rare and badly needed.

Summing up briefly, then, we can say that: research into the probation order is really the story of research into probation with added requirements; we are not much further forward in knowing what is effective now than we were with the 1958 Cambridge report, although the definition of effectiveness has changed with the times and continues to do so (reconviction rates, however, remain the ultimate test); and while innovative methods of research or evaluation are unusual to say the least, the importance of process evaluation is slowly being recognized.

THE COMMUNITY SERVICE ORDER

In contrast to the probation order, the community service order (CSO) has been fairly comprehensively researched from its beginnings. To a large degree this has been because it was introduced in 1973 on a consciously experimental basis and with encouragement from its originators on the Wootton Committee (Advisory Council on the Penal System 1970) for systematic study of its workings.

The first research was carried out by the Home Office Research Unit (HORU) with the aim of informing 'a decision about the viability of the community service scheme and the consequent decision about its extension' (Pease *et al.* 1975). To this end an ambitious research project was designed using a variety of methods: collecting information from files, carrying out sentencing exercises with probation officers, analysing social inquiry reports (now pre-sentence reports), interviewing probation officers and offenders, participant observation, postal surveys of probation officers, etc. Not all of the research effort was carried out equally in the six experimental areas, and one interesting omission is that the views of sentencers were not investigated.

A second HORU report was published two years later (Pease, Billingham and Earnshaw 1977), concentrating on assessing how far the new sentence was used as a displacement from custody and rates of reconviction. Most notable about this report was the care taken in trying to estimate the number of those sentenced to community service who would otherwise have been given a custodial sentence. Four avenues were explored, none of which was conclusive by itself:

probation officers were asked what sentences might otherwise have been passed on those who received CSOs; the sentences that were passed on those who breached their CSOs were investigated (with the implication that if the sentence was being used as an alternative to custody, breach would result in a custodial sentence); the sentences passed on those offenders for whom the courts asked for an assessment of suitability for CS but did not make an order were considered; and those cases where a probation officer recommended CS but the court passed a different sentence were examined. It was concluded that around 45–50 per cent of those sentenced to CS were diversions from custody—a figure which has been relatively consistent in many studies of so-called alternatives to custody in the UK.

Although one cannot be certain, it looks as if the second HORU report draws its conclusions rather more firmly than the evidence suggests and it is notable that the Foreword points out that the text was edited after the departure of the authors from the Unit. Indeed, the whole official basis of the research has been questioned by Ken Pease himself who claimed, some years later, that the idea of the research being critical in the decision to expand CSOs nationally was simply not true; community service orders were going national whatever the research said (Pease 1983).

One key finding from the original HORU research has also continued to haunt the community service order, and that is accusations of wide variations in the way in which the sentence is administered and organized (see Young 1979; W. McWilliams 1980; Read 1980; B. McWilliams and Murphy 1980; Vass 1984; Pease 1985; Skinns 1990). This is usually blamed on the deliberately ambiguous nature of the Wootton report (Wootton 1978), and is one reason why the first set of National Standards—introduced in 1989—were for community service (three years before standards for other community penalties).

Two other studies of community service are worth noting. First, that carried out by Tony Vass (1984), which covers much of the ground of earlier work but included active participant observation by the author (as an offender) in community service work placements. As a result, Vass was able to document clearly the key role of the supervision process for offenders and to show how important was the way in which the supervisor dealt with the offenders carrying out community service:

the major influence on the offender to participate in community service projects without causing disruptions is the *type of supervision* offered. The way supervisors— whether full-time, part-time, qualified or unqualified—intermingle with offenders, express their attitudes, work *with*—not above—the offender and the way they handle discontent, can determine the rate of attendance, how much pride offenders take in their work, how much effort they put in their tasks and how well they behave on site. In other words, the success or failure of a session can often be the function of the supervisor's personality and his actions (Vass 1984: 114, emphasis in original).

Vass does not go into great detail about the methodological issues involved in carrying out such participant observation, although they can be assumed to have been considerable. Today, it would almost certainly be much more difficult to get the agreement of a probation service to allow a researcher to participate in community service as an offender; and it would be a difficult matter to construct a suitable identity and keep it secure. The age and gender of the researcher would be important; women and older offenders are less commonly sentenced to community service which would mean that, in general, it would be easier for young males to adopt such an approach. Despite such difficulties, it is surprising that more studies using this method have not been attempted as the potential rewards are considerable.

Finally, and very much a culmination of the tradition of community service research in the UK, is the work carried out in Scotland in the second half of the 1980s by Gill McIvor and various colleagues (see McIvor 1989, 1990; Carnie 1990; Knapp, Robertson and McIvor 1992; McIvor 1992a; and McIvor 1992b for a book-length study). There is nothing in this research that could be said to be methodologically innovative, but that is beside the point. What we do get is a programme of research carried out carefully and rigorously over a number of years covering key issues in community service (the kind of offenders receiving CSOs, procedural and administrative matters, the comparative costs of CSOs, the views of beneficiaries and sentencers, reconviction rates, and how far the sentence was acting to divert offenders from custody), using a variety of approaches. It is rare for such a comprehensive study to be done and is a direct result of long-term funding (from the Scottish Office, the source of funding for the Ditton and Ford work discussed above) and a real interest in issues after a sentence had moved on from its initial stage of development. McIvor's work confirmed the results of previous Community Service research and raised new questions which require further work—and that is about as much as one could expect from research.

Community service, then, has been better served in research terms than the probation order. There are several reasons for this. It was introduced in the 1970s; it does not involve any 'private' sessions between offender and probation officer; its organizational arrangements are—to a large degree—separable from other probation work (although the arrival of the combination order has changed that somewhat); and the first research study defined the key parameters for study well. Innovative research (with the honourable exception of Vass), however, is lacking and there remain gaps in what we know.

THE COMBINATION ORDER

The combination order (combining probation and community service) was introduced in 1992 as part of the Criminal Justice Act 1991. Although such a hybrid sentence had been available in Scotland for some years, this was a new disposal for England and Wales and it raised important questions: how would the mix of two very different sentences work in practice; what kind of organizational arrangements would be required, given the rather different cultures of those who ran Community Service schemes and maingrade probation officers; and who would the sentence be used for? The initial Home Office view, as promulgated in the first set of National Standards (Home Office 1992), was that the combination order was aimed at the Crown Court (subsequently modified in the revised National Standards—Home Office 1995). This view was shared by probation staff who were—at best—uneasy about the demanding nature of the new order and happy to see it confined as far as possible to the Crown Court. Early Home Office statistical monitoring, however, showed that around 70 per cent of combination orders were made in the magistrates' courts and the latest Criminal Statistics (Home Office 1998a) show that this proportion has gone up to 80 per cent.

Amazingly, despite the significance of the introduction of a major new sentence and the consequent potential for problems, no detailed study of the combination order has yet been published. One reason for this may be the knowledge that the Home Office Research and Planning Unit carried out a research project which attempted to find out how the sentence was implemented, how it was used by the courts, and the practical issues involved in organizing and administering the sentence. However, resource problems within the Unit led to considerable delays in the preparation of the report and it remains unpublished (Mair et al. 1997). Home Office interest seems minimal, yet the combination order now (1997 figures) accounts for almost 20,000 cases per year. This is a subject where there is considerable scope for research.

OTHER 'NON-CUSTODIAL' PENALTIES

The fine remains the most commonly used court sentence, although its use has been declining for some years; even so, in 1997 almost one million offenders were fined. In the same year, almost 100,000 compensation orders were made by the courts. Studies of monetary penalties, however, have not been particularly popular, have tended to rely on documentary research based on files and records, have been very much Home Office-driven and have focused heavily on the courts and their procedures—particularly enforcement (see Softley 1973, 1978a, 1978b; Softley and Moxon 1982; Newburn 1988; Mair and Lloyd 1989; Moxon, Hedderman and Sutton 1990; Moxon, Corkery and Hedderman 1992; Charman et al. 1996; Whittaker and Mackie 1997). Despite the fact that monetary penalties remain popular, studies looking into the ways in which offenders perceive them, how they budget to pay them (or not), and the reasons magistrates give for using them are missing. Absent, too, is any information about how fine enforcement procedures are perceived by offenders and applied by magistrates; and while there is evidence to suggest that the reconviction rates associated with fines are lower than those associated with other sentences (Phillpotts and Lancucki 1979), this is now very much out-of-date apart from a brief mention of 1993 data in Home Office evidence to the House of Commons Home Affairs Committee (House of Commons 1998b). The short-lived unit fines initiative introduced by the 1991 Criminal Justice Act was preceded by experiments with the approach in four courts (Moxon, Sutton and Hedderman 1990) which showed that the new system was viable, although this was not enough to save it from repeal less than a year after its introduction (for an account of events leading to the repeal of unit fines: see Windlesham 1993).

Apart from the probation order, the attendance centre order is the oldest community penalty, having been introduced as a result of the 1948 Criminal Justice Act, although the first senior attendance centre (for 17–20-year-olds) did not begin operation until December 1958. There are fewer than thirty senior attendance centres in England and Wales and they play a minor role in sentencing. Partly as a result of this they have been rarely noticed. One major study has been carried out (Mair 1991), and this attempted to investigate the relationship between the policy and practice of the centres using historical material as well as a variety of social research approaches. These ranged from interviews with offenders and those working in centres; postal questionnaires for those in charge of centres and a sample of magistrates; observations at one centre over a twelve-month period, and visits to other centres; and the collection of standard criminological data on offenders. Although senior attendance centres remain on the periphery they could be incorporated into the other community penalties run by the probation service which might give the centres a higher profile. At present, their significance lies in the fact that they are *not* run by the probation service and therefore represent a wedge in the service's monopolization of community penalties.

A more significant wedge (because the potential to deal with a large number of offenders is much greater) is the curfew order introduced in July 1995 on a trial basis in three areas. Early research into the use of electronic surveillance as a tool for monitoring a curfew imposed as a condition of bail was, at best, equivocal (Mair and Nee 1990). The trials of the new sentence were subject to research by the Home Office Research and Planning Unit using what should by now be recognized as familiar techniques:

Observation, formal interviews and informal discussions were carried out with the contractors; data were collected on all those sentenced to curfew orders; where possible, pre-sentence reports for those so sentenced and where a proposal for a curfew order was made were examined; and semi-structured formal interviews were carried out with 13 offenders sentenced to curfew orders, nine magistrates, three court clerks and two police representatives . . . In addition, a number of informal discussions were also held with people in all these groups, except the offenders, and with 12 probation service staff (Mair and Mortimer 1996: 3–4).

In other words, there was nothing new in methodological terms although it is worth noting that the Home Office Economics Unit was drafted in to assess the relative costs of the new order. Nevertheless, it adopted a fairly comprehensive and solid approach which certainly covered the surface well while lacking the resources to go into detail. The second report on the trials (Mortimer and May 1997) focused on the 'market share' of the curfew order and involved a special 'sentencing choice' exercise for magistrates in sixteen of the twenty courts where curfew orders were an option; more sophisticated estimates of the costs and savings associated with the order were also provided.

The use of electronic monitoring has continued to spread. Trial areas where electronic monitoring is used have been expanded; the Crime (Sentences) Act 1997 has made curfew orders with electronic monitoring available for three new groups of offenders—fine defaulters, persistent petty offenders (for whom a fine might be imposed but for the lack of means to pay it), and juveniles aged 10–15. From the end of January 1999 it is estimated that around 500 prisoners per week will be released under a home detention curfew programme. Because of the trial status of this highly significant development, the Home Office has been able to keep a tight grip on research in the area—a factor which has implications methodologically as well as politically—and it will be interesting to see if this is a development which continues.

WIDER APPROACHES

In the past few years various studies with a rather wider focus have been carried out which have covered community penalties more generally. While, for the most part, these studies have not been especially methodologically innovative, they have looked into aspects of community penalties which have not been addressed previously and they demonstrate changing approaches to measuring the effectiveness of these penalties.

First, postal questionnaires have been used to assess the satisfaction of the courts with the probation service as a result of the need to develop a perform-ance indicator for this issue. As methods texts make clear, postal questionnaires have to be fairly simple, clearly designed, and well targeted if a reasonable response rate is desired. The two publications discussing the results of this work show response rates of over 80 per cent (May 1995) and 62 per cent (May 1997). There is no discussion of the lower response rate for the second and main survey, and it is notable that successive surveys will be carried out not by Home Office researchers but by HM Inspectorate of Probation.

Secondly, one of the spin-offs of the renewed interest in the 'What Works?' question was the realization that a significant finding of much of the so-called 'Nothing Works' literature was that interventions had to be matched to individual offenders and nothing was known about how probation officers actually assessed offenders and allocated them to programmes (so-called interaction effects). Burnett (1996) was commissioned by the Home Office to research this topic and in the process interviewed 120 probation officers. Her main finding was—as might have been expected—that there were important differences amongst probation areas in how offenders were assessed and allocated. Unfortunately, while this might have been the starting point for a much more detailed investigation relating these differences to output and outcome measures, no further work has been carried out (although a study piloting three versions of a needs assessment scale was carried out—see Aubrey and Hough 1997).

Thirdly, as the confidence of sentencers in community penalties became designated as a critical factor in their use during the second half of the 1990s, so interest in how such penalties were enforced became an issue. Yet another Home Office study addressed this topic (Ellis, Hedderman and Mortimer 1996), in which probation and community service staff, magistrates, and police officers (or their civilian equivalents) were interviewed. Again—and not surprisingly—the main finding was that 'enforcement practices differed within and between areas'. Once more, however, this important and tantalizing finding has not been followed up by further research.

Finally, alongside interest in how sentencers perceived community penalties, there was also an interest in how offenders sentenced to community penalties felt about them. Individual probation services began to take an interest in monitoring the views of 'their' offenders and the Home Office, too, realized this was an important topic. Earlier studies had used in-depth interviews with offenders (and sometimes also with their probation officers; see Day 1981; Fielding 1986; Bailey and Ward 1992) in one area. The Home Office, however, carried out a national survey of 1,200 offenders on probation or combination orders aimed at uncovering more detail about their background and circumstances and eliciting views about their supervision, their probation officers, and how helpful it all was in addressing their problems and reducing their offending (Mair and May 1997). There were difficulties with respondents failing to keep appointments which led to a lower response rate than was desirable (only 61 per cent of the effective sample of almost 2,000 were successfully interviewed), and those who could not be interviewed may well have held more negative attitudes than those who participated in the survey. Like the surveys of sentencers discussed earlier, the views about supervision and probation officers tended to be very favourable.

CONCLUSIONS

A considerable number of research studies into community penalties has been discussed (with at least as many—if not more—ignored), but I have argued that the impact of all this research has been relatively minimal. In addition to the reasons given earlier for this lack of potency two others require discussion—the relationship between research and policy (or practice), and the dissemination of research.

Research need not always have a direct pay-off in terms of influencing policy or practice directly. Increasingly, however, with criminal justice agencies such as the probation service under pressure in terms of budget cuts, new responsibilities, and the need to be accountable, access for researchers to staff, data, or offenders cannot be taken for granted. Something has to be offered by the researcher in return for access, and often this is a vague and implicit understanding that the research will contribute to the needs of the organization. In a rather similar way, Home Office research was *understood* to be policy-relevant—although how this was achieved was a matter left to one side (only partly flippantly one could suggest that it was policy-relevant simply *because* it was Home Office-commissioned research, but that only raises more questions).

The policy process involves a series of steps which can loop back to the start and research can contribute at almost any stage of that process. This kind of model, however, was not recognized in the Home Office; nor, I would argue, is it recognized in the probation service. For both of these bodies, research has always been understood as something that might be used when a new policy or practice is about to be implemented in order to find out what the outcomes of that policy or practice are, with the possibility that if things are not happening as expected action could be taken. In reality, even this simplistic model of the research–policy/practice relationship is rarely achieved: as noted above, the Home Office research into community service was never *intended* to validate the decision to make CS available on a national basis; and Home Office research into intensive probation (an initiative seen as having significant implications for national practice) was marginalized because it was decided to introduce the combination order *before* intensive probation was evaluated. If research is to continue in its role of servant to policy/practice (and I have argued that, in fact, it should be seen as equal partner), then precisely what it can contribute needs to be hammered out and clarified anew for every project. The relationship between research and policy or practice is too important to be left to vague, ambiguous understandings which have never been spelled out.

As for the dissemination of research, this is in an even more nebulous state than clarifying the research–policy/practice relationship (but is, of course, closely related to it). It is little wonder that research has such a limited impact upon policy or practice when its results are hardly ever formulated or disseminated in such a way as to make them easily accessible to those who make policy or practice. The lessons of community penalties research are set out with other researchers in mind, not with a view to influencing how probation officers do their work. The increasing use of Executive Summaries, and the introduction by the Home Office of brief distillations of larger studies in the *Research Findings* series, are steps towards making research more accessible to busy non-researchers, but neither translates the results of research into practice recommendations. And even if this were the case, any such recommendations would have to be backed by advice on how they might be implemented and then subject to further research. Academic researchers themselves may not be the most appropriate people to translate the results of their work into nostrums for practice, and others may have to be involved if this is to be done effectively. But, given the fact that so much research into community penalties is grounded on basic ideas about practice, about how such penalties 'work', it is—in one sense—wasted research if results are not actively related to practice.

For the most part, as I hope I have shown, research into community penalties in the UK has followed fairly mundane paths and has had little direct, immediate impact upon policy or practice. The methodologies adopted have been predictable, although they have been applied competently and carefully. Indeed, there may not be very much scope for radically novel approaches; the basic tools of social research have not changed dramatically over the years, they have simply been refined. And innovation simply for its own sake is not necessarily a good thing. It should be emphasized that it is not as a result of 'bad' research that we know so little. It is much more to do with assuming that we know more about the basics of community penalties than we actually do, with pressure to evaluate the outcomes of penalties before we know what they are doing and for whom they are doing it, and with small-scale, limited, fragmented research studies carried out in a vacuum. It is, in short, to do with the lack of a centrally planned, strategic, long-term programme of research which is deliberately targeted and plugged into practice or policy whenever appropriate.[2] This is not likely to change as long as the Home Office keeps such a tight grip on research in this area (although this is not to deny that there is a considerable Home Office interest here). If, however, a National Probation Service is created, as mooted in a recent Consultation Document (Home Office 1998*b*), then the possibility of developing such a research programme may be much improved. Indeed, as I write (April 1999) plans for a new, unified probation service have just been announced; it will be run by a director who will be accountable to the

---

[2] As I was working on the first draft of this chapter, the latest edition of the *Home Office Research Bulletin* was published with an article which, while rather more optimistic than I have been about what we have learnt from probation research, comes to substantially similar conclusions about what is required for the future (Hedderman 1998).

Home Secretary, and the latter will take full responsibility for the performance of the service. How far these changes will lead to the kind of research strategy I have suggested is needed is a moot point.

Finally, then, I would argue that research into community penalties is ripe for serious study. Some interesting new topics have recently been researched, but we still know little about the organization of probation services and how that may relate to the delivery and outcomes of penalties, or how individual probation officers justify what they do and how they do it, to name only two subjects that would seem to be highly relevant to improving the effectiveness of community penalties. A greater willingness to address the politics of community penalties as part of the research agenda is needed; the wider context is at least as important as a narrow-minded obsession with simplistic notions of effectiveness. And it would be invaluable to see more reflection about research on the part of those who study community penalties.

With the Home Office currently committed to the idea of evidence-based practice for community penalties, the time would seem to be right for a renewed push in the direction of research. The main worry here, however, lies in the HM Inspectorate-published report on *Evidence Based Practice* (Chapman and Hough 1998); a look at the references shows a surprising lack of up-to-date, UK-based pieces of work upon which practice may be based. One can only hope that this is not a pointer to the future.

SUGGESTIONS FOR FURTHER READING

Virtually all of the research worth reading has been mentioned, although issues regarding the effectiveness of community penalties are covered usefully in two edited collections: James McGuire's *What Works: Reducing Reoffending* (Chichester: John Wiley, 1995) and George Mair's *Evaluating the Effectiveness of Community Penalties* (Aldershot: Avebury, 1997). A very basic introduction to the work of the probation service can be found in Dick Whitfield's *Introduction to the Probation Service* (Winchester: Waterside Press, 1998). More critical discussions can be found in Ian Brownlee's *Community Punishment: A Critical Introduction* (London: Longman, 1998), Anne Worrall's *Punishment in the Community: The Future of Criminal Justice* (London: Longman, 1997), and George Mair's essay 'Community Penalties and Probation' in *The Oxford Handbook of Criminology* (2nd edition) edited by Mike Maguire, Rod Morgan, and Robert Reiner (Oxford: Oxford University Press, 1997). There are many research methods texts available; my only advice would be never to fall into the trap of thinking that you have to follow their bloodless prescriptions to the letter in order to produce a perfect piece of research. For better or worse, life is a much more messy business.

I would like to thank Roy King and Emma Wincup for helpful comments on the first draft of this chapter; and Peter Raynor and Tony Vass for lending me copies of their books on the Afan Alternative and community service respectively.

REFERENCES

ADVISORY COUNCIL ON THE PENAL SYSTEM (1970). *Non-Custodial and Semi-Custodial Penalties*. London: HMSO.

AUBREY, R., and HOUGH, M. (1997). *Assessing Offenders' Needs: Assessment Scales for the Probation Service*. Home Office Research Study No.166. London: Home Office.

AUDIT COMMISSION (1989). *The Probation Service: Promoting Value for Money*. London: HMSO.

BAILEY, R., and WARD, D. (1992). *Probation Supervision: Attitudes to Formalised Helping*. Belfast: Probation Board for Northern Ireland.

BARKER, M., and MORGAN, R. (1993). *Sex Offenders: A Framework for the Evaluation of Community-Based Treatment*. London: Home Office.

BARR, H. (1966). *A Survey of Group Work in the Probation Service*. Home Office Studies in the Causes of Delinquency and the Treatment of Offenders 9. London: HMSO.

—— and O'LEARY, E. (1966). *Trends and Regional Comparisons in Probation*. Home Office Studies in the Causes of Delinquency and the Treatment of Offenders 8. London: HMSO.

BECKETT, R., BEECH, A., FISHER, D., and FORDHAM, A. S. (1994). *Community-Based Treatment for Sex Offenders: An Evaluation of Seven Treatment Programmes*. London: Home Office.

BOCHEL, D. (1976). *Probation and After-Care: Its Development in England and Wales*. Edinburgh: Scottish Academic Press.

BRODY, S. (1976). *The Effectiveness of Sentencing: A Review of the Literature*. Home Office Research Study No.35. London: HMSO.

BROWNLEE, I. D. (1995). 'Intensive Probation with Young Adult Offenders: A Short Reconviction Study'. *British Journal of Criminology* 35: 599–612.

BURNETT, R. (1996). *Fitting Supervision to Offenders: Assessment and Allocation Decisions in the Probation Service*. Home Office Research Study No.153. London: Home Office.

CARNIE, J. (1990). *Sentencers' Perceptions of Community Service by Offenders*. Edinburgh: Scottish Office Central Research Unit.

CHAPMAN, T., and HOUGH, M. (1998). *Evidence Based Practice: A Guide to Effective Practice*. London: HMIP.

CHARMAN, E., GIBSON, B., HONESS, T., and MORGAN, R. (1996). 'Fine Impositions and Enforcement Following the Criminal Justice Act 1993'. Home Office Research Findings No.36. London: Home Office.

DAVIES, M. (1969). *Probationers in their Social Environment*. Home Office Research Study No.2. London: HMSO.

DAVIES, M. (1970). *Financial Penalties and Probation.* Home Office Research Study No.5. London: HMSO.

—— (1973). *An Index of Social Environment.* Home Office Research Study No.17. London: HMSO.

—— (1974). *Social Work in the Environment.* Home Office Research Study No.21. London: HMSO.

DAVIS, G., CADDICK, B., LYON, K., DOLING, L., HASLER, J., WEBSTER, A., REED, M., and FORD, K. (1997). *Addressing the Literacy Needs of Offenders under Probation Supervision.* Home Office Research Study No.169. London: Home Office.

DAY, P. (1981). *Social Work and Social Control.* London: Tavistock.

DITTON, J., and FORD, R. (1994). *The Reality of Probation: A Formal Ethnography of Process and Practice.* Aldershot: Avebury.

ELLIS, T., HEDDERMAN, C., and MORTIMER, E. (1996). *Enforcing Community Sentences.* Home Office Research Study No.158. London: Home Office.

FIELDING, N. (1986). *Probation Practice: Client Support under Social Control.* Aldershot: Gower.

FOLKARD, M. S., LYON, K., CARVER, M. M., and O'LEARY, E. (1966). *Probation Research: A Preliminary Report.* Home Office Studies in the Causes of Delinquency and the Treatment of Offenders 7. London: HMSO.

FOLKARD, M. S., FOWLES, A. J., McWILLIAMS, B. C., McWILLIAMS, W., SMITH, D. D., SMITH, D. E., and WALMSLEY, G. R. (1974). *IMPACT Intensive Matched Probation and After-Care Treatment: Volume 1 The Design of the Probation Experiment and an Interim Evaluation.* Home Office Research Study No.24. London: HMSO.

—— SMITH, D. E., and SMITH, D. D. (1976). *IMPACT: Volume 2 The Results of the Experiment.* Home Office Research Study No.36. London: HMSO.

HAXBY, D. (1978). *Probation: A Changing Service.* London: Constable.

HEDDERMAN, C. (1998). 'A Critical Assessment of Probation Research'. *Home Office Research Bulletin* 39: 1–7.

HEDDERMAN, C., and SUGG, D. (1996). 'Does Treating Sex Offenders Reduce Reoffending?'. Home Office Research Findings No.45. London: Home Office.

HOME OFFICE (1984). *Probation Service in England and Wales: Statement of National Objectives and Priorities.* London: Home Office.

—— (1992). *National Standards for the Supervision of Offenders in the Community.* London: Home Office.

—— (1995). *National Standards for the Supervision of Offenders in the Community.* London: Home Office.

—— (1998a). *Criminal Statistics England and Wales.* London: HMSO.

—— (1998b). *Joining Forces to Protect the Public: Prisons-Probation A Consultation Document.* London: Home Office.

—— (1998c). 'Probation Circular 72/1998: Motor Projects'. London: Home Office.

HOUSE OF COMMONS (1998a). *Third Report from the Home Affairs Committee—Alternatives to Prison Sentences: Volume I Report and Proceedings of the Committee.* London: The Stationery Office.

—— (1998b). *Third Report from the Home Affairs Committee—Alternatives to Prison Sentences: Volume II Minutes of Evidence and Appendices.* London: The Stationery Office.

KNAPP, M., ROBERTSON, E., and McIVOR, G. (1992). 'The Comparative Costs of Community Service and Custody in Scotland'. *Howard Journal* 31: 8–30.

LLOYD, C., MAIR, G., and HOUGH, M. (1994). *Explaining Reconviction Rates: A Critical Analysis*. Home Office Research Study No.136. London: HMSO.

McIVOR, G. (1989). *An Evaluative Study of Community Service by Offenders*. University of Stirling: Social Work Research Centre.

—— (1990). 'Community Service and Custody in Scotland'. *Howard Journal* 29: 101–13.

—— (1992a). *Reconviction among Offenders Sentenced to Community Service*. University of Stirling: Social Work Research Centre.

—— (1992b). *Sentenced to Serve: The Operation and Impact of Community Service by Offenders*. Aldershot: Avebury.

McLAUGHLIN, E., and MUNCIE, J. (1994). 'Managing the Criminal Justice System', in J. Clarke, A. Cochrane and E. McLaughlin (eds.), *Managing Social Policy*. London: Sage.

McWILLIAMS, B., and MURPHY, N. (1980). 'Breach of Community Service', in K. Pease and W. McWilliams (eds.), *Community Service by Order*. Edinburgh: Scottish Academic Press.

McWILLIAMS, W. (1980). 'Selection Policies for Community Service: Practice and Theory', in K. Pease and W. McWilliams (eds.), *Community Service by Order*. Edinburgh: Scottish Academic Press.

—— (1983). 'The Mission to the English Police Courts 1876–1936'. *Howard Journal* 22: 129–47.

—— (1985). 'The Mission Transformed: Professionalisation of Probation between the Wars'. *Howard Journal* 24: 257–74.

—— (1986). 'The English Probation System and the Diagnostic Ideal'. *Howard Journal* 25: 241–60.

—— (1987). 'Probation, Pragmatism and Policy'. *Howard Journal* 26: 97–121.

MAIR, G. (1988). *Probation Day Centres*. Home Office Research Study No.100. London: HMSO.

—— (1991). *Part Time Punishment? The Origins and Development of Senior Attendance Centres*. London: HMSO.

—— CRISP, D., SIBBITT, R., and HARRIS, J. (1997). *The Combination Order*. Unpublished report to the Home Office.

—— and LLOYD, C. (1989). *Money Payment Supervision Orders: Probation Policy and Practice*. Home Office Research Study No.114. London: HMSO.

—— —— NEE, C. and SIBBITT, R. (1994). *Intensive Probation in England and Wales: An Evaluation*. Home Office Research Study No.133. London: HMSO.

—— and MAY, C. (1997). *Offenders on Probation*. Home Office Research Study No.167. London: Home Office.

—— and MORTIMER, E. (1996). *Curfew Orders with Electronic Monitoring*. Home Office Research Study No.163. London: Home Office.

—— and NEE, C. (1990). *Electronic Monitoring: The Trials and their Results*. Home Office Research Study No.120. London: HMSO.

—— and —— (1992). 'Day Centre Reconviction Rates'. *British Journal of Criminology* 32: 329–39.

MARTIN, J. P., and WEBSTER, D. (1994). *Probation Motor Projects in England and Wales*. London: Home Office.

MAY, C. (1995). *Measuring the Satisfaction of Courts with the Probation Service*. Home Office Research Study No.144. London: Home Office.

—— (1997). 'Magistrates' Views of the Probation Service'. Home Office Research Findings No.48. London: Home Office.

MAY, T. (1991). *Probation: Politics, Policy and Practice.* Buckingham: Open University Press.

MORTIMER, E., and MAY, C. (1997). *Electronic Monitoring in Practice: The Second Year of the Trials of Curfew Orders.* Home Office Research Study No.177. London: Home Office.

MOXON, D., CORKERY, J., and HEDDERMAN, C. (1992). *Developments in the Use of Compensation Orders in Magistrates' Courts since October 1988.* Home Office Research Study No.126. London: HMSO.

—— SUTTON, M. and HEDDERMAN, C. (1990). *Unit Fines: Experiments in Four Courts.* Research and Planning Unit Paper 59. London: Home Office.

—— HEDDERMAN, C., and SUTTON, M. (1990). *Deductions from Benefit for Fine Default.* Research and Planning Unit Paper 60. London: Home Office.

NEE, C., and SIBBITT, R. (1993). *The Probation Response to Drug Misuse.* Research and Planning Unit Paper 78. London: Home Office.

NEWBURN, T. (1988). *The Use and Enforcement of Compensation Orders in Magistrates' Courts.* Home Office Research Study No.102. London: HMSO.

PEASE, K. (1983). 'Penal Innovations' in J. Lishman (ed.), *Social Work with Adult Offenders.* Aberdeen: University of Aberdeen Press.

—— (1985). 'Community Service Orders' in M. Tonry and N. Morris (eds.), *Crime and Justice: An Annual Review of Research Volume 6.* Chicago, Ill: University of Chicago Press.

—— BILLINGHAM, S., and EARNSHAW, I. (1977). *Community Service Assessed in 1976.* Home Office Research Study No.39. London: HMSO.

—— DURKIN, P., EARNSHAW, I., PAYNE, D., and THORPE, J. (1975). *Community Service Orders.* Home Office Research Study No.29. London: HMSO.

PHILLPOTTS, G. J. O., and LANCUCKI, L. B. (1979). *Previous Convictions, Sentence and Reconviction.* Home Office Research Study No.53. London: HMSO.

RADZINOWICZ, L. (1958). *The Results of Probation.* London: Macmillan.

RAYNOR, P. (1988). *Probation as an Alternative to Custody.* Aldershot: Avebury.

—— and VANSTONE, M. (1994). 'Probation Practice, Effectiveness and the Non-treatment Paradigm'. *British Journal of Social Work,* 24: 387–404.

—— and VANSTONE, M. (1996). 'Reasoning and Rehabilitation in Britain: The Results of the Straight Thinking on Probation (STOP) Programme'. *International Journal of Offender Therapy and Comparative Criminology* 40: 272–84.

READ, G. (1980). 'Area Differences in Community Service Operation', in K. Pease and W. McWilliams (eds.), *Community Service by Order.* Edinburgh: Scottish Academic Press.

SINCLAIR, I. (1971). *Hostels for Probationers.* Home Office Research Study No.6. London: HMSO.

SKINNS, C. D. (1990). 'Community Service Practice'. *British Journal of Criminology* 30: 65–80.

SOFTLEY, P. (1973). *A Survey of Fine Enforcement.* Home Office Research Study No.16. London: Home Office.

—— (1978*a*). *Compensation Orders in Magistrates' Courts.* Home Office Research Study No.43. London: HMSO.

—— (1978*b*). *Fines in Magistrates' Courts.* Home Office Research Study No.46. London: HMSO.

—— and MOXON, D. (1982). *Fine Enforcement.* Research and Planning Unit Paper 12. London: Home Office.

SUGG, D. (1998). 'Motor Projects in England and Wales: An Evaluation'. Home Office Research Findings No.81. London: Home Office.

VASS, A. A. (1984). *Sentenced to Labour: Close Encounters with a Prison Substitute.* St Ives: Venus Academica.

—— and WESTON, A. (1990). 'Probation Day Centres as an Alternative to Custody: A "Trojan Horse" Examined'. *British Journal of Criminology* 29: 255–72.

WHITTAKER, C., and MACKIE, A. (1997). *Enforcing Financial Penalties.* Home Office Research Study No.165. London: Home Office.

WINDLESHAM, LORD (1993). *Responses to Crime: Vol.2 Penal Policy in the Making.* Oxford: Clarendon Press.

—— (1996). *Responses to Crime: Vol 3 Legislating with the Tide.* Oxford: Clarendon Press.

WOOTTON, B. (1978). *Crime and Penal Policy: Reflections on Fifty Years Experience.* London: Allen and Unwin.

YOUNG, W. (1979). *Community Service Orders.* London: Heinemann.

10

DOING RESEARCH IN PRISONS

Roy D. King

INTRODUCTION

I have spent a lot of my professional life inside prison walls, if not exactly behind bars, doing prisons research. Most of this has been in England (King 1972; King and Morgan 1976; King and Elliott 1978; King and McDermott 1989, 1990, 1995) but substantial periods have also been spent in the United States (King 1987, 1991, 1999) and some in Russia (King 1994). In this chapter I offer my reflections on the process of doing research in prisons.

My remarks are directed primarily to those embarking upon prisons research for the first time, whether as doctoral students, novitiate researchers whose first rung on the ladder of a research career involves working on a prisons project, or post-doctoral applicants for their first prisons research contracts. But I hope they may also be of interest to undergraduate or postgraduate students whose courses afford them opportunities, however limited, for placements in prisons. My own enthusiasm for researching prisons, particularly maximum security prisons, came about when, as a postgraduate student at Cambridge, I spent a one-week placement in Wormwood Scrubs. There I met George Blake, who had expressed an interest in taking a degree in sociology to while away some of his forty-two-year sentence. Shortly thereafter his escape triggered the Mountbatten Report (Home Office 1966) which in turn started a long-running debate about maximum security custody in the prison system of England and Wales. Today the excitement I get from doing prisons research is directly proportionate to the height of the walls and the number of coils of razor ribbon—not, I hope, simply out of a vicarious association with sensational people and events, but because here are to be found the most intractable problems of imprisonment in their starkest setting.

For reasons of space I will focus on what I regard as the *craft* of doing research *in* prisons, and for the most part I will limit my remarks to prisons in Britain apart from an occasional sideways glance to the United States or elsewhere when it helps to make a point. I begin, however, with some brief remarks on the growth and scale of prisons research, then consider the politics of getting prisons research funded, up and running, and published, before presenting ten nostrums about the process of doing prisons research. It is a highly selective and personal account and I shall finish with some of my reasons for thinking that prisons research is important and worthwhile.

THE GROWTH AND SCALE OF PRISONS RESEARCH

In many parts of the world prisons remain secret places: in extreme cases they are off limits even to the relatives and lawyers of the prisoners held inside, let alone researchers. That is no longer the case in Britain which probably now leads the English-speaking world, which in turn probably leads the rest of the world, in terms of research in prisons. Although many of the early developments in the sociology of prisons, especially in theoretical and conceptual terms, came from the United States, and although many other English-speaking as well as European jurisdictions have invited or allowed researchers inside, it is in the United Kingdom that the strongest tradition of prisons research by academics has developed. This did not happen overnight.

The report compiled by the Labour Research Department on the evidence of suffragists and conscientious objectors (Hobhouse and Brockway 1922) was received with hostility by the Prison Commissioners. In the dying days of the Commission, however, Sir Lionel Fox, and his successor Sir Arthur Peterson, gave their backing to the pioneering case study of Pentonville (Morris, Morris and Barer 1963). This change of heart came about in the context of what Garland (1994) has described as the emerging governmental project which saw major government support for criminology as an administrative aid through the establishment of the in-house Home Office Research Unit and as a scientific discipline through the foundation of the Cambridge Institute of Criminology. Fox was a believer in the policy benefits that would flow from soundly-based criminological knowledge, and these were days of great expectations about the potential of an administrative criminology. The Morrises said little about the origins of their research, although Fox initially proposed a *comparative* study of Pentonville and Maidstone. Had it taken place this would have demonstrated sufficient contrast in conditions between 'local' and what were then called 'regional training' prisons to have helped in at least two areas of Fox's policy agenda—the development of remand centres to take untried prisoners out of local prisons and the need for a prison building programme to improve physical facilities. At about the same time the Prison Commission invited the Tavistock Institute of Human Relations to appraise the implementation of the 'Norwich system'—the introduction of associated dining on the landings for some prisoners previously fed in cells, a longer working week for prisoners (much longer than they work today), and an early version of using prison officers as personal officers—at Bristol local prison (Emery 1970). The price of harnessing this research resource was, unevenly but inexorably, a new level of openness about what goes on in prisons. In any event in the years since then a tradition of criminological research in prisons has been built up, generating a sizeable group of academics with a detailed, first-hand knowledge of what goes on inside prisons which one simply does not find in other countries.

In a reflexive account such as this I make no attempt to list all the studies, still less to review them systematically. For now it will suffice to sketch in the terrain. There have been studies based on work carried out in individual local, training, or high security prisons for men at Pentonville (Morris, Morris and Barer 1963), Bristol (Emery 1970) Birmingham (Sparks 1971), Durham (Cohen and Taylor 1972), Albany (King and Elliott 1978), Grendon Underwood (Genders and Player 1995) and The Wolds private prison (Bottomley et al. 1997); comparative studies that have examined open and closed prisons (Jones and Cornes 1977), prisons from different security categories (King and McDermott 1995) and high security prisons (Sparks, Bottoms and Hay 1996); and studies based on Dover borstal for young male offenders (Bottoms and McClintock 1973), on Cornton Vale prison for women in Scotland (Carlen 1983, Dobash et al. 1986) and a comparative study of women's prisons in England (Smith 1996). There have also been a number of studies of special topics from conditions for remand prisoners (King and Morgan 1976) to the state of race relations (Genders and Player 1989; McDermott 1990); from suicide and self-harm (Liebling 1992) to studies of the mental health of prisoners (Gunn et al. 1978; Gunn, Maden and Swinton 1991); from absconding from open prisons (Banks, Mayhew and Sapsford 1975) to evaluations of special security units and units for difficult prisoners (Walmsley 1989; Bottomley 1995; Cooke 1989; Bottomley, Liebling and Sparks 1994); from the impact of incentives and earned privileges (Liebling, et al. 1997) to the effectiveness of prison work and vocational training (Simon and Corbett 1996); and from studies of prison staff (Colvin 1977; Marsh et al. 1985; Liebling and Price 1999) to the processes of decision-making in Scottish prisons (Adler and Longhurst 1994). There have even been a few studies which have taken an internationally comparative approach with the prison experience in the Netherlands (Downes 1988) and the United States (King 1991). The great majority of these studies has been funded by the Home Office or its Scottish equivalent—a few have been funded in whole or in part by ESRC or its predecessor SSRC (Jones and Cornes 1977; Adler and Longhurst 1994; King 1991; King and McDermott 1995; Downes 1988), one by the Carnegie Trust (Dobash et al. 1986) and one was unfunded (Cohen and Taylor 1972). The list is illustrative, not exhaustive. I am all too aware that I have not included any of the studies done in-house by prison psychologists, for example, or the occasional research done by serving probation officers and medical officers and other members of staff, or accounts by former prisoners, and no doubt there are others which I have neglected. I shall return to some of these studies later when I consider some methodological issues in doing research in prisons.

THE POLITICS AND ECONOMICS OF PRISONS RESEARCH

Although there has been a considerable opening up of the closed world of British prisons this is not to say that access is by any means guaranteed, or that funding is easy to come by, or that the results of research will always be welcomed. If crime is a political issue, so too is punishment. It is also an economic issue: not only do different forms of punishment cost money, but researchers have to live and require reasonable levels of salary or support if they are to do their research. One of the crucial issues for concern here is that the Home Office is *both* gatekeeper as far as access is concerned *and* principal funder of research, which also means that it has considerable control over what is published and when. In the circumstances it is hardly surprising that researchers sometimes have precarious relationships with officialdom: to put it no higher, most researchers will have experienced some degree of ambivalence in their dealings with the Home Office. It is also true that officials will have experienced some degree of frustration in their dealings with researchers, but the relationship is far from symmetrical with real power resting largely in the hands of officialdom.

Ever since Cohen and Taylor (1972) published their appendix criticizing the Home Office-funded study of pyschological deterioration amongst long-term prisoners (carried out by their colleagues at Durham), there have been some criminologists who regard almost everything done with Home Office funding or approval as necessarily tainted. The reality is much more complex and nuanced than that. Compared to Western Europe or the United States, let alone Russia or Eastern Europe, it is remarkable that in England and Wales, a some-times scratchy relationship has evolved between officials and the research community which, in spite of all the difficulties, has fostered a reasonably steady flow of good quality research, which is building a cumulative base of knowledge and understanding.

There have certainly been situations where researchers have found themselves at least temporarily sidelined, where access has been denied, where publication of results has been suppressed or delayed (Bottomley *et al.* 1997), or self-censored for fear of libel-suits (Sim 1990), and where inappropriate policies have been based ostensibly upon independent research findings (as with the closure of Barlinnie following the press misrepresentation of the report by Bottomley, Liebling and Sparks 1994). But there have also been instances of fruitful collaboration between policy-makers and researchers (following King and Morgan 1980, and see the discussion in King and McDermott 1995: 3–15, as well as much of the work done by Alison Liebling and colleagues); where policy-makers have welcomed adverse research findings exposing the consequences of past policies (King and McDermott 1989); and where important scientific research has been carried out in the most unpromising of political circumstances (for example when Sparks, Bottoms and Hay 1996 were able to address the problem of *social order* in prisons in a climate when politicians, though not necessarily officials, were looking for easy answers on the *control* of prisoners).

It is, of course, necessary to cultivate contacts to some degree in order to gain access, but this does not mean that one automatically buys in to an official agenda. In fact the 'official agenda' has not always been very clear. It certainly is not as monolithic as is often assumed and politicians and their official advisors can sometimes be in conflict. Only a few years ago Michael Howard's deputy, David Maclean, wanted to close down the Home Office Research and Planning Unit because even 'in-house' research was seen as subversive. Even where politicians, policy advisers, and research managers see eye to eye their intentions can still fall foul of the micro-politics at institution level where co-operation may be withheld. Nevertheless, the agenda has become more centralized, culminating in the current drive to marshal research to policy needs through the determination to support only evidence-based practice (Home Office 1998). However, research managers have to work together with outside academics who are not always political dupes, but themselves players of politics, sometimes with considerable skill. Researchers can also play to their own agendas once access has been provided, or on occasion use the denial of access to political effect. My point is simply that this is a two-way process and getting access and funds need not mean that one automatically loses any sense of independence, scholarly judgement, or personal integrity. If it did virtually all prisons research could now be written off. In this complex relationship, it is important to maintain a sense of irony, as well as relativism: for what happens in this country may be a great deal less tainted than what happens elsewhere.

GAINING ACCESS

I shall discuss the issue of gaining access under three sets of circumstances: access for doctoral research; access for independently funded research; and access for Home Office-funded research since the processes are inevitably rather different.

Access for research students It is important to recognize that important research can be and has been done in prisons by doctoral students: two of the best recent examples are Ahmad (1996) and Smith (1996), although I shall give an example of some PhD research which did *not* work as a cautionary tale later in this chapter.

Probably the most important element in gaining access will be the track record in prisons research of the supervisor and the university department concerned. In alphabetical order Bangor, Cambridge, Hull, Keele, LSE, and Oxford have probably had the most consistent commitment to research of this kind, but the situation changes with the mobility of academic staff, and this is not to suggest that access would be denied to would-be doctoral researchers whose supervisors had not previously been involved in prisons research. It is probably still possible for a small-scale study in a single prison to be arranged through direct contact with the prison governor concerned, whose approval will in any case be needed before the research can be carried out. Research which involves some comparative dimension—as did both of the studies mentioned above—is likely to be more sensitive and will almost certainly require a more formal application and written approval from Prison Service Headquarters but it would be best, if possible, first to have cleared as much of the ground as possible in an informal way.

The acceptance of PhD research proposals will depend upon a trade-off between the possible benefits and the possible nuisance of having a doctoral student around. Two approaches are likely to have a good chance of success: research which links to self-contained emerging areas of policy where policy divisions have not yet been able to find a place in the larger official research programme (as with Smith 1996) and fairly narrowly defined pure research which offers further exploration of promising leads which have emerged from earlier research (as with Ahmad 1996). Prison officials will probably see most PhD research as potentially the least threatening—if only because work conducted as an apprentice is bound to be limited in scope and unwelcome findings may be easier to dismiss. If anything there seems now to be some official recognition that PhD, MPhil, and even MA students may provide a useful—and cheap, if not free—resource to undertake exploratory studies of various issues. This could be an area for significant growth.

Access for independently funded research With the right credentials, a viable research proposal, and the prospect of some funding of one's own from a Research Council or some other body there is a reasonable chance of a researcher being granted access providing the topic of research is not too currently controversial. It will help if the researcher has a track record, or the backing of someone with a track record. As with PhD research, it is sometimes possible to get small projects off the ground by making direct contact with prison governors, without the need for central approval. In most cases, however, it would be necessary to submit a formal application for access fully outlining the aims and objectives, the methodology, and the kinds of research facilities required. Decision-makers will want to consult policy divisions to see that the research could have some useful pay-off, but with no funding at stake there is likely to be a greater acceptance of longer-term outcomes based on more theoretical exploration and development work. They will also want to consult line managers to ensure the research is not too disruptive. Since the research would be *additional* to the official research agenda the decision may depend more upon whether there are reasons *against* doing the research.

To talk about seeking access on the basis that one *has* independent funding is, of course, an oversimplification. In reality one would be most unlikely to get ESRC or other independent funding unless one had already demonstrated at least a high probability of access. But access can never come with a cast-iron guarantee. Would-be prison researchers should understand that there can be many reasons for saying 'no' or 'not here' or 'not now' which do not always involve 'big' politics. As often as not the problems may derive from the micro-politics of institutions.

Prisons can be volatile places and prior agreement in principle can be undermined right up to the last moment by local tensions, which may mean a change of research locations. This need not be a problem in a large system where the numbers of institutions can allow considerable scope for substitutability, but if one needs access to a more or less unique institution this can be crucial. In a rare case of completing fieldwork early Kathleen McDermott and I once asked that our ESRC-funded research be extended from male prisons to include the women's prison at Holloway. At the time Holloway was at the centre of one its periodic controversies and the Prison Service indicated that, for local political reasons, it could not be made available as a research location. We decided that none of the other women's prisons offered would be an adequate comparator for our work in the men's prison at Birmingham, and chose instead to take advantage of a unique opportunity to use the remaining time for a quick glimpse at the impact of 'Fresh Start' in the five existing research sites. One commentator criticized us for not including women's prisons in the first place, another for not withdrawing from the research process altogether in the face of such a rebuff from the Home Office. It is important in such circumstances for researchers both to be flexible in making the best of their opportunities and to have the courage of their convictions.

However, I am still thinking through which of several possible reasons is the most likely to account for why, in my current study of supermax custody in the United States, also funded by ESRC, I have been twice denied access by the Federal Bureau of Prisons to its administrative maximum (ADX) facility at Florence, Colorado. On both occasions it was known that I had recently been advising the Prison Service of England and Wales on the feasibility of a super-max facility in Britain, and had a letter of recommendation from the then Director General, Richard Tilt. On the second occasion I had also recruited support from some of the luminaries of American criminology, but to no avail. The decision was all the more puzzling given that several years earlier I had been granted access to the Marion Control Unit and other Federal peniten-tiaries. Fortunately, none of the thirty-four states with supermax facilities which I approached denied me access, and it was possible to re-focus the research programme around some of these.

Access and Home Office funding It is a very different matter if one is seeking to do prisons research and one needs funding from the Home Office. Indeed in these circumstances not only are questions of funding and access inseparable, but issues concerning ownership and publication of the results are also likely to be negotiated at the same time. When the Home Office is paying the piper it not unreasonably expects to call the tune (although it has been quite difficult in practice for officials to control *how* the tune is played). The question now becomes one not of whether there are political reasons *against* the research, but whether there are political reasons *in favour*—although the way in which such matters may be determined has changed dramatically over the years. Increas-ingly the scope for real negotiation has become more restricted.

Newcomers to the field of prisons research are now most likely to become involved in bidding for Home Office funding in response to invitations to tender for a given research project in which the aims, objectives, methodology, access to institutions, timing, and reporting procedures have already been closely specified. Researchers, now known as 'contractors', are invited to com-pete on costs and to some degree on methodology. However, their 'customers' in policy divisions, who have already determined the parameters of the research required, are not necessarily bound to accept the lowest bid. Rather, they reserve the right to choose, presumably on the advice of Home Office research managers, the bid which offers best value bearing in mind other matters including the track record of researchers.

It has not always been this way, and it may be helpful before returning to current problems to see how Home Office-funded research has developed. In the early days ministers and their officials might have been vaguely aware of the potential value of research but not known what research offered the best pro-spects, or how to go about it. In these circumstances it was possible for indi-vidual academics, perhaps with the backing of a prison governor, and often with a direct line into the Home Office at a high level, to get particular projects accepted as relevant to policy needs. For example, in 1967, I was able, with the mentorship of the late John Martin, to respond to governor David Gould's invitation to monitor the opening of his new prison, Albany, and to evaluate the effectiveness of its training regime. In fact it was already too late to research the opening of Albany, but with the agreement of Gould, and the support of Martin, I set about persuading the Home Office Research Unit that what was really needed was a comparative study of several prisons which would describe and, if possible, measure prison regimes, using Albany as a pilot to develop measuring techniques. I argued that it would be vital to be able to describe and measure regimes, since too many studies of the effectiveness of treatment at that time failed to describe just what variables were supposed to produce the treatment effects (or lack of them). The Prison Department was then committed to a policy of treatment, training, and rehabilitation and claimed that its allocation policies were intended to send prisoners to prisons where they would get the treatment they 'needed'—but no-one had yet seen this as a priority area for research. Tom Lodge, then Director of the Research Unit, readily agreed and the *Prison Regimes Project* was funded with access to five prisons.

The subsequent history of this research did not run smoothly. The preliminary findings were presented to the Home Office Research Unit in 1972. They showed that it was possible to measure prison regimes in various ways and that statistically significant differences could be demonstrated. However, we found little evidence of anything which resembled treatment, training, or rehabilitation programmes: the principal differences between prisons were in the 'hotel functions'—the food service, the sanitary conditions, the crowding, and so on—and the way these differences were distributed made no sense to prisoners or staff. Our research did not have the protection of a steering group intended to keep us on the right lines, and we were asked by Lodge's successor to justify our results in ways that rather undermined the confidence of the research team. The third and final stage of the project was never approved and the findings of the comparative study were not written up at the time. However, fifteen years later in a quite different climate it was possible to resurrect those findings to demonstrate how prison regimes had further deteriorated over the period since security and control had become such important issues (King and McDermott 1989). These findings were now welcomed by officials since they spoke to a different agenda—already recognized pre-Woolf (Home Office 1991)—in which the Prison Service needed resources to deal with overcrowding and to improve and maintain standards to counterbalance the concerns with security and control. The lesson, I suppose, is that in research it sometimes pays to take a longer view.

Nevertheless, it is important to stress that there was never any interference in the conduct of the research and the absence of a steering group gave us free rein. The relationship with Albany was maintained over several years and close and co-operative relationships were established. It was possible for us to explore the way in which both staff and prisoners developed strategic ways of doing or spending time, and also to attempt an analysis of the breakdown of order once

Albany had become a dispersal prison—none of which had played any part in the original proposals. When this part of the research was finally published (King and Elliott 1978) it contained a strong critique of dispersal policy, and for several years thereafter I was not able to regain access to high security prisons. In 1983 I therefore turned my attention to maximum security prisons in the United States—access to which, in sharp contrast, was provisionally agreed in trans-Atlantic telephone calls to the Federal Bureau of Prisons and the Minnesota Department of Corrections. By the time I returned security and control issues were back on the research agenda following the *Report of the Control Review Committee* (Home Office 1984), and access opened up once more.

Other research (Bottoms and McClintock 1973) has had similar beginnings to the Albany study, and it may still be possible to convince officials of the need for major research initiatives in this way, although increasingly the Home Office has developed priorities for its annual round of research on the basis of bids from its customers in policy divisions. An example of one priority area identified by the Prison Medical Service, but which nevertheless remained in the future programme of research for several years, was the need for research on the therapeutic prison at Grendon Underwood. The relative proximity of the Oxford Centre for Criminological Research to Grendon and professional links between the two institutions led to the submission of successful proposals (Genders and Player 1995). A similar symbiosis has developed between Cambridge and HM Prison Whitemoor—a dispersal prison which has now played host to several Cambridge-based research projects all at the initiative of successive governors.

To some degree the wider Home Office research agenda has been influenced by periodic consultation exercises with the academic research community, either to comment on the existing programme or to help identify the general directions it might take in the future. Prisons research has not loomed large in general Home Office consultations, although academics have sometimes had an input when a crisis has enabled the Prison Service to obtain priority for particular projects in which it had an interest. One such opportunity occurred following the *Report of the Control Review Committee* (Home Office 1984) which emphasized the need for research. Tony Bottoms, John Gunn, and I were appointed to the Research and Advisory Group (RAG) which was concerned with implementing the recommendations of the CRC, especially the small unit strategy to deal with control problem prisoners, but also the circumstances in which control problems arose in the dispersal prisons. At this time I was about to undertake the ESRC-funded *Security, Control and Humane Containment* project, for which members of the CRC had given substantial backing and effectively guaranteed access, not least because it might throw light on some of these issues through a possible comparison between Gartree, then still a dispersal prison, and Oak Park Heights in Minnesota (King 1991).

We took the view that there were two important strands for RAG-sponsored research to pursue from which wider lessons might be drawn. The first was to compare a 'successful' dispersal prison (such as Long Lartin or Wakefield which had survived without riots or serious disturbances) with an 'unsuccessful' one (such as Albany or Gartree which had been plagued with riots and disturbances). Albany and Long Lartin thus became the sites in a Home Office-funded study (Sparks, Bottoms and Hay 1996) whose sociological importance far transcended the simplistic origins just described but which may not have reached its practitioner audience perhaps because of its theoretical weight. The second was to regard the small units as quasi-experiments in which careful description and detailed analysis of staff–prisoner interactions might offer useful lessons about what could be done to promote greater order throughout the dispersal system. This strand was altogether less successful, in large part because of the way it was funded as a series of often retrospective consultancy exercises in which the consultants could do little more than rehearse the obvious whilst regretting they had no opportunity to pursue the more interesting issues (Bottomley 1995).

In recent years, however, the preferred mechanism for allocating research budgets has been for policy divisions to develop research briefs and for these to be put out to tender, and I now return to a consideration of the advantages and disadvantages of these arrangements. On the one hand it has to be said that the process looks fairer and more transparent as well as more systematic than heretofore: it is also clearly more businesslike. On the other hand it can be argued that to some extent these advantages are more apparent than real, and that serious questions have to be raised about whether this system succeeds in getting the best research done or even getting reasonable, let alone best, value for money. Nevertheless, it is important to say that many of the criticisms I raise have to do with practicalities rather than larger political concerns. In good faith they could be met by revisions to existing procedures.

First, it is by no means clear that all interested researchers are made aware of the opportunity in time to prepare a realistic tender. If the Home Office is genuinely interested in opening up research opportunities to the widest audience it needs both to ensure that all media are used to advertise tenders—the press, the Internet, letters to all Departments of Criminology, and so on—and that much longer and more realistic lead times are provided for the preparation of proposals and start dates for the research. As things stand 'inside track' researchers, working in institutions where it is possible to retain researchers who are able to switch activities at short notice, are considerably advantaged. Indeed, if unofficial reports are to be believed, it still happens that individual researchers are telephoned and invited to 'tender' for projects which may not be advertised at all.

Secondly, there seems little point in being business-like when scientific research does not proceed, and cannot proceed, in accordance with business principles, but marches instead to the sound of a different drummer. The present system undoubtedly encourages researchers to overlook the sometimes massive methodological problems which have been inherent in research specifications attached to tender documents and to say that they will deliver what manifestly cannot be delivered within the scope of the time limits and the funding available. Some successful tenders have simply repeated the words of the customer's tender specification as though they had come from the pen of the researcher. Such tenders, as their authors know, would get short shrift if they were submitted as research proposals to the ESRC. In fact it cannot be in the real long-term interests of either customers or contractors for both parties to collude in a process which ignores intractable methodological issues. The best protection for contractors and researchers alike would be to build a serious element of peer review into all tender decision-making.

The net effect of having wider advertising, more realistic deadlines, and real peer review would be to add perhaps four months to start times and, depending on the methodological issues at stake, rather more to finishing times: but it would provide much better guarantees of getting the best research for the money.

Sometimes the Prison Service has put research out to tender in a two-stage process. First, researchers are invited to bid to undertake a literature review on the subject. Only when the outcome of the review is known are researchers invited to bid for the resultant research in those areas where previous research has failed to come up with the answers. There is an obvious and artful economy in organizing matters in this way which inhibits the widening of research agendas once access has been granted. But the treating of the two stages as though they were independent is a kind of legal fiction, because the winners of the first contract could hardly avoid placing themselves in pole position for winning the second (Price and Liebling 1998; Liebling and Price 1999). In the interests of maintaining a continuing research commitment from academe to the changing needs of the prison system, the Prison Service has developed innovative research funding procedures for one of the leading prison researchers—Dr Alison Liebling: it supplied the required 30 per cent of outside funding to secure a four-year ESRC Research Fellowship (1994–8) and then the 50 per cent necessary to support a Leverhulme Special Research Fellowship (1998–2000). Research proposals were required in the usual way, and even the most jaundiced observer would have to say that this imaginative funding arrangement has been very productive, with work of the highest scientific quality.

I cannot really speak to the problems associated with getting materials published, because I have never experienced them. I submitted the text of my only Home Office-funded study to the Research Unit and to prison staff and prisoners for comment (as a matter of courtesy since there was no contractual requirement). It took a long time to get comments back but no strings were attached and many comments were helpful. After carefully considering the disagreements which remained we decided to stick to our version and publish anyway. I know that colleagues have expressed irritation about publication, not so much about censorship but about their reports being Crown copyright, the resultant format of publication, and the often inordinate delay. In today's climate it would be folly to take a publish-and-be-damned attitude if one wanted to gain future research contracts. It seems likely that in the contract-awarding process officials probably have a fair idea of what 'line' different researchers may take. Perhaps the strongest argument for independently funded research is that it puts the matter of who owns the results beyond question.

It should be stressed that initial access is only the first hurdle. In fact negotiating and renegotiating access takes place on almost a daily basis once the research is under way—but that brings me to the research process itself.

THE PROCESS OF PRISONS RESEARCH

I first tried to set out as explicitly as possible my views on the process of 'doing research in prison' in the context of my report on Albany (King and Elliott 1978, ch. 2). As well as trying to be transparent about what we did ourselves I tried to deconstruct at some length what had really happened methodologically in the studies of Pentonville by Terence and Pauline Morris (1963) and of Durham by Cohen and Taylor (1972)—for neither of these monographs devoted any detailed discussion to methodology—although Cohen and Taylor (1977) returned to these matters in a famous reflexive account after I had gone to press. I also reviewed the two other extant studies at that time by Bottoms and McClintock (1973) and by Emery (1970). On re-reading that I find that my views have not much changed, and to some extent have been reinforced by my own experience since and those subsequently reported by others in the field.

TEN NOSTRUMS FOR FIELD RESEARCH IN PRISONS

I shall therefore take the liberty here of providing ten nostrums for doing field research in prisons. They are neither exhaustive—each could be elaborated at some length—nor are they of equal importance: the would-be researcher should ascribe weights to each depending upon the aims and scope of their research project.

You have to be there This may sound obvious. But it does have to be said. It simply is not possible to do research that will tell you much about prisons without getting out into the field. No amount of theorizing or reading in an office can substitute for the hands-on experience of spending your time in prison. The kind of administrative data collection involved, for example, in the Prison Service's in-house regime monitoring (and similar exercises) cannot be taken at face value and can only really be understood in the context of local knowledge, not least of the way the forms are completed at source (see King and McDermott 1995). Postal questionnaires addressed to staff or prisoners, one-off interviews, or diagnostic tests with prisoners, or pencil and paper assessments of involvement in the 'inmate sub-culture' are each likely to have value only in a severely limited way. After some thirty years of doing research in prisons I find myself wedded to a paradox: on the one hand a prison is a prison is a prison in which much the same functions are performed with extraordinary regularity; but on the other hand every prison is unique and its history, structure, and culture influence the way those functions are performed. Even such a small group of institutions as our dispersal prisons, with quite narrowly defined and carefully monitored roles, are far more different from each other than outsiders could possibly imagine. You can only appreciate that if you are there.

You have to do your time I now think that, given good planning in advance, a high degree of co-operation, and more luck than perhaps I deserve, I can, working alone, find out a lot about a prison in a month of concentrated field-work: five and sometimes six days a week. I like to make sure that I work all shifts, including the graveyard (night) shift, and weekends in a relatively high-profile manner. But this is a punishing schedule and is not normally to be recommended. Spreading it out to two months means that one can take regular breaks between bouts of concentrated activity. Three to three and a half days a week in the field is probably about right, because it gives the opportunity for emotional release after playing the researcher role, which necessarily involves controlling one's responses to a degree that is hard to maintain for long periods. As well as recharging one's batteries, the days off allow one to write up notes, consider what one has learned and, if necessary, change strategies for the next period. But these are minimum timings. Longer is almost always better.

Although time is likely to be a scarce resource for the researcher there are several reasons for taking as much time as one can. It permits one not so much to establish a role—I shall argue below that the sooner that is done the better—but to demonstrate the integrity with which one lives it. Being there during the night shift helps to demonstrate to staff that one is prepared to do one of the most unpleasant duties they might have to do. Being there at weekends helps to demonstrate to prisoners that one is prepared to share, at least to this limited extent, their privations. One also sees different things and gets different opportunities to talk at nights and weekends. Having time means you can always wait for a better moment to ask your questions (providing you have remembered to keep good notes) and to put yourself out for others rather than to press people for answers because you are busy. But above all the passage of time changes the nature and quality of information to which one becomes party: as people recognize your presence as relatively permanent, they 'know' you will 'understand' what they say on the basis of what you 'must already have seen'.

In Russia, my hosts could not understand why anyone would wish to spend long periods of time in prison (we were sometimes talking days rather than weeks or months). I explained that getting to know a prison was like peeling an onion, except that each new layer was subtly different from the last—rather like the political *matryoshki* dolls which had just become a tourist item (then it was Gorbachev concealing Chernenko and his predecessors—now it is Clinton concealing Monica Lewinski and her predecessors!). In the ideal world one knows when to stop when the next layer is so little different from the last (i.e. when the probability that the next story you hear is one you have already heard several times before) that saturation has occurred.

You should not work alone unless you have to Ideally fieldwork should be carried out with two (or more) researchers who should sometimes work together and sometimes separately. Not only does this double (or otherwise multiply) the number of person days in the field, but it also provides a sounding board, with the opportunity to test the reliability of each other's observations, and trying out alternative explanations for what has been observed. It also gives staff and prisoners a choice of researcher to whom they can relate, which in turn works to the benefit of the research. Sparks and Hay, who did most of the fieldwork in Albany and Long Lartin (Sparks, Bottoms and Hay 1996) found their identities changed from 'the spies' to 'Pinky and Perky' or 'Bill and Ben' and the 'dynamic duo' as the research progressed. Kathleen McDermott and I became known as 'Dempsey and Makepeace' when we worked at Nottingham and Gartree (and no doubt now would have become known as Mulder and Scully if we conducted the research now). Although we always intended to write up the implications of doing research with different combinations of male and female researchers (McDermott and King 1988: 358, n.3) we have never found time to do so, although others have reflected on gender issues in doing prisons research (Liebling 1992; Genders and Player 1995; Smith 1996).

Just as important it means that it is possible to unwind with someone else who has experienced, albeit also at second hand, the pains and frustrations of prisoners and staff which the prisons researcher absorbs like a sponge. Field-workers coming out of research sites tend to behave like hyperactive children, so it helps if your co-workers are also friends with whom you can share both the highs and the lows. It is impossible to overestimate the value of this mutual support, although these luxuries, of course, are unlikely to be available to the

PhD researcher unless he or she is attached to colleagues working on some wider project. The lone researcher bears a large emotional burden, and there is simply no denying that this is a cross many PhD students will have to carry. The size of the burden can be reduced to the extent that the research itself can be narrowly limited in focus, but otherwise the best advice is to spend short periods in the field at a stretch, spend long periods debriefing with your supervisor, and if possible acquire a long suffering and sympathetic partner who is prepared to share it.

You have to know why you are there One of the most difficult aspects of prisons research is to find a convincing and acceptable research role, which makes it crystal clear why one is there. The really tricky thing about this is that you have to start living the role from day one. Day two is already too late. The most difficult questions will be posed at the very beginning and may be designed to test exactly where you stand. Getting the answers right first time is vital. Redressing the situation later is a steeply uphill task. The research message has first to be transmitted successfully to staff. Their advice can often then be taken about how best to get the message across to prisoners, so long as one never sacrifices research control (written research communications should *always* bear the signature of the researchers, not the prison managers). In my experience, prisoners readily understand why the introduction to the prison is done in that way without regarding the research as compromised or management-oriented. Indeed prisoners would be not a little surprised if researchers were able to by-pass staff and move directly into a dialogue with prisoners: I well recall a prisoner whom I interviewed in Oak Park Heights pat-searching me for a wire (slightly bizarre because I had my tape recorder on the table) and checking the room for hidden microphones because he assumed I must be 'the man' since I had officially, and so readily, been given access to him (of all people).

In my earlier writing on these issues (King and Elliott 1978) I characterized the justifications for the roles claimed by prison researchers at that time as ranging from *independent* (Morris, Morris and Barer 1963), *officially sponsored* (Emery 1970), *mutual prisoner and research interest* (Cohen and Taylor 1972), and *mutual staff and research interest* (Bottoms and McClintock 1973). I argued that each of these was viable, but that each brought with it its own problems— not least in terms of how understandable the researcher seemed in the eyes of potential respondents (or fellow participants). My own approach, then as now, is to state as clearly as I can that my commitment is neither to management, nor to prisoners, nor to scientific objectivity or ethical neutrality, but to the specific nature of my own research problems. For the solutions to these I need the help of staff and prisoners alike, whose respect and co-operation I hope to earn: I try to be what I am—a kind of obsessional boffin who is also a citizen and a person with fads and foibles like others of that breed. I have resisted the temptation here to try to categorize all subsequent research within this kind of classification, but I note that at least one team of researchers since then has found something like my approach the most comfortable to live with (Liebling 1999).

In our more recent monograph (King and McDermott 1995) we, regrettably, devoted all too little space to the research process: this was partly because the research was already widely published and we had included methodological snippets in several papers, but mostly it was because one of us had already written in detail about the general process in the earlier collaboration with Ken Elliott and it almost seemed unnecessary to say it all again. By then this had all become lived experience, almost second nature.

One excellent and nicely expressed recent analysis of some of the problems associated with creating a research identity is given by Sparks, Bottoms and Hay (1996, Appendix A). They point out that the prison researcher starts out with 'few natural advantages' and 'looks naïve "green", uncomfortable and out of place'. Moreover, with 'no uniform' and 'no keys' there is 'no proper job or activity' which staff or prisoners can immediately recognize and so researchers may be confused with other, more familiar roles—probation officers or trainees of one kind or another. Most researchers probably pay some attention to the way they dress or comport themselves so that they avoid these confusions as far as possible, without drawing too much attention to themselves (though for a more self-assertive stance on this see Genders and Player 1995).

Sparks, Bottoms and Hay go on to liken the researcher, at least in the early stages of the research, to 'an ignorant spy' who clearly has some implicit connection to the 'powers that be' or he would not be there, foisted on to the prisoners and the staff whether they liked it or not, and with a free-ish run of their private domains. But they also acknowledge that to deny such connections would not only make the researcher untrustworthy but potentially something worse, someone 'without position or purpose'—'in short a fool' especially as he chooses to spend months at a time hanging around a prison.

I am not at all comfortable with the spy metaphor—because it suggests that the researcher is working on behalf of someone other than him or herself—but I ought to say something about managing one's identity when one clearly does have connections with 'authority'. In my current work on supermaximum security prisons in the United States I explained to Departments of Correction that I had advised the Prison Service on the feasibility of Learmont's proposal for building two supermax prisons in England and Wales (Home Office 1995), and enclosed a letter of endorsement from the Director General of Her Majesty's Prison Service with my research proposals and requests for access and facilities. There is little doubt that this considerably eased the anxieties which Departments of Corrections would otherwise have had about granting me access to these highly controversial facilities (though it cut no ice, as I have already indicated, with the Federal Bureau of Prisons). However, there were obvious dangers in terms of my research role and these played out differently in different circumstances. In two states where I conducted detailed fieldwork over many weeks, and in some others where I spent more than a few days in institutions, nobody had too much difficulty in understanding that my advice to the Prison Service was in the past and that my present role was as a researcher learning how this particular facility functioned and what it was like to be a prisoner or a member of staff there. In several other states where I spent most of my time at Department of Corrections Headquarters and made only brief site visits to institutions which did not involve talking to prisoners, it was sometimes difficult to disabuse my hosts of the idea that I had an office in Buckingham Palace and advised the Queen as to which of her subjects should spend how long in the Tower. Nevertheless, in these instances, I became aware that this was more of a problem for me—because I was anxious not to present myself as something I was not—than it was for them. In practice, given the limited time at my disposal, the residual Home Office connection served to expedite matters and to enhance access on 'difficult' topics. It seems to me that providing there is sufficient time, and sufficient interest, most respondents are able to bring considerable sophistication to the understanding of multiple roles and cross-cutting connections once these are clearly laid out.

I am also slightly puzzled about why Sparks, Bottoms and Hay (1996) suggest that the best one can hope for, as a prison researcher, is 'to move over the course of time, from being a grudgingly tolerated fool to a fairly welcome one' (p. 349). It is puzzling because, as we have seen, they also say it is when the researcher *denies* the institutional connections between the university and the 'powers that be' that he will be seen as having 'no position or purpose' and become 'in short a fool'. Yet it seems clear, by implication at least, that the Cambridge researchers did not deny those institutional connections and so the appellation of fool should not have applied. I would like to suggest that prison researchers can set their sights slightly higher than this—though they will always be seen as slightly odd.

Sparks, Bottoms and Hay's account reinforces the point made in King and Elliott's that academic researchers do not have a great deal in common with either prisoners or prison staff. Whereas most researchers can identify with the pains and frustrations of the prisoner and the fears and boredom of the prison officer, it is extremely difficult for prison researchers to present themselves, in any convincing way, as somehow *representing* prisoners—as Cohen and Taylor (1972) professed to do—or prison officers—as no-one in this country has tried to do. Such improbable identifications are probably best avoided or left to that comparatively rare breed of poacher-turned-gamekeeper: the ex-con or the ex-prison officer who enters the research arena. Amongst American work the excellent and influential writings of John Irwin (1970) on prisoners and Kelsey Kauffman (1988) on prison officers owes much to their prior experiences of those roles, however brief. To the best of my knowledge we have no equivalents in Britain: though there are two cautionary tales to which I will draw attention in the course of setting out subsequent nostrums.

You must always remember that research has costs for staff and prisoners Doing research in prisons is inevitably going to be disruptive of normal prison activities to some degree, and will require greater or lesser input from staff. These inputs will always have some costs, which researchers cannot ignore. It is always best to explain what your needs are up front, and to be as accommodating as possible to the needs of staff and prisoners and to work around the dictates of the daily routine (this is where working nights is so useful—once staff know you are prepared to do that they will much more willingly put themselves out for you). If you get what you need remember to say 'thank you'. If not, be resourceful: there are always alternative ways of getting the information.

The costs of any particular item in the research programme may vary enormously depending on the type of custody. In January 1999 during fieldwork in Colorado State Penitentiary it took seventy-four separate escorts to bring thirty-seven prisoners from their living 'pods' to the visits area for interview and then to take them back again. Since each escort involved three officers and each journey, allowing time for cuffing, shackling, and searching, took about half an hour, this meant not only that the Colorado Department of Corrections was effectively paying the equivalent of one officer's wages for three weeks in order for this part of the study alone to be carried out but also that it constituted a considerable logistical problem. In this case it was important that we allowed the watch commander to come up with an efficient solution to timing and locating the interviews, and that when he found that the programme had to be changed because of staffing needs elsewhere we immediately accommodated his new suggestions. It was also important that we thanked the officers concerned, because they found this a chore, and made sure that we talked to them as part of the research programme later. In this instance the costs for prisoners were minimal: coming to talk to researchers in visits was usually preferable to the alternatives available, but in other prisons that would not necessarily have been the case.

Every activity involving the research will be at the expense of something else. Fortunately, providing one checks out the alternatives and makes arrangements accordingly, most prisoners find it a welcome change to talk to outsiders, and most staff will be glad to unload to researchers who are prepared to take an interest in them as ordinary people doing a difficult, sometimes dangerous, often boring, job and who bother to find out what they think and feel about it. Both may be concerned, however, about what each other may tell the researchers, which leads to my next nostrum.

You must know when to open your mouth and when to keep it closed The rules here are easy to specify but can sometimes be devilishly hard to live up to in practice. It is important to be open and honest about who you are and what you want to do and why you want to do it. In our account of the work in Albany, we described in some detail how we actually *answered* the difficult questions: what's it all about? why here? what's in it for us? what's in it for you? what will you do if (such and such) happens? and what then will you publish?—all of which took up several pages of the main text (King and Elliott 1978: 51–64). Nevertheless, it is easy to explain the general aims of the research though harder to relate the specifics to the generalities: easy to say what information one wants but harder to say exactly why one wants it, sometimes because one is not sure oneself and sometimes because one or another party might find it threatening.

Living day by day in prisons and establishing relationships with both prisoners and staff can put researchers into delicate situations. Establishing a relationship with anybody involves exchanging information between the parties, and researchers ask so much of others they have to give something of themselves. However, one cannot lose sight of the fact that prisons are dangerous places and it would be foolish not to monitor what one gives out—private addresses, personal information about family, perhaps even the specifics of where one goes for holidays could all be dangerous topics.

One of the most difficult dilemmas to resolve is that the researcher typically gives at least limited guarantees of confidentiality, but may be frequently invited to breach them. The problem most usually comes from staff and arises in two ways. Staff frequently tell researchers about a particular prisoner, and then knowing the prisoner has been interviewed, ask for confirmation of their view. Or else staff may be fearful about what a prisoner or prisoners say about them and may ask the researcher what they have said. I have managed to train myself always to say something like 'You must understand that whatever you say to me is confidential and it wouldn't be fair if I did not do the same for (so and so) . . . but I think you would be surprised how often prisoners really appreciate the difficulties that staff have and do not immediately slag them off'. But it is amazing how frequently one has first to bite one's tongue.

You must do whatever you have to do to observe but do not go native Much is talked about participant observation in books on methodology, and the phrase is frequently used to cover all kinds of involvements in the research enterprise. It is my contention that observation is much more important than participation, and that participation has a rather special meaning in the prisons context. My first cautionary tale concerns an attempt to get close to the prison officer in research terms. I once arranged for a graduate student to go through the entire prison officer training programme at Newbold Revel. Careful protocols were put in place. Everyone, both trainers and trainees, knew that he was a graduate student studying at first hand the process of becoming a prison officer which was to be the subject of his PhD under my supervision. In the process the student concerned went so native that he lost all powers of observation and was incapable of making any kind of detached analysis. He became, to all intents and purposes, a prison officer (though without the licence to practise) and he never completed his PhD.

Since observation is of the essence, the researcher needs to do whatever is necessary in order to observe that which is required to fulfil the aims of the project, subject to certain caveats. For prisoners the prison world is effectively, for want of a better term, home. A prisoner will often speak of his cell as his 'house' or 'pad'. Observation of private activities in private spaces by researchers should, it seems to me, be subject to the same kind of restraint one would impose if one were in someone else's home—that is, one does not poke around in drawers and closets. Although, as I argued earlier, the researcher should always think of him- or herself as a guest, and remember to say please and thank you, the same kinds of restrictions do not apply to the public spaces or to the world of work, which are governed by more universalistic criteria. Perhaps I should simply say here that it is important for the researcher to take advantage of whatever opportunities for observation present themselves and then to ask questions about what one has seen. Stretching this principle to its limits I once discovered that I, along with many other academics and virtually all NGOs offering support to prisoners and their families, was on an (outdated) list of persons and organizations to whom information was not to be provided!

The possibilities of *participating* as observer in prisons are strictly limited and in any case not to be recommended, except in the following sense. The researcher inevitably constitutes a new element in the situation, and thereby changes it. Staff and prisoners cannot avoid taking some notice of the researcher even if it is only in the form of avoidance procedures. The researcher cannot help but participate by carrying out the role thus created. But going native, or getting too close to prisoners or staff, will almost certainly be counter-productive. Staff have to learn that one will spend time with prisoners out of sight or hearing: prisoners have to learn that one will similarly spend time with staff. Different researchers will have different views on just where the boundaries have to be drawn. I personally would never conduct prisons research in which I carried keys although some researchers have done so. In my view possession of keys is so symbolic of the difference between freedom and captivity that it would place the researcher too close to staff. I have been offered keys, but refused them, preferring to wait and to be seen to be waiting, at gates and sally ports. It makes it plain that one is in but not of the prison.

For the rest I do not believe there are right answers to where the boundaries are drawn: but each researcher will have to take *some* line and be prepared to justify it. It may seem unduly pragmatic to say that where the line is drawn may depend upon what one is trying to achieve, but that may nevertheless be preferable to a position based on high principles of scientific independence or neutrality which may be difficult to realize in practice. At bottom it is up to the researcher to demonstrate to both staff and prisoners that he or she seeks to learn from and appreciate all points of view, without necessarily committing him- or herself to any of them. I have found that people fairly readily appreciate it when I tell them that I have an obsessive commitment to a research problem which I will only really understand if I listen to all sides. The longer one is there the easier it is to carry this off. Persistence brings its rewards: I have been told to 'fuck off' (in several languages) by prisoners on many occasions and cold shouldered by staff (and on occasion 'grassed up'), but some of those same prisoners and staff came to initiate conversations before the end of the fieldwork.

You should triangulate your data collection wherever possible The virtues of triangulation are well known: if it is possible to get corroboration for an interpretation of one set of data from data collected by other means then one's confidence in the validity of the interpretation is increased. On this basis if what one has seen through observation is confirmed by what staff and prisoners tell one in interviews or in self-completion questionnaires, and this in turn can be verified by what can be gleaned from documentary sources of various kinds, then one can have considerable confidence in the validity of the findings. What is more problematic is what to do when these various sources provide conflicting accounts. Are the data collection instruments flawed and unreliable? Has the situation changed? May the same events mean different things to different people? It is here, of course, that the judgement of the researcher comes into its own, but it is surely incumbent upon the researcher not to select what suits but to report the conflicts as fully as possible so that the reader may also try to form a judgement. But there are much more mundane reasons for using multiple sources of data which go along the lines that it would be foolish to put all one's eggs in one basket. The order in which one uses different data sources can be crucial. As a rule of thumb, begin with observation and records, then proceed to interviews in which what one has seen and read, can be subjected to questioning and fuller understanding, and finally move to questionnaires in which one can test the generality of what one has discovered in the widest population. Proceeding in this way also enhances the chances of getting the best response. Questionnaires will be more likely completed at the end of fieldwork when strong research rapport has been built up: probing questions in depth interviews can only be asked when there is something to ask about on the basis of puzzling events already observed.

You must strike a balance between publicity and anonymity My second cautionary tale concerns the cardinal principle of social research that one should protect the anonymity of one's subjects whose participation in the research is usually sought in return for a guarantee of confidentiality. A few years ago my son was aggrieved to discover, as a sociology student at City University, the dismissive remarks about his father's work by John McVicar, once Britain's 'most wanted' who 'got sociology' in jail. 'One of the books that have recently been published on an English prison', McVicar wrote, 'is almost a treatise on prison management: the only way I can recommend King and Elliott's *Albany* is as a lesson in how not to conduct prison research' (McVicar 1982: 202). On reading the chapter so disconcertingly drawn to my attention I pointed out, in my defence, two things. One, that McVicar never articulated a *single* (not one) further word to explain what exactly it was about the Albany study which breached the rules of how one should do prison research to support his *ex cathedra* judgement. And two, that in this same essay McVicar himself breaches the most fundamental rule of prison research: namely not to identify vulnerable respondents. One of the prisoners he affected to disguise, but in fact very clearly identified, is still in custody and could still be put in threat of his life as a result of what McVicar wrote.

Protecting the vulnerable is one thing but I have never taken the view that confidentiality can be absolute. I *always* tell staff and prisoners that I would not regard as confidential information given to me about planned self-harm or harm to others, for example, or a planned escape, because I always make it clear that I am a citizen and would have my own problems about living with that information. In the event I have nevertheless become privy to information that I would rather not have had but have still kept it secret (cf. the sensitive discussion of this problem in her book on suicide in prison by Liebling 1992). I also make it clear to senior staff that since the prison is bound to be identifiable from the published report it will not be possible to conceal their identities. I have never quite understood why some reports of prison studies go to great lengths to disguise the identities of the prisons (and thence everyone in them?). When I come across such accounts I cannot resist the challenge of identifying the prisons from the contextual data thus supplied. The record, I think, is probably held by Canter and Ambrose (1980) in their study of prison design and use where all sixteen participating prisons can be fairly readily identified from the contextual data supplied. I have always named the prisons in my own research studies since I believe that to be in the public interest: so far it has not been a problem for the senior staff involved or for me, although it has meant that I have occasionally had to impose some self-censorship. Rightly or wrongly I have preferred that to the alternative of leaving such individuals exposed once the translucent veil of anonymity covering the institution has been lifted.

You should try to leave the site as clean as possible It is important to recognize that prisons constitute a very small world in which the reputation of all researchers collectively can depend upon the legacy left behind by any one individually. Providing one has made no promises which one cannot deliver, and providing one takes the time to discuss and explain as one goes along, this should not be too difficult, but it is necessary to be alert to rumours and speculations and to deal with them as quickly and as publicly as possible. It then only remains to make sure that one leaves as few loose ends as possible. Some researchers find it hard to leave the field, mostly because in the course of the research one inevitably makes rewarding relationships, in which confidences are exchanged which seem more than just doing the job. However, this should not be a problem at the institutional, as distinct from the personal, level. Most fieldwork programmes follow a natural trajectory, hard work at the beginning to win support leads to a middle stage of fruitful co-operation, followed by a tailing off as both researcher and researched recognize that the objectives have more or less been achieved and research fatigue settles in. This last period can be difficult, because the researcher often leaves some of the more boring tasks to the end and the researched, sensing the end, can find it more difficult to keep up their end of the bargain. I usually try to leave one loose end hanging, explicitly or implicitly, to provide an opportunity for going back if need be. It is not unusual for contacts to be maintained with individuals, especially prisoners but staff also, long after the fieldwork is done.

CONCLUSION

I hope it will be clear that I have found the process of doing research in prisons endlessly fascinating, though it is not the kind of fascination that is easily conveyed at dinner parties. It does not make good small-talk, at least not for long, and casually mentioning that you have just returned from prison, especially a deep-end maximum security prison, can lead to misunderstandings. I have some friends in France who deal with this by regarding me as a saintly figure graciously descending into dungeons reclaiming the souls of the lost, but in Britain it more usually leads into discussions about prisons being holiday camps, and in the United States about the rights and wrongs of capital punishment. The table talk moves on to other more congenial topics for the chattering classes, but I sometimes find myself wondering whether my dinner companions would cope with the privations of maximum security confinement with the same dignity that I have occasionally been privileged to see in some prisoners.

So why then do I continue with this line of research? In 1973 I went to the United States intending to pursue other areas of interest on sentencing policy and parole decisions. But as young teachers and researchers at Yale in 1973, my colleague Kelsey Kauffman and I were able to take a party of students as 'guests' of the Connecticut Department of Corrections where we were all locked up for seventy-two hours, guarded by professional prison officers in a prison used for staff training purposes. Twelve of those hours I spent in 'the hole' having been 'fitted up' on charges of possessing the paraphernalia for brewing prison 'pruno'. I knew (didn't I?) that I would be released, that my wife would meet me at the end, that my students and I would de-brief on a situation, though 'unreal' much more real than anything dreamed up by Haney, Banks and Zimbardo (1973) in their so-called experiment. But it was a long seventy-two hours and it was sometimes hard not to entertain doubts when I knew that somebody else had the key. Although the Latin did not spring readily to my lips as I was stripped and made to bend over and 'spread em' on being released from solitary confinement, the question did—*quis custodiet, ipsos custodies?* or who guards the guards?

How is it possible for prisoners to survive in the most extreme conditions of overcrowding or prolonged solitary confinement in a world virtually devoid of stimulation? How is it possible for managers and staff to plan and carry out regimes that subject prisoners to an all-encompassing authority without abusing that authority? And how can staff daily go through the grind of locking, unlocking, escorting, searching, and supervising, without themselves becoming demeaned by the process, or taking a delight in the humiliation or torture of their charges? At what point in such a process may moral authority pass from captor to captive? How is it that, despite the obvious divisions, most prisons, most of the time, remain in a tolerable state of order without staff and prisoners, or prisoners and prisoners, constantly at each other's throats?

These are challenging intellectual questions in their own right. But there is no shortage of intellectual challenges, and for me it is also important to believe that even partial answers could make some modest difference to the human condition—otherwise one might as well do something more profitable for a living. I am no longer so sanguine about the capacity of my research, or anyone else's for that matter, to make much of a difference as once I was. The same prisoner identified by John McVicar once told me after I had explained the intention behind my research that the Home Office would 'look at your results, find the one thing they can screw us with and they will implement that—the rest will stay on a dusty shelf'. As the years go by it may be that I become content with smaller and smaller differences—but there is still a challenge in that.

SUGGESTIONS FOR FURTHER READING

There are all too few detailed discussions on the doing of research in prisons, but the following are essential reading: *Albany: Birth of a Prison—End of an Era* (chapter 2) by Roy D. King and Kenneth W. Elliott; 'Talking about Prison Blues', by Stan Cohen and Laurie Taylor in *Doing Sociological Research*, edited by Colin Bell and Howard Newby; *Prisons and the Problem of Order* (Appendix A) by Richard Sparks, Anthony E. Bottoms, and Will Hay; *Suicide in Prison* (chapter 5) by Alison Liebling, and 'Doing Research in Prison: Breaking the Silence', by Alison Liebling, in *Theoretical Criminology* (1999). There is also an interesting chapter on methodology in Genders and Player's account of *Grendon: A Study of a Therapeutic Prison* (chapter 2).

REFERENCES

ADLER, M., and LONGHURST, B. (1994). *Discourse, Power and Justice: Towards a New Sociology of Imprisonment.* London: Routledge.

AHMAD, S. (1996). *Fairness in Prison.* Unpublished PhD thesis, Cambridge University.

BANKS, C., MAYHEW, P., and SAPSFORD, R. (1975). *Absconding from Open Prisons.* London: HMSO.

BOTTOMLEY, A. K. (1995). *CRC Special Units: A General Assessment.* London: Home Office Research and Planning Unit.

—— JAMES, A., CLARE, E., and LIEBLING, A., (1997). *Monitoring and Evaluation of Wolds Remand Prison, and Comparisons with Public-sector Prisons in Particular HMP Woodhill.* Hull and Cambridge: A Report for the Home Office Research and Statistics Directorate.

—— LIEBLING, A. and SPARKS, R. (1994). *The Barlinnie Special Unit and Shotts Unit.* Edinburgh: Scottish Prison Service.

BOTTOMS, A. E., and McCLINTOCK, F. H. (1973). *Criminals Coming of Age.* London: Heinemann.

CANTER, D., and AMBROSE, I. (1980). *Prison Design and Use Study: Final report.* Guildford: Department of Psychology, University of Surrey.

CARLEN, P. (1983). *Women's Imprisonment: a Study in Social Control.* London: Routledge and Kegan Paul.

COHEN, S., and TAYLOR, L. (1972). *Psychological Survival: The Experience of Long-Term Imprisonment.* Harmondsworth: Penguin Books.

—— and —— (1977). 'Talking about Prison Blues' in C. Bell and H. Newby (eds.) *Doing Sociological Research.* London: Allen and Unwin.

COLVIN, E. (1977). *Prison Officers: A Sociological Portrait of the Uniformed Staff of an English Prison.* University of Cambridge PhD Thesis.

COOKE, D. J. (1989). 'Containing Violent Prisoners: An Analysis of the Barlinnie Special Unit'. *British Journal of Criminology* 29: 129–43.

DOBASH, R. P., DOBASH, R. E., and GUTTERIDGE, S. (1986). *The Imprisonment of Women.* Oxford: Basil Blackwell.

DOWNES, D. (1988). *Contrasts in Tolerance: Post-war Penal Policy in the Netherlands and England and Wales.* Oxford: Clarendon Press.

EMERY, F. E. (1970). *Freedom and Justice Within Walls: The Bristol Prison Experiment.* London: Tavistock Publications.

GARLAND, D. (1994). 'Of Crimes and Criminals: The Development of Criminology in Britain' in M. Maguire, R. Morgan, and R. Reiner (eds.). *The Oxford Handbook of Criminology*, Oxford: Oxford University Press.

GENDERS, E., and PLAYER, E. (1989). *Race Relations in Prisons*. Oxford: Clarendon Press.

—— and —— (1995). *Grendon: A Study of a Therapeutic Prison*. Oxford: Clarendon Press.

GUNN, J., ROBERTSON, G., DELL, S., and WAY, C. (1978). *Psychiatric Aspects of Imprisonment*. London: Academic Press.

—— MADEN, T., and SWINTON, M. (1991). *Mentally Disordered Offenders*. London: HMSO.

HANEY, C., BANKS, C., and ZIMBARDO, P. (1973). 'Interpersonal Dynamics in a Simulated Prison'. *International Journal of Criminology and Penology* 1: 69–97.

HOBHOUSE, S., and BROCKWAY, A. F. (1922). *English Prisons Today*. London: Labour Research Department.

HOME OFFICE (1966). *Report of the Inquiry into Prison Escapes and Security* (Mountbatten Report). Cmnd 3175, London: HMSO.

—— (1984). *Managing the Long-Term Prison System: The Report of the Control Review Committee*. London: HMSO.

—— (1991). *Prison Disturbances April 1990, Report of an Inquiry by the Rt.Hon. Lord Justice Woolf (Parts I and II) and His Honour Judge Stephen Tumim (Part II)*. Cm.1456, London: HMSO.

—— (1995). *Review of Prison Service Security in England and Wales and the Escape from Parkhurst Prison on Tuesday 3rd January 1995*. Cm 3020, London: HMSO.

—— (1998). *Crime Reduction Programme Prospectus*. London: Home Office Research, Development and Statistics Directorate.

IRWIN, J. (1970). *The Felon*. Englewood Cliffs, NJ: Prentice-Hall.

JONES, H., and CORNES, P. (1977). *Open Prisons*. London: Routledge and Kegan Paul.

KAUFFMAN, K. (1988). *Prison Officers and their World*. Cambridge, Mass: Harvard University Press.

KING, R. D. (1972). *An Analysis of Prison Regimes*. Unpublished Report to the Home Office, University of Southampton.

—— (1987). 'New Generation Prisons, the Prison Building Programme, and the Future of the Dispersal Policy' in A. E. Bottoms and R. Light (eds.). *Problems of Long-Term Imprisonment*. Aldershot: Gower.

—— (1991). 'Maximum Security Custody in Britain and the USA: A Study of Gartree and Oak Park Heights'. *British Journal of Criminology* 31: 126–52.

—— (1994). 'Russian Prisons after Perestroika: End of the Gulag?'. *British Journal of Criminology, Special Issue*, 34: 62–82.

—— (1999). 'The Rise and Rise of Supermax: An American Solution in Search of a Problem?' *Punishment and Society: the International Journal of Penology* 1: 163–86.

—— and ELLIOTT, K. W. (1978). *Albany: Birth of a Prison—End of an Era*. London: Routledge and Kegan Paul.

—— and McDERMOTT, K. (1989). 'British Prisons 1970–1987: The Ever-deepening Crisis'. *British Journal of Criminology* 29: 107–28.

—— and —— (1990). '"My Geranium is Subversive" Notes on the Management of Trouble in Prisons'. *British Journal of Sociology* 41: 445–71.

—— and —— (1995). *The State of Our Prisons*. Clarendon Studies in Criminology. Oxford: Clarendon Press.

KING, R. D., and MORGAN, R. (1976). *A Taste of Prison: Custodial Conditions for Trial and Remand Prisoners*. London: Routledge and Kegan Paul.

—— and —— (1980). *The Future of the Prison System*. Farnborough: Gower Press.

LIEBLING, A. (1992). *Suicides in Prison*. London: Routledge.

—— (1999). 'Doing Research in Prison: Breaking the Silence?' *Theoretical Criminology* 3: 147–73.

—— MUIR, G., ROSE, G. (1997). *An Evaluation of Incentives and Earned Privileges: Final Report to the Prison Service*. Cambridge: Institute of Criminology.

—— and PRICE, D. (1999). *An Exploration of Staff–Prisoner Relationships at HMP Whitemoor*. Prison Service Research Report, No 6. Cambridge: Institute of Criminology, University of Cambridge.

McDERMOTT, K. (1990). 'We Have No Problem: The Experience of Racism in Prison'. *New Community* 16: 213–28.

—— and KING, R. D. (1988). 'Mindgames: Where the Action is in Prisons'. *British Journal of Criminology* 28: 357–77.

McVICAR, J. (1982). 'Violence in Prisons' in P. Marsh and A. Campbell (eds.), *Aggression and Violence*. Oxford: Blackwell.

MARSH, A., DOBBS, J., and MONK, J. (1985). *Staff Attitudes in the Prison Service*. London: Office of Population and Censuses.

MORRIS, T., MORRIS P., and BARER, B. (1963). *Pentonville: A Sociological Study of an English Prison*. London: Routledge and Kegan Paul.

PRICE, D., and LIEBLING, A. (1998). *Staff-Prisoner Relationships: A Review of the Literature*. Unpublished Report to the Prison Service.

SIM, J. (1990). *Medical Power in Prisons: The Prison Medical Service in England 1774–1989*. Milton Keynes: Open University Press.

SIMON, F., and CORBETT, C., (1996). *An Evaluation of Prison Work and Training*. A Report for the Home Office Research and Statistics Directorate, Brunel University.

SMITH, C. (1996). *The Imprisoned Body: Women, Health and Imprisonment*. Unpublished PhD thesis, University of Wales, Bangor.

SPARKS, R., BOTTOMS, A. E., and HAY, W. (1996). *Prisons and the Problem of Order*. Clarendon Studies in Criminology. Oxford: Clarendon Press.

SPARKS, R. F. (1971). *Local Prisons: The Crisis in the English Penal System*. London: Heinemann.

WALMSLEY, R. (1989). *Special Security Units*. London: HMSO.

PART 4

RESEARCH: FROM PRINCIPLES TO PRACTICE

11

'DOWN AND OUTERS': FIELDWORK AMONGST STREET HOMELESS PEOPLE

Julia Wardhaugh

INTRODUCTION

Street homelessness has proven attractive to successive generations of qualitative researchers, many of whom have engaged in debates concerning the ethics, politics, and morality of their enterprise. My own reflections on my role as an ethnographic researcher are rooted in this tradition, which is briefly reviewed below. Three research scenarios form the core of this chapter, and are preceded by a discussion of the establishment, funding, and direction of a research project; of the wider social, political, and economic context within which the research was conducted; and of the relevance of personal biography to the research process. First, though, I provide a brief review of the literature by way of orientation.

A BRIEF REVIEW OF THE LITERATURE

Social scientific exploration of homelessness has a long history, dating back in Britain as far as the Elizabethan rogue pamphleteers who established what some commentators have interpreted as a proto-sociological perspective, and who certainly pioneered qualitative and ethnographic approaches to the study of vagrancy (Harman 1566; Dekker 1608; Aydelotte 1913; Judges 1930; Kinney 1990). This tradition was later developed by the Victorian and Edwardian 'social explorers': the philanthropists, novelists, and social scientists who regularly went undercover in their investigations of the social world of homelessness, and many of whose methods and perspectives were to influence subsequent generations of ethnographers (Dickens 1853; Higgs 1906; Chesterton 1928; Beresford 1979).

From the early twentieth century onwards, the geographical centre of such enquiries shifted from Britain to North America, with the denizens of the Main Stem and Skid Row quickly becoming established as a major focus of interest for sociological and criminological ethnographers. In the years up to 1965 alone, more than 150 North American studies were published about Skid Row, that real yet symbolic location that came to epitomize marginality, deviance, and social exclusion (Wallace 1965; Russell 1991).

Perhaps the most famous of these early American ethnographers was Nels Anderson (1923), whose Chicago School study of 'hobohemia' proved to be definitive in terms of both theory and methodology. Anderson departed from the conventions of inter-war sociological theory that defined marginal people as dysfunctional deviations from social and economic norms, instead developing a detailed and sympathetic account of the complexities and intricacies of hobo life. Such knowledge derived from his own time spent on the road: 'for a number of years Anderson had not been a participant observer and *bona fide* sociologist: instead he had been an observing participant and *bona fide* hobo' (Watson 1997: x). Moral and ethical considerations notwithstanding, such extended periods spent 'going native' undoubtedly served to produce material that is rich in qualitative detail.

The drive to seek ethnographic authenticity by going undercover, while rarely adopted for such extended periods as was the case with Anderson, was nevertheless a significant part of the North American qualitative tradition of homelessness research from the 1920s until the 1970s, after which time it began to decline in popularity as a research technique (Allsop 1967; McSheehy 1979; Vander Kooi 1973; Wiseman 1973). Those contemporary ethnographers who have attempted to go undercover have encountered both psychological and ethical difficulties:

Psychologically I knew I was not homeless . . . yet I ended my participation after two nights because I was becoming deeply depressed . . . and I began to understand how one's identity can be lost. I also knew that a homeless woman might need my bed (Russell 1991: 28).

Perhaps times had changed, in that researchers were by now more willing to admit to such difficulties, or perhaps as a woman Russell took a different view of the streets. Certainly, female ethnographers have been more likely to acknowledge the psychic and physical dangers of homelessness, and have been less drawn to the romantic imagery of the open road than their male counterparts (Crouse 1986; Garrett and Bahr 1976; Harper 1982; Golden 1992).

The majority of studies up to the 1970s focused on one dimension of Skid Row life above all others: the consumption of alcohol. Although excessive consumption was to be found only among a minority of the homeless, this nevertheless came to serve as a signifier both of the social deviance and the psychological alienation of the denizens of Skid Row. Despite such a focus on marginality and alienation, the criminological dimension of most such studies remained implicit, with only a few adopting an explicit empirical focus on crime and deviance (see for example Bittner 1967; Rose 1965, 1997; Spradley 1970).

Rose provides an ethnographic and ethnonomic account of Skid Row in Denver, Colorado, leading a team of researchers, one of whom 'played the role of a bum' during the course of the investigations (Rose 1965: 3). Unusually for its time, this study of Larimer Street focused on the agents of social control as well as on the men living in this 'unattached society'. Rose added his distinctive methods of analysing natural language to the already diverse and well-developed tradition of homelessness research, emphasizing the need to understand social worlds from the inside by means of first-hand accounts. For Rose language was not simply the means by which social interaction took place, it was the very essence of such interaction. Consequently his report contains extensive narrative accounts taken from the field, accounts such as the 'poignant story of survival' told to Rose by Johnny O'Leary.

Dedicated to 'my friend the tramp', Spradley's (1970) classic ethnographic study of 'urban nomads' is one of the few within this empirical and methodological genre to focus specifically on criminal justice dimensions of Skid Row life. Spradley documents the complex social rituals that take place over time and in space to define individuals as 'tramps' or 'bums', and thus render them liable to arrest for what they are rather than for what they do. The ethnographic power of this text centres around its vivid descriptions of the stages involved in 'making the bucket', that is, being arrested and incarcerated in the 'drunk tank' as a tramp.

In Britain during this period, work on homelessness was mostly written in a social documentary or journalistic style, and was motivated primarily by an agenda of social concern and social change (Deakin and Willis 1976; Erlam and Brown 1976; Wallich-Clifford 1974; Wilkinson 1981; Sandford 1971, 1976). With only isolated exceptions (see for example Archard 1979), an academic ethnographic tradition of homelessness research did not become established in Britain during the second half of the twentieth century, and therefore the present project referred in methodological terms to a mainly North American corpus of work[1] (Russell 1991; Golden 1992; Snow and Anderson 1993; Wagner 1993). In North America the focus shifted during the 1980s towards a mainly quantitative perspective, with an emphasis on a census and survey approach to

---

[1] A few ethnographic researchers were working contemporaneously with us, although they did not necessarily adopt a criminological focus (see for example Hutson and Liddiard 1994).

the enumeration and demographic profiling of the homeless population (Baumann *et al.* 1985; Roth *et al.* 1985; Rossi *et al.* 1987; Lee 1989). By the late 1980s and
early 1990s, however, a small but healthy qualitative tradition had been re-
established, and it was this tradition that was to inform and inspire our work
(Glasser 1988; Kozol 1988; Golden 1992; Snow and Anderson 1993).

THE THREE CITIES PROJECT

The Three Cities Project[2] took place at a time when street homelessness was
high on the political agenda, with particular attention being directed to the
associated incivilities of begging and sleeping rough (Hunter 1985). The Criminal Justice and Public Order Act 1994 was passing through Parliament and both
Government and Opposition were fulminating against those modern folk
devils, beggars and new age travellers; and few could fail to be aware that the
face of 'new' homelessness was becoming ever more youthful and desperate.

Recent economic and social policy initiatives had included radical and detrimental changes to the welfare benefit system for young people (Carlen 1996);
reduced entitlement to rehousing on the part of the homeless; and the instiga-
tion of the Rough Sleepers' Initiative, first in London and then in other English
and Scottish towns and cities (Randall and Brown 1993). On the criminal justice
front, high numbers of beggars were being prosecuted under the 1824 Vagrancy
Act, while police responses alternated between a reluctance to arrest homeless
people for what were essentially status offences, and the undertaking of periodic
special operations designed to clear the city streets of beggars and rough
sleepers.[3]

The Project set out to investigate criminalization, victimization, and lawbreaking among the homeless population from an ethnographic perspective
(Carlen 1996; Wardhaugh 1996; Wardhaugh 1999). Within these general

[2] The Three Cities Project was an investigation of youth homelessness, lawbreaking, and criminaliza-
tion in Manchester, Birmingham, and Stoke-on-Trent, and was based at Keele University from 1992–5.
Funded by the Economic and Social Research Council at a level of £125,000 (reference number
R000233540) the joint grant-holders and co-directors were Dr Julia Wardhaugh (University of Wales,
Bangor) and Professor Pat Carlen (University of Bath); the research assistant was Paul Bridges, who
subsequently went on to become a youth worker. The qualitative fieldwork was conducted by Julia
Wardhaugh and Paul Bridges and consisted of 100 interviews with homeless people, interviews with
statutory and voluntary agency personnel working with the homeless, and participant observation in
venues such as day centres for the homeless. A range of homeless situations was investigated in these
three cities, including people living as new age travellers as well as in hostels and squats, but this chapter
concentrates on research conducted by the author with the street homeless population in Manchester.
[3] For example Operation Cinderella in Manchester and Operation Clean Sweep in Stoke-on-Trent
were police initiatives of the early 1990s designed to clear the city streets of beggars.

empirical and methodological parameters, each member of the research team had a different research role to develop, both in the field and in relation to the others. The research assistant was appointed in the second year of the project and, as a streetwise man who shared many aspects of youth culture with the subjects of his research, he soon developed his own distinct research role. As a junior researcher (having completed a Master's degree, but not yet registered for a doctorate) he was accountable to both the other members of the team, and received general academic supervision from Pat Carlen and more specific field-work training from me.

The roles of the co-directors and joint grant-holders on the project were somewhat different. As professor and head of department, Pat Carlen was involved in a range of other academic activities and therefore engaged in general oversight rather than direct involvement in fieldwork. As a full-time senior researcher on the project my time was spent in intensive fieldwork, in day-to-day supervision of the research assistant, and in detailed planning and development of the project.

In terms of funding, we were invited to resubmit our initial proposal to the Economic and Social Research Council, and were successful with our second, somewhat smaller-scale version. We were confident that we could construct, as requested by the funding body, a successful project around two research workers rather than three as originally requested, but an issue of great concern to us was the question of making payments to interviewees. Our initial request for the (we thought) modest amount of £1,000 was rejected on the ground of lack of precedent, although one of us (Carlen) had made such payments under a previous grant from the same funding body.

It was our strong political and ethical belief that socially and economically vulnerable participants in our study should be paid for their time, and so we contrived in a number of ways to make such payments possible, sometimes in cash and sometimes in kind (food and cigarettes). We understood the possible objection that we were therefore 'buying' people's stories, but were able in practice to ensure willing participation on the part of potential interviewees before the question of money was raised. In paying homeless people for their time we were reversing the more usual emphasis on the researcher entering the world of the researched, and instead brought them a little way into 'our' world, with its emphasis on the dignity of employment and economic reward for labour.

PERSONAL BIOGRAPHY

Many ethnographers talk about having 'paid their dues' by virtue of their participation in the physical privations and social indignities of homelessness, and thus of having earned the right to conduct their research and subsequently to tell their stories. Harper, for example, presented himself 'with the outside trappings of a skid row man' in order to gain rich qualitative data as an 'inside observer' (1979: 26). He recognized the ethical dilemmas involved in such covert participant observation, but failed to anticipate the dangers of 'going native':

As I became more and more integrated into the lifestyle, I realised that it was more attractive to me to experience the life of my informants than it was to produce documents about it (Harper 1979: 27).

For myself, it was not these dangers that deterred me from adopting 'going undercover' as a research technique, but rather some personal and ethical considerations. My own experience of homelessness might have tempted me to feel that perhaps I had already 'paid my dues' and therefore had no need to prove myself in this way. Encounters with homelessness have taken several forms within my personal biography, including several months spent in a hostel as an infant and a period of 'hidden homelessness' in later childhood—a period when our small nuclear family (mother, brother, and me) lived in one household with several members of our extended family, while awaiting rehousing.

However, to use such aspects of personal biography (either past experiences of homelessness or present attempts to enter the social world of homelessness) in order to claim some particular authenticity for one's research seems to me to be of limited validity in both personal and intellectual terms. Personal biography is of course important in bringing us to the point of conducting our fieldwork, and will inevitably influence the quality of our interactions within the field. In my case early experiences undoubtedly affected my motivation to engage in homelessness research, as well as informing the nature and quality of my fieldwork. Nevertheless, leaving aside the tramp authors who may or may not have been homeless,[4] researchers of homelessness are in the privileged position of having a safe and comfortable home to which to return, either after the end of their day's work or following a period spent undercover as a 'homeless person'. I believe it is essential to acknowledge the material and social differences that exist between the researcher and the researched, and thus to recognize the limits that necessarily exist in terms of 'our' entering into 'their' world.

PARTICIPANT OBSERVATION

The predominant method adopted by qualitative homelessness researchers has been participant observation, a significant proportion of which has been covert

[4] The genre of literature produced by the Victorian and Edwardian tramp authors relied for its popular appeal and claims to authenticity on the belief that the texts were genuinely autobiographical. This is something of a contested claim, with at least some such works being produced by novelists and evangelical authors who had no authentic experience of the tramping life (Burn 1855; MacGill 1914, 1985).

in nature, although authors often prefer more romantic descriptions such as 'going undercover' or 'taking the role of a bum'. Without entering into the extensive methodological debates that surround participant observation, it seems reasonable to state in general terms that research roles adopted may vary from complete participant to complete observer, with most researchers occupying a position somewhere between these two extremes (Junker 1960; Gregor 1977; Pollert 1981; Hammersley and Atkinson 1995).

A second dimension relates to degrees of overtness or covertness during the observation process. In my experience 'overt' and 'covert' should be understood as points on a continuum rather than as polar opposites, and perhaps most such fieldwork can best be described as semi-overt (or semi-covert, depending on whether you like to think of your glass as half-full or half-empty) participant observation (Gilbert 1993; Mason 1996; O'Connell, Davidson and Layder 1994). Taken together, these two continua (from covert to overt and from participation to observation) provide innumerable potential positions to be adopted by the ethnographic researcher. The following scenarios describe some of the research roles I adopted within the Three Cities Project, varying from that of semi-overt, semi-participant observer in scenes one and two, to covert complete observer in scene three.

Scene one

> Setting: a day centre for the homeless in central Manchester, entered by means of narrow steps leading down from a side street which borders a canal. A few hundred yards away are the busy rail and coach terminals serving the city, and a short walk further takes you to the main shopping mall. Few shoppers, tourists, or business people come down this street, and if they did they would not notice the centre as there is no sign advertising its presence. Once inside the centre it is warm and noisy, full of people talking, eating, playing pool, or just sitting and staring into space. Food and drink are provided at regular intervals and at low cost, shower and laundry facilities are available, and users of the centre may seek advice and share conversation.

Time spent in this particular day centre proved to be central to the research process both in the establishment of research roles and in the development of research questions and theoretical perspectives. Participant observation took place in a more or less overt fashion, with staff and some key informants consenting to the research, although it would have proven to be very difficult (and probably intrusive) to seek individual permission from each of the dozens of people using the centre over the course of several days of observation (Hammersley and Atkinson 1995). A formula that worked in this situation was to seek formal permission from the central characters in this particular drama, and then to negotiate various roles and relationships with the minor players. For example, I was able to discuss my research agenda with one forthright young man who asked me directly what I was doing, while it seemed more suitable to accept the role of volunteer helper allocated to me by some of the older users of the centre, a role with which we were all comfortable. In practice, the limited adoption of the tasks of a volunteer (for example helping to serve meals) helped me to overcome the awkwardness inherent in conducting research in social settings within which there is no clearly defined role to be adopted.

Days spent documenting the detail of interactions within the centre as well as observing the wider picture led to the emergence of a series of research questions around the use of social space. As an observer, it seemed to me that people entered the centre in waves of movement that were largely determined by temporal factors such as mealtimes, and that they then proceeded to make use of the physical space of the centre in ways that were both regular and socially meaningful. One notable pattern was that young men tended to dominate the prime space adjacent to the small staff office, while women and older men both practically and metaphorically faded into the background. More sociable members congregated in the 'front regions' around the kitchen serving-area and thus received the greater share of staff attention, while lone men and women sat towards the back of the centre, apparently content in their occupation of marginal places (Goffman 1971).

Day centres such as this one can be understood as 'free spaces' within a cityscape that is generally hostile to marginal groups, in that users of the centre are generally free from interventions by the police or by members of the public, but this should not be taken to mean that this is unregulated space (Wagner 1993). Such centres are subject to their own forms of social and spatial ordering, such as differential occupation and use of space according to factors such as age and gender. Furthermore, they are also part of a wider nexus of socio-spatial relations by virtue of their belonging to a network of such locations on the homelessness circuit. For example, it became clear from my wider series of observations of life on the 'circuit' that at least some street homeless people moved in a regular diurnal pattern between day centres, and from day centres to soup-runs and back again, and that in this way their lives were systematically regulated in both temporal and spatial terms (Wardhaugh 1996).

Major theoretical questions around the use of space began to be developed on the basis of these observations, and in particular queries around the binary division of space along two axes: public and private, and prime and marginal (Lofland 1973; Snow and Anderson 1993). A central 'puzzlement' was how significant numbers of stigmatized and marginal street people could effectively disappear from the city streets, and at least part of the answer seemed to lie in the existence of interstitial, marginal locations such as day centres within prime city centre space (Hammersley and Atkinson 1995).

Scene two

> Setting: the same day centre at night. Situated on the borderline between Cardboard City and the red-light district, the centre is used by working girls in the evenings, and is supported at this time by a separate agency: different staff, different clientele, different ambience. The researcher's aim is to talk to any of the working girls who may be homeless, and she musters her courage to approach them 'cold' on the street. Staff have said that she may interview them in the centre, but must make the initial contact herself as they do not want to become known as 'the agency that administers questionnaires to homeless people'. Things do not go exactly according to plan . . .
>
> JW: [Nervous and trying to act streetwise, introduces herself to two women standing on the street corner outside the centre, and makes some general conversation with them. Wishing to make contact with homeless women working as prostitutes, she wonders about the ethics of assuming the nature of someone's profession from their socio-spatial behaviour]
> I'm hoping to talk to some homeless people in connection with some work that I'm doing . . . do you know anyone who might be interested?
> [Wonders whether they will recognize this as a not very subtle ploy to enlist their own co-operation as potential interviewees]
> Two women: The homeless youngsters hang around over in Piccadilly Gardens, you can always find someone there at this time of night [9pm]. We're homeless ourselves [they look at each other] . . . we wouldn't mind talking to you but we're busy just now, we need one more punter each and then we can go, 'cause we've got things to do tonight. But we can talk to you some other time . . . Look, there's Jimmy,[5] he's homeless, do you want us to shout over to him, he knows everyone and I'm sure he'll help you.

Jimmy did indeed prove to be helpful, not only in agreeing to be interviewed himself, but in introducing me to people congregating around the Piccadilly Garden soup-run, several of whom agreed to be interviewed later that evening in the centre. It is impossible for participant observers in such locations to feel safe and contained, or for their work to be planned and predictable. However, it is essential to balance the potentially dangerous nature of such work and questions of personal safety against the drive to conduct research, something rarely mentioned within the often macho world of homeless ethnographers (but see Garrett and Bahr 1976). In this particular instance I did feel relatively safe, partly because daylight lingered far into the summer evening, partly because I had made myself familiar with the contours and boundaries of Cardboard City, and partly because I was working for some of the time within the staffed base of the

---

[5] In order to protect confidentiality this is a pseudonym.

centre. Nevertheless, I cannot think of any other circumstances in which I would agree to wander through the city with a group of young men that I had only just met, nor where I would not resent the role of protector that they adopted in relation to me.

On this occasion, interviews and participant observation shaded into one another as research techniques, in the sense that formal, tape-recorded interviews were conducted within the centre amidst a series of other activities (Hammersley and Atkinson 1995). A degree of privacy was maintained by choosing a quiet corner for conversation while the other men played bar football or 'had a brew', and a steady stream of women came into the centre in search of tea, condoms, advice, and conversation. Nevertheless, during interviews we were in full view (although not necessarily within hearing distance) of several other people, and we ourselves were participants in the ongoing life of the centre.

This was to prove to be an important factor when towards midnight two men arrived and aggressively demanded to be interviewed for payment. This interlude can be read in two ways: they were drunk and abusive men threatening a female researcher (and therefore they were exploitative); or they were needy individuals disturbed by the introduction of a cash exchange into the homelessness circuit (and they were therefore potentially exploited). I think that this situation may be read in both ways: that is, both the researcher and the researched were potentially vulnerable as a result of the complex and unstable balance of power that existed between them. In practical terms the important thing was to defuse a situation that was potentially dangerous or disturbing to all those present, and this was achieved by the quiet offering of cigarettes and a small amount of money (about half the standard amount paid to interviewees) to the two new arrivals. The central dilemma was that payments to interviewees undoubtedly eased the making of contacts on the streets, but at the same time money proved to be a potentially explosive ingredient when introduced from outside into street homeless culture.

A further significant theoretical concern emerged from this fieldwork episode in that the very different purposes to which this centre was put at night and by day highlighted the importance of time as a social variable within the lives of street homeless people. Questions around space had already begun to be addressed, but now a temporal dimension could be added to the regulation of street life (Murray 1986; Rowe and Wolch 1990). Later pursuit of this theme began to reveal the ways in which the daily subsistence round of the street homeless person is structured over time and within space (Wardhaugh 1996).

Scene three

In an ongoing scenario that unfolds over many months, the researcher spends time exploring the contours of Cardboard City and its neighbouring 'urban villages'. She wanders down back-alleys and under canal bridges, noting places where people might sleep at night or by day. Sometimes pieces of cardboard or blankets are left out to mark someone's patch, and on winter days the attraction of the hot-air vents of the restaurants of Chinatown becomes obvious. Both official and unofficial locations used by the homeless are carefully noted, and gradually the social and spatial boundaries of Cardboard City are mapped. These boundaries are clear but not static, in that there is a dynamic interaction between Cardboard City and its three neighbouring districts: the red-light area, Chinatown and the Gay Village, all places where street homeless people work, eat, and sleep. Observations are made of the interactions between street people and other users of the city centre: of hostile or sympathetic exchanges between *Big Issue* vendors and members of the public, or the occasional police questioning of people engaged in begging.

Theoretical questions around the social use of space that arose from scenes one and two led to the adoption of a specific research role in scene three: that of covert, complete observer. By this I mean that no-one else in the settings observed was aware of my presence as a researcher, and there was no degree of social interaction other than that shared by passers-by. Inspired in various ways by social ecological, symbolic interactionist, socio-geographical, and Foucauldian analyses of the cityscape, my intention was to document the cognitive maps used by street homeless people in their efforts at daily subsistence, and to gain along the way a sense of the *genius loci* of Cardboard City (Gans 1962; Pocock and Hudson 1978; Davis 1990; Shields 1991; Sibley 1995).

In terms of methods the choice was clear: covert observations of the spaces and places used by homeless people would allow for the development of a social cartography of Cardboard City in a way that would have been complicated by an overt or semi-overt participant role. Quite simply, an obvious research presence (even if this were possible to negotiate within the ever-changing tableau of street life) would alter the nature of interactions and behaviours taking place. However, for me the role of covert observer was both unfamiliar and ethically questionable.

Looking to academic precedent for guidance on the ethics of covert observation in public settings, Lofland's (1973) excellent micro-sociological study of social interactions in public places, based largely on visual observations conducted through a window looking out on to city streets, appeared to offer reassurance that this was an acceptable technique. However, her study was based on observations of shoppers, business people, and commuters, people for whom the public–private distinction was of relevance. If they enter into public space, the argument reasonably might go, then their actions within such space are by definition public in nature and therefore open to general observation.

For street homeless people, however, there is no such clear separation between public and private domains: their whole daily round is carried out in public places, and they have no private space to which they may retreat, although they may contrive temporarily to define some places as semi-private. My observations were partly of general public space (shopping malls, coach stations, shops, and cafes) but they also inevitably intruded into private or semi-private lives: for example, glimpsing 'back-region' behaviours such as personal grooming or stumbling across someone's bedding in an alleyway (Goffman 1959). The usual conventions of seeking permission to conduct observations seemed impossible to apply within this context (who exactly would give such permission?), yet the ethical dilemma remained difficult to resolve. I wondered whether it was possible to avoid being a 'research tourist' or 'flâneur', someone who voyeuristically enjoys her time spent as an observer without having any substantial contribution to make (Wilson 1995; Cloke and Little 1997).

As is often the case with such ethnographic research, no clear-cut answers were forthcoming, and the resolution achieved in this instance relied on pragmatism as much as on abstract principles. In the end, guidelines for research practice in this type of situation were formulated, based on both my ethical beliefs and research experience over an extended period of time. These guidelines included a commitment to be as unobtrusive and non-invasive as possible during observations; to maintain acceptable levels of personal space between me and those observed; to conduct visual but not aural observations, on the ground that the latter were more invasive than the former; and to respect the usual research conventions concerning confidentiality and anonymity. Above all, the most important objective (successfully achieved I think) was not to violate the already constantly threatened privacy and dignity of people living on the streets.

CONCLUSION

An ethical code adapted from the medical profession might serve well within social ethnography: 'if you can do no good, at least do no harm'. Within the tradition of homelessness research in particular, with its tendency to romanticize its subjects and to observe them in a covert fashion, this principle is of particular relevance. The Three Cities Project was pioneering within the British context of homelessness research in its adoption of an ethnographic perspective and in its criminological empirical and theoretical focus. An ethnographic approach promises the production of richly-detailed fieldwork materials, but brings with it also a range of ethical, moral, and political considerations. In recognition of the complexity of street homeless lives, a variety of participant, observer, and interviewer roles were adopted during the collection of data, and in so doing a number of ethical dilemmas were encountered and perhaps resolved.

The internal and moral coherence of the project cannot be separated from the wider social and political context within which street homeless people were being demonized and criminalized by politicians and the media, a process that was itself a major focus for our research. Just as research and ethical questions were closely related, so too was there an intimate connection between theory and method. For example, 'puzzlements' about the social use of space by homeless people arose from fieldwork observations, and this interest in turn led to the adoption of a role I would not have envisaged at the outset: that of covert observer (Hammersley and Atkinson 1995). The relation between theory and method can thus be said to be cyclical rather than linear, and often to develop in an organic rather than mechanical fashion.

REFERENCES

ALLSOP, K. (1967). *Hard Travellin': The Hobo and His History*. New York: New American Library.

ANDERSON, N. (1923). *The Hobo: The Sociology of the Homeless Man*, Chicago, Ill.: University of Chicago Press.

ARCHARD, P. (1979). *Vagrancy, Alcoholism and Social Control*. London: Macmillan.

AYDELOTTE, F. (1913). *Elizabethan Rogues and Vagabonds*. Oxford: Clarendon Press.

BAUMANN, D. J., BEAUVAIS, C., GRIGSBY, C., and SCHULTZ, F. D. (1985). *The Austin Homeless: Final Report Provided to the Hogg Foundation for Mental Health*. Austin, Tex.: Hogg Foundation for Mental Health.

BERESFORD, P. (1979). 'The Public Presentation of Vagrancy' in T. Cook (ed.), *Vagrancy: Some New Perspectives*. London: Academic Press.

BITTNER, E. (1967). 'The Police on Skid Row: A Study of Peace Keeping'. *American Sociological Review* 32: 699–715.

BURN, J. D. (1855). *The Autobiography of a Beggar Boy*. London: William Tweedie.

CARLEN, P. (1996). *Jigsaw: A Political Criminology of Youth Homelessness*. Buckingham: Open University Press.

CHESTERTON, A. (1928). *Women of the Underworld*. London: Stanley Paul & Co.

CLOKE, P., and LITTLE, J. (1997). 'Introduction: Other Countrysides' in P. Cloke and J. Little (eds.), *Contested Countryside Cultures*. London: Routledge.

CROUSE, J. M. (1986). *The Homeless Transient in the Great Depression: New York State 1929–1941*. New York: State University of New York Press.

DAVIS, M. (1990). *City of Quartz: Excavating the Future in Los Angeles*. New York: Verso.

DEAKIN, M., and WILLIS, J. (1976). *Johnny Go Home*. London: Futura.

DEKKER, T. (1608). *Lantern and Candlelight*. London: John Busbie.

Dickens, C. (1853). 'Home for Homeless Women' in *Household Words, 23 April. Miscellaneous Papers 369*. London, Biographical Edition.

Erlam, A., and Brown, M. (1976). *Catering For Homeless Workers*. London: CHAR and Low Pay Unit.

Gans, H. J. (1962) *The Urban Villagers: Group and Class in the Life of Italian-Americans*. New York: Free Press.

Garrett, G. R., and Bahr, H. M. (1976). 'The Family Backgrounds of Skid Row Women'. *Signs: Journal of Women and Culture* 2: 369–81.

Gilbert, N. (ed.) (1993). *Researching Social Life*. London: Sage.

Glasser, I. (1988). *More Than Bread: Ethnography of a Soup Kitchen*. Tuscaloosa, Ala.: University of Alabama Press.

Goffman, E. (1959). *The Presentation of Self in Everyday Life*. New York: Anchor/Doubleday.

—— (1971). *Relations in Public: Microstudies of the Public Order*. London: Allen Lane.

Golden, S. (1992). *The Women Outside: Meanings and Myths of Homelessness*. Berkeley, Cal.: University of California Press.

Gregor, T. (1977). *Mehinaku: The Drama of Daily Life in a Brazilian Indian Village*. Chicago, Ill.: University of Chicago Press.

Hammersley, M., and Atkinson, P. (1995). *Ethnography: Principles in Practice*. (2nd edn.). London: Routledge.

Harman, T. (1566). *A Caveat for Common Cursitors*. London: William Griffith.

Harper, D. (1979). 'Life on the Road' in J. Wagner (ed.), *Images of Information: Still Photography in the Social Sciences*. London: Sage.

—— (1982). *Good Company*. Chicago, Ill.: Chicago University Press.

Higgs, M. (1906). *Glimpses into the Abyss*. London: P. S. King & Son.

Hunter, A. (1985). 'Private, Parochial and Public Social Orders: The Problem of Crime and Incivility in Urban Communities' in G. D. Suttles and M. N. Zald (eds.), *The Challenge of Social Control: Citizenship and Institution Building in Modern Society—Essays in Honor of Morris Janowitz*. Norwood, NJ: Ablex Publishing Company.

Hutson, S., and Liddiard, M. (1994). *Youth Homelessness: The Construction of a Social Issue*. London: Macmillan.

Judges, A. V. (ed.) (1930). *The Elizabethan Underworld*. London: George Routledge and Sons.

Junker, B. (1960). *Field Work*. Chicago, Ill.: University of Chicago Press.

Kinney, A. F. (1990). *Rogues, Vagabonds and Sturdy Beggars: A New Gallery of Tudor and Early Stuart Literature*. Amherst, Mass.: University of Massachusetts Press.

Kozol, J. (1988). *Rachel And Her Children: Homeless Families In America*. New York: Fawcett Columbine.

Lee, B. A. (1989). 'Homelessness in Tennessee' in J. A. Momeni (ed.), *Homelessness in the United States: State Surveys*. Westport, Conn.: Greenwood Press.

Lofland, L. (1973). *A World of Strangers: Order and Action in Urban Public Space*. New York: Basic Books.

MacGill, P. (1914; repr.1985). *Children of The Dead End: Autobiography of a Navvy*. London: Caliban.

Mason, J. (1996). *Qualitative Researching*. London: Sage.

McSheehy, W. (1979). *Skid Row*. Boston, Mass.: G. K. Hall.

Murray, H. (1986). 'Time in the Streets' in J. Ericcksson and C. Wilhelm (eds.), *Housing the Homeless*. Rutgers, NJ: Center for Urban Policy.

O'CONNELL, DAVIDSON, J., and LAYDER, D. (1994). *Methods, Sex and Madness*. London: Routledge.

POCOCK, D. C. D., and HUDSON, R. (1978). *Images of the Urban Environment*. London: Macmillan.

POLLERT, A. (1981). *Girls, Wives, Factory Lives*. London: Macmillan.

RANDALL, G., and BROWN, S. (1993). *The Rough Sleepers Initiative: An Evaluation*. London: HMSO.

ROSE, E. (1997). 'The Unattached Society: An Account of the Life on Larimer Street Among Homeless Men'. *Ethnographic Studies* 1: 1–93.

ROSSI, P., WRIGHT, J. D., FISCHER, G. A., and WILLIS, G. (1987). 'The Urban Homeless: Estimating Composition and Size'. *Science* 235: 1336–41.

ROTH, D., BEAN, G. J., LUST, N., and TRAIAN, S. (1985). *Homelessness in Ohio: A Study of People In Need*. Ohio: Ohio Department of Mental Health.

ROWE, S., and WOLCH, J. (1990). 'Social Networks in Time and Space: Homeless Women in Skid Row, Los Angeles'. *Annals of the Association of American Geographers*. 80: 184–204.

RUSSELL, B. G. (1991). *Silent Sisters: A Study of Homeless Women*. New York: Taylor and Francis.

SANDFORD, J. (1971). *Down and Out in Britain*. London: Peter Owen.

—— (1976). *Edna The Inebriate Woman*. London: Marion Boyars.

SHIELDS, R. (1991). *Places on the Margin: Alternative Geographies of Modernity*. London: Routledge.

SIBLEY, D. (1995). *Geographies of Exclusion*. London: Routledge.

SNOW, D. A., and ANDERSON, L. (1993). *Down on Their Luck: A Study of Homeless Street People*. Berkeley, Cal.: University of California Press.

SPRADLEY, J. P. (1970). *You Owe Yourself a Drunk: An Ethnography of Urban Nomads*. Boston, Mass.: Little, Brown and Company.

VANDER KOOI, R. C. (1973) 'The Mainstem: Skid Row Revisited'. *Society* 10: 64–71.

WAGNER, D. (1993). *Checkerboard Square: Culture and Resistance in a Homeless Community*. Denver, Colo.: Westview Press.

WALLACE, S. E. (1965). *Skid Row as a Way of Life*. New York: Harper.

WALLICH-CLIFFORD, A. (1974). *No Fixed Abode*. London: Macmillan.

WARDHAUGH, J. (1996). ' "Homeless in Chinatown": Deviance and Social Control in Cardboard City'. *Sociology* 30: 701–16.

—— (1999). 'The Unaccommodated Woman: Home, Homelessness and Identity'. *Sociological Review* 47: 91–109.

WATSON, R. (1997). 'Prologue to "The Unattached Society: An Account Of The Life On Larimer Street Among Homeless Men" '. *Ethnographic Studies* 1: iv–xii.

WILKINSON, T. (1981). *Down and Out*. London: Quartet.

WILSON, E. (1995). 'The Invisible *Flaneur*' in S. Watson and K. Gibson (eds.), *Postmodern Cities and Spaces*. Oxford: Basil Blackwell.

WISEMAN, J. (1973). *Stations of the Lost: The Treatment of Skid Row Alcoholics*. Chicago, Ill.: University of Chicago Press.

12

BREAKING IN: RESEARCHING CRIMINAL JUSTICE INSTITUTIONS FOR WOMEN

Catrin Smith and Emma Wincup

INTRODUCTION

There is no doubt that studying for a PhD, while rewarding and, yes, at times, fun, can also be a lonely and isolated experience, particularly at the fieldwork stage. Working alone in often unfamiliar, perhaps uncomfortable, settings, novice researchers frequently have to make difficult methodological decisions on site and learn how to 'manage' themselves whilst in the presence of those they seek to study. This can be an emotionally and physically exhausting experience, but one which is rarely talked about in any great detail. As May (1993) notes feelings are equated with weakness and thus remain hidden and not articulated. Instead, methodological reflections are often presented as 'heroic tales' (Lee 1993) of how the problems of social research were encountered and overcome. The partial nature of such accounts of the research process can leave the novitiate insufficiently prepared for the *actual* experience of 'doing' research, which can come as something of a shock. Thus, the aim of this chapter, like others in this edited collection, is to provide an 'honest' account of the research process which connects, in particular, with those embarking upon an academic apprenticeship.

The chapter has evolved out of the joint consideration of our separate postgraduate experiences in criminal justice institutions for women: one focusing on bail hostels and women awaiting trial (Wincup 1997), the other on the prison system and the relationship between women's health and women's imprisonment (Smith 1996). Whilst distinct in terms of research focus, the two projects were theoretically and methodologically similar. Both were informed primarily by feminist debates, within and beyond criminology. Both sought to explore the particular experiences and needs of women in secure environments and the patterns of institutional response. Both pieces of research were essentially exploratory in nature, combining ethnographic observation and qualitative interviews with both bail hostel/prison staff and their charges.

We met in 1996, when we were both at the post-completion, pre-viva (so near and yet so far) stage of the PhD. In our discussions of our experiences of conducting research, we identified a number of concerns common to us both. In what follows we highlight some of the complexities of actually carrying out doctoral research in criminal justice institutions for women. In particular, we explore the situational and institutional issues relating to access negotiation, researcher identity, and acceptability that arise for consciously feminist PhD scholars in this setting. In order to communicate this process, the chapter is organized chronologically.

GETTING STARTED: MAKING CHOICES

PhD students are often asked (and ask themselves) why? Why the particular topic? Why the theoretical position? Why the methodological approach? Such questions are certainly old favourites in *viva voce* examinations! In fact, when subjected to systematic consideration, these questions are not easily answered because the PhD is often the consequence of a number of overlapping concerns, academic and otherwise.

The topic of Catrin's PhD very much evolved out of two fundamental concerns: women's health and women's imprisonment. As an ex-nurse (driven out of a National Sickness Service in the late 1980s when Thatcherite policies really began to bite), she was well aware of the major differences between the sexes in terms of ill health and help-seeking behaviour. She had observed, first-hand, not only the power relations in the doctor–patient relationship and the routine medicalization of women's distress (the terminology came later), but also some of the more extreme examples of medical interventions in women's lives, such as electro-convulsive therapy.

The interest in women's imprisonment was aroused when a close friend (somewhat selflessly, with hindsight) received a custodial sentence. By that time, Catrin was an undergraduate student studying criminology and criminal justice as part of a broader social sciences degree. Suddenly things both seemed to make sense and, at the same time, not to make sense and a spark was ignited. She became more involved in reading around the subject of women's imprisonment and, in particular, the critical literature on the penal control of women (see, for example, Carlen 1983, 1985; Dobash *et al.* 1986; Heidensohn 1985). Two texts, in particular, captured her attention: Joe Sim's (1990) detailed study of the then Prison Medical Service and Florence Maybrick's (1905) autobiographical account of fifteen years in prison. Both these books, in very different ways, highlighted that the history of women's imprisonment was one of medicalization and medical interventionism. But was this not also the history of woman? The PhD was conceived and Catrin, finally, embarked on her doctoral studies in 1992, following a Master's degree in health promotion, keen to explore the relationship between women's health and women's imprisonment in the context of an increasing political drive towards health promotion in prison and in society at large.

Emma's interest, similarly, developed when she began to read a number of highly critical accounts of women's imprisonment (e.g. Carlen 1983, 1985; Padel and Stevenson 1988; Peckham 1985) whilst studying for a Master's degree. One in particular held her attention: Audrey Peckham's autobiographical account of her time awaiting trial. Her descriptions of the humiliations and degradations of waiting anxiously for trial in a remand centre where she was denied access to appropriate psychiatric care were disturbing, particularly her suggestion that her treatment on remand was worse than her treatment as a convicted, sentenced prisoner. Peckham's account concluded with a suggestion that where possible defendants should be diverted from the remand system to supportive institutions such as bail hostels. Unsure about the role of bail hostels in the criminal justice system, but having read similar suggestions by penal pressure groups and academic criminologists, Emma selected the study of bail hostels as an alternative to women's imprisonment as her research topic.

Both pieces of research were primarily influenced by what could loosely be termed a 'feminist criminological' perspective. In the 1970s and for some time after, feminist concern was directed at the misrepresentation and/or the absence of women in conventional criminological research (see, for example, Smart 1976). As a consequence, research in Britain and the United States sought to redress the balance and made more visible the issue of female offending, women's victimization, and the treatment of women within the criminal justice process. More recently, studies have attempted to explore the relationship between gender and other social divisions such as ethnicity, social class, and age (Rice 1990; Smart 1990). What has resulted is what Heidensohn (1994) refers to as a 'patchwork' of knowledge. We were aware of the incomplete nature of this knowledge and were keen to address some of the gaps. In addition, both studies were informed, somewhat eclectically, by a number of overlapping theoretical positions on the body, self-identity, risk, power, regulation, and resistance (see, for example, Doyal 1995; Ettorre 1992; Howe 1994; Turner 1984, 1987; Shilling 1993).

Our theoretical framework influenced how we approached our practice as research students. At the outset of our doctoral studies we both spent time reading the methodological literature and taking advice on techniques and practice in the field. We were keen to develop a research strategy, or set of strategies, that could help us to understand women's experiences. Not surprisingly, our approach to our work as doctoral students was very much influenced by the sophisticated debates since the 1970s which have established definitions of 'feminist methodology' and 'feminist research practice' (Harding 1987; Olesen 1994; Stanley and Wise 1983, 1993). Of central importance has been the need to focus on the complexities and problems of women's situations and the institutions that influence those situations (Olesen 1994). A variety of approaches, methods, and epistemologies have emerged and it is generally agreed that there is no exclusive feminist method. However, diverse feminist approaches share a number of common assumptions: the need for academic study *for* rather than *on* women; the rejection of distance and objectivity in the researcher–researched relationship; a preference for, but not an exclusive focus on, qualitative work, and a reflexive approach to issues of power and control.

In both our studies, our aim was not so much to become insiders in our chosen institutional settings but to see the world from insiders' perspectives. Smircich (1983: 164) refers to this as 'empathetic ethnography' and, at the outset of both projects, this strategy appealed to our feminist positions since it did not depend on us consciously manufacturing an objective stance in our researches. Unlike the position adopted by earlier feminist researchers such as Graham (1984), the choice of qualitative techniques was not based on the premise that *only* qualitative approaches can be used to generate the kinds of knowledge that feminists wish to develop, and that *only* qualitative approaches are compatible with the politics of feminism. This viewpoint developed from a critique of quantitative approaches that were seen to represent 'masculinist' forms of knowledge, emphasizing objectivity and the detachment of the researcher. We do not hold this view. As others have also noted (Kelly 1990; Kelly *et al.* 1992, 1994; Pugh 1990), research involving quantification has made an important contribution to our knowledge and understanding of women's lives; for example, through raising awareness of the nature and extent of violence against women. Rather, the choice of a predominantly qualitative approach was based on the apparent appropriateness to exploratory researches that had an emphasis on investigating the subjective experiences and meanings of those that live and work in prisons and bail hostels.

Choices about the most appropriate methodological approach to adopt are, of course, influenced by a range of factors other than one's theoretical position. For Emma, an important influence was being awarded a studentship in the School of Social and Administrative Studies (now School of Social Sciences) at Cardiff University. The strong and well-established tradition of ethnographic research influenced the design of the research a great deal and it evolved from being an interview-based study to an ethnographic one. For Catrin, the methods chosen for the research, while loosely framed at the outset, very much developed from *within* the field. The unique nature of the prison setting as a research field in many respects dictated something of a 'grab-bag' approach that included a variety of different methods (including observation and semi-participation, focus group discussions, in-depth unstructured and semi-structured interviews). In addition, a (with hindsight) wise suggestion on the part of her supervisor to include a questionnaire survey at the conclusion of the fieldwork programme led to a mixed-method study that was born as much out of realism and opportunism as out of any strict adherence to methodological positioning (also see Liebling 1992).

GETTING IN: THE POLITICS OF NEGOTIATING ACCESS

Research settings vary considerably in the extent to which they are 'open' or 'closed' to public scrutiny and these differences, in turn, impact upon the nature and degree of negotiation necessary to secure access. Not surprisingly, getting in to the relatively 'closed' world of criminal justice institutions, particularly prisons, can be a time-consuming and problematic process for outside researchers, not least because of the 'sensitivity' of much criminological research, but also because many areas of interest are surrounded by political controversy. Indeed, Morgan (this volume) argues that criminological research is inherently and integrally bound up with wider political conflict and debate that, ultimately, shape the research process.

Fieldwork for both projects commenced in 1994. At this time, some fundamental changes were taking place in criminal justice policy. The proliferation of community penalties in the 1991 Criminal Justice Act, accompanied by the framework of 'just deserts', was subverted through increasingly punitive approaches to crime control. By 1994 new legislation had been introduced which sought to satisfy the populist rhetoric of Michael Howard, then Home Secretary, and the governing party (Brownlee 1998). Criminological research was increasingly caught up in the party politicization of 'law and order' with implications for the shaping of research questions, design, methods, and, particularly, the question of access. Although not financially sponsored by the state (both of us were awarded university studentships), our research was inevitably influenced by this political context in various ways. Explicitly, we were dependent upon the state for access to the criminal justice agencies we wanted to research. Implicitly, the political context impacted upon our relationships in 'the field'. We had to tread carefully.

Catrin's sortie into the prison world coincided with some of the more controversial events in recent penal history. In response to the spirit of 'toughness' in penal policy, the number of prisoners grew sharply with, in particular, an unprecedented and quite specific increase in the female prison population. Moreover, as the movement away from a mood of social responsibility towards one of greater authoritarianism really took hold, there were increasing demands for security and control for *all* prisoners irrespective of their security risk, evidenced most notoriously by the shackling of pregnant prisoners. Prisoners (and their keepers) were beginning to feel the effects of the changes introduced by Michael Howard under the 'Prison Works' rhetoric, not least the curtailment of temporary and home leave. Mandatory drug testing was being phased in and, for some prisoners, it was made clear that life was to mean life. Prisons were being 'contracted out' to the private sector and the Prison Service was adjusting to agency status and the degree of independence (rhetorically, at least) that it gave from Home Office control of daily operations. The period also saw the increasing politicization of women's imprisonment through a series of 'scandals' around conditions in women's prisons (see Carlen 1998, for a more detailed discussion), and women prisoners, actual and fictional, were receiving a lot of attention.

In order to gain access to prisons for research purposes, the proposed research and the researcher generally need to gain Home Office 'approval'. For Catrin, the familiar problems of 'courting approval', so clearly documented elsewhere (see Cohen and Taylor 1972; Liebling 1992; Smartt 1995; also King this volume), were eased greatly by several factors. First, a supervisor with a long (albeit not uncontroversial) history of prison research proved to be an excellent gatekeeper to the gatekeepers. Secondly, at the outset of the project (1992–3) and throughout the time of the fieldwork, prison health care was undergoing a period of significant reform. A long history of intense criticism of prison health services (Lee 1983; Prison Reform Trust 1985; Sim 1990) had led to various official examinations over a period of some years culminating in a rigorous Efficiency Scrutiny conducted in 1990 (Home Office 1990). The Scrutiny Report recommended a number of key changes in the way that prison medical services operate including that they should take a greater responsibility for the promotion of health and the prevention of illness: Catrin's area of 'expertise'. She was in the right place at the right time and it was the happy coincidence between the needs of the service and the needs of the researcher that removed one of the major obstacles to 'doing' prison research. But, at what price?

No constraints were imposed upon the research (see Liebling 1992) and an informal *quid pro quo* relationship with the Prison Service Directorate of Health Care developed. This had a number of advantages. Regular trips to Prison Service Headquarters in Cleland House, at a 'sensitive' time in penal history, provided an invaluable source of information and advice as well as an insight into the nature of relationships 'at the top'. However, the strategy needed to secure access also provided Catrin with a number of dilemmas: how, for example, did it fit with her values as a feminist and one who has always resisted any association with the formal structures of institutional power (in principle, at least)? What would be the implications for the development of rapport and relationships in the field? Certainly, in the many subsequent methodological discussions (particularly with post-graduates and the research students she now has the pleasure of supervising), she has, at times, been accused of 'selling out'. It has been suggested that the very fact of being allowed in to the prison setting must involve some expression of understanding of the institutional perspective and that the maintenance of access implies a perception on the part of the gatekeepers concerning the researcher's empathy for the institutional stance, or, at least, that the researcher is a non-threatening person that will do the institution no harm. This argument, we believe, is too simplistic and, if this were so, then what would be the point of any outside prison research? However, it does raise fundamental questions about the theoretical and philosophical concessions that might have to be made before (and during) the research process in order to get the research done, complete the apprenticeship and acquire accreditation. Here, there are no easy answers.

For research within bail hostels, a more informal approach can be adopted than that which is required in prison research. Access is negotiated at a local level with individual probation services rather than through a central body, although this is not to suggest that Emma's research was not affected by the political context. The research took place at a time when defendants awaiting trial became the focus of media and political concern. There was a 'moral panic' about offending on bail with the minority who do offend whilst waiting for trial dubbed 'bail bandits'. This was based on the contradictory findings of a number of police research projects. Specifically on hostels there was a closure programme which reversed the previous trend to expand accommodation in approved hostels and the influence of managerialism led to the introduction of limited budgets and Key Performance Indicators. The remand prisoner population continued to rise as a consequence of more restricted use of bail as well as the lengthening of court waiting times and an increase in the proportion of defendants awaiting sentence being remanded in custody (Home Office 1995a, 1995b).

For Emma, the access procedure required negotiation at various levels: the Chief Probation Officer and the Senior Probation Officer responsible for hostels and then the hostel managers and, in one case, a management committee. This proved to be a particularly time-consuming process. Moreover, several conditions were imposed on the research, which could have led to compromises being made. For example, all the probation areas studied by Emma stated that client confidentiality must be maintained, and one area requested copies of all subsequent publications. Additionally, one hostel manager agreed to the research on the condition that Emma was aware of, and took responsibility for, the emotional effects on the women residents participating in the research.

The political context did not, therefore, prevent either of us from physically accessing criminal justice institutions for women: Catrin's study included three prisons for women and Emma's involved three bail hostels. However, as in institutional research generally, there exist layers of gatekeepers to negotiate, with hierarchies of authority and power between them that can help or hinder the research. Once physical access to our chosen research establishments had been secured, we then needed to hone our skills of communication, tact, and diplomacy in an attempt (not always successful) to gain the co-operation, trust, and assistance of *all* the other groups within each establishment. This is the issue of social access and the strategies for 'getting on' after 'getting in' (Liebling 1992).

GETTING ON: ESTABLISHING SOCIAL ACCESS

Sparks (1989, cited Liebling 1992: 119) argues that the researcher entering a prison for the first time appears ' "naïve", "green", uncomfortable, out of place'. This could equally be applied to research in bail hostels. We both found ourselves anxious, alone, and in unfamiliar settings. We were surrounded, in some cases, by individuals who had committed some quite serious offences and we were both unsure how the women and their keepers (who, in the prison setting, at least, could be quite scary) would react to outsiders poking around in their lives. Being 'naïve' and 'green' can, however, be an advantage. Throughout the fieldwork, we both, consciously and unconsciously, projected an image of ourselves as earnest, sympathetic, if slightly naïve research students, grateful to learn about the experiences of others. Being young (both then in our twenties) and being female probably facilitated this. To a lesser and greater extent we both *used* these (and other) aspects of our personal biographies at various times, as perhaps do many female researchers, if only they would admit it (but see Rawlinson, this volume). While feminists have provided detailed reflections on the extent to which variables such as age, sex, and 'race' influence the field researcher's role and, hence, the research process (Easterday *et al.* 1992; Gelsthorpe 1990), and some have even reported on the sexualization of research interaction (Warren 1988), few have actually documented how female researchers might *exploit* such factors to their best advantage without being *exploitative*.

We both found being young and female more enabling than constraining, but in some quite different ways. In general, bail hostels for women can be characterized as 'women-only' spaces. Most of the women residents are young and many have been in relationships with men that could be described as abusive. For Emma, being female helped to facilitate access, not because she was seen as non-threatening *per se*, but because of the very fact that she was female and it is unlikely that a male researcher would have gained access. In contrast, the prison service (like prison research) is largely male-dominated and, even in women's prisons, masculine values dominate. Until very recently, with the formation of the Prison Service Women's Policy Group, women's imprisonment has largely been ignored by politicians and policy-makers (see Carlen and Tchaikovsky 1996; Hayman 1996; Liebling 1991). As a consequence, much of the care and administration of women's prisons has been based on the male world: staff training, work, leisure, security, and control all represent products of the male system, where masculinity is seen as the norm. Moreover, many male officers work in women's prisons and many of those occupying positions of power in the institutional hierarchy are, not surprisingly, men.

For Catrin, like Emma, the very fact of being female was beneficial in her encounters with women prisoners, many of whom had been in relationships with men marked by violence and abuse. For such women masculinity in and of itself represents a threat and it is, perhaps, a harsh irony that for them prison life can be seen as such a 'masculine culture'. Being a young, female researcher may have encouraged them to give so generously of their time, their trust, and their histories. However, it also has to be said that such aspects of Catrin's social identity were enabling in her encounters with prison staff and the representatives of the Home Office. Here, she experienced a range of responses from the generally paternalistic (young female researcher needing help) to the overtly flirtatious, and she frequently found herself engaging in the forms of sexualized social banter she would normally avoid (we very much doubt that this happens to male prison researchers). While, at a fundamental level, such attitudes inevitably conflicted with her values as a feminist, in reality they undoubtedly made it easier to gain access to the data. At the end of the day, the question should be whether or not female researchers can flirt (maintaining access), whilst also holding on to a sense of integrity? Whatever the answer, doors were opened for Catrin, metaphorically at least.

In the main, people welcomed our interest. However, we both occasionally experienced patronising attitudes from staff, which may have had as much to do with us being students as being young and female. Emma's research was, at times described as 'just another student project', which seemed to be a dismissal of its importance, while, in Catrin's encounters with some prison staff she felt a sense of them looking over her shoulder for a wiser, more authoritative (male?) 'boss'. The impact that her own gender identity had on their view of her also varied and, at times, it was assumed that she would see things in a specific way (from the woman prisoner's perspective) simply because she was a woman. This implicit sense of 'sisterhood' needs to be understood against the backcloth of a general suspicion of outside researchers. Prison research has, over the last fifty years, tended to focus on the prisoner's experiences and perspectives, and researchers interested in the prisoner's world have tended to distance themselves from staff so as to develop rapport and credibility with their chosen study group (e.g. Cohen and Taylor 1972). This dissociation from the formal power structures, while understandable, has led to feelings of alienation amongst staff members and a general cynicism of the value of research. For those researchers, like Catrin, who want to capture the experiences of *both* staff and prisoners, the difficulty is avoiding alienating either group. As Liebling (1992: 118) notes, researchers have to learn the 'dos and don'ts' that involve carefully avoiding taking sides and constantly being prepared to explain your presence.

Both staff and prisoners were naturally curious about the nature of Catrin's relationship with the Home Office. She had been allowed in, hadn't she at a time when it was increasingly difficult for outside researchers to gain entry. How? Was she a spy? (see also Liebling 1992; Carter 1995). Staff and prisoners were interested in the purpose of her research and frequently questioned 'who did you say you were working for?' It was, at times, difficult to explain that as a PhD student she did not technically work for anyone and she often found herself re-cast in a number of different roles. In particular, medical staff tended to draw upon her ex-nurse status as a means of explaining her presence (well she was interested in health wasn't she?) and she was often introduced as a nurse rather than as a student or researcher. There is no doubt that this was one important way in which Catrin gained acceptance from medical staff (you're a nurse, you know what it's like) and from discipline staff who seemed impressed that she had not followed the traditional route into academia but had served a form of uniformed (disciplined) apprenticeship. However, implicit in this was a sense of Catrin being 'one of us', which she then had quickly to disclaim in her encounters with women prisoners, many of whom were deeply critical of prison nursing services and staff.

Overcoming the institutional mistrust of outsiders held by both prison staff and prisoners themselves presented something of a challenge. This mistrust also needs to be viewed in the context of penal policy at the time. Staff and prisoners alike represent the sharp end of these policies, resulting in low morale and insecurity amongst staff and prisoners being subjected to increasingly punitive and restrictive regimes. Catrin's motives and independence were occasionally questioned and while all welcomed an 'outsider' willing to listen and attempt to understand what it was really like, they had realistic fears about how their views would be represented and who would have access to the research findings.

To a lesser extent, these issues also applied to Emma's research in bail hostels. Relationships between hostel staff and residents were less antagonistic when compared with relationships in prison. Although inevitably there was potential for tension and conflict, relationships were also characterized by the provision of support (Wincup 1997). Hostels are much smaller than prisons and there were few symbols of institutional power such as uniforms, security measures, and keys. Exacerbated by the political context, however, hostel workers often felt marginalized and at the fringes of probation practice. They felt their experiences were frequently glossed over in research and policy agendas. As a result, they were only too willing to participate in the research and explore issues relevant to them with an interested individual. The women residents, like the women prisoners, were often desperate to outpour to someone willing to listen. Unlike other criminological researchers, Emma was not treated with any real suspicion. Only one woman suggested she could be a 'cop' or a 'screw', although Emma was also at times re-cast as something other than what she was or wanted to be: a social worker, a staff member, a relief worker. Mostly, the women residents found it hard to take on board why she would want to spend time voluntarily in a hostel and why she would be interested in hearing their experiences.

MANAGING DIVERSE RELATIONSHIPS IN THE FIELD

Throughout the fieldwork we both encountered diverse researcher–researched relationships for which our reading of the feminist methodological literature had not sufficiently prepared us. A great deal of feminist work has been concerned with power, power-sharing and the potentially exploitative nature of social research. Feminist researchers who interview women (e.g. Finch 1984; Oakley 1981) have identified power as resting largely with the researcher and much of the early feminist methodological literature deals with redressing this balance. In contrast, feminists interviewing men (see Laws 1990; McKee and O'Brien 1983; Smart 1984) have identified a less clear-cut balance of power. Smart (1984), for example, in her interviews with men in the legal profession, found it impossible to adhere to a feminist methodological approach because this might have endangered the research. This implicit distinction within feminist research—on the one hand, (powerful) women researchers interviewing (powerless) women respondents and, on the other hand, (powerful) male subjects interviewed by (less powerful) women—is, we believe, a false one, and one which perpetuates a whole range of gender assumptions. Whilst in the field, as in everyday life, we experienced a whole range of relationships and, in our many interviews with staff and women inmates, we met the 'powerless' and the 'powerful', although this had as much to do with institutional power relations as gendered ones.

At the outset we were both aware of the potential to exploit our captive audiences. There is a danger in research of this nature that individuals, even if they are not directly involved in the research, can be 'sucked in' unwittingly. The constraints on their liberty, especially in the prison context, make it difficult for them to walk away or to refuse to take part, and respondents may agree to participate in research for a range of reasons (for example, boredom or that it may be preferable to alternative regime activities). Indeed, the ready willingness of the women prisoners and the women hostel residents to participate in our many research interviews could be seen as an indication of their powerlessness. This raises the thorny question of informed consent in secure and semi-secure environments (see Liebling 1992).

In practice, we both had a generally positive reception, although relationships based on trust and rapport needed to be established and could not be taken for granted. Here, we can characterize the different types of relationships we experienced in the field, distinguished by a number of factors including the power differentials between our respondents and us as well as our status as 'outsiders' in their world. The first type of relationship, based on what we have loosely termed *simulated equivalence*, most closely matched our understanding of feminist approaches where rapport and empathy develop through shared interest and mutual experiences, leading to a more authentic interaction. Here, the interview becomes more of a conversation where the topic areas are explored through mutual consent. This was, perhaps, the most enjoyable research relationship although we are aware that such authenticity of action, especially over a prolonged period of immersion in the field, can gloss over the issue of power with consequences for the researcher, the researched, and, ultimately, the research itself. Game (1991), for example, has warned about the problems of over-identification with 'the other' in research and, at the end of the day, these were not equal relationships. We were able to leave the setting at any time. We also had the power to access our respondents' lives and our conversations (however cosy) were the data we needed to complete our researches and build our future careers. So, while we were conscious of the similarities of interest and experience in this type of relationship we also had to keep reminding ourselves of the profound differences.

A second type of relationship, which can be characterized as *researcher-directive*, occurred when we had no shared or comparable experiences with our respondents, or where the respondent had little interest in the topics under discussion, and where we struggled to establish rapport for a range of possible reasons. In these situations the conversation became more of a structured interview, where we set the agenda and asked the questions we felt were important: a more traditional researcher role, but one in which we both felt uncomfortable and actually quite powerless. In contrast, a third type of relationship, which can be termed *respondent-directive*, developed where it was the respondent that very much set the agenda and, while in empathetic ethnographic or feminist terms this is preferable, in that it allows the respondent to identify the issues most important to them, in reality the interview often turned into a monologue with the interviewee keen simply to express opinions on a range of topics, and where there was little space for the researcher to use such communication skills as reflection and clarification. This type of communication occurred most predominantly for Catrin in her interaction with discipline staff (male and female) and with those in a senior position in the (legitimate and illegitimate) pecking order of the institution. Women prisoners actively involved in campaigning also often used the interview as a forum for expressing their concerns on a host of issues, in the hope that Catrin would act as their mouthpiece and actively take their cause further.

A fourth type of relationship occurred when the respondents (intentionally or not) used the interview as a means for releasing emotions or for generally having a good moan, secure in the knowledge that we would not take the issue further and breach their confidentiality. Certainly, many of our interviews were emotionally charged, where respondents revealed the deep complexities of their histories and lives. We were both, at times, shocked by the intensity of emotion expressed and, while we did not find such relationships problematic as such, it was difficult not to become emotionally involved in our respondents' stories. Moreover, we were aware of our ethical positioning and, with hindsight, we questioned our role in this situation: researcher, friend, counsellor, or merely woman (and, hence, provider of pastoral care)? This ethical dilemma in feminist research has been noted elsewhere, not least in relation to emotionally 'hot' or sensitive topics (see Skeggs 1994; Stanley and Wise 1983). Here, the power relations are far from clear-cut and, in many respects, this type of relationship can be defined as *mutually advantageous* and is possibly the most equal. At one level, it can be seen that we (albeit unwittingly) used our respondents' emotional responses to events as part of our research. At the same time, however, we also made some reciprocal attempt to help them to manage their emotions through the very fact of listening to, and sympathizing with, them. Rarely are women prisoners and bail hostel residents given much listening space or their views taken seriously, and it is possible that being given the opportunity to talk in as much detail as they wished was of value to these women. We then had to try to deal with our own emotions in relation to our respondents.

Of course, these different types of research relationships were neither rigid nor mutually exclusive and we found that relationships would shift during the course of an interview and over the duration of the fieldwork. Moreover, emotions and feelings were not restricted to any one particular form of interaction or to only 'hot' topics. On reflection, these relationships and the ways in which we presented ourselves therein were shaped by what we thought would be acceptable to those we were with at the time. This adjustment and readjustment of ourselves to the various individuals we encountered required some work and emotional management on our part and different situations produced quite different research behaviours, for which no textbook could have prepared us. Throughout the fieldwork we moved in and out of a variety of researcher roles (some feminist, others more traditional) in order to manage such diverse relationships, to maintain access, and, essentially, to 'do' the research. We would suggest, then, that 'breaking in' socially is much more complex than 'breaking in' physically. Researchers undergo a process of being 'sussed out' and need to engage in 'impression management' (Goffman 1969) to present themselves as credible researchers. For both of us this was achieved in a number of ways: by earning a reputation as a good listener, by discussing common interests as far as possible, by appearing dedicated through spending prolonged time in the settings and, generally, by creating an atmosphere of interest in people, what they were doing and what they had to say.

GETTING OUT: LEAVING THE FIELD AND LETTING GO

Stanley (1990) has identified the important role of self-reflexivity as a fundamental characteristic of feminist research. This has relevance for all stages of the research process, from theoretical inception through to conclusion. While leaving the field has traditionally been a neglected issue in ethnographic research (Snow 1980), some sensitive reflections have emerged in recent years from researchers about their departures from a variety of research settings (see Shaffir and Stebbins 1991). A common theme is that the process of leaving involves reflecting on when to leave, managing the relationships formed, and deciding whether or not to return, if, in fact, it is possible to return. Here, there is an important distinction between getting out and getting away. For both of us, leaving the field physically was relatively easy. We had made it clear from the outset that our presence would only be for a specific period of time and we 'did our time' (or so it felt). However, getting away from the field emotionally proved more challenging. It was hard to distance ourselves from the settings and the more intensive period of data analysis served as a constant reminder of who we had met, their experiences, and the emotions they displayed when telling their stories.

The very fact of exploring women's experiences of criminal justice institutions was stressful and emotionally exhausting. As we noted in the introductory section, researchers rarely explore the emotional dimensions of their research and thus research practice can be isolating. This was exacerbated for us both because our fieldwork took us away from the university setting, our supervisors, and our networks of support, and so we felt physically isolated as well. On the one hand we were inspired and moved by the strength and insights demonstrated by the women we spoke to and felt privileged to have been permitted access to their emotions and experiences. On the other hand, we became intensely aware of the fact that, given certain circumstances, any woman might find herself in a similar situation. These were not unusual women. We saw aspects of ourselves, our friends, and our families in the women interviewed. In some respects, this realization encouraged us to listen more closely to their accounts, and listening to their stories (we both tape-recorded our interviews) over and over again in the post-fieldwork stage kept them alive and reminded us variously of their distress, hope, courage, and determination. It also made it harder to let go.

Ultimately, our emotions and reactions, recorded in our field notes, led us (we hope) to a fuller understanding of the subjective reality for these women and their keepers. We could not divorce our reactions from the research process and instead utilized them as a valuable analytical tool to deepen our awareness of the issues raised which are discussed throughout our theses. As far as the constraints of presenting a PhD for examination allowed, we included women's voices within the text. This was an attempt not to lose sight of the accounts provided by the research participants. We were careful, too, not to attach spurious meaning to them in an attempt to develop some deeper theoretical framework. However, those we interviewed gave their account from their own perspective and we then had to locate these accounts within our own perspectives. At the end of the day, the stories were theirs, the interpretation of those stories was ours. Did we do them justice?

REFLECTIONS

This volume is testimony to the fact that conducting research can be a 'messy business'. Inevitably, numerous methodological questions are raised throughout the research process which require reflection, and even after the PhD is submitted it is not completed. Data are revisited in the struggle for publications and new research questions emerge. Methodological dilemmas often remain unresolved.

In this chapter we have traced some of our experiences (there are many more) as PhD students researching women in criminal justice institutions. We have presented our doctoral journeys from inception, through methodological organization to the practical issue of 'doing' the research and 'leaving' the field as part of an explicit academic labour process. In so doing, our aim has been to highlight some of the complexities encountered and the compromises made along the way. As we stated in the introductory paragraph, ours is not a 'heroic tale' of how problems were confronted and overcome. Instead we have documented some of the challenges we faced and how we responded to them. No doubt others would have responded differently, and indeed if we were to conduct the same research again as more experienced researchers we might have reacted differently, or even designed it differently (another favourite question in *vivas*).

We have highlighted some of the situation-specific problems of conducting ethnographic research as feminists in secure and semi-secure environments. Negotiating and re-negotiating with diverse groups within such settings can be problematic. This needs to be viewed within the context of an environment characterized by an understandable curiosity about, and certain suspicion of, outsiders, as well as low morale and political change. More generally, we point to the theoretical and philosophical questions and, in particular, the tensions in what we assumed to be a feminist methodological approach. We found feminist research principles inadequate to the task of countering power in various researcher–researched and researcher–gatekeeper relationships. Issues to do with power and the various roles which researchers have to play in the field can constitute an additional emotional burden but one which often becomes disguised (sanitized) in the processes of 'writing up'.

Finally, on reflection, the management of the self in the field in many ways parallels the management of the self as a PhD student attempting to 'break in' to the academic world. There is no doubt that for both of us doing the PhD was a great opportunity. Certainly, we had the sort of academic freedom that we can only now really appreciate. However, doing a PhD requires a high level of emotional management both within and outwith the field. As academics in training, we experienced a whole range of emotions, not least intense academic insecurity, especially at having one's work criticized (however nicely done). We also encountered the same sort of diverse relationships we experienced in the field (some good, some bad, some paternalistic, some patronizing). At the end of the day, doctoral students are in a relatively powerless position within academic institutions and potentially exploitative situations can arise. Rightly or wrongly, as researchers in training, they have to deal with a lot of flack, which raises important questions about the strategies for support and reassurance. For PhD students, the desire to complete the apprenticeship and acquire accreditation and acceptance in the academic world can lead to a whole range of compromises or, at the very least, much tongue biting.

REFERENCES

BROWNLEE, I. (1998). *Community Punishment: A Critical Introduction.* London: Longman.

CARLEN, P. (1983). *Women's Imprisonment.* London: Routledge and Kegan Paul.

—— (ed.) (1985). *Criminal Women: Autobiographical Accounts.* Cambridge: Polity Press.

—— (1998). *Sledgehammer: Women's Imprisonment at the Millennium.* Basingstoke: Macmillan.

—— and TCHAIKOVSKY, C. (1996). 'Women's Imprisonment in England and Wales at the End of the Twentieth Century: Legitimacy, Realities and Utopias' in R. Matthews and P. Francis (eds.), *Prisons 2000.* London: Macmillan.

CARTER, K. (1995). *The Occupational Socialisation of Prison Officers: An Ethnography.* Unpublished PhD thesis, University of Wales, Cardiff.

COHEN, S., and TAYLOR, I. (1972). *Psychological Survival: The Experience of Long-term Imprisonment.* Penguin: Harmondsworth.

DOBASH, R., DOBASH, R., and GUTTERIDGE, S. (1986). *The Imprisonment of Women.* Oxford: Basil Blackwell.

DOYAL, L. (1995). *What Makes Women Sick: Gender and the Political Economy of Health.* London: Macmillan.

EASTERDAY, L., PAPADEMAS, D., SCHORR, L., and VALENTINE, C. (1982). 'The Making of a Female Researcher: Some Role Problems in Fieldwork' in R. Burgess (ed.), *Field Research: A Sourcebook and Field Manual.* London: Allen and Unwin.

ETTORRE, E. (1992). *Women and Substance Use.* Basingstoke: Macmillan.

FINCH, J. (1984). 'It's Great to Have Someone to Talk to' in C. Bell and H. Roberts (eds.), *Social Researching: Politics, Problems and Practice.* London: Routledge.

GAME, A. (1991) *Undoing the Social: Towards a Deconstructive Sociology.* Milton Keynes: Open University Press.

GELSTHORPE, L. (1990). 'Feminist Methodologies in Criminology: A New Approach or Old Wine in New Bottles?' in L. Gelsthorpe and A. Morris (eds.), *Feminist Perspectives in Criminology.* Milton Keynes: Open University Press.

GOFFMAN, E. (1969). *The Presentation of Self in Everyday Life.* London: Allen Lane.

GRAHAM, H. (1984). 'Surveying Through Stories' in C. Bell and H. Roberts (eds.), *Social Researching: Politics, Problems and Practice.* London: Routledge.

HARDING, S. (1987). *Feminism and Methodology: Social Science Issues.* Milton Keynes: Open University Press.

HAYMAN, S. (1996). *Community Prisons for Women.* London: Prison Reform Trust.

HEIDENSOHN, F. (1985). *Women and Crime,* London: Macmillan.

—— (1994). *Feminist Criminologies: Directions for the Future.* Unpublished paper presented to the Institute of Criminology, Cambridge, England.

HOME OFFICE (1990). *Report of an Efficiency Scrutiny of the Prison Medical Services.* London: HMSO.

—— (1995a). *Criminal Statistics 1994.* London: HMSO.

—— (1995b). *Prison Statistics 1994.* London: HMSO.

HOWE, A. (1994). *Punish and Critique: Towards a Feminist Analysis of Penality.* London: Routledge.

KELLY, L. (1990). 'Journeying in Reverse: Possibilities and Problems in Feminist Research on

Sexual Violence' in L. Gelsthorpe and A. Morris (eds.), *Feminist Perspectives in Criminology*. Milton Keynes: Open University Press.

—— Regan, L., and Burton, S. (1992). 'Defending the Indefensible? Quantitative Methods and Feminist Research' in H. Hinds, A. Phoenix and J. Stacey (eds.), *Working Out: New Directions in Women's Studies*. London: Falmer Press.

—— Burton, S., and Regan, L. (1994). 'Researching Women's Lives or Studying Women's Oppression? Reflections on What Constitutes Feminist Research' in M. Maynard and J. Purvis (eds.), *Researching Women's Lives from a Feminist Perspective*. London: Taylor and Francis.

Laws, S. (1990). *Issues of Blood: The Politics of Menstruation*. London: Macmillan.

Lee, B. (1983). 'On Standing Up and Being Counted'. *The Lancet*, 4 June.

Lee, R. (1993). *Doing Research on Sensitive Topics*. London: Sage.

Liebling, A. (1991). 'Where are the Women in Woolf?'. *Prison Report*, 15.

—— (1992). *Suicides in Prison*. London: Routledge.

McKee, L., and O'Brien, M. (1983). 'Interviewing Men: "Taking Gender Seriously"' in E. Gamarnikow *et al.* (eds.), *The Public and the Private*. London: Heinemann.

May, T. (1993). 'Feelings Matter: Inverting the Hidden Equation' in D. Hobbs and T. May (eds.), *Interpreting the Field: Accounts of Ethnography*. Oxford: Oxford University Press.

Maybrick, F. (1905). *Mrs Maybrick's Own Story: My 15 Lost Years*. London: Funk and Wagnalls Co.

Oakley, A. (1981). 'Interviewing Women: A Contradiction in Terms' in H. Roberts (ed.), *Doing Feminist Research*. London: Routledge.

Olesen, V. (1994). 'Feminisms and Models of Qualitative Research' in N. Denzin and Y. Lincoln (eds.), *The Handbook of Qualitative Research*. Newbury Park, Cal.: Sage.

Padel, U., and Stevenson, J. (1988) *Insiders: Women's Experiences of Imprisonment*. London: Virago.

Peckham, A. (1985). *A Woman in Custody*. London: Fontana.

Prison Reform Trust (1985). *Prison Medicine*. London: PRT.

Pugh, A. (1990). 'My Statistics and Feminism—a True Story' in L. Stanley (ed.), *Feminist Praxis: Research, Theory and Epistemology in Feminist Sociology*. London: Routledge.

Rice, M. (1990). 'Challenging Orthodoxies in Feminist Theory: a Black Feminist Critique' in L. Gelsthorpe and A. Morris (eds.), *Feminist Perspectives in Criminology*. Milton Keynes: Open University Press.

Shaffir, W., and Stebbins, R. (eds.) (1991). *Experiencing Fieldwork*. Newbury Park, Cal.: Sage.

Shilling, C.(1993). *The Body and Social Theory*, London: Sage.

Sim, J. (1990). *Medical Power in Prisons*. Milton Keynes: Open University Press.

Skeggs, B. (1994). 'Situating the Production of Feminist Ethnography' in M. Maynard and J. Purvis (eds.), *Researching Women's Lives from a Feminist Perspective*. London: Taylor and Francis.

Smart, C. (1976). *Women, Crime and Criminology*. London: Routledge and Kegan Paul.

—— (1984). *The Ties That Bind: Law, Marriage and the Reproduction of Patriarchal Relations*. London: Routledge and Kegan Paul.

—— (1990). 'Feminist Approaches to Criminology or Postmodern Woman Meets Atavistic Man', in L. Gelsthorpe and A. Morris (eds.), *Feminist Perspectives in Criminology*. Milton Keynes: Open University Press.

Smartt, U. (1995). *Remand Prisons in England and Germany*. Unpublished paper presented to the 1995 British Criminology Conference, Loughborough University.

Smircich, L. (1983). 'Studying Organisations as Cultures' in G. Morgan (ed.), *Beyond Method: Strategies for Social Research*. Beverly Hills, Cal.: Sage.

Smith, C. (1996). *The Imprisoned Body: Women, Health and Imprisonment*. Unpublished PhD Thesis, University of Wales, Bangor.

Snow, D. (1980). 'The Disengagement Process: A Neglected Problem in Participant Observation Research'. *Qualitative Sociology* 3: 100–22.

Stanley, L. (1990). 'Feminist Praxis and the Academic Mode of Production: An Editorial Introduction' in L. Stanley (ed.), *Feminist Praxis*. London: Routledge.

—— and Wise, S. (1983). *Breaking Out: Feminist Consciousness and Feminist Research*. London: Routledge and Kegan Paul.

—— and—— (1993). *Breaking Out Again: Feminist Ontology and Epistemology*. London: Routledge.

Turner, B. (1984). *The Body and Society*. Oxford: Blackwell.

—— (1987). *Medical Power and Social Knowledge*. London: Sage.

Warren, C. (1988). *Gender Issues in Field Research*. London: Sage.

Wincup, E. (1997). *Waiting for Trial: Living and Working in a Bail Hostel*. Unpublished PhD thesis, University of Wales, Cardiff.

13

MAFIA, METHODOLOGY, AND 'ALIEN' CULTURE

Patricia Rawlinson

FROM HERE TO MATURITY

Although much has been written on what is more popularly known as the Russian *mafiya* most of it consists of reports in the Russian and Western media or else is based on those reports. And while law enforcement agencies can be useful sources (assuming access is granted) their data have utilitarian functions, that is to investigate and prosecute those suspected of organized criminal activities, thus providing at best only a partial view of organized crime. As even these two sources were limited when I began my research the only other viable option seemed to be to go to Russia and find out first-hand 'who' and/or 'what' was Russian organized crime. This brief chapter deals reflexively with the trials and tribulations of doing research on Russian organized crime 'out there and in the field'.

In 1990 I registered for a part-time MPhil/PhD. Full-time was out of the question as family commitments (two adolescents desperate to contribute to designer-label profit margins) and the added expense of post-graduate fees demanded a financial contribution to our household income. Research would have to fit around work. Other potential obstacles loomed large in my initial wariness of embarking on a long-term commitment to a PhD: the choice of subject (organized crime), region (the USSR), academic background (no grounding in criminology), and age (I was a tender thirty-seven). All I could offer to counter these negatives was huge enthusiasm for my research topic, a good degree in Russian and English, familiarity with Soviet culture as a result of student placements in Minsk and Kiev, and a commitment to filling in gaps of knowledge by embarking on a Certificate of Criminology at Birkbeck College. Age, however, I was stuck with.

Age plays a part not only in one's own perception of self, but also in the attitude of the academic world, funding bodies, and peer groups. Our present culture encourages us to think, look, and feel young. A constant stream of images, advertising, and role models nudges us towards the altar of rejuvenation where we are divested of time and money in the absurd attempt to stop the clock. And yet in a world dominated by the cost-effective principle, it is logical to question the allocation of funding or jobs to someone with only two or three decades of potential employment when there are so many applicants who could give another ten to fifteen year's value. Further, rapid technological advancement means that many mature students need to acquire computer skills, at a cost, so as to become a part of the academic mainstream. Even if the above obstacles are overcome, peer pressure can encourage self-doubt. Common sense, as friends and colleagues were often at pains to point out, exhorts the 'sensible' approach. 'Now you've done your first degree time to get/go back to work in the "real world"', or, as the other popular discouragement went, 'you'll be forty-something when you finish the PhD, then what?' This kind of 'support' came not only from my well-meaning circle. I felt unceremoniously exiled to the graveyard of employment prospects by an influential academic who assured me that 'at your age', finding a good job, even with a doctorate, would be nigh impossible. Yet the mature student knows more than anyone that time becomes more precious with age, and justifying another three to five years of student status with only the faintest promise of employment makes a PhD a particularly high-risk investment. Few mature students take up a PhD on a whim, hence the choice of research area becomes crucial. If it is linked to former employment and can enhance expertise the advantages are immediately obvious. For me, there was no thematic connection between the research topic—Soviet organized crime—and former employment—motherhood, school librarian, or the odd bits of freelance journalism. What did stand in my favour was the uniqueness of the subject. No-one in the United Kingdom had studied Russian organized crime and the majority of academics were unaware it even existed in the USSR. Here was virgin territory, obviously with the attendant problems that data deprivation brings, but with the distinct advantage of allowing me the first voice. As luck would have it (for me, but not for the Russians), organized crime was to become a major security problem, both nationally and internationally. In 1993 I received an ESRC award and became a full-time researcher, a luxury I only now fully appreciate.

The unique life experience brought to research by mature students should be regarded, potentially at least, as one of their greatest assets. Without even being aware of it, I drew on a multitude of skills gained through life experience. Motherhood taught me how to mediate, listen, offer objective encouragement, and observe meaning in the subtleties of gesture, lessons which became invaluable for interviewing. Multi-tasking, one of the most crucial skills of parenting, was yet another invaluable transferable skill. Work as a librarian helped immensely with literature searches, the collation of data etc. My temporary foray into journalism was instructive on how to think on my feet, conduct interviews in difficult situations, double/treble check 'facts' before committing an opinion, and follow 'leads', even of the most obscure nature. All of which helped gain access to the often impenetrable world of organized crime. The wisdom accumulated from being out in the world, the lessons learned from life's knocks, the insight and sensitivities gained from abundant, disparate levels of interaction over a number of years, whether in the family or at work, provided non-articulated skills, particularly important for an ethnographic methodological approach, but which can also be employed in other areas of research. Mature students possess a cache of resources. Academic institutions and funding councils need to value more this potential and recognize that age is a tool rather than an issue.

MINEFIELDS AND FIELDWORK

The subject of my research challenged every resource available, whether as a mature student or otherwise. Organized crime probably rates as one of the most difficult areas on which to collect data. Its covert nature and high-risk activities have made it necessary for those researching organized crime to construct a defensive response to unwanted intrusions, sometimes involving coercion and even violence. Even when access is granted to a criminal organization there can be no guarantee whatsoever that the information given is an accurate representation of the group and its activities. Nor are there any obvious benefits for those concerned in divulging the *modus operandi* or structure of their criminal group. Consequently it becomes tempting for researchers to limit themselves to data from official sources, thereby providing a skewed approach to the topic. Paradoxically it is this very inaccessibility which favours an ethnographic-based methodology in the study of organized crime. Even if access is not achieved, pursuing access, within a common-sense framework, can reveal the nature of criminal structures, their links with the legitimate world, the strength and weaknesses of defence systems, the nature of individuals who act as gate-keepers, and so on. This is not to say that researchers should deliberately set out to put themselves at risk in the pursuit of primary material. There are, to my knowledge few, if any, academics, certainly in the Western world, who have met with serious physical threats or harm in their investigations of organized crime. Unlike the journalist whose bread and butter is based on getting 'that story', emphasizing the sensational rather than the sober elements of organized crime and hence increasing the risk factor of investigation, the academic is given more time and required to take a measured stance to his or her subject, and to that extent is less vulnerable.

Ethnography is as much part of a self-educational process as it is the collection of data. 'All social research is founded on the human capacity for participant observation. We act in the social world and yet are able to reflect upon ourselves and our actions as objects in that world' (Hammersley and Atkinson 1995: 21). If we are conducting an experiment from inside the test-tube then objectivity can only be subjective. 'Being there' helped me to understand the inherent preconceptions and prejudices that I, as a Westerner, brought to an understanding of organized crime in Russia. There was also a limited but rich tradition of ethnographic work on organized crime from which I could draw support, most specifically from academics in the USA.

The dangerous and sensitive nature of research into organized crime has not deterred social scientists from entering the field and getting their hands dirty. Landesco, one of the leading proponents of the Chicago School, set a precedent in his study of organized crime in Chicago and capitalized on the fact that he 'could speak their language as well as the language of the academic' (Landesco 1968: xv), a privilege also afforded Hobbs in his study of illegal entrepreneurship in the East End (Hobbs 1988). If Landesco and Hobbs *were* native, others like Chambliss (1988), who gained access to criminal networks in Seattle, or Polsky (1969), in his study of poolroom hustlers, *went* native, or at least attempted to. However, there is no obvious advantage in being native to a group other than having fewer problems in initial access. An outsider certainly has fewer conflicts of loyalty. Francis Ianni, as an Italian engaged in an anthropological study of the Lupollo crime family, emphasized his detachment from their world other than in a purely social setting when he was happy to share the ethnic and cultural identity which bound them. In this way he could avoid the ethical dilemmas faced by those who can genuinely become 'one of the lads' (Ianni and Ianni 1972). Other researchers of organized crime and gangs have either continued the tradition of participant observation (Armstrong 1993) or won the trust of underworld figures to record the inner workings of organized crime groups and professional criminals (Inciardi 1975; Douglas 1972; Sutherland 1956).

Unlike Landesco, Hobbs, and the Iannis I experienced no cultural or regional areas of common identity in my study of organized crime in the USSR and Russia. It was impossible even to attempt to go native, despite speaking the language. Sex, nationality, culture, and history created a total divide. Nor was it possible to win the complete trust of members of an underworld which changed as rapidly as the country within which it operated. I was, in short, an outsider.

The demands of work in the early days of the project, before funding, meant that I could tackle the subject from three different perspectives: journalist, academic, and informal police liaison. (I had acted as interpreter and networker during the initial stages of the training programme for Russian police cadets in the St Petersburg–Hendon exchange programme which facilitated access to police data in St Petersburg.) At other times I was simply 'that Western woman who hangs around in bars'. These different hats provided a diversity and, in darker moments, a perversity of approaches to this elusive subject. My shifting identities were in many ways a reflection of the shifting realities to which the Soviet Union, and, in its post-coup incarnation, the Commonwealth of Independent States were subject. Indeed the appropriateness of differing identities was more an expedient use of certain opportunities which presented themselves at different times and which I grabbed in an *ad hoc* manner, hardly the ordered ethnographic approach prescribed by Burgess (1993). The research methodology often reflected the *modus operandi* of those I was studying, that is, organized criminals who made their living by responding to the changing scenario and turning it to their advantage. Opportunism played an important part in my acquisition of data, in the same way that the subjects of study made their money from opportunist ventures. Their success rate was notably higher than mine.

NEGOTIATING THE LOOKING-GLASS WORLD

As if the study of organized crime was not difficult enough, I had compounded the problem by wanting to research *Russian,* or as it was in the early stages of investigation, *Soviet* organized crime. No cultures tease the sensibilities of the foreigner so much as does that of Russia, which rests between the European and the Asian, neither the one thing nor the other, but with pretensions of both. The writer Alexander Zinoviev offers the following rebuke to non-Russians who study his native society: '[w]hat is the reason for such monstrous mistakes that Westerners make when they evaluate the phenomena of our own life? The reason is that they measure our life too according to their own yardstick' (Zinoviev 1986: 128). Even during periods of relative political and social stability Russian reality has consisted of half-truths, embellishments of the truth, or total reconstructions of the truth, always managing to steer just clear of blatant mendacity (Marquis de Custine 1989). For foreigners to be able to grasp even a modicum of understanding of this world of shifting realities, they need an understanding and appreciation of behaviour and symbols unique to Russian culture. Kremlinologists, the Western observers of the dark world of Soviet politics, drew great significance from the theatre of public performance played out by the country's leaders. The hierarchy of power and party machinations which went on secretly behind the Kremlin walls could be divined by observing which Party members attended official occasions and where they stood in proximity to the General Secretary, whether he was speaking from a podium or, as occurred with embarrassing frequency in the early 1980s, lying in state. What media propaganda obscured, the semiotics of tradition exposed. On a more mundane level, the quality of contacts and friendship between Russians and foreign visitors, was displayed in a variety of symbols of status. Those Soviet 'friends' with easy access to western goods, an ability to overcome the manifold bureaucratic obstacles of daily life or fluent in one or more foreign language, could usually be categorized as being 'big brotherly', in other words, KGB minders. The informed visitor would know to act with amicable caution.

All this changed from 1985 onwards with Gorbachev's reforms of *perestroika* and *glasnost*, the courageous challenge to a legacy of hollow ideological and political conventions. For many Soviets these were positive changes, but from the perspective of the researcher they dismantled a hitherto reasonably reliable framework within which some kind of 'truth' could be established. As Gorbachev encouraged the democratization of politics Kremlinologists found themselves bereft of familiar behaviours and traditions upon which decades of political analysis and prognosis had been based. 'Spotting the spook' became equally difficult as the KGB underwent a series of metamorphoses whilst keeping a lower profile in the new democratic environment. In the beginning *glasnost* allowed the media to speak with limited openness about the state of the country. But for a people who for so long had been silenced by authoritarianism, the relaxing of constraints soon led to their total eradication. Voices not only spoke, but shouted. Data on the most taboo of subjects, including crime and organized crime, flowed from unofficial and official sources. Many of us were perhaps blinded by this hitherto unknown quality of sincerity, allowing it to eclipse the dubious methodologies upon which the plethora of information was based. The problem shifted dramatically from data acquisition to data interpretation. It was in this world of cultural mutation and social and political disquiet that I began my research.

JOURNALISM, INTERVIEWS, AND 'JUST LOOKING'

The diversity of approaches—from investigative journalism to archival work—employed in the research, not surprisingly, had its advantages and disadvantages. Opportunities which arose from journalistic experience tended to focus on visual and easily assimilated phenomena, ignoring the more subtle details of interaction which constitute a significant part of ethnographic research. Nonetheless, journalism has been both an important experience and a source for the doctorate. Nor, in the future, would such sources be spurned.

Soviet and Russian journalism provided much material, particularly in the early days of my research. Held back for so long by the constraints of ideology and heavy-handed censorship, I was able to take advantage of the new freedoms exercised by the media during *glasnost*. However, journalism did not change overnight and it still indulged in the Soviet practice of wordiness and high-flown rhetoric. On the positive side, the experience of being silenced for so many years meant that now investigative journalists really could investigate, they brought to their work an idealism and courage that only the most stalwart of editors and journalists under the former repressive regime had dared to show. There is an irony in the fact that authoritarian regimes can bring out the better qualities of human nature and give the pursuit of truth a noble ring. In the investigation of organized crime in Russia a handful of journalists, such as Vladimir Glotov, Dmitri Krikoriants, and Dmitri Kholodov, have lost their lives in the pursuit of 'truth'.

Admittedly courageous journalism does not necessarily make for good journalism, but it does stand as a reminder that good investigative journalism is a cornerstone of the free press which need not degenerate into prying sensationalism or voyeurism. In the West the opprobrium poured onto a lot of journalism is justified. However, the neglect of journalistic sources by academics often makes for a one-sided and diluted analysis of certain areas of research. Lack of in-depth analysis in journalism need not detract from the usefulness of material collated by the investigator. As Hobbs points out 'the intransigence that colludes so closely with administrative analysis ignores narrative accounts at the considerable loss of detail, tone and depth' (Hobbs 1994: 443). The level of cynicism which is brought to many anecdotal accounts used in journalism could equally be levelled at official documentation. It is worth remembering that in the study of organized crime official documentation has been partisan and ill-informed. The Valacchi tapes, the recorded official testimony of a low ranking mafioso, formed the evidence upon which Cressey (1969) based his book, *Theft of the Nation*, for many years the definitive text on the Cosa Nostra. Subsequent research has found the evidence to be spurious in a great many places. It is also methodologically dubious to form conclusions on the evidence of one individual, what Furstenberg calls 'an uncritical acceptance of local mythology' (Block 1978: 12), a technique more appropriate to tabloid journalism than serious academic study. Exploiting lessons learned as a freelance journalist I set off to 'get the story' through interviews and observation.

The interview can create as many problems as it solves. Hammersley and Atkinson comments that 'the quality and relevance of the data produced by interviews can vary considerably, and is not always predictable' (Hammersley and Atkinson 1995: 139) The extent to which an informant is prepared to divulge information is usually determined by external and internal constraints based on cultural, psychological, and professional factors. Russians, for historical reasons, can be acutely ill at ease with the idea of expounding uncomfortable truths in a formal setting. It became obvious that none of the recorded interviews was going to reveal as much as off-the-record conversations, a fact by no means limited to Russians. However, the semiotics of communication—hesitancy, a slight nodding of the head, eye contact, and so on, added another dimension to the data collection. Perhaps I was more conscious of this because most of the interviews were conducted in Russian. In order to follow more closely the often detailed and rapid discussions I would anxiously observe physical gestures of the respondent as an aid to better understanding. Many of the interviews were non-directive, as much by accident as design, but as other researchers on sensitive subjects have found this approach can serve to lessen the inhibitions of respondents and provide more accurate accounts (Burgess 1993; Lee 1993). An interview, for example, with Oleg the pimp and low-level mafioso often moved away from the framework within which I wished it to develop, but in doing so it brought in whole areas of information about which I previously knew nothing and which became important fragments of the picture I was trying to describe.

The interviews provided a significant, albeit small, contribution to the study. The social context, colours in the background, so to speak, was acquired simply by 'watching' and living with Russian friends and colleagues. Although seeing is not necessarily believing, especially in Russia, general observation and a degree of interpretative analysis of the observation was crucial. To understand deviance and crime one needs to be aware of what constitutes normality, a task which became increasingly difficult as social upheavals continued through the early 1990s when the fieldwork was conducted. The most disturbing evidence of social change could be found in the growing number of homeless people, of all ages, living on the streets. Where once the only children seen begging were gypsies, now they came from all backgrounds and were of all ages, a pitiful spectacle in a country which once prided itself on its care and vision for its youth. Such sights also rang alarm bells where organized crime was concerned. Here, among the disenfranchised young, were prospective gang members, youngsters who had nothing to lose and everything to gain from a life of crime, particularly from an economic gain point of view. Here too were prospective customers, a generation whose disillusionment would make them prey to what organized crime could offer: prostitution as an alternative means of employment, alcohol and drugs as a release from the drudgery of everyday life, 'protection' as a means of ensuring that their own forays into the world of business were 'safe'. So too was the fear and distrust amongst ordinary people an indication of changing times. Where once the 'enemy' had been the authorities and only the closest of friends were to be trusted, where people had to stick together as a way of making ends meet, now in the competitive world of business the enemy became the friend or colleague against whom individual interests were pitted.

In the absence of the rule of law, restraint and legitimate redress for unfair practice were also absent. Innovative means to stay ahead of the game in a society where shortage of goods had been replaced by shortage of money meant that the majority of the Russian people were 'on the take' in varying degrees. This was not the old Soviet practice of ripping off the state but the new Russian practice of grabbing and selling, from friends, neighbours, and customers. The price of freedom was higher than many could afford. And so, whilst acknowledging that 'we should interpret what we observe with caution' (Whyte 1984: 95), there is nevertheless a lot to be said for academic voyeurism of the mundane, of treasuring those prosaic vignettes of Russian society.

BENDING GENDER

Finally, the question of sex and gender has to be addressed, and not from a purely feminist perspective. As a female researcher I was under no illusions about the gender-related problems I would confront during the study: organized crime and law enforcement are all indisputably male dominated. It came as no shock to confront ill-placed paternalism, cultural misogyny, or chauvinistic hostility which formed a constant, but thankfully limited, resistance to the research. I was prepared for the worst and set off with the premise articulated by Warren that 'for a female to become a significant other in a community in which maleness is the main status criterion is not easy, and the researcher should be aware that she may have to put considerable effort into becoming the type of person that the community will value' (Warren 1972: 152). The problem lay in discerning the nature of the values of the different communities I inhabited. Russian law enforcement has few women in high-ranking positions (much the same as in Britain) and presents an inbuilt resistance to accepting women as anything more than low-status administrators. It helped being a *foreign* woman in so far as a non-Russian passport had been (until recently) a symbol of fear and opportunism (the highly regarded ticket to the West *via* a marriage certificate).

If Russia's patriarchal culture created obstacles for the female researcher it simultaneously presented ways of getting round them. The positive side of paternalism manifested itself in a concern for my safety when 'out and about', a willingness to help a damsel in 'intellectual distress' by offering access to material, and a trust that, as a woman, I would not betray some of the more sensitive information to which I was party. The negative side persistently informed me that this was not the type of work for a woman, which meant that I was constantly having to assert the academic purpose of my trip and suffer the embarrassing opportunities that were taken to display me as a 'curiosity'. There was also the persistent hidden agenda, often not so hidden with Russian men, which expected female gratitude to be expressed in sexual terms. The perceived singularity of my position is also apparent in the UK, confirming that certain areas of study remain a male preserve even in allegedly progressive cultures.

Most frustrating was the inability to gain access to relevant sites for data collection purely on account of gender. Many of the meeting points for members of organized crime are exclusively male environments such as the gym and *banya* or bath house. Such venues offer a haven and security for Russian men and allow a freer exchange of ideas and information between groups than the more restrictive public spaces. On one occasion I was allowed into a section of a gym in Moscow but this rare acquiescence was in deference to the presence of the British television crew with whom I was working. On balance, however, gender *and* nationality served the research advantageously. Physical vulnerability meant that I was less likely to become a victim of violence as assaulting a female (Russian wives and partners excepted) was, in a world of warped chivalry, still regarded as shameful. Cosmetics and jewellery could allow me to blend in to the environment or stand out.

There is of course always a certain amount of guilt accompanying the exploitation of one's sexuality, which I invariably did whilst in Russia. Cosmetics and coquetry might enable a woman to get past the gatekeeper or soften the hardened bureaucrat in the pursuit and acquisition of data but unfulfilled, albeit non-articulated, promises and mixed messages play an unfair hand in the complex game of women in the field of men. One part of me feels that such strategies were demeaning to my sex, another part can justify them as redress for the restrictions on the data-collection process and personal humiliation suffered by a woman in a patriarchal society and male dominated domain. Perhaps the latter scenario could be interpreted as expedient use of disadvantage, the rejection of 'methodological Puritanism' in the search for truth (Douglas 1972: 8) without betraying principles and personal relationships outside the study.

CONCLUSION

The manifold approaches used in the research reflect the complexity of the subject as well as the biography of the researcher. Indeed all PhDs are a reflection of their authors' lives, the freedom to conceive, develop, and write up ideas of one's own, the creative act which reflects back its creator. And yet freedom is a double-edged sword. The freedom to express ideas has also to be contained within a framework of rules—style, format, deadlines, and so on. So too will the ideas and hypotheses which drive the PhD also be contained within the relationship formed between researcher and researched. External factors greatly facilitate the process. Supportive supervisors, families, and colleagues and a certain amount of luck all play a crucial part. Ultimately, however, researching and writing a PhD is rather akin to an endurance test, the overcoming of a series of obstacles the majority of which (financial aside) are placed there by the researcher him/herself. Whether the researcher is a mature student or a bright young thing the PhD is a personal high-risk investment, but well worth taking. For myself, I have not been exiled to the graveyard of unemployment. Writing and completing the PhD has simply been the beginning of another phase, a new career. The learning process continues.

REFERENCES

ARMSTRONG, G. (1993). 'Like that Desmond Morris'? in D. Hobbs and T. May (eds.), *Interpreting the Field: Accounts of Ethnography*. Oxford: Clarendon.

BLOCK, A. (1978). 'History and the Study of Organized Crime'. *Urban Life: A Journal of Ethnographic Research*. 6: 455–74.

BURGESS, R. (1993). *In the Field. An Introduction to Field Research*. London: Routledge.

CHAMBLISS, S. (1988). *On the Take: From Petty Crooks to Presidents*. Bloomington, Ind.: Indiana University Press.

CRESSEY, D. R. (1969). *Theft of the Nation: The Structure and Operations of Organized Crime in America*. New York: Harper and Row.

DOUGLAS, J. (1972). *Research on Deviance*. New York: Random House.

HAMMERSLEY, M., and ATKINSON, P. (1995). *Ethnography: Principles in Practice*. London: Routledge.

HOBBS, D. (1988). *Doing the Business*. Oxford: Clarendon.

—— (1994). 'Professional and Organized Crime in Britain' in M. Maguire, R. Morgan and R. Reiner (eds.), *The Oxford Handbook of Criminology*. Oxford: Oxford University Press.

IANNI, F., and IANNI, E. (1972). *A Family Business: Kinship and Social Control in Organized Crime*. London: Routledge & Kegan Paul.

INCIARDI, J. (1975). *Careers in Crime*. Chicago, Ill.: Rand McNally.

LANDESCO, J. (1968). *The Illinois Crime Survey 1929, Part 3, Organized Crime in Chicago*. Chicago, Ill.: Illinois Association for Criminal Justice.

LEE, R. (1993). *Doing Research on Sensitive Topics*. London: Sage.

MARQUIS DE CUSTINE (1989). *Empire of the Czar*. New York: Anchor Books.

POLSKY, N. (1969). *Hustlers, Beats and Others*. New York: Anchor Books.

SUTHERLAND, E. (1956). *The Professional Thief*. Chicago, Ill.: Phoenix Books.

WARREN, C. (1972). 'Observing the Gay Community' in J. Douglas (ed.), *Research on Deviance*. New York: Random House.

WHYTE, W. (1984). *Learning from the Field. A Guide from Experience*. Beverly Hills, Cal.: Sage Publications.

ZINOVIEV, A. (1986). *Homo Sovieticus*. London: Paladin Books.

14

SAD, BAD, AND (SOMETIMES) DANGEROUS TO KNOW: STREET CORNER RESEARCH WITH PROSTITUTES, PUNTERS, AND THE POLICE

Karen Sharpe

The central concern of this chapter will be to highlight a number of method-ological issues encountered whilst conducting street corner research with female prostitutes, their punters, and their pimps, in their natural setting of a red-light district. The principal aim of the discussion will be to present a per-sonal reflexive account of the fieldwork experience, highlighting some of the problems—and pleasures—of handling ethnographic research with a number of groups whose behaviour and activities are perceived, categorized, and classi-fied by many in wider society to be immoral, anti-social, and legally 'deviant'.

Whilst many academic studies of prostitution are loosely grounded in theor-etical, ideological, and political analyses, reference to these works rarely offers much of a glimpse into the world of the sex industry as experienced by the observing researcher (recent exceptions are McKeganey and Barnard 1996; O'Neill 1996). Studies of prostitution tend to fall into one of three distinct categories: historical texts (Acton 1857; Benjamin and Masters 1964; Davis 1965; Finnegan 1979; Mahood 1990; Roberts 1992; Walkowitz 1980); socio-criminological studies providing both international profiles (Bryan 1965, 1966; Cohen 1980; Hoigard and Finstad 1992; Kapur 1978), local British studies (Cun-nington 1980; McKeganey and Barnard 1996; McLeod 1982; Rolph 1955); or the personal semi-autobiographical accounts of sex workers themselves (Anon 1959; Jaget 1980; St Clair 1993). Similarly a seemingly endless diet of television documentaries, fictional programmes, and daytime and late-night discussion shows about prostitution reveals surprisingly little about the reality of the sex industry and the people who are involved in it.

Douglas (1972: 13) has characterized prostitutes as a stigmatized and criminalized group with a 'profound public relations problem'. The central objective of my research was to understand why and how women entered the world of prostitution: to discover the motivating factors, the dynamics of the introductory process, and how they learnt the skills, values, and codes of conduct of the business. I wanted to explore the importance and impact of prostitution on their lifestyles and to put the 'deviance' of prostitution into context with other aspects of their criminality. I also wanted to discover how the women themselves, and their families and friends, subjectively defined, perceived, and rationalized their activity. If I could develop relationships with a number of actors over a long enough period of time, I hoped it would also be possible to paint a broader picture of a year in the life of a red-light district and the people who shape it—the prostitutes, punters, pimps, and the police (Sharpe 1998).

To facilitate the fieldwork, I spent a year attached to the police vice squad responsible for policing street prostitution offences. As an 'honorary' member of the vice squad, I was expected to suffer the same delights and indignities that they were subjected to in the course of their daily duties. Where they went, I went. What they saw, I saw (we may have viewed it differently but that's another matter). As their remit covered a wide variety of crimes and misdemeanours ranging from drug offences to missing persons, sexual assaults, obscene publications, indecent exposure, and importuning in public places such as parks and toilets, a fair percentage of the fieldwork year was spent in some strange and not entirely exotic locations.

It should be recognized at the outset that many complications arose from the complexity of the networks in which I was involved. Not only did I have to endeavour to forge a relationship with the police and learn how to cope with their cop culture (a generic term for a wide range of behavioural traits), but I also had to cultivate an entirely different type of rapport with the prostitutes and their various associates in order to gain their confidence and trust. Just to complicate things further, of course, the prostitutes and the police were involved in their own highly ambiguous relationship with each other (Sharpe 1997). As Neff Gurney (1991) points out, in the process of collecting the best possible data for the study, the researcher faces the problems of developing a 'professional detachment' whilst at the same time cultivating a deep involvement with members of a different culture (Neff Gurney 1991: 53).

My own fieldwork experience required a flexibility bordering on the schizophrenic to deal with these issues. On a number of occasions, the entire research process with all its interrelationships became extremely tense—almost to the point of total collapse—particularly when the police embarked on one of their periodic high-profile cautioning and arrest operations on the patch. This could make life very difficult indeed for me as each group would expect me to be on 'their side'. Much is written about the need for objectivity in the research

process. When conducting research with individuals and groups who are mutually suspicious and ostensibly opposing each other (the perennial game of 'cops
and robbers' as Reiner 1994: 705 describes it), neutrality is almost impossible. As
Vidich comments:

Neutrality, even to the point of silence is a form of reaction ... but also implies a
specific attitude towards the issue—being above it, outside it, more important than it,
not interested in it (Vidich 1955: 358).

IN THE IVORY TOWER: PLANNING THE CAMPAIGN

One of the immediate issues confronting the research was the wide disparity
between the plethora of material informing research methods and the real lack
of useful practical guidance on how to deal with the day-to-day (or in my case
night-to-night) reality of conducting fieldwork, particularly with individuals or
groups whose culture and lifestyle was vastly different from anything I had
previously experienced or encountered.

In numerous research monographs, the emphasis is on outlining how the
research was done, justifying the theoretical frameworks and the presentation
of the results. Frequently any exposition of the experience of actually doing the
research is relegated to the footnotes or the appendix almost as an afterthought.
Whether this is because academics, once they have their PhDs, develop selective
amnesia and become rather coy in admitting to making mistakes in the process
of doing research, or simply that the PhD is seen as a tiresome obstacle that has
to be overcome, never thereafter to be spoken about in polite circles, it is
nevertheless a stark fact that the literature on the practical realities of
conducting criminological research with deviant groups is remarkably scant. As
Sjoberg and Miller (1973) point out:

The problems encountered in actual practice are often glossed over in the presentation
of the findings and researchers are unable to benefit from one anothers' experiences
and, above all, their failures (Sjoberg and Miller 1973: 130).

When, as part of my literature review, I finally did trace an article with what
seemed like promising advice, it offered the following wise words:

Insofar as the investigator is interested in studying potentially dangerous kinds of
behaviour he should understand the risks. ... Do not stay too late at night and avoid
Friday nights altogether (Berk and Adams 1970: 111).

As it transpired, my research was to involve numerous late nights—including a
lot of Friday nights. I endured winter blizzards, biting gale force winds, pouring
rain, fog, hailstones, and the energy-sapping humidity of midsummer. I spent

endless hours hanging around the sterile corridors of the police station. I engaged in mundane chit-chat and constantly asked dumb questions to just about anyone who happened to be loitering (literally) in the vicinity. The research process was not a dull experience. It was hard work. It was sometimes dangerous, it was frequently soul destroying. It was often extremely funny and enjoyable, and it was too often very sad.

ON THE PATCH

No matter how carefully one plans in advance, the research is designed in the course of its execution. The finished monograph is the result of hundreds of decisions, large and small, made whilst the research is underway (Becker 1965: 602).

When I first embarked on the research I was armed with only a very vague strategy and a lot of high hopes. Following a preliminary sortie to assess the feasibility of the research proposal, I started to face the reality of the task and realized that the interview schedule which had seemed so workable on paper might not figure a great deal in the research itself. It became clear that it would take some considerable time, patience, and ingenuity to gain the confidence and establish rapport with the women working as prostitutes. Moreover, I would have quickly to acclimatize myself to the ways of the police. Until then cop culture had been something that was primarily about men, written by men, for men. I was about to become that rare phenomenon of a female researcher in a male dominated setting (Neff Gurney 1991).

The fieldwork did not get off to a promising start. By only the second night it seemed that I had managed to confuse, irritate, and alienate the entire red-light district. There was considerable confusion about who I was and what I was doing which, fuelled by the gossip and rumours of the patch, had me designated as being anything from a social worker to a newspaper reporter with hidden cameras and microphones. One irate prostitute even walked across the city to the central police station and reported me to the police; when she was told by a rather perplexed officer at the front desk 'but she's with the police—she's a student' she assumed this to mean I was a student policewoman and returned to the patch to subject me to the usual barrage of expletives reserved for rookie police officers. It then seemed imperative that I made my own introductions to the women, outlining my status and what I was doing rather than let the rumours and misunderstandings snowball out of control. However, I was still prone to being undermined. The women on the patch had just started to come to terms with the fact that I was 'a researcher writing a book' when, a few weeks into the research, a new police officer on the team told anyone who would listen that I was 'an official from the Home Office' (the research was actually funded by the ESRC).

At first the women would have nothing to do with me. Some of the women were indignant that I had the audacity to go on to their patch—it was their territory and I was seen as the intruder. Cultivating relationships—the need systematically to establish, maintain, and develop rapport through what may be several phases of acceptance is the most time-consuming and complex aspect of the research process (Janes 1970; Denzin 1970; Weinberg and Williams 1972). Let's face it, most of the people involved in crime or anti-social deviant activity, as well as those who are part of the criminal justice process, are sensitive in one way or another to being researched or exposed.

When the central focus of the research involves people whose behaviour and lifestyle are generally vilified, and whose lives are dominated by abuse and violence, they are likely to react to intrusions with aggression. The problems facing the researcher move from the mundane issues of what to wear and what to take out in the field, to the more vexing problems of how to survive asking sensitive questions of frequently unwilling and hostile respondents.

Throughout the fieldwork period I kept a research diary which provided a barometer of the ups and downs of my research experience. One month into the fieldwork and I had written:

The women are practically ignoring me as if I do not exist. Some of them look straight through me, some of them look me up and down, some of them leave me in no doubt that if looks could kill . . . I have the feeling that any other intelligent person doing this kind of research would know exactly what to do and would say all the right things and everything would be fine, but I seem to be having to make this up as I go along and adapt to whatever situation I find myself in. I have been sworn at, spat at, laughed at, ridiculed and threatened. This is much harder in reality than I ever imagined it would be.

Initially the concern of the women was that their names would be published or that they would be recognized by their description, and that this would lead to various people, most notably their partners, social security or tax officials, finding out about their nocturnal activities. Some of the women had constructed elaborate stories, or had contingency plans organized, to explain their nightly absences ranging from a nightly baby-sitting job to attending an evening class. I regard this as the paradox of being a prostitute, actively working to attract attention and yet desperately seeking to maintain a degree of secrecy about working in the profession. The issue of respecting privacy and not revealing personal identities was one of the paramount aspects of the research which I was determined to uphold. I promised total anonymity in any subsequent publication; to this end I gave all the women pseudonyms (compiled from various soap opera listings) and I never made any descriptive references to their

physical appearance or gave any other details which could in any way compromise them.

There are numerous pitfalls to conducting research in an established red-
light district. For a non-prostitute woman, standing in an area with such a
reputation is a strange and not altogether pleasant experience. The area in
question was very secluded, not particularly well lit in places, and was situated
on a one-way system; as the cars were constantly passing round the circuit it was
pretty obvious what the occupants in the cars were looking for. Even if they
were not punters looking for sex, everybody who lives in the city or who drives
round the area knows what it is famous for, so any woman who stands there is
automatically thought to be a prostitute. On reflection, I think that one of the
worst features of having to stand in the area was having to endure the reaction
of the public. During the course of the fieldwork I had potatoes thrown at me, I
had supposedly 'decent' members of the public walk past on the way to a
concert in the nearby city hall and spit at me and hurl abuse, and I had obscen-
ities shouted, and objects thrown, at me by gangs of youths driving past at
speed. At such times it was difficult to remain calm; but when you are being
verbally abused and find the situation physically threatening and when you
know that people twice your size are deliberately trying to provoke you into
responding, you have no choice but to tough it out. When such incidents
occurred on the patch the women would tend to rally round each other in a rare
example of solidarity. Whilst it was widely believed that if the women stood
together it put the punters off, it was also recognized that there was safety in
numbers and that standing together in difficult times acted as a deterrent to
potential troublemakers. On a number of occasions when I was talking to one
of the women and we started experiencing difficulties from punters or from
members of the public, other women would wander over to 'share the situation'. Eventually, when all the regulars knew that I was not 'one of them' or out
to poach their customers, they would actually be very useful allies adept at
seeing off unwelcome attention.

On the positive side, standing my ground in the district and absorbing the
abuse and threats eventually earned me a grudging sort of respect from the
prostitutes because it showed I had courage. It also gave me credibility as
being prepared to be seen as 'one of them'. It signified that I had an interest
in them that was not judgemental or condemnatory. But this all took some
time.

Although there was no large-scale organized network of pimps in the city, the
women would often come onto the patch with their boyfriends or partners who
acted as their minders whilst they were conducting the business. When I first
appeared on the scene I was sometimes aware of their presence when I was
speaking to the women—shadowy figures lurking around in the dark of the
alleyways protecting their investments. After a time, once they recognized me,

they seemed to revert to their usual habit of spending the night in the local pub just occasionally stepping outside to check on proceedings.

Once I had reached what was ostensibly a workable level of acceptance by my hosts, there were still obstacles to be overcome and certain things which had to be accepted as part and parcel of my lot conducting research on prostitution. Inevitably, approaches were made to me and I had to learn evasive tactics without being obviously offended or irritated by the requests. This is not romantic Mills and Boon territory you understand, this is some bloke choosing whether or not he wants to spend ten minutes of his time and his hard earned cash having cold clinical sex.

Initially I was surprised at how 'ordinary' the punters were—I do not know what I was expecting. Most were embarrassed—mortified—at having being stopped by the police. Some cried, one appeared to wet himself, and one put his hand on my knee when in the back of the police car and said he was not doing what we thought he was doing but please 'not to mention it to the missus all the same'. As the research progressed, I listened patiently and with as much non-judgemental incredulity as I could muster to some of the kerb crawlers' explanations for their presence in the area. I heard men construct the most bizarre and implausible stories in an effort to get themselves out of a pickle. This is not to say that I did not come out with some absolute howlers myself. To one man, who had travelled from outside the city and was found in *flagrante delicto* with a prostitute, I innocently asked 'do you come here often?' to which he replied in a broad Yorkshire accent 'I haven't cum' at all love—you buggers have put a stop to that'.

Six months into the fieldwork and the research began to develop its own momentum—the women were now readily agreeing to be interviewed—they wanted to be included in the study and some even came over to the police car when we were parked up on observations to arrange interviews, indeed some of the women became quite cross with me for not having interviewed them already. On the whole, all the women were extremely patient in answering my endless questions and they talked with extraordinary candour and depth about their lives and experiences. It was not always easy listening.

In a strange way the study, and I the student, became the studied and the focus of some interest. However, the patch was a volatile and changeable place and on some nights the atmosphere could be extremely hostile. When the police embarked on one of their high-profile caution and arrest operations I was frequently seen as being in some way responsible and would receive the cold shoulder from the women. Sometimes the frosty silence would be broken only by a return to a liberal dose of abuse by the women.

Research of this nature takes patience and perseverance. One woman only finally allowed me to interview her after eleven months of refusing to acknowledge my presence. Since she was built like a shot-putter on steroids, I was relieved when she chose to speak to me rather than beat me up as she had previously threatened—even though she had a voice louder than any I had ever encountered before.

Prostitution takes place in a dangerous and violent world. For the prostitutes, the violence can emanate from a number of different quarters—the pimps, the customers, other rival prostitutes who are seeking to reduce the level of competition, the public who do not want the activity of prostitution on their doorstep, and the police who are tasked with the almost impossible mandate of keeping prostitution under control and containing it to 'manageable' or acceptable levels. If stress is a constituent element of policing and potential violence is an occupational hazard of prostitution, then the occupational dangers and physical, mental, and emotional stress of the research process for the researcher should not be lightly dismissed. I met characters whom I really do not wish to meet again, although I think on further reflection that it was their dogs that caused me most alarm. These were not cute little Disney Dalmations or helpful 'Lassies' but great big salivating hounds with names like 'Satan' and barks that could pierce eardrums within a twenty-mile radius. I have had to face the grim reality that some of the people I came to know in the course of the fieldwork have since been murdered or have been subjected to serious violent assaults. In the ensuing media coverage they are always discussed simply as 'vice girls' with the most unflattering of mug shots of them splashed on the front page—images which portray them as inhuman or unimportant as individuals.

The fieldwork was demanding and time-consuming. I found it to be both physically and mentally exhausting having constantly to adapt to another culture. The threats and dangers associated with being in 'alien' territory, and the idiosyncratic expectations of my various hosts proved extraordinarily stressful. My almost total obsession with the work and a manic desire to collect every possible piece of data, meant that I worked long and very anti-social hours so that my own friendships were neglected. Indeed, the very nature and topic of the research caused a number of people to doubt my sanity—some were concerned at my placing myself in the potentially very dangerous world of the red-light district, others at the relationship I forged with the police. There seems to be this peculiar notion in certain research circles that, whilst it is appropriate to expect to be able to cross the thin blue line for the purpose of collecting data it is actually not the done thing to take the relationship one step further and actually get on and mix with them as living, breathing, mortgage-paying human beings. These pressures were compounded by the constraints of the time limits imposed on the fieldwork, the necessity to produce results, and the expectations of the funding body and the academic institution.

CONCLUSION

After one year, 95 per cent of the women working regularly as prostitutes in the city were contacted and interviewed. Towards the end of the fieldwork period as I was about to sign off and return to the ivory tower to learn the process of writing up, I asked some of the women why they had participated in the study and why they had talked to me with such extraordinary honesty and openness. One response was both simple and yet profound and it came from one of the younger women working on the patch: 'because you listened'. Perhaps that is the key to doing research with 'deviant' groups. It seems to me that one should expect the unexpected and remember that the people one meets are not objects or subjects or clients or samples; rather they are human beings with families and friends and feelings and frailties. We should not use them or abuse them for many of them already lead lives that are full of abuse, violence, and fear. We should not betray the trust that they place in us when we step into their lives even for a fleeting moment. We should listen to what they say—for without them there is no 'research process'.

REFERENCES

ACTON, W. (1857). *Prostitution Considered in its Moral, Social and Sanitary Aspects in London and Other Large Cities: With Proposals for the Mitigation and Prevention of its Attendant Evils.* London: MacGibbon & Kee.

ANON. (1959). *Streetwalker.* London: Bodley Head.

BECKER, H. (1965). 'Review of "Sociologists at Work: Essays on the Craft of Social Research"'. *American Sociological Review* 30: 602–3.

BENJAMIN, H., and MASTERS, R.E.L. (1964). *Prostitution and Morality.* New York: Julian Press.

BERK, R. A., and ADAMS, J. M. (1970). 'Establishing Rapport with Deviant Groups'. *Social Problems* 18: 102–17.

BRYAN, J. H. (1965). 'Apprenticeships in Prostitution'. *Social Problems,* 12: 287–97.

—— (1966). 'Occupational Ideologies and Individual Attitudes of Call Girls'. *Social Problems,* 13: 441–50.

COHEN, B. (1980). *Deviant Street Networks: Prostitution in New York City.* Lexington, Mass.: Lexington Books.

CUNNINGTON, S. (1980). 'Some Aspects of Prostitution in the West End of London in 1979' in D. J. West (ed.), *Sex Offenders in the Criminal Justice System.* Cropwood Conference Series No. 12. Cambridge: Cambridge University Press.

DAVIS, K. (1965). 'Prostitution' in R. Merton and R.A. Nisbet (eds.), *Contemporary Social Problems.* New York: Harcourt Brace Jovanovich.

DENZIN, N. K. (ed.) (1970). *The Research Act: A Theoretical Introduction to Sociological Methods.* London: Macmillan.

DOUGLAS, J. D. (1972). *Research on Deviance.* New York: Random House.

FINNEGAN, F. (1979). *Poverty and Prostitution: A Study of Victorian Prostitutes in York.* Cambridge: Cambridge University Press.

HOIGARD, C., and FINSTAD, L. (1992). *Backstreets: Prostitution, Money and Love.* Oxford: Blackwell.

JAGET, C. (ed.) (1980). *Prostitutes: Our Life.* Bristol: Falling Wall Press.

JANES, R. W. (1970). 'A Note on the Phases of the Community Role of the Participant Observer' in Norman K. Denzin. (ed.) (1970), *The Research Act: A Theoretical Introduction to Sociological Methods.* London: MacMillan.

KAPUR, P. (1978). *The Life and World of Call Girls in India.* New Dehli: Vikas.

MAHOOD, L. (1990). *The Magdalenes: Prostitution in the 19th Century.* London: Routledge.

McKEGANEY, N., and BARNARD, M. (1996). *Sex Work on the Streets: Prostitutes and their Clients.* Buckingham: Open University Press.

McLEOD, E. (1982). *Women Working: Prostitution Now.* London: Croom Helm.

NEFF GURNEY, J. (1991). 'Female Researchers in Male Dominated Settings' in W.B. Shaffir and R.A. Stebbins (eds.), *Experiencing Fieldwork: An Inside View of Qualitative Research.* New York: Sage.

O'NEILL, M. (1996). 'Researching Prostitution and Violence: Towards a Feminist Praxis', in M. Hester, L. Kelly, and J. Radford (eds.), *Women, Violence and Male Power.* Buckingham: Open University Press.

REINER, R. (1994). 'Policing and The Police' in M. Maguire, R. Morgan, and R. Reiner (eds.), *The Oxford Handbook of Criminology.* Oxford: Oxford University Press.

ROBERTS, N. (1992). *Whores in History: Prostitution in Western Society.* London: Harper Collins.

ROLPH, C.H. (1955). *Women on the Streets: A Sociological Study of the Common Prostitute.* London: Secker and Warburg.

SHAFFIR, W. B., and STEBBINS, R. A. (eds.) (1991). *Experiencing Fieldwork: An Inside View of Qualitative Research.* New York: Sage.

SHARPE, K. (1997). 'Working With Prostitutes'. *Policing Today* 3: 38–41.

—— (1998). *Red Light, Blue Light: Prostitutes, Punters and The Police.* Aldershot: Ashgate.

SJOBERG, G., and MILLER, P. J. (1973). 'Social Research on Bureaucracy: Limitations and Opportunities'. *Social Problems* 21: 129–43.

ST. CLAIR, L. (1993). *My Sensational Life Story.* London: Pan Macmillan.

VIDICH, A. J. (1955). 'Participant Observation and the Collection and Interpretation of Data'. *American Journal of Sociology* 60: 354–60.

WALKOWITZ, J. R. (1980). *Prostitution and Victorian Society: Women, Class and the State.* Cambridge: Cambridge University Press.

WEINBERG, M. S., and WILLIAMS, C. J. (1972). 'Fieldwork Among Deviants: Social Relations with Subjects and Others' in J. D. Douglas (ed.), *Research on Deviance.* New York: Random House.

15

GOING AROUND THE HOUSES: RESEARCHING IN HIGH CRIME COMMUNITIES

Lynn Hancock

BACKGROUND

This chapter examines some aspects of my experience of researching 'Neighbourhood Change, Crime and Urban Policy', between April 1996 and March 1998. The origins of the project can be found in the latter part of 1994, when a number of biographical factors coalesced. First, after just over a year of teaching criminology at Keele University (on full-time but temporary contracts) and finishing my doctoral thesis (in Urban Sociology, University of Liverpool), it seemed important to develop new research interests in criminology. Secondly, whilst teaching criminology, I realized the value of a background in urban social theory. Thirdly, I thought I could make a contribution by developing research where urban sociology and criminology meet: in environmental criminology. Such a project would allow me to combine the comfort of the familiar with the excitement (but sometimes awesome task) of developing new research directions. So, following the successful presentation of my PhD thesis, I set about putting together a research proposal. My colleagues at Keele were encouraging: some were working on 'community'-related research and informal discussions with them greatly assisted the development of the proposal.

THE RESEARCH PROJECT

THE PROPOSAL

Of course, many researchers had turned their attention to the urban context of crime over recent years. Studies in the UK had examined why crime and/or offenders were concentrated in particular areas of cities; and why the crime rate in a community changed over time (see Bottoms 1994; Bottoms and Wiles 1997 for references). The role of the housing market was pivotal to explanations of these phenomena. However, with few exceptions, these studies were oriented towards local authority housing estates. The deviating cases were rather dated; little research examined the impact of changes in the political economy of housing on 'community crime careers' in the contemporary (1990s) context. Some writers had urged researchers to examine these and related phenomena (Bottoms and Wiles 1992, 1995), but there were few empirical studies examining these processes.

My research proposal aimed to develop such an approach in three ways. First, an examination of the impact of 'structural processes', such as housing market, labour market, social policy, and population changes upon residential communities and their sense of 'place' in the inner city. Secondly, an analysis of the interpretation of the role of these processes in crime prevention and other urban policies. And thirdly, through an investigation into how these processes are understood and responded to by actors in high-crime areas at the community group level.

The proposal was submitted to the Leverhulme Trust, in 1995, to be considered for an award under their Special Research Fellowship Scheme; these fellowships were targeted at researchers in the early stages of their careers and provided support, for up to twenty-four months, to enable a substantial piece of publishable research to be pursued. I was fortunate, despite keen competition, to be awarded a fellowship. Fellows were required to provide end-of-year reports but, other than that, the scheme did not require formal *supervisory* structures to be in place. I felt especially pleased because the research would be funded independently of national and/or local political agendas.

DEVELOPING THE RESEARCH

This is not to say that local or national political agendas did not influence the research. They clearly did. There were a number of changes made to my objectives during the early stages of the research. The nature and place of 'disorder' in neighbourhoods experiencing change became more important than originally envisaged, because of academic, political, and public (especially policing) policy debates, during 1995 and 1996. Some research attention was focused on policing incivilities in this context. Likewise, I had prepared for community-based respondents, perhaps a little naïvely, to report a greater amount of 'change'; regeneration initiatives had been present in, or near to, the neighbourhoods selected for study for a number of years. Early investigations revealed that some urban policies were undermined by the contradictory effects of other urban or social policies or by conditions that remained unresolved. This led to more complicated ideas about 'neighbourhood change', and the decision to investigate the nature of these contradictory processes in the study areas. The election of the (New) Labour government in May 1997 and the publication of the Crime and Disorder Bill also influenced the project. Although I had expected to contribute to community safety debates, these developments fortuitously coincided to make my research rather timely, since it was well placed to comment on emerging developments; ones I could not have foreseen when the proposal was developed. Furthermore, it probably facilitated access to policy-makers during the later stages of the research. As in most research of this nature, the research questions evolved as data were collected and analysed; ideas were clarified, some avenues of investigation were widened, others diminished in importance. When different kinds of methods generated data that suggested potentially contrasting findings, further research questions were generated as shown below (see also Hancock forthcoming).

THE COMPARATIVE APPROACH

The study employed a comparative approach examining two inner-city neighbourhoods in the Merseyside conurbation where I lived and had experience of community-based research for my doctoral study. My review of the literature told me that some of the most important work had employed this method. My doctoral research had also illustrated the value of comparative work. That said, the approach requires that researchers are able to identify the variables to be present, to compare, so that the research questions can be investigated.

The study areas are both high-crime areas. Regeneration initiatives were present in each area at the time of the research. Each neighbourhood has features that can be argued to indicate 'social disorganization' and has signs of social and physical disorder. Each has the following social and spatial characteristics: a heterogeneous population (regarding social class and/or ethnicity, for example), living in relatively high densities, and in a mix of housing and tenure types. Each is in an area controlled by a different local authority, but sharing the same regional administrative boundaries. Both are close to their respective town centres. A number of community groups are present in each area. Although some characteristics are more amenable to identification than others, I have preserved the anonymity of the neighbourhoods by giving them pseudonyms—Earleschruch and Edgebank.

The research benefited from the assistance of colleagues at the Urban Research and Policy Evaluation Regional Research Laboratory (URPERRL) at the University of Liverpool. Their Social, Demographic, and Land Use Profiler was an important tool for identifying crime patterns, social, demographic, and some spatial features. However, it was unable to identify 'real' 'neighbourhoods' because the 'Profiler' uses enumeration districts, police beats, and like categories of households and spaces. Qualitative techniques were required to identify the 'character' and 'boundaries' of the neighbourhoods.

As the research progressed from the selection of research sites to data collection, a number of issues germane to the collection and interpretation of data were raised; these are discussed below. Nonetheless, in the context of discussing the comparative approach, one further point is worth noting. Earleschurch had a more developed community group infrastructure than Edgebank. In this environment, using community groups as the main points of access for the ethnography, as I had intended, would have resulted in unacceptable disparities in access and research attention. To some extent this is unavoidable. However, by using interviews, drawing on the 'snowball method', and supplementing these data with less intrusive observation activity, some of its injurious effects could be limited. The decision to glean data in this way was justified early in the study, on appreciating the considerable demands that current urban policy frameworks place on community groups. (For a more developed account of these issues, see Hancock forthcoming.)

COLLECTING THE DATA

The study employed a range of data collection methods (see Table 15.1 opposite). The strength of such an approach is impossible to overstate in a study of this kind. An illustration will make the point clearly; command and control data (calls to the police) for 1992–4 were compiled according to the small area Enumeration Districts, using the Geographical Information System facility at URPERRL. These data, in Earleschurch, showed a disproportionately high number of calls about sexual offences—twenty-one times the regional average in the neighbourhood as a whole, and eighty-nine times in one sub-section of the area. Other data indicated that these were mainly associated with prostitution—kerb crawling and soliciting—which inevitably take place in 'specialized' areas of cities. It may be inferred from these data that 'the community' was intolerant of street-walking sex workers and/or prostitution-related activities in Earleschurch or sections of it. However, the validity of such a claim would be questionable; the most we can glean from these data is that an unknown number of people have reported sexual offences, which are likely to be prostitution-related. We cannot assume that calls to the police (the indicator) is appropriate for shedding light on more difficult to observe phenomena (intolerance).

Table 15.1: A Summary of Data-collection Methods

Data to be collected	Main and Supplementary Methods
A profile of crime and disorder in the study areas together with information regarding their changes over time.	Official or officially derived sources. Interview, observations, other secondary materials.
Material sufficient to enable an assessment of long and short term movements in the housing and labour markets.	Census, Documents, Interviews.
Data regarding the kind of regeneration projects that were present at the time of research, and information concerning those that have existed in the past, where available.	Interviews and Documents.
Data concerning the nature of population change in the localities, and the ways in which residents regarded such changes.	Census and Interviews.
Data regarding the ways in which individuals, community groups, businesses, policy-makers, planners, housing agencies, the police, regeneration initiatives, and other agencies with interests in the neighbourhoods, regarded the neighbourhoods and changes in the phenomena noted above.	Interviews, Documents, Observation.
Information about residents' groups' responses, in each area.	Interviews, Observation, Documents.

Indeed, interviews with community groups, business pressure groups, and other agencies throughout Earleschurch, almost without exception, suggested contrary assumptions. By asking quite general, open-ended questions, and allowing the respondents to take their answers in whichever ways they chose, and by adding 'anything else?' it was possible to gather many interesting data. Their answers made evident the complexity of community perceptions of, and responses to, incivility and disorder in Earleschurch. Local people talked about issues associated with prostitution but also about (more important neighbour-hood) problems—and how to resolve them. Further questions were raised:

who, then, is reporting prostitution-related activities, and why? Indeed, how can we explain the relatively high levels of toleration? In pursuing data to address these questions, further anomalies emerged and yet more questions were generated. For example, some respondents thought prostitution had declined over recent years. Others regarded the number of sex workers on the street to be increasing (though relatively tolerant responses were still evident). Further inquiries revealed that the geography of prostitution had changed. Though there appeared to have been a decline in the numbers of sex workers in total, from the late 1980s, some residents observed an increase in the numbers concentrated in their immediate area.

This discussion illustrates the importance of cross-method triangulation for 'testing' some inferences, in some contexts. It shows the importance of allowing respondents the freedom to elaborate their responses in a relatively unstructured way, in response to a carefully constructed question, and in a context where the research task has been presented in such a way that it should not influence respondents' answers. Moreover, it offers a cautionary tale for policy-makers who may consider examining command and control data for indicators of community perceptions of crime and disorder as they undertake audits and move towards developing community safety plans under the Crime and Disorder Act (1998). Unfortunately, some local authorities (at least in the short term) are using existing (sometimes outdated) data derived from such sources; they lack the resources, skills, or political will to undertake the kind of research that is sensitive to these problems.

THE COMMUNITY SETTING

I was beset by a number of quandaries attendant upon the process of conducting a criminological research project in a community setting. There are several factors that make such research different from other types of research, and some difficulties and dilemmas are almost unavoidable. For example, on the one hand, some respondents often talk to each other (sometimes about the research and the researcher). On the other hand, historical conflicts between different groups, organizations, and sections of the community can mean that some groups avoid talking to each other! Researchers, therefore, need to be mindful of the sensibilities that exist in a community and consider their implications for: (a) the ways in which access is negotiated; (b) how the research task is presented to potential respondents; (c) confidentiality during the research process; and (d) ethical issues at the stage of writing up. Of course, the first problem to be confronted is that the 'sensibilities' of the community to be studied are often unknown to the researcher. This was the case in one of the neighbourhoods, though I had some experience of researching in the other (during research for my PhD).

Since a number of agencies with interests in the neighbourhoods were to be included in the study (see Table 15.1) it was necessary to consider the order in which access would be sought. I found it prudent to conduct interviews with members of the community before conducting interviews and observations with the police for example. This way, the problem of being (wrongly) identified as part of the organization diminished, and with it the danger that access to some groups may be closed off. Similarly, one had to be mindful of the ways that the research was presented to the different agencies. Different respondents were approached to elicit data that would illuminate different aspects of the research questions, so it is not surprising that some aspects of the research were presented in contrasting ways to some respondents (see Table 15.1). Respondents often anticipated their role in the research, and it was sometimes necessary to explain the rationale for approaching them in a particular order. Quite often during the fieldwork I would be greeted with: 'I was wondering when you would be contacting me. I was talking to [whoever] and they said they had been talking to you'. Respondents were sometimes disappointed that they had not been contacted earlier. Prior experience provided a degree of preparedness. In my doctoral research some respondents wanted to participate precisely so that they could put a different point of view to that of other respondents they knew had been interviewed!

Because respondents do communicate with each other in this way there are concerns about confidentiality which must be remembered. However, sometimes, despite best efforts, protecting respondent confidentiality lies beyond the researcher's control. For example, a while after the fieldwork I attended a local event where I met one of my respondents. In a group setting she asked (loudly) whether I remembered interviewing her and her (named) friend, and then proceeded to talk about what she and her friend (who was absent) had discussed. In such situations it is not research skills so much as particular social skills that are required.

Throughout the project I considered it appropriate to maintain anonymity for the neighbourhoods; the stigma associated with high-crime areas can have grave and lasting effects and I wished to avoid contributing to this process. Therefore, pseudonyms have been used and, very occasionally, some features have been omitted. Nevertheless, the task of maintaining anonymity for research sites is difficult in community studies; respondents have occasionally disclosed the identity of one or other of the neighbourhoods to other parties. Some features stand out, and in some instances they cannot be disregarded easily because of their importance to the research questions.

Professional guidelines on ethical practice in sociology (BSA 1992) provide standards to which we should aspire. However, in the 'community study', the task of implementing them straightforwardly is challenging. For example, the convention of ensuring that individuals are not recognizable is less easy to achieve than might be supposed. Some individuals and organizations are, because of their position in the local social structure, recognizable by those with even a little knowledge of the community (Bell and Newby 1971). Changing the names of respondents is not enough in this context; it is difficult to disguise the identity of some informants or organizations without changing the meaning of their roles. Some measures can be and have been taken in my work, but I necessarily fall back upon the need to render anonymous the research sites, and I have been forced to grapple with the problems accompanying this process. Even so it is necessary to acknowledge that the work may offend some respondents or organizations who may sense that they are able to self-identify. As other writers have noted, in studies where power, class, and status are principal parts of the research, it is likely that someone will be displeased with their portrayal (Bell and Newby 1971).

I was able to gain some insights regarding these problems through the work of other authors and through conversations with colleagues at Keele, later Middlesex, and beyond. Methodological discussions in similar studies (where they existed) were useful, though not always directly. Similar research projects can offer interesting leads but one cannot set too much store by them. Questions about access provide a good case in point because the kinds of access that researchers need will be determined by the research questions. For example, Xanthos's (1981) *modus operandi* would not have been adequate for this research (see also Bottoms, Mawby and Xanthos 1989). Polii Xanthos worked as a taxi driver, as a football pools collector, and as a helper at a youth club to reach local people in her study. But, because 'my' neighbourhoods were near to town centres, few residents used cabs regularly. Some respondents, when asked about the 'reputation' of their part of Edgebank—a small local authority-controlled scheme—spontaneously indicated that they tell people, such as taxi drivers (when they do use them), that they live near, but not in, the estate. They are 'ashamed' to tell them their addresses. Furthermore, respondents indicated that there had been conflicts over the 'ownership' of youth clubs (in each study area); and many young people are self- or otherwise, excluded from youth centres.

By consulting the published work of other researchers, and through conversations with colleagues and respondents, the most appropriate methods of 'sampling', in qualitative studies, can be assessed: decisions about where, when, and what or whom to observe (Burgess 1982a). Each depends upon a range of factors beginning with the research questions, relationships with respondents, the research setting, and the opportunities that arise. But it also helps to have a fair share of 'luck'. The chance encounter with a useful contact when visiting a respondent's organization or home, for example, or the discovery that a community organization has carried out a local survey and is prepared to hand over the completed questionnaires for a few weeks.

However, one can also have a fair share of luck of the adverse kind. Fairly early in the research I came across a particularly obstructive gatekeeper, while I was trying to identify resident organizations in, and close to, one of my proposed study sites. 'The profiler' was, of course, unable to identify community associations. So, libraries, the local authority, and regeneration projects were my first points of reference. Library information was notoriously out of date because tenants and residents' groups go through cycles of activity. The gatekeeper was responsible for involving community groups in regeneration. She told me about two such groups in the area but 'warned' me that, in her discussions with them, 'crime' had not been an issue for them in her experience. Moreover, she insisted on approaching groups before passing their contact addresses to me. This was irritating because it deprived me of the opportunity to exercise control over the way my research would be presented to potential respondents.

It was very important to me that crime and disorder were not unduly highlighted in case community-based respondents adjusted their replies accordingly. My concern was to examine the 'place' of crime and disorder in perceptions of change in the neighbourhoods, that is, in the context of other neighbourhood problems. In other circumstances, I would be able to convey the nature of my research in such a way that this would be possible. On meeting a respondent the first question would usually be: 'could you start by telling me about living in Earleschurch/Edgebank'? I believed that the data would benefit from allowing respondents to 'tell their own stories', but this routine brought with it some ethical concerns. Respondents had not been fully informed that the research was about the nature and place of disorder in neighbourhoods experiencing change.

The ethical ideal to inform *all* individuals about the research project is more complicated in the field than the textbooks would have us believe. It is impossible for all individuals to understand and anticipate their roles in the research in exactly the same way as other respondents and the researcher, despite best efforts to present the research in a meaningful way (Burgess 1984). Moreover, in public settings it is impossible to indicate to all the participants even that research is being conducted (Burgess 1982*b*: 46) although the use of community-based newsletters went some way towards this aim. That said, despite my anxieties, the episode provided interesting insights not least about how little some of the agencies knew about the communities in their area. As a representative of one of the groups recounted in our first meeting:

People actually call it Beirut or the Bronx round here you know. There have been drugs' raids and drug-related family feuds . . . where windows were smashed and cars were dumped. One time, all the windows were smashed in the flat above. I phoned the police because I was terrified . . .

Not only was crime 'an issue', but crime and disorder had led to the formation of the community group and, arguably, to a decision to demolish and redevelop the housing scheme the following year.

CONCLUSION

I have attempted to provide an account of some of the processes involved in researching neighbourhood change, crime, and disorder in two high-crime neighbourhoods. In so doing, some of the practical and ethical issues accompanying such a study have been discussed, albeit briefly. I hope the chapter provides some insights that may be of interest to future researchers and policy-makers. I cannot end without reference to the emotional aspects of the study. I was inspired by the tenacity of some individuals and groups as they contended with difficulties; and, equally, I was angered, disappointed, and frustrated by some organizations, individuals, and groups as well as, occasionally, by the research process itself. These aspects of the research experience are important because they have implications for the data-collection process, the data themselves, and therefore the conclusions that may be drawn. Suffice it to say that not only did the research develop as I 'went around the houses' but the activity shaped me, personally and academically.

REFERENCES

BELL, C., and NEWBY, H. (1971). *Community Studies: An Introduction to the Sociology of the Local Community*. London: George Allen and Unwin.

BOTTOMS, A. E. (1994). 'Environmental Criminology' in M. Maguire, R. Morgan, and R. Reiner (eds.), *The Oxford Handbook of Criminology*. Oxford: Oxford University Press.

—— MAWBY, R. I., and XANTHOS, P. (1989). 'A Tale of Two Estates' in D. Downes (ed.), *Crime and the City: Essays in Memory of John Barron Mays*. Houndmills, Basingstoke: Macmillan.

—— and WILES, P. (1992). 'Explanations of Crime and Place' in D. J. Evans, N. R. Fyfe, and D. T. Herbert (eds.), *Crime, Policing and Place: Essays in Environmental Criminology*. London: Routledge.

—— and —— (1995). 'Crime and Insecurity in the City' in C. Fijnaut, J. Goethals, and L. Walgrave (eds.), *Changes in Society, Crime and Criminal Justice in Europe*, i. The Hague: Kluwer.

—— and —— (1997). 'Environmental Criminology' in M. Maguire, R. Morgan, and

R. Reiner (eds.), *The Oxford Handbook of Criminology* (2nd edn.). Oxford: Oxford University Press.

BRITISH SOCIOLOGICAL ASSOCIATION (1992). 'Statement of Ethical Practice', *Sociology* 26: 703–7.

BURGESS, R. G. (1982a). 'Elements of Sampling in Field Research' in R. G. Burgess (ed.), *Field Research: A Sourcebook and Field Manual.* Contemporary Social Research Series. London: George Allen and Unwin.

—— (1982b). 'Some Role Problems in Field Research' in R. G. Burgess (ed.), *Field Research: A Sourcebook and Field Manual.* Contemporary Social Research Series. London: George Allen and Unwin.

—— (1984). *In the Field: An Introduction to Field Research.* London: George Allen and Unwin.

HANCOCK, L. (forthcoming). *Community, Crime and Disorder: Questions for Community Safety and Regeneration.* London: Macmillan.

XANTHOS, P. (1981). *Crime, the Housing market and Reputation.* Unpublished PhD thesis. University of Sheffield.

16

SUSPECT DATA: ARRESTING RESEARCH

Carole Adams

INTRODUCTION

The principles governing the research process are clean, well-ordered, and rational when they appear on crisp white paper in black text. The practice of research, however, is, in my experience, altogether different. As a PhD student entering the everyday travail of the research process I encountered a multi-coloured, multi-textured, mind-altering river that stretched ahead of me, seemingly without direction or end. The waters engulfed me and tossed me about until the rational became irrational, the clean and ordered became dirty and disordered, and what I knew became what I no longer knew or could take for granted. This was my first experience of conducting an academic research project from beginning to end, although the end was never in sight until the completed thesis went to the binders.

I was a PhD student in the Law (and Sociology) Department at the London School of Economics (LSE) when I conducted the research discussed in this chapter. My first year's studies were funded by the LSE's Kahn Freund Award in Law, with subsequent years being funded by an Economic and Social Research Council (ESRC) award. Two professors in the Law Department (one of criminology and one of law) and a professor in the Sociology Department (also a criminologist) supervised my research. Initially, the thought of three eminent professors looking at my first musings on research was daunting to say the least, but my gratitude and thanks go to my supervisors[1] for providing supervision that enabled me to move from the bookish principles of research to the practice of research, and completion, i.e. supervision that allowed for independence and self-directedness as well as providing friendliness and approachability, valuable

[1] Professors Robert Reiner, Paul Rock, and Michael Zander. Note, however, that the thoughts and ideas expressed here are entirely my own, and are not in any way a reflection on my supervisors or the supervision I received.

insights, thoughtfulness, and provocative discussions when needed—strongly backed by a dynamic and vibrant research seminar and peer group.

My research (Adams 1995) investigated suspects' responses to rights when detained in police custody. My interest in this area of research was first aroused when as an undergraduate, I investigated the current position of the 'right to silence' in England and Wales and asked in respect of the abolition of the right 'Is there Cause for Concern?' (see especially Criminal Law Revision Committee 1972). I was taken aback to discover, in the many parliamentary papers, Reports of Committees and Commissions, and statements on 'law and order' by Home Secretaries which I consulted, that much of what was written about the actions and motivations of suspects in the pre-trial criminal process was based on rhetoric, assumption, and anecdote—and certainly not on systematic investigation and analysis. From here, the subject and broad aim of my doctoral research was born, i.e. to ascertain what suspects do, and do not do, when detained in police custody and, most importantly, why?

The modern law governing the investigation of crime by police officers, as contained in the Police and Criminal Evidence Act 1984 (PACE) and accompanying Codes of Practice, is based on the philosophy and 'balanced' recommendations of the Royal Commission on Criminal Procedure (RCCP 1981). But, as my analysis of the Report shows, the RCCP did not investigate, from the viewpoint of those on whom rights are conferred, the workability in procedural terms, or the efficacy in due process terms, of the operation of suspects' rights in practice (Adams 1995). This begs the question which the research investigated: 'Is PACE in practice the balancing Act which it was conceived to be in theory, in the experiences of those on whom rights are conferred by its provisions?' Theoretically, then, the essentially qualitative socio-legal research on which I embarked was concerned with the dominant ideological approaches to the criminal justice process and the models of the criminal process which underpin the 'balancing' of police powers (crime control) and suspects' rights (due process) in the PACE Act. The 'law in books' confers rights on suspects detained in police custody, and the research aimed to investigate the extent to which the 'law in action' and suspects' own motivations made the exercise of rights possible, or even desirable, from the suspects' own vantage point.

In essence, I am going to tell four short reflexive (and in places, self-critical) stories about my doctoral research practice; each of these is presented in an extremely frank and honest way. I have not done this because I wish to heap the reader's ridicule upon myself and what I have written, but in order to facilitate discussion about research practice as it really is, and not as it is most often packaged in books and journal articles. I hope that new and would-be researchers will thereby be encouraged to continue working through their research problems, feelings, and frustrations, safe in the knowledge that these are in fact commonplace. It is, in my experience, the ongoing work on the problems and frustrations encountered during the research process, the insights gained, and contacts made that makes research so captivating and ultimately fulfilling. If I may be forgiven the play on words I found the work involved in obtaining suspect data to constitute particularly 'arresting' research, in all senses of the word. At times I was literally halted in my research process even as it continued to engage my whole-hearted attention.

GAINING ACCESS TO CRIMINAL SUSPECTS: PROBLEMS, FRUSTRATIONS, THOUGHTS OF PERSONAL ILLEGALITY, AND BREAKING THROUGH

How does a new, student researcher obtain a sample of criminal suspects? My reading of the relevant literature informed me of the successful efforts of other criminal justice and criminological researchers in gaining the co-operation of suspects and defendants in research (see Brown 1989; Brown, Ellis and Larcombe 1992; Sanders *et al.* 1989; and Zander 1972), but none of these options seemed available or desirable to me. I did not, for example, have the financial wherewithal to approach potential respondents by post including an honor-arium in the initial introductory letter (Zander 1972) and, not being a Home Office researcher or conducting research for the Lord Chancellor's Department, I did not have access to suspects detained in police custody as a few researchers have in previous studies (Brown 1989; Sanders *et al.* 1989). Moreover, I did not in any event consider that the aims of my research would be well served by my being seen by suspects to have negotiated access *via* the police as gatekeepers. This would not only raise negative suspicions toward me in the minds of suspects and detrimentally affect my interview data, but it would also be unlikely that suspects who readily waive their rights at the police station in an effort to secure their early release would remain longer in order to provide me with worthwhile research data. So what was I to do?

I had, in my darkest 'no suspects, no data, no thesis' moments, considered drinking in pubs frequented predominantly by the criminal fraternity or 'join-ing' (I hope, in the participant-as-observer way) a criminal gang in order that I could find out first-hand about gang members' experiences in police custody and their responses to rights at the police station, but acceptable strategies these were not. Instead I started by approaching solicitors and barristers known to me to seek access to their clients. Since my essentially qualitative research strategy did not require my obtaining a statistically representative sample of suspects, and since in the final research report I could consider and discuss the likely biases introduced in obtaining respondents from solicitors and barristers I knew, I felt this to be a useful starting point—not least because I had no other acceptable strategy at my disposal. In the event it was not as useful as I hoped. Although initially most of the barristers and solicitors I approached were keen to assist me in the research by providing access to their clients, this did not in the long term prove very effective for a variety of reasons.

For example, the clients on whom details were provided by one barrister turned out not always to be clients known personally to her, nor had they all been detained in police custody within days (and at most a few weeks) of meeting with me, as I had specified. One respondent had not even been arrested and detained in police custody under the provisions of the PACE Act, and this only became known to me in a stark and frightening way. I went to interview the respondent, whom my barrister contact informed me was a depressed petty criminal. I arrived at the locked, guarded hospital wing to interview him. I was taken through several locked doors and a glass viewing area into an inner sanctum occupied by poorly dressed, unkempt men. My respondent led me along a corridor off the main sitting area to an interview room. On entering the room, he quickly moved a large armchair in front of the door. With my heart thumping, I asked as calmly as I could why he had done that. He said that the door did not close properly and he did not want anyone to hear the research interview. I accepted this explanation, but was uneasily aware that I was dealing with more than a depressed petty criminal. In fact, he explained that he was a 'technical lifer following three machete attacks on women'; knowledge of this did not ease my sense of fear when he lunged at my neck every time he tried to explain how angry he became before committing these offences. This respondent suffered from 'bi-polar disorder', had been detained since 1979, and had met my barrister contact for the first time a few weeks previously when she was visiting one of her clients, which he was not. In other cases pilot questionnaires were simply not returned by the agreed deadline, and whenever I telephoned to enquire about them the barrister was in court.

These setbacks left me in a near catatonic state in which I returned to chanting my now familiar 'no suspect, no data, no thesis' mantra, and thought of personal acts of illegality that would bring me into contact with those suspected by the police of having committed offences contrary to criminal law.

Following these experiences I then set about in earnest identifying, contacting, and seeking the co-operation of persons initially unknown to me but from whom further contacts and access to respondents could be gained—a so-called 'blind snowball'. My 'gatekeepers' to suspect respondents were primarily in the voluntary sector and the Inner London Probation Service. This process, although worrying, and at times fear-inducing, and always time-consuming, proved to be a very useful strategy. I eventually built up sufficient contacts and outlets to spend over six months in the field on data collection for my main study. This time was spent in bail hostels, probation service day centres, and voluntary sector organizations interviewing suspects and, when asked, playing pool and sharing discussions over lunch with the wider group.

METHODS, LANGUAGE, AND KNOWLEDGE: REFLECTIONS ON LEARNING TO LEARN WHAT IS KNOWN

Broad methodological principles governing the research process can be ascertained from the ever-increasing number of publications on 'doing research' (see especially Denzin and Lincoln 1994; Jupp 1995; and Robson 1995). Starting from the epistemological and ontological stance of the major paradigm within which one is working, and moving to the theoretical principles of the associated methodology, the researcher soon reaches the point of considering the research strategy. By this time many options in respect of methods are foreclosed; and the methods to be employed can be selected from the 'tool box' of methods listed in familiar fashion in the various sources on the research process. There is a danger at this stage of feeling too secure in the knowledge that now all one has to do is pilot the research instruments, make minor changes, enter 'the field', and 'collect' or 'generate' data. This was not my experience; and I learnt valuable lessons between piloting my questionnaire on 'Detention at the Police Station' and commencing the main study data collection. The questionnaire was checked in the usual way for ease of completion, problems with question wording, and problems relating to layout and format; and following the piloting stage I was sure I had a good, well-calibrated research instrument. However, an impromptu discussion with a respondent who had completed a pilot questionnaire caused me seriously to doubt the usefulness of this research tool in my research study. The reasons for this are best illustrated in the following example.

I was in conversation with the respondent about his views on the tape-recording of formal interviews at the police station. He mentioned several reasons why he thought it was useful, and then sighed and exclaimed that it made no real difference in his case as his interview had not been tape-recorded. I was surprised by this statement and reminded him that on his questionnaire he had ticked to say he had been formally interviewed at the police station. He told me that was correct, he had been in a formal police interview, but that there was no tape-recorder available at the time to tape his interview. 'No tape-recorder?' I exclaimed. 'No', he said 'they don't put them in the back of the van and the cells you know.' It transpired that this (and later other) respondents believed they had been formally interviewed by the police when they were asked questions about the offence for which they had been arrested and detained. The definition and conduct of police interviewing as defined by PACE and the accompanying Codes of Practice was of no consequence to these suspects, and so when they encountered a question on my questionnaire asking whether or not they had been formally interviewed by the police at the police station they answered positively even though the 'interview' had taken place outside a police station interviewing room with no tape-recording equipment. Clearly, answers given in good faith on the questionnaire, which was structured from legal definitions and concepts, did not always tally with the suspects' actual experience as defined and structured by them. This, and other similar examples, raised my awareness of the need in my in-depth interviews with suspects to focus upon ascertaining and clarifying my own and their taken-for-granted assumptions, concepts, and definitions.

The next stage in discovering what suspects knew of their legal entitlements when detained in police custody, which they act upon in respect of rights, involved my learning to learn what was known by suspects. This is because that knowledge could, as I discovered in the field, only be ascertained once the language used by suspects to express their knowledge of the formalities at the police station was understood by the would-be-knower/researcher. For example, in interviews with suspects, many spoke about their 'right to a phone call' when detained in police custody. Since suspects have a 'right to notification' (where a police officer telephones a nominated individual on the suspect's behalf to inform him or her of the suspect's arrest and detention), I could simply have assumed that suspects were referring to this right to notification when in their language they spoke about their 'right to a phone call'. To have done so, however, would have resulted in data lacking in validity, and the overlooking of a vital misunderstanding held by many suspects, which often gives rise to acrimonious conflicts between suspects and the police. By not assuming that language between the researcher and the respondent shares the same meaning, and by always probing and asking for clarification of concepts, events, and definitions used, I was able to discover two things. First, some suspects had confused their 'right to notification' (which they can expect to be fulfilled) with the 'phone call privilege' (which is discretionary) and so believed they literally had a 'right to a phone call'. When their insistence on this 'right' was denied this brought conflict between them and the police. Secondly, some had in their minds fused the provisions of the 'right of notification' and the 'phone call privilege' into one notification phone call which they believed they had a right to make themselves, which, again, when demanded wrought conflicts between suspects and the police.

'DRESSING UP' AND 'DRESSING DOWN': CRITICAL REFLECTIONS ON THE PRESENTATION OF SELF IN INTERVIEWS WITH SUSPECTS, SOLICITORS, AND POLICE OFFICERS

In interviews with suspects I wore blue jeans, pumps, and socks, a sweat shirt and no make-up. In interviews with police officers I wore a skirt, blouse, tights, shoes with a slight heel, and a little make-up. In interviews with criminal defence solicitors I wore a two-piece Planet skirt suit, co-ordinated blouse, tights, shoes with a heel, and make-up. Why?

Clearly, given my 'dressing up' and 'dressing down' in research interviews, I had given some thought to the possible import of dress in meetings with respondents, but on reflection I must confess this was not very sophisticated. I was aware at the time of wanting to get alongside all of my research respondents, i.e. I wanted to be able to meet with them and be acceptable to them, and ensure that dress did not pose a barrier between us. My rationale for 'dressing down' in interviews with suspects was that I did not want to appear as a well-dressed, well-to-do 'official', and consequently as someone who would be divorced from their life circumstances and experiences. I reasoned that the more I dressed as I perceived suspects would dress, the more acceptable I would be and the more comfortable they would be in research interviews with me (although I soon discovered that suspects' expensive designer jeans were not the same as those I had purchased on Walthamstow market). My rationale for 'dressing up' in interviews with police officers was that I wanted to appear simply as a 'normal', 'law-abiding' 'woman' who was divorced from sexual overtones, in the hope that this would abate fears that I might be rooting for the 'other side' and remove any sexualized glares or comments. My rationale for 'dressing up' in interviews with solicitors was simply that I felt I needed to appear professional and well-dressed as I assumed they would be, in order to facilitate comfort in conversation with me.

In retrospect, I am critical of this 'dressing up' and 'dressing down' in my research practice. I now take the view that my 'dressing' for interviews with research respondents raises serious questions about my authenticity and integrity in research interviews. This is because my experiences suggest that what I wore did more than simply change my surface appearance—it changed me. When I 'dressed up' I felt uncomfortable, unreal, constrained, and not myself in interviews with police officers and solicitors. In short, I was being something I was not. It strikes me that the presentation of an 'unreal' or 'false' self in research interviews is an ethically questionable practice, and certainly one that requires considerable thought and ongoing debate among social researchers. In any event, the experiences detailed in the following paragraph suggest that my original thoughts on the import of dress in research interviews were in some cases at least misguided.

On one occasion poor planning meant that I was due to conduct interviews with suspects in the morning, and interviews with solicitors on the afternoon of the same day. The question arising, then, was 'what should I wear?' I decided to wear my 'dressing up' outfit to suit my afternoon appointments. I arrived, as I had done over the previous few weeks, at the probation day centre and went to the common room where most of the clients gathered. Without so much as a second glance, a respondent I had interviewed in the early weeks asked if I would play a game of snooker with him. Indeed, I did not perceive any difference in interviews with suspects on that day from when I had been wearing my 'suspects' outfit. On another occasion I had just finished interviewing a male police officer, in an office in a police station, when the next male police officer I was to interview knocked on the door. I asked the police officer who was about to leave to invite the next interviewee in. As I sat waiting for him to enter, I heard the incoming officer whisper to the outgoing officer 'what's she like then?' I am in no doubt this question referred to what I was like as a woman, and not as a research interviewer. To judge from the sigh, the tutting, and the exclamation 'oh bloody-'ell' I must have received the thumbs down. My dress had not impacted on this situation in the way I had naïvely envisaged. Lastly, on another occasion I attended a rather plush-looking solicitors' firm to conduct an interview. The solicitor came to collect me from the waiting room. He wore a suit that looked to have several years' creases embedded in the cloth. He said a cheery hello and started to lead me out of the building. As we walked down the stairs he explained it would be nice to get away from the office and conduct the interview in a restaurant nearby. To my astonishment, the solicitor took me to a 'greasy spoon' cafe. He munched on a large crusty bacon roll so noisily that his munching imprinted on my tape-recording of the interview, as did the orders and conversations of the other patrons. 'Dressing up' had not prevented this situation occurring, and I would have felt a good deal more at ease interviewing this respondent in this setting wearing jeans and a tee-shirt.

MY BOYS—LOVE 'EM, HATE 'EM, LOVE 'EM: FLUID EMOTIONS AND SHIFTING MIND SETS IN THE RESEARCH PROCESS

My stance on beginning the research was very much civil libertarian. I was worried by what appeared to be the imminent abolition of the right to silence in the face of substantial police powers of arrest, detention, and interviewing.

Moreover, I genuinely wanted to understand and comprehend from the suspects' point of view why so few suspects detained in police custody exercise the rights provisions made available to them. However, during the process of this research I was horrified to discover in me, as a result of my contact with suspects, a deep-rooted streak of utilitarianism that was directly opposed to the civil libertarian stance that had pervaded my consciousness until this point. At first, I found difficulty in living with the conscious knowledge of the diametrically opposed 'abolitionist' and 'retentionist' tendencies I discovered inside me when in interviews with suspects. On some days, these interviews were exhilarating and informative; I felt I really understood the suspects' 'plight', I loved 'em and my research, they were boys not men, they had gone astray, they needed understanding and protection from further harm. On other days, I felt angry and annoyed and could not understand why some suspects whinged incessantly about poor treatment from the police, especially in the face of what they had done to others: I hated 'em and my research, they deserved what they got, they were scheming, horrible, cowardly little men who, for example, committed house burglaries several times a week and then complained bitterly when the police 'turned me place over, smashed in me doors and left a right royal mess everywhere'. The fluid emotions of 'love' and 'hate', and the shifting mind sets between 'crime control values' and 'due process values', caused me much consternation, even though I have never subscribed to the view that the principle of objectivity in the researcher is desirable or possible in any research venture.

Ongoing analysis of these personal phenomena provided me with answers to what I perceived as a problem, and a strategy for continuing in the field. I decided that I needed to ensure that in interviews with suspect respondents I did not act on either extreme emotion or mind set. I ensured that I continued in all interviews to hold a positive regard for my respondents, which entailed monitoring and containing my extreme emotions and thoughts in research conversations with them. This, I found, enabled fruitful interviews to continue taking place, thus providing the data I sought to address my research question. Furthermore, I discovered that the analysis of my extreme feelings and thoughts alongside the analysis of associated typed interview transcripts facilitated my appreciation of the heterogeneous make-up of my suspect sample, my understanding of suspect 'types' (ideal, in the Weberian sense) and the import of 'types' on responses to rights provisions at the police station. Here, in these findings, the end of my journey began to come into sharp focus, and my appreciation of the 'arresting' nature of obtaining 'suspect data' in the research process came finally to fruition.

CONCLUSION

While my research experiences were at times vivid and colourful, engulfing, and ever-changing, more mature reflection on them suggests that the practice of research is really about the everyday, the banal, and the commonplace. In the research process we have to connect the principles of research and our research strategy to our personal resources and biography. The strategies and insights born from our life experiences help us deal with the everyday issues that are inevitably thrown up, and which could not have been envisaged at the outset.

REFERENCES

ADAMS, C. (1995). *'Balance' in Pre-trial Criminal Justice: Suspects' Experiences in the Nick Under the Revised PACE Code of Practice C.* Unpublished PhD Thesis. LSE: University of London.

BROWN, D., ELLIS, T., and LARCOMBE, K. (1992). *Changing the Code: Police Detention Under the Revised PACE Codes of Practice*, Home Office Research Study No 129. London: HMSO.

CRIMINAL LAW REVISION COMMITTEE (1972). *Eleventh Report: Evidence (General)*. Cmnd. 4991. London: HMSO.

DENZIN, N. K., and LINCOLN, Y. S. (eds.) (1994). *Handbook of Qualitative Research*. Thousand Oaks, Cal.: Sage Publications.

JUPP, V. (1995). *Methods in Criminological Research*. Contemporary Social Research: 19. London: Routledge.

ROBSON, C. (1995). *Real World Research: A Resource for Social Scientists and Practitioner-Researchers*. Oxford: Blackwell.

ROYAL COMMISSION ON CRIMINAL PROCEDURE (1981). *Report*. Cmnd. 8092. London: HMSO.

SANDERS, A., BRIDGES, L., MULVANEY, A., and CROSIER, G. (1989). *Advice and Assistance at the Police Station and the 24 Hour Duty Solicitor Scheme*. London: Lord Chancellor's Dept.

ZANDER, M. (1972). 'Legal Advice and Criminal Appeals: A Survey of Prisoners, Prisons and Lawyers'. *Criminal Law Review* 132–73.

17

BEING 'A NOSY BLOODY COW': ETHICAL AND METHODOLOGICAL ISSUES IN RESEARCHING DOMESTIC VIOLENCE

Carolyn Hoyle

INTRODUCTION

By the early stages of a doctoral programme the sagacious student has chosen a topic which can sustain interest over the subsequent years. The next step is to adjudge how to research that topic. For those planning to carry out empirical work this means deciding which institutions and people are appropriate for investigation. Choice of research topic does not necessarily prescribe this. There are usually various different people who could shed light on an issue. It is necessary to determine *which* and *how many* of these to speak to and, of course, what questions to ask. Once this has been decided the student must secure co-operation from those in control of the information. Gaining access to data is not typically a 'one off' exercise. Indeed it is generally an on-going commitment which can last the duration of the project and present the student with multifarious dilemmas. This chapter will look at the ethical minefield that is negotiating access to research subjects. It will also consider the importance of adopting a rigorous and thorough methodological approach for doctoral work. As my own experience suggests, this is particularly crucial for work in sensitive and politically contentious areas.[1]

My thesis (Hoyle 1996) was based on an in-depth study of policing domestic violence in the Thames Valley. When it was published (Hoyle 1998a) I found that my methods were denigrated by critics who were not sympathetic to my findings.

Over a two-week period my book was lambasted by high-profile columnists. They criticized my methods because the book did not espouse their extreme normative position on responding to domestic violence. In other words, I failed to condemn all men involved in domestic disputes as beyond, or unworthy of, rehabilitation and I resisted advocating blanket arrest and prosecution policies and custodial sentences for all convicted abusers. In attacking me for this, these critics put their feet firmly in the right-wing feminist camp, which one might crudely caricature as 'hang 'em and flog 'em feminism'. I was prepared for informed academic criticism, but not for politically driven denunciation relayed through the media. I found myself pressed into attending radio talk-shows to debate the issues with my critics (one of whom admitted that she had not even read my book prior to writing her critical review of it), and I wrote rebuttals for two national newspapers (Hoyle 1998*b*, 1998*c*).

Whilst the publicity certainly had a positive effect on sales of my book, it was not an experience I wish to repeat in a hurry. It is never agreeable to have one's theoretical or political position censured, but it is particularly frustrating when methods are criticized because the findings are not considered to be acceptable. I learnt from the negative publicity around my book that to challenge any political orthodoxy can bring erroneous criticism of the motives and the methods of the researcher. This is something that any student embarking on research in a 'sensitive' or 'political' area—however these may be defined—should bear in mind when designing research tools. Perhaps people assume that those who research subjects such as domestic violence are peddling a specific doctrine. However, in choosing this subject, I pursued no political ideology. As a social scientist, I sought to explain a very interesting fact: that there are relatively few prosecutions in cases of domestic violence. One critic of my work, who was clearly disappointed by my findings, argued that I had 'asked the wrong question of the wrong people' (Bindel 1998). Her protest urges consideration of just who are 'the right people' to talk to, and what are 'the right questions' to ask in order to understand fully the criminal justice response to domestic violence?

In this chapter I will explain who I considered to be the appropriate subjects and what I considered to be the appropriate means of gaining information. To do this it is helpful to detail briefly the theoretical framework within which these questions were grounded.

THEORY-DRIVEN DATA COLLECTION

My research examined the factors which shape the criminal justice response to domestic violence in the light of policy changes at the beginning of the 1990s which aimed to increase arrest rates. In its attempt to analyse police discretion, this project shared the feminist theoretical understanding of police decision-making as operating in a gap, created by discretionary powers, rather than being determined by law. However, it attempted to move away from purely cultural theories which saw police behaviour firmly rooted in misogynistic assumptions. Many explanations of policing driven by this gendered perspective have either ignored, or paid only lip-service to, other cultural or structural explanations of police action at the scene of domestic disputes.

Moving away from simple 'police blaming', my research aimed to understand the context within which police make decisions. It united different theoretical approaches in order to satisfy a range of aims, drawing on both interactionist and structuralist perspectives. This approach is based on the recognition that whilst social structures influence how people act, this power is not total: people are active—they can, to a greater or lesser extent, manipulate and attach meaning to their environment. I sought to understand how the significant actors (those with some sort of a role or an interest in the offence and its resolution—usually the police, the victims, and the perpetrators) negotiate and often re-negotiate an outcome. It makes little sense to assume that such interactions take place within a vacuum. Therefore, I tried to understand how this interaction, and therefore to some extent the outcome, was shaped by certain organizational factors. Mainly, I considered the extent to which changes in policy impact on the response of operational officers and how the shifting role of operational officers influences decisions. To unite such approaches seemed to me—and, not surprisingly, to the officers I interviewed—a fairly obvious way to understand decision-making. Yet, as if to obfuscate the role of the sociologist, the approach is saddled with the label of 'theoretical triangulation' (Denzin 1970).

In order to achieve theoretical triangulation, an eclectic approach to methods was necessary, combining qualitative and quantitative methods, and involving scrutiny of official documents and interviews with various people: the officers who answered the telephone calls reporting an incident; those who attended the disputes; the victims, and occasionally the perpetrators; the custody officers; and the Crown prosecutors. In these interviews use was made of structured and semi-structured interview schedules.

I chose not to restrict myself to using either positivist or interpretive methods, but to adopt a pragmatic approach to data collection. I used any appropriate method in as accurate a way as possible to unite holistic analysis, which is characteristic of the positivist school of sociology, and atomistic analysis, characteristic of the interpretive sociologies. Again, the labels 'methodological triangulation' and 'data triangulation' shroud in mystery straightforward and sensible means of looking at the social world (see Denzin 1970; Hammersley and Atkinson 1995). 'Within-method' methodological triangulation involves the use of different strategies within a broad research method (see Webb *et al.* 1966)—in this study the use of semi-structured interviews with officers which generated quantitative data and qualitative descriptions. 'Cross-method' triangulation refers to the procedure of using different types of methods to study the same phenomenon (Webb *et al.* 1966)—in this study interviews with police officers and victims, observation of officers on duty, and examination of official records were all used to understand (amongst other things) the police response to incidents of domestic violence.

The use of different sources of data within one study is know as 'data triangulation' (Denzin 1970). This study generated data sets on police officers, prosecutors, and victims in order to consider what the role of the criminal justice system is, and should be, in relation to victims of domestic violence. I interviewed victims after I had interviewed the officers who had responded to their particular incident, partly to ensure that the police officers had given me an accurate version of the incident and of the wishes of the victims. However, data triangulation does not necessarily provide a straightforward check on reliability and validity. Whilst each discrete data set provides a unique perspective and therefore can be considered in isolation from the others, two (or more) sets of data on the same situation permits one to explore the relationship of 'accounts' to what people are actually observed to be doing, thereby generating a further account in relation to data already gathered (Fielding and Fielding 1986). When outcomes are seen as products of interactions, the question of who are the right people to talk to is easily answered: to understand the criminal justice response to domestic violence it is necessary to talk to all of those involved in disputes and their resolution.

WHAT ARE THE RIGHT QUESTIONS TO ASK AND WHO ARE THE RIGHT PEOPLE TO TALK TO?

It is not possible in this short chapter to explain how I sought access to all the various actors involved in domestic disputes. Therefore I will concentrate on the role of police, victims, and perpetrators. I will explain the approach I took to questioning these actors, and some of the ethical issues raised by the research.

THE RIGHT QUESTIONS TO ASK

By analysing officers' own accounts of their actions and decisions, I attempted to discover the 'working rules' which routinely inform their decisions; their links with legal rules and official guidelines; and the extent to which 'working rules' prevail over legal rules (see Smith and Gray 1983; McConville, Sanders and Leng 1991). The responding patrol officers were interviewed in almost 400 incidents of domestic violence and the victims in just over one in ten of these cases. Most prior studies have chosen only to examine one or the other. Semi-structured interviews were preceded by an invitation to the interviewees to offer their own interpretation of events and their response to others' 'behaviour'. This method enables people to identify those variables which they believe determine their behaviour and yet also allows for direct comparison between cases (Hammersley and Atkinson 1995).

I decided to interview patrol officers about their response to *specific* incidents of domestic violence because I believed that interviewing officers about their *general* response would, at best, yield limited information and, at worst, provide a distorted picture. Semi-structured interviews were preceded by a general opening comment informing interviewees that they would be asked about domestic disputes. Officers were given the time to offer an initial reaction, which was frequently quite negative. Many looked exasperated, commenting that 'domestics are so much trouble', or that they hated responding to them because they are 'so griefy', or that they did not have the time or inclination to deal effectively with them. Other comments indicated that domestic disputes are still, to some extent, trivialized by officers within 'canteen culture' discourse. However, when then asked questions about the specific disputes they had recently attended their replies almost invariably contradicted their initial response. Most went on to assert that they had listened carefully to the disputants and that they had taken the time to try to deal sympathetically and effectively with the situation. These contentions were borne out by my direct observation of the police handling of numerous disputes.

This methodological approach secured a more accurate picture of the police response to domestic violence than would have emerged from discussion of domestic violence in general. It illustrates the divide between certain negative cultural attitudes and what officers actually do in practice. Other researchers (e.g. Edwards 1989) have asked questions about general attitudes only and have assumed that officers' behaviour is entirely consistent with their espoused attitudes. As the social psychology literature shows (Ajzen and Fishbein 1980; Eiser 1986), action and attitudes are often inconsistent. Hence researchers need to be careful that they understand both, and attempt to explore the complex interaction between the two.

THE RIGHT PEOPLE TO TALK TO

To ask genuinely open questions is not so tempting to researchers who believe that they know the answers before they conduct the empirical work. Of course, many logical positivists, in their attempts at verification, claim to seek data which could falsify their hypotheses. However, the extent to which their methods are capable of achieving this, and the degree to which many positivists even aspire towards this, has been questioned by various interactionists since Kuhn (1962). At the extreme some publications on domestic violence read as if the conclusions were reached before any data were collected. Whilst academics need a theoretical framework before deciding who to talk to and what to ask them, it is contrary to good scholarship to enter the field looking exclusively for evidence consistent with a preferred explanation. It is, for example, unacceptable to discount *a priori* the views of women who may challenge the researcher's normative position.

In investigating domestic violence, it is tempting for academics to speak to only those more easily accessible women who are resident in refuges, rather than other victims. This is a legitimate method of inquiry, but it tells a partial story. Such data cannot shed light on the lives of victims who choose to stay in violent relationships. I decided to interview both women who were resident in refuges and those who were still in their homes. In the main, the refuge women were at different stages in their violent relationships from the women still living with their partners—most were nearer to ending permanently the relationship, if they had not already done so. This suggests that refuges provide a distinctive sub-sample of victims.

Whilst I would recommend that researchers of domestic violence talk to both samples of victims, students have to be pragmatic in deciding whom to interview. Whilst it is not easy to gain access to refuges, interviewing women in their own homes, who cannot be approached through an organization, poses even more onerous logistical and ethical problems. I decided that the best chance of persuading a woman to talk to me was to turn up uninvited on her doorstep. 'Cold calling' is a controversial method. It undoubtedly improves dramatically the 'hit rate', but it does so by making it difficult for women to say no. Whilst some of the women I wished to interview were not at home on repeated visits, this part of my study had an 80 per cent success rate. However, this was not achieved without facing some difficult ethical dilemmas.

THE DIFFICULTIES IN ASKING THE RIGHT QUESTIONS OF THE RIGHT PEOPLE: ETHICAL DILEMMAS

On my visits to victims' homes I was accompanied by a police officer, not in uniform but carrying identification. This assistance was volunteered by the police, rather than sought by me. The shift inspectors whose officers I had observed on patrol over many months offered either to escort me personally or provide a constable for the purpose. This arrangement was made because of their concerns for my personal safety but it almost certainly had the effect of increasing victim co-operation. It could be argued that using a police officer to help to secure access to research subjects could lead those subjects to believe that they had no choice but to agree to be interviewed.

Although the British Society of Criminology and the British Sociological Association provide statements of ethical practice, the most thorough and clearest of such statements is by the Socio-Legal Studies Association (SLSA 1993) and it was this which informed my empirical work. In accordance with this statement I tried to ensure that victims, as other participants, were aware of their right to refuse participation whenever and for whatever reason they wished. Furthermore, in order that the consent was freely given and informed, victims were told who I was, what the research was about, how it was funded, and how I would use the data. They were also told that their 'stories' would be anonymised in order to protect their privacy. However, as will be discussed below, this rigorous approach to consent did not rule out ethically dubious practice and, furthermore, it was not extended to perpetrators.

Whilst police officers who accompanied me were required not to become involved in the interviews with victims, indeed to keep a discreet distance, they were required to assist in those cases where the perpetrator was at home. It was thought that men might be antagonistic or dissuade victims from being truthful. Hence a separate interview schedule was devised for these occasions. Men were told that the research was intended to examine public perceptions of the police handling of any disputes—not just domestic disputes—and they were taken by the officer into a different room to be interviewed. This ploy enabled me to speak to victims alone. Clearly this was being economical with the truth. However, I went further than this in seeking reliable information from victims. I told a lie in persuading perpetrators of domestic violence to leave me alone with their partners. I told them that they were to be asked the same questions as their partners. Whilst some of the questions were the same, many were not, and, more importantly, their partners were asked questions about the men's behaviour which were not asked of the men. Whilst some of these men were surprisingly honest and volunteered information about their abusive behaviour, they did so in ignorance of the fact that their partners were being asked specifically about such behaviour. Hence, they not only consented to interviews with officers without fully understanding all of the reasons behind the interviews, but without knowledge of what questions were being asked in the next room. Can such duplicity be defended if the end-result is research findings which may prove to be highly beneficial to victims? I believed that minimizing the risk of further violence to the victim and having the opportunity to talk openly and

honestly to a victim whose opinions may not have previously been taken seriously by anyone justified this duplicity. But this is an ethical question. All social
scientists 'have a responsibility to ensure that the physical, social and psychological well-being of research participants is not adversely affected by their
research' (SLSA 1993). This is particularly important when the interviewees are
relatively powerless and when they may be vulnerable to further abuse.
However, the nature of domestic violence means that any 'intervention' from
outside the family may be considered by the perpetrator to be unacceptably
intrusive. This cannot mean that such studies are not contemplated, as good
research can benefit the general victim population, if not these specific victims.
It does mean, though, that interviewers need to be sensitive to the dangers to
which victims may be exposed as a direct result of the interviewer's presence.
The interviews with perpetrators provided some valuable data and allowed
them to 'present their side of the story'. They did not seem to 'damage' the
interviewees in any way. Nonetheless, they had not been carried out with their
informed consent.

The two principles of 'informed consent' and 'non-damage' may cut against
each other once it has been decided to conduct research into a topic. One
therefore has to decide which should be given priority in any given situation
and one should do this in a principled way. Principles are not absolutes, but
have to be given a weight. The weighting should not be based on a researcher's
desire to progress her own career but could be based, for example, on the social
desirability of obtaining reliable evidence on a controversial topic. This may be
especially so if that evidence can help to bring about changes which could
improve the lot of the research subjects. The greater the social problem, the
more it may be justified to attach less weight to particular methodological
principles, whilst never abandoning them completely, nor ignoring them. The
alternative is not to research the topic at all. Ethical considerations should
inform our thinking about choice of research topic as much as it should our
choice of methods. Is it ethical to avoid those research topics that can only be
researched by giving less weight to (or breaching, if one prefers) ethical principles concerned with means, such as those of the SLSA? Should the SLSA have
guidelines about ethical choice of topics too? If it did, the ethical dilemmas
would be revealed more starkly and the simplistic view that we must be 100 per
cent obedient to every SLSA principle would be revealed as unrealistic. To weigh
conflicting principles and decide how to prioritize them in an ethical and
principled manner is not an unethical enterprise, but its opposite. Social scientists tend to gloss over ethical dilemmas, but few of us complete an empirical
project without facing at least one difficult decision about priorities.

At this point a specific example may prove illuminating. On two occasions in
my study the perpetrators returned home whilst the victim was being interviewed. In one instance the man was easily persuaded to co-operate with the

research and was interviewed by the officer who accompanied me. In the other the victim told the perpetrator what we were doing before we had the chance to be duplicitous. He was clearly furious and, despite our efforts to distort the truth, he told his wife not to speak to us any further. She insisted that we stayed, at which stage he became verbally aggressive, threatening both me and the officer and then left the home to sit in his car, parked outside. It was clear that our presence was provocative and according to strict ethical standards we should have aborted this interview. However, the victim asked us to stay. She wished to tell us 'her story' and wanted us to provide her with information about how she could leave the relationship. We decided that, on balance, it was in her best interests to continue and it was in the best interests of victims of domestic violence in general. In this example it seemed to be appropriate to give less weight to strict ethical principles and more to the desirability of gathering reliable evidence. This evidence could both help this particular victim, by listening to her and providing relevant information, and help victims of domestic violence in general by gathering data from a woman whose experiences and aspirations mirrored those of many others. In the event outstaying our welcome did not seem to cause any further violence to the woman. I had reason to telephone her the following day to provide further contacts she had asked for. She assured me that she had not been the victim of any further retaliatory abuse. This was lucky. It could have turned out differently. Most of the women I interviewed—even those few whose partners were at home during the interview—were not contacted again. I do not know what effect, if any, my visits had in those cases.

One other interview I conducted involved a rather more difficult balancing act. This interaction certainly breached ethical standards, as currently written. The incident about which I wanted to interview the victim was unusual in that the victim's son had called the police and the victim had told the police, in no uncertain tones, to leave. When the officers insisted on talking to the son the woman attacked one of them, by throwing a plate of hot food at him. When I visited her she told me on the doorstep that she did not wish to be interviewed. She was angry with the police and considered me to be yet another interfering 'authority figure', or, to put it in her words, 'a nosy bloody cow'. She added that she hated the police and thought that they should not intervene in rows between couples. However, she proceeded, still on the doorstep, to tell me why 'people should not have the right to interfere between husbands and wives who choose to batter each other.' With this 'encouragement', I continued to ask her the questions on the interview schedule without looking at the schedule and without immediately recording her responses. We 'chatted' for about fifteen minutes, after which she realized that I had, as she put it, 'got my bloody interview'. She told me I was 'a cheeky cow', smiled at me, and said 'now piss off'. I thanked her profusely and asked her if I could use her comments for my research, to which she replied 'I don't care what you do with them' and shut the door.

In no way could it be said that I had secured her consent before the interview, and even if we were to translate 'I don't care what you do with [my comments]' as consent to use the data, it was not informed consent. And yet I did continue to ask her questions and I did use her interview to inform the research analysis. Perhaps I should have walked away following her initial response without my interview. I did not do so. I persisted in asking her questions—literally on her doorstep, as shamelessly as some tabloid journalists. Should I have done this? Although in a brief piece this question cannot be answered satisfactorily, I wish to use this forum to suggest certain reasons for believing that my behaviour may have been justified.

The woman in the above example was, initially at least, unwilling to talk to me. One might argue that if we only ever talk to 'willing participants' we are not asking the 'right questions' of the 'right people'. If we do not try to persuade those who are reluctant to talk we are in danger of missing out on the opinions or experiences of a specific, very important sub-group of those for whom we profess to speak at the end of empirical enquiry. My justification for breaching ethical standards by analysing and discussing the interview is founded in the atypical nature of her opinions. With a subject such as domestic violence, where so much has been written based on the opinions of small selective samples, we need to be aware of the danger of assuming that these victims are a homogenous group. Like victims of all types of offences, they vary in their experiences and wishes. To believe that all want state interference and tough penalties for their perpetrators is as arrogant an assumption as the standard police position up until the late 1980s which regarded any interference in disputes between intimates as necessarily unwise. However, whilst accurate and truthful reporting may serve the integrity of the discipline of social science, and may even help the very group one is focusing on, is it right to give precedence to domestic violence victims in general over specific individual victims? With an important issue such as domestic violence, is there a greater tension between searching for 'the truth' and not abusing the 'rights' of those whom we seek to understand than with other subjects of social science enquiry? This question is crucial to an important debate on empirical protocol. We need to ask ourselves if sometimes the ends justify the means? And at what point do the 'means' stray into the boundaries of ethically unacceptability?

I would like to suggest that it is acceptable to place less weight on a protective principle of an individual if we believe that to do so may help the wider victim group. Occasionally academics' work, most notably the work of criminologists, does make a difference to certain groups of people. My own work on domestic violence helped to inform changes in policy and practice within the Thames Valley Police which I believe have benefited this particular group of victims.

Hence, the occasional abuse of our positions of power may be justifiable even when we are concerned with victims who, in the main, are vulnerable to the abusive behaviours of others. As in all areas of social life, priorities must be balanced. Whilst it may seem easier to compromise ethical standards in dealing with perpetrators of crimes, sometimes academics will decide it is just as necessary to do so with victims.

CONCLUSION

In discussing methodological approaches to understanding the criminal justice response to domestic violence, I have identified two issues which should be of concern to students hoping to research this and other sensitive areas. The first is the political context within which such research is undertaken and, perhaps more importantly, received. When gender cuts across criminal justice matters, and, in particular, when the subject involves women as victims of male perpetrators, the student who refuses to sign up unquestioningly to a hard-line feminist agenda may find herself denigrated or, even worse, ignored. As long as there are critics who prefer dogma to reasoned argument, and anecdotal evidence to in-depth research, social scientists who engage with issues such as domestic violence will need to be especially careful to ground their arguments in rigorous data. Those who challenge widely accepted orthodoxies, believing them to rest on sand, will need to ensure that their own challenges have secure foundations.

The second issue may be particularly pertinent to sensitive topics but has a wider applicability. Students need to work out what empirical practices they consider to be acceptable and where they will draw the line in the search for data. This, I have learnt, is best done in advance of commencing fieldwork but cannot be achieved simply by reading and mentally signing up to a statement of ethical practice. Students should consider fully the many potential situations they may find themselves in and try to work out how they would want to respond. But, perhaps more importantly, academics in general need to start being more honest when writing about their methodological approach. They should not only record what they intended to do, or what they believe they ought ethically to have done, but also what they actually did. I have not set out to be controversial for the sake of it; I believe that many researchers will have come across similar situations in their fieldwork and, whilst most have previously endorsed a code of ethical standards, they may at times feel ambivalent about it. If this chapter provokes a debate about these issues it may encourage students to think in advance how they may wish to respond in similar situations.

I would like to thank Richard Young and David Rose for commenting on the earlier draft of this chapter.

REFERENCES

AJZEN, I. and FISHBEIN, M. (1980). *Understanding Attitudes and Predicting Social Behaviour.* Englewood Cliffs, N.J: Prentice Hall.

BINDEL, J. (1998). 'On a Hiding to Nothing'. *The Guardian,* 8 September.

DENZIN, N. (1970). *The Research Act.* Chicago, Ill: Aldine.

EDWARDS, S. S. M. (1989). *Policing 'Domestic' Violence: Women, the Law and the State.* London: Sage.

EISER, J. R. (1986). *Social Psychology: Attitudes, Cognitions and Social Behaviour.* Cambridge: Cambridge University Press.

FIELDING, N. G. and FIELDING, J. L. (1986). *Linking Data.* Qualitative Research Methods Series 4. Newbury Park, Cal.: Sage.

HAMMERSLEY, M. and ATKINSON, P. (1995). *Ethnography: Principles in Practice.* London: Tavistock.

HOYLE, C. (1996). *Responding to Domestic Violence: The Roles of Police, Prosecutors and Victims.* D. Phil Thesis. University of Oxford, Bodleian Library.

—— (1998*a*). *Negotiating Domestic Violence: Police, Criminal Justice and Victims.* Clarendon Studies in Criminology. Oxford: Oxford University Press.

—— (1998*b*). 'Let the Victims Speak'. *The Independent on Sunday,* 13 September.

—— (1998*c*). 'Crime After Crime'. *The Guardian,* 14 September.

KUHN, T. S. (1962). *The Structure of Scientific Revolutions.* Chicago, Ill.: Chicago University Press.

MCCONVILLE, M., SANDERS, A. and LENG, R. (1991). *The Case for the Prosecution.* London: Routledge.

SMITH, D. J., and GRAY, J. (1983). *Police and People in London, Vol. 4, The Police in Action.* London: Policy Studies Institute.

SOCIO-LEGAL STUDIES ASSOCIATION (1993). Statement of Ethical Practice by the Socio-Legal Studies Association in *Directory of Members.* London: Butterworths.

WEBB, E. J., CAMPBELL, D. T., SCHWARTZ, R. D., and SECREST, L. (1966). *Unobtrusive Measures: Nonreactive Research in the Social Sciences.* Chicago, Ill.: Rand McNally.

18

THE NUMBERS GAME: QUANTITATIVE RESEARCH ON ETHNICITY AND CRIMINAL JUSTICE

Bonny Mhlanga

INTRODUCTION

The debate surrounding the strengths and weaknesses of qualitative and quantitative approaches to social science research has been ongoing for several decades (Silverman 1998). Writing at a time when qualitative research has taken over so much of the field (Bryman 1988*a*), I explore within this chapter the value of quantitative research on ethnicity and criminal justice. This chapter has two main aims; first, to explore the way in which quantitative research fits into the research process and, secondly, to reflect upon my own experiences of using quantitative methods in a recent study on the role of ethnic factors in decisions made by the Crown Prosecution Service (CPS) to prosecute young offenders (Mhlanga 1999).

My interest in carrying out this research was prompted by a growing concern about the position of ethnic minorities in the criminal justice system in Britain (Hood 1992; Gelsthorpe and McWilliams 1993; Mhlanga 1997; Smith 1997). One of the most salient issues arising from this body of work is an awareness of the responsibility of persons engaged in the administration of criminal justice to avoid discriminating against any person on the ground of race. The responsibility of central government in this area was recognized specifically in the 1991 Criminal Justice Act, of which section 95(1)(b) obliges the Home Secretary to publish information relating to the treatment of ethnic minorities in the criminal justice system (Home Office 1992, 1994, 1995, 1997, 1998). Moreover, the Royal Commission on Criminal Justice (Fitzgerald 1993) recommended that ethnic monitoring should be conducted routinely by all agencies in the criminal justice system, and that further research on ethnic minorities and the criminal justice system should be conducted. As a consequence of these obligations and recommendations, the treatment of ethnic minority people in the criminal justice system promises to remain a critical issue in criminology and public affairs, if not the most crucial issue, for many years to come.

My research, funded by an Economic and Social Research Council (1995–8) Post-Doctoral Research Fellowship award, was conducted against this backdrop. It set out to assess the effect of ethnic factors on decisions made by the CPS relating to all the 6,144 young offenders aged under 22 who came to their notice during a two-month period (September–October 1996), and the prosecution of cases in the Youth, Magistrates', and Crown Courts. The CPS is a single independent and nationwide authority in England and Wales, which is now organized into forty-two CPS areas that match Police Force boundaries. During the period of the study, however, there were only thirteen CPS areas. Cases were selected from at least one branch in each area. The duty of the CPS is to review cases at every stage of the prosecution process, and it has the power to discontinue prosecutions (see Davies *et al.* 1998 for a more detailed overview of the work of the CPS). The Code for Crown Prosecutors published in 1994 is a public statement of the guidelines to be applied to the decision on whether to prosecute an offender or not. The bulk of the code is concerned with the two tests involved in the decision to prosecute: the evidential sufficiency test and the public interest test. As a result, the factors most likely to influence CPS decision-making relate to legal criteria. However, the project aimed to explore the relationship between these factors and the ethnic origin of the defendants controlling for the influence, if any, of gender, age, socio-economic status, area of domicile, principal offence charged, offences taken into consideration, previous cautions and convictions, plea, and police bail. It was intended that this method of analysis would enable me to delineate factors affecting CPS outcomes for different ethnic groups and to test a differential outcome hypothesis between Asian, Black, White, and other minority defendants.

The findings of my study (Mhlanga 1999) were in some respects surprising. The research evidence available to date suggests that ethnic minorities receive harsher treatment from the police and the courts (see Smith 1997 for a detailed literature review). However, the evidence uncovered by my research shows that at the prosecution stage of the criminal justice system Asian, Black, and other minority defendants were more likely than White defendants to receive favourable outcomes from CPS lawyers, in the sense that these lawyers acted as a sifting and diversionary mechanism for these defendants. For example, cases involving Asian defendants were found to be significantly more likely than cases involving White defendants to have been discontinued on evidential grounds during the two-month period of the study. In addition, cases involving Black defendants were found to be significantly more likely than cases involving

White defendants to have been discontinued on public-interest grounds. Moreover, the existence of some significant interactional relationships between CPS decisions, the ethnic origin of the defendants, and the areas of their domicile or the type of primary offences with which they were charged was also discovered. However, the study concluded that CPS lawyers should sift more cases involving Asian and Black defendants on evidential grounds because higher proportions of ethnic minorities are acquitted in both Magistrates' and Crown Courts on the grounds of insufficient evidence when compared to White defendants.

Furthermore, it was found that the number of Asian young people who came to the notice of the CPS during the two-month period of the study was marginally higher than that of Black young people. This finding is new and contradicts previous studies which claim an overwhelming discrepancy in the numbers of Asians and the Afro-Caribbeans who are charged with criminal offences (Fitzgerald 1995). With the exception of a small number of studies (Mawby and Batta 1980; Graham and Bowling 1995; Wardak 1995; Webster 1995, 1997) little criminological research has explored Asian offending.

The above conclusions are drawn from a research study which adopted a quantitative approach within the positivist tradition. In fact, the majority of the research on the relationship between ethnic origins and criminal justice outcomes, especially in the USA, adopts a straightforward positivist position. A positivist approach can be characterized by a number of key stages such as testing of the theory(ies) or hypotheses, operationalization of concepts, sampling of respondents or subjects, formulation of a survey or correlational design, collection of data, data analysis, and interpretation of findings. Although these stages provided me with a very useful model, there are grounds for doubting whether research always conforms to a neat linear sequence (Bryman 1988a, 1988b). However, for the purpose of this chapter their relevance to my quantitative research experience is discussed in turn.

DOING QUANTITATIVE RESEARCH

THEORY AND METHOD

At the outset it is important to spell out the theoretical or conceptual framework informing or underpinning one's study, as it will later provide a framework within which one interprets the findings during the final stage of the research. As many social scientists have argued (Bottoms, this volume; Clegg 1990; Fox Keller 1990; Harvey 1990) all research is 'theory dependent'. Indeed as O'Brien (1993) argues, whether the theory is acknowledged or not, theoretical ideas influence the work and pure 'empirical' research is impossible.

Those wishing to explore the relationship between ethnic origins, criminal behaviour, and criminal justice could draw upon a wide range of criminological theories including 'control', 'strain', 'sub-cultural', and 'labelling' theories (see Downes and Rock 1998) which are designed to help us to understand the nature of the link between the ethnic origins of offenders, their criminality, and the type of treatment meted out to them by the criminal justice system. These theories are in the main derived from broader theoretical traditions and also developed from empirical research. However, it should be noted that there is ongoing debate and controversy between the various theories and/or perspectives in their quest to provide a 'true' explanation of social phenomena. Moreover, it should also be noted that it is legitimate and some would argue desirable to use a mixture or triangulation of perspectives and methods in one's research (see Hoyle, this volume).

Once a theory has been formulated, it is likely that researchers will want to test it in order to discover whether the theory holds water when confronted with empirical evidence. As has been pointed out by Bryman and Cramer (1990), it is rarely possible to test a theory as such. Instead, researchers need to construct a more specific hypothesis relating to a limited facet of the theory which can then be subjected to searching inquiry. In connection with my own research, the hypothesis tested was one of differential treatment of defendants on the basis of ethnic origin. As is very often the case, the hypothesis took the form of the association between two or more variables; that is, the ethnic origin of the defendants and CPS decisions to discontinue or to prosecute cases while taking into account the influence of gender, age, socio-economic status, area of domicile, type of primary offence allegedly committed, offences which were taken into consideration (TICs), previous cautions, previous convictions, type of plea, and type of police bail. In this way, it was possible for me to think systematically about what I wanted to study, and to structure my research plans accordingly.

RESEARCH DESIGN

Once the researcher has decided on the theoretical or conceptual framework informing or underpinning the study and has formulated the research question(s), the next step is to decide on the data-collection strategy and the precise methods to be used. Whilst the general nature of the research design is known at the outset, the research design may evolve as the study progresses. The degree of statistical manipulation that can be performed depends on the nature of the data collected. Whilst a wide variety of methods can be used to generate quantitative data, those wishing to test hypotheses usually make use of surveys, experiments, structured observation, and the analysis of secondary data such as official statistics.

My own research adopted a survey approach which allows the researcher to use methods which can generate data to make sense of relationships between variables. My research was designed to explore the relationship between CPS decisions and the ethnic origin of defendants, controlling for a wide variety of variables (see below). This is more problematic than it first appears, precisely because in survey research variables are not manipulated (and often are not capable of manipulation), and the ability of the researcher to impute cause and effect is limited (Jupp 1989; Bryman and Cramer 1990; de Vaus 1996). However, this problem can be alleviated by employing a multivariate analysis of the data which allows the researcher to explore connections between more than two variables. This technique was used in my study to examine the relationship between CPS decisions and the ethnic origin of the defendants while simultaneously taking into account the influence of gender, age, socio-economic status, area, primary offence, TICs, previous cautions or convictions, plea, and police bail.

Using predominantly CPS files, I was able to collect statistical data on a number of variables. A paper coding frame was used as my data-collection instrument which consisted of pre-coded independent variables (race, gender, age, socio-economic status, area, primary offence, TICs, previous cautions, previous convictions, plea, and police bail) and dependent variables (discontinuances on evidential grounds, discontinuances on public-interest grounds, charge reductions, caution or bind-over recommendations, prosecutions, committals to the Crown Court for trial, withdrawals because lawyers offered no evidence at Court, acquittals in Magistrates' Courts, and acquittals in the Crown Court). I found that using a paper pre-coded coding frame was extremely useful as a method of collecting such quantitative data because it helped to ensure accurate data collection and entry into the computer before analysis.

Social researchers, including me, are frequently faced with the fact that they cannot collect data from everyone who is in the category being researched (Denscombe 1998). Whilst 100 per cent sample sizes are preferable to representative samples due to the methodological difficulties of estimating the true population value from the sample value, researchers for practical reasons have to use sampling techniques. Addressing these concerns, I had to find ways of making my own project a manageable task for a single researcher to complete within a limited period of time. Thus my study examined CPS decisions relating to all under 22-year-old defendants who came to the notice of the CPS, but only during a two-month period in 1996. Attempts were made to ensure the sample was nationally representative, and to this end data were collected from at least one branch in each of the then thirteen CPS geographical areas in England and Wales. Altogether, the total number of CPS branches from which data were collected was twenty-two. The branches selected were those situated in the locations with the highest proportion of ethnic minorities for each area. For example, the London locations were those with an ethnic minority population of 29 per cent and over. Nonetheless, in practice there was substantial variation in the size of ethnic minority populations between the samples for different areas.

DATA COLLECTION

The primary sources of data for my study were official statistics from CPS and police records. Prior to the study commencing I had to seek permission to gain access to CPS files. Permission for the study to go ahead was eventually granted subject to the oversight of a steering group consisting of senior representatives from CPS and the Home Office, together with academic representation from the University of Hull. It was also agreed that a pilot study should be conducted first at one of the branches. This piloting stage had three main aims: first, to determine the extent to which information on the independent and dependent variables to be examined in the main study would be available from CPS files; secondly, to estimate precisely how many cases would be generated using the proposed method; and, finally, to ascertain any potential practical problems of data collection. Overall the aim of the pilot study was to determine what would be feasible after examining CPS files, so that an appropriate coding frame for the main study could be constructed.

The process of data collection for the pilot study proved more problematic than had been anticipated, as it took more time and resources than originally planned. This was due to the fact that the data storage and retrieval system at the branch where the pilot study took place was being upgraded at the time. However, I managed to complete the data set for the pilot study by matching information obtained from CPS files with that kindly provided by the local Youth Justice Team and by the local police force. The results of the pilot study were perceived to be positive by the CPS, and I was invited to present a revised proposal. This was accepted by the steering group subject to the necessary additional funds for travel/subsistence costs being made available by the Economic and Social Research Council to enable me to carry out the survey on the scale now required by the CPS. The revised proposal had a much larger sample size. Consequently, an application for supplementary funding was made to the ESRC by Professor Bottomley (Hull University), on my behalf. Although requests for such additional funds are now highly exceptional, the ESRC agreed to grant a supplementary award to meet the additional expenses because of the considerable social scientific and 'political' interest in the issues raised by the project.

The data collection for the main study itself went smoothly, with only very minor local hiccups. My visits to the respective branches across the country had been facilitated by the CPS through the steering group. At an early stage 'familiarization' visits to three London branches were arranged for me to enable me to acquaint myself with the current CPS data storage and retrieval system which at the time of the research was being standardized. The familiarization visits also helped me to become aware of local variations in the way information was recorded on files.

DATA ANALYSIS

At the design stages of the research project, it is crucial to think ahead to the data analysis stage, and in particular to consider whether one has sufficient skills and training to analyse the data satisfactorily. Potential doctoral students and their supervisors are required to consider this in detail when completing application forms for Economic and Social Research Council Studentships. For instance, if the research is designed to gather quantitative data, one needs to consider some training in computer-assisted data analysis. Similarly such training may also be required for those who aim to gather predominantly qualitative data since it is becoming increasingly common to use dedicated computer software to facilitate data management and analysis (see Coffey and Atkinson 1996; Fielding and Lee 1991).

Even quantitative data collected in small-scale studies are frequently analysed with the help of dedicated computer software. It is generally recommended that if you collect more than twenty questionnaires and you have asked more than five questions, then you should be using a computer to help analyse the results (Fielding 1993). For bivariate and multivariate quantitative data analysis, the most commonly used computer software packages are SPSS for Windows and GLIM (version 3.77 or 4.0) on the Main-Frame Computer or PC. Using these packages, statistical calculations such as cross-tabulation and regression analyses can be performed. However, it should be pointed out that statistical analyses of this kind are often criticized for reducing interesting questions to totally incomprehensible numbers. Packages such as SPSS are not a panacea for those who feel uncomfortable with statistical manipulation because it still requires an understanding of the logic involved in these statistical analyses.

The analytical method adopted by my study encompassed a multivariate examination of the data using the most appropriate technique, namely the special case of the loglinear model or the so-called logit model. The model allows us to estimate the likelihood of an event happening or not happening, such as a decision by the CPS to discontinue or not to discontinue cases on evidential grounds or public interest grounds when a range of explanatory factors are taken into account. Most importantly, it was also possible to carry out analyses of the interaction effects between each CPS decision made, the ethnic origin of the defendants, and their areas of domicile or the type of primary offences with which they were charged.

INTERPRETATION AND WRITING UP THE RESULTS

Statistical analyses of criminal justice practice invariably attempt to establish discrimination by seeking to show that there is a residual element of differentiation in the treatment of ethnic minorities which is not explicable by 'legally relevant' factors. For instance, they seek to demonstrate that Black people receive harsher treatment which is not due to their greater criminality or other deviance by holding constant such 'legally relevant' variables as type or seriousness of offence or previous convictions (see, e.g., Hood 1992). However, Reiner (1993) has argued that this approach is unlikely to establish discrimination conclusively, since it is practically impossible to hold constant more than a few 'legally relevant' variables. He suggests that under these circumstances it is always open to analysts of different persuasions to characterize any remaining differences in treatment as (so far) unexplained variation rather than discrimination.

It is a valid criticism that statistical studies cannot control for all relevant variables apart from ethnic origin which might affect differences in outcome between cases. Nevertheless, the analysis carried out for my CPS inquiry was based on a substantial number of cases and can be regarded as the best quantitative data on the issue to date. It is always hazardous to move from correlation to explanation, and the marked differences in the apparent treatment of Asian, Black, and other ethnic minority defendants by the CPS when compared to the treatment of White defendants clearly required further explication. For example, the apparent association between ethnic origin and CPS decisions to discontinue cases, in favour of ethnic minority defendants, may have resulted from transmission from an earlier stage in the process rather than reflecting 'positive discrimination' in favour of minorities on the part of the CPS.

Researchers often hope that the results of their research are statistically significant and will thus confirm the hypothesis stated by the researcher at the beginning of the study. Researchers tend to pride themselves on finding statistically significant results because significant results are more difficult to ignore. Such findings can indeed have implications for social policy, and that includes changing and introducing legislation. For example, in relation to the issue of ethnic minorities and the criminal justice system, it is clear that earlier research highlighting discrimination influenced the introduction of section 95(1)(b) of the Criminal Justice Act 1991, which arose as a House of Lords amendment to the 1990 Bill. Under that section of the 1991 Criminal Justice Act, the Home Secretary is obliged to publish, each year, information relating to the way in which ethnic minorities and women are treated in the criminal justice system in England and Wales.

LINKING QUANTITATIVE AND QUALITATIVE DATA

While quantitative data are thought of as 'hard' and qualitative data as 'soft', it is also now widely accepted in criminological research that quantitative and qualitative data can complement one another, each shedding light on the other. Thus statistical correlations derived from quantitative research can be further explained using qualitative techniques. For example, quantitative research on people's attitudes to crime and the criminal justice response may find that they correlate with age, gender, and social class. Whilst this is an important finding in itself, more in-depth approaches may help to explain why people hold the attitudes they do and why they vary according to age, gender, and social class.

The view that statistical correlations in quantitative research require further explication using more intensive methods of research is held by many researchers (Bottomley and Pease 1986; Fielding and Fielding 1986; Hudson 1989; Reiner 1993; Coleman and Moynihan 1996) and it informed my research design. I had initially planned to revisit selected areas/branches in order to conduct in-depth interviews with a sample of lawyers for the purpose of eliciting their comments on the quantitative data. However, I did not pursue this plan because of concerns that I would have difficulty in tracking down lawyers at a time when the CPS was undergoing major organizational change. As a compromise, a group of lawyers and their senior managers was eventually invited by the steering group to attend a 'brainstorming' session to which I presented the preliminary findings of my research, and this provided valuable interpretive material in the course of discussions. For example, with respect to the finding of Asian, Black, and other minority defendants as more likely than White defendants to have their cases discontinued on evidential grounds, some lawyers summarized their discussion group as follows:

The statistics point in the direction of the police getting it wrong, but we said that we would have to bear in mind there might be alternative explanations, and it could be said that perhaps the CPS could be using positive discrimination. So we needed to be aware of those alternative explanations.

Although the brainstorming session provided some useful qualitative material and feedback, there is clearly scope for much more detailed exploration of the meaning of the main findings from the research. In any future research on this topic, it would be highly desirable to conduct individual face-to-face interviews with CPS lawyers.

CONCLUSION

In the light of qualitative research coming increasingly to the fore, we might ask why should social science students be trained in the use of quantitative approaches? On this question, Bryman and Cramer (1990) point out that an extremely large proportion of the empirical research undertaken by social scientists is designed to generate, or at least draws upon, quantitative data. They conclude:

In order to be able to appreciate the kinds of analyses that are conducted in relation to such data and possibly to analyse their own data (especially since many students are required to carry out projects), an acquaintance with the appropriate methods of analysis is highly desirable for social science students (Bryman and Cramer 1990: 1).

Moreover, in everyday life in which people are deluged with statistical data from opinion polls, market research findings, attitude surveys, health and crime statistics, and so forth, an awareness of quantitative data analysis greatly enhances the ability to recognize faulty conclusions or potentially biased manipulations of the information.

The usefulness of official statistics to criminological researchers has been explored in detail (Coleman and Moynihan 1996; Maguire 1997). A common theme is that researchers need to acknowledge the limitations of their data sources but official statistics can still be used as an important resource. With reference to statistics which can shed light on the relationship between ethnic origin, criminal behaviour, and criminal justice response, it has been argued that such statistics are an important tool for highlighting discrimination, as well as targeting and monitoring services (Anwar 1990) and gaining 'race' equality in the new formalized, bureaucratized forms of anti-racism (Ahmad and Sheldon 1993). With the issue of racial discrimination, particularly in relation to criminal justice, receiving unprecedented attention following the murder of Stephen Lawrence and the publication of the MacPherson Report (Home Office 1999), there are many opportunities to conduct meaningful research using quantitative approaches, particularly when combined with qualitative techniques.

REFERENCES

AHMAD, W., and SHELDON, T. (1993). '"Race" and Statistics' in M. Hammersly (ed.), *Social Research: Philosophy, Politics and Practice*. London: Sage.

ANWAR, M. (1990). 'Ethnic Classifications, Ethnic Monitoring and the 1991 Census'. *New Community* 16(4), 606–15.

BOTTOMLEY, A. K., and PEASE, K. (1986). *Crime and Punishment: Interpreting the Data.* Milton Keynes: Open University Press.

BRYMAN, A. (1988*a*). *Quantity and Quality in Social Research.* London: Unwin Hyman.

—— (1988*b*). 'Introduction: "Inside" Accounts and Social Research in Organisations' in A. Bryman (ed.), *Doing Research in Organisations.* London: Routledge.

—— and CRAMER, D. (1990). *Quantitative Data Analysis for Social Scientists.* London: Routledge.

CLEGG, S. (1990). *Frameworks of Power.* London: Sage.

COFFEY, A., and ATKINSON, P. (1996). *Making Sense of Qualitative Data.* London: Sage.

COLEMAN, C., and MOYNIHAN, J. (1996). *Understanding Crime Data: Haunted by the Dark Figure.* Buckingham: Open University Press.

DAVIES, M., CROALL, H., and TYRER, J. (1998). *Criminal Justice.* London: Longman.

DENSCOMBE, M. (1998). *The Good Research Guide.* Buckingham: Open University Press.

DE VAUS, D. A. (1996). *Surveys in Social Research.* London: UCL Press.

DOWNES, D., and ROCK, P. (1998). *Understanding Deviance.* Oxford: Oxford University Press.

FIELDING, J. (1993). 'Coding and Managing Data', in N. Gilbert (ed.), *Researching Social Life.* London: Sage.

FIELDING, N. G., and FIELDING, J. L. (1986). *Linking Data.* London: Sage.

—— and LEE, R. M. (1991). *Using Computers in Qualitative Research.* London: Sage.

FITZGERALD, M. (1993). *Ethnic Minorities and the Criminal Justice System.* The Royal Commission on Criminal Justice: Research Study No. 20. London: HMSO.

—— (1995). 'Ethnic Differences' in M. Walker (ed.), *Interpreting Crime Statistics.* Oxford: Oxford University Press.

FOX KELLER, E. (1990). 'Feminist Criticism of the Social Sciences' in J. McCarl Nielssen (ed.), *Feminist Research Methods: Exemplary Readings in the Social Sciences.* Boulder, Colo.: Westview.

GRAHAM, J., and BOWLING, B. (1995). *Young People and Crime.* London: Home Office.

GELSTHORPE, L., and MCWILLIAMS, W. (eds.) (1993). *Minority Ethnic Groups in the Criminal Justice System.* Cambridge: Institute of Criminology.

HARVEY, L. (1990). *Critical Social Research.* London: Unwin Hyman.

HOME OFFICE (1992). *Race and the Criminal Justice System.* A Home Office publication under section 95 of the Criminal Justice Act 1991. London: Home Office.

—— (1994). *Race and the Criminal Justice System.* A Home Office publication under section 95 of the Criminal Justice Act 1991. London: Home Office.

—— (1995). *Race and the Criminal Justice System.* A Home Office publication under section 95 of the Criminal Justice Act 1991. London: Home Office.

—— (1997). *Race and the Criminal Justice System.* A Home Office publication under section 95 of the Criminal Justice Act 1991. London: Home Office.

—— (1998). *Statistics on Race and the Criminal Justice System.* A Home Office publication under section 95 of the Criminal Justice Act 1991. London: Home Office.

—— (1999). *The Stephen Lawrence Inquiry.* Report of an Inquiry by Sir William MacPherson of Cluny. London: HMSO.

HOOD, R. (1992). *Race and Sentencing.* Oxford: Oxford University Press.

HUDSON, B. (1989). 'Discrimination and Disparity: Researching the Influence of Race on Sentencing'. *New Community* 16, 23–34.

JUPP, V. (1989). *Methods of Criminological Research.* London: Unwin Hyman.

MAGUIRE, M. (1997). 'Crime Statistics, Patterns and Trends: Changing Perceptions and their

Implications' in M. Maguire, R. Morgan, and R. Reiner (eds.), *The Oxford Handbook of Criminology* (2nd edn.). Oxford: Oxford University Press.

MAWBY, B. I., and BATTA, I. D. (1980). *Asians and Crime: The Bradford Experience*, Published for the National Association for Asian Youth, Southhall, Middlesex: Scope Communications.

MHLANGA, B. (1997). *The Colour of English Justice: A Multivariate Analysis*. Aldershot: Ashgate, Avebury.

—— (1999). *Race and Crown Prosecution Service Decisions*. London: HMSO.

O'BRIEN, M. (1993). 'Social Research and Sociology' in N. Gilbert (ed.), *Researching Social Life*. London: Sage.

REINER, R. (1993). 'Race, Crime and Justice: Models of Interpretation' in L. Gelsthorpe and W. McWilliams (eds.), *Minority Ethnic Groups in the Criminal Justice System*. Cambridge: Institute of Criminology.

SILVERMAN, D. (1998). 'Qualitative/Quantitative' in C. Jenks (ed.), *Core Sociological Dichotomies*. London: Sage.

SMITH, D. (1997). 'Ethnic Origins, Crime and Criminal Justice' in M. Maguire, R. Morgan, and R. Reiner (eds.), *The Oxford Handbook of Criminology* (2nd edn.). Oxford: Oxford University Press.

WARDAK, A. (1995). *Predicting Delinquency Among Young People in the Edinburgh Pakistani Community*. Paper presented to the British Society of Criminology Conference, University of Loughborough (July).

WEBSTER, C. (1995). *Youth Crime, Victimisation and Racial Harrassment: The Keighley Crime Survey*. Bradford: Centre for Research in Applied Community Studies, Bradford and Ilkley Community College Corporation.

—— (1997). 'The Construction of British "Asian" Criminality'. *International Journal of Sociology of Law* 25: 65–86.

19

RESEARCHING THE POWERFUL:
TOWARDS A POLITICAL
ECONOMY OF METHOD?

Dave Whyte

INTRODUCTION

This chapter draws upon my own experience of researching 'powerful organizations' in the UK oil industry. This research, an analysis of the regulation of health and safety on offshore oil platforms, involved an examination of the role of the regulatory authority, the Health and Safety Executive (HSE), and the activities of oil companies operating in the North Sea—companies which are arguably amongst the most criminogenic of all private corporations (Clinard and Yeager 1980: 119). The research involved conducting qualitative interviews with offshore workers, managers, and HSE inspectors between Spring 1995 and Summer 1998. It was informed by a Marxist theoretical framework which drew upon the literature on regulation, state theory, and hegemony.

'Independent' research within this framework is unlikely to be popular with either the powerful organizations or their regulators, and the findings contrast markedly with those from officially sanctioned studies. It is important to note that the neo-liberal project has, over the past two decades, been successful in assimilating social research into the 'official' or business-friendly policy environment which rewards those who are 'one of us' (Hillyard and Sim 1997: 58). This has implications for those who wish to conduct research which requires access to government departments and institutions, and even private corporations. Researchers who are not deemed to be 'one of us' (and I count myself as one of *them*) face a series of tactics to frustrate and obstruct their inquiry and marginalize their viewpoint. In the case of the regulatory agency HSE, some may even be placed under surveillance if they 'become persistent in their inquiries' (*The Guardian*, 21 May 1998: 22).

Although very little has been written which has a methodological focus on the process of 'researching the powerful', this chapter does not attempt to redress the balance in any systematic way. It merely seeks to reflect upon and identify some issues that I was faced with during the course of my fieldwork and locate them within the political and economic context of the time. Since part of that context is a *specific* political economy of researching the regulation and organization of safety in the off-shore oil industry I present a brief description of how that works with particular reference to one group of researchers.

FUNDING AND ACCESS TO THE POWERFUL

In my own experience, access to the HSE was welcomed until the point that I actually published my (critical) findings. In December 1995, a colleague and I were granted access to the HSE Offshore Safety Division to conduct interviews with offshore inspectors in the Operations Branch at one of the HSE's office buildings. After the interviews were finished, a senior civil servant in the HSE invited us to his office for a 'chat'. Our host commenced with a polemical attack upon a paper that we had presented a few weeks earlier to an industrial audience. He pointed out that we were giving a 'distorted view', adding that 'some people have a hidden agenda, so we (HSE) have to be careful'.[1] The senior civil servant was visibly angry about the views that had been presented in our paper. He then added that there was a great deal of money available from the HSE for this type of research: '[w]e have a large pool of research funds. Six million pounds is a lot of money, you know.' It was made clear, however, that this money would not be made available unconditionally, adding that he would be in support of 'winning this money for Merseyside' but 'obviously you would have to be very careful about *the way you put things*'. In other words, government funding would be forthcoming only for research that would be constructed around the HSE's agenda. Integration into the HSE's programme of research and the possibility of wider access would have been on their terms, and, judging by the senior civil servants' comments, it would have substantially restricted our freedom to publish and disseminate findings. This was an offer we most certainly could, and did, refuse.

I was subsequently denied access to other branches of the HSE Offshore Safety Division. In terms of my own research, this access was not essential for the survival of the project. I had already completed my qualitative interviews with HSE inspectors. However, others may not find themselves in such a fortunate position. A research project may stand or fall on the gatekeeper's decision

---

[1] All quotations here are taken from fieldwork notebooks. The meeting referred to took place in the HSE's Bootle offices on 11 December 1995.

to grant or refuse access. Of course, there is often a strong link between funding and access. For, if a researcher is funded by the organization that he or she wishes to research and is also deemed to be 'one of us', then this may also entail privileged access to sources of data. For particularly ambitious or career-minded researchers, such an offer may be highly seductive.

Once a group of researchers, or a university department, enters into a grant-holding relationship with either government or corporate funders, then it must accept that its research activities will, to some extent, be structured by those who hold the purse strings. For many university departments that rely upon external funding, their future success may be gauged by their ability to secure and retain future financial support from government and corporate sources. Given the value increasingly placed by research panels upon the securing of external research grants, loss of funding may also effectively have a 'double' impact in terms of a department's ability to win funding from Research Assessment Exercises. It follows that, since loss of this funding may have implications for the long-term sustainability of a university department's research output, the 'success' of a department's research may be measured ultimately by the degree to which its funders are satisfied with its output. With this measure as one of the primary performance indicators it may become difficult to distinguish between the role of management consultancies and the role of some groups of researchers in universities.

THE UNIVERSITY AS MANAGEMENT CONSULTANCY: THE CASE OF THE ROBERT GORDON UNIVERSITY

One example of university researchers assuming the role of management consultants can be found at the Robert Gordon University in Aberdeen. This institution received between £325,000 and £600,000 from the HSE Offshore Safety Division research budget in 1996 alone (figures estimated from HSE 1996), a large slice of which was match-funded by oil company grants. A major departmental beneficiary of these monies is the Offshore Management Centre[2] at the university. The Centre was launched in November 1993 with the purpose of 'carrying out research, training and consultancy for the offshore industry' (*Petroleum Review*, February 1994: 92) and was set up with funding commitments from a range of operating and contracting companies including: AMEC, BP, Brown and Root, Hamilton Oil, and Shell. In return for this funding, it was promised that '[c]onsultancy services will be offered to business arising from the research activities and from staff experience' (*Petroleum Review*, February 1994: 92). The total value of research grants attracted by the centre since its

[2] The main body of researchers at the Robert Gordon University Offshore Management Centre moved to a new centre at the University of Aberdeen in the summer of 1997. For purposes of clarity this group is referred to throughout the text as the Offshore Management Centre.

inception is not known, but one project commissioned in October 1995 provides an indication of the type of funding involved in the centre's work. This project was set up to establish the link between 'accidents' and 'human error' and was thus based upon conservative, business-friendly assumptions of the causes of accidents. Research which locates the causes of industrial 'accidents', injuries, and deaths in the failings of individual workers neglects structural and systematic factors: productive and market pressures; managerial regimes; the labour process; and so on (see Nichols 1975; Tombs 1991). The 'human factors' or 'forensic' approach to research thus allows some fundamental questions surrounding the activities of the oil companies to be circumnavigated. It is primarily for this reason that this type of research remains hugely popular to funders in the offshore oil industry. A total of £140,000 was provided by HSE, British Gas, BP, Conoco, Coflexip Stena, Elf, Texaco, Total, and the Offshore Contractors' Association (Aberdeen's *Evening Express*, 5 September 1995) to fund the project.

Research agendas and the methods used in projects such as this one are discussed and approved at a steering committee where the funders of the Centre's research are represented (personal communication with Offshore Management Centre, 10 October 1996). The success, and thus the survival, of the centre relies almost entirely upon ensuring it is able to continue to attract industry funding. This point has been made in public by the head of the Centre, Rhona Flin, who, on receiving another round of funding from the industry, remarked: 'I can only presume that through this latest award, the companies are very happy with the work we're doing' (*Evening Express*, 5 September 1995).

With this in mind, it is perhaps unsurprising that the published work of the centre presents the industry as one which has safety as its primary concern, and one which is constantly (and successfully) striving to improve its safety record. The published material is based upon a flawed and narrowly managerialist perspective. It tends to locate safety problems in terms of 'human factors' or presents them as the failures of individual workers on the one hand, and as the abilities of managers on the other (for a comprehensive collection of this work see Flin and Slaven 1996).

In contrast, 'unofficial' research which is not funded by oil company or HSE sources presents a rather different picture of the industry. This work reveals the UK oil industry to be one of the most dangerous, if not the most dangerous, in the country, with an appalling history of: unsafe working practices; regulatory non-compliance; manipulation of HSE reportable data; and routine criminal breaches of health and safety law (Beck *et al.* 1998; Carson 1982; Cavanagh 1998; Lavelette and Wright 1991; Woolfson *et al.* 1996).

The unpublished work of the Centre, research produced for internal company circulation only, also presents a very different picture from that found in the Centre's published research findings. One example of this is a report leaked to the press by offshore union OILC in early 1997. This report was commissioned to examine the 'safety climate' on one of Shell's North Sea platforms, Brent Charlie (Flin *et al.* 1996). The Brent Charlie report identifies serious safety problems and includes evidence of: 'massaged' accident figures (Flin *et al.* 1996: 7 and 12); and routine management disregard for workers' safety concerns (Flin *et al.* 1996: 7). Significantly, the leaked report locates these problems not in the responses and abilities of individual managers, but in the *systematic* economic and productive demands of management. Moreover, 'senior management were overly focused on productivity and had lost sight of safety' (Flin *et al.* 1996: 9).

Remarkably, the unpublished consultancy work of the Centre tends closely to resemble some of the most critical of the 'unofficial' work listed above. It is the incongruity between the Centre's published work, and its work which is for oil company eyes only that seriously damages the integrity of its output: for the output that is deemed suitable for a public audience remains uncritical, unreflective, and benign. Those who work within these constraints are well aware of the not-so-subtle way in which their work is compromised. One researcher at the Centre told me:

When I ask these guys [oil company senior managers] about why the accident rates are changed for their own records, they tell me to shut up. Of course I do. Because you can't challenge what they say if you want to keep credibility (personal communication with a researcher at the Offshore Management Centre, 10 September 1996).

All of this sheds serious doubt upon the validity of work conducted with the co-operation of the oil companies generally and, in particular, the output of the Offshore Management Centre. Since corporate interference in the research process can be understood as a potential symptom of the economic power relationship between funder and researcher, it does lead us to ask some fairly basic questions surrounding the integrity and accuracy of university research financed by external funders more generally.

A MUTUALLY BENEFICIAL ARRANGEMENT

Professor C. Duncan Rice, Principal and Vice Chancellor of the University of Aberdeen, recently indicated the extent to which his institution is tied to oil industry funding in an open letter to Chancellor of the Exchequer Gordon Brown. In the letter, published in the Aberdeen-based *Press and Journal*,[3] as part of an oil industry campaign to oppose a Treasury review of North Sea

---

[3] The *Press and Journal* is a local broadsheet with a readership concentrated in the North East of Scotland. Due to the importance of the oil industry to the area, the *Press and Journal* carries detailed news of the offshore scene on a daily basis. Uniquely for a provincial local newspaper, it also has a wide circulation in oil company headquarters, and in the Department of Trade and Industry in London.

taxation,[4] the Vice Chancellor appealed to Brown to reconsider his plans to tax the oil companies: '[t]he North Sea tax issue is of immense importance to the whole of Scotland, especially the North East. The University of Aberdeen is inextricably linked to the oil industry and to the local economy. A dynamic oil industry creates employment for our graduates and funds our research activities' (*Press and Journal*, 29 June 1998: 'The Dead Sea?' supplement: 2).

It is remarkable that the head of a public institution evidently feels that his relationship with the private oil companies is important enough to justify a political attack on the government (generally, Vice-Chancellors are not known for their willingness to confront governments in this manner). Given the fact that the government review was ostensibly aimed at recouping a proportion of the super-profits extracted from North Sea oil production to redistribute this wealth into education (*Scotland on Sunday*, 31 May 1998), the irony of the Vice Chancellor's intervention on behalf of oil capital is not missed.

Within this context, it becomes easier to understand exactly why there is a dearth of social research in universities with a *critical* focus upon the activities of large corporations. After all, university managements are hardly likely to encourage researchers to produce work which may offend the sensibilities of a current or potential funder. Indeed, this was the very dilemma that faced Edwin Sutherland in the 1940s. Sutherland was forced into a protracted battle with his university management and publisher over the naming of companies analysed in his seminal text, *White Collar Crime* (1949), since some of these companies exposed by him were university benefactors. Sutherland was eventually forced to back down and the corporations in his text remained anonymous (see Geis and Goff 1983).

However, the relationship between universities and their corporate backers is not simply based upon the flow of research monies into university coffers. There are also considerable benefits for companies. In the oil industry, university-based 'organic' intellectuals play an important role in the struggle for hegemonic domination (Gramsci 1996: 5–14). In this way, companies partially rely upon researchers in universities to provide the authority and justification for their activities. A current example of how this relation can have a substantial mutual benefit is the work conducted by the oil industry's favourite economist, Alexander Kemp,[5] and his colleagues at the University of Aberdeen.

[4] This campaign was successful, and the Treasury abandoned its review in the summer of 1998. The UK continues to take a lower proportion of profits than any other oil producer state in the world (Rutledge and Wright 1996; *Petroleum Review*, September 1997; *Lloyds List*, 20 April 1998).

[5] Alexander G. Kemp is Professor of Economics at the University of Aberdeen where he is Director of Aberdeen University Petroleum and Economic Consultants, an organization which provides consultancy services on petroleum economics to the international oil industry. He has longstanding links with the oil industry, having previously worked for Shell, and has built a considerable reputation as an expert in oil economics, with special reference to licensing and taxation. It was a paper jointly authored by Kemp and MacDonald (1993) that provided the academic rationale for the launch of the North Sea cost-cutting campaign, CRINE (see Whyte 1999). Alexander Kemp is currently European editor of *Energy Journal* (biographical details from *World Oil*, v. 217, No. 12, December 1996).

This work plays a significant role in the development of (and moral justification for) corporate policy in the industry (Whyte 1999).

At a crude level, the importance of university research to oil companies is also indicated by the regular and consistent reference to the Offshore Management Centre (see, e.g., Potter 1998; Cresswell 1998) and Aberdeen University (see, e.g., HSE 1998) research in industry publications, and in public statements by industry representatives. These references to academic research are used as evidence to demonstrate good practice such as the oil industry's improving safety record or its positive contribution to environmental protection (see, e.g., UKOOA 1995).

All of this tells us that the process of conducting research in universities can (far from being an objective and value-free enterprise) be a highly politicized one, particularly for those who are funded by corporate and state grant-holders. Yet those who conduct this 'management-consultancy style' work for powerful interests are rarely accused of being partisan, or accused of bias: 'the thin disguise of a special interest afforded by foundation names or government agency labels permits relations with such entities to be used as badges of honour rather than as suggestions of bias' (McClung Lee 1978: 90).

UNOFFICIAL BARRIERS

Coming into the industry as an 'unofficial' researcher undoubtedly created barriers for me in my study of the industry, particularly in terms of seeking interviews with senior oil company personnel, or gaining access to company records and data sources. After a number of failed attempts, I quickly discovered that I was not going to gain access to oil companies via the normal channels. I did not have the necessary credentials of the officially sanctioned researcher. Numerous requests for interviews with managers were refused after 'cold' contacts to companies at various levels of the hierarchy and the industry trade association UKOOA. I was eventually able to reach managers only by using a complex and often contrived network of contacts. Initially, I made the most of a list of contacts given to me by two former oil company managers. This network was developed by using 'snowballing' techniques, and subsequent interviews were successfully arranged by mentioning the name of a colleague or associate of the respondent.

At first it may seem paradoxical that I also experienced difficulties when I attempted to arrange interviews with offshore workers. In the absence of official backing it was impossible to secure access to off-shore platforms. I therefore sought interviews with off-shore workers in the places where they gather in transit to and from the heliport—in hotel bars, public bars, train stations, and on trains. However, in the context of the preceding discussion, it is perhaps unsurprising that off-shore workers were suspicious of the process of research in their industry, since it is a process that tends to reflect management agendas, and rarely represents their views or reflects their experiences in anything other than a tokenistic manner.

A significant majority of offshore workers I approached immediately declined to participate in the study. Indeed it has to be said that, despite the overtly stated guarantees of anonymity and my introductory statement to the interview which made it clear that they would not be asked to give the name of the platform on which they worked, or even the name of the company, all of those interviewed expressed some sort of suspicion about the notes that I was taking, and what they would be used for. Now, these were not the normal types of suspicions that a social researcher might be faced with. They were not simply concerns about why someone from a university was snooping about with a notebook approaching strangers to ask questions about their work. Their concerns were, without exception, related to the possibility that their names, or even my notes, might become known to their employer, and that they had been shooting their mouths off about safety conditions. Even after my standard introduction, which stressed that I had no backing from any oil company or government department, it was not unusual to be asked repeatedly to reveal which company I was working for. I had to work extremely hard to convince workers that I was not conducting 'official' research on behalf of the industry. On one occasion, I was actually asked to leave a public house because the clientele (every one of them either currently worked, or had worked in the past, on an offshore platform) did not trust me and thought I was either a journalist or was working for one of the oil companies.

The reluctance to discuss such matters is symptomatic of the highly secretive treatment by the operating oil companies and their contractors of issues of worker safety, whether it be in terms of their own accident and injury statistics or the (in)effectiveness of their safety strategies. This treatment is especially sensitive when it comes to the views and opinions of workers themselves, whether these views are expressed in public or in private to colleagues. The sacking of offshore workers, and even their safety representatives, for speaking their minds on matters of workplace safety is commonplace, indeed routine, on many platforms in the North Sea.

Clearly, all of this is important context for anybody who wishes to conduct corporate crime-related research in the industry: both in terms of the politics of the subject matter, and in terms of the methodological problems that might be encountered in a climate of secrecy. Yet, this is context that is often ignored by those who conduct research within the boundaries of the 'official' domain.

CONCLUDING REMARKS: A POLITICAL ECONOMY OF METHOD?

The preceding discussion suggests that not only is 'official' and 'unofficial' research likely to differ in terms of its political and/or theoretical orientations, but it may also generate entirely different empirical observations of social phenomena. This is not a new revelation. Feminist theorists have for many years now advocated the use of alternative sources of data to counter dominant masculinist perspectives and construct a new and indeed more accurate body of knowledge (see, for example, Cain, 1990).

The discussion presented in this chapter suggests that an understanding of the political economy within which research is structured is of incalculable value to understanding how knowledge is constructed. This point is particularly crucial for understanding our relationships with the populations, institutions, and organizations that I study. It is one that has to be considered as central to the research process, since these relationships have a defining methodological impact and, to a great extent, structure the procedural methods we are able to use to generate empirical research findings. Yet this is an area that is largely unexplored in the literature on research methods. There is very little methodological work on the study of powerful organizations generally (Tombs and Whyte, 1999). There is also very little that examines methods within the wider political economy of research in any detail. Given the evidence and observations presented here, it seems that such a literature could prompt a re-examination of some basic assumptions that we make about the nature and purpose of university research.

The commentary on the relationship between university researchers and their oil industry funders that has been presented here sheds serious doubt upon the validity of work conducted with the co-operation of the oil companies. If this point can be generalized to other industries (and evidence from some preliminary research conducted by a colleague and me at Liverpool John Moores University suggests that it can, Tombs and Whyte 1999), then this raises some fundamental questions surrounding the integrity of much of the research conducted in our universities.

In this context, then, it is no coincidence that some of the most important research in the social sciences continues to be conducted without corporate or government funding (Hillyard and Sim, 1997), and, at the same time, 'official' studies continue to produce a body of social research that is anodyne, unreflective, and contributes little to our understanding of the world. Given current attempts to undermine and marginalize the former (for example see ibid.; Hunt, 1994; Sanders, 1997; *Times Higher Educational Supplement*, 20 November 1998; Tombs, 1999), it is now more important than ever to resist this process and to place the 'powerful' under intense scrutiny. At the heart of this process, approaches to studying the powerful must be theoretically reflexive (Cain, 1990), and, as a central methodological concern, consider the political economy within which university research is structured.

For their comments and advice during the preparation of this piece, thanks go to Pete Gill, Steve Tombs and Joe Sim, and to the editors of this volume.

REFERENCES

BECK, M., FOSTER, J., RYGGVIK, H., and WOOLFSON, C. (1998). *Piper Alpha—Ten Years After*. Glasgow: Centre for Regulatory Studies, University of Glasgow.

CAIN, M. (1990). 'Realist Philosophy and Standpoint Epistemologies or Feminist Criminology as a Successor Science' in L. Gelsthorpe and A. Morris (eds.), *Feminist Perspectives in Criminology*. Milton Keynes: Open University Press.

CLINARD, M., and YEAGER, P. (1980). *Corporate Crime*. New York: Free Press.

CARSON, W. (1982). *The Other Price of Britain's Oil*. New Brunswick, NJ: Rutgers University Press.

CAVANAGH, M. (1998). 'Offshore Health and Safety Policy in the North Sea: Policy Networks and Policy Outcomes in Britain and Norway' in D. Marsh (ed.), *Comparing Policy Networks*. Milton Keynes: Open University Press.

CRESSWELL, J. (1998). 'Improving North Sea Safety'. *Petroleum Review*, September.

FLIN, R., MEARNS, K., FLEMING, M., and GORDON, R. (1996). *Safety Climate on the Brent Charlie Platform*. Report prepared for Mr G. Birnie of Shell Exploration and Production UK and Mr A. Sanvor of Wood Group Engineering Contractors Ltd. Unpublished report produced by the Robert Gordon University Offshore Management Centre.

—— and SLAVEN, G. (eds.) (1996). *Managing the Offshore Installation Workforce*. Tulsa, Okla.: Penn Well.

GEIS, G., and GOFF, C. (1983). 'Introduction' to E. Sutherland, *White Collar Crime: The Uncut Version*. London: Yale University.

GRAMSCI, A. (1996). *Selections from the Prison Notebooks*. London: Lawrence and Wishart.

HILLYARD, P., and SIM, J. (1997). 'The Political Economy of Socio-legal Research' in P. Thomas (ed.), *Socio-legal Studies*. Aldershot: Dartmouth.

HEALTH AND SAFETY EXECUTIVE (1996). *Offshore Safety Research and Development Programme Project Handbook*. 1996, London: HSE Books.

—— (1998). *Minister Emphasises Key Role of Workforce in Offshore Safety*. HSE News Release, 21 May.

HUNT, A. (1994). 'Governing the Socio-legal Project: Or What Do Research Councils Do?' *Journal of Law and Society*. 20: 114–28.

JUPP, V. (1989). *Methods of Criminological Research*. London: Unwin Hyman.

KEMP, A., and MACDONALD, B. (1993). *Economic Aspects of Cost Savings in the UKCS, Strategies for Cost Reduction in the New Era*. CRINE Conference organized by UKOOA and the Department of Trade and Industry, Queen Elizabeth II Conference Centre, 2 and 3 December.

LAVELETTE, M., and WRIGHT, C. (1991). 'The Cullen Report—Making the North Sea Safe?'. *Critical Social Policy*, 34: 60–9.

McCLUNG LEE, A. (1978). *Sociology for Whom?* New York: Oxford University Press.

NICHOLS, T. (1975). 'The Sociology of Accidents and the Social Production of Industrial Injury' in G. Esland *et al.* (eds.), *People and Work*. Edinburgh: Holmes McDougal.

POTTER, N. (1998). 'Total Management Commitment Needed for Safe Operations'. *Petroleum Review*. April.

RUTLEDGE, I., and WRIGHT, P. (1996). *Taxing the Second Oil Boom: A Fair Deal or a Raw Deal?* Unpublished paper, University of Sheffield.

SANDERS, A. (1997). 'Criminal Justice: The Development of Criminal Justice Research in Britain' in P. Thomas (ed.), *Socio-legal Studies*. Aldershot: Dartmouth.

SUTHERLAND, E. (1949). *White Collar Crime*. New York: Dryden Press.

TOMBS, S. (1991). 'Injury and Ill Health in the Chemical Industry: Decentring the Accident-prone Victim'. *Industrial Crisis Quarterly*. 5: 59–75.

—— (1999). 'Official Statistics and Hidden Crime: Researching Safety Crimes' in V. Jupp, P. Davies and P. Francis (eds.), *Criminology in the Field: The Practice of Criminological Research*. London: MacMillan.

—— and WHYTE, D. (1999). 'Researching the Powerful: Problems, Possibilities and Praxis'. Paper presented to British Criminology Conference, Liverpool, July 1999.

UNITED KINGDOM OFFSHORE OPERATING ASSOCIATION (1995). *An Assessment of the Environmental Impacts of Decommissioning Options for Oil and Gas Installations in the UK North Sea*. London: UKOOA.

WHYTE, D. (1999). *Power, Ideology and the Regulation of Safety in the post-Piper Alpha Offshore Oil Industry*. Unpublished PhD thesis. Liverpool: John Moores University.

WOOLFSON, C., FOSTER, J., and BECK, M. (1996). *Paying for the Piper: Capital and Labour in Britain's Offshore Oil Industry*. London: Mansell.

INDEX